GW00722524

Gardening Complete

A peaceful corner of the vegetable and flower garden at Crittenden House

GARDENING COMPLETE

R. H. W. Brown

illustrations by
Irene Hawkins
from drawings by the author

FABER AND FABER
24 Russell Square
London

First published in mcmlxviii
by Faber and Faber Limited
24 Russell Square London WC1
Printed in Great Britain by
Ebenezer Baylis and Son Limited
The Trinity Press, Worcester, and London
All rights reserved

Standard Book Number 571 08332 3

© *1968 by R. H. W. Brown*

Contents

Plates

Plates 1–7, 13–17, 19–22, 25, 27, 28, 31 and 33 are reproduced by
courtesy of H. Smith; frontispiece and plates 18, 23, 24, 29, 30,
32, 34 and 35–39 are reproduced by courtesy of J. E. Downward;
plates 8–12 are reproduced by courtesy of Oakworth Greenhouses; plate 26 is reproduced by courtesy of Samuel Dobie
and Son Ltd.

Introduction

This is a complete book for all gardeners. Although it is written principally for those who are new to gardening it will also help all those who seek additional information.

It is mainly an instructive book which covers all fields of this fascinating and absorbing hobby, but I hope it will also make enjoyable reading.

This book covers town gardens as well as country ones and I hope I have included enough for all those who love gardening.

The book will show you how to construct a colourful and attractive garden without too much expense involved, and with the very minimum use of artificial manure and poisonous insecticides.

The emphasis is on good garden compost and farmyard manure—the natural plant foods. Much benefit can be gained from growing our own food in the right way and from eating unadulterated vegetables and fruit.

Good exercise in the fresh air and relief from much mental stress and strain can be ours when we are working among our beautiful plants and observing the rich variety of our bird and insect life.

1
Making a Start

How to tell the nature of soils by the weeds growing on them—
improving different kinds of soil—crops which suit particular soils
—soil testing—clearing rough land

You may have acquired a garden for the first time, having moved
from the city to the country. You may have moved to a new house
with a waste piece of land just as the builders have left it. You may
have taken over a garden from another owner and do not like what
is in it or the design.

Before making a plan on paper it will have to be decided which
crops are to be grown. Everyone has something special in mind. The
particular soil you possess really decides what you can grow and what
you cannot grow. Every soil will grow something if it receives the
necessary cultivation. Try to grow the crops which suit your soil the
best. A good way of discovering the nature of your soil is by examin-
ing the kind of weeds which are growing there.

If there is plenty of chickweed, fat hen or short annual nettles then
they indicate a good soil and almost anything can be grown. If some
of the following plants are found growing on the same piece of land
it is a sure sign of lime deficiency: spurrey, corn marigold, sheep sorrel
and foxgloves. On a gravelly or sandy soil there is usually plenty of
gorse together with broom and ragwort. The latter is poisonous to
animals. Chalk soil provides wild mignonette, wild clematis and
chicory. Badly drained and waterlogged ground will have some
rushes, sedges and horsetail growing together.

Chickweed, when found, usually grows in profusion. It is a low-
growing plant, the stems trail along the ground, and it has many
rounded leaves ending in a point. They are light-green in colour and
are quite small. The plant bears many tiny white flowers which have
eight petals and a yellow centre. It is in flower all the year round. Fat
hen, or goosefoot, is an annual which grows to two feet in height with
leaves of pale green. These are bluntly toothed, gradually becoming

narrower as they reach the top of the plant. The flowers are whitish-green and are arranged in spikes. This weed quickly goes to seed when the spikes appear a blackish colour. Spurrey grows from one to two feet in height. It has thin stems and the very thin grass-like leaves fan out from joints spaced at about two inches all the way down to ground level. The flowers are minute with five white petals. Corn marigold is just like a small garden calendula, and is golden yellow. Sheep sorrel is a smaller plant than common sorrel and only grows to about a foot in height. The leaves lie close to the ground and are spear-shaped with two basal lobes turned outwards. They become conspicuous in autumn by turning a bright red. The flowers are small and resemble the dock. Ragwort is a handsome flower with its rich golden blossoms which are like a small yellow daisy. It grows from two to four feet tall on a stout erect stem. The leaves are broken up into toothed lobes, about five of these on each side of a leaf stalk. Broom and gorse are too well known to need description. Wild mignonette is very similar to the sweet mignonette of our gardens, but is scentless. It has a hard stiff stem with flowers of a yellowish-green packed closely on either side. The leaves are lance-shaped. It grows to about three feet high. Wild clematis is a climbing shrub clambering freely over hedges everywhere on chalk lands. The feathery appearance of its seed vessels is very noticeable during autumn. The flowers are slightly fragrant and are greenish-white. It is known by many other names such as 'traveller's joy', white vine and 'old man's beard'. Chicory is one of our most beautiful wild flowers. It has clear blue flowers of a most unusual hue; these are stalkless and the petals are strap-shaped with a straight end notched into five teeth. The flower buds are pink on the outside. The leaves are shaped like those of the dandelion and they spread themselves out on the ground. Horsetail looks like a miniature fir tree with bright green thin leaves and a rounded stem.

Of course it is possible to have annual nettles, chickweed, fat hen and spurrey all growing on the same patch. Then you can just carry out sufficient liming of the land and know that all will be well.

If you are unable to identify these weeds, look for them in a good wild flower book.

TYPES OF SOIL

Some people may have a piece of land which is solid chalk with only a thin covering of soil. These soils generally lack iron and it is useless to waste time, money and effort trying to grow peas and beans or apples. Neither can one expect good Russell lupins or rhododendrons, both of which are lime intolerant. However, bearing in mind that all soils will grow something, if this land is manured and well cultivated very good vegetables and flowers can be produced. These will be described later on. Chalkland brings out nice colours in the flowers that like lime. It is also good land for livestock such as poultry, the calcium content being beneficial for bone formation and for producing egg shell. If one's favourite flower is the lupin, then the thing to do is to grow some from seed each year and re-plant as the old ones deteriorate. The beautiful Russell lupins are very easily grown from seed in the open ground.

Peaty soils are absolutely devoid of lime and are very sour. They can be made into valuable growing soils once they have been sufficiently limed. Celery grows well on them, being a native of Britain and found on marshy land.

Clay soils are one of the best types, containing most of the plant foods. Once clay has been properly drained, broken down and given the necessary substances for improving its texture, almost anything can be grown on it.

Very sandy soils which dry out so quickly are very poor in plant foods. They have to be well manured regularly to produce good crops. They have some advantages however: the soil warms up quickly, enabling early crops to be grown, and the ground can be worked at almost any time of the year.

The fortunate person coming into possession of a plot of medium loam in which there is enough chalk for the plants to take advantage of, can go ahead and plan to grow anything he wishes. Medium loam is land which has equal parts of sand and clay, has some humus, and if manured from time to time, contains all the plant's requirements.

Badly drained land easily becomes waterlogged and only certain aquatic plants, especially adapted through years of fighting against adverse conditions, can live here. This land will have to be drained if anything worthwhile is to be grown.

IMPROVING DIFFERENT KINDS OF SOIL

Let us now take each kind of soil in turn and see what can be done to improve them. On the solid chalklands which only have a thin layer of soil, deep digging is essential. The bottom of the trench must be broken up and plenty of good compost or farmyard manure incorporated. Try not to bring too much chalk to the surface. If plenty of nettles are available and are well rotted down, they make a valuable contribution to the compost for they contain iron, one of the plant foods which is generally missing from this type of soil. Do not remove too many stones during tillage operations as they help to retain moisture. These soils should not be over-watered as the chalk becomes very sticky and difficult to work. Plenty of work with the Dutch hoe is preferable.

Peaty soils have to be limed each year until the sourness has gone. They have to be drained and well manured and then become quite fertile.

Heavy clay soil is cold and late. This means that it is difficult to obtain early and late crops. It needs to be well dug in the autumn and then left rough on the surface. The frost, snow, wind and rains of winter are valuable agents for the breaking down of the stiff clay particles. The operation of digging year after year will gradually let air in and water out. Sometimes this kind of land will need to be properly drained. When digging add plenty of compost or rotted farmyard manure, together with any straw obtainable, sand and gritty materials. These all help in the breaking up of the large pieces of soil and they make it more porous. The land must also be limed; lime acts upon the clay, making it much finer in texture. It is very important, however, not to put lime on at the same time as the manure, otherwise the valuable plant foods will be given up to the air in the form of gases. Do not work on clay soil during wet weather otherwise the clay will be trodden into a solid mass and difficult to work if a spell of hot sunshine comes along to bake it still more solid. Clay is a good soil when properly worked and it has the advantage of being able to retain moisture during drought periods.

On sandy soils the most important task is to provide plenty of moisture-retaining material, as rain quickly percolates through the sand. The amount of improvement which can be given to a very sandy site is limited. Plenty of leaf mould, peat, compost, farmyard manure and watering are called for.

Waterlogged land will need to be drained. There are several ways of carrying out this work. Few people will be able to afford a complete drainage system employing agricultural drain-pipes. A cheaper way is to dig drainage trenches about three feet deep and two feet wide and fill the trenches with stones, rubble, clinkers, broken bricks or old tins, covering over with grass turves turned upside down to prevent soil trickling through and blocking the drain. Bundled brushwood, heather or willow thongs can also be used. But there is no point in carrying out a complicated system of drainage if there is nowhere for the surplus water to go. If there is not a convenient ditch at the bottom of the garden then a sump will have to be built. Dig a well-like hole up to six feet wide and twelve feet deep, penetrating into porous sub-soil. Fill with rubble and clinkers to a level of three feet below the surface of the plot. Cover the drainage material with turves turned upside-down and finish with top soil. It is best to put the drains under pathways where possible and this can be worked out best when

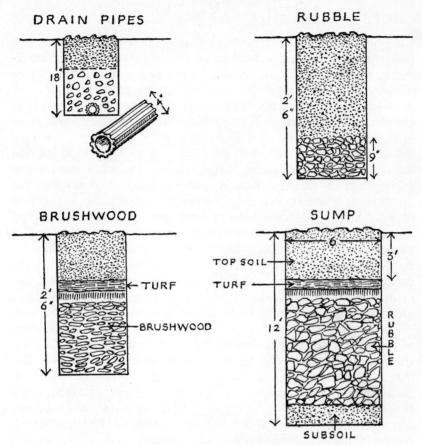

DRAIN PIPES

RUBBLE

BRUSHWOOD

SUMP

Various forms of Drainage

planning the garden. The slope of the whole drainage system, or 'fall' as it is called, should be one foot in a hundred feet for main drains and one foot in seventy-five feet for sub-mains. Always begin to lay drains from the lower end as this is the only way to ensure an even fall. Another method of drainage is to try and raise the surface of the plot and then dig a ditch all the way round it. If your garden is naturally situated at a lower level than gardens surrounding it, it would be a waste of time building a system of drainage until you could be assured that water from other gardens was not running into yours. Some method would have to be devised whereby water from other gardens ran into a suitable ditch, or neighbours built their own sumps.

CROPS WHICH SUIT PARTICULAR SOILS

Everyone can grow some worthwhile crops in his garden, whatever the nature of the soil, if he has carried out the necessary soil improvements. The individual cultivation of the plants mentioned in this section will be given in a later chapter. It is no good trying to grow good plants which will not tolerate the particular soil in which they are placed when there are plenty of excellent plants which will grow in the soil you have.

For vegetables which will grow on chalky soils most of the brassicas, or cabbage family, spring readily to mind. These include cabbages of all varieties, kale, sprouting broccoli and savoys. Not much success can be expected, however, with Brussels sprouts or summer and winter cauliflowers; they need a deeper, richer and wetter soil. Field swedes, garden swedes, turnips and radishes can all be grown well. Some lettuces can be grown but they do not heart up very well. Some good crops of potatoes can be obtained if the right varieties are planted, 'Arran Pilot' for an early one and 'Majestic' for main crop are the most suitable for this type of land. Globe beet is grown but not long beet, as there is not usually sufficient depth of soil.

There are many beautiful flowers grown on the chalk lands; some of the best for the herbaceous border and for cutting are as follows: *Achillea* or Yarrow, *Acanthus, Aconitum, Anchusa, Anemone, Anthemis, Campanula, Centaurea, Coreopsis, Chrysanthemum maximum, Delphinium, Dianthus* (all varieties), *Erigeron, Gypsophila* (called 'the chalk plant'), *Gaillardia, Geranium* (Crane's Bill), *Geum, Helleborus orientalis* (Lenten Rose), *Helianthus, Iris, Kniphofia* (Red-hot poker), *Nepeta* (Catmint), *Scabiosa, Sidalcea, Solidago, Statice* (Sea lavender) and *Verbascum.*

Good annuals for chalk are *Aster*, Larkspur, Annual Chrysanthemum, Annual Anchusa, Candytuft, *Calendula, Calliopsis, Campanula* (Annual harebell), Cornflower, *Clarkia*, Carnation, *Eschscholtzia*, Annual Gypsophila, *Hibiscus, Nigella, Scabiosa*, Virginia stock and *Zinnia.*

Half-hardy annuals include *Antirrhinum*, Carnation, *Dahlia* ('Coltness Gem'), *Dianthus* (all varieties), *Petunia, Phlox drummondii, Salvia* and stocks.

Biennials very easy to grow are Canterbury Bell, Sweet William and wallflowers. Sweet peas can be grown on well-prepared land, and the chalk seems to bring out very beautiful colours, but they tend to become short-stemmed rather quickly. Gladioli will also produce wonderful, colourful blooms on a well-prepared section of the plot.

An indication of trees and shrubs which suit these soils will be given in Chapter 6.

Chalk soil is not one of the best ones for roses but some can be grown if plenty of compost has been dug in during the preparatory stages. They will also need top dressings in spring. The rambler rose 'American Pillar' has grown quite well in chalk.

The fruits you can grow are the stone fruits, not apples or pears. These will include cherries which do particularly well, apricots (on a south wall), nectarines, peaches and plums. Some strawberries will grow (although they prefer an acid soil) if peat, leaf mould and compost are put into the soil. It is sometimes difficult trying to grow rhubarb. Cultivated hazel nuts or filberts do extremely well with a chalky sub-soil.

Once a peaty soil has been well limed and worked for a number of years it becomes very fertile. Very good celery and celeriac can be grown. Most varieties of potatoes do well; rhubarb and tomatoes are other good suitable crops.

Most of the flowers which originated from woodlands are the ones to try. Some of the bulbs, *Astilbe, Aquilegia,* primrose, polyanthus, lily of the valley, heathers, anemones, foxgloves, lupins, Michaelmas daisy, violets, lilies and spiraeas.

Generally speaking apples, pears and strawberries are the fruits that grow on acid soils (which will include soils which contain a lot of natural peat).

When heavy clay soils have been prepared in the manner described earlier, they will grow almost any kind of plant well. Roses do particularly well and any plants which need a lot of moisture during drought periods, in order to keep producing flowers, like sweet peas, are good crops for clay soils. All vegetables can be produced including all the brassicas. The ground needs to contain sufficient lime for this crop. All fruits can be grown, again, after attending to their individual requirements.

Herbaceous flowers which can be grown on sandy soils, providing adequate moisture-retaining material has been put in, are *Aconitum, Anthemis, Armeria, Catananche,* carnations, geraniums (crane's bill), geums, *Hemerocallis* (the 'Day lily'), *Heuchera, Lychnis* (campion), *Monarda, Montbretia, Nepeta* (catmint), *Oenothera* (evening prim-rose), Michaelmas daisy, penstemons and salvias.

Many annual flowers can be grown if copious watering is given during drought periods in addition to the compost. Antirrhinums will tolerate fairly dry conditions and so will mesembryanthemums, both sown under glass and then planted out after hardening off.

Vegetable growing on sandy soils is somewhat difficult and the best course is to concentrate primarily upon those crops which are specially suited to these conditions. These will include asparagus, carrots, parsnips and some potatoes. The land for the potatoes will

2

have to be well-limed if a profitable crop is to be hoped for. Most bush fruits may be tried, with the possible exception of black currants.

It is important to have a section on seaside planting in the book as those who live on the coast have some very special problems not met with elsewhere. There are some advantages for seaside gardens, for the absence of severe frosts, the presence of high temperatures and humidity are all conducive to the growing of some of the less hardy plants. When we are on holiday by the seaside and see the wonderful displays in the parks and on the front we are apt to forget the phenomenon of nature which seaside gardeners have to contend with at other times of the year—the wind. It has the ability to produce mountainous waves and to bear along salt-laden spray which will kill many ordinary garden plants. The flowers by the sea which we see in summer are all grown in pots in the greenhouse or cold frame and then planted out very firmly at the end of April or May, when danger from gales is largely over. Even evergreens should be planted during late April.

Planting by the seaside and choice of plants will be governed by the distance you actually live from the sea front. The most violent seaside storms usually bear along salt spray for a distance of twelve miles. During normal conditions of high wind we shall find a layer of salty moisture covering all plants up to 400 yards, in gale force up to three miles. It is common sense to begin by devising some sort of protection and shelter from the wind for our seaside gardens. The special varieties of trees and hedges which can be used as windbreaks will be mentioned in Chapter 6. A combination of semi-permeable fencing together with the windbreaks is the best answer to the problem of protection from the salt-laden winds. A temporary form of wind guard needs to be erected at planting time when the hedges and trees are put into their permanent quarters. A small-meshed wire netting fencing will filter the wind quite well; when considering bedding plants after the windbreaks are in position, it is best to confine yourself mostly to low-growing subjects which have more wind resistance. We can at once think of pansies, violas, primulas, petunias, nasturtiums, French marigolds, lobelia, double daisies, dwarf godetias and *Phlox drummondii*.

The following list of herbaceous flowers and flowers for cutting shows that the seaside grower has many beautiful plants to choose from. It must be emphasized that a most careful selection of seaside plants would be quite useless if the rules for seaside planting were ignored. Do not plant in late autumn and subject your poor plants to six months of gales and salt spray. Erect a semi-permeable fence. One of the best for this purpose is a lathe structure of wooden slats one inch wide with similar-sized spaces. Plant in late April and plant more closely together than is usual. The plants will then give each other protection. Adequate staking and tying must be rigidly attended to. Firm planting is essential. Every now and then the plants must be further firmed in the soil, as winds will often move them after planting.

Most of these border plants will grow well by the sea. *Catanache,* blue, good for cutting; *Cistus,* the rock rose; two climbing plants are *Clematis calycina,* the fern-leaved clematis with bronze foliage in autumn, and *Solanum crispum,* purplish-blue flowers with prominent orange stamens and very free flowering. *Echinops* (globe thistle), which is wonderful for floral decoration, *Eryngium* (sea holly), lovely steely blue and purple stems, *Euphorbia wulfenii* (spurge), very decorative with dense glaucous foliage, *Helichrysum angustifolium,* good for dry walls and rockeries, *Kniphofia* (red-hot poker): these will grow almost to the water's edge; and *Lavatera olbia rosea,* loose sprays of hollyhock-like flowers on long branching stems, for the back of the border. *Polygonum affine,* or Knot grass, is liked by some as an excellent ground coverer, but it has to be kept in check. 'Lowndes' Variety' is a nice one, with dainty red flower spikes followed by copper leaves in autumn. Statice (sea lavender) is well known as an everlasting; and thrift (sea-pink) is another delightful plant. Both of these are found growing wild on salt marshlands, especially in Essex and Suffolk.

When we turn to the vegetable plot, runner beans and tall peas are out, of course. The leaves of runner beans are not salt-tolerant and bean rods and pea sticks would be difficult to keep in position. French beans, dwarf runners and dwarf peas could be grown in a sheltered spot, perhaps behind a hedge which was facing the sea. All the cabbage family can be well grown for the wild cabbage plant is a native of the sea cliffs. Very firm planting would be needed for taller varieties and Brussels sprouts might need staking. Beet is a good plant for the seaside and so is asparagus, a native of the sandy coasts all around Britain. Near the coast it is possible, owing to the absence of severe frosts, to grow early potatoes, if a sheltered part of the garden is available. Carrots and parsnips can be grown, also leeks. The dwarf outdoor tomato called 'The Amateur' is a worthwhile crop, especially in a hot summer, but one of the vegetables which is sure to give a good account of itself is sea-kale. This plant is found wild on most of the sea coasts of Western Europe and it grows in abundance on the shingle in East Sussex. It is possible to dig up crowns of wild sea-kale and cultivate them in a seaside garden.

SOIL TESTING

Let me first of all describe what is meant by humus. Humus is decayed or decaying organic matter found in the soil. Mostly of vegetable origin, with some animal, it is the centre of bacterial activity leading to the general well-being of the soil. A test to show if any or very little humus is present in your soil is as follows:

1. Place some soil collected from various parts of the garden into a jam jar.

2. Add a quantity of solution of caustic potash to cover the soil (one part of potash to ten parts of water).

3. If mixture turns black humus is present, otherwise it is absent. Caustic potash can be obtained from the chemist.

After humus, lime is a big soil improver. It can provide a good texture and help in general fertility. It corrects acidity, breaks up clay particles (allowing for better drainage), liberates other plant foods and checks fungoid diseases. The disease of club-root in the brassica family is not found in chalky soils. There are several tests for lime deficiency which the amateur gardener can carry out for himself. Throughout this book I shall refer to the relevant scientific matters in a simple manner, which I hope every reader will fully understand. The simplest way to test for soil acidity or alkalinity is by using the B.D.H. (British Drug House) Soil Indicator. This is in addition to taking note of the indicator weeds. The indicator is obtainable from any good chemist's shop. It consists of a porcelain boat with two sections and a bottle of soil-indicating liquid. The largest section of the boat is filled with the garden soil which is to be tested and then the indicator is added to the soil drop by drop. When the boat is tilted the liquid drains from the soil into the smaller section. By looking at the colour of the liquid we can quickly tell the degree of acidity or alkalinity of our soil.

1. A red colour shows a strongly acid soil.

2. An orange colour shows moderate acid.

3. A green colour shows a neutral soil.

4. A blue colour shows an alkaline soil.

(An alkali is the opposite of an acid.)

Practical application can be made from the knowledge gained by the soil testing. Having decided on the crops we wish to grow we now know whether to lime heavily, moderately or not to lime.

The term pH is always used when the chemistry of the garden is under discussion. It is only a shorthand way of expressing the degree of acidity or alkalinity. For example, the pH of pure water is 7. The pH of all acids is denoted by numbers less than 7, whilst the pH of alkalines is by figures greater than 7.

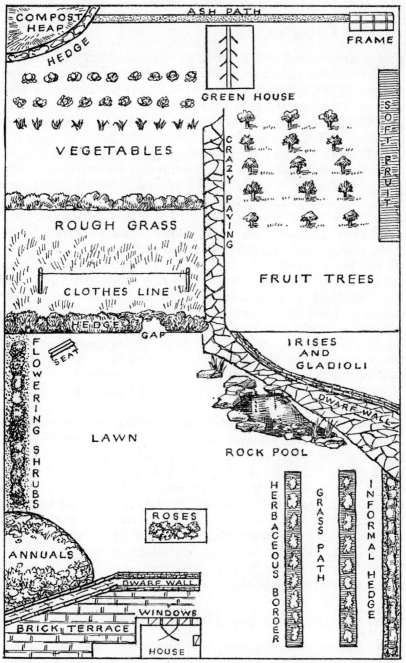

MAKE A PLAN ON PAPER

The Garden Plan

THE GARDEN PLAN

Having decided which of the soils we have and what we can grow in our particular soil we are ready for the drawn plan. No one plan will suit all the readers of this book, so I shall concern myself with some of the main features of a garden and hope to give some useful guidance. Before beginning to draw up our plan on paper we must know our garden measurements in feet, we must decide on any parts to be levelled, and we must know the aspect. We can then proceed to mark in the main features, remembering to reserve for early crops a border which is warm and sheltered. If we are taking over some established garden we can mark in that which we wish to retain and that which we wish to dispose of. The least productive area, which is out of sight of the house, will be used for compost heaps, sheds, pea-stick storage, stakes, pots and potting soil. We will put in the permanent main parts such as the herbaceous border, shrub border, lawns, paths, orchard, rockery and a large piece devoid of trees and shrubs suitable for vegetable growing. Do not have a water garden or ponds if you are one of those people who are greatly allergic to mosquito bites. These insects can take a great deal of pleasure out of the work we like to do during the summer evenings. Never discourage insect-eating birds such as swallows, house-martins and spotted flycatchers from nesting on your property. They are invaluable for destroying large numbers of harmful insects which infest the garden.

We want to try to arrange our garden so that the best views are from the living-room windows. We shall require good paths from the kitchen to the vegetable site. When considering grass-land it is important to remember that the lady of the house will need a good drying spot, hidden from view, on which to have her clothes-line erected. This spot will need to be firm and dry underfoot so that a large amount of mud is not brought into the house after she has hung out the washing. The completed plan can be altered and improved as the garden develops and it usually takes a year or so before a planner is satisfied that he possesses a garden of which he can be proud, without reservations.

HOW TO DEAL WITH ROUGH LAND

If you have taken over a newly-built house, sometimes the disorder left in the garden by the builder can be very bad. All kinds of rubbish may be scattered over the surface of the garden site. You can remove the old paint tins, buckets, and odd timber without much trouble, but there may be innumerable articles buried beneath the surface, such as old piping, lumps of concrete, bricks and broken glass. Do not be tempted to cover the whole with soil and sow a few annual flower seeds to hide the ugliness. You must dig over your site and remove all rubbish systematically. It will probably take you a long time but you will be very pleased with your work in the end. It is only when this task has been completed that the garden can be planned, levelled, dug and manured.

If you have a lot of rough grass you can either borrow a rotary or other motor scythe or cut it with a sickle. Few people will know how to use a hand scythe these days. Using a hand scythe is very laborious work unless one is used to it. If you are using a sickle or rip-hook it would be best to choose one of the long-handled type as these are much less tiring to work with. Have a good sharpening stone with you and use it frequently. As with digging, try not to do too much to start with. Do not take hold of tufts of long grass with the hands and then make a fierce stroke with the sickle; this is much too dangerous. Use a hooked stick, not your bare hands, for this purpose. Small trees and brushwood can be removed by sawing down and grubbing out the roots. Very large trees are best dealt with by experienced tree-fellers. After sawing away the side branches they grip the main trunk with chains and with the aid of heavy machinery and various types of winch, drag the tree out of the ground. (If you have several trees for removal it would be best to get an estimate for the work to be done.)

If the land to be cleared is almost covered with large thorn bushes and scrub it would be best to enlist the aid of a friendly farmer. Three ropes may be wound round three separate bushes and a tractor may pull out the whole simultaneously. Bulldozers can be used for levelling, and for getting out small bushes a mattock hoe is a useful implement.

The first crops grown on such reclaimed land are generally potatoes, known as a 'cleaning crop'. This does not mean that the good old potato actually cleans the ground. It means that by growing a good crop of potatoes, you are automatically cleaning the land by the many cultivating operations required. First you dig and plant, disturbing many weeds in the process. Then you flat hoe and bank hoe and finally harvest your crop, at the same time disposing of any weeds. Also during the growing season the potato haulms or foliage do a certain amount of smothering of surface weeds.

A word or two for those who may be taking over very old neglected gardens. These days many old estates are being divided up into various plots when the large house is split up into flats. Each flat dweller is often allotted some part of the former large garden. On his acquired piece of land the new owner may find some permanent features that are worth reclaiming. Lawns, orchards and borders which are so overgrown that they are hardly distinguishable are often met with. It will sometimes be difficult to bring these features back to something like their former glory. Neglected lawns can be cut early in spring by hand or motor scythe. Further treatment should consist of seeding any bare patches and hand weeding. Follow this up by monthly applications of lawn sand containing sulphate of iron and sulphate of ammonia. It is very important not to use selective killers if the subsequent mowings are going to be used for compost. Soon, with regular cutting and rolling, the lawn will begin to take shape. Often a first-class lawn can be obtained in this way without all the work entailed in digging it all up and re-seeding. Overgrown borders need to be forked over very carefully and slowly, keeping a look-out for any choice or rare plants that may be there. All the very old, overgrown and weak specimens should be disposed of.

Many fruit trees found in an old orchard may not be worth keeping; they may be diseased, the fruit might be of poor quality, and the whole site might be better cleared and used for a vegetable plot. Sometimes, however, some very good trees may be growing there: perhaps a 'Gascoyne's Scarlet', one of the best eating apples I know, or a 'Devonshire Quarrendon', two varieties which seem unobtainable today. Some of these fruit trees will need drastic surgery. All ingrowing, weak and tangled branches must be removed and the cuts treated with lead paint. Often with these large houses, which have the flats adjoining, one has to erect some sort of fencing for privacy. A wattle or interlaced board fencing usually fits into the landscape and offers some shelter if one wants to sit outside and enjoy the garden view.

THE BEST WAY TO DIG THE PLOT

We must dig and pulverize the soil so that free circulation of water and air may be assured. What we actually do by digging is to expose fresh portions of soil to the action of frost, rain, wind, alternations of heat and cold, atmospheric oxygen and carbonic acid. The effect of these weathering agents is seen in the most striking manner on ground which has been dug in the autumn and left with a rough surface. This soil can be raked into so fine a tilth that without any further cultivation the most minute of seeds can be sown in the spring.

There are many other advantages of digging; the chief of these is the burying of grass and weeds which will rot and turn into valuable plant food. Digging exposes many pests on to the surface where they are soon devoured by birds. We are able to put our compost or farmyard manure into the bottom of the trench as we proceed.

Any piece of new ground, or a piece that has been neglected, will need double-digging. This means that it will need to be dug two spade depths. (One spade depth is the length of the blade sunk into the soil.) There is no need to dig any deeper except for growing such special crops as sweet peas.

We begin our digging by taking out a trench two feet wide and two spade depths deep. Fill the wheelbarrow with this soil and take it to the end of the plot where the digging will finish. We must keep this same width of trench in front of us throughout the whole process. The reason for this is to enable all the top weeds and turf to be buried in the bottom of the trench with ease. After the first trench has been opened up it is best to take another two feet width and proceed to thrust the end of the spade blade into the top turf making an indentation all along the row. Then, standing in the trench, cut back to the indentation by skimming off all the top turf and weeds; place them earth-side up into the bottom of the trench. Then, facing the trench, turn over with the spade all the remaining soil up to the indentation line into the trench and on top of the upturned turf. If, after the first trench has been taken out, the sub-soil at the bottom is very hard, then it could with advantage to the roots of any following crop be broken up with a garden fork. Just dig along the trench with the fork; this will greatly assist with drainage. You will proceed in like manner until you have reached the end of the plot, then fill in the final trench with the soil you deposited there from the wheelbarrow. Some people might find it easier to face the trench when skimming off the top turf or even standing sideways. As the digging proceeds the roots of perennial weeds must be removed, also any harmful pests can be destroyed. The work is made easier if a basket is handy for putting these roots into before wheeling them away to be burnt. While digging do not slice off too big a lump of soil at a time and then find it too heavy to lift into the trench. Be sure you hold the spade correctly. Place the left hand downwards and grip lightly, using the right hand as a lever and pushing downwards when lifting the laden spade. Push the blade down into the soil in an upright position and not at an angle. Do not rush at the job, work steadily and slowly. Leave some for the next day but make sure you do dig the next day if the weather is suitable. When you feel you have had enough for one day, clean your tools and pack them away in the toolshed. Many a newcomer to digging has rushed at the job and has soon caught a chill or contracted lumbago. When taking a rest between labours put on your jacket or pullover. Do not stand about with a perspiring body exposed to a cold wind; this is the easiest way of becoming a sufferer from lumbago.

If there are no surface weeds or turf, good garden compost or farmyard manure can be placed into the bottom of the trench instead. Try to keep the plot level as you proceed; if you find you are getting into little hills and dales stop for a while and do a little levelling with the garden fork.

On a new plot it is best to dig in the autumn so that the frosts of winter can pulverize and sweeten it. Success depends upon tilling the soil when it is in the right condition. Do not try to dig when it is very wet or very dry. If you take it at the right moment your task will be a pleasant, enjoyable exercise in the fresh air.

A word about suitable clothing for digging may be included at this point. Do not dig for long periods wearing Wellington rubber boots. The blade of the spade will cut into the rubber soles and spoil an expensive pair of rubbers in no time. Also they tend to make the feet perspire overmuch and make the feet sore and the legs ache. The best possible footwear for digging is a pair of ordinary Army boots. If these are regularly dubbined, and soled and heeled from time to time, they will last a lifetime. Wear a pair of old, strong trousers which are loosely fitting to allow plenty of movement, and tuck the bottoms into your socks.

2

Tools and Equipment

Selecting suitable tools and how to use them — other tools and appliances — mechanical cultivators — layout of the toolshed — maintenance of tools — garden furniture

The old saying, 'A bad workman always blames his tools', does not seem to fit in where gardening is concerned. For good work in the garden can only be carried out with the best tools which the gardener can afford. A set of essential garden tools need not be too expensive. There is no need to buy stainless steel or chromium-plated implements unless the gardener so wishes. The tools which the gardener must have for a start are two spades, a fork, a rake, three hoes, a trowel, a dibber, a pair of secateurs, a sickle and sharpening stone, a garden line, a pair of shears, edging shears, lawn mower, watering-can, wheelbarrow and a syringe. Only a fussy gardener will insist on a large variety of tools. This list can be added to as the need arises. If really good-quality tools are purchased at the outset they can last almost a lifetime.

It is very important to choose tools which will absolutely suit the user in weight, shape and length. How often have we seen a short, slightly-built man working on his allotment with a huge spade which looks as though it were made for a giant? If the workman is using unsuitable tools he is making the work twice as hard for himself.

When selecting tools from the shop, lift them, examine them, and then go through the motions which you will use when working with them in the garden. Try several of each sort in this way, until you have found those which will suit you the best. Think mostly about the weight when choosing spades and forks and about length of handles when selecting hoes and rakes. All the tools purchased should be those made by well-known manufacturers. I have a spade which has been in continuous use for the past fifteen years, and it is almost as good today as when it came from the shop.

The spade for turning over and trenching rough land and for many other digging operations should have a smooth handle made of ash, and the blade should have a flange or ridge on top so that the instep of the boot will not be cut into when the gardener thrusts the blade into the soil with his foot. The blade should be $7\frac{1}{2}$ inches in width and 11 inches in length. I have purposely mentioned the necessity for having two spades and I recommend the second smaller one as the best tool in existence for planting potatoes, assisting with bank hoeing, lifting out small plants and general transplanting. It also should possess a smooth ash handle and the blade should be $6\frac{1}{2}$ inches wide and 9 inches long. It is a much lighter tool than the first spade mentioned.

The best all-round purpose garden fork is the one known by various names, such as border fork, boy's fork or lady's fork. This, as most other tools, has an ash handle and should have pointed tines $6\frac{1}{2}$ inches of total tine-width and 10 inches in length. This is a light-weight tool and is used for lifting potatoes, levelling land, forking over borders, spreading compost or manure, and for putting garden rubbish, weeds and compost into the wheelbarrow. It can be used for digging purposes after the garden has been initially dug with a spade.

The rake should have a 6-foot handle. For normal garden use a twelve-toothed rake will be sufficient. The teeth should be riveted to an iron bar with the ends slightly curved. Avoid buying a rake which has the head, teeth and the piece which fits on to the handle, all made in one section. These soon buckle and bend and the teeth close together. The rake is used for raking stones from rough land, raking up hoed-off weeds, preparing seed beds and levelling soil. The best use is made of the rake when it is employed for making a fine tilth on the seed bed preparatory to seed sowing. Do not dig the teeth of the rake too deeply into the soil. The rake should glide lightly through the earth and it should be pushed and pulled. It will take a lot of practice for the gardener to gain a good eye for levelling when using this tool. After a while he will be able to use it for a variety of jobs with great skill.

The three hoes which will be found necessary are the draw hoe, the Dutch hoe and the 'onion', or short-handled hoe.

The draw hoe has an upright blade set at right angles to the handle. The handle should be about $5\frac{1}{2}$ feet or longer depending upon the height of the user. The draw hoe is used with the gardener walking forwards as with a chopping or dragging action he cuts off large weeds. It is also used for making seed drills and for earthing up potatoes and other plants.

The Dutch hoe is one of the most useful gardening tools ever invented. It should have a length of handle to suit the user's height.

There are many widths of blade and the worker will be able to choose the width which suits his purpose. A most useful width is $4\frac{1}{2}$ inches. When using a Dutch hoe the blade should be parallel to the ground. This time the work is done by proceeding backwards and the hoe is glided through all the small weeds, cutting them off at ground level. The soil is filled with pockets of air and water, and much of this water is drawn to the surface by the capillary action of the sun and atmosphere. If the tube-like structures carrying the moisture to the surface are cut off with the hoe and blocked by a film of soil, then much moisture is conserved. This condition will be brought about by the constant use of the Dutch hoe. Whether weeds are present or not the hoe should be in action especially during very dry weather. This incessant work saves much watering and is very beneficial to plant life. It prevents weeds getting a hold, and helps to aerate the soil.

The 'onion hoe', so called because of its suitability for weeding onion beds, is a short-handled swan-necked hoe. It is best used when one is kneeling on a piece of sacking or other material and working among seed-beds. It can be used where the distance between rows of plants is quite narrow. It is used in conjunction with hand weeding when seedlings are small. Firstly work forwards, scraping the soil and cutting all weeds off at ground level close to the sides of the plants. The weeds should then be gathered up to the ends of the rows with the aid of the hoe and taken to the compost heap. The weeding is carefully completed by hand, by pulling out the weeds between each seedling. All hoes need to have a sharp cutting edge, and in particular the 'onion' hoe.

The trowel is used for transplanting and for carrying small plants a short distance. It is also useful for mixing potting soil and for filling pots and seed boxes. The short-handled one is preferable. It needs to have plenty of strength in the metal part where the blade joins the handle. Its main use is for transplanting, especially for bedding plants and sweet peas. The correct depth and width of planting hole can easily be made. After planting and hand firming of the soil around the plant the trowel can be turned upside down and the handle used for further ramming of the earth. Finish the planting by making a shallow depression round the plant so that when watering in, the water will run into the centre and not away to waste.

The dibber is like a short spade handle with a rounded end. Do not have a pointed end. It is used for making planting holes and for making the soil round the transplanted subjects very firm. Wooden dibbers are preferable to trowels for some jobs because they are quicker in action, especially in loose soil. They are particularly well suited for planting out cabbages and Brussels sprouts. It is important to make the hole for receiving the plant roughly the same diameter all the way to the bottom, and to make a flat bottom. Do not leave the plant suspended, let it rest firmly on the base. Complete by firming with the dibber. Any broken spade or fork handle can quickly be made into an excellent dibber.

The most useful secateurs are those of the 'Rolcut' type with a removable blade. These should be kept sharp and well oiled.

The short-handled sickle can be used if preferred, but the long-handled one makes the work easier as there is less stooping. When using the sickle for cutting long grass or weeds do not bring the blade too near to the legs. Great care must be taken when sharpening the sickle; it needs constant sharpening while in use. Do not let children use it, or any inexperienced or irresponsible person.

A garden-line can easily be made from a medium-thickness clothes-line and two stout pieces of wood creosoted for preservation and sharpened to a point for insertion into the ground. Make sure the line is long enough for all widths of the various plots on the garden or allotment and do not leave it outside to rot.

Garden shears will need to be of fairly good weight and made of good-quality steel if they are to be used for hedge trimming as well as for grass clipping. The central bolt and nut must be of a good design and strong, for ease of tightening and for wear. There is nothing more exasperating in the garden than trying to cut through tough grass with a pair of shears when the blades do not meet in a proper manner. It is very useful to have at the bottom of the blades a semi-circular nick which is sharpened and which will act as a pruner when any really thick branches are encountered in the process of hedge trimming.

Long-handled edging shears seem essential when the garden contains a lot of lawn and many flower beds. It is tiring and it causes back strain if a large amount of lawn edge trimming is done with short-handled hand shears. With the long-handled edging shears it is possible to do the job in a semi-upright position which is far less tiring. It is very important that these shears should be of extra good quality as the blades come into contact with lumps of soil, tough grass and stones. Poor blades are soon deflected and become useless.

Lawn mowers will be described and discussed in Chapter 9, 'Lawns and Grassland'.

It is best when choosing a watering-can to have one which can be used for a variety of watering requirements. One made of strong galvanized metal, and with a long spout and a cross-bar as well as a handle, is the best type. It can be used in the greenhouse and cold frame to reach high plants and those at the back of the staging. It can be easily dipped into a tank. Several 'roses' will be required. A rose is a metal attachment which is screwed on to the end of the spout;

some have very tiny holes punched in them for creating a mist-like spray of water over boxes of tiny seedlings; others have larger holes for use where a greater amount of water is needed. These cans should be rinsed out thoroughly after being used for any poisonous liquid. They should be stood upside-down to drain after use or hung up in a safe position, where they will not be knocked continuously and so become punctured.

There are many types of wheelbarrows and garden transport on the market. Wooden wheelbarrows with movable backs (a piece of wood which lifts out just where the handles begin) are the most useful. In this type the potting soil, pots, manure or other material can more easily be removed from the barrow. The wheel should have a pneumatic tyre so that the barrow can be easily moved without leaving marks on lawn, path or garden plot. The wheel bearings need constant oiling. If a galvanized iron or other metal type is chosen it is important not to have one which is too heavy for the user. Often these large iron barrows are quite weighty even before anything has been put into them. Wooden barrows should be painted or creosoted regularly, and all barrows and other transport should be stored under cover.

Many other forms of garden transport can be devised. A good stout box mounted on the axle and wheels of an old push-chair or perambulator, with handles fixed to the sides of the box, makes a good conveyance for old flower stalks, weeds and general garden rubbish destined for the compost heap.

A hand garden syringe, usually made of copper, is often the only spraying equipment necessary. It is used for spraying roses against greenfly and black spot, for spraying the few fruit trees the garden may have and for spraying potatoes against potato blight.

Pieces of useful garden material which townsfolk can collect are a few of the empty containers which have held washing-up liquid. Those which have screw tops make very good syringes for spraying the rose bushes. Take off the lid and fill with spray, replace the lid and squeeze the sides of the container; a nice thin jet of spray will result. This saves buying a garden syringe when there is only a small amount of spraying to be done.

OTHER TOOLS AND APPLIANCES

In addition to the essential tools the gardener may from time to time feel the need for some others, not strictly necessary but of great help in certain situations.

A tool known as a hand cultivator is sometimes very useful on heavy land. It is used like a draw hoe. It has three or four prongs instead of a blade, and is most usefully employed where the land is baked hard and difficult for hoeing. If one should take over a piece of land which has been 'rough' dug (where some weeds have been buried and some not) it is a very good tool for levelling this land and dragging out the weeds. It may also be used for breaking down and tilling the soil where there are many hard lumps of soil, or for bank-hoeing potatoes.

A pruning knife and a sharp penknife will be often in demand, also a pair of long-bladed scissors for cutting flowers for the house and for cutting away dead flower heads.

A half-moon shaped tool called an edger is used for making a nice clean cut to the edge of the lawn where it meets flower border or path.

A long-handled tree pruner may be required where there are many established fruit trees. It has a curved head which can be hooked over branches and the blade is operated by a lever at the end of the handle.

Everyone appreciates the need for a good garden broom or two. A sound all-purpose broom can be obtained with bristles of tapering whalebone, ideal for lawns or paths. An ordinary birch broom or besom will do a lot of good work on a lawn but will soon wear away. For terraces of brick or stone, tarmac drives, crazy paving or concrete surfaces an ordinary stiff-bristled yard broom is best.

A hose pipe is often required where there is a large garden. Rubber ones are best although the plastic ones are serviceable if handled and packed with care. They all need a good attachment where the hose fixes to the tap. Never leave a hose scattered all over the garden for long periods; this causes the rubber or plastic to deteriorate. Dispose of the surplus water lying in the pipe, coil up the hose and hang up in a convenient spot away from direct heat.

TOOLS WHICH CAN BE MADE AT HOME AND ELSEWHERE

Very many useful gardening tools can be made at home by the gardener himself. A good handyman with a set of efficient tools can soon make himself several wooden cold frames. He can make tool racks for the garden shed; can make the whole of his required stock of wooden labels and paint them white. Window boxes, wooden spade scrapers, garden lines, measuring sticks and baskets are other items which come to mind.

If the keen gardener has a son who attends a secondary modern school where metalwork is on the curriculum, he can obtain many very well-made garden tools from this source, by persuading the son to make them himself during metalwork lessons. These are much cheaper to purchase than if they came from a shop, because there is no middleman, no transport or other extra costs involved. I have seen some very fine tools made in school workshops. They are often better made and stronger than those obtainable from a shop. Being of hand work, they can often be made to the gardener's own design. Tools which can be made at schools are onion hoes, ornamental brackets for hanging baskets, hand cultivators, Dutch hoes, draw hoes, metal garden lines, trowels, hand forks, scrapers and half-moon edging irons. Wooden grass rakes can be made in the wood-work room.

MECHANICAL CULTIVATORS

Today there is a bewildering list of mechanical aids for the gardener. In a recent catalogue I saw thirty-six different types of motor lawn mower and twenty-five types of powered cultivator.

When you are thinking of buying a garden motorized cultivator there are several points to consider seriously. Is your garden large enough? Is the saving in time and labour sufficient to warrant the initial cost? What about cost of petrol, oil, maintenance and repairs? Are the various attachments fitted easily and quickly? Will it be too heavy for a lady or some less robust helper to operate if the regular user is unable to use it for a time? Will it have frequent use or stand idle for long periods? Does it require much mechanical knowledge and skill? Is there a suitable shed in which to keep it?

I will comment on each question in turn. It is no use purchasing a mechanical cultivator unless you possess a large garden where long rows of plants either way can be grown. You need plenty of room at the end of each row to enable you to turn and come back up the next one. This applies when tackling mechanical hoeing, digging between rows or loosening and aerating the soil. Some cultivators have a reverse gear to enable you to get out of trouble if you run into a hedge or something of similar nature; these gears are not much used, however, in actual practice. You must measure the width of the widest part of your cultivator, add a few more inches to avoid over-hanging foliage, and then plant accordingly. This should be the rule down and across so that you can get between the plants either way without cutting them off or trampling them underfoot.

If the owner of a large garden cannot spare enough time to devote to his land, he might well consider a powered cultivator. He must decide between two alternatives: whether it will be best to employ a man to help him for a few hours per week, or to buy a cultivator. It must be pointed out that a cultivator will not tackle virgin soil or unploughed grassland. Neither will any rotary cultivator do a digging job as well as a man with a spade. A cultivator will not stop and pick out the roots of perennial weeds, it just churns them over and over. It often leaves a hard pan of earth at the bottom of its digging depth and, of course, a man with a spade can go much deeper.

A rotary cultivator does very good work on land which has been previously ploughed by a friendly farmer. It can provide a very good seed bed on land that has been well cleaned, and it is good for hoeing off annual weeds between rows of plants. When making a seed bed it is best, first of all, to run over the land using the first gear; this is the slowest speed and it enables the rotating tines to dig well into the soil and break it up. An excellent tilth, ready to receive the seed, can be gained if, in order to complete the operation, the cultivator is run over the bed several times at top speed and set at a shallow depth.

It is a good plan to find out how much work can be done with the cultivator best suited for your particular purpose, on a gallon of petrol. Discover how much oil is used and the likely running costs, then weigh this against a man's wages. Then a final decision is more easily made.

Some of the many attachments which can be fitted to a mechanical cultivator may be required. A cutter-bar to be fitted to the front for cutting long grass is a most likely one. Here one has to consider simplicity and speed of removal and attachment. On some machines very heavy rotary equipment has to be lifted from the rear of the machine before the cutter-bar can be assembled on to the front. Often the nuts and bolts are in very inaccessible positions. It generally requires the efforts of two men to lift off the heavy machinery. On other machines the job is done much more quickly and easily, often by merely unscrewing one nut at the front of the machine. Again, with some machines, the parts most likely to break down are in such awkward positions that the engineer can attend to them only with difficulty.

The weight and durability of the equipment are important points to think about. Many machines are well-balanced, and in their case the weight is not unduly noticed. When choosing a machine the age, strength and agility of the purchaser have to be considered. One which all adult members of a family can use will be more satisfactory than a heavy cumbersome machine. These are difficult to use on sloping ground.

Most engines can be started easily if the cultivator is attended to in a routine manner. No powered equipment should ever be left outside when not in use, but should be stored in a dry shed or garage. Petrol should be put into the tank through a wire gauze-filter. Do not work the machine during wet weather. All working parts must be regularly oiled. Keep the engine and gear oils to the correct level at all times.

Drain the sump and replenish at frequent intervals. Inspect and clean the air filter. Only in very cold weather is the choke needed and the 'tickler' rarely needs to be operated. No engine really needs to have the carburettor flooded. If the engine fails to start after the attention suggested, the probable cause is moisture on the sparking plug insulator which will short-circuit the current. Wipe the plug with a dry, non-fluffy cloth. There is usually a book of instructions issued with each machine, and these should be followed carefully. If the machine has been lying idle for some time, and starting difficulties have arisen, it is a good plan to stand the machine outside in strong sunlight for a couple of hours. The warmth of the sun will often dry out all parts and the machine will then start without trouble.

Once a machine has been acquired it will want plenty of use if the initial cost is to be worth while. Cultivators soon depreciate in value if left idle; and if the owner wants to sell the machine eventually as second-hand, a big loss could be incurred.

After use the machine should be well cleaned. Weeds such as long grass and bindweed often twine around the axles and in between the axle and wheels; these can be removed with a long, sharp-pointed knife.

Before purchasing a machine study all the foregoing points carefully and try to make sure you have the right type of machine for your particular garden and purpose. Beware of high-pressure salesmen who will try to convince you that the particular machine they are trying to sell is the right one for you. Go and see for yourself several different machines in action and handle them yourself, preferably on your own land.

Another mechanical device which a gardener will find very useful is an electric hedge trimmer. This is for the person with a considerable length of well-grown hedges and who can afford the outlay. There are two kinds of electrical trimmer: one with reciprocating blades, and another which has a chain of cutter-blades that move at high speed round a guide bar. The latter embodies the same principle as the chain saw used for timber cutting.

LAYOUT AND CONTENTS OF TOOLSHED

Every gardener requires a good toolshed. It need not be a very large one, for many tools can be stored in a small space if they are hung on the shed wall with each tool in its allotted position.

It is desirable to have all the forks together, then all the spades and so on: it is then easy to see if any tool is missing. Such sharp tools as sickles or pruning implements should be out of the reach of children. Any poisons which have to be used in the garden are better locked away in a separate container. Raffia can be hung on a hook for easy access. Soft tying string, tarred string, thin wire, nails, staples, and a sharpening stone are best kept in a drawer in the shed table or in a wooden box.

A small table is very useful if there is room in the shed. Small jobs such as painting of labels or even pricking-out of seedlings can be done here. Seed boxes can also be stacked on a table neatly. Some white paint, putty and turpentine and a paint brush should be found in a toolshed for renovation of cold frames and the greenhouse.

Some garden trug baskets, which are baskets of convenient shape with a handle and two stout pieces of wood fixed to the bottom, can be used for carrying vegetables or flowers. Seed boxes may be used for the same purpose, or cardboard mushroom boxes with metal handles, or any strong box which may be to hand.

The gardener will need plenty of labels. Stout wooden ones painted white and clearly lettered with one of the flow-type waterproof felt-tipped pens with a fine point are most suitable for the herbaceous border. Smaller metal ones with the name of the variety scratched on, and which can be wired to the plant, are best for roses, trees and shrubs. Small wooden white-painted ones very clearly marked with some indelible ink which is waterproof and fadeless will be the ones for seed beds. It is most frustrating when the gardener comes to transplanting time and finds the names of his varieties all washed away by rainfall. This is especially the case when he is growing many varieties of cabbage and cauliflower and is not sufficiently experienced to recognize them by the variations in foliage.

Every good gardener keeps a notebook and pencil handy in the toolshed. Very many observations which he will make in his garden from year to year will be invaluable in future years.

An oil can and waste oil and rags are obvious occupants of a toolshed. If a heavy lawn mower or cultivator is kept in a shed the floor will have to be of concrete or extra-strong material of some kind. Petrol is best stored away from wooden buildings.

MAINTENANCE AND CLEANLINESS OF TOOLS

Keep the toolshed clean and tidy. Give it a brush out with the stiff broom from time to time. Very many gardeners will be able to make for themselves wooden scrapers for use with dirty spades. One needs to be taken to the allotment or garden when any work with the spade or fork is in process. Edges of hoes and spades should be kept sharp with a coarse file. Rakes must never be put into such a position that their teeth can be readily trodden upon.

Broken tools need to be repaired or disposed of frequently.

Nothing looks worse than a toolshed littered with broken equipment. A little welding can often make a damaged tool almost as good as new. Tools should only be used for the purpose for which they were intended. Never try to heave up huge boulders with a spade or fork, it will soon become bent and useless for digging.

All metal parts of tools should be thoroughly cleaned and dried and then smeared with oil before being put away. Waste engine oil is admirable for this purpose. Seed boxes which have been well cleaned and left to dry in the sun can be stacked away one on top of another on the shed table or other suitable position.

With the gardener who raises his own bedding plants, there is always the problem of securing enough seed boxes for his needs. One cheap source of supply is the local fishmonger; you can usually obtain plenty of very suitable seed boxes from him. These boxes have contained kippers, herrings and sometimes other fish, so they sometimes need washing to destroy the smell; but very often they are usable just as they are. The local fishmonger will often deliver a large quantity for a small charge.

Other supplies can be obtained from any local travelling greengrocer. These are boxes which have contained soft fruit and tomatoes. Often boxes with corner pieces that rise above the sides, which are ideal for potato sprouting, can be collected in this way. Boxes of many kinds, so useful to the gardener, can be obtained from canteens where food is delivered in bulk. From these three sources of supply, wooden boxes can be obtained either free or at a very small charge. If these boxes are not collected by the gardener they are only used for firewood, which seems such a waste of useful material.

If you buy bedding plants, wash out and save the seed boxes for your own use. Preserve all boxes you can obtain by washing them out after use, drying them in the sun and storing them under cover.

GARDEN FURNITURE

During the summer months what is more pleasant than a meal in the garden? Usually a tall hedge on the north side and some sort of shelter on the east side are necessary for privacy and comfort. If there are no hedges or suitable trees for shelter then it is worth while erecting a trellis covered with a creeper.

When a good sheltered spot has been selected some chairs and tables which suit the surroundings will have to be found. These can often be purchased cheaply from a second-hand dealer or from an auction room. They can be made of suitable height by sawing down the legs. If given a coat of paint of pastel green, grey or white a very attractive set of garden furniture will have been produced.

Three or four deck chairs are always welcome. It is very easy to renew the canvas from time to time and to keep the woodwork brightly painted. Never leave them out in the rain.

Garden seats look very inviting if placed in the right setting. In a woodland scene they look best if of a rustic design made of lengths of log with the bark left on. If a seat is near the house it can be constructed of the same material as the walls of the dwelling. If there are plenty of wrought iron fences or gates nearby, then a seat of iron construction would be suitable. In formal parts of the garden, seats can be more obvious. At the end of a lawn bordered by many-coloured herbaceous flowers or bright annuals, a conspicuous white-painted wooden seat can look very effective.

3

Manures and Composts

The only manures needed — making a compost heap — saving of kitchen refuse — a few insecticides and pesticides — friends and foes — plant diseases

Why do we manure the soil? Because manure is a plant food, and a plant must have food, moisture and air in order to live, grow and come to maturity. Nature strives to build up the humus content of the soil year after year and particularly at leaf-fall. So if we follow nature by adding organic matter we shall not go far wrong. Why do we need such a large quantity of compost or farmyard manure—a good dressing of well rotted manure is dug in at the rate of a good barrow-load to ten square yards?—because this manure has to be broken down and diluted to a liquid form. A plant can only take in liquid food from the soil through the very minute root-hairs.

Plants extract from the soil each year all the food they need and the gardener must replace that which has been taken out. Some plants take more of one sort of food than another, and some plants (legumes) give back plant food to the soil while they are growing upon it. This situation is balanced by practising a system called crop rotation. This means, simply, that we sow or plant crops which need the unwanted food left in the soil by the previous occupants. In order to achieve this objective, we move crops to a different part of the plot each year. The gardener need not worry too much about having a complicated plan of crop rotation: the important things to remember are not to have brassicas (members of the cabbage family) growing on the same piece of land year after year because of risk of club-root disease; to follow beans and peas with leaf-forming plants to take advantage of the nitrogen left in the soil by them; and to move potatoes around. Years ago gardeners thought it best to grow onions and shallots on the same site year after year. It is best, however, to move these crops to a new position each year in order to discourage the fungus diseases called Onion Downy Mildew and Onion White Rot.

Throughout this book the emphasis will be on the use of organic rather than artificial manures. The main organic manure for our purpose will be well-made garden compost with the addition of farmyard manure if obtainable. The only artificial manures which we may need are those used as activators for our compost heaps.

The three main plant foods are nitrogen, phosphates and potash. Good garden compost will supply all the plant foods as well as providing moisture-retentive material. Sometimes we may have to use other organic manures as supplements to the compost, as top dressings, and as quick-acting fertilizers.

Nitrogen helps to speed growth and is an essential element for the production of leaves and stems. Phosphates encourage flowers and fruit, promote ripening and help with root growth. Potash gives good colour and flavour and assists healthy growth.

Just as we need vitamins to keep us healthy so there are many other plant foods which the crops need in minute quantities. These are known as trace elements. If the garden is regularly manured with some form of organic manure these trace elements will nearly always be present. They are boron, cobalt, copper, iron, magnesium, manganese, sulphur and zinc.

The organic manures to use in addition to the two most important ones (compost and farmyard manure) are as follows: poultry manure, rabbit manure, wool shoddy, hop manure, seaweed, fish manure, guano, bone meal, soot, wood ashes and dried blood.

Poultry manure is rich in all the plant foods. It is best used when dry and should be stored in a bin. It is very concentrated and must be used with great care. Its most useful contribution to the manuring programme is its suitability as an activator on the compost heap. Owing to the great increase in poultry keeping today this valuable manure is fairly easily obtained. Many owners of deep-litter houses are glad when someone offers to take it away, and they will often let them have it free of charge.

Only those who keep a few rabbits will have a sufficient quantity of rabbit droppings, and these are best used on the compost heap as an accelerator.

People living in the north of England can sometimes obtain waste products from the woollen trade known as wool shoddy. It should be free from oil. It will take a long time to rot down and is best heaped separately and then mixed with the compost heap gradually as it decomposes.

Different organic manures can be obtained in different parts of the country. In Kent and around the Alton district of Hampshire much hop manure is available. This is the vegetable material left behind after the beer has been made. It contains some nitrogen but hardly any potash or phosphate. It may be dug in during autumn or spring and it makes a good top dressing or a mulch as it is light in texture.

Seaweed, sometimes obtainable on the coast if permission to collect has been given, is a very good manure. It can be used fresh as a substitute for compost or dried as a fertilizer. It contains a certain amount of potash and is good for potatoes. This is why it is collected and much used in the Channel Islands, where early potatoes and tomatoes are grown on a large scale.

Fish manure is generally used as a fertilizer and is excellent for a top dressing for fruit trees in the spring. It should be lightly raked into the surface. It is very rich in nitrogen and phosphate but not in potash; sometimes this is added in manufacture.

Guano, which is really an accumulation of sea-bird excrement, is a very concentrated fertilizer and needs to be used with caution. It can be used as a top dressing, but not at a more liberal rate than three ounces to the square yard. It is expensive and although it gives a good supply of nitrogen over a long period, pigeon manure, if obtainable, is almost as good.

Bonemeal is usually raked into the surface soil at the rate of three ounces per square yard. It is very slow-acting and it therefore provides continuous food for the plants during the growing season. It can be used for almost any crop as it contains about 20 per cent of phosphoric acid and 4 per cent nitrogen. It is an excellent food for roses and fruit trees. Very many fruit trees, once established, get very little manure. This part of fruit cultivation is often neglected although most people will carry out some form of pruning. It is quite an easy task to supply each fruit tree with about three ounces of bonemeal sprinkled around the tree in early spring, and any wood ashes available for the potash requirements. This would ensure the tree or bush having enough food to produce its fruit in the autumn.

Soot contains from 1 to 6 per cent nitrogen and it makes a good fertilizer. It must be old soot however. It is no use obtaining some soot from the sweep after the chimney has been swept and then applying it directly as a fertilizer. Fresh soot contains poisonous sulphides, so leave it in a heap outside to 'weather'. Thereafter it is best used as a top dressing or raked into the top few inches of soil prior to sowing or planting. Never put soot into a planting hole which is to receive a fruit tree or rose bush or any other bush or tree. Keep all fertilizers away from the stem of a tree.

Wood ashes and seaweed are two of our few sources of organic potash so we must save all the wood ashes we can obtain from the bonfire or elsewhere. Hedge trimmings which contain much hard wood are no good for composting and are best burnt in order to obtain the natural potash. If a good log fire is kept going during the winter, collect the ashes and either store them in a bin with a lid on, or spread them on to the compost heap, as they become available. Cover the layer of ashes with vegetable waste or soil. The valuable potash content is very soluble and therefore quickly lost if left on the garden uncovered during wet weather.

If the land is ready the wood ashes can be immediately raked into the surface. Potash helps the plant to build and store carbohydrates so it is particularly valuable where the intention is to grow root crops and potatoes. It also improves quality of fruit and flowers and helps to prevent leaf scorch in soft fruits. The rate of application of wood ashes is half a pound per square yard.

Dried blood is a nitrogenous plant stimulant and must be used with great caution as it can contain up to 20 per cent of nitrogen. It can readily be seen that it is better to apply too little rather than a lot. If used in the right manner it can make a very noticeable difference to the rate of growth, especially with pot plants. It can be applied in the powdered state or as a liquid manure. In the dry state it can be given to growing crops in spring and summer at the rate of two ounces per square yard. When making a liquid manure with dried blood use it at the rate of one ounce to two gallons of water. Pot plants need half a teaspoonful about once a fortnight during the growing and flowering season. There is no need to feed pot plants during the dormant period. Do not mix a liquid manure and use it right away, leave it to soak for a day. It is better to have a liquid manure too weak rather than a strong solution. The rule with all fertilizers is to apply little rather than too much. Too much will soon kill any tree, bush or plant. The only manure which can be used in fairly large quantities is well-rotted garden compost.

MAKING GOOD COMPOST

Good garden compost is just about the gardener's best friend. It will enable him to grow wonderful crops and it is practically free. With its aid he will grow vegetables and fruit with real flavour and without poisoning his land with anything artificial.

Organic vegetable compost is the best substitute for farmyard manure. It contains all the plant foods, it is very cheap to make, it is easily obtained, and it is a way of using waste materials so that there never *is* any waste. Compost provides humus, conserves moisture and improves the texture of the soil, making it easier to work. Above all, it maintains fertility.

Do not burn any unwanted vegetable refuse; this is a great waste of valuable plant food. Grass cuttings, lawn mowings, pea, bean and potato haulms (those which are not diseased), outer leaves of all vegetables, annual weeds, soft hedge clippings, faded flowers, discarded straw and most kitchen refuse can all be turned into good garden compost.

Do not use thick woody stems like apple tree prunings; do not use coal ashes, sawdust, any chemicals (other than artificial manures), or the roots of perennial weeds such as couch grass, docks or bindweed. No cabbage stumps with the disease known as club root should be incorporated, but must be burnt.

There are many ways of making good garden compost, but whichever method is employed, it is very important to construct the heap so that the heat engendered is kept in. A well-made compost heap can generate heat up to 160°F. and with good ventilation will go beyond this. The heat of a properly constructed compost heap will prevent it from becoming a breeding-ground for flies and vermin and there will not be any offensive smell. Weed seeds and disease spores will also be destroyed.

The temperature of a compost heap is best kept at between 140°F. and 160°F., for a temperature much higher than this might destroy some of the vitality of the manure. The temperature can be measured by the use of a dairy thermometer or any thermometer that will measure this temperature and beyond, such as those used in a school science room.

A high enough temperature is essential in a compost heap in order to promote proper decay, for without this, much plant food in the form of nitrogen is lost. It is not enough to make a heap of vegetable matter and leave it to rot as best it can. Use one or more of the methods which will be described here. The final value of composted material depends upon the management and proper construction of the heap.

There are some general principles for all compost methods. A suitable site should be selected. Although the place chosen needs to be out of sight of the house, it should, if possible, be where the following conditions prevail. The site should not receive too much strong sun, wind, excessive rain or drippings from overhanging trees. Strong sun dries the material too quickly. The winds both dry and cool the heap. Excessive rain and drippings wash away a proportion of the plant nutrients and also interfere with a good building up of heat.

Trees and shrubs which are not overhanging the site provide good shelter against winds. Where the heap has to be constructed in the open, some form of windbreak erected while a quick-growing hedge is maturing, will be very helpful. Chestnut fencing, corrugated iron (painted pastel green), or canvas could be used.

There must be free access to the heap for the wheelbarrow or other garden transport. In very large gardens it might be more sensible to have several heaps in various places, to save labour.

The foundation for the compost heap should have the soil forked over and then a layer of decayed compost, straw or peat spread onto this. This will allow useful earthworms to enter the heap. If the first covering next to the forked soil is grass clippings or green vegetation it often forms an acid layer which prevents earthworms and micro-organisms from entering. The adverse conditions of hot sun, winds and excessive moisture already mentioned are also unfavourable for the activities of the living organisms which carry out the process of decomposition. Never make a solid foundation, say of concrete, brickwork or corrugated iron, for a compost heap. Always build the heap on forked soil.

We need the earthworms in our compost heap. They do a great deal of the mixing for us and help to prevent an undue accumulation of one kind of vegetation, such as grass mowings. This mingling of ingredients encourages a more even decaying process. Organic matter swallowed by worms is thoroughly pulverized and then deposited in the heap again. An abundance of earthworms tells us that our compost heap is decaying satisfactorily and their withdrawal will indicate that the compost is ready for use.

In a well-made compost heap, there will be tens of millions of micro-organisms. These organisms will be working for us. They break down and convert into simple substances many complex plant and animal tissues. These simple substances are then turned into suitable plant foods.

Those gardeners who use organic manures, the chief of which are well-made garden compost and farmyard manure, are supplying their plants with natural food. This is plant food which has profited from the action of all the beneficial organisms.

There are several important points to bear in mind when making a compost heap by any of the methods described:

1. All materials should be moist when put onto the heap. Any dry matter should be moistened, preferably with rain water which has been exposed to the sun.

2. Lawn mowings and fallen leaves (if used) should be placed in thin layers or mixed with the coarser material, otherwise they become matted and then prevent good aeration of the heap. Aeration is essential for proper decay. Thick stalks of cabbage or other plants should be cut into small pieces. If there is a large amount of thick, resistant material for composting, then it is best composted separately. If it is put into the general heap, it will slow down decomposition and necessitate more turning of the heap.

3. Retention of heat is most important. This heat is mainly provided by newly added refuse. Failure to generate a proper degree of heat is the commonest explanation of poor results.

4. Weeds should, if possible, be put onto the heap before they have gone to seed. If they have seeded, put them into the centre where the heat will be greatest.

5. The inclusion of some animal manure when available is advisable for all compost making. This can be in a solid or in a liquid form. It speeds up decay and makes for a more balanced compost.

6. It is better not to try to make compost during the bad months of winter when only frosted material is available. Materials can be collected but made into compost later when conditions are more suitable. With an alternation of freezing and thawing temperatures, no consistent build-up of heat is possible.

BUILDING A COMPOST HEAP

Prepare the foundation by forking over the soil. For aeration at the bottom, a six-inch layer of coarse material can be laid. This might consist of chopped-up cabbage stalks, hedge trimmings, prunings or tough pea or bean haulm.

Spread layers of vegetable refuse and mix these as you go along. If coarse and fine materials, young and old, wet and dry and many kinds of material are thoroughly mixed together, the more evenly will the heap decay. The final compost will be of better quality also. The thickness of the layers of refuse should vary from a few inches in small heaps to about a foot in large heaps.

On each layer of vegetable refuse spread some organic manure containing an ample amount of protein. This can be animal manure, poultry droppings, residue from deep litter houses, fish meal or other organic activators which will be mentioned later.

In proportion to the vegetable matter in the heap, add approximately one-quarter of farmyard manure (if obtainable), one-eighth of pig or horse manure, or one twenty-fourth of fresh poultry manure. As with all top dressings of manure, it is better to add too little of the activator than too much. Animal manure layers should not exceed three inches in thickness, otherwise they interfere with aeration.

On the layer of manure a sprinkling of soil should be spread, about a half to one inch thick. This may have mixed with it natural ground chalk or wood ashes. Fairly good garden soil should be used and not very poor clay or sandy soil. This soil is needed for the introduction of organisms and minerals which help the decaying process. Not too much soil should be used if there are only thin layers of vegetable refuse. The heap should never be so weighted down with any material that air is excluded. As the heap is gradually built, slope the sides to a ridge shape if the heap is a rectangular one, or to a cone if it is rounded.

Moisture and heat need to be conserved as the heap is built up; this is effected by covering the heap with old sacking, old carpets, straw, rushes, bracken or even corrugated iron.

A completed heap, that is one which has reached a manageable height, should be covered by a quantity of peat, moss or soil, in a layer about three inches thick. Never use any soil, for covering or for mixing in the heap, which has been chemically sprayed. This may completely prevent the rotting of the refuse and it will certainly retard it.

As part of the after-management of the compost heap, an inspection should be made of the coverings and interior of the heap. A spade or trowel can be thrust into the heap at about one-third from the bottom. If the compost scooped out has a pleasant earthy smell, and plenty of earthworms present, and if it is of about the consistency of a moist sponge, then all is going on well. If it is sour-smelling, slimy or wet, it would be best to remove the coverings and turn the heap. While doing this, thoroughly mix the ingredients and as far as possible place the outside of the old heap into the centre of the new one. Some sprinkling of soil and dry refuse at intervals of about a foot would be helpful.

If a heap is too dry it will feel brittle and give off a musty smell, and it may have a greyish growth; also, wood lice may be present. Sometimes this condition can be remedied by pouring on limited supplies of water, or dilute liquid manure. Several holes can be made into the heap and the liquid can then be poured in. It is sometimes much more satisfactory to rebuild the heap, moistening the materials as you go along.

One turning of the heap should be enough in ordinary circumstances, when it should hasten decay by providing better aeration and destroy weed seeds and diseased vegetation which may have been on the outside, and are now put inside. To judge when a heap needs turning, the temperature of the heap should be studied. It should fall naturally to about 100°F. before being turned, otherwise heat may be dissipated before it has had time to be fully effective. A very slow-rotting heap will need to be turned twice, first after six months and again a year later. After turning the heap, allow it to settle down a little before putting on the covering.

Garden compost is ready for use when it has a pleasant earthy smell and when it hardly shows any of the original constituents. It is important when using mature compost in the garden not to bury it too deeply: not more than four inches deep for best results. It can also be used as a mulch, as a top dressing almost everywhere, including lawns.

SOME SPECIAL COMPOST METHODS

The Q.R. or Quick Return method of compost making is a rapid way of making good compost by using a herbal mixture as an activator. The herbal mixture can be bought in packets of powder and is mixed with water. The Q.R. method prevents nitrogen losses during the rotting process, and the finished product from a Q.R. compost heap is a fine, crumbly, dark, sweet-smelling material.

The same vegetable refuse, with added animal manures, is used with this method as with other compost heaps. The heap in this method is built in a similar way to that just described, with the same general principles of keeping in heat, mixing refuse, keeping the heap just moist enough, and attending to aeration.

When beginning to build the heap, it is first necessary to make sure that drainage of the site is good. Then mark out the site. Build each layer of vegetation by starting on the outside and working in towards the centre. Perennial and seeded annual weeds should be in the centre of the heap. Mix the materials well and place in four- to six-inch thickness of layers. If there is only one kind of material the layers should be divided by a scattering of soil. Long stems should be cut into lengths of about one foot. If the materials can be shredded, then very quick results are obtained. This can only be done by gardeners who have suitable equipment for this purpose.

You activate the heap as you build it, by lightly sprinkling the Q.R. solution over the surface of each four- to six-inch layer of refuse. You must cover the sprinkled layer at once with fresh material. Add a scattering of good garden soil on to the top of every foot of fresh material. A sprinkling of garden lime is optional, and will not be required where the soil is chalky.

The top of the last layer of material must be kept covered with sacking or some other protection to keep in the damp heat. Construct the heap with straight sides until it is about three feet high, then finish the work by rounding it into a dome or ridge shape at the top. Cover the top with a little soil.

After-building care consists mainly of keeping in the heat. The rise in temperature in a Q.R. heap depends on the protection afforded and the speed of building. Damp heat always escapes very rapidly, thus it is very important to have sacking or other covering on the top as building proceeds.

When heat reaches the surface it means that the micro-organisms are working in the top layer of refuse. If you add a fresh layer they pass quickly into it and within twelve hours the new addition will be hot like the layers below. If you wait some time before adding a new layer, the micro-organisms withdraw and it would take several days to restart the heat in the added material.

If the heap begins to have an unpleasant smell and becomes soggy, it means that it needs air. Open out the heap and loosen it, add a few spadefuls of good garden soil, and reactivate with Q.R. solution. If the heap is dry and grey with powder, loosen it, add soil, reactivate with Q.R. solution, and drench with a compost solution (a trowel full of ripe compost to a gallon of water).

A spring and summer heap made by the Q.R. method will be ready in about six weeks. A late summer or autumn heap will take about twice the time. Compost heaps break down very slowly during the winter months.

The Q.R. solution can be used in deep litter houses and stockyards. Used in these cases it banishes smell and the final product is much improved. For deep litter houses and stockyards, make up a Q.R. solution at normal strength and allow one pint for every fifty square feet of surface area. Wet the whole area by watering on the solution with a fine-rosed can. Repeat once a month. The resulting compost will be richer and easier to use than untreated deep litter.

The Garotta system of making garden compost provides a manure rich in humus which can be used in three ways. It can be dug into the soil in a rough condition, it can be sifted before use, or used as a liquid. A Garotta compost heap must be carefully made and it must not have a roof on it. It should be built straight up from the open ground. The heap can be enclosed by walls of brick with air spaces between them, wire netting or boarding. We shall come to descriptions of some enclosures later on. Most kinds of compost heaps are better, on the whole, if they are enclosed to keep in the heat and so avoid too much turning. Compost heaps in gardens are generally small enough to permit the building of some kind of enclosure.

A Garotta heap is made rectangular in shape so that an even surface can be acted upon by the Garotta. A Garotta heap can be compressed more than heaps made by other systems. Mix the materials as in other methods. After treading heap down firmly, Garotta powder is dusted lightly and evenly over the refuse, at every nine inches thickness of layers. When the heap has been completed, a light covering of earth goes on the top of the last sprinkling of Garotta. No other earth and no lime are ever put inside the heap, as they are with many other methods. No other chemicals can be used, as they would upset the Garotta recipe.

When starting a fresh heap, use some of the ready-made compost for the first layer. Unlike heaps made by other systems, the Garotta heap does not require watering or turning. If left alone, it will work up to a temperature of 140°F. and even beyond. House flies are not attracted and vermin are repelled.

The usual materials are used, except that all roots are shaken free of soil. Wood ashes can be put on to the Garotta heap to increase the potash content. Never put on mowings from lawns which have been treated by a hormone weed killer. This applies to all methods of composting. Spread treated mowings to dry and then burn them.

Animal manures of all kinds can be used with the Garotta process. Mix them well with the refuse. If straw is being used, small quantities should be thoroughly mixed with green material. Thick stalks of cabbage stumps are very slow to rot down and are best chopped into small pieces. The manure made by the Garotta system is suitable for all plants, including those which are lime intolerant.

Garotta-made compost is used for general purposes by digging in when it is ready. It should be dug out of the heap and chopped into pieces with a spade. It can be sifted for seed boxes, seed beds and lawn dressings. It should be passed through a half-inch sieve and mixed with the potting compost wherever a fairly rich mixture is needed.

To make liquid manure from Garotta-made compost, fill a sack with the compost and submerge it in a water butt or other container filled with water. Cover the receptacle with a board to exclude air. Within a week the water will have become liquid manure. After liquid manure has been withdrawn, replace with clean water and keep the same sackful of compost in it. Keep this process going for six weeks, then restart with a fresh sackful of compost.

I have already spoken of seaweed as a manure for digging into the soil and as a fertilizer when used in the dried state. It supplies the garden with natural potash. Marinure is a powdered seaweed manure, an efficient organic fertilizer and soil conditioner, containing most of the trace elements. It is seaweed which is collected from the Galway Bay area, dried and ground into powder. The whole plant is used with nothing extracted except moisture, and nothing added. It has been established, during recent years, that dried and powdered seaweed has the same manurial properties as fresh, raw seaweed. Marinure stimulates soil bacteria and makes available to the plant nitrogen, phosphates and potash. As well as the trace elements seaweed contains plenty of minerals such as phosphoric acid and salts. This is because minerals are taken from the land by rain and rivers and carried to the sea, where some of them are absorbed by seaweed.

The use of Marinure as an activator on the compost heap is quite a recent development. During composting trials carried out in 1966,

4

it was found that Marinure used as an activator raised the temperature of mixed garden refuse to between 120°F. and 140°F., sufficient to kill weed seeds and disease spores. These temperatures were maintained for several days and excellent compost resulted. To use Marinure, make a compost heap in the manner first described in this section of the book. The temperature mentioned above was for an average compost heap of about one yard square which was enclosed by a New Zealand Box or similar enclosure. Sprinkle on two ounces of Marinure at every foot thickness of refuse layers.

The Fertosan process is yet another way of making good garden compost. It is simple to carry out and the compost is soon ready. The makers say that the powder used contains nitrogen-fixing and cellulolytic bacteria and micro-fungi. The usual way to use this activator, which is supplied in powder form, is to dissolve it in water to make a stock solution. It is then further diluted according to instructions. The makers are now preparing sprinkler canisters, from which the powder is just sprinkled on, but this is for fresh green waste only.

The vegetable matter is built into a pyramidal heap, about six feet square, on ground which has been forked over. A sprinkling of garden lime is put on first. The heap should be built above ground level, because the process of decomposition in this method depends upon free access of air. It is built up of six-inch layers of refuse with a sprinkling of garden lime between each layer. After the lime, a sprinkling of the Fertosan Accelerator is applied, and then a half-inch of good garden soil over each second layer of refuse. The first heap can be extended by adding fresh material at the back of it and treating in the same manner. No turning is required in this process, and it is claimed by the makers that garden refuse can be converted into good compost in about six weeks. The makers also supply what is known as Fertosan Modern Septic Tank Conditioner. This dissolves solid waste, kills unpleasant odours, and is harmless and non-corrosive.

Another organic accelerator for making compost is Murtonic. In this method, a compost heap is made by the first method described. Four level teaspoonfuls of Murtonic are mixed with a gallon of water, and after every foot thickness of refuse, this solution is watered on to the heap. After each watering, about an inch of good garden soil is put on.

Alginure is an organic accelerator which is also used for producing good garden compost.

The method of composting known as the Indore process, which was initiated in India, was very much favoured and recommended by the Ministry of Agriculture during the last war. It is still much used (with variations) but the Indore method can only be practised by gardeners who have a few poultry, pigeons or rabbits or who have access to animal manure of some kind.

First find a shaded spot, dig a trench a foot deep, six feet in width and as long as is convenient. Leave the excavated soil along the sides of the trench. Thoroughly mix the vegetable refuse, chopping up small any long cabbage stalks or stems of other plants. Place a layer of the well-mixed refuse, six inches thick, over the base of the trench, then well wet the whole with water. Cover the layer with an inch thickness of animal manure. If a mixture of different animal manures is available, so much the better. Now cover the manure with a thin layer of refuse, then sprinkle this with garden lime. Never use quick lime. The next step is to put on a layer of soil, taken from that which has been placed along the sides of the trench. This layer of soil should be an inch thick. Water the soil if very dry.

Continue the same process until the heap is five feet high; do not have it any higher. Make the layers progressively narrower so that when the heap is completed there will be a slope all the way round. Finish off with a coating of soil one inch thick.

If you have not enough material to build the heap to five feet it does not matter, build it to the height you think you can reach and then finish off in the way described. Start another heap later as the material becomes available.

In a few days the heap should become warm and then hot. This heat should destroy any perennial roots or weed seeds which may have got in. After about five weeks the heat will probably be greater than can be borne by the bare hand; at this stage the heap should be turned over, putting the original outside of the heap inside. A heap which does not become hot should be left for ten weeks or more before being turned over.

The time taken for the refuse to decompose completely varies greatly, and after the final turning it may have to mature for something between three weeks and six months before being ready for use. When it is ready it will be of a uniformly dark colour and with an agreeable earthy smell. For the plants to gain most benefit from the compost it should not be buried more than one spit deep.

Another compost-making method which has been used for many years now is the Adco process; this involves the use of proprietary chemicals. This is ideal, of course, for people living in large towns or cities where there is no animal manure of any kind available. The usual practice is to make two heaps, one of tough materials such as cabbage stalks, pea and bean haulm and hedge clippings, another consisting of soft materials such as lawn mowings, annual weeds or cabbage leaves. The tough material is sprinkled with a grey powder called Standard Adco and the soft with Adco Accelerator, a pink powder. You can, however, make one heap with 50 per cent of each type of material, well mixed, and treat with Adco Accelerator. The makers now state on their packets that the chemicals contain trace elements.

To make a compost heap embodying the Adco principles, select a site which will not become waterlogged, and dig a pit two feet deep with the excavated earth banked up around the sides. The making of the heap is simplicity itself. Mix well the garden rubbish, spread a six-inch layer over the bottom of the trench, thoroughly wet it if dry, and then sprinkle with Adco. Spread another layer of refuse and repeat the process until the heap has reached a manageable height. Turn the heap at least once during the rotting-down period. As with all other methods the time taken for complete decomposition varies. Never apply chemicals or fertilizers with the bare hands: use a trowel, as sensitive skins may be affected by them.

If green bracken can be obtained, it is valuable for all kinds of compost heaps. When rotted down, it is rich in natural potash. Green bracken can be cut from forest land with permission or collected after being cut by foresters. Those who can borrow a trailer for their car might be able to take advantage of this source of organic potash.

COMPOST HEAPS ENCLOSED TO KEEP IN HEAT

With the exception of the Fertosan process, most compost heaps are better managed where it is possible to erect some sort of enclosure for them. This is especially so in the case of very exposed areas. The important reason for these enclosures is that they help to keep in the heat. We must have a temperature of between 120°F. and 140°F. in order to prolong a proper decomposition process, with a resultant retention of nitrogen and destruction of weed seeds and diseased spores. Enclosed compost heaps also look and keep tidy.

In New Zealand, much use is made of what is known as a New Zealand Box, which can be made in many ways. These enclosures are very widely used in many countries.

The Indore method of composting can be carried out in a New Zealand Box. When using such an enclosure for this method, vertical holes are made with a crowbar or other instrument at three-feet intervals through the top of the compost. This is done to ensure aeration.

To make the box, a wooden frame is constructed, the sides of which can be four feet six inches long and about three feet high. The box has neither top nor bottom, only four sides. The boards at the sides have gaps for free circulation of air. One of the sides of the New

Zealand Box made in this manner is detachable, and fastened by thumbscrews or hooked together, for easy removal. After about a month, this side is detached and the box is taken from the heap and moved to a fresh position on to soil which has been forked over. It is then put together again. The refuse is put back into the framework, beginning from the top of the heap. After another month the process is repeated, and this completes the work.

With the New Zealand Box and other enclosures, the heaps may not need turning if enough constant heat is engendered. Enclosing of heaps will certainly cut down the number of times the heaps will need turning, compared to a heap which is not enclosed.

There are easier ways of making a New Zealand Box and other

A NEW ZEALAND BOX

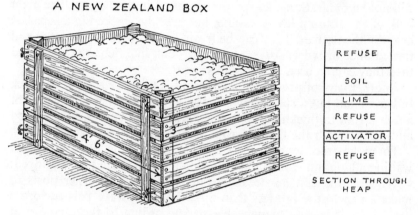

SECTION THROUGH HEAP

One good method of making garden Compost

enclosures, and the gardener will be able to enclose his heap according to the time and the materials he has available. Chestnut fencing erected around the compost heap with the gaps stuffed with newspaper will help keep in heat, or even wire netting with paper. In the Garotta process, loose bricks around are suggested or just wire netting. For the Q.R. process a wooden enclosure is recommended. For this kind of enclosure, grocers' packing cases can be utilized to make a surround of about three feet square for a small garden. A large garden can have an enclosure made from old railway sleepers. These bins should be about three feet high. Old railway sleepers are heavy and awkward to handle, but they make a fairly permanent enclosure. They can sometimes be obtained from the stores department of the nearest large railway station.

With all boxes, bins or enclosures of any kind, it is important to remember that aeration is essential, therefore leave spaces between boards or other building materials used. Roofs may have to be provided in districts of very heavy rainfall to prevent saturation of the refuse. These can be sheets of corrugated iron and can be removed when heavy rain has ceased.

When converting straw and other vegetation on a large scale by the Garotta process, enclosing walls of bales of straw, old pieces of board or corrugated iron are suggested.

LEAF MOULD

Some autumn leaves added to the compost heap help to produce that desirable dark colour, but these must be mixed with the other refuse as are the lawn mowings, otherwise they become a soggy mass and will not let in air. Some leaves can be put on in thin layers. The main bulk of the autumn leaves should, however, be stacked in a separate heap by themselves. They can be treated with Adco Accelerator and turned once or twice. After a time they look like rich, black soil and then they can be used as a top dressing.

Another way of producing leaf mould is to make a separate stack of leaves and put a sprinkling of good garden soil between layers of about a foot in thickness. This stack is left until spring, then turned and treated with the Q.R. Herbal Solution and stacked again.

To make traditional lasting leaf mould (if one does not mind waiting a long time for it) the following method should be employed:

Wire netting can be stretched taut around four corner posts to make an enclosure not less than three feet each way. This enclosure can be made to any manageable size according to the quantity of leaves available. Leaves in layers about a foot thick are placed in the enclosure directly on to the earth base. These should then be really consolidated by treading and should be well soaked with water. The layering, treading and watering are continued until the bin is full.

The best leaves to use are those of oak and beech, but others will do. No other vegetable matter must be added as it will bring in weed seeds and possibly perennial roots. The heap should have no protection from rain, as added moisture will prevent fungal decay from the base. The aim is not fermentation but slow decay over a long period. Leaf mould made in this way improves with age and the finest leaf mould will be about ten years old, although it can be used after two years.

If we can manage our gardens as nearly as possible in Nature's way we shall benefit accordingly. Therefore it is advisable to use rotted leaves as a top dressing for subjects which in their natural habitat live in or near woodlands, such as primroses, primulas, polyanthus, violets, lily of the valley and bulbs. If a considerable amount of potting is done the rotted leaves will form one of the chief constituents of the potting and seed box soil.

THE SAVING OF KITCHEN REFUSE

All waste in the kitchen should be saved for the compost heap and other garden purposes. If everyone saved the kitchen refuse and used it for the good of the garden the cost of collecting and disposing of dustbin contents would be greatly reduced. This could mean a saving on the rates and the money saved here could very well go towards that gardener's dream—a greenhouse.

Here are some of the materials which can be saved and turned into valuable plant food all from rubbish which is very often put into the dustbin. Tea leaves, coffee grounds, beetroot skin, leek, radish, turnip, swede and carrot tops, potato, turnip, swede, apple, bean, orange and lemon peelings, rhubarb leaves, cabbage leaves, lettuce waste, banana and onion skins, empty pea and bean pods, fish waste, bones, egg shells, dust from vacuum and carpet cleaner, soot, small cuttings from dressmaking and odd wool, dog fur (when animal is shedding coat), feathers, dead flowers and leaves, tomato skins, and wood ashes; the list is endless. Even coal ashes and clinkers can be utilized to make splendid foundations for paths. If coal ashes and clinkers are spread level with a rake before putting on gravel they assist greatly with drainage and help to bind the gravel. Empty tins can be flattened with the coal hammer and used for the same purpose.

So now we only have waste paper left. Some of this can be used in the garden for covering pots and seed boxes in greenhouse and cold frame prior to germination. The rest of the newspapers and magazines can be bundled and tied and taken to the nearest scrap merchant. Odd small pieces of paper can start the bonfire and be burnt with it. So you see there is no need for the refuse collector to call often, he need only come to collect the accumulation of ashes and tins, as they could not be all used once the paths were established. Some coal ashes could be kept in a heap, however, as they make an excellent slug deterrent when used as a base in the cold frame on to which the pots or seed boxes are placed. They can also be used for the same purpose to cover bulbs outside in pots, which will be later brought into the house for forcing.

Thus kitchen refuse can easily be saved by installing, in the kitchen, two medium-sized bins with lids. Into one, all material for the compost heap is put; into the other go paper, tins, etc. Ashes can be taken straight outside and made into a heap ready for use. Tea leaves in the compost heap help considerably towards increasing the worm population.

A FEW INSECTICIDES AND FUNGICIDES

For successful gardening there is no need to buy or use the abundant poisonous sprays now flooding the horticultural market. The beautiful butterflies that were once so numerous in this pleasant countryside of ours are slowly being exterminated. Hosts of birds and bees are meeting with the same fate. Some of this dearth is due to the encroachment of towns upon the countryside, houses appearing where once grew the plants which fed the caterpillars. Even so, much of the scarcity of our insect population is due to careless use of poisons. If we destroy nature in this way then we shall have to pay for it. What would a garden be without the charm of bees, butterflies and birds? In addition to their decorative attributes, we could not grow anything without the fertilizing work of bees, butterflies and moths, and the pest destruction effected by many birds.

The pesticides, fungicides and insecticides which I think necessary, are only ten in number; most of these are non-poisonous and they are not used on the blossoms of plants. They are: Bordeaux Mixture, Cheshunt Compound, Derris Dust, Calomel Dust, Colloidal Copper, Flowers of Sulphur, Soot (well weathered), Garden Lime, Pepper Dust, and some form of Slug and Snail killer containing metaldehyde.

Bordeaux Mixture is used to spray potatoes and tomatoes against a fungus called potato blight. *Cheshunt Compound* is a fungicide used to prevent damping-off disease and as a mild soil sterilizer prior to seed sowing. *Derris Dust* is a general insecticide now much preferable to D.D.T. in view of the recently discovered lasting poisonous properties of D.D.T. It can be used as a dust or as a liquid spray when it is mixed with soft soap in the following proportions: 1 to 2 oz. of derris powder, 4 oz. of soft soap, and 5 gals. of water. Derris is non-poisonous to human beings and it is most valuable when used to dust brassica seedlings against flea beetle, and beans and peas to control the weevil.

Calomel Dust is both an insecticide and a fungicide. When used as an insecticide it controls onion fly, cabbage root fly and carrot fly. Sprinkle the dust on to the surface soil close to the stems of the plants. It is used as a fungicide against club root of brassicas. Sprinkle seed drills before sowing and when planting out mix with the soil in the planting hole. This treatment will at the same time deter the cabbage root fly.

Some form of *Colloidal Copper* must be used as a fungicidal spray chiefly to control black spot on roses. It can also be used for antirrhinum rust, hollyhock rust, potato blight and other fungal diseases. When using a proprietary brand follow the makers' instructions carefully.

Flowers of Sulphur can also be used as an insecticide and as a fungicide. Its chief use is against mildew on roses and members of the pea family. It will also control strawberry leaf spot, foot root (a soft decay of the stem) which attacks cucumbers, melons and tomatoes, red spider and fungal diseases generally.

Well-weathered *Soot* is a valuable deterrent to slugs, snails, cut-worms and wireworms when lightly forked into the soil. It will also act as an insecticide against aphides, flea beetle, leaf miners and insects generally. Dust on to foliage when damp.

Garden Lime is used for the prevention of club root and against soil insects generally. It is useful for controlling slugs, snails, cut-worms, wireworms, millipedes, and as a deterrent—against destructive birds.

Pepper Dust will keep stray cats from seed beds and also deter earwigs and slugs. Some *Slug Killer* containing metaldehyde completes our list and is the most effective destroyer of slugs and snails. More will be said about these aids to the gardener later on, when individual crops are being discussed.

GARDEN FRIENDS AND FOES

Although many garden foes are described in this section it does not mean that a garden will be attacked simultaneously by all of these. If the methods of control advocated are carried out and a good system of garden hygiene is practised, the gardener need not fear that he will be overwhelmed with pests and diseases. He need not be discouraged from attempting to grow any crop, neither need he despair of being able to save a crop once it has been attacked.

Ants are only a nuisance in the average garden and are not really a pest. If they are too numerous in the greenhouse the staging can be dusted with derris dust. Also greasebands may be placed around main trunks of trees up which ants are swarming.

Aphides are one of the serious garden pests, and can only be controlled effectively if tackled early. These lice-like insects, some winged and others wingless, are of many species varying in colour from green through bluish grey to black. The ones most commonly met with are the greenfly on roses, sweet peas, lettuce, cane fruits and many flowering plants; the grey fly on brassicas, pears and apples; the black fly (most commonly found on broad beans), also on other beans, chrysanthemums, ferns and nasturtiums. The woolly aphis attacks the bark and roots of apple trees and covers itself with a white substance which resembles thin cotton wool. The rosy apple aphis and currant aphis cause the leaves to develop red patches and blisters.

All the aphides suck the sap from the plant or tree and besides causing leaves to shrivel, buds to disintegrate and fruit to drop prematurely, they can cause some plants and bushes to be totally destroyed if no counter-measures are taken. One of the most important reasons for destroying aphides is that in addition to the damage mentioned they also spread virus infection.

Most of the large family of plant lice pass through two cycles in their life history. They live on one plant to begin with, known as the host plant, and then move to a second plant. You can often see plants of the weeds 'fat hen' and dock covered with black fly. The spindle tree also is a host plant. So we can see why garden hygiene is so important. We must rid our garden of docks, 'fat hen' or other host plants, remove and burn any badly infested shoots of beans, currants or raspberries, spray or dust with derris to control all aphides. If the tops of broad beans are pinched out at the first sign of a single black fly they will seldom be affected. These tops should be burned immediately.

Wireworms are the larvae of click beetles (they make a clicking noise with their wings) and they are most destructive pests, attacking the roots of many plants. They are found in abundance where old grassland has been turned over. They live in the larval state for about four years. They are yellow, slow-moving, about an inch long and with hard, shiny skins. Their bodies are divided into segments and have three pairs of legs near the head.

To control them it is best to grow (in the spring on newly turned turf) broad beans or brassicas, as these crops seem less vulnerable. The greatest activity of the wireworm takes place during autumn so it is best to choose, in danger areas, crops which seem able to resist this pest better than root crops. Runner beans, peas, onions and shallots seem the least susceptible. Discourage the wireworm by digging over the soil and exposing the pests as often as possible to the attacks of rooks and blackbirds, who are particularly fond of them. Grow second early potatoes and harvest them in August. Garden lime is a wireworm deterrent. After some time this foe can by such means be almost eradicated.

The *flea beetle* is a great nuisance every year, particularly during dry weather. To the gardener who likes to grow his own brassica plants they are a menace. It is much better and cheaper to grow your own plants if you have club root under control. Flea beetles attack all young seedlings of brassica including all the cabbage family, turnips, swedes and radishes. They are small blackish beetles which jump about when disturbed, and as they start on the seedlings just as they are pushing through the soil a constant watch has to be made for their appearance. These seeds quickly germinate, so the rows

WIREWORM AND CLICK BEETLE

Destroy these and expose
them to the birds

The Spindle Tree: do not
grow this in your garden

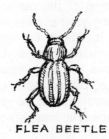

FLEA BEETLE

Showing the damage caused
by the Carrot Fly

Dust with Derris Powder
to kill and discourage this pest

PEA AND BEAN WEEVIL

LEGLESS LEATHER JACKET

Encourage strong growth
and dust with Derris Pow-
der to destroy this enemy
of peas and beans

The larva of the Crane Fly: the
destroyer of much grassland

must be looked at every day. As soon as seedlings show through, dust the rows with derris powder. A second application about a week later is usually required.

The *pea and bean weevil* is discussed at some length in the section on the growing of garden peas. There has been so much published about the Colorado beetle that it only needs to be mentioned briefly here. These beetles feed on the potato foliage and they are orange and black striped. Any specimens discovered must be reported to the Ministry of Agriculture, with all details of where they were found.

The larvae of the *crane fly* or *daddy-long-legs* are known as leather-jackets on account of their tough skin. They vary in colour but are mostly dark grey. They feed on the roots of plants throughout the spring and summer, but in winter they are completely dormant. For their control keep turning the land over for the birds to dispose of them, hand pick any you see, and destroy any rough grass which provides a site for egg-laying.

The eggs of the *carrot fly* are laid below the surface of the soil, so when young carrots are thinned the soil needs to be firmed, thus making it difficult for egg-laying. This is a small, greenish-black fly about a quarter of an inch in length, and is best controlled by moving the carrot bed each year to a different spot and by delaying the sowing of carrots until mid-June. This is for the main crop. Some early carrots might be gathered before the attacks usually start, in early June. The maggots of this pest cut into the roots.

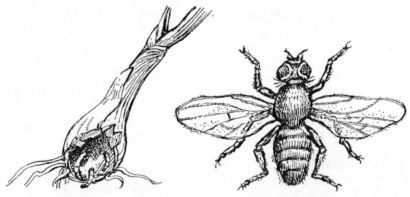

The Onion Fly and the damage it causes

The *onion fly* is sometimes a serious foe. It looks like a small, dark-grey house fly. In late spring it lays its eggs on the neck of the onion or nearby in the soil. It is a troublesome pest if not deterred, because in some years there may be three generations, and a complete onion crop can be destroyed by the white maggots. Soot sprinkled along the rows is a good deterrent, but 4 per cent calomel dust, at the rate of one ounce per ten yards on either side of the rows, seems to be better. This should be applied when the seedlings are about two inches high, and a second application is given ten days later.

Sometimes gardeners are troubled by minute insects called *gall-flies*. They generally have bodies and wings of bright metallic colours, and cause malformations on the ends of twigs, sometimes attacking brassicas, beet and tomatoes. Dusting with derris is the best control measure.

There are a number of *saw-flies* which attack fruit. The apple saw-fly also damages plums and damsons as it produces a white maggot which finds its way into the centre of the fruit, causing premature falling. The gooseberry saw-fly eats the leaves of gooseberry and currant bushes. The green caterpillars, marked with black and orange, are easily seen and can be hand picked if not too numerous. There is a saw-fly which attacks pears and cherries and is known as a slug worm. It is first a pale yellow in colour and then turns black. Dusting with derris dust is the best control measure for all these foes.

The *codling moth* attacks apples and the larvae eat their way to the centre of the fruit. After a month they eat their way out and seek a

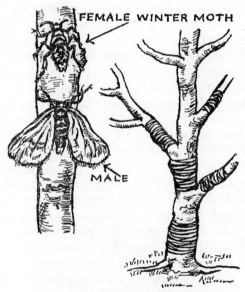

GREASE BAND TO STOP
THESE PESTS AND KEEP
RENEWING THE GREASE

The Winter Moth

sheltered place, often in a fold of bark. The adult insect emerges in May and lays eggs on tiny fruit or on leaves. The codling moth caterpillar always feeds in or near the core of the fruit. The moth itself is rarely seen as it is a night-flying insect. To control this pest, spray with derris from the end of June to early July and search for pupae on the trunks of the trees or in garden sheds where apples have been stored. Greaseband the trees to capture caterpillars.

There are several species of *winter moth* and the wingless females creep up the trunks of apple trees during winter. This is a very common moth. Sometimes up to two hundred eggs may be laid by each female, consequently there is much damage to the leaves and flowers. The eggs hatch in March and the caterpillars, which feed on foliage and blossom, can lower themselves to the ground by a silken thread where they bury themselves just below the surface. Pupation then takes place and the wingless females emerge in early winter, unless checked, to continue egg laying. This is why all your apple trees should have grease bands affixed in autumn, and the grease should be renewed when necessary. The trees can be dusted with derris, but after petal fall, so that the bees are not injured. Keep the ground underneath the trees stirred with a hoe to give access to the birds, especially poultry if they are running in an orchard on free range.

The *magpie moth* has black and white markings and it lays eggs on gooseberries and currant bushes during June or July. The larvae have black heads and whitish-yellow bodies covered with dots. These pests have two feeding periods, one in the summer and another during the following spring; in the intervening period they bury themselves in the soil. The pupae can be found on leaves and twigs during late May and June, and the moth emerges during August. The control measures are hand picking, dusting with derris, and hoeing round base of bushes to kill with the hoe and to expose for the birds; also useful is application of soot to the soil.

The *cabbage white butterfly* is of two species, the large white and the small white. The caterpillars of the large white are bluish green above and yellowish underneath. There is a long yellow line along the back, with black dots and a yellow line at each side, and the head is brown. The caterpillars are covered with fine hairs, and they eat away at almost every part of the cabbage plant for six or seven weeks: one of the most destructive pests we have. There are two broods, one in spring and one in late summer. The chrysalids are grey with black dots and yellow dashes, and can be found in almost any sheltered spot fastened by silken threads to tree trunks, fences, garden sheds, window sills, under eaves and often just attached to a plain brick wall. Control measures are hand picking and killing all larvae

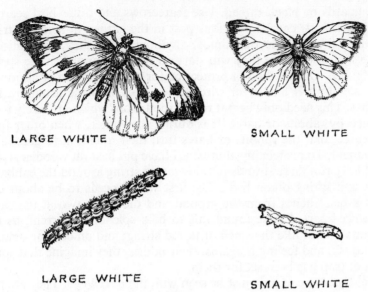

LARGE WHITE   SMALL WHITE

LARGE WHITE   SMALL WHITE

The only harmful butterflies

and pupae and crushing all eggs. The eggs are straw-coloured and are found in clusters, usually on the undersides of the leaves. Spraying or dusting with derris is to be recommended, and a salt solution can be used. A search for caterpillars should be made at all times while working in the garden. If this is done regularly this foe will be kept at bay and no serious damage to brassicas sustained.

The small cabbage white butterfly has a similar life-history but the caterpillars are a velvety green and have a faint yellow line down the middle of the back. They are very difficult to see when they are on a cabbage plant. Damage to the leaves should be looked for, also the dark-coloured excrement. These do not seem to be so numerous as the large white.

The natural enemies of these caterpillars are insectivorous birds, such as starlings, lapwings, gulls, rooks and cuckoos. Here in the New Forest I have also observed stonechats and spotted fly-catchers snatching up the adult butterflies and carrying them off while on the wing. All of these birds should be encouraged. Wasps and small ichneumon wasps which lay their eggs within the bodies of the caterpillars are also ruthless enemies of these garden foes.

Any *harmful birds* in the garden can be prevented from doing a lot of damage by using the following methods. Cover soft fruit plantations with fine mesh netting (not more than half-inch mesh) or erect permanent wire netting cages. Cover seedlings with wire pea guards or black thread. Use scarecrows and other bird scarers.

Wild rabbits can be a serious pest in the garden in some districts because they will devour almost anything. After they have finished off a bed of cabbage they will start on the leeks and then the spring onion bed. One method of protection for a small garden or allotment is a small-mesh barrier of wire netting sunk into the ground a few inches. This need only be put round food crops which are likely to be visited by rabbits or hares. It is during the winter, when other food is scarce, that the rabbits or hares turn their attention to garden or allotment. To protect my allotment I have put in stout wooden stakes and have run three strands of thick tarred string around the cabbage, leek and spring onion beds. The first strand needs to be about one and a half inches from the ground and the other two at the same distance apart. I have found this to be a splendid deterrent, as the rabbits do not like the smell of tarred string; and on coming against it at dusk, and feeling it against their bodies, they imagine that some sort of trap has been set for them.

Red spiders can only just be seen with the naked eye. They are not true spiders, but mites. They do most damage in the greenhouse with their sap-sucking habits. Frequent syringing with water is most effective as they only thrive in very dry conditions.

Slugs and *snails* are the best-known garden pests. They can easily be controlled by putting down heaps of meta-bran baits; the best form seems to be the slug-killer pellets. Soot sprinkled along rows of seedlings acts as a deterrent and so does garden lime. Encourage members of the thrush family.

There are other pests to be found in the garden but I have only mentioned the main ones which are likely to worry the average gardener.

GARDEN FRIENDS

Never, never let any harm come to a member of the *owl* family. Never let boys take the owl's eggs. The owl is one of the gardener's greatest friends, an unpaid night worker who never takes any time off. All owls destroy thousands of mice, voles, rats, beetles and other injurious vermin every night. The owl protects everything that rats and mice destroy, not only our growing crops but also our vegetables, fruit and seed in store.

Other birds which are friends of the gardener include blackbirds, robins, rooks, hedge sparrows, thrushes, members of the tit family, chaffinches, and spotted flycatchers; many of these birds can be seen in and around the garden. Other friends among the birds include the insectivorous swallows, swifts, house martins, wrens, stonechats

1. Taking out the first trench and wheeling the soil to the end of the plot

2. Applying a layer of manure or compost to the bottom of the first trench

3. Taking out the first spade-width of soil and placing it on to the manure. This is the beginning of a new trench

4. Taking out the second spade-width of soil and placing it on the soil and manure

DOUBLE DIGGING

5. Taking out the third spade-width of soil and placing it on the soil in the trench to keep a continuous level throughout the plot

6. Removing loose soil or 'crumbs' from the bottom of the new trench and placing it on the top of the previous one

7. Loosening the bottom of new trench before applying manure. This can be done with spade or garden fork

DOUBLE DIGGING

and cuckoos. The green woodpecker occasionally visits the garden in search of ants, its chief food.

The blackbird's food consists of caterpillars, leather-jackets, wire-worms, slugs and snails. We must not be harsh towards the blackbird on account of the little fruit it takes, as we cannot stop natural instincts, and must protect our fruit by netting the bushes effectively.

The robin consumes harmful flies, daddy-long-legs, cabbage butter-flies and their larvae, and numerous other pests. This friendly creature also keeps the gardener company.

The damage attributed to rooks is often overrated and they help the gardener and farmer by keeping down harmful grubs of many kinds, including wireworms, leather-jackets, slugs and snails. They will even tackle mice.

Hedge sparrows are principally insect eaters and they are always searching for caterpillars and grubs around the base of trees and shrubs. Starlings devour an untold number of wireworm, leather-jackets, weevils, slugs and snails, but like the blackbird they are also fond of fruit.

The mistle thrush and song thrush both like fruit too, but are great destroyers of snails, being continuously at work cracking the shells and eating the contents. They also destroy some harmful insects.

All members of the tit family are great helpmates in the garden. They are one of the principal exterminators of aphides and scale insects. The chaffinch, although a seed eater at other times of the year, feeds on insects during spring and summer. It is particularly fond of aphides and it will catch other insects while on the wing.

The spotted flycatcher, a spring migrant, is working unceasingly all day, ridding the garden of harmful flies, gnats and mosquitoes. All these birds should be encouraged, not only for their valuable work in the garden, but also because many of them delight us with their beauty and songs as well.

There are many beneficial insects to be found in the garden as well as harmful ones, and these must not be mistakenly destroyed. There is no need to say much about the bees except to mention perhaps that there are in the world about 600,000 species of bee. The honeybee is virtually the only insect that is domesticated by man, and the value of the bee to orchardists for pollinating is incalculable. How attractive during spring and summer the humble bee is, as it flits to and fro among the gaily coloured flowers. Some queen bees may be found in the garden shed or house during their winter hibernation; these should be left undisturbed as they are fertilized bees carrying eggs, ready to start a new colony in the spring. Any red admiral, peacock or tortoiseshell butterflies found hibernating should be left alone also, but destroy cabbage whites.

5

The *ladybird* beetle is one of our greatest friends. It feeds on greenfly and never seems to have its appetite satisfied. The adult beetle may be red with black spots, black with red spots, or yellow with black spots. The larva of the ladybird is a voracious hunter of aphides. After it has destroyed one colony it will travel in search of more. It is an ugly little creature, and to save it from being destroyed in mistake for a pest a short description of it seems necessary. It is about half an inch in length, of a greyish-black colour and with six yellow spots on the back of its body and with two near the head. The body is divided into segments and it has rows of about eight black spots lengthways. The three pairs of legs are situated near the front part of the body. The pupae are rounded, black and grey and orange-yellow. The yellow and orange usually predominate. They are fixed by their tail ends to a leaf

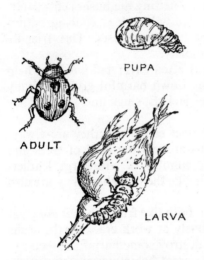

PROTECT THESE

PUPA

ADULT

LARVA

The Ladybird Beetle: one of the gardener's greatest friends

stem or some other object. There are over forty kinds of ladybird beetle in this country which are predatory, and they are all of similar construction. Ladybirds vary in their habits; some are scale insects, but all do wonderful work for the gardener. They often winter together in colonies and a favourite place is behind ivy, which is clinging to the bark of a tree. So wait until spring before clearing ivy away from trees.

The *hover fly* is another friend and the name is derived from the remarkable ability of the flies to stay motionless in the air and then suddenly dart away. They might be mistaken for wasps but they are smaller and of a different shape. They have generally yellow bodies with alternately thick and thin bands of black. There are many species, and colours vary. The hover fly lays eggs upon shoots of roses or other plants which have greenfly upon them. In a few days the eggs produce little maggots which feed chiefly upon aphides. The colour of the maggot is variable but the skin is transparent and the creature is legless, but it still moves about rapidly. On reaching an aphis it seizes it and devours it, leaving the skin. It has been calculated that one hover fly maggot will, during the course of its life, kill about one thousand aphides.

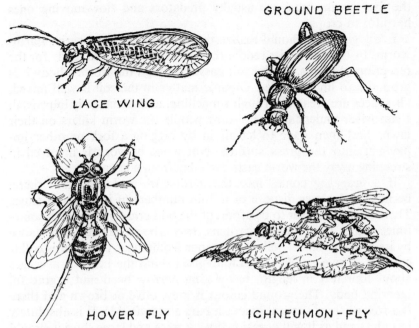

GROUND BEETLE

LACE WING

HOVER FLY

ICHNEUMON-FLY

Some other garden friends: do not destroy these

Another predatory insect is the beautiful *lace-wing fly*. These are greenish-yellow in general colour with golden eyes, and have four wings and fly with a slow fluttering movement. They often come into the house at night, attracted by light, but they should be looked after carefully and not injured as they are one of the greenfly's greatest enemies. The eggs of the lace-wing fly can rarely be mistaken as they are pearl-like and oval and each one has a stalk-like filament about half an inch in length attached. These eggs are usually in groups of about a dozen fixed to stems or leaves. When the eggs hatch, very active larvae are seen attacking and destroying aphides in much the same manner as the hover fly maggot. They also attack and eat scale insects, thrips and leaf hoppers.

Other parasitic insects such as *ichneumons, chalcids* and *brachonids* are also the gardener's friends. With the aid of their long ovipositor (which looks like a sting but is an egg-laying apparatus) they deposit eggs within the living tissue of a caterpillar. The grubs feed upon the host which is quickly killed.

The list of predaceous insects, parasitic insects and helpful beetles together with their life history and study would fill another book. The main ones have been mentioned and these should be preserved. The general rule regarding the beetle family found in the soil, is that the fast-moving type are usually predators and slow-moving ones harmful to crops.

Every gardener should realize the value of the *earthworm*. Earthworms by their activities render the soil more fertile and ready for the reception of plants. As the soil passes through the worm's body it is ground into fine particles. Organic matter in the soil is well mixed, air spaces are created through tunnelling, and drainage is improved. I can never understand why some people use worm killers on their lawns and then have to let air in by digging a fork or other implement into the grass surface. Not a lot of work is involved in sweeping away the worm casts each day from a lawn.

If a *hedgehog* comes into the garden try and keep him there, because hedgehogs dispose of untold numbers of insects and slugs. There is no need ever to be afraid of the odd *grass snake* which sometimes comes into country gardens. It can be recognized at a glance by its bright collar of yellow or orange (sometimes white); this collar consists of two patches of colour just behind the head. It averages about four feet in length, has a long narrow head and a graceful tapering body. The ground colour is grey, olive or brown and there is a row of short vertical blackish bars along its side. It is absolutely harmless and as it will occasionally eat mice and large slugs it should not be harmed in any way. It will make a loud hissing noise while being examined but this should be disregarded. Keep away from all other snakes which have not the yellow collar, as one might be the poisonous adder.

PLANT DISEASES

There are many plant diseases but the average gardener will only need knowledge of some of the main ones. The vegetable grower will almost certainly come up against potato blight at some time or another. This is more prevalent during wet summers. *Potato blight* is recognizable from the state of the leaves. If it is present, the leaves will lose their green colour and become spotted with yellow patches which soon turn brown and then black. Look at the underside of an infected leaf; a white cottony growth will be seen around the margin of each brown spot. This growth contains spore-bearing branches of the fungus. If spores (the seeds) fall on to other leaves it may cause a new infection by germinating immediately. It will only do this if conditions for growth are suitable. All fungi will only multiply if the weather is damp. Sometimes a very dry spell comes along after the first infection and the progress of the disease is arrested. The spores are carried by wind and rain from one plant to another and the whole crop can soon become infected. Sometimes the spores are washed from the leaves to the tubers and they also become affected. These tubers develop brown or purplish areas and when the potato is cut the flesh is usually a rusty red. It is very important not to put any of these diseased tubers into the seed tray for sprouting, and careful examination of each seed potato before planting is desirable. This appears to be the reason for the disease living from year to year, because diseased tubers have somehow got into the seed tray.

No potatoes should be left in the ground to over-winter, for the disease does not live on the dead foliage but remains in the tubers. It is most important when harvesting the potato crop, the early varieties as well as the main crop, to dig over the vacant land several times to ensure that all tubers are removed before planting other crops. If every gardener and farmer did this the infection chain would be broken.

Stored potatoes should be examined frequently for any sign of disease, any diseased tubers found should be burnt. Digging should take place on a dry day, there is then less chance of spreading spores. The tines of the fork and the gardening boots could be dipped in a solution of a copper fungicide after harvesting the crop. A strict rotation of planting must be carried out with potatoes and outdoor tomatoes. A regular spraying programme is very desirable. Spray with full-strength Bordeaux mixture, beginning in late June and repeat three times at fourteen-day intervals. Use a fine nozzle on the sprayer and see that the fungicide is directed at the undersides of the foliage as well as making a mist above the plants. See that the potatoes are well earthed up so that none are exposed. This lessens the chance of tubers becoming infected. If you have come back from a holiday and you observe that your plants have been attacked by blight, cut off all the haulms and burn them. This may prevent the tubers from becoming affected. Cut the haulms carefully so that you restrict the spreading of spores as much as possible. Leave the tubers for a fortnight, then lift them on a dry day, dry them well in the sun, and examine for signs of blight before storing. Similar control measures apply to outdoor tomatoes because they may be attacked, as they are members of the same family.

Always buy seed potatoes from a well-known seedsman. Beware of unknown advertisers offering cheap seed. Very often a consignment of these tubers will arrive and on inspection about half of them may be suffering from *dry rot*, another fungus infection. Bad storage seems to encourage this fungus to grow but as it attacks the tubers only it would appear that damaged tubers are most likely to be affected. This fungus lives in the soil so it is doubly important to carry out a good rotation for this important vegetable. To avoid this trouble when you have started off with good seed, try to prevent damage to tubers while harvesting; put any damaged ones to one side and use them in the kitchen first. Only store sound potatoes and avoid damp, stuffy conditions in store. Examine stored potatoes periodically, burn any found to be suffering from dry rot, or cut away the damaged part for burning and use the rest of the potato for immediate cooking.

The disease shows itself by a shrinkage of affected tissue, a characteristic wrinkling of the skin and the appearance of whitish or pink pustules on the brown decaying patch.

Club root of brassicas, including all cabbage family together with turnips, swedes and radishes may be encountered by the gardener taking over a garden or allotment which is lime deficient, and which has been supporting brassicas for some years. This is another fungus which destroys the fibrous roots and causes the larger roots to swell and decay, giving off a strong smell. When it is widespread it is advisable to refrain from growing any of the crops likely to be affected for a year or so. Thoroughly lime the land and use calomel dust in the seed drills when it seems possible to attempt brassicas again. Also put about a teaspoonful into each planting hole before transplanting.

Damping off, another fungus disease, is very common but easy to combat. It attacks seedlings which are growing in seed boxes or pots in greenhouse, cold frame or living-room. It may be present in the water used for watering, or in the soil, and the little seedling stems shrivel up and topple over. Water the soil in seed boxes or pots prior to sowing, with a fungicide called Cheshunt Compound, which is another copper preparation. Use this solution made up according to the maker's instructions on the tin, for watering all small seedlings, using a fine rose. To help prevent the disease ventilate as freely as possible, sow thinly and prick out early.

From time to time the gardener will hear a lot about a disease called *Botrytis* which is also a fungus. It is very widespread and abundant and it attacks a great variety of growing plants and also dead vegetation. It causes softness followed by decay and blackening. The most recognizable point is the later appearance of an outgrowth of grey fluffy mould. It will attack tomatoes, melons, vines, lettuces, strawberries, geraniums, roses, cucumbers and is also responsible for *chocolate spot* on beans. Control measures are to dust with flowers of sulphur; try to promote vigorous growth and avoid stuffy, damp conditions in greenhouse, frame and store.

White rot of onions and shallots sometimes puts in an appearance where these crops have been grown in the same piece of land for a number of years. This is identified by the ease with which bulbs can be pulled from the soil, as they have no roots. The leaves droop and turn yellow, and such roots as there are have a growth of fluffy white mould. The remedy is to burn all affected crops and not to grow onions or shallots in the same place for a few years. When growing the next crop of onions or shallots, work into the top soil 4 per cent calomel dust at the rate of two ounces per square yard before sowing or planting. This is yet another of the fungus diseases.

A great nuisance to those who like to grow a nice bed of roses is another fungus disease called *black spot*. Circular black spots appear all over the leaves and often on the stems as well. Leaves wither and drop off and if the disease is not checked the rose bush quickly becomes a mere skeleton. The treatment is to spray thoroughly with some kind of colloidal copper, but be careful to carry out the maker's instructions. Spray frequently from pruning time through the summer. Gather up all prunings and fallen rose leaves and burn them.

Mildew on roses, sweet peas, late culinary peas and many other plants is easily controlled by dusting with flowers of sulphur.

The most important tasks for the gardener to carry out in order to control pests and diseases is a rigorous destruction of all weeds which may act as host plants, together with good cultivation to promote vigorous growth in all plants so that they are stronger and able to resist disease. The burning of all infected prunings, foliage and in some cases whole plants, trees or bushes is essential. So is good crop rotation, so is attention to storage conditions; and, finally, it is possible in some cases to grow varieties which are resistant to particular diseases.

4

Gardening under Glass

Types of greenhouse — heating arrangements — the cool greenhouse — half-hardy bedding plants — starting vegetables under glass — cacti and succulents — cold frames — cloches

On any train journey one can see many derelict glasshouses. Some have numerous glass panes missing, others are covered with green scum and moss. There are many which are in good condition with spotless glass and newly painted timber, but for a greater part of the year they are empty. The purpose of this chapter is to show how these empty greenhouses can be filled to the great advantage of the owner. I wish that all the derelict ones would not remain so, that the owners would take an interest in them and clean and repair them. If they have been taken over by that minority who detest gardening, then instead of letting them remain an eyesore let them be given or sold to some keen gardener who is longing for a greenhouse, but who cannot afford to purchase a new one.

With the recent upsurge of interest in gardening, many more green-houses are being acquired. This is partly due also to the fact that higher incomes have brought the small greenhouse within the range of many more people.

Some gardeners may have taken over an old greenhouse or a conservatory on moving into a fresh house, others may have bought a new one, and many will be considering the benefits to be gained by possessing one. We shall see how the different types can best be used and how the various systems of heating will suit different growers.

There are five main types of greenhouse in use today. These are the glass-to-ground span roof, the span roof with a brick, asbestos or timber base, the Dutch type span roof, the lean-to and the three-quarter span. Before deciding on the type of house to be purchased consider which crops one wants to grow.

The greenhouse must be correctly sited so that it receives all the light possible. Plant growth is proportional to light intensity. The amount of light entering a greenhouse during the less favourable months, from October to April, is a very important consideration. We do not want the occupants of the greenhouse to stand still, we want them growing. To admit the maximum light as well as good siting, we must have the correct roof angle. The average grower is best equipped with a building which has high glass sides and a low angle roof slope. The best orientation for a well-designed house up to twelve feet by eight feet is from north to south but for longer houses, east to west is better, so that the plants can obtain the maximum benefit during the shortage of light in the winter months. Span-roof houses admit much more light than lean-to. We know that metal is a good conductor of heat, so an all-metal house has the disadvantage of rapid heat losses and heat gains. Metal supports can, however, be made very narrow, thus offering less obstruction to light. If a timber construction is chosen, some shelter against strong winds on the north and east side should be provided. The greenhouse should be built where the greatest light is obtainable but at not too great a distance from the dwelling-house. It is not convenient for the attendant to have to go some distance to attend to ventilation, heaters or plants during very bad weather. Greenhouses can be obtained which combine strength with the minimum of light obstruction and heat loss by using both metal and timber in the same building.

A greenhouse should be in use all the year round. Many gardeners still use it only for tomatoes in summer, followed by chrysanthemums. We should not discourage the growing of these two fine subjects, but there are many additional uses to which a greenhouse should be put.

To take full advantage of a greenhouse one or two cold frames should be acquired. Half-hardy flowers and vegetables can then be germinated in the glasshouse and gradually hardened off in the cold frames. One should not try to grow too many plants in a greenhouse, as greenhouse plants do not grow well in overcrowded conditions. It is advisable to try to grow species which require more or less the same treatment. Do not try to bring vegetables to maturity unless a large well-heated greenhouse is available, and do not mix vegetables and flowers or pot plants, only in the small seedling stage.

The greenhouse owner can profit in many ways from his possession; he can pursue a worthwhile hobby in a comfortable atmosphere, when in winter all outside gardening is at a standstill. He can get a good start when the weather is suitable by having brought forward his vegetables and flower seedlings under glass.

During a hard winter the gardener with a glasshouse can calculate what heating he will need to meet every emergency. The most efficient heating apparatus can only produce a known amount of heat from

coal, coke, gas or electricity. It is unsatisfactory to install heating
equipment that is incapable of giving a 20° Fahrenheit rise in temperature if required. This temperature may have to be maintained
sometimes for several days. If a heating system of this nature is too
costly, then one must not try to grow the tender variety of plants.

Adequate ventilation should be looked for in the new modern
greenhouses. Choose one with roof ventilators and with side ventilators. Although side ventilators can be fitted at any time, it is
cheaper in the long run to have them right from the outset.

TYPES OF GREENHOUSE

The *glass-to-ground span-roof* greenhouse has high eaves and vertical
sides. It is the best kind of house for growing tomatoes, chrysanthemums, carnations and many other plants which need plenty of
light. The maximum light is admitted and the ground is warmed, thus
conserving heat. Staging can be used for pot plants and there is a
growing space beneath the staging for raising seedlings of all kinds
or for propagating cuttings. This ensures a high growing capacity
to the house because every part can be used.

There are in existence, nearly everywhere, brick-based span-roofed
greenhouses. These were built before the universal growing of tomatoes, chrysanthemums and carnations for which they are entirely
unsuitable. The staging which is usually permanently constructed all
the way round the house was used in Victorian times for a hetero-
geneous collection of pot plants. These greenhouses are still quite
suitable for growing many beautiful flowering plants in pots and for
starting half-hardy plants which will later be transferred to the cold
frame and open garden. Owners of these houses who have taken them
over, have to make the best use of them, because their conversion
into a glass-to-ground house would present many constructional
problems. This type of house can be purchased today but instead of
bricks often a timber or asbestos base is used. These houses are used
by people who just want to grow some pot plants for house decoration, but as nothing can be grown below the staging they are wasteful
of space. The base can be used for storage of fuchsias, dahlia tubers,
gladioli corms and pots, seed boxes, watering-can and labels.

The *Dutch-type span-roof* is so named because its appearance is
similar to the Dutch Light structures which are more like very large
cloches and are used as such in Holland for the bulb industry. It has
sloping sides which slope outwards. Some people have preferred this
design which has appeared since the last war. It is usually glazed to
the ground and is most suitable for crops which must have plenty of
light such as chrysanthemums, tomatoes and carnations. There is the

one disadvantage of not being able to plant tall subjects near the glass sides.

The *lean-to greenhouse* is now only recommended where there is no suitable site for a span-roof type. This greenhouse is best erected against the south wall of a dwelling-house, for this gives protection from wind, and as the walls of an occupied house radiate some warmth, advantage can be taken of this also. As with the span-roof one on a brick base, there are a great number of lean-to houses, and in these, if large enough, can be grown figs, grapes, peaches and nectarines. Pot plants can also be grown if the staging is erected in tiers so that the plants get as much light as possible. There are today some very attractive conservatory-type greenhouses built on to the south wall of a residence with an entrance door leading from the dwelling-house. Some of these are glass-to-ground and some have a timber base. Many people grow beautiful house plants in them, others, besides growing plants, use them as sun porches or as an extra sitting-room. The *Dutch-type lean-to greenhouse* gives a good width and can be fixed against fairly low walls.

The *three-quarter-span greenhouse* is just a modified lean-to which allows some northern light to enter. It is used mainly as a vinery in large gardens. If one has taken over a large house with one of these gardens there are often a span greenhouse and frames as well. In the three-quarter span, fruit trees such as peaches and nectarines or ornamental climbers can be trained against the high wall.

Where tomatoes, chrysanthemums or a few carnations are to be grown as well as pot plants, a *dual-purpose greenhouse* can be obtained. These houses are glazed to the ground on one side only, the other side being boarded up to the level of the staging for pot plants. This also provides winter storage space for begonias, fuchsias, gladioli corms, dahlia tubers and other plants.

HEATING ARRANGEMENTS

There are many systems of greenhouse heating in use today. The temperatures to be maintained depend on the plants being grown. For the plants growing in what is known as a cool greenhouse, where just enough heat is provided to exclude frost, the grower should aim at a temperature of 50° Fahrenheit during the day and 40° at night. To measure this, a good quality maximum and minimum thermometer is absolutely essential. One can then see at a glance if the temperature has fallen below the figure required during the coldest part of the night.

Whichever system of heating is employed, we have to face the fact that all types of fuel are expensive today. Therefore if we are using heat we must try to make the best possible use of it and manage our greenhouse to the best advantage we can. We might be able to cover our heating costs if we can bring on early vegetable plants, harden them off and grow them to maturity when they are scarce and expensive in the shops. Also by growing our own bedding plants a considerable saving is effected.

There are various kinds of electrical heating equipment for greenhouses. If a solid fuel boiler type has been inherited there are usually two four-inch hot water pipes, a flow and return, which run the length of the house. Into these can be fitted electric immersion heaters with thermostatic control. This is a very useful device because if there is an electricity cut, the solid fuel boiler can be started up, provided that it has been maintained in good condition. In all greenhouses some alternative heating arrangement should be at hand should there be a power cut or an electrical fault. A greenhouse paraffin heater will sometimes overcome these difficulties.

Electric tubular heaters are most efficient, and extra heaters can easily be added if required. The actual heat source is dry heat and the desired humidity is obtained by damping down the inside paths of the house. These tubes are usually made of aluminium and they are long-lasting. Each apparatus consists of the lengths of tubing required according to the size of the greenhouse, brackets for mounting them, a length of cable for plugging into the power point and a thermostat for automatic temperature control. This form of heating is relatively cheap to run because the heat only comes on when actually wanted.

Another method of electrical heating is by a fan which blows warm air through the house. In the summer it can be used merely to circulate air. This is a system to be recommended as a safe frost protection, but not for a house whose plants need a high temperature. This heater is thermostatically controlled and it reduces condensation and damping off. It circulates air evenly, eliminating any cold corners. It is supplied with cable and thermostat.

Electric water heaters, sometimes called heater-humidifiers, consist of two copper tubular troughs filled with water. These are connected to three larger upright tubes. An advantage of these is that they are portable and require no fixing. They are supplied with a cable which is just plugged in and they are thermostatically controlled.

There are two further pieces of electrical heating equipment for greenhouses which can also be used for heating garden frames. One is a warming cable for direct connection to a mains supply. It can be run round anywhere in the greenhouse, on bench or staging. These cables usually consist of a flat, flexible, glass-shrouded element encased in some heat-resisting material.

The final electrical heating device is a soil-warming unit. This is an outfit where the cable to be heated is laid under the soil giving bottom warmth. This takes the place of the old hot bed so much favoured by gardeners in the past. This was made of fermenting manure or compost, but the great drawback to these was that it was difficult to control the temperature. These soil-warming units can be thermostatically controlled.

If one is making use of a lean-to greenhouse with the back door of the dwelling-house adjoining and a point plug is handy, an ordinary convector heater could be used to heat the lean-to. It is best when wiring or installing any electrical equipment to have the work carried out by a fully qualified electrician.

For large heating installations, a solid fuel boiler which burns anthracite or coke is economical to run, but entails fairly constant attention and cannot be automatically controlled. It is not the sort of heater for a busy man who is away from home all day, unless someone else on the premises is willing to attend to it. It has to be stoked, ashes must be kept clear, clinkers removed and damper adjusted to meet the needs of changing weather. Also it has to be made up last thing at night. It is still a very good heating system, however, for someone who is on the spot for long periods, and able to meet all these requirements.

Where a solid fuel boiler has been taken over and one has not the time to attend to it, it can easily be converted to an oil-fired boiler. An oil storage tank will then be necessary. The amount of oil consumed can be controlled at the turn of a knob.

There are many firms who make paraffin greenhouse heaters. They are of many different designs and sizes. On some there is a removable humidity tray which lies on top of the heater and is filled with water. These oil heaters are very cheap to run and are very good where no electricity is connected. Today they are well designed and do not emit an excess of fumes if well attended to. Many gardeners are finding them most successful, especially in the growing of tomatoes. As frost excluders they are most valuable and for any crops which need only gentle heat.

A small propagating frame which can be about three feet by four feet is always required in a greenhouse for rooting various soft cuttings like chrysanthemums and for germinating seeds quickly. This can be in the form of a box with a sheet of glass on the top and kept on the staging nearest the boiler or the particular form of heater. There are today many electrically heated propagating frames and they are worth installing if they can be afforded. Most of them are made of fibre glass or one of the plastics. Some are thermostatically controlled. These propagators may be used apart from the greenhouse, in the living-room or elsewhere, and they can be used by people without a greenhouse. In these cases boxes of seeds are put into the propagator, the current is switched on, and with those which are self-humidifying the seeds are soon germinated. The resultant seedlings can be kept near the window in a warm room, then gradually transferred to a cold frame.

While on the subject of heating it may be mentioned that sometimes in a particularly hot summer some form of shading for the greenhouse may be necessary. Shading is often needed for orchids, cucumbers, ferns, melons and some primulas. If some of these crops are grown in

ROLLER LATH BLINDS

A good form of greenhouse shading

the same house as vines which clamber among the greenhouse rooftops, then, of course, the vines will provide enough shade. The other forms of shading used are white-washing of the roof glass or using a special wash called 'Summer Cloud', which is green and less conspicuous; but remember to remove these at the end of summer. Lath blinds on rollers may be utilized, or a green mesh material which separates from the sun's rays while allowing a free circulation of air.

THE COOL GREENHOUSE

When preparing potting and seed sowing composts a convenient place for this work must be found. If a good floor is available in a garage or shed this would do for the mixing of the potting soil. Then a bench is required for the actual seed sowing and potting operations. Sometimes this work will have to be done in one corner of the greenhouse. Then a portable potting bench or tray can be provided. A convenient tray made of wood could be about three feet six inches wide and three feet long with back and sides a foot high.

The gardener will hear and read a lot about John Innes potting and seed composts. At the John Innes Horticultural Institution they came to the scientific conclusion that seed sowing and potting composts must be made up to a certain formula. This was evolved after many years of experiment and it has proved highly suitable for most plants and seeds. The details are as follows:

No. 1 *Seed Sowing Compost:* two parts medium loam, one part good garden peat, one part silver sand. To each bushel of this mixture are added $1\frac{1}{2}$ oz. superphosphate and $\frac{3}{4}$ oz. ground limestone or chalk.

No. 2 *Potting Compost:* seven parts medium loam, three parts good peat, two parts silver sand. To each bushel of mixture are added $1\frac{1}{2}$ oz. superphosphate and $\frac{3}{4}$ oz. ground limestone or chalk.

Although garden peat is to be preferred, because it is free from any injurious organisms and sources of disease, thoroughly decayed leaf mould could be used if the peat is too expensive. If the gardener has made his own leaf mould as outlined in the last chapter, so much the better. Sand for potting composts is difficult to find and silver sand has generally to be purchased. If some coarse, clean sand can be discovered it can be used, but ordinary builders' sand is practically useless. If this is used pots will dry out quickly and set hard.

The most important ingredient of these composts is the medium loam. The roots of a plant growing in a well dug and cultivated garden can ramble to an almost unlimited extent in search of plant food. A plant whose roots will be permanently encased by a pot will have its root run very restricted, so careful consideration must be given to the preparation of the soil for a pot plant which will be very largely a permanent occupant of the greenhouse. For the medium loam use the very best soil you have in the garden and mix with it a good proportion of well-rotted garden compost. The kind of loam or soil which the gardener can use will dictate the amount of lightening-up material to be added until the loam becomes suitable for potting soil. Some will have to add more sand, leaf mould or well-rotted compost until the loam acquires the correct texture. With experience the gardener will soon discover for himself a suitable loam to use.

When a quantity of turf is taken from the lawn, paddock or

grassland it should be stacked with the earth-side uppermost in layers. If a little soil, leaf mould, sand and some rotted manure is sprinkled over at intervals between the layers it will rot down after about a year into excellent potting loam. The heap should be built to about five feet in height. If this sort of loam is used together with well-decayed leaf mould or garden peat, I do not think there is any need to sterilize soil. Too much soil sterilization may well destroy the helpful bacteria.

Although the sieve has not been mentioned in the list of tools in Chapter 2 the greenhouse owner will need one of quarter-inch mesh for most pots and seed boxes, although an additional one of half-inch mesh would be very useful for larger items. After the ingredients for the potting compost have been thoroughly mixed with a shovel, they will have to be put through the sieve.

Pots and boxes must be absolutely clean before they are filled. The good gardener always has a collection of well-scrubbed clean pots of different dimensions stacked ready for use. Pots may be obtained in different sizes from one inch across the top to eighteen inches.

All plants in pots and boxes need a drainage system which will fulfil the following conditions. It must not let the soil out through the hole in the bottom of the pot, it must not let the water through too quickly, but it must let it through gradually. A few crocks, which are broken pieces of pots, are first put loosely over the hole, and then some rough material like partly decayed leaf mould or lumpy peat is laid on the crocks. If some seedlings or small plants are being potted up for growing in the cool greenhouse, the procedure is as follows. Put some compost into a 3 inch pot and make firm, place the plant to be potted in the centre, making sure that it is level. Do not bury too deeply or plant too shallowly. Add more compost and make firm with thumb and fingers all round the plant, leaving a space below the rim of the pot for watering.

The newcomer to a greenhouse will learn by experience how to manage it well. When the plants are flagging it may be due to the need for water or to over-watering. There may not be enough air circulating or the temperature may be too high or too low. When in doubt about ventilation it is best to give air. With watering the gardener can obtain a piece of bamboo cane about a foot long and insert tightly on one end an empty cotton reel. If a pot is tapped in the centre with this and a dull heavy sound is emitted then the plant does not need water. Similarly if a high-pitched ringing note is received then watering is required.

It is very convenient to have a tank to catch the rain water from the roof of the greenhouse and to use this for watering as far as it will go. In some greenhouses these water tanks can be under the staging

Glass-to-Ground Span-roof

Span-roof, boarded all way
round and with staging
for pot plants

Span-roof, boarded on
one side only

GREENHOUSES
All those illustrated on
this and the following
page are constructed of
timber and metal

Span-roof 'Dutch Light'
type, boarded on one
side

Lean-to greenhouse.
More staging could
easily be erected

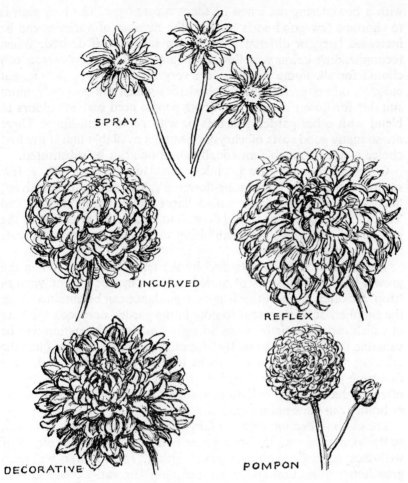

SPRAY

INCURVED

REFLEX

DECORATIVE

POMPON

Types of Chrysanthemums

where the water will run inside the house, thus ensuring that the water is fairly tepid. Where possible always use water which has been raised to the temperature of the house. Never water with ice-cold water from a tap. In the summer, watering is normally done in the evening unless one spots a plant which is needing a drink. In the winter, water at about ten in the morning or when the outside temperature begins to rise.

When speaking of a cool greenhouse we mean one which has sufficient heat to exclude frost. Most greenhouse owners will want to grow a few chrysanthemums which they can have in flower at Christmas-time or after. The varieties of chrysanthemums abound in great numbers and a newcomer to a greenhouse is often confronted

6

with a bewildering list when he scans a catalogue. The best plan is to choose a few good sorts at first; the number of varieties can be increased later, or different ones grown each year if desired. When recommending colours of flowers of any kind, no one person can choose for all. Some people adore very bright or even flamboyant colours, others prefer soft pastel shades which are generally more suitable for flower decoration. Some people need certain colours to blend with other garden schemes or with room furnishings. There are so many good sorts of chrysanthemums available that if the first choice is not obtainable an equally good one can be substituted.

Chrysanthemums grown under glass are divided into a few sections; these are 'anemone-flowered', 'cascades', 'decoratives', 'incurves', 'Japanese' (now called 'large exhibition'), 'singles' and 'charm'. The newcomer would do well to confine his attention to the growing of one or two large exhibition varieties, a few incurved sorts and some decoratives.

The amateur is often mystified by the term 'stopping'. When the grower buys his first stock of rooted cuttings, instructions of when to 'stop' are often given. If this is not so, guidance can be obtained from the supplier. It is important to note in the garden notebook the date at which certain varieties were 'stopped', as this information will be valuable the following year. By 'stopping' we mean pinching out the growing point of the plant to make it more bushy and to delay the flowering period. A flower bud developing too early or too late will often produce a flower of deformed shape. Many varieties will 'break' or branch out quite naturally.

The chrysanthemum enjoys a fairly rich soil with plenty of humus, so the loam used with the John Innes No. 2 compost needs plenty of well-decayed garden compost mixed with it. These flowers will need greenhouse protection and some heating if late varieties are grown, so it must be remembered that a space must be available where the plants can stand outside during the summer. They are taken into the greenhouse before the first autumn frosts.

Select your rooted cuttings from the list of a reputable firm. A chrysanthemum specialist is best, but well-known seedsmen can be relied upon. Many will advertise their cuttings as 'heat-therapy treated'; this means that the cuttings have been immersed in hot water at a temperature of 110°F. in order to kill any eelworm, one of the chrysanthemum pests. This is an operation best left to the experts for it is difficult for the amateur to maintain the exact temperature required. Anything higher is likely to kill the cutting and anything lower will not exterminate the eel worm.

Have enough soil and pots ready to receive the cuttings. Three-inch pots will be most suitable. When the cuttings arrive, unpack as soon

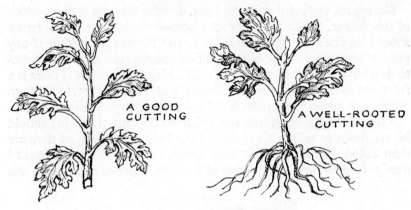

A GOOD CUTTING

A WELL-ROOTED CUTTING

CHRYSANTHEMUMS

How good cuttings should look.
Some side leaves may be trimmed before potting up

as possible and submerge the roots in tepid water for an hour or so.
Pot firmly in the manner previously described and space them out so
that there is plenty of air circulating between the plants to encourage
sturdy growth. After a few weeks' growth transfer the pots to a cold
frame. If there is a severe frost imminent the frames must be covered.

Transfer to larger pots as necessary, the first being a six-inch pot.
Deal with the most forward-looking plants first. When all danger of
frost has disappeared, the plants may stand outside, preferably on a
bed of ashes. Each plant should be tied to a bamboo cane. When the
tips of white roots are seen protruding from the base of the pot, put
the plants into their final ten-inch pots. Do not delay re-potting
at any stage as the plants become starved, take some time to recover,
and may produce inferior blooms. Watch out for aphides at all stages,
and take measures to control them.

'Stopping' depends upon variety and nurseryman's instructions;
some sorts need no stopping. The first is usually done in April, and
the second, if needed, in early July. Disbudding is the removal of
side shoots and flower buds, leaving the crown bud or one bud per
shoot. Select the largest and healthiest-looking bud and pinch
out the others carefully. This operation must be done gently because
the crown bud is very easily dislodged in the process.

Weeding must be done carefully so that no damage is caused to the
roots which will soon be filling the pots. Plants may be brought into
the greenhouse at the end of September or beginning of October.
Watering should be carried out in the usual manner, taking care not
to over-water but also making sure that no plants dry out.

During the days of decreasing light, dampness is one of the enemies of this flower. When the plants are housed the interior of the house should be dried out gradually. Dust with flowers of sulphur if any mildew appears. A large bloom will sometimes take about six weeks to develop fully, but do not try to hold a high temperature if there is a frost outside. During the developing and flowering period 45° to 50°F. with some ventilation will be a high enough temperature.

After the chrysanthemum has finished flowering the stems should be cut down to within six inches of the base, the stools, as they are then called, being placed in deep wooden boxes with loam packed firmly around them. They should then be watered and put in the

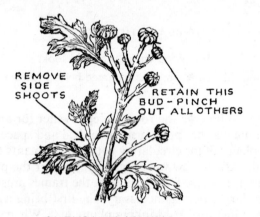

REMOVE SIDE SHOOTS

RETAIN THIS BUD - PINCH OUT ALL OTHERS

CHRYSANTHEMUM

Disbudding and removing side shoots

greenhouse. After about a month, most varieties will send up new shoots from the roots. Different kinds of shoots will be seen, some growing from the stems, but the ones to be used for cuttings are the fresh young shoots from the base of the stool. This is the way in which the chrysanthemum is propagated each year. These shoots should be about three inches long and are usually ready for taking in January or early February. The shoots should be cut cleanly just below a joint and any bottom leaves removed. Cuttings can be inserted firmly around the edge of a three-inch pot or in boxes with the soil being an equal mixture of loam and silver sand. Water them after firming, but not again until they have rooted. When they have rooted they should be potted singly as soon as possible. The cuttings may be dipped in a hormone rooting powder and put into a propagating frame if obtainable, but they will usually root quite well in an ordinary greenhouse atmosphere with the temperature at 50°F. They will flag while they have no roots but they will soon pick up again.

Do not sprinkle with water in the hope of reviving them while they have no roots.

Once the gardener has purchased an initial stock of rooted cuttings he can go on increasing his plants by taking cuttings each year. Each stool will usually provide at least six good cuttings.

For those who would like to try to grow from seed there is now a mixed strain called 'Autumn Happiness', which if sown early in the year will bloom the same season. From the best plants cuttings can be taken the following year. Larger flowers will be provided from the cuttings. The mixture contains double, semi-double, needle-petalled and incurves of various colours and forms.

Here are some chrysanthemums well worth growing in the cool greenhouse. When purchasing cuttings it must be remembered that the latest varieties are always more expensive than others.

The first on my list are varieties which will flower from late October to the end of November without heat. They need greenhouse protection. 'Charles Rowe', a 1962 introduction, is a fine incurving yellow. 'Dick May', 1964, deep crimson, purple sheen. 'Evenglow', golden-amber, with spiky petal formation. 'Snowclad', large white, green-tinged centre. 'Virtue', soft rose-pink. 'October Dazzler', crimson. 'Marie Brunton', tight incurving blooms, deep yellow, tinged orange.

Next is a list of incurved varieties, which also flower in late October and November, but require slight heat in damp, foggy weather. 'Alice Rowe', white, award of merit, 1961. 'Audrey Shoesmith', a perfect pink incurved. 'Connie Mayhew', pale creamy-primrose. 'Coronation Gold', beautiful crimson, with gold reverse. 'Leo', rose with purple sheen (a new colour). 'Mme. E. Roger', for floral art, an incurved green. 'John Rowe', 1962, a wonderful example of perfect incurved yellow.

The large exhibition varieties flower in November and require slight heat in damp or frosty weather. The first of these which I would grow would be 'Cossack', a magnificent crimson. 'Green Goddess' is sea green. 'Margaret Shoesmith', a lovely pink. 'Peter May', rich purple, with wine colour shading, an unusual colour. 'Surrey White', incurving blooms of fine quality, and 'Shirley Primrose', large primrose-yellow.

For the late decoratives, those which require heat from November onwards, the following are really magnificent flowers. Some will provide flowers during January. 'Elizabeth', 1963 introduction, is a beautifully shaped variety with pointed petals, in a lovely pastel colour of lemon, primrose and cream. 'Snowshine', 1962 award of merit, a wonderfully shaped, incurved white. 'Firecracker', brilliant crimson. 'Glenshades', red-gold incurved. 'Apricot Fred Shoesmith', rosy-apricot with gold centre. 'Christmas Wine', a broad-petalled, wine-coloured. 'Goldplate', 1964, large decorative, deep gold and 'Primrose Fred Shoesmith', a beautiful shade of primrose.

The high price of tomatoes throughout the year makes them a worthwhile crop for the owner of a cool greenhouse. Tomatoes have been grown in many types of houses, but the best type is the glass-to-ground span roof. Plenty of light is needed, not only for the growing plant, but also for the ripening of the fruit. They may be grown in pots or boxes or in a border in the greenhouse with staging removed altogether or from one side, if pot plants are to be grown as well. Tomatoes, unlike carnations, are tolerant of other crops growing in the same house.

The seed-sowing compost should be John Innes No. 1, again having plenty of good, well-rotted garden compost mixed with the loam. This mixture should be placed in the greenhouse about a week before it is required. The temperature of the house at sowing time should be 60°F. Fill the seed boxes, making the soil firm, and then water with Cheshunt Compound. This fungicide is to prevent damping-off disease and is a mild soil sterilizer. It is made up in the following manner. One ounce of the mixture is dissolved in a little warm water and made up to two gallons with cold water. This should be used immediately after being made. It should not be mixed in any vessel made of iron, tin or zinc. After some experience in using this compound the gardener will be able to mix without measuring. The right strength is usually a pale sky blue colour. The seeds should be spaced at about an inch and a half apart after the excess water has drained away. Only a slight film of compost is needed to cover the seeds and then each box should be covered with a pane of glass, and over this a sheet of brown paper. Each morning the glass should be turned over to prevent condensation from dripping on to the seedlings as they are germinating. When the seedlings appear, remove the glass and paper. When two leaves have grown, transfer the seedlings to three-inch pots using John Innes No. 2. Again when watering is required, use Cheshunt Compound until the plants are growing away strongly. Handle the small seedlings very carefully as the stems are very easily bruised. Keep the temperature at 60°F. When the plants are about six inches high and have made a good root system, plant them into their permanent quarters. When planting out, do not disturb the roots and plant firmly, retaining the soil from the pots pressed around them. Tomatoes may be planted a little deeper than they were, for new roots will form from the stem.

If the tomatoes are to be grown in the greenhouse border (provided that the owner has a large enough space) the border should be dug over early, adding plenty of well-rotted garden compost or farmyard manure. Flood the trenches as digging proceeds to ensure that the sub-soil is really wet; the rotted compost will help to retain this moisture. In addition to the compost an organic fertilizer, like fish manure, and a quantity of wood ashes to give potash should be forked into the top soil.

Plant out at about twelve inches between the plants and eighteen inches between the rows. The soil for receiving the plants should be at 58°F. Water the plants for two or three days until they become established. Water a week later and then try and withhold water until the flowers of the second truss are opening. Then the watering programme should be to water only when the plants really need it, when the leaves look dull or appear to be drooping. Let in as much air as possible during the day, at the same time trying to keep the temperature at 60°F.

A top dressing of fish manure can be given every fortnight after the fruit has begun to set. The plants may be tied to six-foot bamboo canes or trained up lengths of string or wire suspended from the roof of the house.

The night temperature should be kept at 63°F. but the higher temperature in the daytime due to sun-heat does not matter as this is natural heat. It is usual to keep the plants cool during June by over-head syringing. From June onwards it is nearly always possible to keep the ventilators open at either end of the house to ensure a free movement of air. These can be kept open at night providing it is not an exceptionally cold June. The grower must try and see that his plants do not suffer from any check during their entire lifetime.

Side shoots must be removed regularly and the growing point of the plant pinched out when it has reached the roof. If the plant has produced an excess of foliage it will not hurt to carefully remove some here and there where the leaves are shading the fruit.

The gardener will learn from experience when and how to water his plants. Care must be taken with all watering, sometimes insufficient watering or over-watering can cause uneven ripening of fruit and cracking of fruit. If the plants are watered about once a week from June onwards there should not be any serious trouble. If mildew appears, dust the foliage with flowers of sulphur. One word of warning. No one should ever smoke in a greenhouse, particularly in a tomato house. Smoking can cause plants to turn yellow and die back.

The method of growing tomatoes which has been described is for those people who have a fair-sized greenhouse. Tomatoes are not a good crop to grow where one has only a very small box-like structure and where the owner is away all day with no one to attend to watering and ventilation. These small greenhouses where only a few plants may be housed are nearly always short of ventilators, and tomatoes must have adequate air to grow well.

We have talked about the two favourite crops for most owners of a cool greenhouse, but there are many other subjects which will make it possible for the greenhouse to be filled all the year round.

Bulbs are one of the most useful and most beautiful flowers to grow in the cool greenhouse. Their culture is fairly easy and they fill the gap between the chrysanthemums and the tomato crop. Bulbs in the greenhouse can be brought into flower from December to March. The best way to ensure a succession of bloom is to start planting from early September until the end of October at weekly intervals. Bulb fibre can be used in bowls but better results are obtained if the bulbs are planted in pots with drainage holes, using good medium loam, leaf mould and silver sand; a little bone meal is a welcome addition for hyacinths, as they are big feeders. For all kinds of bulbs use deep pots which will hold about three bulbs, and pot up in the usual manner. Bury the pots outside in the garden in a shady spot. The pots may be first covered with garden peat or straw and then soil. I always finish off with a layer of ashes to deter slugs, and I put down a few slug-killer pellets. Often slugs will go for the young shoots as they appear and then, later on, the foliage will look rather disfigured. Well water the spot where they are put and then subsequent rain should provide the required moisture. After about eight weeks the pots ought to be well filled with roots and the bulbs making top growth. The cool conditions outside are essential for root production. No bulbs must be forced into flower until a good rooting system has materialized. The many insignificant blooms one sees in many houses and some shops during the winter are mainly due to lack of good root function.

When the pots or bowls have been lifted from their outdoor position they should be gradually given more light but not put straight away into the greenhouse. They must be grown on for a week or two in cool conditions. A cold frame which at first has been partially shaded, is a good place for them, then a room in the dwelling-house which has little or no heating, such as a spare room. Place the bulbs at this stage near the windows. After about a week or ten days of this treatment they may be placed in the greenhouse to be brought into flower at a temperature of 55°F. They can be left in the greenhouse for a colourful display there or distributed in all rooms in the house, where they are perhaps best appreciated.

Hyacinths are about the most popular bulb for indoor flowering today. This is easy to understand when one thinks of their wonderful perfume and the lengthy flowering period. One type of hyacinth

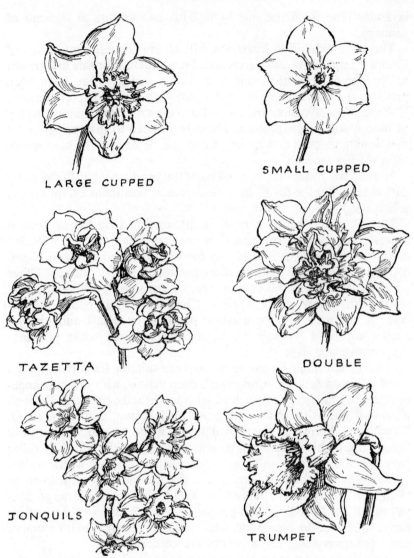

LARGE CUPPED

SMALL CUPPED

TAZETTA

DOUBLE

JONQUILS

TRUMPET

Types of Narcissi grown under glass

which should be grown more extensively is the miniature hyacinth called 'Cynthella'; it has lovely loose spikes on graceful stems and can easily be forced into bloom for Christmas. They can be obtained in almost the same colour range as the large-flowering hyacinths.

The 'Roman hyacinth' can be in flower by Christmas even in an ordinary heated living-room. Then there is the 'multiflora' hyacinth which gives from five to seven small dainty spikes of a bright lavender blue from the one bulb. This one flowers at the end of January.

The large exhibition hyacinths will all give magnificent spikes of bloom if large bulbs are purchased. Some offered for sale are known as 'prepared hyacinths', and will flower earlier. They have been pre-cooled to give the bulb winter and early spring-like conditions. If some of each variety mentioned are grown, a continuous display of bloom will be guaranteed. There is no need to take up space by mentioning colours and names, these can be seen in the seedsman's shop during autumn.

Next to the hyacinths, narcissi seem the most popular, followed by daffodils. All bulbs for forcing need similar treatment except crocus which need no heat.

The 'Poetaz' type of narcissi is distinguished by having several flowers on a single stem, and they are very fragrant. 'Paper White' can easily be brought into bloom for Christmas, and so can 'Soleil d'Or' which has rich golden-yellow petals and a tangerine cup. Other good varieties from this section are 'Cheerfulness', double creamy-white with yellow centre, 'Yellow Cheerfulness', a yellow counter-part, 'Cragford', with pure white perianth or petals and orange-scarlet cup, and 'Geranium', large-flowered, pure white perianth, deep orange-red cup.

Most of the single large-cup narcissi are suitable for forcing, and a good selection follows: 'Carbineer', deep yellow, with bright orange-red cup, 'Cavaliero', deep yellow, with bright red cup, 'John Evelyn', creamy-white, with widely expanded apricot cup, and 'Mrs. R. O. Backhouse', known as the pink daffodil, white with an apricot-pink fluted cup. If this variety can be afforded, and at the time of writing they are about fifteen shillings a dozen, they are well worth trying.

Daffodils suitable for forcing are the double daffodil known as 'Van Sion', 'Beersheba', pure white, 'Golden Harvest', a large golden-yellow, 'King Alfred', golden-yellow, 'Golden Spur', a golden-yellow early, 'Queen of the Bicolours', white perianth, canary-yellow trumpet and 'Unsurpassable', the largest of all, golden-yellow.

Early single tulips are a good subject for bringing into bloom in the cool greenhouse. Their bright colours are very welcome in any household. Suitable varieties with about three or four bulbs to a pot or bowl are 'Bellona', rich golden-yellow, 'Brilliant Star', vermilion-scarlet, for Christmas forcing, 'Joffre', pure yellow, Christmas forcing, 'Cramoisie Brilliant', rich glowing scarlet, 'Proserpine', brilliant rose, flushed carmine, 'Van Der Neer', rich purple-mauve, and 'White Hawk', pure white.

Early Double tulips are good for pot work, their massive blooms on strong stems giving a most pleasing effect. Some of the best varieties are 'Dante', rich blood-red, 'Maréchal Niel', soft canary-yellow, 'Electra', rosy-carmine, shaded violet, 'Murillo', soft pink, 'Schoonoord', pure white, and 'William Kordes', orange, shaded yellow and flame red, a very colourful variety.

Darwin tulips may be forced if the grower would like some but they are more suitable for the commercial grower who grows a large quantity for the cut-flower trade. They are tall, so they would need staking and tying if grown in the greenhouse in pots. They will not grow with any measure of success in fibre alone. There is a wider range of colour in this section of the tulips than in other kinds.

We can include crocus in the bulb section although classed as corms. They are most effective when planted in a round bowl with about fifteen corms to a bowl. The yellow variety blooms about a fortnight before the other colours. They do not need heat to be brought into flower, just protection from frost.

One or two other showy plants for the cool greenhouse which may be mentioned at this point and may be grown if there is room for them, are Hippeastrum or Barbados Lily, Arum Lily, Freesias, Lily of the Valley and Tritonia.

The Hippeastrums can be propagated from offsets or from seed. They are bulbous plants and can be obtained in shades of red, orange, salmon, rose and white. They make glorious pot plants growing to a height of two to three feet with strap-shaped leaves and large funnel-shaped flowers which appear in March, April and May. The off-sets should be potted up singly in six-inch pots of John Innes Compost No. 2 and water should be given sparingly until growth has started. These plants are usually re-potted every three years in January and it is at this stage that the off-sets can be potted up. Seed is sown in the usual way in early spring. The Hippeastrum is a useful plant to start off in the cool house, because if there is a shortage of space it will grow afterwards in a sunny window or in a cool or heated conservatory.

The Arum Lily is a choice subject, very good for flower arrangements and equally admired for flower and foliage. In addition to the well-known white variety which flowers at Easter-time, there are yellow-flowered varieties with variegated leaves which adorn the greenhouse in August. All varieties are propagated by root divisions or off-sets after flowering and should be put into six-inch or eight-inch pots. The roots are then kept at a temperature of 55° to 60°F. keeping the soil moderately moist at all stages of growth. The established plants of the white varieties are best put out of doors from June to September, plunged into a bed of ashes or soil.

Another charming bulb flower is the popular Freesia which can be grown by planting corms or from seed sowing. It is particularly suited for the cool greenhouse as it is almost hardy and only needs protection from frost. A long flowering period can be ensured if successional weekly plantings of the corms are made, beginning in August and completing the work by November. A five-inch pot will accommodate six corms and they are placed just below the surface of the soil. They must be kept in good light throughout growth. When the buds begin to show the plants can be given an organic liquid manure.

Freesias grown from seed are sown in large boxes from March until June and after the germination and pricking out stage, again using Cheshunt Compound; the seedlings are grown on out of doors during the summer months. They are brought into the greenhouse from mid-September onwards, keeping the temperature at 50°F. This beautiful fragrant greenhouse flower can be obtained in separately named coloured hybrids ranging through blue, mauve, pink, red, white, cream and yellow.

When the corms of Freesias are potted up, they are brought into the greenhouse. They do not need a temperature higher than 52°F. It is advantageous to the growing of Freesias if a little lime is incorporated into the potting soil. All the potting soil needs plenty of well-decayed garden compost in the loam used with leaf mould or peat and silver sand. Water sparingly and keep the plants under cool conditions. As the plants grow they will require supports; early on, small twigs will be suitable, followed by canes of sufficient height.

Anyone possessing a shady spot in the garden where, growing in profusion, is the lovely Lily of the Valley, can obtain some early blooms by forcing. A strong clump should be selected during early summer and not allowed to bloom outside during the flowering time of June and July. They are put into bowls or pots with sandy loam and leaf mould and then brought into the greenhouse during October for flowering in November and December. They are put underneath the staging (if provided) and surrounded by damp ashes, and when the shoots are about five inches high they are moved to full light and given plenty of water. During the time they are beneath the staging the temperature required is 60°F. and this is reduced to 55°F. when the plants are given the light. When in flower they can be moved into the rooms of the dwelling-house where their lovely perfume will be much appreciated.

No one with a cool greenhouse should be without some of the greenhouse primulas. They are easily grown from seed and it is not difficult to fit them in with most greenhouse arrangements.

Primula malacoides are at their best if allowed to flower in February and March, but if a few are needed for Christmas flowering, they can be obtained by sowing in February. Use John Innes Compost No. 1

and sow thinly with the temperature at 55°F. The seedlings are then transplanted singly to three-inch pots and grown on at the same temperature. As with all transplanted subjects, and especially with pot plants, success depends largely on avoiding a check to growth at all times. The soil must be always moist while primulas are germinating so this means the seed sowing compost must have plenty of moisture-retentive material, such as well-rotted garden compost, leaf mould or garden peat.

A common mistake with many gardeners is wastage of seed. Many more plants are grown than are actually needed. Sow just enough seed for your required number of plants, allowing for some non-germination. In the case of primulas do not throw out the smaller seedlings, as they often make the best plants later. Pot on the plants as soon as white roots are discernible.

After May frosts have ceased, the seedlings can be placed in the cold frame. This will be the general rule, although in my sheltered garden in the New Forest, I have managed *Primula obconica* outside in a shady part of the garden. They should be growing away nicely in their final six-inch pots when brought into the greenhouse during September. Keep soil away from the crown of the plant as they are susceptible to damping off in this part of the plant. *Primula malacoides* when housed in autumn will only require enough heat to exclude frost.

This lovely primula is at its best if the seeds are sown in mid-July and germinated in a cold frame, from then on receiving the same treatment as those grown for Christmas flowering. All primulas should be given some shade during very hot days in June and July. Rush mats are placed on the top of the cold frames but any light material which will provide partial shade will do. The covering should be removed at about 5 p.m. in summer. *Primula malacoides* hybrids give a colour range from lavender and mauve to deep rose and crimson.

Primula sinensis, called the 'Chinese Primula', since in China it once grew wild, has a wide range of types and varieties. It will require the same treatment as *malacoides*, but it gives of its best if sown in June. If needed for mid-winter flowering, it can be sown in February. The mixture called 'Giant-flowered Hybrids' have large fringed flowers in shades of pink, salmon, scarlet, crimson and blue.

Another form of *Primula sinensis* which is becoming popular is *Primula stellata* which has tiers of star-like flowers in shades of pink, orange, scarlet and blue. Both the last two forms of primula will enjoy a slightly higher temperature, so if grown with other primulas they may be put in the warmest part of the greenhouse.

Primula obconica is the easiest one to grow. Seeds can be sown at any time of the year according to when the flowers are required. It gives best results if sown in early autumn and germinated in a cold frame. From then on treatment is much the same as for *Primula malacoides*, except that *obconica* can be put into the coolest part of the house and is quite at home in a temperature of 45°F. The plants will flower at an early age but the first small flowers should be pinched out. *Primula obconica* can take advantage of a slightly richer compost than the other sorts and an organic liquid manure can be given. A mixture called 'Giant-flowering Mixed', includes light and dark blue, pink, crimson, salmon and white. There is a large-flowering variety called 'Goliath' with individual bloom measurements of sometimes two and a half inches across. The colour of this variety is cerise-red with variations.

Another primula needing similar treatment to *Primula malacoides* is *Primula kewensis*, only obtainable in yellow. Seeds are sown in March for winter flowering. It is a very attractive plant, more loosely flowering than the other varieties of primula. *Kewensis* 'Sungold' has large and fragrant golden-yellow flowers with nice clean foliage.

A good subject for the cool greenhouse is the Cineraria, particularly useful because it can be in flower from December to April, and as with bulbs, can be used to help bridge the gap between chrysanthemums and tomatoes, if these are grown. For succession they should be sown from April until August. Very hygienic conditions are needed in the growing of cinerarias as they seem to be attacked by more pests than other greenhouse plants. If a number are being grown, several cold frames will be needed, as these showy subjects need plenty of space on account of their more spreading foliage. One of the pests that may be encountered are leaf miners whose larvae attack the interior tissues of the leaves. Spray with derris for control. Greenfly is almost certain to put in an appearance; the same control measures apply. A virus disease called 'spotted wilt' may appear. This disease is spread from plant to plant so any affected plants should be burnt. This disease shows itself in its early stage by a tiny brown or black ring. This ring enlarges and more rings appear, growth is retarded and the plants ultimately die. These pests and diseases do not always appear, however, and the gardener should always go ahead and try to grow any plant he fancies and has the facilities for. A lot of the fun in gardening is the continual fight with weather, pests and diseases. In some years there will be more setbacks than in others but in every year the gardener will be able to produce a wonderful display of many garden species.

The cineraria seed is very small, and it is a good plan to sow about three seeds spaced out around the centre of a three-inch pot, then after germination discard all the seedlings but one; select the strongest for growing on, and this might well be the smallest. If sowing is done in April, the cool greenhouse is the best situation, but from May onwards, a cold frame, with all the glass shaded, is more suitable for germination. Even those which are started in the greenhouse will be moved to the cold frames, and all the cinerarias will remain there until brought into the greenhouse during October. Eight-inch pots will be needed for the final potting. The plants must not be forced into bloom and the night temperature should not be above 45°F. A medium-rich potting compost is required and the plants must be kept shielded from bright sunlight at all times. They need plenty of air and moisture. Cinerarias are very beautiful greenhouse subjects, possessing a wonderful range of colouring and combination of colours, reminding one of rich tapestries and old-time pageantry.

The large-flowered section, sometimes with blooms measuring three to four inches across, can be obtained in shades of pink, carmine, crimson, light and dark blue, purple and white. The intermediate strain has very large trusses of medium-sized flowers with about the same colour range. Then there is the *stellata* or star variety which is taller and of lighter growth. They are very free-flowering and produce a great number of starry blooms on a single plant. Practically all the colours found in cinerarias are within this group.

If the greenhouse owner is fond of cyclamen it would be best for him to purchase corms and pot them up in August for winter flowering. This is less difficult than growing them from seed, because with seed sowing a constant temperature of 68°F. has to be maintained and they are often difficult to germinate. When potting up, always leave the crown of the plant exposed, otherwise the plants will wilt and die off. Winter temperature needs to be about 53°F. They need plenty of water, especially when coming into bud. The plants should be dried off after flowering, and if well taken care of will last for several years. They are useful plants, having a flowering period of at least a month and supplying a wealth of colour during the winter months.

We must not omit the beautiful schizanthus which is sometimes called the 'poor man's orchid' or the 'butterfly flower'. They usually flower in mid-May and a well-grown plant forming a pyramid of wondrously coloured bloom is a sight to gladden any gardener. They are grown in the same manner as cinerarias but they are great feeders, with an extensive root action, so they are generally potted finally into ten-inch pots. This potting compost needs to be fairly rich with plenty of well-decayed garden compost mixed into the loam with the addition of a five-inch potful of hoof and horn meal, fish manure or bone meal to each barrow load of potting compost. When the plants have settled down in their final pots they can be top-dressed at weekly intervals with an organic fertilizer. Schizanthus soon require supports, first thin twigs and finally stout bamboos to which the central and lateral shoots can be lightly tied.

Schizanthus can be obtained in several strains, including the large-flowered, dwarf bouquet (of more dwarf and compact growth) and pansy-flowered. Most of the varieties have colours ranging from blush-pink and white to deep rose and crimson, with blotching and markings resembling those of orchids.

In the summer months, if the greenhouse owner does not grow tomatoes he can grow some annual flowers. This is of course more suitable for someone with a greenhouse who has only a very small garden, because annual flowers are better grown in effective masses outside for garden display and cutting. Any of the well-known annuals, hardy or half-hardy, can be grown in pots in the greenhouse. According to the annual grown, a suitable-sized pot will be chosen. A few seeds are sown into a fairly rich compost, reducing to a final strong-growing seedling. Annuals grown in pots need a weekly application of an organic plant food. They will require a great deal of water, otherwise in the heat of summer they will soon collapse. Plenty of supports must be provided, for annuals under glass grow much taller than those grown outside.

People who only wish to grow one crop in their greenhouse, and who want a continuation of cut flowers, would do well to consider perpetual-flowering carnations. It must be understood that these flowers need a house to themselves and the best house is a glass-to-ground span roof. They will not tolerate other plants growing with them. Perpetual carnations are grown entirely under cool conditions and the night temperature should never be above 50°F. They are propagated from cuttings taken yearly. Once the initial rooted cuttings have been purchased, a good stock can be built up over the years. A few cuttings may be bought at a time, whatever the gardener can afford, or has room for.

The best cuttings are taken from halfway up the stem of a two-year-old or three-year-old plant. These cuttings are better if they have a heel, and when the lower leaves are removed they should be about four inches long. They are usually inserted into a box containing coarse silver sand and granulated peat and put into a propagating case in which a temperature of 50° to 55°F. can be maintained. Growers who live in sheltered spots in the south of England can take cuttings in mid-August and root them in a cold frame using the same medium.

The rooting medium should be made moist just before inserting the cutting. Do not bury the cuttings too deeply, and press the rooting compost around the stem firmly. After the cuttings have

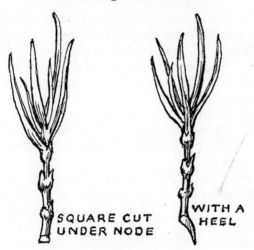

SQUARE CUT UNDER NODE   WITH A HEEL

Taking Carnation cuttings

rooted they can be put into two-and-a-half-inch pots, using a compost of two-thirds turfy loam, one-third peat and a little silver sand. Always when re-potting or planting handle with great care as the carnation plant is easily severed from the root. Do not plant the stem too deeply when re-potting. For the final potting, good loam, with plenty of well-decayed garden compost and some silver sand, is the best medium. A little lime is required if the garden is not on chalky soil for the carnation will not be at its best where there is acidity in the soil. Eleven- or twelve-inch pots can be used for the final potting and good supports are needed when the plants have become established. The greenhouse carnation needs plenty of light, air and sunshine but no draught. The ventilators must be thrown open during summer and even in winter should not be entirely closed except in times of severe frost. The carnation house should be fitted with adequate ventilation. It would take a lot of space to mention named varieties. These, together with the colours, can be selected from the catalogue of the specialist grower.

Begonias can give an all-the-year-round display in the cool greenhouse. The gardener usually begins with some purchased tuberous varieties in March and starts them into growth under glass. Place them with the round, smooth side downwards into boxes of soil containing peat or leaf mould and silver sand, with their flat tops showing above the soil level. When the tubers start to sprout, transfer them to smaller individual pots and pot on in the usual way. Their final potting soil should contain plenty of well-decayed garden compost and some well-rotted leaf mould. They do well in a temperature of 50° to 55°F. and should be kept moist but not saturated with

7

water. Only the strong shoots should be retained and the weaker ones removed with a knife. When the plants are in bud they will appreciate a once-weekly application of an organic plant food.

When flowering has finished, begonias should be dried off by withholding water. Take them from the pots, clean them, and let them lie dormant by storing in sand until needed for re-potting in early spring. In addition to the large showy bloom, tuberous begonias will produce some very insignificant blooms; these are the female flowers and they should be pinched out, leaving room for the large male flowers to develop.

If a little more heat can be provided, very beautiful greenhouse plants, the fibrous-rooted begonias, can be grown. There are valuable winter-flowering varieties, although some fibrous sorts are used for summer bedding displays in the open garden. The fibrous-rooted begonias grow from ordinary roots, their leaves are often colourful and their small blooms are usually pink, crimson, scarlet, cerise or white. They are produced in abundance.

Winter-flowering varieties are usually propagated from cuttings taken in early April. They are put into a mixture of peat and silver sand around the edge of three-inch pots and placed in a propagating case; the temperature is maintained at 60°F. When rooted they are potted on to individual pots. For the final potting use a four-inch pot with the usual good mixture of potting compost. Weekly applications of organic plant food can be given. Some kind of staking will be necessary, split bamboos will be inconspicuous with soft green string. As with the tuberous begonia, these plants can be gradually dried off, trimmed back and rested before being started into growth again.

RAISING HALF-HARDY BEDDING PLANTS

Buying bedding plants from a nurseryman in the spring is a costly affair, because most people like a variety of plants and several boxes are usually required even for a garden of moderate size. The owner of a cool greenhouse will save himself a lot of expense by raising his own plants. For this purpose he will need some cold frames for hardening off. At least three will be necessary, especially if autumn-sown sweet peas are being grown, for these lovely plants will occupy a cold frame all to themselves from October to the end of March.

For sowing half-hardy annuals for bedding out, select good seed boxes, attend to the drainage, and use John Innes Compost. No. 1 Water all boxes of soil with Cheshunt Compound prior to sowing.

There are very many kinds of bedding plants and I shall deal with those which I think every gardener will want to grow at some time or another. As with other flowering plants it is best to grow a few kinds one year and then from year to year have a change and grow other plants. Some varieties will perhaps be grown every year, antirrhinums and petunias for instance. Also, once they have been grown Unwin's Dwarf Hybrid Dahlias, grown from seed, will, I expect, be wanted most years.

In a good summer, antirrhinums seem to go on blooming for ever if the dead flower spikes are removed regularly. Some in my garden during 1964 began to bloom in early June, and were still in flower during early January. This was in a very sheltered spot in the south. Petunias also have a very lengthy flowering period.

The antirrhinum is really a perennial but it is usually grown as a half-hardy annual. It is almost hardy and will never need a lot of heat during the raising and hardening-off periods. The seeds should be sown at the end of January, and very thinly. As they are very tiny, great care must be taken. For germination, a temperature of 55°F. is required and as soon as the seedlings are seen the glass covering the boxes must be removed as these plants are very susceptible to damping-off; water with Cheshunt Compound as soon as possible, and thereafter water carefully. As soon as they are large enough to handle, the seedlings need to be pricked out two inches apart each way into John Innes Compost No. 2 and given slightly cooler conditions and a free circulation of air at all times. At the end of March they can be put into the cold frame and gradually hardened off and planted out about the end of April.

Many colours of antirrhinum are available, and there are tall varieties growing to three feet, some with double flowers, also bedding varieties (one-and-a-half feet to two feet), intermediate, rust-resistant, floral carpet (a miniature strain), 'Tom Thumb', and 'Magic Carpet' (a dwarf, of trailing habit, for rockeries). If the flowers are to be used in formal arrangements, a bed of mixed colours of the intermediate type would be suitable. Most antirrhinums can be used as cut flowers for floral art, and they are not used nearly enough for this purpose.

Petunias look very effective in a bed of their own, and are valuable as edging plants and for window boxes and hanging baskets. The seed is sown in a similar manner to antirrhinums during February. The seed is exceptionally small so some gardeners mix a little sand with a small quantity of seed as this helps to distribute the seed more thinly. Some seedsmen offer what is called pelleted seed; this is the technique of applying an inert coating to each seed, thus making it larger and more easily seen for sowing. There are not nearly so many seeds in a packet, of course, and for petunias the packets average about 1s. 6d. for fifty seeds. The seeds will only need a very light covering of soil and then a piece of glass covering the seed box followed by brown paper; glass and paper will be removed immediately after germination. Prick off into boxes and water with Cheshunt Compound until established. Gradually harden off by removal to the cold frame. Plant out from end of May onwards.

There are many varieties and colours of petunia. The new F.1 Hybrids are superior to the old kinds, on account of their greater vigour, complete uniformity of habit and growth, and the brilliance of their colouring. These seeds are produced by isolating two parent strains and hand-pollinating them for several generations. They are then cross-pollinated to produce F.1 hybrids. Seeds from F.1 hybrid itself will not breed true to colour or type so each cross has to be repeated when further seeds are required. F.1 hybrids have been produced with many kinds of flower. In the petunias, one named 'Brass Band' is outstanding. It has flowers of deep primrose-yellow, which are weather-resistant. In the double-flower section, one called 'Cherry Tart', which is also a F.1 hybrid, has double flowers of rose-pink and white; this is another one well worth growing. F.1 hybrid 'Bonanza' is a mixture of the double multiflora sorts and is especially suitable for pots and window boxes; they can also be used for bedding. These double varieties are made up from shades of red, rose-pink, salmon, white, purple and some bi-colours.

Like petunias, there are many types of aster to choose from. By glancing through the seedmen's catalogues the gardener can select a few kinds to grow and try others in following years. If an all-yellow aster is wanted there is one called 'Duchess', but it is rather late flowering and so needs to be in a bed by itself. The single varieties are the best for cut flowers and floral art. All asters are best grown in a bed where there are asters only, as they blend excellently together but not so well with other flowers. The seed is sown during March and April, watering with Cheshunt Compound after germination. It is easy to sow the seeds thinly because they are light-coloured and of fair size. Prick out in the usual manner and harden off in the cold frame. Outdoor sowings in their flowering positions can be made from May onwards.

One of the easiest and most satisfying half-hardy flowers to grow for those on chalk lands is the Giant Double Chaubaud carnation. It can be grown on other soils if the ground has been limed. This carnation also enjoys a fairly rich soil, so plenty of well-rotted garden compost should be dug into the site where they are to flower. Seeds should be sown early in the year, February is late enough, and a temperature of 55°F. maintained. The plants will bloom within six months of sowing. Damping off should be avoided with the use of Cheshunt Compound and the usual pricking out and hardening off processes must be carried out. As with perpetual carnations care is needed when handling the seedlings and young plants, because of the thin piece of root which joins the stems. These flowers will give a great display lasting well into November. Some will burst their calyx but there will be a wealth of beautiful flowers in all the colours known for carnations. They have very attractive fringed petals and there are some bi-colours. If they are dis-budded early, very large blooms can be obtained and they will fill the air with a delicious fragrance. They also attract the humming-bird hawk moth, a day-flying moth, whose flight and probing tongue are so fascinating to watch. If room can be found in the cool greenhouse, some of these plants can be lifted from the open ground, potted up into large pots, and put into the house where they will continue to flower.

Unwin's dwarf hybrid dahlias are other easy-to-grow half-hardy annuals that can be raised from seed. They are wonderful subjects for bedding and for cutting. They give double and semi-double blooms in shades of salmon, crimson, apricot, purple, bronze, yellow, orange, scarlet and white. Seed should be sown in March in a temperature of 60°F., and be watered in the initial stages with Cheshunt Compound, pricked out early and hardened off via the cold frame. If planted out at the end of May in ground that has been liberally composted they will give a magnificent display until winter frosts come along.

Lobelia, though not so popular as it once was, is still a valuable half-hardy bedding plant. It has been mainly used as an edging plant, but it is far more effective massed in a bed and planted out at six inches intervals. If a blue lobelia and a white one are interplanted with the French marigold 'Petite Yellow', a lemon yellow, the effect created can be really startling. Dark blue and light blue are obtainable and the white variety is called 'White Lady'. There is also a wine-red variety with a white eye. A temperature of 55° to 60°F. is suitable for lobelia and early February is the sowing time. The usual system of watering, pricking out and hardening off is required. The seeds are very tiny and only need a slight covering with peat or silver sand. The pricking out is rather tedious as they need this treatment very early in life. Plant out at the end of May. The *pendula*, or trailing type of lobelia, is nearly always planted in hanging baskets. The varieties for this work are 'Blue Cascade' and 'Sapphire'.

African marigolds are very valuable in a garden because of their long-lasting qualities and their brilliant yellow and orange hues. They are also most suitable as cut flowers and are very free flowering. They grow from one and a half feet to three feet in height so are better placed more towards the back of a border or bed. All of these showy plants, including the French marigold, come from Mexico and not from Africa or France. The seed is fairly large and easily seen, so thin sowing can be practised. Sow in a temperature of 55° to 60°F. and carry out pricking off, the usual watering system and hardening off. Plant out into flowering positions at the end of May. Seed may also be sown out-of-doors from late May onwards.

The French marigolds which grow from six to eight inches in height need the same treatment as the African marigolds. To ensure a continuous display of bloom from early summer right through to November, cut off all dead flower heads frequently. Consult catalogues for colours and varieties.

The beautifully perfumed bedding stocks are well worth growing; they are easy to cultivate, fragrant and of delicate colouring. The variety called 'Hansen's 100 per cent Double Stocks' are the best for the amateur gardener to grow. Raise in a temperature of 55°F. and then lower the temperature to 50°F. after germination. While they are growing at this lower temperature it will be noticed that the plants can be divided into two sections, light green foliage and dark green. Discard all those with dark green leaves as they will only produce single flowers. Grow the others on and harden off in the usual way, planting out during May. The seed should be sown in February or early March.

Zinnias are generally raised under glass in the same way as Asters but better results can sometimes be obtained by sowing the seed directly into their flowering quarters at the end of May. To grow and flower to perfection, Zinnias need a really hot sunny summer, and are often very disappointing during a dull, wet, short one. They need rich soil where planted out and a good soaking of water around the roots from time to time. They must not be continuously watered however, as they like a dry atmosphere. Although grown in the same way as other half-hardy annuals, a later sowing is preferable because they grow rapidly. April will be soon enough. They seem to resent root disturbance more than other bedding plants, so care must be taken while pricking out and transplanting. Try to grow Zinnias without check, not letting the greenhouse temperature drop on a cold night. Zinnias make very good cut flowers because they have long-lasting qualities and brilliant colouring. There are many types of Zinnias which come from Mexico. Almost every colour is available except a true blue.

A selection can be made from the following list and descriptions. 'Burpee Hybrids' are large with curled and quilled petals resembling chrysanthemums. 'Super Giants' are large quilled-petal types; then there are giant 'Dahlia-flowered', 'Lilliput', dwarf and compact, 'Merry-Go-Round', quilled petals with the bases being one colour and the tips a contrasting shade. 'Mexicana' has miniature double flowers in shades of yellow, orange, red, maroon and mahogany. 'Old Mexico' is mahogany red, overlaid and tipped with varying shades of gold and yellow. 'Peppermint Stick' has red and yellow, pink and white, orange and yellow, and purple and white striped petals. 'Thumbelina' is dwarf, about one and a half inches across the bloom, and is in various colours.

Phlox drummondii needs good soil where it is to be planted out and fairly moist conditions. An early April sowing is best and they should be grown without check. They can be obtained in very many beautiful pastel shades and are always sold in mixed colours. They are suitable plants for hanging baskets as well as for bedding. The variety called 'Twinkles' is particularly arresting when seen massed in a bed. This variety bears large clusters of star-like blossoms.

Salvias, although not so popular as of old, are still good half-hardy subjects with a variety of uses, including growing in hanging baskets. They can be sown from January to March in a temperature of 65°F. and pricked off early. Salvias soon become box- or pot-bound so they may need more transplanting into larger boxes than is usual with other bedding plants. Put into flowering positions during late May. There is a half-hardy perennial salvia, which can be raised as an annual and flowered in the same way. It is called *Salvia patens* and has beautiful gentian-blue flowers. It has tuberous roots which are taken up and stored in a frost-proof place during winter, divided in spring and started into growth under glass; they can also be grown from seed. So can the variety called 'Farinacea' which has long blue-coloured stems bearing flowers in lavender and violet-blue. The familiar red bedding salvias, which come into flower as soon as they are planted out, can now be obtained in many shades of red, including scarlet, rose-cerise and rich deep purple.

A very lovely Dianthus, raised and grown in the same manner as Chabaud carnations, is *Heddewigii*. There are single and double varieties, but the singles give a more brilliant display. They are essentially sun lovers and should never be tried in the shade.

There are many other half-hardy annuals, perennials and biennials which can be raised in the cool greenhouse using the same growing methods as those already mentioned. These include such lovely subjects as Nemesia, Arctotis (African Daisy), Annual Gaillardia, Gazania, Kochia (burning bush), Nicotiana (flowering tobacco), Pentstemon, Rudbeckia, Salpiglossis, Tagetes (miniature French marigolds), Ursinia, Venidium fastuosum (Monarch of the Veldt), and Verbena.

STARTING VEGETABLE SEEDLINGS UNDER GLASS

There is much to be gained from an under-glass start for early vegetables, especially during a wet, late spring, such as the spring of 1965. As I wrote this, my garden was covered in snow and the date was March 8th, so the man who then had some vegetable seedlings coming along in his greenhouse promised to be a long way ahead of those who would have to wait for suitable sowing conditions outside.

Cold frames are essential for raising vegetable seedlings as they should not be left in the greenhouse too long, otherwise they become drawn and weak. They also dry out very quickly in boxes, unless frequently watered. If the gardener has only a small amount of frame space he would do best to content himself with a sowing of a few cauliflowers, Brussels sprouts (as these really need this treatment for the long growing period required for the production of good, firm sprouts), some early cabbage and lettuce. If the gardener has plenty of room some early peas, runner beans and onions can also be sown for planting out later. For raising vegetable seedlings in this manner, use deep seed boxes, at least three to four inches in depth. Proper drainage is essential and the boxes should be filled with John Innes Compost No. 1. All the vegetable seeds mentioned can be thinly sown as they are all large enough to see clearly. For germination only gentle heat is needed; about 45°F. should be maintained. The end of January and during February offer the best sowing time. When the seedlings are about two inches high they should be grown on in the cold frame and gradually hardened off. Cheshunt Compound will prevent damping off. Do not allow the boxes to become overcrowded, and prick out early.

Suitable cauliflowers for early work are 'Early Snowball' and 'All-the-Year-Round'. For early cabbage sow 'Greyhound', 'Primo' or 'Golden Acre'. The amateur gardener will not go far wrong by sowing the cabbage lettuce called 'All-the-Year-Round'. Half-hardy vegetables such as ridge cucumbers, tomatoes and sweet corn, which always need an under-glass start, will be described and discussed in the chapter on vegetable growing.

HOW TO GROW GOOD GRAPES

A dwelling-house may have been taken over with a three-quarter span greenhouse containing an established vine. Try to ascertain from the previous owner the name of the variety and the kind of crops that were harvested. The border soil in which the grape is growing must be well-drained and it must contain some old lime rubble. Turfy loam should be used, and mixed with it should be some well-decayed garden compost or well-rotted farmyard manure. The turf which is mixed with the loam should also be very old and well-rotted; never use new turf. Plenty of bone meal is necessary, and this is incorporated into the whole of the soil to a depth of three feet. About fourteen pounds of garden lime to each ton of soil are necessary, in addition to the limestone rubble.

There is some very important work to carry out on a vine during winter, and pruning must be completed by the third week in January. After this the sap begins to rise and vines start to bleed very easily. The old loose bark is removed from the main trunk or rod of the vine. Then all laterals, or side-growing branches, are cut back to within a bud of the main trunk, weak laterals are cut back to within two buds. When the pruning and removal of old bark are completed, the whole of the vine should be gently scrubbed down with soap and water. On established vines, flood the border at this time with water that has had the chill taken from it. Give a mulch of well-rotted garden compost or decayed farmyard manure. Only very gentle heat is needed at this time. As the weather becomes warmer and the sap rises more heat can be given gradually. With the continuation of the growing season very careful attention must be given to ventilation, and a stuffy atmosphere must be avoided. When the fruit is beginning to colour ventilation should be given day and night. Temperatures to be maintained are during the growing season between 50° and 60°F. and when the vine is in flower it may be at 70°F., but when the fruit has set, lower to 60°F. When the grapes start to colour a temperature of 65°F. is about right.

Well-grown vines will set their fruit quite freely if the rod is tapped during the day to disperse the pollen. Grapes must be thinned if they are to grow and develop properly. About half the grapes which are first seen on the bunch will have to be cut away with a pair of long-pointed scissors. When thinning a bunch of grapes, first remove all

GRAPES THINNED CORRECTLY

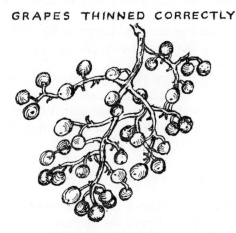

The thinning of greenhouse grapes

those berries which are badly placed, then thin out those which cluster too thickly towards the centre of the bunch. The first thinning should take place when the grapes are about the size of a sweet pea seed and another thinning is carried out when they are about twice this size. They should be looked over each week, as further light thinnings may be necessary. At all times grapes must be managed very carefully. Try not to touch any of them while removing the surplus berries, as any slight damage will spoil the whole look of the mature bunch.

During hot weather a syringing of the vine night and morning will help to keep down red spider. Do not syringe during flowering or fruiting stage. If any mealy bugs are seen (they have a shiny wax-like form) destroy them by covering with a small brush dipped in methylated spirit.

Vines are propagated from 'eyes'. These are cut from laterals with about an inch of wood on either side. These 'eyes' are inserted into a hole in an old piece of turf which has been filled with silver sand. See that the eye is exposed and the wood on either side just buried. Place these into seed boxes in the cool house with the temperature at 65°F. Never allow them to become dry, and syringe with tepid water. After they have become well rooted they can be planted directly into the border of the vine house. These young vine cuttings should be planted during the dormant period and should be five feet apart. Muscat varieties need a space of six feet between the plants. From these cuttings during the first summer, only one shoot should be trained up towards the roof of the house. All side growths are taken off when the plants are eighteen inches high. One bud is left at the base from which will grow spurs; these are also cut back to one bud. When the main stem reaches the top of the house, it is stopped, detached from the wires supporting it, and slightly bent down to arrest the flow of sap and to provide more strength for the laterals lower down the stem. For the first two years the vine should not be allowed to carry any fruit but during the third year one bunch of fruit per lateral is usually allowed.

Good strong wiring is needed for supporting vines and the bunches of fruit also have to be supported and tied with raffia. Mildew can be controlled by dusting with flowers of sulphur. Vines may be fed with liquid manure after the first thinning at once a fortnight, but young vines must not receive any feeding whatsoever.

CACTI AND SUCCULENTS

We could not leave this section of the book without a word or two about cacti, so popular are they at the moment. I could not attempt to describe them all here as there are over two thousand varieties known to English gardeners. The popular variety known as Opuntia alone has over a hundred kinds including a yellow-flowered one, otherwise known as the Prickly Pear, which will grow out of doors.

Seedsmen usually sell cacti seed in two divisions, one a mixture of large-seeded kinds and the other of small-seeded varieties. It is fascinating to sow a mixture of cacti seed, to watch them grow, and then wonder what sort of flowers they will produce. Some bloom only once every ten years, some only in the dead of night. Some have many small flowers, and some bear very large blooms. Very many colours are obtainable.

It is best to sow the seed in summer so that a temperature of around 70°F. can be supported. The seeds must have plenty of moisture in order to germinate and this usually takes about a week with some kinds, but others may take up to two months. Seed boxes should be well-crocked and the compost consists of coarse silver sand with about a handful of garden peat to each box. Cover boxes with panes of glass and brown paper, removing when seeds have germinated. When large enough, seedlings should be moved to small pots and a small amount of loam is then added to the compost. Many varieties can be propagated from offshoots, giving the same treatment as for seed sowing. Cacti need plenty of root room so they should be frequently potted on until the final potting stage is reached. Make the soil for potting on gritty and porous. As the plants grow reduce the temperature then keep at 50°F. Give plenty of ventilation and water during summer, about once a fortnight.

Packets of mixed succulent plant seeds are sold by seedsmen and these need the same treatment as cacti except that they are able to store up moisture in their fleshy leaves and so do not require so much watering during the autumn and winter. Water during warm weather, when they will take up sufficient moisture to carry them through a long period. There are many different species of succulent plants of very many different shapes, colours and sizes.

A plant which is better if kept in a heated greenhouse is the brilliant foliage plant called 'Coleus' or 'Flame Nettle'. These have self colours and wonderful combinations of red, copper, yellow and green, and many are beautifully variegated. They like the sun but do not like to be over-watered. The seed should be sown during spring in John Innes No. 1, pricked off early and moved to individual pots when about three inches high. The first leaves are green but the brilliant colouring appears as the plants develop. Pinch out the small, insignificant flowers. A temperature of 60°F. is needed for germination and the seed wants only a very light covering of soil. The young plants must be pinched back once to make them bushy—just take out the growing tip.

MAINTENANCE OF THE GREENHOUSE

When considering which type of greenhouse to purchase there are one or two points worth remembering about a glass to ground house. Are there likely to be any children playing around in the vicinity of the glasshouse? If so, a glass to ground house might easily be damaged. The same applies where there is a dog which might be scampering around. Glass cloches should not be situated near a brick wall, for cats often jump from these walls at night and soon break a few panes of glass.

Portable staging is most useful in a greenhouse of any size, for when not in use it can be taken away to permit the growing of tomatoes or other plants in the borders.

At some time every year a greenhouse should be given a thorough cleaning inside and out. All woodwork inside should be well scrubbed, and a little Jeyes Fluid is mixed with the water. Hot water pipes should be brushed to remove any rust and dirt, and then given a coat of lamp black mixed with linseed oil. Interior brick walls should be white-washed or distempered to deter pests and diseases and to help reflect the light. In autumn all white-wash or 'Summer Cloud' must be removed from the roof, if it was used during the summer, to allow the maximum light to enter during the winter. All the glass inside and outside should be well washed.

Paint the exterior and interior of a timber house every three years with a good-quality white lead paint. Attend to any necessary glass repairs or puttying before painting. If shingle is being used on greenhouse benches, it should occasionally be removed and washed and the staging washed down, before replacing.

Garden frames should be cleaned, repaired and painted in the same manner. Do not leave any broken glass from cloches scattered about the garden. Small pieces often easily find their way into the ground and cause cut hands during weeding at a later date.

COLD FRAMES

If the gardener does not possess a greenhouse some cold frames are the next best thing. A cold frame is absolutely necessary for the growing of good sweet-peas. There is no comparison between autumn-sown sweet-peas nurtured through the winter in the frame and those sown in spring.

Cold frames are of two types, the span and the half-span. Some sides are made of wood, some of brick or concrete. There are metal frames with glass to ground all the way round. These of course let in the maximum light, but are very easily damaged.

The site for the frames should be an open one, and not shaded by trees or hedges. Some shelter on the north and east sides, so that the frames are not exposed to biting winds, is desirable.

The ground beneath the cold frames needs to be well drained. Clay soils should be excavated to about a foot and drainage materials, rubble, stones or clinkers are filled in to the top. Pots in all frames should stand on a bed of ashes, as this helps drainage when watering and also helps to deter slugs and snails.

The interior of a frame should always be kept beautifully clean, free of weeds and with no dead vegetation of any kind allowed to remain. When watering try not to spill any water, because without heat is is difficult for excess moisture to be expelled. Continual dampness within the frame will help mildew and other fungus diseases to develop.

Before the owner of a cold frame fills it with plants a collection of

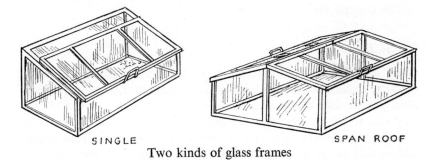

SINGLE   SPAN ROOF

Two kinds of glass frames

protective materials for placing on the top of the frame during cold weather needs to be acquired. Old mats or rugs are useful for this purpose. Sacking and straw or bracken can also be used. In very severe winter weather the sides of the frames will have to be covered as well. This is especially the case during the cold nights, but the coverings should be removed as soon as possible next day. At other times ventilation can be afforded by sliding the light or lid forward a little or by putting wooden wedges under the lights at the front end. Very little watering will be needed during winter and then only a light application should be given. Glass should be kept clean at all times as admission of the maximum amount of light is important, especially during the short winter days.

A number of seeds can be sown in boxes directly into the cold frame. Autumn-sown sweet peas are sown in pots and are over-wintered in the cold frame and planted out in spring. Then, if there is no greenhouse available, many of the half-hardy bedding plants can be germinated in a cold frame, including antirrhinums, asters, cosmos, kochia (burning bush), morning glory, African and French marigolds, scabious, stocks and zinnias. Most of the seeds of biennials, or plants grown as such, can be germinated in a cold frame. Among these are double daisies, aquilegias, Canterbury bells, dianthus, foxgloves, Russell lupins, pansies, polyanthus and violas. Cuttings of many herbaceous plants can also be rooted in a cold frame, delphiniums, Michaelmas daisies and phlox can be propagated in this way. Violas are often grown from cuttings rooted in a cold frame. If one is keen on growing Alpine plants many choice varieties can be wintered in a cold frame.

A good supply of slug-killer pellets is nearly always necessary, especially when the frame occupants are in the seedling stage. Scatter them around and in between seed boxes and pots.

There are electrically heated frames in which the air can be warmed inside for frost protection and bottom heat can be switched on for germination and for producing early salad crops. The air temperature can be thermostatically controlled.

CLOCHES

Glass cloches are used extensively in Britain for protecting plants growing outside from cold, wind and excessive rain. They are cheaper than greenhouses and they can be moved from place to place. In this way soil which has been under cloches is exposed to the elements and can regain its fertility. There is practically no shade from cloches and as with the glass-to-ground greenhouse, light penetrates from all angles. Cloches give adequate ventilation because you cannot close them entirely. The necessary moisture reaches the roots of plants under cloches from the rain which runs down the side of the glass.

When sowing seeds in the open for cloche protection, measure the widest part of the cloche and make the seed drills far enough apart to allow the cloches to be put over and to allow walking on either side of the row of cloches. As with frames and greenhouses, cloches should be used in the sunniest part of the garden and not in the shade of houses, hedges or trees. Cloches are a very useful aid to gardening for those who live near the sea shore, protecting the plants from wind and salt-laden spray. In industrial areas they guard the plants against injurious chemical deposits. They offer a complete protection from birds and rabbits if the ends of the rows are blocked securely with a pane of glass and with a block of wood or pegs holding this piece of glass solidly. Among the greatest hazards of gardening are the late spring frosts which we nearly always get in one part of the country or another. Cloches give a good measure of protection against this enemy. The cloches have trapped any small amount of warmth which may have been present during the day, and during the night this is usually enough to combat the frost. It is better, however, if the foliage of plants under the glass is not touching the roof of the cloche where the glass will be covered with frost on the outside. Plants actually touching the glass are often affected by frost; this becomes particularly noticeable with sweet peas growing in a cold frame. The tall plants become frosted while the smaller ones below the lights are untouched.

In a garden where cloches are going to be continually used, the soil must be kept very fertile. Every opportunity must be taken of digging in well-rotted garden compost.

There are three types of cloche now in general use; these are the

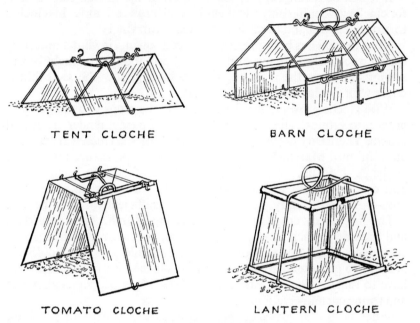

TENT CLOCHE   BARN CLOCHE

TOMATO CLOCHE   LANTERN CLOCHE

Types of glass cloches

tent cloche, the barn cloche and the tomato cloche. Tent cloches are used for seed raising and are suitable for bringing single rows of lettuce to maturity. The barn cloches are of two kinds, the low barn and the large barn. As the cloches graduate in size so do their prices. As with all implements, glass, plants, trees, shrubs and seeds, the gardener is best advised to obtain a little at a time, what he can afford for a start. But with cloches, this principle does not apply, for as is implied in the term 'continuous cloches', enough for one whole row at least must be purchased. Perhaps enough of them to cover a row of strawberries will do to begin with, and then as progress is made, and according to the space available, the number can be added to. The tomato cloches are so arranged that one pane of glass is removable, so that the gardener can attend to the plants growing underneath.

To make the best use of the cloches available, a cropping plan is necessary at the start of each gardening season. Try to discover an all-the-year-round use for your cloches. The first crop of the season may be protected by cloches for perhaps two months and then the cloches are removed to another crop, and then to a third crop. Cloches are best used for helping crops through the initial stages of growth: although with subjects like October-sown lettuce, they can, of course, remain on the crops until maturity is reached.

If it can be arranged, a special section of the garden can be used for cloche gardening only. This enables the grower to move his cloches to crops near at hand to save a lot of extra carrying.

After the soil has been prepared for seed sowing, in winter and early spring, the cloches are put over the seed bed about a fortnight before sowing. Remove the cloches for seed sowing, sow the seed thinly, cover with cloches and block each end.

With cloche growing, it is best to divide the crops you are going to grow into groups. These will be hardy, half-hardy, tender crops and others. The hardy crops will be occupants of the cloches from early autumn until March, and can include early peas, lettuce and spring cabbage. I do not see a lot of advantage of sowing broad beans and covering them with cloches as some gardeners do. The main crop from an ordinary outdoor sowing is sufficient for most people.

The half-hardy crops are cloched during March, April and May, and include French beans, runner beans, sweet-corn, tomatoes and cucumbers. I do not suppose that many readers of this book will attempt to grow tender crops which are cloched during summer and have to remain cloched. These are melons, sweet peppers, egg plants and frame cucumbers.

Other crops for growing under cloches can consist of potatoes, strawberries, turnips, beetroot, carrots, radishes and spring-sown annual flowers. Strawberries are cloched from February to June.

If the gardener has only a few rows of cloches they would best be employed for starting early sown peas, French beans and strawberries. If French beans are sown and cloched in early March (provided that a seed bed can be prepared) beans can be gathered when they are about 4s. 0d. per lb. in the shops. The glass of cloches should always be kept very clean.

5

Simple Stonework

Construction of a small rock garden — some rock plants — sinks and troughs — dry walls — water gardens and pools — paths and terraces

Very many people like to create a rock garden and no garden is too small for this charming feature. Stonework made from stone which suits the locality and is in harmony with the dwelling can be made to suit a variety of garden purposes and it looks pleasing in almost any garden.

Although limestone or hard sandstone is the best choice for rockeries and other garden stonework, it is sometimes very costly. If the gardener resides within a few miles of a quarry where natural stone can be acquired, he may be able to afford some good rockery materials. The cost of transporting stone over long distances sometimes makes the purchase of a quantity of stone out of the question. By all means obtain some good stone wherever possible, and be sure to get different sizes of stone when ordering. Some large rocks must be included, but not too many for a small garden.

If garden stone is found to be too expensive, many other materials that are to hand may be used. It is very important, though, to keep to one type of stone. Whatever is constructed, by all means avoid one of those rubbish heaps that we see about the country—a pile of soil in an odd corner, dotted with lumps of concrete, bricks, clinker or other mixtures. They are called 'rockeries' by their owners, but they are entirely unsuitable for growing Alpines and other rock plants. They usually only grow weeds and provide well-protected homes for snails, slugs, woodlice and other garden pests.

If no limestone or sandstone is available, some rough, porous concrete blocks of various sizes can be used. Uneven slabs of stone and broken paving stones can also be utilized. Try to have them all well weathered, of the same colour, and choose material that will blend in with the surroundings. If some are covered with moss they will be even more suitable.

8

Sometimes granite is supplied and used for rockeries but it should be avoided if possible. It looks very hard and out of place on arrival from the quarry, and is non-porous. If it must be used it should be left as long as possible to 'weather'.

The site for a rockery should be open and away from trees. Any shade which is needed for some alpine plants is provided by the special placing of the rocks.

The important point about the soil on the chosen site for the rock garden is that it must be well-drained. All the soil should be excavated to a depth of about two feet and a layer of clinker is spread over the bottom, followed by a layer of inverted turves. A lime-free soil is to be preferred as many rock plants are lime-intolerant. Lime can be added to soil pockets where chalk-loving plants are to be grown. The soil will need to be arranged in some system of mounds and depressions. Whenever further excavations are made, always attend to drainage.

The most difficult task for the beginner will be the setting of the stones in a natural, artistic and pleasing arrangement. Although the novice will be best advised to confine himself to the more easily grown plants, before attempting cultivation of some of the choice alpines, he may have to provide shade for some of his subjects. This is achieved by placing a fairly large rock in front of the soil pocket or crevice where the particular plants are to grow.

It is sometimes a good plan to have a look at some good rockeries which have pleasing designs before attempting to build your own rockery. When perplexed by the problem of which side of a particular stone is to be embedded, if one can throw it up into the air, the side on which it lands is often the one to choose.

Another useful measure is to make a sketch on paper of how your rockery should look when completed. Put in the areas for any paths, stepping-stones or natural steps. You will arrange pockets of soil for the reception of plants as you go along.

An important point to remember when constructing your rockery is that all soil put in must be rammed in solidly behind and around each stone placed in position. No subsidence must take place after the plants have been put into their final quarters. It is sometimes difficult to fit in some plants into a crevice where they will look their best while in flower. In these cases it is advisable to plant them during the construction of the stone work.

When using dwarf conifers which are such useful subjects for the rock garden, giving illusions of height, providing shade and offering contrasts of shape and colour, it may be found that they are difficult to get established. They must be firmly planted with as little root disturbance as possible and they must be frequently heavily watered.

Dwarf conifers should be planted where the water will run into the roots and not on an incline where it will run away.

The shape of the rockery will depend upon the other features of the garden. If the garden is absolutely flat, do not build a high rockery at one end of a lawn for this will look very much out of place. In this case make a rockery with very gentle slopes.

Bury the stones well into the soil, do not have them just sitting on the top of a mound. Place them so that they have an inward and downward slope, so that rain may be diverted to where it is needed, among the roots.

Each rockery builder will discover his own method of construction. Some place all of their large stones in position first, but with this method gardeners often find that they have a lot of small stones over, and have to fit them in somewhere. Paths among the rockery need to be as informal as possible; they may be of grass, limestone chippings or perhaps of a crazy paving nature, with a few plants here and there growing between the stone slabs Any steps should be made from roughly hewn rock. Try to make the rockery look as natural as possible: have a look at those in botanic gardens, zoological gardens, etc., where rock strata are so well reproduced.

Where there are some high natural banks, they may be found to be a suitable site for a small rock garden of one face The site will be of no use if it is under trees. The perpetual shade would not suit many plants and the drips from the trees after rain or during fog would kill most. According to the aspect of the site, whether it faces north or south, suitable plants will be selected. When dealing with a very steep slope, rocks can easily be arranged so that a flat terrace of soil is provided for the plants, and the moisture will not drain straight to the bottom of the bank. Again stones should be placed sloping inwards, for directing the rain where it is most needed.

When preparing a slope of this nature for use as a rockery, it should be well dug and drainage should be attended to, as in the building of all rockeries. Start from the base and insert well into the soil an uneven row of large rocks to establish a firm foundation. Ram the soil well in for planting.

Sometimes in town gardens one sees rockeries of one face built against a wall. This is all right so long as there is not too great a weight of soil for the wall to support. On no account should a rockery be built against the walls of a dwelling-house. This would interfere with the damp course and cause rising dampness on the inside walls.

The beginner with rockery work need not be over-awed by all he hears about choice alpines, or the special soil needed to grow them. Three of the main occupants of the rockery, golden alyssum, aubrietia and white arabis, will grow almost anywhere if the site is well drained.

Nor need one always stick to alpines in a rockery. Confine yourself to the number of simply grown alpines which you can afford, or grow them from seed, and then, if you like, other dwarf-growing subjects can be added. Violas and sometimes Tom-Thumb nasturtiums do not look out of place. Many dwarf-growing bulbs and flowers from corms can also be planted in the rockery.

Although we do not hear very much about colour-harmonizing in rock gardens, I believe that this should be encouraged in all forms of gardening. With aubrietia, arabis and alyssum, we have three plants of rapid growth which can be allowed to run into each other, within reason. Here we have the correct colour combination. Aubrietia and arabis, where overgrown, will need to be cut back after flowering so that they do not smother smaller subjects which may be planted near them.

When planting the rockery with pieces from established plants, make the portions small as these settle themselves in more easily than large clumps. Pot plants can be obtained from nurseries. These can be used initially, and friends with established rockeries usually have a surplus of cuttings or seedlings to spare. Plenty of future plants will be available through natural propagation.

Before allocating a position for a particular rock plant, find out its habit of growth so that it is not growing where it will soon smother a small, slow-growing plant. March or September are the best times for rockery planting. If plantings are done from pot-grown plants, when these are knocked from the pots it will sometimes be seen that more than one can be obtained by careful root division. Better results are obtained by planting in this manner. The rules for all garden planting apply to rock planting. Have the planting hole large and deep enough, spread out the roots carefully, make the soil firm around the plant, and water well in.

The maintenance of the rock garden consists of a good spring and autumn clean up, weeding and replacement of any plants that may be lost during the winter.

In early spring remove all rubbish from the rockery and put down slug-killer. Divide all plants that require division and apply a top dressing. A mixture of fine garden peat and coarse gravelly soil will do for most plants. A coating of fine limestone chippings is best for lime lovers. All plants which have spread rapidly and have over-run their allotted space will have to be cut back severely.

In the autumn, some derris dust may be sprinkled along rock cracks where woodlice are seen to lurk. All weeds seen should now be removed, otherwise the job will become hard work during the spring when weeds increase so quickly. Some form of protection may be necessary for the less hardy plants. Any plants which will be submerged beneath the soil during winter must be well marked to show their position.

For weeding the rock garden, I have found a kitchen fork of the old type, with three prongs, a most valuable tool. An old, short, pointed kitchen knife is another useful weeding implement.

Watering of the rockery must be carefully done. Individual watering of plants is often necessary. More water is needed for plants with long penetrating roots. Never have a sprinkler on continually, showering the whole rockery with cold water. This will be harmful to many plants and will also wash away much of the soil which you have carefully placed in position.

No artificial manures or feeding of any kind, apart from the annual top dressing, should be given to rockery plants. As with the flower beds and borders, faded flowers and dead stems should be removed from rock plants. Cut away all straggly growth and aim at a fairly neat appearance.

Aubrietias frequently become brown and withered after flowering. Do not trim them immediately after flowering, but wait for some signs of new growth. Then give a top dressing and trim back with shears. Treated in this way they will often give a second show of bloom. *Saponaria ocymoides, Arabis* and *Gypsophila repens* can be given the same treatment.

Many rock plants can be increased by root division. Take up the whole plant carefully when the soil is fairly moist. Break off small pieces with some roots attached. Re-plant firmly where required and water in. Some rock plants such as the sempervivums, popularly called 'house leeks', send out runners like a strawberry plant. At the end of these is produced a rosette, or young plant; it is a simple matter to sever the runner from the parent plant and re-plant the young rosette where required.

Some shrubbery rockery plants which will not readily root from

PEG DOWN SIDE SHOOTS IN SANDY SOIL. COVER WITH STONE TO RETAIN MOISTURE

One method of propagating rock plants

cuttings may be increased by the gardening operation known as layering. Pin down a few of the lower branches until they reach the soil. Make a diagonal cut into the stem, which will then form a tongue. Choose a position for the cut which is near a joint. With a piece of wire of hairpin shape, peg the cut branch down firmly to the soil. Cover the branch where it is cut and pegged down with some gritty compost and leave intact until it is seen that this part of the branch is producing new foliage and appears to be growing away. When you are sure that roots have formed, sever the layer from the parent plant, dig up the rooted portion and transplant.

Many rock plants may be propagated by cuttings. They need to be set in pots or boxes in an unheated cold frame, and should be taken in early autumn or in spring. They should be embedded in about four inches of sharp, clean sand with a little compost (John Innes No. 2 will do). Drainage crocks are needed at the bottom of the boxes or pots.

Seed sowing of some rockery plants is another way of increasing stock or of starting a collection. If gardeners are sowing some of their own seed saved from their own rock plants, then the best time to choose is when the seed has ripened on the plant. The time of year when they are ready will decide where the seed sowing spot is located. If it is in midsummer, then a cool shady spot will have to be chosen. For autumn sowing, put them in a cold frame, mainly for protection against heavy rain. If it is not convenient to sow in autumn, the seeds may be kept in store. Put them in the dry but not near artificial heat, and sow in the open ground in spring.

Seeds of alpines sown in pans or boxes need no special treatment. Cover with a piece of glass and brown paper; be sure to remove these as soon as the seeds germinate. Often seeds fail to germinate in the first year, but if left out in the frost and snow during the next winter, they are often found growing away sturdily during the following spring. The conditions of their natural habitat have been reproduced. Seeds of many rockery plants can now be obtained from well-known seedsmen, and will have full sowing instructions on the packets.

Rock plant seedlings should be pricked out very early in life. The rockery enthusiast who sows his own saved seed will need to discard any inferior plants and only retain the best colours and those which are equal or superior to the parent plant.

SOME PLANTS FOR THE ROCKERY

Here are some rockery plants which are easy to grow and are very suitable for someone constructing or taking over a rockery for the first time. The plants can be obtained from nurserymen and many can easily be grown from reasonably priced seed.

The *Achillea* or Yarrow family, so well known in the herbaceous border, has a number of dwarf species used as rock plants. Like all the Achilleas, the rock variety will grow in the driest and hottest position. *Achillea tomentosa* should be the first choice, for it is a fine dwarf-growing perennial, suitable for the front of a herbaceous border as well as the rockery. It is in flower from July to September and gives masses of golden-yellow blooms in the typical *Achillea* shape, which is a flattened, circular head of blossom. *Achillea clavennae* grows to a height of six inches and becomes a miniature shrub with white flowers. *Achillea ageratifolia* produces clusters of white flowers during July and August.

Golden Alyssum is one of the best-known rock and dry wall plants. *Alyssum saxatile* is the most usual variety grown, but there are two others which can be grown from seed. These are *Alyssum montanum*, which is a miniature alpine species with masses of small, bright yellow fragrant flowers, and *Alyssum saxatile citrinum*, lemon yellow. Both flower in early spring until about June. Alyssums are excellent plants for the tops of rockeries or walls.

There are several anemones suitable for rockery work. The *Anemone pulsatilla* (or Pasque flower), a native species, has violet flowers and silky foliage. Flowering time is from April to May. It can be grown from seed obtainable from well-known seedsmen. A pale blue variety with single flowers is *Anemone robinsoniana*. Our native wood anemone, *Anemone nemerosa*, is very suitable for rockery work, but it will have to be kept in check, because it very quickly spreads. There is also a double white form, called *Anemone albaplena*.

The common white *Arabis albida* very quickly covers the ground and rocks and although a very useful plant to grow in conjunction with alyssum and aubretia, it has to be cut back ruthlessly, fairly frequently, or it will soon cover the whole rockery. Propagation is easy from cuttings. There are two varieties easily grown from seed, *Arabis alpina* and *Arabis rosea grandiflora*. The latter has attractive pink flowers.

Armeria (Thrift) is an easily grown plant and very useful as it does not spread. The globular flower heads stand up well above the foliage. This is very suitable for growing by the sea, for the native thrift or sea pink grows close to the seashore on the marsh lands. *Armeria formosa* can be grown from seed. *Armeria maritima* has white and rosy forms and is quite dwarf. *Armeria latifolia* grows to a height of twelve inches, and there are white, pink and red varieties. *Armeria plantaginea* is a long-flowering variety which is in flower from May until the end of August. In addition to growing from seed armerias may be increased by root division.

Aubrietias are found everywhere and have a place in every rock garden, and are an ideal plant for dry walls. They can be grown from seed sown in John Innes No. 1 compost, with good drainage, from March until June. Grow on in a cold frame and plant out during late summer and autumn. Aubrietias can also be propagated from cuttings in the cold frame. Early autumn and spring are the best times for taking cuttings. Aubrietias come in shades of lilac, lavender, purple, rose, crimson and carmine.

A useful aquilegia for the rock garden is 'Hensol Harebell' which is a dwarf form of *Aquilegia alpina*. It has blue flowers with white centres, can be grown from seed, is a foot high, and flowers from May to June.

Dwarf campanulas in many shades of blue are easily grown rock plants. They should be planted on the lower and cooler slopes of the rockery and the bottom parts of dry walls. Three which are fairly easily grown from seed are *carpatica*, in shades of blue, lavender and white, *garganica*, which is a trailing species with masses of bright violet-blue flowers, and *pusilla* in shades of blue and white.

Cheiranthus, one of the wallflowers, is a very good rockery and wall plant which does not require too rich a soil. When well established it thrives for years, setting its own seed. It is best to sow the seeds where the plants are to bloom. *Cheiranthus linifolius* is the mauve alpine wallflower with evergreen foliage. It will begin to bloom in April and often continues until October. *Cheiranthus alpinus* has small spikes of yellow flowers. *Cheiranthus mutabilis* has a good variety of colour, with flowers of uncommon shades of puce, red, purple, wine, lemon and sulphur.

There is one Dianthus which beginners can handle well: *Dianthus deltoides*, free flowering and vigorous in growth. It is of low habit and looks at its best if planted where it can hang over the edge of a rock. The bright green foliage becomes overlaid with a mass of carmine blossoms. Growers might also try *Dianthus caesius*, sometimes called *Dianthus glaucus*, the pink which grows near the Cheddar Caves. It has bluish-green foliage and fragrant fringed flowers of rose-pink. Both varieties can be grown from seed.

Most people have heard of the romantic edelweiss, but not many people are aware that it is an easily grown rock plant. It just needs a compost containing plenty of stone and grit and a position high on the rockery where it is exposed to plenty of sunshine and air. It can be grown from seed, and the flowering time is from July to August.

A plant for the base of the rockery, where there is a little more soil, is the *Epimedium*, with beautiful foliage. In spring it is of various shades of chestnut bronze and pink with wonderful veinings. There are small, elegantly-borne flowers, of white, yellow, pinks and reds.

Erinus alpinus is a pretty rock plant, grown from seed, with rosy-mauve flowers. Flowering time is from March to June. Seeds should be sown in the previous April in their flowering positions. There is a white form called *Erinus alpinus albus*.

Among the herbaceous geraniums are several dwarf types suitable for the rock garden. All are easy to grow. A favourite, *Geranium sanguineum*, has bright rose-pink flowers.

Dwarf geums are suitable rock plants and about the best one is *Geum borisii* which is a brilliant orange-scarlet. *Geum montanum* is a rich yellow. Geums bloom throughout the summer, starting in April, and can be increased by root division every two or three years. When dividing in this way, plant only the outer parts and discard the centre portion. They can also be grown from seed.

Gypsophila repens trails prettily over the edge of a rock. It has a glaucous foliage and during July and August will produce a cloud of minute white blossoms. There is a pink variety, *Gypsophila repens rosea*. Both can be grown from seed, but cut back all old growth in the spring.

The *Helianthemum*, or rock rose, must have plenty of sunshine. Rock roses can be grown from seed and are usually sold in packets of mixed colours including yellow, orange, pink and scarlet. The flowering time is from May to July. These are well-known plants which spread quickly and have to be thinned out from time to time.

Iberis sempervirens, or perennial candytuft, is an easily grown rock plant, evergreen, with pure white, very pleasing flowers which are on view for most of the year. They require a very well-drained position. *Iberis gibraltarica* is a neat evergreen with flower clusters of pale mauve or lilac during spring and summer. Both varieties can be grown from seed.

Linum, or flax, has a variety called *Linum arboreum*, bright yellow and very floriferous. It requires a sheltered spot but also plenty of sun, and can be grown from seed.

Mesembryanthemums are very useful subjects for the rockery. There are many kinds. The well-known one (usually treated as a half-hardy annual), known as the 'Livingstone Daisy', is often planted near the aubrietias to provide some summer colour after the aubrietias have finished flowering. This one should be sown under glass in March and hardened off. It likes sunny, well-drained positions and appreciates a little lime or chalk in the soil. There is another half-hardy annual variety, *Mesembryanthemum crystallinum*, or ice plant, which has inconspicuous white flowers, but very striking foliage with glistening silver hairs. The annual varieties of this genus are propagated by seeds sown in spring, the perennial sorts by seeds sown in spring or by cuttings taken in September.

Oxalis is a suitable rock plant because it is dwarf and has attractive foliage. There are both annuals and perennials. The hardy annual produces deep golden flowers in profusion from July onwards throughout the summer. Of the perennials, one has rose flowers and another yellow flowers and brown foliage. Annuals can be raised from seeds sown in the open ground in spring and the perennials from seeds sown in the cool greenhouse during March.

There are very many varieties of primula which are fairly easily grown for the rockery. The majority of primulas prefer shady, moist conditions. *Primula japonica*, 'Millar's Crimson', is a vigorous plant with tall stems bearing tiers of bright crimson flowers. It is usually grown from seed initially and can be split up by root division when established. This is a good plant to put by the edge of a pool. *Primula pulverulenta* hybrids have flowers set in tiers and in shades varying from blush to deep pink. This is a very choice plant, but beginners can grow it from seed, and it needs a moist shady position. *Primula juliae* is a very early-flowering primula and only grows to a height of about two inches. It very quickly spreads and needs to be given plenty of room for a good display of gaily coloured blossom. *Primula violi* has unique poker-like flower spikes which are scarlet in bud and opening to rosy-pink. It grows to a height of eighteen inches and flowers from June to August. *Primula rosea grandiflora* does well in sun or shade if the soil is moist or even wet. It has bright pink flowers and is another good plant to put by a pool or stream. It grows to a height of nine inches and flowers during March and April. Most primulas are best grown from seed and can afterwards be propagated from root division.

Saponaria ocymoides is a useful rock plant, also very suitable for dry walls. It is of trailing habit and bears pretty rose-pink flowers from June to August. It is easily grown from seed.

The Saxifrages belong to a very extensive range of plants and some varieties are always included in a collection of alpine plants. Two classes which can be grown from seed are known as 'encrusted' and 'mossy' varieties. The encrusted varieties need lime added to the soil and a sunny position, and the mossy varieties need a shady position. The encrusted varieties have rosettes of silvery foliage with dainty sprays of white or pink flowers, are from four to six inches high, and the flowering time is from May until July. The mossy varieties make compact green cushions with sprays of pink, rose or white flowers from March to June. The height varies from six to twelve inches. Several seedsmen can offer a good choice of seeds, and *Saxifraga* plants which can be obtained from nurserymen include *Saxifraga aizoon lutea*, nine inches, which has soft yellow flowers in June; *muscoides densa* with tightly packed foliage and a height of four inches is April- and May-flowering; and *muscoides* 'Lovely Rose' has evergreen foliage and large rose-pink flowers.

The Sedums or Stonecrops are other plants with an extensive range of varieties, and packets of seed of mixed varieties are available. These are fleshy-leaved plants with flowers of yellow, pink or white. Heights vary from three to twelve inches. The place for them is the driest and sunniest part of the rockery or wall. If you do not wish to grow them from seed, they are very easily propagated by root division. These are plants which have to be kept in check by drastic thinning each year once they become established, or they will soon swamp other rock subjects. *Sedum acre* is the common golden stonecrop, three inches high, flowering in June. *Sedum sieboldii,* six inches, has lovely pink flowers in August. *Sedum spathulifolium atropurpureum* has beautiful red foliage and yellow flowers in May and June; the height is from three to four inches. *Sedum spectabile*, twelve inches, has upstanding blossoms of pink during September. *Sedum spurium coccineum* is six inches high with large heads of ruby-red flowers in July and August.

Of *Sempervivum* (house leek) mention has already been made. There are many varieties of these attractive plants, with their neat rosettes of thick fleshy foliage. Packets of mixed varieties should be tried. On page 130 there is more about sempervivums and veronicas for trough gardens.

In the large *Veronica* family there are several dwarf varieties, suitable for the rockery. One of the most popular is *Veronica rupestris*, with a height of only three inches. It is an evergreen and during May to July carries a wealth of beautiful blue flowers. *Veronica incana* has grey leaves and spikes of blue flowers during summer. *Veronica allionii, alpina, aphylla, chamaedrys, repens and teucrium* are dwarf-growing veronicas with flowers of various shades of blue. *Veronica caespitosa* is a pink variety with white downy leaves. *Veronica gentianoides variegata* is a pretty variety with variegated foliage. *Veronica spicata rosea* has beautiful heather-like pink spikes of blossom.

Some of the many violas are used as rock plants and among these is *Viola calcarata*, of white, lilac or yellow. *Viola cornuta* has many varieties which can be grown from seed, as can almost all the violas. Seed should be sown in boxes in the cold frame during spring. Prick off when large enough to handle and plant into flowering positions during late summer and autumn. Violas are best planted in the rockery where there is shade and moisture. They appreciate some leaf mould and a well-drained soil. The *cornuta* varieties are compact and exceptionally free-flowering, with medium to small flowers of a very wide range of viola colours. The usual height is six inches. *Viola pedata* is a charming rock viola with fairly large flowers of purple, violet and mauve.

A beginner with rock plants might like to also try some of the alpine phloxes. He may be able to obtain cuttings of one or two varieties and strike them in well-drained soil and a sunny position. If they can become established they will grow into very beautiful trailing rock plants. The flowers are borne in profusion. *Phlox amoena* has pretty rose-pink flowers during April and May. *Phlox douglasii* is covered with lilac stars in May and grows only to a height of two inches. There are numerous varieties of *Phlox sublata*, 'G. F. Wilson' is mauve-blue, 'Margery' is a pink variety, 'The Bride', white with a pink eye, 'Sampson' a clear rose-pink, and 'Temiscaming' has masses of brilliant red flowers on cushions of dark green foliage. All of these flower during May and June.

CONIFERS FOR THE ROCKERY

Evergreen coniferous trees, of dwarf habit, look very charming in the rockery when placed in the most effective position. Careful planting is needed for conifers. A hole of suitable size should be dug, the roots are spread out, then the soil should be put back carefully and made very firm. A heavy soaking of water is required as the final operation, then a watering every day around the roots until the trees have become established. A daily over-head watering is also called for. Some trees may have to be staked and supported temporarily. Dwarf conifers can be planted in the autumn or in spring. It is very important to see that the roots do not come into contact with any fresh manure at the time of planting. Here are some conifers suitable for rock gardens:

Of the *Chamaecyparis,* I recommend four. These are *lawsoniana ellwoodii*, with erect branches covered with feathery glaucous foliage, a charming, slow-growing variety; *lawsoniana fletcheri* is bluish-grey, also slow-growing; *lawsoniana forsteckensis* is of a dwarf globular form with dense branches of deep moss-green; *lawsoniana nana glauca* is also of dwarf globular form.

Of the *Juniperus, chinensis Pfitzeriana* is a wide-spreading tree with glaucous branchlets pendent at the tips; *Juniperus cupressifolia* is a semi-erect form with green glossy foliage; *Juniperus hibernica,* the Irish *Juniperus,* is a close-growing, columnar variety frequently used in formal gardens.

Thuya 'Rheingold' is a beautiful, dwarf-growing tree of a broad pyramidal shape, golden in summer and bronze in autumn.

SINKS AND TROUGHS

Old stone sinks and troughs can be used for several purposes in the garden. A well-weathered old sink can be sunk into the ground on the rockery, or some other part of the garden, filled with water, and used as a bird bath. It can be made to harmonize very well with a natural-looking stone or two in the water for the birds to alight on. A good, well-fitting stopper must be provided, so that the water can be let out and fresh water added. If some aubrietia is allowed to trail towards the stones and around the sink the effect can be very beautiful.

Many people with a small town garden or only a courtyard can grow some alpine plants or other rockery flowers in one or two old stone troughs or sinks. It is better if a sunny position can be found in the courtyard for them, yet if only a shady position is possible, some shade-lovers may be coaxed into flowering.

Drainage is very important in trough gardening. Holes will have to be made in the bottom of the sink or trough. This operation has to be carried out very carefully indeed. Use a sharp small cold chisel, then the stone may be gradually chipped away until a small hole is seen. Be careful not to strike too vigorously and so crack the whole of the base. Once it is there, the hole can be enlarged. A handyman will know how to use a hand-drill with a copper tube packed with carborundum, obtainable from garages where grinding is done.

Cover the drainage holes with large crocks placed concave face downwards, then cover the whole of the bottom of the sink with small crocks. Lay over the crocks a layer of turfy fibre and partly decayed leaf-mould. The rest of the compost for the container will consist of fibrous loam, a little garden peat, some well-rotted garden compost, a little leaf mould, plenty of grit and silver sand and some porous stone or brick chippings. The ingredients should be well mixed and made firm. A trough containing lime-free soil could be used for lime-intolerant alpines.

Watering must not be neglected; because of the limited amount of soil which can be put into a trough, plants can soon dry out. A miniature rockery effect can be created if a few stones are embedded in the soil for a few inches. Try to achieve a natural setting, as with all such work, and do not dot the soil with a pattern of stones.

The selection of plants for a trough garden will be a matter of personal choice as there are so many to pick from. Some people may like to grow plants from just one family, and here the miniature roses would be good subjects for a tiny garden of this nature. 'Baby Masquerade' is a miniature floribunda, 'Perle de Montserrat' is soft rose-pink, 'Perle D'Alcanada' is carmine, 'Pour Toi' creamy-white and like a tiny hybrid tea rose, and 'Rosina' is of a lovely deep yellow.

The miniature bulbs make another good subject for this kind of gardening. This selection of spring-flowering crocus species embraces many kinds seldom met with, and they are quite outstanding in colouring:

Susianus, 'Cloth of Gold', is yellow, feathered with dark purple; inside is a deeper golden yellow. *C. chrysanthus*, 'Blue Pearl', is a soft pearly blue and a globular-shaped flower. *C. chrysanthus*, 'Cream Beauty', is an unusual and very attractive shade of soft primrose. The flowers have rounded petals and a deep orange stigma. *C. chrysanthus*, 'Snow Bunting', is white, slightly feathered purple, with orange throat. The variety 'Zwanenburg Bronze' is a deep orange crocus feathered on the outside with purplish bronze. 'Goldenbunch' is orange-yellow with many flowers from each bulb. *C. imperati* is a very lovely crocus, inside violet, outside fawn and very early. *C. tomasinianus* produces numerous flowers of silver-grey opening to sapphire lavender *C. tomasinianus* 'Whitewell Purple' is a bright reddish-purple, with a conspicuous orange stigma. *C. vernus* 'Vanguard' is a bright mauve.

For autumn flowering, *speciosus* is a brilliant deep blue, veined violet with a showy orange stigmata, and *zonatus* is rosy lilac, a beautiful flower.

Miniature *Narcissus* (daffodil) species should be planted during September and left undisturbed as they do not flower freely during the first year of planting *N. bulbocodium conspicuus*, a yellow hoop-petticoat type, is rich golden-yellow and six inches high; *minimus* is the smallest of daffodils, of a very rich yellow and only three inches high; *nanus lobularis*, the 'Lent Lily', has a cream perianth and a yellow trumpet; it is early flowering, six inches high. *N. triandrus albus*, 'Angel's Tears', has a creamy-white globular cup and reflexed petals, is six inches high. 'W. P. Milner' is sulphur-yellow and nine inches high. All of these miniatures are also very suitable for rockeries.

There are some lovely dwarf irises suitable for trough gardening and for rockeries. *I. danfordiae* is deep lemon and sweetly scented, flowers in February, three inches; *I. reticulata* is a charming dwarf iris, rich violet-blue with an orange blotch on the lower petal, flowering in February, six inches. *I. tuberosa* is a unique species, purplish-black and green, flowering in June. *I. pumila*, with all its named hybrids, is of shades of lilac and purple, the flowering time is April and May, heights from three to eight inches.

The tulip species offers flowers of very rich colours suitable for trough gardening and for rockeries. Most of them flower during March and April. 'Goudstuk' is deep golden yellow, the inside petals with a crimson ring, height ten inches. 'Red Riding Hood' is oriental scarlet with reddish-brown striped foliage, height eight inches. 'Shakespeare' is a blend of salmon, apricot and orange, seven inches high. 'Stresa' is a rich golden yellow with a red band on the outside, interior with red markings. *Kaufmanniana* Hybrids are called the 'Water Lily Tulips' and attractive mixtures in many of the tulip colours can be obtained. Heights from twelve to fifteen inches.

When growing alpines or other rock plants in troughs it is important not to plant those which are of straggling growth. A trough of various primulas would be very suitable, placed in partial shade. *Primula denticulata* and its hybrids, *Primula pulverulenta* hybrids and *Primula viali* could all be tried; *Primula obconica* would succeed in a warm part of the country.

Other alpine or rockery plants for trough gardening are *Aethionema coridifolium*, 'Warley Rose', which is an alpine candytuft forming a neat twiggy bush of blue-grey leaves with bright rosy-pink flowers in April and May, growing six inches high. *Erodium chamaedryoides rosea*, 'Heron's Bill', is only three inches in height and has pink-veined flowers which resemble miniature pelargoniums and delicate fern-like foliage. Some small fuchsias could be planted and one called *pumila* 'Tom Thumb', twelve inches, is in summer and autumn smothered with relatively large red and purple flowers. It needs protection from frost.

Mimulus 'Fireflame' and *Mimulus* 'Queen's Prize' are compact plants, the first with flowers of coppery scarlet from June until September; they need fairly moist conditions.

Penstemon heterophyllus has long spikes of rich blue tubular flowers from July to September. *Zauchneria latifolia*, six inches high, has long tubular flowers of brilliant scarlet with silvery foliage; it is a lovely autumn subject, flowering in September and October.

If the courtyard where only sink or trough gardening can be undertaken is entirely in the shade, a collection of ferns could be grown. These will need plenty of moisture. The soil for ferns must contain plenty of leaf-mould for moisture retention. Any of the following ferns would be suitable: *Adiantum pedatum*, 'Maidenhair Fern', has bronze-tinted foliage when the plants are young. The foliage is useful for flower decoration and mixes very well with sweet peas and carnations. *Athyrium felix-femina*, 'Lady Fern', has lovely lacy foliage. *Onoclea sensibilis*, 'Sensitive Fern', needs quite moist conditions. *Polypodium angulare* is easily grown in shade or sun, and is evergreen in a sheltered position, such as a courtyard. *Scolopendrium vulgare*, 'Hart's Tongue', is a most adaptable fern that will thrive with the minimum of attention.

The following are also suitable trough plants. Some of these may be used as a mixture, but if the gardener has several sinks he may like to fill some with various plants of one species, such as saxifrage or dianthus.

Asperula suberosa is one of the best of the Woodruffs but it needs protection from heavy rain during the winter. It has silvery-grey foliage and the pink trumpets are borne from May to August. It is three inches in height.

There are a vast number of *Dianthus* varieties suitable for the rock garden but the following are the best for troughs, as they are only miniature: *Dianthus freynii* has little tufts of blue-grey leaves and is covered in summer with very small rose-pink blossoms. The flowering time is from June onwards and the height is two inches. *Dianthus myrtinervis* is like a condensed form of our native *Dianthus deltoides*. It has stemless pink flowers, and needs a poor soil in order to preserve its compact habit. The flowering time is from June onwards and the height is one inch. *Dianthus subacaulis* produces carmine flowers with dark-green foliage, flowers from June onwards, and grows to two inches.

Draba or 'Whitlow Grass' has many varieties but the following will be suitable for the miniature garden: *Draba bryoides imbricata* produces compact dark green domes with yellow flowers during March and April. The height is two inches. *Draba dedeana* has white flowers in March and April and is two inches high. *Draba rigida* makes neat green cushions of foliage with yellow flowers in April. The height is three inches.

One of the Cranesbill family is suitable for large troughs: *Geranium farreri*. It has scalloped red-green leaves with relatively large apple-blossom pink flowers and black anthers. It blooms through the summer and is three inches high.

Morisia monanthosis is a good subject for a trough garden but it likes a sandy soil; although a plant of the seashore, it associates well with other small rock plants. It has curiously notched leaves in the form of a rosette, and clusters of bright yellow flowers nestle in the centre during April and May; height, one inch.

The Kabschia section of the Saxifrages is the one for sink and trough gardening. These are the Saxifrages which form cushions. They enjoy a very gritty soil with plenty of limestone chips and ample supplies of water during summer and some shade from hot noonday sun. All produce neat cushions about two inches through. The main flowering period is during March, but some are earlier and some later.

Saxifraga burseriana, with spiny grey rosettes, has white flowers. *Saxifraga* 'Aubrey Pritchard' has grey rosettes and rosy-mauve flowers. *Saxifraga* 'Cranbourne' is a good hybrid with grey-green rosettes and bright pink flowers. *Saxifraga* 'Faldonside' has spiny grey rosettes and sulphur-yellow flowers. *Saxifraga* 'Grace Farwell' has wine-red flowers, *Saxifraga* 'Iris Pritchard' apricot flowers. *Saxifraga Jenkinsae* is very free-flowering and has pale pink flowers with darker eyes. *Saxifraga marginata* has green rosettes margined with silver-white flowers.

All the above plants are from the Kabschia section of Saxifragas, and apart from these there are only two others suitable for miniature gardening. These are commonly known as the 'silver saxifrages'. *Saxifraga aizoon baldensis* has small rosettes and white flowers in June. *Saxifraga cochlearis minor* needs a little more space with its larger and flatter rosettes. It bears white flowers during May and June.

Sedums are best grown in a trough of their own. The following are the smallest of over five hundred different varieties of this succulent. All mentioned are easy to grow in fairly dry soil and in full sun.

Sedum brevifolium, one of the smallest, has tight green and red foliage and white flowers during June and July and is one inch in height. *Sedum hispanicum* has grey-green leaves shaded pink, white flowers with black anthers during June and July, height two inches. *Sedum nevii*, with grey-green rosettes shaded orange, has white starry flowers during June and July. *Sedum spathulifolium* has rosettes of grey leaves and yellow flowers on pink stems. *S.s. capablanca* is smaller, and *S.s. purpureum* has leaves of reddish purple. The flowering period is June and July and the height from two to three inches.

SOME SHRUBS FOR THE TROUGH GARDEN

Some of the dwarf Genistas are small enough for trough gardening. They enjoy light soil and a sunny position. *Genista delphinensis* forms a dense plant with curiously winged branches. At the tips of these are clusters of golden-yellow flowers in June. The height is two inches. *Genista villarsii* is a compact shrub with masses of grey-green branches and bears yellow flowers in June. It is three inches high.

Polygala chamaebuxus is a small evergreen; the pea-shaped blossoms have bright yellow keels. The flowering time is from May onwards, height about six inches. *Polygala chamaebuxus purpurea* is an attractive form where the wings of the flowers are reddish-purple. The flowering time is from May onwards and the height about six inches. *Polygala vayrediae* has narrow leaves and crimson flowers with yellow bells. Flowering from May onwards, three to four inches high. These plants like a peaty soil with some sand.

There are several dwarf Spiraeas suitable for the miniature garden. All need ample supplies of water during the summer. *Spiraea caespitosa* is the smallest, with downy grey foliage and racemes of white

9

flowers in July, height two inches. *Spiraea decumbens* bears flat heads
of white flowers throughout the summer. Well drained soil in full sun
is required, height six inches. *Spiraea pectinata* forms a prostrate mat
of bright green foliage and fluffy white flower heads on erect stems.
Well drained soil in part shade will suit this plant.

The Sempervivums or house leeks appreciate similar growing
conditions to the Sedums. The following are some suitable dwarf
species. *Sempervivum allionii* has pale green rosettes and greenish-
white flowers during June and July. *Sempervivum arenarium*, with
small reddish-green globular rosettes, produces creamy flowers in
June and July, with a height of three inches. *Sempervivum hirtum*
resembles the last-named plant but is slightly larger with flatter
rosettes and yellow flowers. It also flowers during June and July and
is four inches high.

One or two of the Veronicas are suitable for troughs and a light
gritty soil suits them best. Both of the varieties described need protection from heavy or continuous rain. *Veronica bombycina* produces
neat tufts of white woolly foliage and pale blue flowers. The flowering
time is June, height three inches. *Veronica caespitosa* is smaller, with
grey leaves and large pink flowers. It flowers during May and June
and grows to two inches.

The Wahlenbergias are attractive plants for the miniature garden.
They are sometimes listed as *Edraianthus*. They need a light gritty
soil containing plenty of limestone chippings or crushed mortar
rubble. *Wahlenbergia pumilio* has a neat spiny tuffet of silvery leaves
and in June these become covered with stemless upturned lavender
cups. The height is two to three inches. *Wahlenbergia serpyllifolia* is
more straggly, has mats of dark green leaves, and in May and June
deep purple bells. It has a short flowering period and the height is
two to three inches.

There are some dwarf conifers suitable for trough and sink gardening. *Chamaecyparis obtusa caespitosa* only grows to three or four
inches, and *Chamaecyparis obtusa minima, compacta, intermedia,
juniperoides* and *nana* are also very small trees.

Chamaecyparis pisifera nana and *Chamaecyparis pisifera plumosa
compressa* are more spreading in habit but are delightful trees for the
miniature garden.

Juniperus communis compressa will make a lovely miniature tree
with densely packed grey-green foliage of symmetrical shape. It will
grow to a height of two feet, but this will take a few years as it is
very slow growing.

These midget trees are easily cultivated but they should be well
watered for some time after being planted; do not allow them to
become waterlogged. They appreciate a little peat or leaf mould mixed

with the soil at the time of planting. Place the trees as artistically as possible in the troughs.

DRY WALLING

Dry walls serve many purposes besides being a very attractive feature of the garden in their own right, enlivened with plants which are happy growing in soil pockets in the crevices. A dry wall can be employed as a retaining wall at the end of a paved terrace and it can be used wherever a change of level occurs. If a lawn is higher than the paved entrance and surrounds of the dwelling-house, then a dry wall will prevent the soil from falling on to the paving, and it looks better than a high grass bank which is difficult to mow. A sunk garden also needs a dry wall as a retaining wall.

A dry wall can be constructed of flat pieces of walling stone, such as that which is used for crazy paving. This sort of stone, usually sandstone, is handsome and durable when properly laid and with suitable plants growing and flowering from the soil pockets.

If the walling is to be built against a bank of soil, the face of the bank needs to be made flush with a spade, so that the stones can be laid against it with the minimum of trouble.

Prepare a large heap of soil, by mixing old turfy loam, some silver sand, leaf mould, grit and well-rotted garden compost. When this has been thoroughly mixed with a shovel, it should be passed through a sieve. The soil should not be too dry, for when moist it can be worked between the layers of stone and rammed tightly more easily than dry, powdery soil. Have plenty of walling stone near at hand, and use it as it comes; do not try to arrange all the large pieces first and then have a lot of small pieces left over which will be difficult to use; part of the skill in dry-walling lies in the successful combination of large and small, thick and thin.

SECTION OF DRY WALL   FRONT VIEW OF DRY WALL

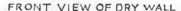
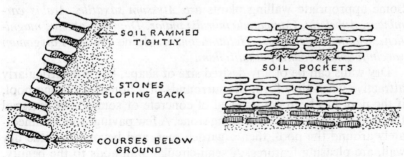

How to construct a dry wall

First, excavate the soil where the base of the wall will come, to a width of about twelve inches. Two courses of stone should then be laid on firm, level ground and these, below ground level, will constitute the footings. It would be best to use the thickest stones for the foundation, as these will have to bear the whole weight of the wall without subsiding.

Put down the first layer of stones which are above ground level with the straightest edges to the front, but bring them forward far enough for each succeeding layer of stones to be set back a little. They should also be slightly tilted, so that each stone slopes slightly towards the bank behind them.

After seeing that the first row of stones looks nice and level, cover them with about two inches of the sifted soil and ram the soil in very firmly at the back of the stones. The next layer of stones should overlap the crack where two stones below are joining each other, using the same method here as a bricklayer with his bonding.

If some stones are placed with a wider crack between them, little pockets of soil can be created for the planting of rock or walling plants later. Every now and then a stone can be turned with its narrow edge as facing and its length tucked into the soil behind; this will make for extra strength. The top layer of stones is sometimes joined with cement to give stability to the wall and to prevent the top stones from being knocked over when mowing or weeding are being done.

If there is a lawn immediately above the top of the wall, it would be best to arrange the top layer of stones a little below the edge of the grass to make mowing and edging easier.

The planting of the wall can be undertaken as building proceeds, or after the wall has been completed. It is best done during spring or in autumn. After insertion in the soil pockets or in crevices, the plants should be firmed and watered.

Suitable plants for dry walls are those of trailing habit, and free-flowering subjects. Plants in these situations generally make quick growth and the wall soon becomes an object of beauty and colour. Some appropriate walling plants are *Alyssum saxatile*, *Arabis carmineus*, *Aubrietia*, *Campanula muralis major*, *Dianthus caesius magnifica*, *Dianthus deltoides*, *Helianthemum*, Alpine Phlox, *Polygonum vaccinifolium*, *Sedum spathulifolium*.

Dry walls can be of any desired size or shape, but are particularly attractive when they form the surrounds of a home swimming-pool, if the pool has been constructed of concrete or some other material that will blend in with the walling stone. A few paving stones immediately around the pool, then a garden seat, and beyond that the dry wall, are pleasing features. A semi-circular wall adds to the beauty, and beyond the wall could be a lawn with a bed of floribunda roses.

On the other side of the pool could be grass, with a bed of the same shape as the pool, filled with irises of various varieties, interplanted with butterfly gladioli. Both of these plants would look appropriate by the side of a swimming-pool. The irises would flower in June when bathing would begin, followed by the gladioli throughout the summer. Early, mid-season and late gladioli could be planted. A rockery would also look well at the end of a pool, opposite to the swimmers' entry.

GARDEN ORNAMENTS

If one is fond of garden ornaments, some will not look out of place if used in conjunction with stone work. Only those in keeping with the general scene should be used. Avoid those grotesque painted gnomes one frequently sees for sale in some garden shops; stone herons, white storks and artificial frogs also give an absurd impression, but a well-weathered old sundial will fit in well with a sunk garden that has a dry wall. Old wells and stone urns can also be used and a nicely sculptured figure with nothing bizarre about it could be standing at the edge of a garden pool of reasonable size.

THE WATER GARDEN

Not very many people will have a stream running through their garden. If they have, and if the garden is large enough, it gives scope for several attractive features. Waterfalls could be arranged to run through parts of the rockery, or some of the stream could be dammed to form a pool and bog garden. One disadvantage of pools and bog gardens is the presence of mosquitoes and gnats. Some people are not very much troubled by these insects, some become more or less immune, but some are very badly bitten. If you are one of the many who are allergic to the bite of a mosquito, and have as a result, to take penicillin tablets or have injections, then forget a water garden unless some effective means can be found of destroying the insects.

When just a garden pool is to be made, the nuisance will not be considerable if the pool is stocked with fish. Besides being ornamental, these help to keep a pool clean and they feed on mosquito larvae.

Before constructing a water garden, make sure that there will be a continuous supply of water and that the local authorities are not going to impose water restrictions just when the water lilies or some other choice aquatic plants are in full bloom. If all conditions are appropriate, the next step is to decide which material to use. A pool can be made of concrete, or some of the ready-made pools may in suitable cases be easily installed.

A natural pool must be situated in a low-lying part and should blend in well with the rockery, if there is one. Do not have too regular or too irregular an outline, try to copy nature as far as possible. All pools and water gardens should have an uninterrupted view of the water and the plants growing in it. In formally laid-out gardens, the pool which may be near the house should, however, be rectangular or square, and have definite edges usually constructed with paving stones.

If you wish to make your own pool of concrete it will be found that the task is not too difficult. If there is a low-lying part of the garden which is naturally boggy, and if it is your wish to create a full water garden as well as a pond, then this will be the correct site.

A natural pool without a bog garden would ideally be situated near, or be part of, the rock garden. It should also be in an open position where it will receive plenty of sunshine, and away from trees which will choke the pool with fallen leaves.

Mark out the site, and mark with pegs where different levels are to come. Where a more shallow trough is required for growing bog plants, it is made outside the area of the main stretch of water. Although water lilies and other aquatic plants, in their natural habitat, can be found growing in very deep water, if a home-made or ready-made pool is about three feet at its deepest point, this will be found sufficient for all plants and fish. The ready-made pools of plastic materials which are so popular today are very much more shallow, and seldom of pleasing colour.

After deciding on the position for a concrete pool, excavate the soil to a depth of 3 ft. 9 ins. to allow for hard core and concrete. Fill the bottom with hard material and fill in cracks with sand and make quite level.

Mix the concrete, using two parts *washed* sand, one part cement and two parts aggregate. Do not use any sea sand as it will have a bad effect on fish and plants. The concrete base of the pool should be about 6 inches thick for small ponds and 9 inches for large ones.

If the soil walls of the site of the pond are dry and crumbly, boards will have to be used to build the concrete against. These can be taken out later. The walls will probably have to be made in stages. Build up so far and then allow to set. Build another section on top later on, and leave the top of each section of walling rough, so that the next layer will unite with it. After all the cementing has been completed, a coating of a substance called Gandersil will have to be applied. This material has merely to be dissolved in water and brushed on to the surface. It neutralizes the free lime which would be harmful to fish and plants, and converts it into an insoluble compound (silica), making the concrete waterproof.

Although the pond can be stocked twenty-four hours after treatment, there is usually no hurry and it would be better to wait a week or so. During this period the rockery stones can be placed in position to hide the concrete and to make the pool look natural.

Now we come to the ready-made pools which can be purchased and easily installed. Most of them are made of some form of plastic. Some are in sheets which are sunk into the excavated ground and some are ready constructed in various sizes.

Always buy these materials from a reputable firm as there are many cheap plastic pools on the market which are quite useless. Polythene sheet is the cheapest pool lining but is not durable. P.V.C. Pool Liner is a reliable product at an intermediate price range. Blue Atoll Pool Liner is a special grade of thick P.V.C. sheeting which is strong and long-lasting. Plastolene sheet is an extremely strong, laminated, flexible plastic, consisting of terylene coated with P.V.C. It has a greater degree of elasticity than polythene. Ready-made pools of this material are on the market. Glass-fibre, bonded with resins and shaped on a mould, is the only material from which rigid pools are made. They are more expensive than the flexible materials, but can be of good design, appearance, durability, and easy to install. All of these materials are unaffected by frost.

Glass-fibre pools are very light in weight and can easily be installed by one adult. Besides the conventional manner of excavating a hole and sinking the pool to ground level, the pool can be sunk only halfway or to other depths. This saves digging where a bank for a rockery slopes away from the sides of the pool. Such pools are very easily cleaned.

Plastolene pools come in three colours, blue, green or stone. Plastolene sheeting can be used to make a pool of your own design. An excavation is made of whatever shape is required to a depth of 15 inches for a small pool and 24 inches for a large one. A shelf of about 9 inches wide and at a similar depth below the surface should be incorporated for marginal plants. All walls must slope at an angle of 20 degrees. All stones should be removed from the bottom and a covering of fine soil applied.

Then the Plastolene liner is stretched over the hole and held in place by stone slabs. Water is run in and its weight gradually pulls down the liner until it is moulded to the shape of the excavation. A flap is left all round and is concealed with rock or paving stones. Plastolene sheets can be used to line a leaking concrete pool. For making a pool with Polythene, P.V.C. or Blue Atoll liners, the same method as for Plastolene is used.

Waterfall units can be obtained in various materials, shapes and sizes. Some are replicas of natural rock pools, complete with stone surrounds. Some are in one-piece moulding, and some are in separate pieces. The one-piece units are just set firm and level in the soil of the rockery adjoining the main pool. A submersible pump can be employed to lift water from the pool through concealed plastic hose and taken to the rim of the upper rock pool to pour from between rocks like a mountain stream.

Those who like fountains to combine with their pool or waterfall can install them by using a submersible pump and fountain adjuster. In pools more than 4 feet wide these two parts of the apparatus remain accessible at the side of the pool with the jet mounted in the centre.

Fish like water movement, and it can be provided by a fountain. It helps oxygenation and cools the fish in hot weather. Water lilies, however, do not flower well if they are over-cooled, so a fountain must not spurt out too violently. There must be no introduction of cold mains water. The fountain and waterfall must be produced by re-circulation of the pool water itself, which will be of even temperature and the water which the fish and plants have become accustomed to.

It is advisable to introduce fish to any pool. As already pointed out, they are interesting and handsome and they check infestation by mosquitoes as well as feeding on many injurious insects which will damage the water and marginal plants. It is best to let a few weeks elapse between the planting of the pool and its stocking with fish.

Initial stocking should allow three inches of fish length, or less, for every square foot of surface area. This will leave room for growth. The fish which are mentioned will all mix together and they are all hardy. If the pool freezes over during the winter, bore one or two holes in the ice to allow the escape of gas from decaying matter in the pool. In no circumstances must the ice be broken with heavy blows, as the concussion can kill or injure the fish.

Golden and silver orfe, salmon-orange or silver in colour, are beautiful fish, suitable for all but the very smallest of pools. They are lively surface feeders. Goldfish are too well-known to need description.

Shubunkins are almost scaleless relatives of the goldfish, and with a wonderful mixture of brilliant colours, red, white, blue, black, yellow and silver. Both goldfish and Shubunkins come in a form with extra-long tails and are then known as 'comet longtails'.

Silver and golden russ, also active surface feeders, have a body colour of reddish-gold and silver. Fins are reddish in both forms.

Green tench remain at the bottom of the pool, where they feed. They are seldom seen but carry out a useful job as scavengers. On no account introduce cat fish which are frequently mentioned as scavengers. They will eat other fish as large as themselves.

No rules can be laid down for the feeding of fish. It depends largely on the amount of natural food which is present. Fish are more hungry in the summer, when they are more active, but need hardly any food in the winter. Never over-feed, as food not consumed soon decays in the pool. Feed daily in the summer, and do not give more food than the fish will clear in about ten minutes. Vary the diet as much as possible. Purchased fish are usually sent to the customer, nearly always by passenger train, in sealed containers which contain water and pure oxygen. Dispatch is notified by post, and using the same method as for the collection of day-old chicks, the purchaser should make frequent enquiries at his local station about their arrival. The fish should be released into the pool at the earliest possible moment.

In addition to fish, some ramshorn snails may be introduced to a pool or aquarium, as they are important scavengers and help to keep the water clear.

AQUATIC PLANTS

The soil mixture for all water plants should be a good medium loam, with not too much organic matter in it. Leaf-mould, peat and horse manure tend to ferment in the water and so pollute the whole pool.

With the plastic pools, it is best to plant in plastic planting crates, made from moulded polythene, and then lower them into the pool. If it is a large pond and the intention is to plant a number of water lilies, it would be best to wrap the ball of soil in sacking and then drop the plants carefully over the side of a boat into the desired position.

Many water and bog plants are very rampant growers, so the major work with a water garden of any size is the drastic thinning of these subjects. No one wants the pool or pond covered with green growth to the exclusion of colourful flowers. Neither do the fish, who need light and air.

April to June is the best time for planting aquatic plants. The hardy water lilies or nymphaeas come in many varieties, and a suitable collection can be acquired to suit many different depths of water. First on the list are the miniature Nymphaea, which need only from three to twelve inches, and are very suitable for small shallow pools. These include *froebelii,* with rich, red, fragrant flowers. *Laydeckeri lilacea* is sweetly scented, and of a soft pink turning to deep rose. *ellisiana* is vermilion red and *graziella* coppery red with bright orange stamens.

The following sorts will grow in seven to fifteen inches of water and eighteen to twenty-four inches of water. 'Escarboucle' is glowing crimson, with crimson-stained stamens, 'James Brydon' has large paeony-shaped flowers of rosy red, *marliacea chromatella* shapely yellow blooms with mottled foliage. *marliacea rosea* is a very free-flowering kind with soft pink flowers and golden stamens. *N. odorata* 'Turicensis' has sweetly scented, star-like pink flowers. *N. odorata* is white, with a delicious scent, a very attractive plant. 'Virginale' has large, white, sweetly-scented blooms.

These water lilies will flower from May to October. When planting into baskets, the crowns of the plants should be just above the soil level. Line the baskets with moss. Allow about eight inches of soil in the planting crate.

Marginal aquatic plants add greatly to the beauty of the water garden and from the following list plants can be selected for the actual pool, for the margins and for a bog garden, if one is being included.

Aponogeton distachyum or 'Water Hawthorn' has sweetly-scented white flowers in spring and autumn and with its oval, floating, shiny leaves needs twelve inches of water.

Astilbe is not strictly a water plant but is very valuable for planting in a damp spot by the water. They range in height from four inches to four feet and their colours are dark crimson, rose, white, purple and scarlet.

Butomus umbellatus or 'Flowering Rush' is rose-pink and three feet high; it needs four inches of water. *Caltha palustris plena* is a double yellow marsh marigold, six inches in height, and will grow in a boggy part near the water. *Cyperus longus* is a beautiful rush with tufts of grass-like foliage terminating in plumes of reddish-brown. It grows to a height of from two to four feet and it needs four inches of water. *Glyceria maxima variegata* is a beautiful grass, striped white, yellow and green, and is tinted deep rose in spring and autumn.

Many irises are suitable for water gardens and they look very natural growing there. Among the best are *Iris kaempferi,* Enfield hybrids. These are the very lovely clematis-flowered Iris embracing both single and double forms. They need no depth of water. *Iris laevigata* is a brilliant violet-blue and requires two inches of water. *Iris albo-purpurea* has white and blue mottled flowers, also needing two inches of water. *Iris sibirica,* 'Emperor' is a cornflower blue, 'Perry's Blue' is sky-blue, 'Snow Queen', white. All *Iris sibirica* will grow out of the water. *Iris variegata* has striking green and white foliage with blue flowers, and needs two inches of water.

Juncus ensifolius is a rush with red tufts of dwarf iris-like foliage and dainty brown flowers, for from three to five inches of water. *Lythrum salicaria* or 'Purple Loosestrife' has graceful spikes of blossom and there are red and rose varieties. It will grow well in any damp situation.

Menyanthes trifoliata, the 'Bog Bean', has trefoil leaves and pink flowers, is nine inches high, and the plant wants three inches of water. *Mimulus luteus*, 'Water Musk', is invaluable for giving colour at the water's edge, with its rich golden flowers throughout the summer. It will grow in four inches of water. *Myosotis palustris*, the 'Water Forget-me-not', thrives at the water's edge or in a few inches of water.

Nymphoides peltata, also known as 'Water Fringe', has green, floating leaves mottled with reddish-brown and golden flowers, needs twelve inches of water. *Pontederia cordata*, the 'Pickerel Weed' from North America, produces large china-blue flowers; and like the Musk it gives some nice colour near the edge of the pool. It is very suitable for small stretches of water, and there should be three inches of water over the roots.

Many of the primulas make charming waterside plants. They will often seed freely and make many more good plants which could be used elsewhere in the garden if desired. The species and varieties are: *Primula bulleyana*, with buff-orange flowers, *Primula denticulata*, with round heads of lilac colour, *Primula denticulata alba*, white, *Primula florindae,* soft-yellow flowers, *Primula japonica,* white, pink, and crimson varieties, *Primula waltoni,* heads of crimson, pendulous flowers and stems covered with fine white hairs contrasting with the leaves and bloom.

Ranunculus lingua has dark green foliage and large golden flowers and it will grow in from three to eighteen inches of water. *Sagittaria sagittifolia*, or 'Japanese Arrowhead', has white flowers resembling those of annual stocks with handsome leaves in the shape of an arrowhead. Two inches of water are enough. *Saururus cernuus*, called 'Lizard's Tail', gives nodding white flowers and wants two inches of water. *Scirpus tabernoemontani albescens* is a rush with green and white vertical variegations. *Scirpus zebrinus* has green and white bands. Both varieties grow to a height of three feet and grow in four inches of water.

Floating plants provide shade and help to control various weeds which infest ponds, and they provide food for fish. One to every ten square feet of surface water is enough. *Azolla caroliniana*, 'Fairy Moss', is a floating fern of greeny-bronze colour. *Hydrocharis morsus-ranae*, commonly known as 'Frogbit', resembles a tiny water lily. *Lemna triscula*, the 'Ivy-leaved Duckweed', is used for clearing the water, and *Stratiotes aloides*, 'Water Soldier', has star-shaped spiky leaves.

In addition to some of the water, marginal and floating plants mentioned, a pool will require some submerged oxygenating plants, essential for preserving the pool balance. The usual method is to put in a dozen plants for every 24 square feet of water surface area.

These plants take in carbon dioxide emitted by the fish and return life-giving oxygen.

A few hardy ferns can be used for the water garden, if you like. *Osmunda regalis* is one of the best for this purpose and it grows to a height of from four to six feet. *Blechnum spicant*, known as the 'Hardy Fern', is a small one of only a foot in height.

Although a good number of aquatic plants have been mentioned here, the final choice must be governed by individual taste and size of pool. All water plants grow much more quickly than land plants, and some should be avoided because they would soon get out of hand in the ordinary water garden. Where space is limited it would be unwise to plant any of the ordinary wild yellow iris, any of the reeds, including the Great Reed Mace, *Typha*, a tall plant with numerous cat's tail brown spikes, *Gunnera rheum*, the ornamental rhubarb, bamboos, dogwoods or any of the larger ferns. With small pools, perhaps the flowering rushes could also be omitted.

For an average pool of about thirty square feet, a dozen marginal plants of different varieties would be sufficient.

Water gardens are fascinating, as they seem to provide something different from ordinary gardening. To watch the colourful fish darting here and there, to hear the delightful sound of a waterfall, to see the exotic water lilies in bloom and the beautiful reflections of the marginal plants, all this gives another dimension, a new range of experiences.

PATHS AND TERRACES

The materials chosen for a terrace should blend with the house and plants grown. A terrace is a hard, wide path, which can be in front of the house, part of the way round, or even surrounding it. It should be at least eight feet wide and where there is a large garden it would be better to have it much wider. There should be room for some chairs and tables, for it is very pleasant in the summer to sit and look at the garden from a sheltered terrace.

One of the nicest materials to use is well-weathered old brick. These bricks look attractive whether the house is constructed of brick or stone. If a new terrace is to be laid, take out the soil to a depth of about eight inches. If this is a good soil, use it for potting or put it to one side for sprinkling onto the compost heap.

Put in some wooden pegs with a floor-board on top of them and then a spirit level. Tap in the pegs until the foundation is absolutely level. See that the tops of the pegs are below the damp course and fill in the cavity with hard core material in order to ensure good drainage. Broken bricks, stones, clinkers or any hard material through which water will drain will be suitable. Put a layer of coal ashes or sand on the top of the hard core so that the bricks can be bedded in and laid more easily. Use the board and spirit level repeatedly to get the terrace really level.

Have a quantity of cement mixed ready and place it between the brick joins. This will help to make the terrace firm and will prevent weeds growing through for some time.

Squared stone can be laid in this way, and crazy paving. Measure the distance from the house to the edge of the terrace and then put down a garden line for guidance.

With crazy paving, some stones with straight edges will have to be picked out for the outer edge. Crazy paving stones often vary in thickness and a little sand or ash may have to be taken out from the bed in order to firm them in correctly.

If the gardener wishes to grow some small rock plants or scented thymes between the paving stones, then the stones need to be bedded on to a covering of soil, and soil will have to be packed between the joints. If no plants are to be grown then cement is better between the joins; as already mentioned, it stops weeds from coming through.

There are many other materials which can be used for a good-looking terrace and there are many processes which can be employed. Old, grey, broken paving stones can sometimes be purchased fairly cheaply from the local council. It is quite easy to find perfect straight edges among these. Try to keep away from broken concrete slabs, however, and at all costs avoid pure concrete terraces and too many concrete paths. Concrete in a garden always looks wrong and very unnatural. Asphalt is not very suitable, either. Terraces and paths need to serve some useful purpose, and many are essential, but they should never be too prominent.

Some of the following suggestions may be found pleasing and suitable.

A paved terrace with steps of the same material leading down to a lawn could be enhanced by two brick tubs on either side of the steps filled with petunias or other colourful plants.

A combination of paving and cobblestones will give plenty of scope for interesting pattern work if desired. For a cobbled terrace, stones or pebbles from the beach can be put into mortar which has a concrete base. The concrete can be of about three-inch thickness.

Slabs of stone can be of some uniform shape such as hexagonal, triangular or rectangular, or a combination of many shapes. The joins can be filled with cement of the same colour or a contrasting shade, or the joins may be filled with soil and some rockery plants grown in the crevices. Terraces of this nature are more interesting if you introduce small beds of flowers here and there.

Dwarf conifers or a fish pond where rectangular or square paving stones are used can also break up a terrace effectively. Stone urns, large earthenware pots or wooden tubs filled with geraniums or other free-flowering and colourful plants may also be employed. The terrace may be further beautified by climbing plants on the walls of the house and hanging baskets by the doors. The doors of the house should be painted in some pastel shade of blue, yellow, grey or green, or some colour which tones with the general setting.

GARDEN PATHS

I have already spoken briefly about garden paths in connection with garden planning but a little more detail should be provided here.

In a new garden the sooner the paths have been decided upon and made, the better. The paths will be one of the first garden features in constant use by those walking from one point to another when engaged on planning and cultivating a new garden. If you have taken over an old garden with poor paths, you will soon want to renew them and perhaps add others.

All paths should be in keeping with the particular garden layout. They can be straight, curved, winding, informal or formal, but they should all lead somewhere.

Having decided where the paths are to be located, the next step is to determine their width. Main paths should be at least three to four feet wide and in some large gardens they will need to be wider. The width should be appropriate to the size of the lawn the path will lead through, the size of the garden or the plots the path crosses or surrounds, and the width of barrows, etc., which will be pushed along it.

There is a wide choice of materials for garden paths. A selection may be made from the following: gravel, bricks, stone, concrete (plain or coloured), ash, tiles, cobbles, crazy paving, grass or one of the recent asphaltic compounds.

Gravel is comparatively cheap to lay; it is long-lasting, and after it has weathered it looks pleasing combined with most garden layouts. Once it needed a lot of weeding, but now, with two applications per year of weed killer which can be sprayed on with a watering-can, it does not give much trouble.

Bricks are fairly reasonable in cost and they can be laid to form a pattern. Different colours may be used.

Stone is clean and hard-wearing and harmonizes with other stone work in the garden. It is rather costly, however.

Some people may like concrete paths, which can be plain or

coloured. These are cheap to lay, but difficult to embrace in a natural setting.

Ash paths are the least expensive and plenty of material is always available. They need plenty of rolling.

Tiles are suitable for formal gardens, and they can be obtained in many colours, but are slippery in wet weather.

Cobbles give a nice appearance to the garden path, but they have an uneven surface. They can be combined with other materials, such as stones or bricks, to form many patterns.

Crazy paving has much to commend it, and if rock plants are not grown in the joins, they can be watered with weed killer or the joins can be cemented.

Grass paths are mainly used on rockeries and a wide grass path is the best kind of path to have dividing a double herbaceous order.

A fairly new method of making a path or drive is by using a cold bituminous macadam. This material is supplied in handy half-hundredweight bags. Some makers supply two colours, black and a maroon red. Also with some, coloured granite chippings can be rolled in to break up the black or red. The leading proprietary brands are Colas, Easimac, Durive, Decopath, Rezmatt and Synthacold.

In making a new path of gravel, excavate the soil in the same way as suggested for a terrace. If the path is to run across a lawn, put down a line and edge the lawn on both sides before laying the hard core. A gravel path should come below the lawn for ease of mowing and clipping. After ten inches of soil have been taken out, place the brickbats, rubble, clinkers or stones about six inches deep in the bottom, cover with two inches of fine material. Coal ashes are best, and finally, put on two inches of binding gravel.

When removing the soil, dig out any tap-rooted weeds, such as docks or dandelion. Give a sprinkling of weed killer according to maker's instructions. After raking, level the top layer of gravel and give a good rolling. Two applications of weed killer per year, watered on with a watering-can between rainy spells, will usually stop weeds growing on a gravel path. If the path has been neglected and weeds are growing fairly thickly, hoe them out first, rake the gravel level, and then apply the weed killer.

Always be sure to rinse the watering-can well several times with clean water after the weed killer has been used. All kinds of path should have a slight curve to the edge to allow water to drain away after heavy rain.

For a brick path, the construction work should be carried out in the same way as for a brick terrace. If the path is to go between two areas of lawn, carry out the edging of the lawn as for a gravel path.

If weeds start growing through between the bricks at a later stage, then the weed killer can be applied to the bricks.

If on either side of any kind of path there are flower beds or soil, then you have the problem of providing a suitable edging to the path to keep the soil back. Tiles, bricks set at an angle, low concrete walls or the special pre-cast concrete garden kerb units can be used. Wooden boarding is not to be recommended, as it soon rots and always encourages all sorts of pests. The old-fashioned box hedges also offer shelter to thousands of snails.

The bricks on the path can be laid in several ways to create patterns. Sometimes, instead of laying the bricks on to sand and ashes, a more satisfactory method is to lay them on to cement mortar of one part cement to four parts of fine builders' sand. Fill in the joins with the same mixture.

To summarize: all new paths should have the soil excavated and the hard core drainage material put in. All tap-rooting weeds should be dug out. See that the hard core is absolutely level by using boards, pegs and spirit-level. You can lay tiles, stone slabs, crazy paving or any kind of stone on to a bed of sand or finely sifted soil. You can also bed them on to pats of mortar, one at each corner and one in the centre for large stones. The joints between slabs, etc., may be filled with mortar permanently or left open and filled with sandy soil for the growing of low rock plants.

Cobble paths are very hard-wearing and shingle paths and drives have a pleasing colour. The weeds can usually be very easily raked out of the shingle because of its loose surface.

A very satisfactory way of making a path or drive is to use the cold-setting bituminous macadam. It has a long life and it is oil fluxed to give ease of handling. The first essential in laying one of these paths is to provide a very firm foundation. About three inches of stones, broken brick, clinker or other hard material, well rammed in and rolled, will be required.

If a concrete path or any other kind of path with a firm foundation is already in existence then the tar macadam can be easily laid on the surface. The material comes in convenient half-hundredweight paper containers and two bags will cover eighteen square feet of path. If people like this kind of material for paths and drives they will find it an easy way of making a surface which is smooth, level and durable. Sometimes very persistent weeds such as docks, dandelion or bramble will push their way through the tarmac and crack the surface. This is unlikely to happen, however, if all perennial weeds are dug out thoroughly before laying the hard core, and a non-creosote weed-killer is applied.

A price and quantity calculator can be obtained from one of the

A formal pool, showing how it can look very natural with the right setting and suitable plants

A dry wall, showing how it will harmonize with crazy paving, lawns and surrounding beds and borders

A delightful informal pool and rockery

A colourful shrub border so arranged to give a good view from the house

many firms supplying the macadam. With this it is quite simple to order the correct number of bags required for any given area.

After well rolling and ramming the hard foundation, wheel the half-hundredweight paper bags to convenient positions for opening and spreading. The macadam is raked over the surface with an ordinary garden rake to a thickness of three-quarters of an inch. The roller should be wet to prevent the material sticking to it. Roll over the tarmac a few times to consolidate it until it looks solid, smooth and level. Coloured granite chippings of green, white and buff can be rolled into the tarmac at the same time, if desired. Some people may like a combination of red and black macadam in patterns or stripes. This type of drive is easily constructed with the aid of boards when laying the tarmac, to separate the colours, and the boards are removed after each colour has been put down.

6
Trees and Shrubs

The cultivation of trees and shrubs — wall shrubs and climbers — flowering trees that attract butterflies — easy shrubs and trees for all soils and positions — taking care of hedges

Most flowering trees and shrubs are not hard to grow and maintain. Many people are mystified by what they have heard about part-hardy and lime intolerant species. Pruning also is rather obscure for beginners, but need not present any difficulties. I hope to show that everyone can grow a good number of beautiful shrubs and trees, whatever his soil or garden position. A few simple rules need to be followed. When planting, dig a hole wide enough to spread out all the roots comfortably. Avoid planting too deeply; it is not difficult to observe where the soil mark comes, when the trees arrive from the nursery. Plant just deep enough for the soil to come up to this mark when planting has been completed.

Provide adequate staking. Drive the stakes into position before planting. This precaution means that you will not drive it through one of the main roots.

Put the tree or shrub into the position in the garden which best suits it. And think of probable size after ten years: you must not plant huge forest trees in a small patch of garden.

Plant as soon as possible after arrival from the nursery. If unable to do so, unpack, dig a hole somewhere, put the trees or shrubs in, and cover the roots with soil; follow this by a good watering. In severe frosty weather it would be better to put them in a shed and cover the roots with sacking, straw or bracken, until planting can be proceeded with.

After completion of planting, a good watering is required and this should be carried out every evening unless there is heavy rain or frost. Water the tree or shrub until it is growing away nicely and looks strong and healthy. Never let the roots of a newly planted tree or shrub come into contact with fresh farmyard manure. Some well-

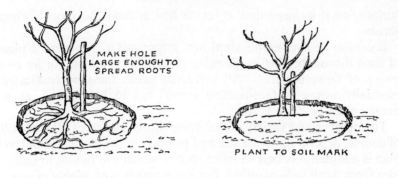

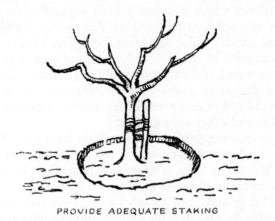

PROVIDE ADEQUATE STAKING

The correct way of planting a tree or shrub

rotted garden compost, thoroughly mixed with the planting soil, is best. But of course your shrubs and trees can be planted in well-dug ground that has been manured the previous autumn.

Tie all trees and some shrubs to the stakes carefully after planting. Affix a good metal label with the name printed clearly; thin, cheap, tin labels are useless, for the name is very soon obliterated.

Information on pruning certain varieties can be obtained from the nurseryman supplying. Generally it is best to under-prune rather than go in for too much severe cutting.

Never let grass grow around the base of a tree until several years have elapsed.

Weeds are best kept down by providing a good mulch of leaf mould. A mulch is a covering of wet straw, manure, grass clippings, soil or other material used for the protection of the roots or to conserve moisture. A mulch of leaf mould will also help to feed the soil in nature's way.

The roots of the rhododendron and azalea families feed at the soil surface, so it is important never to hoe around the base of these shrubs.

It cannot be over-emphasized how important it is to clean a piece of land thoroughly before planting a shrubbery, mixed border or a group of flowering trees. All perennial weeds must be eradicated, especially where surface-rooting shrubs are to be planted, as no hoeing must be done here.

The number and variety of flowering shrubs and trees planted will, of course, depend upon the size and position of the garden. Whatever plan is adopted it is best to select species which will bloom in succession from April to September. For those people with plenty of space, there are varieties which will flower from September onwards.

For those who are keen on floral art, there are two subjects among the trees and shrubs which are ideal for foliage effects. One is the copper beech, with its magnificently coloured copper-purple leaves which make a wonderful background for gay flowers like gladioli or zinnias, and *Elaeagnus pungens aurea variegata,* or 'Wood olive', whose beautiful yellow and green variegated foliage combines so well with daffodils and other spring flowers.

Do not go into the garden and cut from trees and shrubs indiscriminately for flower decoration. A tree or shrub needs to be well established before any twigs or branches are cut from it and then they must be cut carefully to avoid spoiling the shape.

Although the possessor of a chalky garden will not, without going to much trouble, be able to grow azaleas, rhododendrons and heaths, there are plenty of flowering trees and shrubs which can be grown on the chalk land.

Flowering trees and shrubs can be used in a variety of ways, and one or two trees or shrubs in even a very small garden will add interest. Just a few years ago it was fashionable to plant a thick shrubbery down one side, or both sides, of a drive leading to the front gate. These shrubberies were very uninteresting as they mainly consisted of laurels, privet, conifers and other non-flowering subjects.

The modern flowering shrub can be used to make up a pure shrub border with nothing but shrubs growing in it. In this case, several shrubs of the same species but with different colours are massed together. If it is to be a fairly large border several different species of shrubs can be grown to provide colour for a long period. For a flowering shrub border of this character it is advisable to have (as far as possible) a naturalistic background. The shrubs or trees used for this purpose will vary according to soil and position. In a lime-free soil rhododendrons with their dark evergreen foliage are very suitable. In a very windswept area, or at the seaside where shelter is needed, some of the conifers would be better.

When planning a flowering shrub border, always include a few evergreens as they will offer contrast to the deciduous (leaf-losing) shrubs, especially if these are planted in front of the evergreens or nearby. A border can be made consisting of evergreen flowering shrubs only. These will give you interesting foliage and flowers for the whole year.

Flowering shrubs can be used to brighten up a shady corner of the garden; a dozen or so shrubs which will flower in shade can be grown here.

Another way of using flowering shrubs is to provide an island site on a lawn. Here again shrubs need to be chosen which will give an all-year-round display, with low-growing subjects to the front. Be wary, though, of creating mowing problems for yourself.

One of the most pleasing way of using flowering trees and shrubs is to create a mixed border. A mixed border today will consist of flowering trees and shrubs, bulbs, herbaceous border flowers, biennials and even perhaps a few annual flowers. There should be something of interest here from January to December.

With a careful selection and judicious placing of the shrubs and trees, a really wonderful display can be created by interplanting with Russell lupins, Shirley foxgloves, some of the tall campanulas and delphiniums. If the shrubs used include *Cornus kousa chinensis*, *Philadelphus* 'Belle Etoile' and *Philadelphus delavayi*, what is known as the June Gap can be overcome. There is generally a distinct shortage of flowers during June, although in some districts roses are then at their best.

All shrubs need to be informally grouped, and they need to be so placed in the garden that their massed colour can be viewed from the dwelling-house windows.

For all kinds of shrub borders it is wise to make a plan on paper and to mark in the names of the various species. This is especially necessary when planning a new garden where a house has just been erected. Make a list of the trees and shrubs you will require, and order them early from the nursery. It is often a good idea to visit a good nursery which specializes in trees and shrubs and see them in bloom at the various flowering seasons, as well as ascertaining their probable future girth and height.

The site for the planting of flowering shrubs and trees must be ready by October, when the first planting will be made. If individual trees or shrubs are to be placed in various parts of the garden, a prepared planting hole will have to be made for each. Dig out the soil to a depth of about two feet and a diameter of about four feet. Thoroughly break up the sub-soil with a fork but be careful not to bring any to the surface. Mix in plenty of well-rotted garden compost with the sub-soil, but not fresh manure (see page 146). Drive in a stake of adequate length and thickness.

Take the shrub or tree and fit it into the centre of the planting hole and see that the soil ring showing around the main stem does not come below the soil surface. If it does, take the shrub out and put some more soil on the planting bed. When the correct planting depth has been found, spread out the roots carefully and work in some fine top soil around them. Make firm with the hands, fill in the remainder of the top soil, and tread in firmly. Give a good soaking.

Many shrubs, of course, would not need to be staked; but all standard trees must be securely tied and staked.

There are many ways of tying trees. The stake should be parallel to the main trunk of the tree at a distance of two or three inches, and it should not reach up into the branches. One good method of making a tie is to obtain a piece of old rubber hosepipe about six inches long and thread a twelve-inch length of galvanized iron wire through the pipe. Place the rubber round the tree stem, cross the ends over, and twist the wire ends round the stake. This kind of tie can easily be adjusted at any time. A piece of old cycle tyre could be used in the same way. Sometimes several thicknesses of sacking are placed round the trunk and the tree is secured to the stake by the means of tarred string. Special rubber tying gadgets can be purchased. Never tie string or put wire round the bare stem of a tree without some protective material. As the tree grows and the trunk thickens, the tie must be adjusted every so often to allow for this growth.

When one is planting a whole border of shrubs or a shrubbery, the site should be dug two spades' depth and plenty of well-decayed garden compost should be dug into the bottom of each trench.

Trees and shrubs planted in spring often suffer from dry conditions. Give plenty of water during this period and follow immediately with a mulch of damp, strawy, well-decayed manure, well-rotted leaf mould or bracken. Lawn mowings are not very satisfactory for mulching as they ferment and heat up the ground, which is detrimental to surface-rooting subjects.

Firm planting is essential in all cases, but no planting should be carried out when the ground is waterlogged or even very wet. Planting distances for shrubs generally are three shrubs to five square yards. Low-growing shrubs are planted fairly close together in groups with a wider space between the groups.

General rules for pruning are as follows. Basically, pruning ensures that bushes are kept in good shape and do not reach unmanageable proportions. Most deciduous flowering shrubs fall into three groups:

First, winter-flowering shrubs. Remove only very old wood during the spring and any dead wood.

Second, shrubs flowering from March to July on growth of the previous year. Immediately after flowering, remove completely worn-out stems, cut back old flowering shoots to fresh young growths on the main branches. Thin crowded shoots, remove weak, thin twigs and any twisted or shapeless ones. Well-known trees and shrubs needing this treatment are *Deutzia, Diervilla, Philadelphus, Ribes*, early flowering *Spiraea* and Lilac.

Third, shrubs flowering from July onwards on growths of the current year. Cut back hard in February and March, to within two inches of the old wood, the young shoots which bore flowers the previous summer and autumn. Shrubs needing this method of pruning are *Buddleia davidii*, varieties (also shorten by one-third the longest shoots during autumn), *Caryopteris, Ceanothus* (but not evergreen varieties), *Hibiscus, Hypericum* (except *calycinum*) and *Tamarix pentandra*.

Another section of shrubs which cannot be included in the above are *Ceratostigma* and *Hypericum calycinum*; these should be cut to ground level each year in early spring.

Shrubs which are pruned immediately after flowering are the strong-growing varieties of broom, which should be lightly pruned to prevent them becoming straggly, and lavender bushes which can be trimmed with shears.

The longest branches of newly transplanted evergreens should be cut back to two-thirds of their lengths. Established specimens need very little pruning except for the removal of twisted, weak or dead shoots in early spring. Pruning should be deferred until after spring-flowering varieties have flowered. Evergreens which are bare at the base or have outgrown their position should be cut back hard in April. New shoots will soon cover the cut stumps. Arbutus, box, lavender, *Phillyrea, Olearia haastii* and rhododendrons respond well to this treatment.

Apart from the pruning mentioned, very little other pruning is necessary. Trees and shrubs sometimes have to be very lightly pruned if they have grown too large for the position allotted to them. Very often such trees as flowering cherries and flowering almonds, which will ultimately grow to a height of thirty feet if unchecked, have to have the tops and other branches shortened. This should be done soon after flowering. To stop the sap running out, and to discourage disease entering the wounds, the ends of the cut branches should be painted with a preparation called 'Arbrex'; or use white lead paint.

Many flowering shrubs can be propagated by cuttings taken during August and September and by layering during October. For cuttings the cold frame will come into use. The cold frames are best placed in a position where they are sheltered from drying winds and out of direct sunshine. Dig over the ground where the frames are to be installed, taking care to remove all perennial weeds. Mix a compost using equal parts of well-decayed garden compost, finely sifted medium loam and silver sand. Add some sifted garden peat. Fill the bottom of the frame with about six inches of this rooting compost and make firm. Water well and allow to settle for a few days before inserting the cuttings.

When taking the cuttings, use short pieces of non-flowering shoots of new growth. The length of cutting will depend on the type of shrub selected. Pull the twig selected from the parent plant to secure a heel,

Taking a shrub cutting, showing the heel

and trim the end neatly with scissors. Strip off the lower leaves and put the cuttings into the soil by making a planting hole with a pencil. Do not plant too deeply, and firm well around each cutting. Space them about three inches apart. Give the cuttings a good watering with the fine rose on, and close the lid of the frame. Examine the cuttings every few days, and if necessary give them another watering. It is important to see that they do not dry out. They should root in three or four weeks. When signs of rooting are apparent by growth of the tips, let air into the frame and gradually continue to give more air, finally removing the light altogether except in severe storms or frost.

Layering of shrubs can take place from October onwards. Do this work during mild spells only, when it is warm enough for rooting to take place. Choose a low outward-growing branch that will easily touch the ground. Make a hole with a trowel about six inches deep and provide a good rooting medium, consisting of silver sand and sifted moist peat. Fill the hole with this, bend the branch into it, put some of the medium on top, and peg the branch down with a piece of bent wire, or put a large heavy stone on to the top of it. About six inches of stem should be emerging from the hole. Choose young shoots for this method of propagation. When the branch has rooted, sever it from the parent plant. Transplant the rooted branch where wanted during suitable growing periods, but not during the middle of winter.

When one consults a catalogue of flowering trees and shrubs and notes the hundreds of varieties, it is often difficult to decide which ones to grow, especially if space is limited. Here is a short list of easily grown trees and shrubs which will suit most people and will provide colour for most of the year.

First the shrubs. For winter flowers, jasmine, both yellow and white forms should be grown. *Daphne mezereum* is another good winter-flowering shrub. *Forsythia* for early spring flowers. *Camellia* for flowering in early spring and sometimes in the winter. *Ceanothus*, a beautiful blue-flowered shrub, for growing in the sheltered south only. One of the Chaenomeles, of which there are many varieties; these are spring-flowering. *Clematis* is a beautiful climber. *Cornus kousa,* flowering in June. Brooms of various varieties and colours, which are May and June flowering. *Escallonia,* an evergreen, flowering from June to August. *Fuchsia,* hardy outdoor varieties. *Hibiscus,* or 'Tree Hollyhock', flowering during August and September. Hydrangeas, which are flowering throughout the summer. Tree lupins, flowering in June. *Philadelphus* or Mock Orange, June- and July-flowering. *Ribes,* the flowering currant, with early spring flowers. *Spartium* or 'Spanish Broom', flowering July to November. Lilacs, especially the new varieties. *Wistaria,* the beautiful climber. Some of the *Berberis* for spring flowering and autumn berries. *Buddleia* which attracts the butterflies, and *Pyracantha,* the shrub with the beautiful winter berries.

More will be said about these shrubs later, but for someone with limited space, these would be the ones to choose from.

When considering the best trees to grow, it depends very much again on the space available. It is unwise (see page 181) to plant a large-growing tree in a town garden, however beautiful it may look when young.

Here is a short list of recommended trees to choose from. One of the *Crataegus* or Hawthorn would be a valuable tree, as it will thrive in almost any soil. Many give good autumn colour and also retain decorative berries. One called *C. coccinea plena* has double scarlet blossoms. *Laburnum* is a very showy tree with yellow blossoms but it should not be planted near most of the hawthorns, as the colours may not blend. Magnolias are among the most beautiful flowering trees, but they take a few years to become established and produce enough blossom. *Malus*, the flowering crab apples, are very suitable small garden trees. The flowering almond, with its lovely pink blossom, is a very welcome sight in early spring. Flowering cherries are very ornamental and free flowering.

CLIMBING PLANTS AND WALL SHRUBS

Where climbers are to be planted in a border against a wall or fence, ordinary preparation of the soil, with the digging in of plenty of well-decayed garden compost, will be sufficient.

Where the climber is to climb the wall of a dwelling-house, and the planting position is bounded by a gravelled or paved terrace, a space of about two feet wide and two and a half feet deep should be prepared. The planting position should also be about a foot and a half away from the base of the wall, otherwise the plant will not receive enough moisture. Thoroughly fork over the sub-soil and put in a good thickness of well-rotted garden compost. Fill in the remainder of the planting hole with good top soil of medium loam, if this kind of soil is available.

Whenever climbing plants are mentioned, the two that first spring to mind are *Wistaria* and *Clematis*.

Wistaria (or *Wisteria*) is one of the most admired of all climbing shrubs. They all climb by twining and will quickly cover walls, sheds or pergolas. Wistarias can be so planted that they ramble through laburnum trees, giving two colours which harmonize so well. They look attractive if well trained to grow on a wall of a large house, but as they are very strong growers they are not very suitable for a small house. They show up better when trained to a wall, if the wall is cream in colour, or climbing a stone wall. Perhaps they are better seen where the long racemes of flower are displaying themselves along a pergola. In all cases they need a large space to cover and plenty of attention with training and tying. I have seen a beautiful combination of wistaria and *Clematis montana* growing on a south-west wall. Both are in flower during May, bearing hundreds of blooms, and combine to provide a most glorious spectacle. Wistarias must be growing where they can get plenty of sun, and good ordinary garden soil will suit them. They need plenty of moisture at the roots. For pruning, the current year's lateral growths should be shortened back to about six inches at the end of July to early August. If plants are not pruned, they develop into a thick tangle of stems which will not flower. After transplanting, wistarias sometimes remain dormant for a long period. Spraying overhead with water on warm days encourages the buds to begin growing.

Two varieties are *sinensis*, with purplish-lilac flowers and trusses of eight to ten inches in length and sweetly scented. This variety flowers in May and June. *W. venusta* produces broad, white trusses of flowers in May and June.

Clematis, like wistaria, is in the forefront of climbing shrubs. It will thrive in any normal soil which has been well prepared by digging in plenty of well-decayed garden compost as recommended for the wistarias. The soil must be well drained and as the clematis grows very well on chalky soil, some garden lime mixed in with the sub-soil would be beneficial. Two ounces of bone-meal per plant should be added, well mixed with the soil.

Clematis plants are usually pot grown at the nurseries and can be transplanted at any time between late September and May, during suitable weather. Some bonemeal and a mulch of well-rotted garden compost should be given every spring after rain. North and west aspects are preferable, and it must have its roots shaded by some low-growing shrubs or other plants.

The clematis supports itself by twining its leaf stalks around any support which is available. It can be grown in a variety of ways. Some poles can be erected towards the back of the herbaceous border and surrounded with wire netting, or some pea sticks can be pushed into the soil and the plants allowed to ramble over them. They can be grown on wooden trellis work anywhere in the garden, or up walls provided with pig-netting. They grow well when allowed to twine into other climbers. A good combination for clambering over a porch or

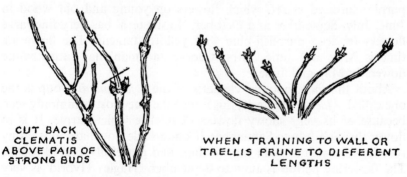

CUT BACK
CLEMATIS
ABOVE PAIR OF
STRONG BUDS

WHEN TRAINING TO WALL OR
TRELLIS PRUNE TO DIFFERENT
LENGTHS

The correct way to prune a Clematis

other archway would be one of the honeysuckles and a June-flowering variety of clematis with blue or purple blossoms.

Pruning is important for the clematis. Newly-planted specimens of the large-flowered group should be pruned in the first spring to a healthy bud, within six to nine inches of the ground. Tie the growth to a support leading to whatever is to be covered.

Clematis are divided into five groups: *florida, ×jackmanii, lanuginosa, patens* and *viticella*. Then there are several *Clematis* species. A few of the best of each group will be mentioned here, but many more varieties are listed in the catalogues of good shrub nurserymen, and many can be seen in flower in numerous nurseries throughout the country. One could plant different varieties so as to have one in flower in almost every month of the year.

The *florida* and *patens* groups flower on short growths from the previous season's wood. Spread out the main branches and train them so that each one has plenty of growing space. Remove the rest of the straggling and overcrowded thin shoots in February. After flowering, cut the flowering shoot back to just above a pair of strong buds.

For the *×jackmanii* and *viticella* groups, hard pruning is necessary. Prune back in February almost all the growth made the previous season, making the cuts just above a joint. The *lanuginosa* group can be pruned in the same way.

Two good varieties of the *florida* group are 'Duchess of Edinburgh', which is rosette-shaped with fragrant double white flowers, and 'Belle of Woking', rosette-shaped with double pale mauve flowers. Both flower during May and June.

Of the *patens* group the well-known 'Nelly Moser' is one of the best. It is striped blush white with a carmine red bar and flowers in May, June and September. 'Bee's Jubilee' is an improved variety of 'Nelly Moser'. It is deep mauve suffused pink with a red bar down each sepal, and it flowers during May and June. 'The President' is purple, suffused claret, which flowers on young and old wood in June, July, September and October. 'Lasurstern' has very fine large flowers of deep purplish-blue with yellow stamens. The flowering time is May and June. 'Mrs. George Jackman' has satiny white flowers in May and June.

About the most popular clematis of the *×jackmanii* group is the one called *×jackmanii* itself; this is also the one most commonly seen because of its very showy flowers of intense violet-purple. It is in flower through July to September. 'Comtesse de Bouchard' has satiny rose flowers with a slight mauve tinge and gracefully curved sepals. The flowering period is June to September. 'Hagley Hybrid' is very free-flowering and a vigorous grower with deep pink flowers which has pointed petals. It flowers from June to September. 'Madame E. André' is a rich crimson-claret flowering in July and August. *Jackmanii superba* is an improvement on ×*jackmanii,* of dark violet-purple with a fuller flower, and blooming in July and August.

'Ernest Markham' has beautiful large glowing petunia red flowers from August to October and it belongs to the *viticella* group, which also has 'Ville de Lyon', a bright carmine-red of medium-sized flowers showing from July to October. 'Lady Betty Balfour' has violet-blue flowers with yellow stamens, blooming in September and October.

In the *lanuginosa* group is 'Mrs. Cholmondeley', a delightful shade of light lavender, very free-flowering in May and June. There is also 'Madame Le Coultre' with large pure white flowers and yellow stamens from June to August; and 'Crimson King' which is bright rosy-red with a paler shading down the centre of each sepal, flowering during July and August. 'Henryii' is a beautifully formed large creamy-white which flowers during July and August. 'Lord Neville' is a rich deep blue with deeper markings, and it flowers from June to August.

Of the many small-flowered species and varieties of *Clematis, montana* is the best known. It is very vigorous, often reaching a height of forty feet when well grown. It is covered with hundreds of lovely almond-scented white flowers, shaped like those of the wood anemone. It flowers during May. *C. montana rubens* is a rosy-pink variety with purplish leaves in spring and early summer. Newly-planted specimens of these two varieties should be pruned by cutting back shoots to about a third after flowering. On established plants, cut out old flowering stems in June and train shoots intended to form the framework.

Clematis macropetala or the Downy Clematis, is a beautiful form. The semi-double, nodding flowers are deep lavender-blue, produced in May and June, and it will sometimes flower again in the autumn. It should be pruned in February, cutting out weak shoots and shortening others.

There are bush and evergreen forms of clematis species. The bush forms can be used to good effect in the herbaceous border or in the shrub or mixed bed. They have erect growths and produce fragrant hyacinth-like tubular flowers in clusters from August to October. They are pruned back to the previous year's wood every spring. Two bush forms which are obtainable are 'C. Cote d'Azur' and *C. heracleifolia.*

A beautiful climber which everyone admires for its wonderful scent, is the *Lonicera* or honeysuckle. Honeysuckles like a good loamy soil and plenty of moisture, and are best grown so that they can ramble over a porch, archway, pergola or trellis work. This climber is ideal for covering a summerhouse or garden shed. The roots like to be shaded and not much pruning is required, merely the cutting away of old wood, thinning out a little and trimming back, if the plant has outgrown its allotted space. Most varieties begin to flower in June. Evergreen honeysuckles are pruned in spring and the late-flowering types in autumn. They are fairly easily propagated by cuttings.

A very popular and easily grown climber or wall shrub is the jasmine. There are both winter- and summer-flowering varieties. Jasmines are easily propagated by layering. *Jasminum nudiflorum* is the winter-flowering sort, bearing bright yellow flowers from late autumn until April. Avoid planting this fragrant shrub on the eastern side, as the sun will damage the frosted blooms. After flowering, shorten strong shoots which have flowered, and prune back others close to the old wood. Tie in the main shoots.

Jasminum officinale grandiflorum is a summer-flowering kind with pink shaded buds and bearing sweetly scented white flowers from June to August. *J. beesianum* has deep red small flowers which are borne during the summer. Jasmines are best trained up a sunny wall.

Passiflora caerulea, or blue passion flower, is perfectly hardy except in extreme cold positions in the north of England. It likes a sunny position. This most unusual flower is three to four inches wide with white petals and a distinctive ring of slender purplish-blue growths, which are about two inches high. It is a fragrant shrub, flowering from June to September. Orange egg-shaped fruit are sometimes borne. Propagating is by cuttings.

There are a few other climbing shrubs, but the best and easiest to grow have been described here. Others may be selected from specialists' catalogues, but care should be taken to ascertain if the ones chosen are hardy and if they will suit the particular soil and position in which it is intended to grow them.

There are many shrubs which, although not classed as climbers, grow very much better when trained against or planted in the shelter of a wall. Some of the best for all purposes will be taken account of in the following paragraphs.

One of the Buddleias, *Buddleia colvillei*, which is a Himalayan species, grows well as a wall shrub. It has bell-shaped flowers in pendulous clusters of a rich rose colour, with white centres. Thin and train after flowering.

The *Ceanothus* or Californian Lilac, of which there are several varieties, is one of the most beautiful flowering shrubs which we have growing in this country. There are deciduous and evergreen varieties, and the evergreen varieties all need the protection of a warm wall.

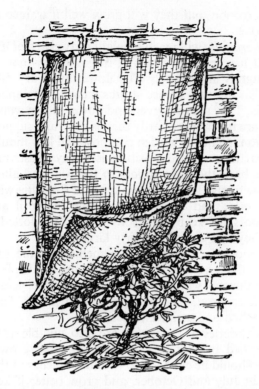

A method of protecting wall shrubs from frost with sacking and straw

They will grow in any well-drained soil, and are lime tolerant. Most of the evergreen varieties flower during May and June and the colour of the flowers is a most wonderful steely, powdery blue. The flowers are borne most profusely and almost hide the foliage. Little pruning is necessary, but if needed it should be done when the flowering season is over.

Cytisus battandieri, one of the brooms, comes from Morocco. The leaves are covered with silky down and are a contrast for the pineapple-scented, golden-yellow flowers in July. A very handsome plant for a sunny wall. Train and prune after flowering.

An evergreen magnolia, called *grandiflora* 'Exmouth', has glossy, green leaves and large fragrant, creamy-white flowers about eight inches across, and appearing from July to September. Prune fairly hard in late summer. This is an excellent wall shrub.

Viburnum macrocephalum has huge hydrangea-like white flower heads in May. It is semi-evergreen and needs a good soil with plenty of well-decayed garden compost incorporated.

The flowering shrubs of the following section do not necessarily need wall protection, but they will grow well if trained to a wall or sheltered by one.

Buddleia alternifolia will reach a height of twelve feet if trained to a warm wall. It has graceful sprays of fragrant rosy-mauve flowers in June. Prune lightly immediately after flowering. A dry site is suitable.

The camellias are very choice shrubs indeed, but cannot be grown in chalky soils. They are evergreen and flower in late winter and early spring. They are much more hardy than is generally supposed. During soil preparation, plenty of garden compost and leaf-mould should be dug in. A partially shaded position is always best, but avoid an east wall. Tie back the main shoots to the wall and allow the front shoots to grow freely. There are two types of Camellia which concern us here, *japonica* and ×*williamsii*. Prune in April any weak or straggling shoots and keep the shrubs within the allotted space, as in a few years they will grow into fairly large shrubs.

There are too many varieties of camellias for me to be able to mention all of them here. There are single and double forms and the colours range through white, soft pink, salmon, rose, geranium, blood red, light red, crimson, pale blush pink and peach. There are also marbled, splashed and striped varieties.

Deciduous varieties of *Ceanothus* are also suitable as wall shrubs. These are pruned in March. Cut away all weak growths and the strong shoots should be cut back to within six inches of the old wood. They flower in July and October, and grow better if kept to a size of about six feet by six feet.

Chaenomeles, or Flowering quinces, are often known as *Japonica* (see page 175). They are completely hardy, will grow in any soil or site, are quick growers and will effectively clothe a north or east wall. They bear golden-yellow, edible quinces in the autumn. The long shoots produced in summer should be pruned back in early autumn. There are many varieties, but 'Knaphill Scarlet' and *simonii* are the best ones for low walls. Other colours are white, salmon, crimson, scarlet and pink. Suckers should be dug out and propagation may be from cuttings, layering or seed sowing.

Those who would like a delightful fragrant winter-flowering shrub should choose the *Chimonanthus* or 'Winter Sweet'. This shrub takes a few years to reach flowering size. The flowers are small and there are ivory, yellow and primrose varieties. Cut sprays of blossom last well in water and will fill the house with their very beautiful perfume. They need a sunny wall and a good well-drained soil. The foliage is also scented in summer. This shrub is easily propagated from seed.

There are many varieties of *Escallonia*, with flowers of pink, red and white. They grow well by the sea. The ones most suitable for wall growing are *Escallonia edinensis* and *Escallonia* 'Slieve Donard'.

The graceful
Buddleia alternifolia

Clematis montana,
showing its very floriferous
habit

Choisya ternata, the Mexican Orange, growing against a sheltered wall

Betula pendula, a very attractive form of Silver Birch

The first has arching sprays of bright rosy-pink flowers and the second large apple-blossom pink blooms, and the foliage is very glossy. All escallonias do well in warm positions and they will grow on chalk land. They can be increased by cuttings.

Forsythia suspensa is at its best when it is grown against a wall. It has deep primrose pendulous flowers along the stems. It is suitable for a north wall. The branches of this shrub will root freely if allowed to touch the ground. It does not object to a chalky soil. All forsythias strike very easily from cuttings put into the open ground.

Garrya elliptica is a lovely evergreen wall shrub, bearing pale green catkins in autumn. In February, these catkins elongate into beautiful graceful tassels which are most useful for floral arrangements. It is a vigorous grower suitable for a dry, sunny position. The male plant gives the tassels, and usually nurserymen supply this male plant only. It can be trimmed in May.

If I could choose only one wall shrub, I would decide on the *Pyracantha* or Firethorn. It would not be everyone's choice, but I have several reasons for liking it. It is easy to grow in any good garden soil, even on chalk land. It has a neat habit of growth. It is very hardy. It is covered with white flowers in summer, followed by a most magnificent display of brilliant berries, which in most varieties are often retained in their full beauty until the spring. If the shrub has not kept possession of its berries, then some of them may have provided food for the beautiful crested waxwing, one of our charming and infrequent winter visiting birds from Scandinavia and Russia. This is another good reason for growing it. Finally it is a wonderful subject for winter floral arrangements. There are several varieties of *Pyracantha*. *P. atalantioides* has large, brilliant crimson fruits, *P. coccinea lalandii* produces large bright orange-red berries, *P. rogersiana* displays bright red berries, while *P. rogersiana* 'Flava' has glowing yellow berries. Pyracanthas can be propagated from seed sowing. They also make good specimen shrubs on lawns and elsewhere.

Viburnum burkwoodii 'Park Farm Hybrid' is a superb wall plant. It has delightfully fragrant white flowers opening from pink buds. This shrub likes a good well-drained soil but it does not object to chalk.

The necessity for watering and mulching in the growing of wall shrubs cannot be over-emphasized. The soil is always very dry beneath a wall.

FLOWERING TREES AND SHRUBS WHICH ATTRACT BUTTERFLIES

A garden would not be complete with just the growing plants and lawns within it. We must have the birds, bees and butterflies. The birds keep down pests and the bees and butterflies help in the important work of fertilization. This is not the only reason why we need their presence, for with them nature adds her own adornments not at our command—a source of pleasure to all who love beautiful creations.

The vision of a butterfly is good but short in range, so its sense of smell is very highly developed in order that it may detect its food. The butterfly's only food consists of nectar from the flowers; and as it has only a short life, up to a few weeks (except in the case of those which hibernate for the winter), it will not waste time visiting a garden which has no flowers. If it is flying along below a hedge, it will smell the flowers beyond and will soon alight upon the blooms and spread its wings, to the delight of the beholder.

Small Tortoiseshells and Peacocks are the most common of the garden visitors but others, including the Red Admiral, Painted Lady, Comma, Orange Tip, Green-veined White, Brimstone, Small Copper, Speckled Wood, Wall, Meadow Brown, Clouded Yellow, Pale Clouded Yellow, Common Blue and Holly Blue have all been seen in my garden from time to time.

Those who enjoy watching butterflies will need to grow some flowering trees or shrubs or other flowers which are in bloom when certain kinds of butterflies are on the wing. The most sweetly scented flowering trees and shrubs seem to attract the butterflies more than other kinds. These may well offer them a larger quantity of nectar, or the strong scent may be its own inducement: some early-flowering fruit trees attract early butterflies and also among these are the flowering almond, peach, plum and cherries.

The Brimstone is the first to appear on the wing in early spring, followed by the Red Admiral, Peacock and Small Tortoiseshell. This is because they are hibernating insects and the first warm day awakens them; this is usually some time in March. If we are to see these welcome harbingers of spring in our garden, we must have some early flowering subjects. Although some bulbs and hardy outdoor primulas are in flower during March and through April and May, when many of the early butterflies are prevalent, these are more likely to alight on a flowering tree or shrub, which are more in their line of flight.

One shrub which has sweetly-scented flowers in early spring is the *Corylopsis*. This is a beautiful shrub and there are two varieties. *Corylopsis spicata* has flexible branches lined with drooping spikes of scented primrose-coloured flowers in March. It grows to a height of six feet. *Corylopsis willmottiae* bears greenish-yellow blossoms with a strong cowslip scent, and is of erect growth. It will grow from six to eight feet high. *Corylopsis* needs a sheltered border with plenty of decayed garden compost and leaf mould or peat worked into the soil prior to planting. It will grow in full sun or in partial shade.

Daphne is popular also for its fragrant flowers in early spring. This shrub needs a cool, moist, yet well-drained root run. Partial shade is preferred although it will tolerate full sun. *Daphne mezereum* is an erect branching shrub with purplish-red sweetly-scented flowers in February and March followed by scarlet berries in May. It grows to four feet. An evergreen variety, *D. odora variegata*, has lance-shaped leaves with apple-green and yellow variegations. Exquisitely scented soft reddish-purple flowers are borne during February and March. It prefers shelter from north and east winds. Height five feet. *Daphne* 'Somerset' has sweetly-scented flowers of soft mauve-pink during May. It is very free flowering and forms a dense bush spreading to a width of about four feet, and will be about four feet high.

Osmanthus is an evergreen which is not particular about soil. It has very fragrant white flowers. *Osmanthus delavayi* has masses of tubular flowers during April. This variety needs wall protection in the colder areas.

Osmarea burkwoodii is an evergreen of compact habit, with pointed and toothed leaves of a lustrous green, and small tubular fragrant white flowers during April and May.

The lilacs or syringas begin flowering in spring and attract the early butterflies. By planting early, mid-season and late varieties, the flowering season can be extended. If some of the new Canadian hybrids are planted as well, the season is further prolonged, as these come into flower after the ordinary lilac, or *Syringa vulgaris*, has finished flowering.

With the Canadian hybrid syringas in flower, we are now advancing well into June, with the appearance of such butterflies as the Wall, Holly Blue, Common Blue, and Clouded Yellows, which have migrated from the Continent. These butterflies will be with us, together with other broods of the earlier butterflies, until the autumn.

The shrub to which butterflies are attracted more than any other is the *Buddleia* with its sweetly scented panicles of flowers. It is often known as the 'butterfly bush', and is a very vigorous-growing shrub; it likes the full sun. It will thrive on most soils, including chalk lands. There are many varieties. The *davidii* group is outstanding because it contains the varieties which have immense panicles of flowers during July and August. These are pruned by cutting back the previous season's shoots to within about four inches of the old wood in February. They grow to about eight feet. 'Black Knight' is a fairly recent introduction, with very dark purple flowers. 'Empire Blue' is rich violet-blue with an orange eye. 'Fascination' is a richly coloured lilac-pink. 'Ile de France' has long heads of deepest violet. 'Royal Red' is not a red, but of a reddish-purple, a rather exceptional colour. Some of the white varieties ought to be grown, as they are really beautiful, and one of the best white-flowered shrubs that can possibly be grown. Both 'Peace' and 'White Cloud' have very graceful white heads, and *fallowiana alba* has pure white flowers with an orange eye; it is a most attractive shrub, but requires some slight shelter to be provided by other shrubs. *Buddleia globosa* is a very robust tree of loose-growing habit, with flowers on short stalks. These are of a much different shape to the previously mentioned varieties, being in the form of a tangerine orange and of the same colour. 'Golden Globe', of the same type, has globular golden flowers in June and July.

There are very many varieties of *Philadelphus,* or Mock Orange; all have a most beautiful scent, and are worth a place in any garden. They flower during June and July and will grow in almost any soil. Thin out the shoots immediately after flowering and cut out old wood which has borne flowers. Leave the young lateral growths which will bear flowers the following year. These grow well in full sun or partial shade; flowers are white, cream or yellowish-white.

Veronica or *Hebe* are small or medium evergreen shrubs which succeed in most soils in the warmer counties and especially near the coast. As noticeably scented shrubs with a long flowering period, often from July to October, they attract the summer and autumn butterflies. There are many varieties, and the colour range is bright pink, white, violet, pale mauve, lavender, lilac, and rich purple. Any hard pruning that is needed to keep the shrubs from outgrowing their allotted space should be done in April.

Some members of the *Genista* family, which are related to the brooms, give us later-flowering shrubs to attract the second brood of late summer butterflies. These lovely insects are the progeny of the early spring Brimstones, Peacocks, Tortoiseshells and Red Admirals.

Genista aetnensis, the Mount Etna Broom, is a large shrub with pendulous rush-like growth bedecked with golden-yellow flowers in July. It is of very graceful habit. The best way to grow it is to prune it very early in life to a single stem and make it form a weeping standard. Cultivated in this manner it makes a very beautiful specimen tree. It can be propagated from seed but needs to be transplanted when very small. All members of the Broom family are difficult to transplant if allowed to get too large.

Genista virgata, the Madeira Broom, has masses of fragrant flowers in June and July. *Genista cinerea* has long slender branches with small grey-green leaves and countless sweetly-scented flowers in July. The genistas prefer light to medium soil and full sun.

If some varieties of the *Hibiscus* or Tree Hollyhock are included in our collection of flowering shrubs, then we have flowers to attract the butterflies right through from August until October. A good well-drained soil, enriched with decayed garden compost, and a sunny warm corner are the requirements of this valuable shrub. It can be grown on chalk, and very little pruning is needed.

Hibiscus 'Bluebird', with flowers measuring three inches across, is a vigorous new variety. *H. coeleste* has lovely deep blue blossoms, and 'Hamabo', pale blush with a crimson blotch, is one of the most beautiful. 'Woodbridge' is a well-known large crimson variety with five deeper red blotches in the centre. *H. monstrosus* 'Dorothy Crane' is an improvement on 'Hamabo', opening better to display the crimson centres. 'W. R. Smith', with large white flowers and crinkled petals, is of compact habit.

One other fragrant shrub which completes our list for butterfly attraction is the *Clerodendron trichotomum,* or Glory Tree. It is an outstanding late-flowering shrub, with white star-like flowers in August, September and October, followed by china-blue berries surmounted by crimson calyces, on an outer circle of floral leaves. It needs a well-drained soil.

EASY SHRUBS AND TREES FOR ALL SOILS AND POSITIONS

Flowering trees and shrubs not already mentioned occupy the next few paragraphs. They can all be grown by amateur gardeners without difficulty, and all of them are reasonably hardy.

The evergreen, *Arbutus unedo,* commonly known as the Strawberry Tree, is a shrub well worth growing. The fruits are attractive and so is the unusual bark. The flowers are pendent, of a cream, white or pinkish colour, and pitcher-shaped, appearing in October and November, often together with the previous year's fruit in various stages of ripening, some yellow and some red. Seedlings can be raised from the fruit.

Berberis varieties offer a large and important group of easily grown evergreen and deciduous shrubs. The deciduous ones have colourful berries and foliage in autumn. The evergreen sorts will grow in shade, and all varieties will tolerate a chalky soil. All make spiny bushes. The flowers are in various shades of yellow, orange, apricot, straw and scarlet. Propagation may be from seed sowing or cuttings. The deciduous varieties will grow well in full sun or partial shade.

Berberis rubrostilla has beautiful translucent berries in autumn which are white varying to carmine, carried on arching sprays. The yellow flowers are produced in May and June. *B. thunbergii* has pale straw-coloured flowers in spring and brilliant red foliage and berries in autumn. *B. darwinii* is an evergreen and outstanding for its brilliant rich orange-yellow flowers. There are bluish-purple, round berries in autumn; this shrub can be planted near the sea coast. *B. linearifolia* 'Orange King' is a very beautiful evergreen. Deep orange flowers darkening to red appear in April, followed by purple berries with a greyish bloom.

Berberis verruculosa is one of the best evergreen shrubs, having dense glossy green foliage and pendent golden flowers in May. Handsome black fruits, covered with a rich purple bloom, come in late summer. There are many other varieties of *Berberis* in cultivation. Some are very suitable for hedging, and will be mentioned later on in this connection.

There are a very large number of species of *Cornus,* or Dogwood, but I shall only mention four varieties for a particular purpose here. The chief value of these lies in the cheerfully-coloured stems produced in winter and early spring. These stems look very beautiful in association with berries and dried flowers of other plants for winter floral decoration.

Cornus alba is wide spreading, producing a thicket of beautiful crimson-red stems in winter. *Cornus sibirica elegantissima* has prettily marked foliage and bright red winter stems. 'Westonbirt' variety has sealing-wax-red bark, which is brighter than that of *alba*, but the two harmonize well together. Steel-blue berries follow the flowers. *Cornus stolonifera flaviramea*, with its striking butter-yellow bark, provides a pleasing contrast to the red varieties.

Cytisus (Brooms as they are known to most people) offers lovely shrubs of very many colours, flowering during May and June. The strong-growing varieties should be lightly pruned immediately after flowering. *C. andreanus* is rich yellow and chocolate. *C. burkwoodii* is very free-flowering, with masses of maroon and red blossoms. 'Cornish Cream' has ivory-cream standards and pale yellow wings. 'Goldfinch' has crimson and yellow standards, pink wings, with a lemon base outside and creamy-yellow within.

The *Cytisus* species comprise low-, medium- and tall-growing sorts. *C. kewensis* has low-spreading branches covered with sulphur-yellow flowers. *C. purgans* is chalk-tolerant and requires no pruning, with flowers of a rich golden-yellow. *C. purpureus incarnatus* produces flowers of soft mauve-pink in June and July and is of spreading habit.

The medium- and tall-growing species include *albus* or the white Portugal Broom, which is very free-flowering; *nigricans* is a later flowering variety coming into bloom during July and August. It has long racemes of sweetly scented bright yellow blossoms. Prune hard in spring to encourage young flower-bearing shoots. The Brooms succeed best in sandy loam and do not need a rich soil. A place in full sun is best.

Forsythia is a shrub worth having in any garden, and it is nice if it can be planted near a road, where the passers-by can see it. I know of no more cheering sight, for someone on his way to work in early spring, than a glimpse of massed *Forsythia* blossom. It thrives in ordinary soil, in full sun or in partial shade. If small branches are cut from a well-established shrub, after Christmas, and placed in water, they will bloom perfectly well indoors. After flowering, the shoots should be shortened to encourage new wood.

Two new varieties, 'Beatrix Farrand' and 'Spring Glory', are improvements on the older varieties. 'Beatrix Farrand' is an American introduction which makes a symmetrical bush, smothered with deep golden-yellow flowers with striking orange markings in the throat. Each flower may be about an inch across. 'Spring Glory' is a very lovely variety, with masses of large bright yellow flowers which completely hide the branches.

Hardy outdoor fuchsias need plenty of well-rotted garden compost underneath them in order to retain plenty of moisture. They also demand a well-drained soil and are lime tolerant. Hard pruning is required in spring. They can easily be propagated from cuttings. *F. gracilis* has scarlet sepals and a purple corolla and is five feet in height. *F. magellanica alba* becomes a twiggy bush with pale pink flowers. 'Madame Cornelissen', with large flowers of scarlet and white, grows to six feet. 'Tom Thumb' is only two feet in height, with flowers of clear violet and carmine.

The hydrangea is one of the most important flowering shrubs for any garden. One or two of them in a garden will provide masses of colour in late summer, when most flowering shrubs are over. They strike very easily from cuttings and prefer a well-drained soil and a fairly sheltered spot. The best blue-coloured hydrangeas can only be grown on a fairly acid soil. There is not sufficient iron and aluminium in a limy soil to produce the blue colouring for the flowers. All hydrangeas have a need for iron, and this can be added to the soil by mixing a solution of a quarter of an ounce of sulphate of iron to a gallon of water. If the special turquoise-blue blossoms are required, a further treatment with blueing powder, obtainable from nurserymen, must be carried out. This will be watered in weekly or fortnightly.

A good loamy soil, enriched with plenty of decayed garden compost, is the best soil for these shrubs. Cuttings should be taken in July for propagation. There are two kinds of hydrangea commonly grown in this country, one the well-known *macrophylla* which is often seen in florists' shops, and the other known as Lacecap types.

H. macrophylla 'Hamburg' is deep pink, but it can be changed to deep blue on an acid soil with the addition of iron and 'blueing' powder, which is really a form of aluminium sulphate. Instructions for its use are given on the packets. 'Pride of Aalsmeer' has large red flowers and blooms during midsummer.

Of the Lacecap types, 'Blue Ware' has large plate-like heads, with an outer ring of pink, and central florets of purplish blue, height six feet. *H. mariesii* has large mauve-pink marginal flowers with small centre blooms (the colour varies according to soil conditions). *H. veitchii*, with large pure white flower heads and blue central florets, is a very strong-growing shrub, height six feet. *H. involucrata* is a charming dwarf shrub producing small brilliant-blue flowers and larger bluey-white ray florets on long stalks. *H. villosa* is a late-flowering shrub with porcelain-blue umbels starred with lavender florets, well displayed. It will grow on chalk. *H. serrata* 'Grayswood' has white flowers in July, which change to deep crimson-maroon by autumn. Leave all old flower heads on Hydrangeas (except those used for cutting) until the spring, as they protect the young buds during winter, and provide excellent material for winter floral art.

Pruning for the *macrophylla* types consists of just removing old wood periodically in spring to encourage new wood from the base. For the Lacecap varieties, pruning is carried out in March by taking away all weak shoots and reducing by half their length the previous year's shoots. A watch must be kept for slugs when the young shoots are beginning to grow in spring.

There are many varieties of lavender, valued for its scent and long period of flowering. All succeed in a light, well-drained soil in full sun. They grow well by the sea shore. Trim the young growth immediately after flowering. There are white, purple and blue sorts.

Tree Lupins, which are really shrubs, are well worth growing, with flowers which are slightly smaller than those of the border lupin. They will grow up to six feet high and are admirable subjects for the June Gap period (see page 149). They make fine lawn specimen shrubs. The perfume of the tree lupin in full sun is wonderful, and anyone who has cycled along the east coast road between Aldeburgh and Leiston in Suffolk, where hundreds of these shrubs are growing wild, will never forget the sight or the marvellous scent, which fills the morning air. A poor, sandy, well-drained soil, in full sun, is best for this subject. It is easily grown from seed or from cuttings with a heel attached. Remove all unwanted seed pods when flowering has finished.

As rhododendrons are usually included with azaleas in nurserymen's lists, they will be described together here. Gardeners with chalky soil cannot grow either shrub because of the lack of iron.

All soils have to be well prepared for these noble shrubs. Rhododendrons are surface rooting, and after the shrub has been received from the nursery, the ball of soil containing the roots should be thoroughly soaked in water prior to planting. When setting in these shrubs, make sure that the soil does not come above the soil mark. After planting, keep them well watered.

The soil on the planting site should be thoroughly prepared, and all weeds eradicated, as hoeing or forking around the plants must be avoided after planting. Enrich the soil with plenty of well-decayed garden compost and plenty of leaf mould. An annual mulch of six inches of fallen leaves is required for good healthy growth. Most of the rhododendrons do well in light shade. Propagation is easily carried out by layering.

Provided that the annual mulch of fallen leaves is given, rhododendrons are practically trouble free. They, and the azaleas, are easily moved from place to place, if the ball of soil containing the roots is intact, and if they are well watered.

Some of the hardy hybrids are listed here, but there are so many varieties that we only have room for a few of the best.

'Britannia' is a glowing scarlet-crimson of a spreading semi-dwarf habit. 'Cynthia' has rosy-carmine flowers in large compact trusses. 'Madame de Bruin', a very free-flowering sort, produces brilliant carmine blossoms. 'Gomer Waterer', a pale blush with yellow eye, is a compact plant with large trusses of bloom. 'Pink Pearl' is well knownand popular, with enormous clusters of flesh-pink flowers and very vigorous. *Fastuosum* has large double mauve flowers and is a fast-growing kind. 'Loder's White', with white, paling pink flowers, is of compact habit with a large amount of bloom.

Of the low-growing, small-leaved varieties, the following can be recommended. 'Blue Tit' is lavender-blue with open bell flowers in April and May, three feet high. 'Elizabeth' has glowing orange-red, trumpet-shaped flowers in clusters. 'Praecox' has delicate mauve flowers in February and March. 'Sapphire' is a small shrub with clear blue flowers and dark stamens.

Azaleas need the same treatment as rhododendrons and require a peaty soil. Many people plant azaleas too deeply: the ball of roots needs to be barely covered with soil and a mulch of fallen leaves should be given annually. They are among the most brilliantly coloured of all flowering shrubs. The tall-growing varieties are usually deciduous, the low-growing evergreen. The deciduous kinds have fragrant flowers of gay colours and autumn leaves of pleasing reddish hues.

'Koster's Brilliant Red' is glowing orange-red, flowering in May, five feet; 'Mrs. Peter Koster' is a beautiful deep red, May-flowering, also five feet. 'W. S. Churchill' is mandarin red, with a signal-red blotch, flowers in May, five feet.

'Bouquet de Flore', a salmon-pink variety, is double, and flowers during May and June, five feet. 'Mrs. J. Dykhuis', a glowing salmon-orange, five feet, flowers in mid-May. 'Directeur Morelands' has golden-yellow flowers in May, also five feet high. 'Nancy Waterer' is a rich golden-yellow, May and June flowering, eight feet. *A. narcissidora* is a double yellow, flowers in May and June, eight feet in height; *flaviesii*, a creamy-white, has a yellow blotch and grey-green foliage, May- and June-flowering, five feet. *A. pontica* is a very useful kind as it flowers in drier and poorer conditions than the other deciduous azaleas. It also has superb autumn tints and masses of fragrant clear orange-yellow flowers in May and June. Yet another that goes to five feet.

The Japanese Azaleas, which are evergreen, have been grown in Japanese gardens for centuries and are among the oldest of cultivated garden subjects. Most of them are May-flowering. Lime-free soil is essential and partial shade is ideal. They are highly successful shrubs for large pots or tubs. 'Addy Wery' is a rich vermilion, 'Hinodegiri', bright crimson, and 'Vuyk's Scarlet' has huge carmine flowers. Of the orange-red varieties, 'Alice' is salmon-red with a dark blotch and 'Orange Beauty' more of a salmon-orange. Pink varieties include 'Blaauw's Pink', with double, soft-pink blossoms, 'Helana' has clear translucent pink flowers, and 'Kerin', an early, bright rose, has a deeper mark at the base of the petals. 'Adonis' is pure white, and 'Palestrina' ivory-white.

Under the name of *Ribes* are usually grouped the flowering currants and gooseberries. These useful shrubs are in flower in April, filling the air with their pungent scent when there is little else in flower. The odour is not enjoyed by everyone and many people do not like to have sprays of flowering currant indoors. *Ribes* will thrive in most soils and they are very easily grown from cuttings. They can be grown in shade or partial shade. Pruning consists of just thinning out in May. *R. alpinum* has greenish-yellow flowers, followed by scarlet berries and orange-red autumn leaves; *aureum* is known as the 'golden currant' and has bright yellow, spicily fragrant flowers and black berries, and the foliage has rich colours in autumn. *R. sanguineum* 'Pulborough Scarlet' is a vigorous shrub producing deep red flowers and it is an improvement on the old red varieties.

R. speciosum, or Fuchsia-flowered Gooseberry, has spiny branches clothed with evergreen foliage and pendent clusters of rich red flowers resembling small fuchsias. It makes a good wall shrub in cold areas. Full sun should be given.

Spartium, or Spanish Broom, is a very beautiful shrub, especially in warm localities or near the coast. It will thrive on light or chalky soil which should be well-drained. An open position is best. The almost leafless rush-like stems carry large yellow flowers shaped something like small sweet peas. It is fragrant and enjoys a long flowering period. Prune in March, remove straggling shoots and trim the previous season's wood. This shrub is easily grown from seed.

The short flowering period of the syringa, or lilac as it is better known, can be partly overcome by planting one or two varieties of the Canadian Hybrids (see page 172). These are not yet as well known as they should be. In some ways different from the ordinary lilacs, they have great charm and a habit of growth which is quite characteristic. These Canadian Hybrids come into flower after the ordinary kinds of lilac have finished.

The common lilac has been cultivated in England for over three hundred years and it has lost none of its popularity through all this time. It is easily grown on all soils, including chalk. They are very long-lived shrubs and will tolerate light shade. The ordinary lilac takes two or three years to become established after being transplanted, so not many flowers can be expected at first. During the first year it is best to remove all unopened flower buds and in the second year to leave only one or two. The dead flowers of all lilacs should be removed.

Strong-growing varieties should have the shoots reduced by about one-third of their length. Thin twigs and any crossing each other should be cut away after flowering. When cutting lilac sprays for the house, cut the stalk immediately above a pair of shoot buds.

An annual dressing of bone meal or other organic fertilizer is beneficial in autumn or in spring. A top dressing of well-rotted garden compost is also helpful in spring as there is nearly always a dry spell when the lilac is in flower. This is best applied after a good fall of rain, as it then acts as a mulch as well as providing plant food.

Sometimes lilacs are attacked by a fungus disease called 'lilac blight', with effects similar to frost damage. Shoots develop a black, frosted look and leaves shrivel and die. A black staining is apparent in the stems. Remove isolated damage and spray with Bordeaux Mixture. Spray each spring as well, if there is danger of attack. Keep bushes healthy and well grown. On acid soils apply garden lime annually.

There are many different-coloured lilacs, both single-flowered and double. Here are some of the best of each colour:

'Blue Hyacinth', raised in 1942, is mauve in the bud and opening to blue flowers in May. The flowers have very long tubes and petals like those of a hyacinth. 'Firmament' is pinkish-mauve in bud, opening to sky-blue flowers in mid-May. 'Katherine Havemeyer' has deep purplish-lavender trusses of double flowers with a very lovely scent. 'Esther Staley', with carmine buds opening to bright pink, is very free-flowering and a vigorous grower. 'Edward J. Gardner', raised in the U.S.A., has semi-double flowers of light pink and it flowers in late May. 'Prodige', with large heads of single deep, purplish-red petals, which are incurved, has a strong perfume. 'Maréchal Lannes' is violet-flowered and a very free-flowering variety in late May. 'Congo' is a single-flowered dark red, with a delightful scent. 'Mrs. Edward Harding', a semi-double red, is also sweetly scented. 'Souvenir de Alice Harding' is the best double white variety, heavily scented. 'Sensation' is an unusual colour, purple-red edged with white, and it creates a lovely effect.

The Canadian Hybrids extend the lilac season by several weeks and are a vigorous hardy race. 'Bellicent' is a beautiful rose colour and very fragrant. 'E. M. Webster' has flowers of a delicate shade of pink. 'Fountain' is well-named as it really does produce a fountain of pink blossom. All of the Canadian Hybrids need full sun.

There are many species of Syringa. *S. chinensis rubra,* the Rouen Lilac, is a natural hybrid between *Syringa persica* and *S. vulgaris* (the common Lilac) and was first grown in the Botanic Garden at Rouen round about the year 1777. The foliage and flowers are smaller than with *vulgaris,* and it has fragrant reddish-purple flowers. *S. persica,* the Persian Lilac, has small, fragrant, lilac-coloured blossoms of a lacy appearance. *S. microphylla superba* is a small-leaved and small-growing lilac, only reaching about four feet in height, with erect panicles of fragrant pink flowers in May and June and again in September. The slender branches are rarely without flowers until November, however.

Viburnums are easily grown decorative shrubs, many with fragrant blossoms. Any good soil will grow Viburnums, even a chalky one. Enrich the planting site with plenty of good garden compost and see that it is well-drained. There are winter-flowering and spring-flowering sorts. The winter-flowering kinds need a position in full sun. One of the most valuable of these is *Viburnum tinus* which is well known by the name of Laurustinus. I have often used the flowers of this variety for Christmas decorations, as they are nearly always in full blossom at this time of the year and blend well with holly and other berried shrubs. It is about the easiest of the Viburnums to grow and it is one of the best winter-flowering evergreen shrubs we have. Pink-tinted buds open to flat, open, lacy white flower heads. The berries are blue, turning to black, and it makes a very charming hedge. The flowering period is from October until March. *V. fragrans* has sweetly scented flowers borne in clusters of one and a half to two inches across from November onwards. It is pale pink in bud, opening to white. The flowers will stand quite a lot of frost, and scarlet berries follow. *V. opulus sterile,* the Snowball Tree, is a spring-flowering variety. The flowers are greenish-yellow at first, and then develop like snowballs. *V. tomentosum* 'Lanarth' is a very vigorous shrub with large blossoms of snow white. Sterile flowers surround the fertile central flowers. *V. tomentosum plicatum* is known also as the Japanese Snowball. It has large white sterile flowers. The clusters are borne in two opposite rows along the branches, providing a wondrous display.

The spring-flowering groups will tolerate partial shade. *Viburnum lantana,* the Wayfaring Tree, has wrinkled leaves which colour well in autumn and produce red berries which eventually turn black.

The *Vinca,* or Periwinkle, is a good evergreen shrub for ground cover, banks, shady sites, the wild garden, woodland; and small rooted pieces make good hanging basket subjects. It will grow in any soil and it will tolerate partial shade as well as full sun. The lovely bright blue flowers appear in May. There is a white variety, *V. alba.*

Yucca filamentosa has ivory-white pendulous flowers borne in panicles, and grows from three to six feet high. The flowering period is through July and August. The stiff green leaves are covered with curly white threads. It grows best in shade or partial shade.

OTHER SHRUBS AND TREES

So far we have mentioned only flowering trees and shrubs, but there are a number of other useful shrubs and trees which are not usually classed among the flowering section. Some of them do have small, but not showy, blooms.

One shrub which will be treasured by all who are interested in floral art is the *Elaeagnus* or Wood Olive (see page 274). This is one of the best hardy evergreens that can possibly be grown. It will thrive in almost any soil and does well in coastal regions. Only slight pruning to shape is required in April. *Elaeagnus pungens aurea-variegata* is a striking variety with large leaves having prominent yellow centres. This is a most beautiful colour, daffodil yellow on some leaves, deep chrome on others, and almost orange on one or two other leaves. A few twigs from this shrub, mixed with Forsythia and daffodils in spring, is a floral arrangement to cheer the gloomiest corner. *Elaeagnus ebbingii* has foliage which is deep glossy green above and silvery grey beneath. It is a vigorous shrub. The *Elaeagnus* looks well in a mixed border, as a specimen shrub, grown in hedges by the sea, or introduced to lighten up any dense evergreen background.

Ligustrum aureum, Golden Privet, is a good evergreen shrub, useful for floral decoration. *L. aureum variegatum* is a variety with opaque yellow foliage. A new sort from America, 'Golden Wax', has leaves with golden hues of varying intensity. One has to be careful with privets, however, as they are big feeders with spreading roots, and take much plant food from the soil. They also, when used as a hedge, need a lot of clipping and harbour quite a few pests.

Some of the shrubby willows (*Salix*) are useful shrubs for almost any soil, and the early catkins are wonderful for early spring floral displays.

When you are thinking of a tree, other than a flowering variety, for the garden, the noble copper beech immediately springs to mind. What a marvellous colour the foliage is, a delight to any artist and an indispensable element in floral art. *Fagus purpurea*, as it is called, does well on chalk, but it dislikes wet soils. And its likely size must be borne in mind.

The Mountain Ash, *Sorbus*, is another popular tree. The foliage is fern-like and fresh green, but some varieties have glaucous-tinted leaves. There are orange, red, white- and yellow-berried kinds.

If you are looking for beautiful autumn foliage, and do not mind a little clearing up of fallen leaves for leaf-mould or compost, then a planting of some of the Maples (*Acer*) is called for. They are a large group of foliage trees with varying colours, thriving in a fairly moist but not waterlogged soil. Two medium-growing sorts are *A. hersii*, with young red wood and the older wood striped yellow-green, and with three-lobed leaves which turn to a brilliant red in autumn, and *A. negundo variegata*, which has leaves margined with silver.

We must not forget the evergreen conifers which add an air of stateliness to any garden. They can be grown as specimen trees or as windbreaks. Conifers do much to cheer up the landscape during dull days of winter. I shall exclude such conifers as make tremendous trees, appropriate only for parks and very large gardens.

Some people are fascinated by the *Araucaria araucana,* Chilean Pine or Monkey Puzzle tree. You can call it by either of these names. This tree grows to a height of twenty feet or more, but it is included because of its interesting form. It is wind resistant, and when purchased from the nurseryman it is usually about eighteen inches high; so some years will elapse before it reaches full stature.

Some of the *Cupressus*, or *chamaecyparis* which cover the family of conifers with round branches and large cones, will be useful and they can be kept to the desired height by clipping.

C. lawsoniana is very hardy and thrives almost anywhere. When grown as a specimen tree, it can be kept to a cylindrical shape. It is also used for hedging and screening. *C. l. columnaris glauca* has that desirable bluey foliage which is a colour difficult to describe, being a mixture of green, grey and blue. *C. l. lanei aurea* has dense golden foliage, and a cone-like habit of growth. 'Wissellii' is an attractive variety with short branchlets of glaucous foliage in tufts.

Cryptomeria japonica elegans is unique among conifers on account of its rosy-red foliage in autumn.

Junipers cover a large genus with very many varied forms. Most have aromatic foliage and grey-green berries. The leaves are generally poisonous to cattle. *J. chinensis pyramidalis* is of bright yet glaucous colour, with a dense pyramidal habit of growth. It will grow to twelve feet.

Libocedrus decurrens is the Incense Cedar. It has a stiffly columnar mode of growth and is a very handsome tree: dark green foliage of flattened sprays.

Anyone with some spare ground and enough room might like to grow a few Christmas trees. They are *Picea abies* or Norwegian spruce, and will usually grow in most soils, including fairly cold, wet ones. *Picea glauca kosteriana* is perhaps the best blue-coloured spruce. It has really beautiful, richly glaucous-blue foliage. No one could fail to be impressed by the sight of this marvellous tree, which also grows to twelve feet.

The Thuyas are trees of shapely pyramidal outline, and a strong cedar-like aroma comes from the trunk or branches when they are touched or crushed. They grow well in most soils. *Thuya zebrina* has very striking variegated yellow and green foliage and it will stand clipping well.

A suitable selection of low-growing conifers has already been discussed in the rock garden section.

A List of Shrubs and Trees for a variety of soils, positions, and purposes

Chalk Soils

NAME	COLOUR	SEASON	REMARKS
Acer, but not Japanese varieties	Autumn tints	Oct. & Nov.	Grown for coloured foliage
Aesculus	Cream	July	Horse chestnut
Azara	Yellow	March	Vanilla scented
Berberis	Yellow	May, June	Autumn berries
Buddleia	Purple shades	July	Butterfly bush
Cercis	Purple	May	Judas tree
Chaenomeles	Red	March	Japonica
Choisya	White	May	Mexican Orange
Clematis	Various	Various	Climber

NAME	COLOUR	SEASON	REMARKS
Clerodendron	White	August	Blue berries
Cornus	Cream, white, red	Early summer	Coloured winter bark
Cotoneaster	Pink-tinted	May, June	Brilliant berries
Crataegus	White, red, pink	June	The hawthorns
Daphne	Rose, pink, purple	April, May	Fragrant
Deutzia	Pink or white	June	Like mock orange
Diervilla	Red shades	May, June	Good soil
Escallonia	Red, pink	June	Wall shrub
Forsythia	Yellow	Early spring	Floriferous
Hibiscus	Various	Aug., Oct.	Tree hollyhock
Hornbeam	Foliage tree	—	Retains leaves during winter
Juglans	—	—	Walnut tree
Laburnum	Yellow	May	Popular
Lilac	Various	May, June	Very fragrant
Magnolia 'Kobus'	Cream	April	Pyramidal
Malus	Pink, white, red	April, May	Ornamental crab apples
Philadelphus	White	June	Mock orange
Pittosporum tenuifolium	Purple	May	Evergreen—pale green, wavy leaves
Pontentilla	Yellow	June–Sept.	Like a miniature rose
Prunus	Red, pink	Spring	Almonds, cherries, peaches, plums
Rhus	Pinkish-grey	June	Smoke tree
Ribes	Red or pink	April	Flowering currant
Senecio	Yellow	July	Silvery foliage
Sorbus	Cream	Spring	Mountain ash
Spiraea	White, pink, crimson	May	Feathery spikes
Symphoricarpus	Pink	Oct.	Waxen white berries
Veronica	Various	July–October	Fragrant spikes

Peaty and Woodland Soil

Acer, including Japanese	Autumn tints	October	Autumn foliage

NAME	COLOUR	SEASON	REMARKS
Amelanchier	White	April	Crimson fruit
Arbutus	White	April	Evergreen
Azalea	Various	May	Brilliant colours
Berberis	Yellow	May	All varieties
Betula	Silver stems	—	The silver birch
Callicarpa	Pink	August	Violet berries
Calluna	Purple	August	Scottish heather
Camellia	White, pink, red	Dec.–April	Conspicuous blossom
Clethra	Cream	August	Moist soil
Cytisus	Various	May, June	The brooms
Daboecia	White, purple	June, Oct.	Irish heath
Erica	Pink shades	All year	Heathers
Eucryphia	White	Summer	Large flowers
Hamamelis	Yellow	Winter	Witch hazel, very scented
Hydrangea	Various	Summer	Long flowering
Ilex	—	May	The holly
Kalmia	Rose	June	Mountain laurel
Laurus	—	—	The bay tree
Liquidambar	—	Autumn	Crimson and gold leaves
Magnolia	Cream, white, pink	Mar.–Sept.	Very aristocratic trees, fragrant
Mahonia	Yellow	Winter	Winter flowers
Parrotia	Red	Jan.–March	Autumn tints
Rhododendron	Various	May, June	Showy flowers

Hot Dry Places

NAME	COLOUR	SEASON	REMARKS
Artemisia	Grey	—	Grey-green fragrant leaves
Berberis	Yellow	May	Will grow on banks
Caryopteris	Blue	August	Blue spiraea
Chaenomeles	Red, pink, white	March	Japonica
Colutea	Yellow	All summer	Pea-shaped flowers
Cotoneaster	Pink tinted	May	brilliant berries
Cytisus	Various	May, June	Fragrant brooms
Erica	Pink shades	All year	Heathers
Genista	Yellow	May, June	Resembles broom

12

NAME	COLOUR	SEASON	REMARKS
Hebe	Various	June	The veronica
Hedysarum	Magenta	June	French honeysuckle
Hippophae	White	Spring	Masses of orange berries
Hypericum	Yellow	June	St. John's wort
Lavendula	Blue shades, white	July	Lavender
Olearia	White	July	The Daisy bush
Perowskia	Blue	July	Russian sage
Phlomis	Yellow	June	Grey-green leaves
Pontentilla	Yellow shades	June	Like miniature rose
Rhus	Pinky-grey	June	Smoke tree
Robinia	White	July	Good foliage
Rosmarinus	Lilac	May	Aromatic leaves
Santolina	Yellow	June	Aromatic, evergreen
Senecio	Yellow	July	Silvery foliage
Spartium	Yellow	Summer	Spanish broom
Spiraea	White, red, pink	June	Free flowering
Ulex	Golden	April	Double-flowered gorse
Vinca	Blue	May	The periwinkle
Yucca	White	July	Pendulous flowers

Shady Positions

NAME	COLOUR	SEASON	REMARKS
Acer, Japanese	Autumn tints	—	Col. autumn foliage
Acuba	—	—	Scarlet berries
Berberis	Yellow	May	Various berries
Camellia	White, pink, red	Dec.–April	Conspicuous flowers
Chaenomeles	Red, pink, white	March	Japonica
Choisya	White	May	Mexican orange
Cornus	Cream	June	Coloured bark
Cotoneaster	White	May	Brilliant berries
Danae	—	—	Will grow under trees
Daphne	Purple, pink	April	Fragrant

NAME	COLOUR	SEASON	REMARKS
Garrya	Greenish-yellow	February	Decorative
Hydrangea	Various	All summer	Showy
Hypericum	Yellow	June	St. John's wort
Ilex (Not golden varieties)	White	May	Holly
Jasmine	Yellow, white	Oct.–April	Winter flowering
Kerria	Yellow	May	Pretty foliage
Laurustinus	Pinky-white	Oct.–March	Winter flowers
Leycesteria	Claret	August	Red bracts, then purple berries
Ligustrum	White	August	The privet
Lonicera	Cream or red	May	Honeysuckle
Mahonia	Yellow	Winter	Winter flowers
Olearia	White	July	Daisy bush
Osmanthus	White	April	Fragrant
Osmarea	White	April	Evergreen
Phillyrea	White	May	Purple berries
Pyracantha	White	Spring	The Firethorn
Ribes	Red and pink	April	Flowering currants
Rhododendrons and Azaleas	Various	May	Showy and colourful
Spiraea	Purple	—	Some variegated
Symphoricarpus	Pink		The Snowberry tree

Waterside Shrubs

Bamboo	—	—	Decorative evergreens
Cercidiphyllum	—	—	Small foliage tree
Cornus alba	White	Spring	Crimson stems
Cornus stolonifera	White	Spring	Yellow bark
Cortaderia	—	—	Pampas grass
Crataegus	Various	May, June	Hawthorn
Diervilla	Red, pink	May, June	Weigela
Hippophae	White	Spring	Orange berries
Leycesteria	Claret	August	Red bracts, purple berries
Philadelphus	White	June	Mock orange
Salix	Yellow and grey	April	The willow

NAME	COLOUR	SEASON	REMARKS
Spiraea bumalda	Purple	July	Flat clusters of blossom
Viburnum opulus	White	April	Snowball tree

Trees and Shrubs for large towns

NAME	COLOUR	SEASON	REMARKS
Acer, except *negundo* and *palmatum*	—	—	Col. autumn foliage
Aesculus	Crimson, pink, white	May	Horse chestnut
Ailanthus	Greenish-white	Spring	Yellow autumn leaves
Amelanchier	White	April	Autumn tints
Berberis stenophylla	Yellow	May	Purple berries
Cercis	Purple	May	Flowers on naked stems
Chaenomeles	Red shades	March	Japonica
Cotoneaster	White	May	Brilliant berries
Crataegus carrierei	White	May	Retained orange berries
Crataegus oxycantha	Red, pink	—	A native hawthorn
Deutzia	Pink, white	June	Like mock orange but scentless
Diervilla	Red, pink	May, June	Weigela
Forsythia	Yellow	Early spring	Floriferous
Hypericum	Yellow	June	St. John's wort
Juglans regia	—	—	The walnut
Kerria	Yellow	May	Jew's mallow
Laburnum	Yellow	Early spring	Very showy
Magnolia stellata	White	March, April	Floriferous
Malus (All var.)	Red, pink	April, May	Crab apple
Olearia haastii	White	July	Daisy bush
Osmanthus delavayi	White	April	Fragrant wall shrub
Philadelphus	White	June	Mock orange
Prunus (various)	—	April–June	Flowering cherries, etc.
Rhus typhina	—	—	Autumn tints
Symphoricarpus	—	—	October berries
Syringa (Lilac)	—	May & June	Fragrant

NAME	COLOUR	SEASON	REMARKS
Viburnum (All var.)	—	Spring, winter	Many uses

Small Specimen Lawn Trees

NAME	COLOUR	SEASON	REMARKS
Acer ginnala	Cream	May	Fiery red in autumn
Acer henryi	Blue green bark	—	Bronzy red shoots
Acer hersii	Red wood	—	Green and yellow old wood
Acer negundo variegatum	Pale green silver margins	—	Very striking
Acer nikoense	—	—	Orange-flame in autumn
Acer negundo 'Elegantissima'	Pale green leaves	—	Bright yellow variegations
Acer palmatum	—	—	Japanese maple
Betula youngii	—	—	Weeping birch
Fraxinus pendula	—	—	Weeping ash
Magnolia (All var.)	Various	—	Showy flowers
Prunus 'Okame'	Rose	April	Flowering cherry
Prunus incisa	White	March	Flowering cherry
Prunus persica 'Cardinal'	Red	April	Flowering peach
Prunus atropurpurea	—	—	Purple leaves
Prunus 'Pissardii'	White	—	Very beautiful plum
Prunus spinosa 'Rosea'	Bright pink	—	Purple foliage
Prunus, weeping var.	Pink	April	Slender pendulous branches
Pyrus salicifolia 'Pendula'	White	April	Weeping pear
Sorbus Americana decora	White	May	Mountain ash
Sorbus bristolensis	White	May	Grey leaves, orange berries
Sorbus sargentiana	White	May	Orange scarlet fruit

NAME	COLOUR	SEASON	REMARKS
Syringa (Lilac) (as a short standard)	Various	May	Floriferous
Tilia euchlora	—	—	Beautiful dome-shaped lime
Viburnum (All var.)	Various	Spring and winter	Showy blossom

SHRUBS AND TREES FOR SEASIDE PLANTING

Two lists of trees are necessary here, the first of suitable shrubs or trees for the first line of defence, or those which can be planted nearest to the coast. They are fairly tolerant of salt-laden and high winds.

The second list will contain trees and shrubs which will do for the second line and can be planted anywhere near the coast, but not as screens to take the first direct winds.

Trees and shrubs for the first line of defence

NAME	REMARKS
Atriplex	Semi-evergreen with long silvery leaves
Aucuba japonica	Scarlet berries
Berberis in variety	Yellow flowers, coloured berries
Colutea arborescens	Pea-shaped yellow flowers
Crataegus in variety	Hawthorns
Hebe salicifolia	One of the veronicas
Hebe speciosa	Very popular
Hebe traversii	Medium growing
Hippophae rhamnoides	The sea buckthorn
Sambucus in variety	The elder
Spartium junceum	The Spanish broom
Symphoricarpus in variety	The Snowberry tree
Tamarix in variety	Pink flowers
Ulex	The double gorse

Other seaside Trees and Shrubs

Abelia	For a sunny site
Abutilon	Suitable for south of England
Arbutus	Pink bell flowers
Azara	Vanilla-scented flowers
Buddleia davidii	The Butterfly bush

NAME	REMARKS
Bupleurum	Yellow flowers
Buxus	The Box, grows in chalk
Caryopteris	Blue Spiraea
Choisya ternata	Mexican orange
Cistus in variety	The rock rose
Convolvulus	Evergreen, pink flowers
Corokia	Orange-red berries
Coronilla glauca	Yellow pea-shaped flowers
Cotoneaster	Brilliant berries
Crataegus in variety	Hawthorns
Cupressus macrocarpa	The best seaside conifer hedge
Cytisus	The brooms
Diervilla	Floriferous tubular flowers
Erica	The heathers
Escallonia in variety	Good seaside hedges
Eucalyptus	Handsome trees
Fraxinus excelsior	The ash
Fuchsia in variety	Very popular
Garrya elliptica	The tassel bush
Genista hispanica	The Spanish gorse
Griselina littoralis	Salt tolerant evergreen
Hibiscus	Hollyhock tree
Hornbeam	Retains foliage in winter
Hydrangea hortensis	Showy blooms
Ilex in variety	The holly
Lavendula	Lavender
Ligustrum	The privets
Mahonia in variety	Yellow winter flowers
Olearia haastii	The Daisy bush
Perowskia	Russian sage
Phlomis	Jerusalem sage
Pittosporum	Shiny pale green leaves
Potentilla	Like miniature roses
Prunus cerasifera	The Myrobalan plum used for hedges
Romneya	The Californian poppy shrub
Rosa spinosissima	A shrub rose, grows well in sandy soil
Rosmarinus	Rosemary, aromatic
Santolina	Dainty, silver foliage
Senecio in variety	Silvery leaves, daisy-like flowers
Skimmia	Male and female bushes required for berrying
Viburnum tinus	The laurustinus
Yucca filamentosa	White pendulous flowers

THE HEATHER FAMILY

Many people have thought that they could not grow any of the splendid heathers, if they were on a chalky soil. There are, however, varieties of *Erica carnea, darleyensis, mediterranea* and *terminalis* which will thrive where there is a certain amount of lime.

Where the heathers are to be planted, perennial weeds must be eradicated, otherwise they will grow faster than the heathers. When the heathers are well-established, they will suppress most annual weeds.

Heathers should be planted in bold drifts of one variety and not isolated plants of several varieties. Space them a foot and a half apart during the initial planting. A fairly open situation is best. They look very well when planted in conjunction with any rock garden. During nearly every month there are some heathers in flower; that is why they are such useful plants for any garden, often providing bright colour when there is little else. Heathers can be used as edgings to paths or borders and also as low hedges, being trimmed at intervals.

The following winter- and spring-flowering kinds are all evergreen and are tolerant of lime. *E. carnea aurea*, with bright golden foliage in spring and early summer, has deep pink flowers from February to April. *E. carnea* 'Springwood White' is the finest white winter-flowering heath. It has white flowers with attractive chocolate anthers, and its dense trailing habit makes it a good ground coverer, blanketing out all weeds. It is in flower from January to March. *E. carnea vivellii* is the deepest red winter heath with dark bronze foliage.

E. darleyensis produces rose-pink flowers from November to April. *E. mediterranea* 'Brightness' is a compact growing sort with bright rose-pink blossoms from March to May. *E. mediterranea* 'W. T. Rackliff', a fine white variety, flowers from January to March. It is free-flowering and it has a dense habit of growth.

The following summer and autumn evergreen varieties need a lime-free soil. *Daboecia cantabrica* is the Irish heath, flowering from June to October. There is a white and a purple variety.

Erica vagans 'Lyonesse' is a good white sort with brown anthers, flowering from August to October. *E.v.* 'Mrs. D. F. Maxwell' is a beautiful cerise variety flowering from July to October. *E. vulgaris alba-plena* is the double white Scottish heather with flower spikes up to eighteen inches in length. Flowering from August to October, it makes a good cut flower lasting for weeks. *E. vulgaris* 'J. H. Hamilton' is a lovely dwarf sort with bright double pink flowers.

There are some heathers called 'tree heaths' and they make specimen shrubs from five to eight feet in height. They have a very long flowering period, from December to September. *E. arborea alpina* has bright green foliage and scented white flowers every April. *E. lusitanica*, with pink buds and white blossoms, flowers freely from December until April. *E. mediterranea superba* flowers during April and May with deep rosy-pink, honey-scented blossoms. *E. terminalis*, the Corsican Heath, has pink flowers from June to September. It will grow on a chalk soil.

HEDGES AND HOW TO CARE FOR THEM

A hedge can be formal or informal. A formal hedge is clipped closely several times a year and kept to a uniform height and width. An informal hedge, usually of some flowering shrub, is just kept in check by the removal of a few very high shoots or straggly and dead wood with secateurs.

Hedges in a garden have many advantages and some disadvantages. The points against formal hedges are that they provide a lot of unproductive work when they have to be clipped with shears, usually at least twice a year. This work can be considerable where there are lengthy hedges all round the garden or house. Even if an electric or other powered clipper is employed, the trimmings still have to be cleared up and taken away afterwards.

Hedges also make shade and take a lot of plant food from the surrounding soil. There is usually a strip of wasted land on the garden side of a hedge, because a certain width must be kept to make room for the owner to stand and place his step-ladder while clipping.

Most gardens must have hedges somewhere. The alternatives would be expensive stone or brick walls or some closely woven wooden fencing. If fencing is chosen, it could be of willow or osier wattle hurdles, either fixed or movable. Interweave fencing is also useful.

Hedges are used for many purposes. They form boundaries, and if they run along the side of a road, they act as barriers against invading ponies, cattle and dogs. They form a good protection for flowers against adverse winds. If a garden has a part which faces east or north, a good thick hedge on these sides is absolutely necessary if anything worth while is to be grown.

If one is a bird lover, then a hedge will provide suitable nesting sites for some species. These birds can then dispose of very many pests from the garden. Finally, a well-kept hedge can look very attractive, especially if it is a flowering one. Formal hedges need plenty of attention if they are to look well. Never let them get higher than is essential to the purpose for which they are grown.

A great variety of subjects can be used for hedges and in a large garden several different sorts of hedge can be established. When planting a new hedge, think ahead and imagine what it will look like in a few years' time. Will it be taking too much light away from the house or garden? Will it grow high enough, or thick enough, to screen the lawn, where perhaps meals are taken in the summer or sun-bathing is indulged in? Can you achieve these ends without too much labour and expense?

When preparing the site for a new hedge, the ground should be dug at least two spits deep. Fork over the bottom of each trench and then add a good layer of well-decayed garden compost. This will encourage the young hedge to root deeply, will provide plant food, and will help to retain moisture. Make sure that the right variety of shrub is chosen for the particular kind of soil you have. Deciduous hedges can be planted during autumn and early spring, provided that the ground is not frozen or waterlogged. Evergreens should be planted in September or early October.

It is important during the first spring and summer to see that the plants do not dry out. Give plenty of water during dry periods.

When clipping or pruning hedges, the first principle is to establish a close, dense base. Hedges must not be allowed to increase too rapidly in height. During the first years, three or four clippings annually will be necessary, but mature hedges will only need clipping once or twice a year. Where one hopes for a closely-clipped formal hedge of yew, holly, privet or quickthorn, trimming should begin in June and be repeated two or three times. For beech and hornbeam delay the clipping until August. A mature hedge which is only clipped once a year is best attended to in August.

Hedges are all too often neglected and left to their own devices. They need as much care and attention as other more showy occupants of the garden. An annual dressing of good garden compost, leaf mould or old manure used in conjunction with a slow-acting organic fertilizer, will keep a hedge in good health and help it make luxuriant growth. Never throw weeds or any other uncomposted garden rubbish into the bottom of a large mature hedge. This does the hedge no good, as it encourages weeds, pests and diseases.

Always keep the hedging shears and secateurs well sharpened so that nice clean cuts are made. Use the secateurs when pruning a hedge which has large leaves, such as laurel. Half-cut leaves will die back and give the hedge unsightly brown areas.

Newly planted hedges in coastal areas, which are subject to strong sea winds, will need some support while they are getting established. When setting out the plants for a new hedge, they should be spaced so that each one almost touches its neighbour.

Here are a few planting distances as a rough guide. Young privet could be set at a distance of 6 to 8 inches, quickthorn 6 to 12 inches, beech 1 foot to 1 foot 3 inches, holly 1 to 2 feet and laurels and rhododendrons 2 feet 6 inches to 3 feet.

To describe all the subjects which could be used for hedges and their cultivation would take another book, so I shall deal briefly with some of the important ones and some of the most beautiful. It is a matter of personal choice for the owner of a garden, whether he plants some of the old-fashioned but still very useful shrubs such as laurels and privets, or whether he would prefer a rather informal hedge of *Philadelphus* or one of the *Berberis*.

The gardener's choice is governed largely by the amount of time he can spare for clipping, the position of his garden and the nature of the soil. Then the purpose of the hedge has to be considered. For formal hedges, a beech hedge is most attractive at all seasons, as in winter it retains its orange-brown foliage. It may be allowed to grow up to eight feet, but as it will stand repeated clipping, it can be kept much lower. A mixture of the green beech and the copper beech makes a most delightful hedge. Avoid heavy, wet soils for this shrub. The hornbeam, which is similar to the beech because it also retains its leaves during winter, is better for a heavy soil and will thrive in most soils, either in full sun or shade.

The hawthorn is a hedge for a large garden. It grows quickly and will stand a lot of severe clipping. It forms a very good barrier against trespassers of any kind. When clipping the hawthorn, care must be taken to avoid the thorns. A wound from one of these often quickly festers and it is advisable to wear protective gloves when clipping any thorny hedges.

Holly is a slow-growing evergreen, and again a good barrier. *Ilex aquifolium*, the common holly, is most frequently used for hedges. *I. argentea marginata*, which has silver variegated broad leaves and good berries, is handsomer, and 'Golden King' has broad leaves with bright golden margins.

Privet, plain, oval-leaved, golden and variegated, is about the commonest form of hedge to be seen. It is easily raised from cuttings and these hedges will stand a lot of clipping. A good, fairly high privet hedge offers a good deal of privacy to a garden but also a good deal of work of clipping and clearing up. Then privets have roots which roam all over the place, taking up a lot of plant food from other occupants of the garden.

Another common hedge, especially suited to coastal areas, is the evergreen coniferous *Cupressus macrocarpa*. These are best grown in the southern half of England, as sometimes a severe winter brings casualties. Often one sees parts of these hedges brown and dying. This is sometimes caused by over-clipping. The *macrocarpa* likes a fairly rich soil.

A fairly new hybrid which is very suitable for hedging is *Cupressus leylandii*. It does not have a large brittle tap root thrusting down into the soil to get broken by wind rocking. So it does not leave dead brown gaps in the hedge, as sometimes happens with *Cupressus macrocarpa*. It is a fast-growing hybrid fairly tolerant of even salt-laden spray. For rapid screening it is admirable; of columnar habit with a dense growth of very pleasing foliage, an evergreen of a grey-green colour. For the first trimmings secateurs should be used.

Cupressus lawsoniana is a hardy evergreen tree which also make a good hedge. A rich, deep loam will suit it. It is a most popular hedge and very suitable as a wind screen. It stands clipping well and is very hardy. It has deep to glaucous-green foliage. When planting *Chamaecyparis lawsoniana* as a hedge, good preparation should be given to the soil. Trench the site and add a fair amount of good garden compost. Plant the shrubs when about two feet high and two feet apart during September or October. The variety 'Green Hedger' is the best one.

Thuya is another conifer suitable for hedges. It has bright lustrous green foliage and is fast-growing. The young plants are put in the ground about two feet apart. Secateurs should be used for trimming during the summer. It will grow as a hedge to fifteen feet in height. It differs from *lawsoniana* in that it has thicker foliage, and emits a strong cedar-like scent when the wood is crushed. It will grow well in most kinds of soil.

The Yew is the finest of all evergreens for hedges. It will take quite a few years to establish a good hedge however, although yews are not so slow-growing as it is generally thought. They are very long-living shrubs. A well-drained soil is required. Trim in late summer and taper the hedge towards the top.

Where a hedge is running by a road, or where privacy is required, it would be best to plant an evergreen. The deciduous hedges can be planted for their beauty and autumn tints elsewhere in the garden.

For informal evergreen hedges *Berberis darwinii* is one of the best. It bears rich orange-yellow flowers in April and May, followed by bluish-purple berries. Prune after flowering, trying to leave some flowering shoots to produce the berries.

Cotoneaster lacteus is another evergreen, with milky white flowers in June and long-lasting red berries. Plant them three feet apart and prune off long shoots during summer.

Olearia haastii, already mentioned, also makes a good informal evergreen hedge. Plant three feet apart and prune lightly after flowering.

Pyracantha rogersiana seedling is an evergreen making a grand hedge. Plant twenty-one inches apart and prune lightly in spring and summer if necessary.

The common rhododendron will make a good evergreen hedge. Plant only in a lime-free light or sandy loam, three feet apart.

Other informal hedges can consist of some of the deciduous shrubs. *Prunus pissardii nigra* is a very beautiful subject with deep purple foliage and bright pink flowers in spring. When the leaves fall, the deep purple of the branches is revealed. Plant two feet apart and trim in late March after flowering. Restrict the annual rate of increase to eighteen inches.

The flowering quince, or Japonica, will make a beautiful flowering informal hedge. 'Rowallane Seedling', bright crimson, and *umbilicata*, a rosy salmon-pink, are the two most suitable varieties. Plant three feet apart and prune after flowering.

Cytisus albus is a free-growing hedge with cascades of white flowers in May and June. Plant two feet apart and trim after flowering.

Escallonia is very popular as a hedge in the south, especially near the sea. Plant two and a half feet apart and prune after flowering to encourage a second production of blossom.

Forsythia intermedia 'Lynwood' produces a mass of yellow flowers in early spring and will make a very attractive hedge. Plant two to three feet apart. Prune lightly after flowering.

Philadelphus coronarius is a fine hedge subject with richly scented, yellowish-white flowers in June and July. Plant three feet apart and prune lightly after flowering.

Ribes, or flowering currant, can be kept to a beautiful shape when grown as a hedge. 'Pulborough Scarlet' is one of the best varieties for this purpose. Really deep red flowers hang in racemes during May. Plant a foot and a half apart and trim after flowering during late summer.

A list of varieties of roses, suitable for hedges, and for shrub borders, will be given in the next chapter.

7

Annual and Perennial Flowers

Hardy and half-hardy annuals — biennials — bulbs and corms — perennials — sweet peas — roses — dahlias and chrysanthemums — some other flowers

An annual flowering plant is a plant which germinates when you put the seed in the ground, under favourable conditions, produces roots, shoots, stems, leaves, flowers and seed, all during the year of sowing. When it has produced the seed, and winter comes, it dies away and if the same variety of plant is required the following year, seed sowing must take place again in the spring.

There are two classes of annual grown in gardens in this country, hardy and half-hardy. Gardeners include under the term of annuals any plants which may be treated as annuals. Some of these are half-hardy perennials which would not survive our winters, but flower easily from seed sown in the same year. All types will be referred to as 'annuals' so that the reader will not be confused.

Hardy annuals are those flowering plants which can be sown direct into the open ground during spring in their flowering position. But most of the half-hardy annuals must be sown under glass and spend their early life as seedlings with glass protection, finally being hardened off and planted into their flowering positions when all danger of frost has passed. However, some half-hardy annuals may be sown in the open ground where they are to flower, at a much later date than the hardy annuals. Hardy annuals are usually sown some time in March or April, but the half-hardy varieties which can be sown into the open ground are not sown until late May or early June.

Here is a list of half-hardy annuals which may be sown in the open ground in their flowering positions: *Anagallis* (pimpernel), aster, balsam, cosmos, dianthus (annual pinks), felicia, gourds (ornamental), helichrysum, *Kochia* (burning bush), marigold (African and French), *Molucella* (Bells of Ireland), *Nolana* (Chilean Bellflowers),

Portulaca, Phlox drummondii, Rhodanthe, Rudbeckia, scabious, *Ursinia, Venidium* and Zinnias.

There are a few hardy annuals which may be sown during late August and early September in the open ground where they are to flower and left to stand the winter. They will give a magnificent display during the following spring and early summer, and will flower much earlier than those sown in the open ground during spring. This is a fairly successful method in the south of England and in sheltered spots in other parts. In cold districts it would be best to protect the seedlings with cloches.

The following are the flowers which can be sown in this way: *Calendula,* Candytuft, *Cheiranthus* (Siberian Wallflower), *Clarkia,* Cornflower, *Godetia,* Larkspur, *Nemophilia, Nigella,* Shirley Poppy, Virginia Stock and *Viscaria.*

Annuals can be used in many ways in the garden and no matter how they are used they always make a brilliant splash of colour and add greatly to the beauty of any garden.

For formal beds near the house half-hardy annuals are often planted. These will have been raised in the greenhouse or cold frame. For annual borders, usually long plots of ground with straight or curving outlines according to taste, hardy annuals are usually sown into their flowering positions. Here you may sow your annuals in any design you please and use as many varieties as you desire. You could sow in drifts or in straight rows, either way is very effective. It is best to plan the border on paper beforehand and to work out a colour scheme. An annual border is much more pleasing if the colours are harmonizing or contrasting but not clashing, and with patches of white to enhance the vivid hues.

An annual border often looks very much more colourful than a herbaceous border, for most of the hardy annuals will be flowering together from June until October. Annuals are sometimes used to fill gaps in the herbaceous border, for edgings to paths, and in the front of shrubberies. Annuals for use in the cut flower border will be discussed in the next chapter under 'Flowers for Display'.

A still further use for annuals is in window boxes, tubs, the rockery and water garden.

A good well-drained soil is best for annuals and there is nothing they like better than a good thickness of well-decayed good garden compost. The site for annual flowers should be well dug in November if possible and have a good layer of compost incorporated into the bottom spit. If the work cannot be done in late autumn, then as early in spring as possible is the next best time. If annuals are to follow the spring bedding subjects, and there is only time to fork the bed over, a sprinkling of bone meal at the rate of two ounces to the square yard will be adequate preparation of the soil if it was also well prepared in the previous autumn.

After digging the site in autumn, leave the surface rough for the frost to pulverize it during winter. Some time in early spring tread the soil and rake it level and down to a fine tilth suitable for seed sowing.

Although the packets of annual seeds usually carry instructions for the gardener to sow in March, it is a mistake to follow this advice too rigidly. One must wait until the soil is damp enough and, more important, warm enough. A soil condition where germination is effected quickly is usually more likely to be found some time in mid-April.

Many a gardener has blamed the seed and thought it to be inferior when he has sown too early. If a long cold wet spell follows seed sowing, then often instead of germinating, the seed just rots in the ground. This is not the fault of the seedsman who supplied the seed. Do not put the seed into ground which is too wet, as after the drills have been drawn, the seed sown and covered, and the soil firmed, the surface often settles down into a compact hard mass through which no air or further moisture can penetrate. If seeds are to germinate successfully, the correct temperature, good aeration and a suitable degree of moistness are all essential.

Generally we have had some sunshine in the middle of April, enough to warm the soil a little, and we have had some showers of gentle rain. So if the soil has been raked down to a fine tilth, to admit some air, we can think about sowing our seed in the conditions specified a moment ago.

Before sowing, it is often helpful if a long-range forecast of the weather can be ascertained. If a warm spell is likely to follow, and the soil is in the right condition, then this is the time to sow. Never sow seed during a prolonged spell of cold weather; it is always better to be a little late with the sowing of hardy annuals than too early.

Never sow too deeply; this is a very common mistake. When we think of these flowering plants in their native habitat, whatever their method of seed dispersal might be, most of the seeds drop on to the surface of the soil and are unlikely to be buried very deeply by nature.

Follow the instructions on the seed packets for correct depth of sowing, and sow no deeper. The general rule is, the smaller the seed, the shallower should be made the seed drill.

If it is almost the end of April, and seed sowing has not been done owing to the very dry conditions, then the drills can be drawn and watered while they are open, using the fine rose and water which has had the chill taken from it. Leave the drills open for a short while, then sow the seed and cover quickly with soil. The moisture thus provided is usually enough to ensure germination. Try not to give any further water until the seeds are showing above the soil.

Whichever way the seed drills are drawn, always label each flower clearly, with small but legible labels. If this is not done it is often difficult for a newcomer to gardening to ascertain which are his precious seedlings and which are weeds. If the exact position of all flower seedlings is known, it makes weeding much easier.

Many a gardener has asked, 'How do I know which are flower seedlings, and which are weeds?' This knowledge of the difference between weeds and flowers will gradually come with experience. The gardener will remember the appearance and characteristics of his different seedlings from year to year. A good plan for a beginner is for him to visit a friend's garden where seeds of the same kind have been sown and where the friend can point out the differences. He could also visit a local nursery with the same object in view.

After the appearance of the seedlings above ground, a very careful watch must be kept for slugs and snails. Slug killer pellets must be put down along the rows.

Always sow seeds thinly. The best method is to empty a few seeds from the packet into the palm of the left hand. Take up a few with the right forefinger and thumb and work them carefully and sparingly along the length of the row. Some seeds are more easily spaced than others, because of their larger size and their colour. In this group we have calendulas, annual chrysanthemums, cornflowers and nasturtiums. At the other end of the scale are the minute seeds of Shirley poppies and foxgloves.

The seed drills can be drawn with the corner of the hoe, the rake, or a stout pointed stick. Use a garden line for any long straight drills. Cover the drills carefully with soil, using the rake lightly. Press the soil down firmly with the rake head, but do not ram it down.

When the seedlings are about two inches high, they should be thinned out first to a few inches apart, and a final thinning is made later on to leave them at a spacing apart equal to three-quarters of their eventual height. These thinnings can be transplanted to other parts of the garden, or to fill in any blanks, during showery weather. If a lot of surplus plants are available, they can either be exchanged with neighbours for something else, sold, or given away. Never destroy good flowering plants.

A most important task, when the plants are a few inches high, is to provide them with supports in the form of brushwood or small branching twigs of some kind. Strong winds are usually experienced with thunderstorms and heavy rain just when the plants are near their flowering period. Any gardener who has surveyed the wreckage in his

13

annual border after one of these storms will not neglect to support his plants in all following summers.

The owner of a small garden may have a bright display of annual flowers each year for the outlay of a very moderate sum of money. This year in my garden I have nearly three hundred calendulas, giving a wonderful display of bright colour, and they cost me exactly one shilling for the seeds.

By trying different varieties each year, the gardener can grow a very large number of different annual flowers eventually. Annual flowers are chosen for giving a brilliant burst of colour in many places. In London and in other large cities and towns, annuals are seen in the parks and private gardens. They succeed under so many different growing conditions because the whole of their growth is made during the best months of the year.

Of course the choice is extremely wide. Send for a seed catalogue from a well-known firm before Christmas, and you can have great fun during the winter months looking at the coloured plates and making plans for the garden. Grow about a dozen different varieties every year if you can, according to how much room you have to spare for your annual flowers. Sow in bold drifts of colour rather than in small patches here and there. Be careful about arranging the colours. Try to avoid any discordant note.

In a small garden it would be best to be moderate with orange or flame, unless this colour appeals particularly to you. Yellow, cream and white can be used with all the blues including lavender and violet. Keep yellow and orange away from pink, rose, carmine, vermilion or any similar red shade. Put all the reds, scarlets, crimson, rose and very pale pinks together with white and pale cream or buffs.

Although it has always been advocated that dwarf plants should be in the front of the border and all of the tallest at the back, do not adhere too rigidly to this plan. In the main, this will have to be so, but the border will look more natural and interesting when a few of the taller sorts are allowed to drift towards the centre of the plot, with a few of the front-rank flowers creeping back towards the middle.

When thinning out the annuals, preferably during showery weather, firm the disturbed soil around the plants left in position by pressing with the hand and trowel handle. Plant firmly and water well any transplanted seedlings. When the plants are in full bloom remove regularly all dead flowers and seed heads to prolong the flowering period.

If there is a space in the garden which can be used for the autumn sowing of some hardy annuals, where they are to flower, then they are well worth growing. Larkspurs seem to like this treatment particularly well, especially on a soil which contains some natural chalk. From an autumn sowing of these lovely flowers, some wonderfully vigorous plants can be grown. When the centre spike of flower has been used for cut flowers, many other good lateral branches of flowers are freely produced.

For autumn sowing, dig the soil and incorporate plenty of well-rotted garden compost into the bottom spit. Leave the soil to settle down for a few days and then tread it firmly. Rake level and to a fine tilth, draw the seed drills and sow thinly. The seed can be sown in late August or in September, whenever conditions are right for sowing. Autumn-sown hardy annuals are better set in straight rows, so that cloches can be placed over them in winter, if necessary. A sheltered spot should be chosen for these sowings and they usually come through the winter with the minimum of losses.

The raising and growing of half-hardy annuals has been fully described in Chapter 4, 'Gardening Under Glass'. Here again correct colour harmonizing may be mentioned. For planting out the half-hardy annuals, select a mild, showery day if possible, when the soil is in the correct state for transplanting. It should not be too wet, or too dry, but moist and crumbly. Plant out when all danger of frost seems to have passed and when the plants have been thoroughly hardened off.

Give the seed box containing the half-hardy plants a good watering prior to planting. Put the finger and thumb around the wet soil in the box, and squeeze it gently around the roots of the first plant in the box to be planted. Put the plant into the planting hole made by a trowel, and then firm the soil around the plant, first with the hand and finally by using the trowel handle. Leave a slight depression in the soil around the plant. This will enable subsequent watering to be done in such a way that the water runs into the centre of the plant, rather than away from it. Well water all plants upon the completion of the transplanting.

Some of the taller-growing varieties of half-hardy annuals will need supporting with brushwood in the manner described for hardy annuals. When transplanting half-hardy annuals, plant with as little root disturbance as possible. If one solid mass of colour is desired in a bed of half-hardy annuals, fairly close planting can be carried out; but leave enough room for each plant to develop.

We now come to that group of half-hardy annuals which may be given a start under glass, but can also be sown in the open ground at a later date than the hardy annuals. They are best sown towards the end of May.

Zinnias grow well when given a warm, sunny, sheltered position in good soil, with plenty of good garden compost in the bottom trench. The successful flowering of good zinnias will largely depend on the summer we get.

The growing of the single asters sown in the open does not usually present much difficulty. They grow on without check and appreciate an early thinning. Asters will look at their best grown in a bed on their own or in front of, or associated with, Michaelmas daisies. While none of the aster colours look out of place in company with their fellows, they are sometimes difficult to fit in with other flowers.

There are very many different types of aster. The gardener would be best advised to grow only one or two varieties each year; he can then try out the others from time to time and discover which he and his friends prefer. The single-flowered sorts make ideal cut flowers. Accurate descriptions of each type will be found in the catalogues of good seedsmen.

Kochia, or Burning Bush, is another half-hardy annual which germinates quite well in the south from a May sowing in the open ground. It is like a miniature cypress tree of conical shape with very feathery foliage. It is of a bright light green colour all summer and then during autumn it changes its colour to a brilliant scarlet bronzy hue. It grows to a height of two feet.

The giant African marigolds, those lovely orange, gold and yellow flowers, sometimes germinate well from a May sowing outdoors in their flowering positions. A very careful watch must be made for slugs, however, as the pungent scent of the leaves seems to attract these pests. The same applies to French marigolds and *Tagetes*; these can both be sown outdoors in late May in the south.

Although the annual sweet scabious is usually listed as a half-hardy annual, anywhere in the south it can be treated as a hardy annual. I have grown them for years and I always sow them in the open at the same time as the other hardy annuals. They always put in an appearance and grow well.

Here is a list of hardy annuals which are easy to grow and they will give lasting pleasure from June until the frosts come along, provided that all dead flowers and seed heads are removed regularly. There is one exception: the annual candytuft. This usually flowers from the end of May until mid-August. As these very free-flowering subjects are put in the front of the border and bear seed heads which are rather attractive, it does not matter a great deal if they do finish flowering before the other annuals. There are colours here to suit every taste and many subjects for those keen on flower arranging for the house and elsewhere. The date given under the heading 'Season' means the time of the year when the flowers first appear.

NAME	COLOURS	SEASON	HEIGHT
Anchusa	Gentian blue	Early July	15 ins
Calendula	Shades of orange, yellow and cream	Early July	2 ft
Candytuft	Shades of pink, carmine, lavender and white	Early July	15 ins
Chrysanthemums (Annual)	All colours and combinations except blue	Early July	2 ft
Clarkia	Shades of red, pink, purple, white	Late June	2 ft
Convolvulus (Major)	Various excepting yellow (climber)	Early July	—
Convolvulus (Minor)	Blue, white, rose	Late June	3 ft
Cornflower (Tall mixed)	Various, excepting yellow	Early July	3 ft
Cornflower, Polka Dot	Shades of purple, red Mauve, maroon, pink, blue and white	Late June	18 ins
Eschscholzia	Shades of yellow, orange, mahogany and crimson	Late June	1 ft
Eschscholzia (Miniature)	Primrose	Late June	6 ins
Gypsophila	Shades of pink and white	Extended by frequent sowing	6 ins
Larkspur (tall)	Various except yellow	Late August	4 ft
Larkspur (dwarf)	Various except yellow	Early July	1½ ft
Layia	Yellow with white edging	Late June	15 ins
Nemophila	Sky blue	Early June	6 ins
Nasturtiums (dwarf jewels)	Various except blue and white	Early June	6 ins
Nasturtiums (climbing)	Shades of red, yellow and orange	Early July	—
Nigella ('Persian Jewels')	Blue, rose, pink, white	Early August	1½ ft
Phacelia	Deep blue	Early June	1½ ft
Poppy, Shirley	Various	Early July	2½ ft
Salvia horminum	Pink, violet, blue	Early July	2 ft
Sunflower (autumn sunshine)	Combinations of red, yellow, orange	Late July	4 ft
Sweet Sultan	Various	Early July	1½ ft
Virginia Stock	Various	Late June	9 ins

Here is a list of half-hardy annuals which need sowing in the cool greenhouse or heated frame. They need pricking out early into seed boxes and they must not be allowed to dry out. Thorough hardening off is essential and firm planting into their final flowering positions generally at the end of May or early in June. These plants need glass protection during their early life because they are not hardy enough to withstand spring frosts or cold winds. They also need a longer period of growth than the hardy annuals in order to flower well.

Most of the half-hardy annuals prefer a fairly rich soil, and again nothing is better for them than good garden compost.

Antirrhinums, everyone's favourite half-hardy annual—and deservedly so, on account of their very long flowering period—may be planted out earlier than the other half-hardy annuals. There is a very wide range of varieties in this most useful flower and there are kinds to suit almost any kind of garden or section of the garden, including the rockery.

NAME	COLOUR	SEASON	HEIGHT
Ageratum	Lavender blue	June	7 ins
Amaranthus	Carmine, crimson, bronze, scarlet	June	18 ins
Anagallis	Scarlet, blue	July	6 ins
Antirrhinum	Various	June	6 ins– 3 ft
Arctotis	Various, excepting blue	July	2 ft
Asters (all types)	Most colours	Late August	1½–2 ft
Carnations ('Chabaud')	Various excepting blue	August	1½ ft
Carnations ('Enfant de Nice')	Shades of red, striped and white	End July	1½ ft
Cosmos ('Goldcrest')	Orange, yellow	July	2 ft
Cosmos	Crimson, rose, white	July	2 ft
Dahlia (all types)	All, except blue	July	2½–5 ft
Delphinium (annual)	Blue	July	1 ft
Dianthus	Shades of red and pink, white	August	6 ins– 18 ins
Gaillardia (annual)	Crimson, yellow, bronze	July	15–18 ins
Gazania	Yellow, orange, carmine, bronze	August	12–15 ins
Lobelia	Blues, wine red, white	July	6 ins

NAME	COLOUR	SEASON	HEIGHT
Mesembryan-themum	Various	July	3 ins
Marigold, African	Yellows and orange	August	22¼ ft
Marigold, French	Yellows, orange, mahogany	July	6 ins– 1 ft
Nemesia	Most colours	July	9 ins
Nicotiana	Various	July	2½ ft
Petunia	Most colours	June	12–18 ins
Phlox drummondii	Various	August	10–15 ins
Salpiglossis	Various	July	1½–2 ft
Salvia (splendens)	Purple and red shades	June	1 ft
Stocks (All var.)	Various	July	1½ ft
Tagetes	Yellows	July	9 ins
Venidium fastuosum	Orange marked, maroon	July	3 ft
Verbena	Various	July	6–18 ins
Zinnias	Most colours except blue	Late July	6 ins– 3 ft

BIENNIAL FLOWERS

Among the biennial flowers, which are not a large group, are some very beautiful subjects. Who does not love the wallflower for its rich colours and superb scent? Biennials are all those flowers which are sown one year, to flower the next.

Some biennials are difficult to fit into general garden schemes, flowering too late for the beds to be used for anything else before the autumn. This must be borne in mind when you are thinking of growing some of these hardy biennials. The old-fashioned and much loved sweet william, for example, often goes on flowering into early August. Canterbury bells are often in flower during July. Against these disadvantages, if they can be called this, is the fact that most of these biennials overcome the so-called 'June Gap', when there are not many flowers to be seen in the garden.

A spare plot of ground must be found to act as a seed bed for the sowing of the biennials, for most of them are sown during May and early June.

The wallflower, one of the most popular flowers in Britain, has much foliage and a shallow rooting system. Therefore transplanting has to be carefully done. It should take place during rainy weather.

To transplant wallflowers during a dry period, unless continuous watering could be given, would be fatal to the plants. The soil around the roots must be damp and with as much original soil as possible from the seed bed retained around the roots. So do not shake off any of the soil. Plant very firmly, pressing the soil around the roots with the handle of the trowel. Give a good watering afterwards.

Wallflowers should be sown at the end of April; and to get good bushy plants, it is usual to transplant them to a nursery bed, to grow on during the summer and to build up a good root system, before being planted out during September or October.

Although many people have their individual choices of wallflowers and colours, 'Blood Red' and 'Cloth of Gold' being about the most popular, anyone who has ever seen a large bed of mixed wallflowers of all colours will want to grow them in this manner. They can easily be associated with other flowers in spring bedding displays, then special colours will be required. A mixture of 'Golden Bedder', 'Primrose Bedder' and 'Ivory White', together with forget-me-nots, would make a charming picture. The best mixed variety, for a mixed bed of wallflowers, is 'Monarch Fair Lady Mixed'. They are bushy and very uniform in height. Some wallflowers tend to throw up a tall central spike of foliage. This should be pinched out when the plants are growing away strongly, in order to induce further bushiness.

Remove all weeds in the site chosen for the seed bed, rake down to a level, fine tilth, and sow thinly in straight rows. The seed can be seen clearly, which enables thin sowing to be done. Hoe frequently between the rows, as the wallflower plants will be growing when weeds are in abundance.

If the wallflowers are to be grown where the soil is fairly acid, work in a little garden lime before planting out. Wallflowers are subject to the brassica disease of Club Root. They should not be planted in too exposed a position. North and east winds coupled with severe frosts sometimes destroy most of the wallflower foliage during bad winters. It turns a whitish straw colour and the beds look rather unsightly.

Sweet Williams have a long flowering period and are very long-lasting as cut flowers. They also appreciate some lime. Separate colours or mixed colours can be obtained. Seed should be sown in May, and they should be treated in a similar manner to wallflowers, except that pinching out is not necessary. They should be planted into their flowering quarters during October. Sweet Williams make a very colourful garden display.

Myosotis, or forget-me-not, should always be planted in a mass. It is only when planted in this manner that their real beauty can be seen. They are good subjects for undercarpets for Early Single, Darwin or May-flowering tulips. Again, careful thought must be given to the colour scheme. Yellow, orange or white tulips would combine well, or a mixture of these. Light pink and white would also look well. Forget-me-nots are best sown later than the other biennials, about mid-July is better, otherwise they make too much growth and are then not so suitable as bedding plants.

An old-fashioned plant which adds a note of cheerfulness to the garden is the Canterbury bell. Seed should be sown in May, bedding out taking place in early October. These showy flowers are at their best in June. There are cup-and-saucer varieties and single- and double-flowered sorts, in shades of mauve, blue, and pink, together with white.

The foxgloves can be very beautiful when planted in the right setting. They look well when associated with Russell lupins and campanulas in a mixed border with shrubs. They also are wonderful subjects for woodlands, where they are in their natural setting.

Although the Excelsior hybrids have in some way superseded the other kinds, the Shirley foxgloves have a charm all of their own. Excelsior hybrid foxgloves have flowers carried horizontally all around the stems and their colours include creamy-primrose, pink shades and purple with spottings and blotches of maroon. The flowering period is during July and August. Seeds of foxglove are very tiny, so thin sowing is most important. They can be sown in the open ground or in boxes in a cold frame in early spring. If sowing in the open ground, June would be a good month to choose. May would do for cold-frame work. Foxgloves usually germinate easily. Anyone who has seen the thousands of wild foxgloves growing in the New Forest will readily believe this.

Polyanthus, which are really perennials often succeed better when treated as a biennial. The seed should be thinly sown in boxes in early October and wintered in cold frames. On a warm day in spring, after rain, plant the seedlings out six inches apart in drills into a nursery bed, and then transplant them into their flowering quarters during October. For the nursery bed choose a partially shaded spot for these flowers. Enrich the ground where the final planting is to be with good garden compost and leaf mould.

Hollyhocks are other good perennial plants which grow and flower well as biennials. Sow in the open ground during May and plant into their flowering positions during September or October. 'Chater's Double Mixed' is a special strain producing double flowers, resembling small paeonies, in crimson, rose, pink, salmon, scarlet, yellow and white. 'Triumph Supreme' are early-flowering and rust-resistant with frilled and fringed double flowers in very many different shades of hollyhock colours.

The double daisies, listed in catalogues as *Bellis*, are very good when used as spring bedding plants. They should be sown in the open during April, pricked out into a nursery bed, and planted into their flowering quarters during October. A cool, moist position is the best site for these plants. The varieties of these daisies are 'Giant-flowered Red', crimson-scarlet, 'Giant-flowered mixed', 'Fairy Carpet', with compact flowers of rose and white, uniform in colour and height, 'Pomponette Pink Buttons' with quilled blossoms, and 'Pomponette Red Buttons'.

Double Brompton stocks are fine biennial flowers, with a lovely perfume, and flowering outdoors from March to May. Sow from June to August and remove the dark-green seedlings as soon as they appear, for these are the single-flowered plants. In mild districts in the south, they can remain in the open ground during winter with cloche protection if possible. In cold, exposed areas, they are best sown in boxes and wintered in a cold frame, and planted out after hardening off in March. They come in colours of light blue, rose-pink, white and mixed.

East Lothian stocks can be sown under glass during February and March when they will flower the same year from July until September. They can also be sown in October, wintered in a cold frame and planted out for summer bedding during the following spring. The colours include crimson, scarlet, rose, pink, purple, lavender and white. All stocks need a rich soil, and plenty of well rotted garden compost is the best plant food for them.

Pansies give best results when grown as biennials. Sow in boxes in a cold frame from May to June and plant out into their flowering positions during September and October. Outdoor sowings can be made on a well-prepared seed bed in May, and the seedlings pricked off into a nursery bed. Final transplanting can be done either in early spring or in the autumn following the sowing. Pansies enjoy a rich, moist soil, so plenty of garden compost is again called for. They will do well in an open position, or in a partially shaded one.

Violas, which are like small pansies, need similar treatment. Outdoor sowings can be made from April onwards, the seedlings being transplanted to nursery beds. Plant out into their flowering positions in autumn. There are very many varieties and an extensive colour range, both in pansies and violas.

BULBS AND CORMS FOR OUTDOOR FLOWERING

For someone making a fresh garden, there is nothing like a collection of bulbs for giving a quick display of colour. They are particularly trouble-free and it is an easy task to plant them into their allotted positions during September and October, and then wait for the lovely display which will come in the spring.

Unfortunately, buying named varieties of bulbs in a large enough quantity to give a good display can be quite costly initially, but against this is the fact that the bulbs can be used again for several years afterwards.

If the owner of a garden who wishes for a lavish display of bulbs cannot afford the quantity he requires, then it is a good plan to purchase some of those collections which are listed as for naturalizing and cutting. Parcels of daffodils and narcissi mixed can be obtained, or all daffodils or mixed tulips. I have grown these on several occasions and I have always found them to be very satisfactory. I have even grown them for the cut-flower trade. They are most inexpensive, and at the time of writing they are listed as follows: Daffodils and narcissi mixed at 250 bulbs for £1, or 500 for £1 17s. 6d. All daffodils at 250 for £1 10s. and mixed tulips at 250 for £1 or 500 for £1 17s. 6d. These prices vary very little through the years.

No one must make the mistake of only planting a few bulbs here and there, in isolated patches. They must be massed if they are to provide any satisfactory picture. Even in a small garden at least a hundred daffodils are really required.

The greatest problem of bulb growing for many people is knowing what to do with the bulbs after they have finished flowering. The space occupied by the bulbs is usually needed for summer bedding. Never cut down the foliage with shears, as I have seen some people do. As with all plants, the bulb manufactures much of its food by the aid of sunlight and the green colouring matter in the leaves called chlorophyll. The bulbs must be allowed to let their green leaves die down naturally, when much of the plant food contained in the leaves passes down to the bulb. This plant food enables the bulb to take a resting period and then produce further leaves and flowers during the following season.

When the owner of a garden has a convenient woodland or wild garden no problem as to how to dispose of the bulbs arises. Just dig them up carefully, keeping the roots as intact as possible; make a hole with a trowel and replant them in natural drifts in the woodland or wild garden, and water them well if conditions are dry.

Where no such easy way out exists, then a spare plot somewhere in the garden must be reserved for them, preferably in partial shade. Draw a drill across this plot to a depth of about four inches, then replant the bulbs here, putting in a prominent label to mark the spot. The bulbs can be planted here fairly close together and can be carefully taken up in September for replanting into their spring flowering positions. Never remove any foliage or cause damage to roots or bulb.

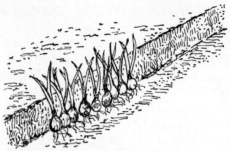

PUT INTO TRENCH THEN
COVER WITH SOIL

How to replant bulbs after flowering

Most of the bulbs are not particular about any special type of soil
and they will grow in most, including thin chalky ones, although here
the flowers do not usually attain a large size. I have found that bulbs
grow and flower better if all soils for them are improved by the
addition of a good quantity of garden compost, not buried too deeply,
and a good top layer of leaf mould. Larger flowers of finer texture,
with a longer flowering period, are produced in this way.

One of the most important points to remember in the growing of
bulbs for outdoor flowering is to get them planted early enough.
Daffodils need to be in the ground at the first opportunity in early
September and tulips by early October. They need time to settle down
before winter comes and to build up some further food supply. The
late planting of bulbs only results in short-stemmed specimens with
inferior flowers.

Bulbs can be used in a variety of ways in the garden. They can be
planted in formal beds with a carpeting of other flowers. They can be
used in masses by the side of a lawn or in natural drifts in woodlands
or on the edge of the wood. They also look very effective when planted
towards the front of a mixed border, that is a border of perennial
plants and flowering shrubs. Another suitable spot for bulb planting
is in the front of an established shrubbery, or at the sides of a long
drive to the house. One of the most natural settings for daffodils is in
grassland, or beneath trees in a cool, sheltered position.

Daffodils and tulips should be planted with a trowel, about four
inches deep. Daffodils are best spaced from nine to twelve inches
apart and tulips from six to eight inches apart, except for the fairly
new Giant Darwin Hybrid tulips which should be planted from eight
to ten inches apart.

Although some growers call all daffodils narcissi, I shall call
'daffodils' all those with long trumpets, and those with short cups
I shall refer to as 'narcissi'. This is how gardeners generally have

distinguished the two types for very many years and it will be more easily understood. People who call daffodils narcissi are quite correct, for the wild daffodil of the English woodlands is known as *Narcissus pseudo-narcissus*, but in a book of this nature, the generally accepted names will be preferred.

Something has been said of using bulbs for spring bedding displays in conjunction with other flowers. If wallflowers are chosen for carpeting with daffodils the dwarfer kinds would be the most suitable. Yellow and white daffodils with a carpeting of *Myosotis* (forget-me-not) or mauve and blue aubrietia, would be charming. Other suitable carpeting plants would be double white arabis, yellow, blue or white polyanthus, yellow, white or blue primroses, yellow alyssum, yellow, white or blue pansies or violas and the Siberian wallflowers, yellow or orange.

Daffodils, narcissi, tulips and other bulbs which have been used for forcing in the cool greenhouse or dwelling-house may be planted outside, when they have finished flowering. The woodland, wild garden, orchard or grassland suggests itself for these, where they will gradually build up into reasonable blooms. Not much can be expected from hyacinths so treated, as they rarely make any large flower spikes. They might do for the rock garden.

A bed consisting entirely of tulips is very striking, especially if it is composed of mixed colours. The early single tulips are very good for this purpose and a collection of Early Single Mixed Tulips will contain many fine varieties in an infinite array of colours. These all flower during April.

Tulips can be associated with other spring flowers, and forget-me-nots make a good carpeting subject. For combining tulips and *Myosotis* the following varieties of tulips can be used: of the single early tulips, 'Bellona', a sweetly-scented deep yellow; 'General de Wet', scented yellow flowers flushed with orange red; 'Rising Sun', buttercup yellow, and 'White Hawk'. Another arrangement would be *Myosotis*, with 'Pink Beauty', a carmine pink, and 'Van der Neer', which is rosy-violet.

Darwin tulips for association with forget-me-nots could be 'Clara Butt', an old variety but still very popular, deep rose pink; 'Princess Elizabeth', oval-shaped rosy-cerise, with a silver margin; 'Pandion', rosy-mauve; 'Queen of Bartigon', salmon-pink; and 'Snow Peak', pure white. Then the yellow shades, 'Niphetos', a lovely soft primrose; 'Sunkist', rich golden; 'Sweet Harmony', butter-yellow, edged with white; 'Mamassa', buttercup-yellow, with 'Snowpeak' as a neutral shade.

Aubrietia could be used in these schemes instead of forget-me-nots. Choose the blue shades.

Here is a list of some of the best daffodils, tulips and narcissi arranged in their different classes. The six petals at the back of the trumpet or cup are known as the perianth.

Trumpet Daffodils

NAME	COLOUR	REMARKS
'Dutch Master'	Golden yellow	Flowers turned upwards
'King Alfred'	Golden yellow	Later flowering
'Golden Harvest'	Deep golden	Large trumpets
'Fortune'	Orange trumpet, yellow perianth	Good contrasting variety
'Beersheba'	Creamy white	All over white
'Soirée'	Primrose trumpet, white perianth	Unusual

Pink Daffodils

'Louise de Coligney'	Narrow apricot trumpet, white perianth	Fragrant
'Mrs. R. O. Back-house'	Apricot-yellow flushed pink trumpet, white perianth	Small

Large-cupped Narcissi

'Armada'	Golden perianth, tangerine cup	New variety
'Binkie'	Lemon perianth, pale lemon cup turning white	Good type for floral art
'Birma'	Yellow perianth, scarlet cup	Flowers face upwards
'Red Rascal'	Yellow perianth, brilliant red cup	New variety
'Rustom Pasha'	Large yellow perianth, orange-red cup	Long lasting
'Duke of Windsor'	White perianth, apricot cup	Large flowers
'Ice Follies'	Creamy-white perianth, primrose cup	Early flowering
'John Evelyn'	White perianth, lemon cup, flushed orange	A popular sort

Narcissi with extra-large flowers

NAME	COLOUR	REMARKS
'Alverado'	White perianth, lemon cup	Frilled cup, deep lemon edging
'Aruba'	Creamy-white perianth, golden cup, edged orange	Deep lemon edging. A beautiful form
'Golden Spray'	Yellow perianth, golden cup	Free flowering
'Orange Monarch'	Creamy perianth, tangerine cup	Early

Small Cupped Narcissi

'Apricot-Attraction'	Creamy apricot, terra-cotta-red cup	A new colour
'Chunking'	Deep golden perianth, orange-red cup	Upward facing
'La Riante'	White perianth, scarlet cup	Good cut flower

Bunch-flowered Narcissi

These produce several fragrant flowers to each stem and are later flowering than the other narcissi.

'Cheerfulness'	Creamy-white with dash of yellow	3 or 4 blooms on tall stems
'Cragford'	White with orange-red cup	Very fragrant
'Primrose Beauty'	Primrose	Double, scented
Triandrus 'Silver Chimes'	Cream perianth, pale lemon cup	5–8 pendent flowers

Double-flowered Daffodils

'Golden Ducat'	Golden-yellow	Large
'Mary Copeland'	Creamy-white, gold centre, orange and lemon	Very attractive
'Snowball'	Snowy-white	Delicious perfume
'Texas'	Primrose, orange-red inner petals	Large blooms

Poeticus Narcissi

These are best known as the Pheasant's Eye Narcissi.

NAME	COLOUR	REMARKS
'Actaea'	White perianth, yellow cup, edged scarlet	Small cup
'Pheasant's Eye'	White perianth, greenish-yellow eye, edged crimson	May flowering

Jonquils

Single Jonquil	Golden yellow	Clusters of 3–5 flowers on 12-inch stem
'Trevithian'	Lemon	18 ins stem, 2–3 blooms

EARLY SINGLE   DOUBLE   LILY FLOWERED.

PARROT   DARWIN   COTTAGE

Types of Tulips

Single Early Tulips

These are April-flowering, have short sturdy growth and are especially useful for massing in beds and borders.

NAME	COLOUR	REMARKS
'Bellona'	Yellow	Sweet scent
'Brilliant Star'	Crimson-scarlet	Early
'Coleur Cardinal'	Deep crimson	Dark foliage
'General de Wet'	Yellow flushed orange-red	Good scent
'Pink Beauty'	Carmine-pink	White base stripe
'Van de Neer'	Rosy-violet	Large flowers

Early Double Tulips

'Electra'	Cerise-red yellow centre	Large
'Mr. Van der Hoef'	Canary-yellow	Long lasting
'Paul Crampel'	Crimson-scarlet	—
'Peach Blossom'	Rose-pink	Gold centre
'Purity'	Snow-white	

Giant Darwin Hybrid Tulips

The largest tulips, with brilliantly coloured flowers carried on erect, strong stems.

'Gudoshink'	Yellow, stippled with small flecks of cerise-red	A novelty
'Holland's Glory'	Orange-scarlet	Long petals

Lily-flowered Tulips

These have gracefully reflexed and pointed petals, and they are suitable for bedding and cutting.

'Aladdin'	Crimson-scarlet	Petals have narrow white ribbon
'Alaska'	Soft yellow	—
'Golden Duchess'	Bright yellow	.
'Marietta'	Cerise-pink	—
'White Triumphator'	White	—

Parrot Tulips

These have quaint, irregularly shaped flowers. The petals are laciniated or fringed, and they have a brilliant colour range.

'Black Parrot'	Glossy, almost black	Tall, stiff stems
'Blue Parrot'	Lavender-blue	Curled and puffed

14

NAME	COLOUR	REMARKS
'Fantasy'	Cerise-pink	Feathered and splashed emerald
'Red Parrot'	Brilliant red	Broad, fringed petals
'Texas Gold'	Golden-yellow edged red	Later flowering
'Van Dyck'	Cerise-pink	Lightly touched with green

Darwin Tulips

'Clara Butt'	Rose-pink	Popular
'Elizabeth Arden'	Cerise-scarlet	Early
'Excellent'	Cerise-red	Very large
'King Harold'	Blood-red	Dusky violet base
'Niphetos'	Soft primrose	Very graceful
'Pandion'	Rosy-mauve	Early
'Paul Richter'	Crimson-scarlet	—
'Perry Como'	Cerise-scarlet	Recent
'Pilot Light'	Scarlet, yellow centre	—
'Princess Elizabeth'	Rose-cerise, silver margin	—
'Queen of Bartigon'	Salmon-pink	—
'Queen of Night'	Maroon-black	The darkest tulip
'Sunkist'	Golden	—
'Snow Peak'	Pure white	—
'Sweet Harmony'	Butter-yellow	White edging

Cottage Tulips

These are May-flowering. They comprise a very wide range of beautiful colours.

'Artist'	Terra cotta with green and salmon-pink	A unique variety
'Dido'	Cerise-red	Fragrant
'General De La Rey'	Salmon-orange, lilac and lavender shading	Long lasting
'Golden Harvest'	Yellow	—
'Ivory Glory'	Creamy-white	Turning pure white
'Magician'	White picotee with edge of violet	Unusual
'Marjorie Bowen'	Cerise-pink, edged orange	Elongated flowers

NAME	COLOUR	REMARKS
'Marshal Haig'	Crimson-scarlet	Often 2 flowers per stem
'Mirella'	Old rose, edge apricot	—
'Mrs. John T. Scheepers'	Canary yellow	A large yellow
'Northern Queen'	Rose-pink	White base
'Smiling Queen'	Salmon-cerise edge, silvery pink	Long lasting

OTHER BULBS FOR THE GARDEN

People who like hyacinths flowering outdoors in early spring, as well as some forced flowers in pots in the house, should plant them in a sheltered position near the house, where their wonderful fragrance can be enjoyed to the full.

It must be remembered that during their second and subsequent flowering seasons, they do not produce so fine a spike of blossom as during their first year of flowering. They are expensive, and perhaps just a few near the house windows would suit most people. Second-size bulbs can be purchased at a lower price, and these will give quite a good display in the garden. They should be planted in well-prepared soil that contains plenty of good garden compost and leaf mould. Plant during September about five inches deep and from six to eight inches apart. Water well in spring if there is a dry spell.

Here is a list for outdoor flowering, giving the colours and flowering season:

'King of the Blues'	Violet-blue	Late
'Myosotis'	Azure-blue	Mid-season
'Ostara'	Deep-blue	Mid-season
'City of Haarlem'	Yellow	Late
'Innocence'	White	Mid-season
'Anne Marie'	Salmon	Early
'Lady Derby'	Shell-pink	Late
'Jan Bos'	Crimson	Mid-season
'Orange Boren'	Apricot-pink	Mid-season

Crocuses are inexpensive, when it is considered that if they are planted on lawns and in grassland where they can remain undisturbed, they will multiply and flower for many years. Who does not welcome the first gay crocus which does so much to dispel thoughts of winter, and heralds the spring? At first they should be planted in September about four inches deep and six inches apart. They also appreciate some well-rotted garden compost and leaf mould. They are good subjects for drift planting in woodland areas. Here is a list of varieties with their colours:

'Giant Purple'	Deep purple
'Golden Yellow'	Deep yellow
'Queen of the Blues'	Silvery lavender
'Remembrance'	Deep violet
'Snowstorm'	White, orange stigma
'Striped Beauty'	White, striped purple

The irises, grown from bulbs, consist of Dutch, Spanish, and English Species. Prepare the flowering site by digging well and adding plenty of good garden compost.

The Dutch varieties will flower and thrive almost anywhere from early June onwards and are another splendid subject to fill the 'June Gap'. Plant three or four inches deep and six to eight inches apart in partial shade or in full sun. They make wonderful cut flowers. The following is a list of the best varieties:

'Blue Champion'	Bright blue, yellow blotch
'Golden Harvest'	Glowing yellow
'King Mauve'	Lavender-mauve, yellow blotch
'Wedgwood'	Porcelain blue
'White Excelsior'	Snow-white, yellow blotch

The Spanish varieties flower just after the Dutch sorts, are a little smaller, but very fragrant. Plant and cultivate in the same way as for the Dutch varieties. Here is a short list of varieties:

'Canjanus'	Clear yellow
'King of the Blues'	Deep blue, yellow blotch
'Prince Henry'	Standards, purple-brown, bronze falls with golden blotch

English irises are beautiful flowers and very easily grown. They flower in July and the same treatment as for the others is required. They are usually listed in mixed varieties, which include some colours and shades of blue and purple, together with white.

Muscari, or Grape Hyacinths, are very charming spring-flowering subjects. They will grow near trees or shrubs and are a grand sight when seen planted in masses in grassland, in full sun. They should be planted in September three inches deep and three inches apart. 'Blue Spire' is a new variety and very free-flowering. 'Heavenly Blue' is fragrant and of a gentian-blue colour. *M. plumosum,* the Feather hyacinth, has plume-like clusters in an unusual shade of violet. *M. tubergenianum* is a free-flowering species known as the Oxford and Cambridge grape hyacinth. When in full bloom, it has two colours, light blue and dark blue.

Ranunculus is usually planted outdoors during February and March, but in mild districts they may be planted in October. The small roots are like little claws, and they need to be planted firmly six to eight inches apart and two inches deep with the claws pointing downwards into the soil. A well-drained soil with plenty of garden compost and a sunny position are the requirements for the cultivation of this colourful plant.

Scillas are charming bluebell-like flowers which greet us with their beauty and bright colours early in spring. They are splendid subjects for naturalizing in grassland where they can remain undisturbed. The best is *Scilla sibirica* which only grows to a height of four inches, but is a lovely shade of bright blue. *S. amethystina* is a lovely variety with broad-based tapering spikes of many florets. It is lavender-blue. *S. tubergeniana* produces three or more stems with four-inch flower spikes. It is light blue with a darker stripe, and flowers in the open at the same time as the snowdrops. *Campanulata* hybrids are really giant bluebells. They should be left undisturbed in their flowering positions. 'Myosotis' is sky-blue and 'Queen of the Pinks' a soft rose-pink.

Snowdrops (*Galanthus*), such a welcome sight when not much else is in flower, struggling to give a show of blossom even in January, are everyone's favourite. Plant four inches deep and leave undisturbed. There is a double snowdrop, and one called *Galanthus elwesii*, the largest one, besides the ordinary single snowdrops.

Anemones are easily grown and very popular. The site for them should be well prepared with plenty of good garden compost worked into the soil, which should be well-drained. Plant the corms from September to November, three inches deep and six inches apart. A fairly sheltered position suits them best. For a succession of bloom plant the corms at fortnightly intervals. In very cold districts anemones can be grown well with the protection of cloches. Here is a short list of anemones, with their colours mentioned:

fulgens	Vivid scarlet, yellow centre
'De Caen'	Rose, scarlet, lavender, purple and white varieties
'His Excellency'	Vermilion-scarlet
'Syphide'	Rosy-mauve
'St. Brigid'	Various colours

Chionodoxa, Glory of the Snow, shows its flowers at the same time as the crocuses and should be planted in September two inches deep with about eighteen bulbs to the square foot. If left undisturbed the masses of blue and white colour will appear year after year, increasing in size and beauty. *C. gigantea* is a lovely lavender-blue with white centres. *C. luciliae* is a brilliant blue with white centres, and *C. sardensis* is a vivid, rich royal blue.

EARLY-FLOWERING CROCUS SPECIES

There are a number of Crocus species which bloom very much earlier than the ordinary large crocus. They have elegant blooms which give many distinctive, delicate colourings. Each corm will give several flowers and once planted they will multiply from year to year. These have already been mentioned in Chapter 5, together with their varieties.

HARDY CYCLAMEN

The hardy cyclamen prefer semi-shaded positions and are suitable for planting under or near trees. The plants grow together and form an attractive carpet of ornamental foliage. Plant one to two inches deep and from four to five inches apart. Varieties are as follows, with names and colours:

C. atkinsii	Crimson
C. coum	Crimson, white and pink
C. neapolitanum	Pink and white
C. repandum	Crimson

Allium is an ornamental garlic; it will grow anywhere and is long living. It will make a lovely show of bloom in early summer. The tall varieties are excellent subjects for use in flower decorations. *A. azureum* has compact heads of cornflower blue during June and July, and grows to a height of two feet. *A. moly* has bright heads of yellow blossom. *A. ostrowskianum*, with large circular heads of pale pink flowers, is only six inches in height. The long pointed buds of *A. pulchellum* make good cutting sprays of reddish-violet flowers during July and August. Their height is from one to two feet.

GLADIOLI

Many people give up growing gladioli when they lose all their corms during a very hard winter. It is only occasionally, however, that we get a winter of a severity which makes the storing of gladioli corms and dahlia tubers extremely difficult. Gladioli corms need to be very carefully attended to and stored at all times. Dampness is a sure cause of losses, and so is frost. Let the foliage die right down and become nearly brown before lifting the corms from the ground. When cutting flower spikes for the house be careful not to cut the remaining foliage. This is needed to build up the new corm forming below in the soil. After the corms, together with the withered stems (see later, page 217), have been lifted in autumn, lay them out in the sun for a few days to thoroughly dry and ripen. This is one of the important stages of preservation, for many corms rot during the winter because this stage has been skimped. Turn them over several times during the course of drying and bring them into the shed or other shelter in late afternoon, before dampness starts to appear. Put them out again on following days during dry periods.

Gladioli should be grown in every garden, for they are extremely easy. They will flourish in almost any type of soil, including those with a solid chalk sub-soil. They respond best to a deeply worked one which has been enriched with plenty of good garden compost. They should be planted where they can be sure of plenty of sunshine, as most of the garden varieties have been developed from corms which originally grew in South and Central Africa. There is a rare gladiolus which is native to Britain and only found in parts of the New Forest— and, according to records, was once found in parts of the Isle of Wight. I have been very fortunate in finding one specimen of this lovely wild plant in the summer of 1965, in an area of the New Forest where it has not been found before. This is *Gladiolus illyricus* and its colour is a bright magenta with cream blotches. They are spread by wind-borne seed and take about four years to come to flowering size. The single plant which I saw in flower was growing eight miles from its nearest neighbour, with high belts of conifer trees between them, so it gives some idea of how seeds are spread and germinated in their wild state.

Gladioli should be planted together in a mass where they can make a brilliant show. They are not good bedding plants, for when in flower not all of the blooms face the same way. There is no way of finding out which way they will face when planting the corms. They are also too tall for bedding work, except perhaps in a large park, associated with some groundwork flowers. They make wonderful cut flowers, but for flower arranging in the home or for competitions generally it is best to grow the *primulinus* hybrids, Butterfly type or the Miniature gladioli. The large-flowering class are good for splashes of colour in the border by themselves, with backgrounds of hedges, shrubberies, or some other arrangement of flowering shrubs. They are also suitable for the mixed border. Another good spot for the large-flowering gladioli, when grown for cut flowers, is in a portion of the kitchen garden where they can be grown in rows supported by bamboo canes or other stakes.

Gladioli are not hardy and so the corms cannot be left in the ground throughout the winter, although they have come through safely during mild winters in some areas. They should be lifted and replanted annually.

Prepare the ground for gladioli thoroughly in the autumn by digging deeply and adding plenty of good garden compost; this will suit gladioli better than farmyard manure, although this can be used if it is available and there is no compost. On no account must fresh manure be used. Gladioli will grow in a little shade although full sunshine is much more preferable.

The ideal soil for gladioli is a cool, fairly damp soil, but well drained. The corms must never be planted in waterlogged soil. When planting the corms the soil should be very friable so that moisture and air can enter. The corms will not start into growth if moisture is not available at the time of planting and for a few weeks after.

Obtain gladioli corms from a good seed or bulb merchant to start with. They can then be saved from year to year, and if an increase of corms is wanted, the tiny cormlets which are clustered around the new corm when it is removed from the soil, can be saved. These can be sown during the following spring on a spare bed and will grow to flowering size in about three years.

The planting of the corms can take place at any time from March until the end of May when weather and soil conditions are suitable. There is a wide choice with the spacing of the corms, which can be placed about three inches apart for a massed display, but better results would be obtained if they were put about one foot apart each way. Make the planting hole with a trowel and let the corm lie flat on the soil at the bottom of the hole. Plant four inches deep; this will allow room for the new corm which will grow on the top of the old one.

If gladioli are planted at weekly intervals, and early, mid-season and late varieties are used, a continuous display of bloom will be assured, until the frosts come.

When the gladioli are well above the soil, keep the Dutch hoe fully employed, destroying the weeds and creating a dust mulch on the surface. Keep the site free of weeds at all times, because weeds in any part of the garden will rob the legitimate plants of much-needed plant food, besides acting as host plants for many pests.

If a long drought is experienced, gladioli must be given a thorough soaking of water. All gladioli will need staking and supporting, especially when beginning to show flower spikes. Natural hazel or other staking material cut from a copse, or gathered from the forest floor, is the most inconspicuous staking for gladioli, but bamboo canes could also be used if the flowers are being grown in the kitchen garden for cut flowers. The stakes must be as high as the gladioli will grow, and sometimes several ties with green soft string are necessary, beginning near the base of the foliage and finishing carefully somewhere near the top of the flowering spike.

If the large-flowering or other gladioli are left to flower without cutting, the dead flower spike should be cut from the plant before the seed has had time to develop, and all the leaves left intact. When the time arrives for the gladioli to be lifted from the ground, cut down the withered foliage to within six inches of the ground and lift carefully with a garden fork. Good tie-on labels should be affixed to each plant or bunches of the same variety.

Follow the drying process mentioned earlier and then lay the plants in a cool and airy frost-proof shed or room, but do not attempt to dry off the plants or corms by artificial means or too quickly. After about a month has elapsed, the foliage will part from the corms easily and then the old corm will also part from the new one. Take nothing away which will not part easily from the corm. A light dusting of flowers of sulphur is sometimes advisable if any damp conditions are likely to be encountered while the corms are in store.

When the corms have received their final cleaning, lay them in seed boxes or other suitable receptacles, so that they are not touching each other, and make sure they are stored where air can circulate freely and where frost and dampness are excluded. Go over the corms at frequent intervals, discarding any which have rotted or are diseased.

Here is a list of some of the best varieties of each section. Early, mid-season and late varieties are indicated by the initial letter E, M or L after each variety.

Large-flowering Gladioli

'Chanson'—M	Light cherry-pink
'Dr. Fleming'—E	Salmon-pink, creamy throat
'Summer Pearl'—M	Shell-pink and orange, cream throat
'Toulouse-Lautrec'—M	Apricot-salmon, yellow throat, marked chestnut
'Mata Hari'—E	Creamy-white, lemon lip, carmine blotch
'Leif Erikson'—M	Ivory-sulphur, cream throat
'Wembley'—M	Pure white
'White Angel'—M	Paper white
'Green Woodpecker'—M	Lime-yellow, wine-red throat
'Flower Song'—E	Bright golden-yellow
'Pactolus'—E	Apricot-yellow, cherry blotch
'Bohemienne'—M	Primrose, faint cerise markings

'Ardent'—E	Brick-red, deeper tips and throat
'Rotterdam'—M	Scarlet-vermilion
'Sans Souci'—M	Brilliant scarlet
'Victory Day'—E	Light cerise-scarlet
'Blue Conqueror'—L	Deep violet-blue, light centre
'Flying Dutchman'—M	Rich violet-blue, blue-black blotch
'Lavender Giant'—M	Silvery lilac
'K. & M.'s Blue'—M	Deep violet-blue
'Tintoretto'—E	Soft lavender, small white throat
'Jamaica'—M	Scarlet, maroon tips
'Marshal Montgomery' —L	Deep reddish-maroon
'Keukenhof'—M	Light carmine-rose, creamy throat
'Uhu'—M	Ash-grey and salmon, mahogany, yellow throat

Primulinus Hybrid Gladioli

'Chrysantha'	Rich yellow, small scarlet throat
'Grace'	Soft coral-pink and white, yellow falls
'Loveday Holman'	Cerise-suffused salmon, golden throat
'Lemon Drop'	Pale primrose
'Red Bay'	Rich glowing chestnut
'Pamela Mummery'	Biscuity salmon, cream throat
'Rosy Maid'	Apricot-salmon, yellow falls

The above gladioli are smaller and more dainty in appearance than the large-flowered kinds.

Miniature Gladioli

These flowers are a little smaller than the butterfly varieties. A very attractive and distinctive feature is the frilling and ruffling of the petals.

'Leprechaun'	Mimosa-yellow, deeper falls, crimson lines
'Greenbird'	Sulphur-yellow, small marked throat
'Southport'	Ivory, cream throat
'Dancing Doll'	Cream, flushed salmon
'Hyprose'	Salmon, flushed rosy-carmine
'Coral Reef'	Deep salmon-orange sheen, scarlet and cream throat
'Zenith'	Rich shell-pink

Butterfly-type Gladioli

These have florets which are about half the size of the large-flowering types and they are not so tall. Most of them have very attractive throat markings and blotches and they remind one of some of the world's most exotic butterflies.

'Donald Duck'	Lemon, orange, scarlet blotch
'Walt Disney'	Sulphur-lemon, red blotch
'Little Diamond'	Deep amber, overlaid rich reddish-orange
'Gipsy Love'	Orange-flame, crimson-scarlet blotch
'Ice Follies'	Ivory-white, cream throat
'Topolino'	Canary-yellow, cherry-red blotches
'Madam Butterfly'	Shell-pink, salmon and violet throat
'Melodie'	Salmon-pink, vivid scarlet throat
'Mickey Mouse'	Deep cream, cherry throat
'Bibi'	Pale rose, feathered carmine, cerise-carmine throat
'Ariso'	Pale primrose, crimson-purple throat
'Euterpe'	Rosy-purple, dark blotch of garnet-red on lower central petal
'Happy'	Flame-scarlet, deep scarlet centre blotch
'Roulette'	Apricot-yellow, cerise blotches

It is much better to plant one or two of each variety of gladiolus than to have a dozen or so of the same colour. The mixed colours give greater interest and look more showy. A fascinating way of growing gladioli is to purchase a dozen or so of mixed unnamed varieties. It is delightful to watch them coming into bloom and not to know what colours they are going to show. Often many unnamed seedlings are included as well as the named sorts. Try to grow some gladioli of various colours from each section. The Primulinus, Butterfly and Miniature types are the best ones for indoor floral decoration, but the large-flowering types can be used in large containers, in conjunction with foliage like that of copper beech. These are suitable for large rooms, in the hall, or for public functions, but are rather large and heavy for ordinary vases and are easily toppled over.

THE HERBACEOUS BORDER AND PERENNIAL FLOWERS

Perennial-flowering plants flower each year and their roots do not die during winter. Just a few years ago, it was fashionable in all large gardens to have what was known as a herbaceous border. This was a wide border of perennial-flowering plants. Today much use is made of the mixed border. This is a border of any shape which the owner of the garden fancies, and it is stocked with flowering shrubs, bulbous plants, and perhaps some annuals as well as perennials.

The herbaceous border still has much to offer however, for a well-planned and planted border of perennial plants can be a truly magnificent spectacle. The herbaceous border must be fairly wide and as long as a medium or small garden will allow. It must be boldly conceived to give any satisfaction. Perennial plants growing on their own, in any odd spot, would not be tolerated in a well-managed garden.

Perennial plants need plenty of room in which to develop; a minimum width of seven feet is essential for any beautiful effect to be created. A double border with a grass path running through the centre is an ideal way of making this permanent feature of the garden. The grass path should be at least four feet wide, so if the garden is not large enough to provide all this space, then one single border would be better than two narrow ones, where every plant is cramped and struggling for growing room.

The site for the perennial border should be open, sunny and sheltered from east and north winds. If possible, put it where it can be viewed from the house, and so that you can look along it, or be able to look down the grass path.

The border can be straight, or it may curve round at the end, or it may have curves here and there along its length. A double border looks more effective if it has a grass path running through the centre, lawns on either side, with a hedge or a collection of flowering shrubs planted back some distance from the border. This will give a background to show up the flowers, and to provide shelter from the winds. The hedge must not be too close to the border, or it will take valuable plant foods from the flowers. In this connection, try to avoid heavy feeders such as laurel or privet. A well-weathered stone or brick wall could be used instead of a hedge, or in conjunction with one.

When choosing plants for the border, we must consider their time of flowering and distribute the colour along the entire border accordingly. So if we have, say, a subject which flowers in May, we must plant several of these at various stages along the border, although they need not all be of the same colour.

One of the most important features of a perennial border is the method of blending our colours. By choosing carefully, as described for the annuals border, we can create something really beautiful in colour harmony and contrast.

Before making a plan of the proposed border on paper it would be advisable to have a look at a really good herbaceous border in some large garden nearby. To see the actual growing flowers, with all their different habits of growth and diversity of colour, is the best way of learning how to plant a border. The border seen will give plenty of ideas of colour combination, but originality can still be the keynote, and your own border can actually be an improvement on the one observed.

Do not necessarily place all of the tall plants in the back row. Bring one or two a little forward, and try to create as natural an appearance as possible. When planning the border, have a good nurseryman's coloured catalogue in front of you. Order your plants in plenty of time for an October or November planting. Make sure that you order flowers which will suit your particular soil, although there are plenty of plants to suit almost every kind, excepting perhaps a waterlogged one.

Make a plan on paper, allowing three to six plants of the same sort to each grouping. Have the measurements of your site written down and allow for adequate space between the various plants. Make the grouping as informal as possible and the distances between each plant will vary according to the subject. Small plants to the front of the border will need about a foot of space between them, and taller ones in the middle and at the back, according to height, will need more space. Hollyhocks and delphiniums and like subjects need up to two and a half feet of space.

When choosing the subjects for the herbaceous border, some of those which are really the backbone of any perennial border should be used. These generally include such well-known favourites as delphiniums, Russell lupins (in non-chalky soils), Michaelmas daisies, iris, phlox, *Chrysanthemum maximum* (single and double), helenium, paeony, pyrethrum, *Achillea*, *Echinops* and *Scabiosa*.

I have not given a plan for a herbaceous border as is seen in most gardening books. Once the general principles of preparation, planting and culture have been laid down, gardeners will like to make their own designs, remembering correct colour harmony or contrast. Here are some good perennials which are not included in my other lists:

Monarda 'Croftway Pink'	*Salvia virgata nemorosa*
Campanula 'Telham Beauty'	*Echinops* 'Taplow Blue'
Heliopsis incomparabilis	*Doronicum plantagineum excelsum*
Helleborus orientalis	*Sidalcea* 'Elsie Heugh'
Catananche caerulea	*Kniphofia* 'Lord Roberts'
Nepeta mussini	*Geranium ibericum*
Anchusa 'Opal'	*Astilbe* 'Etna'
Eremurus himalaicus	*Geum* 'Lady Stratheden'

One may not be able to afford a complete collection of the plants which I have suggested for the herbaceous border. Get what you can and gradually extend and build up the border, by adding plants year by year, or by propagation, by seed sowing of perennials, or by root division. Do not accept root divisions and rooted cuttings from friends unless you have seen the parent plant growing and in flower. If you can obtain some selected young growth from the outside of a clump of a good, fairly new variety, then all is well if the plant fits into your border plan and colour formation. Too often, little pieces chopped from someone's border plant are put hopefully into the garden, but the person who does this is soon disillusioned.

Remember that the stocks held by experienced nurserymen are specially chosen for vigour, freedom from disease, and ability to make rapid root growth. Also, only the best or newest varieties are supplied.

If the whole border intended for perennials cannot be filled for a couple of seasons, the gaps may be filled in with annuals and biennials until sufficient stock has been built up. Do not expect a brilliant show from the perennial border during the first year; give it time for the plants to become established and used to their new surroundings. A common mistake with many is that they divide their perennial plants and replant the divisions much too early. No root division or thinning out will be needed for at least four years. This is one of the reasons why it is important to give the plants plenty of space during the initial planting and also why it is equally important to prepare the soil thoroughly at the start.

Having selected the most suitable site, dig the plot at least two spits deep and put into the bottom of the trench plenty of good, well-decayed garden compost. Farmyard manure can be used instead, but it must be well-rotted; on no account must the roots of young herbaceous plants come into contact with fresh manure.

All perennial weeds must be removed during the digging of the plot. The plot will need to be dug in early spring in readiness for an autumn planting, but it may be dug during the autumn previous to planting. Before the consignment of plants arrive from the nurseryman, have sufficient labels prepared. Stout wooden white-painted labels still seem to be the most serviceable for herbaceous borders. Do not have them too large or they will look out of place, but make them large enough for the names to be quite legible. Put the lettering on neatly in block capitals, using either one of the Flomaster-type black felt-nibbed pens or ordinary black oil paint. Of course, whatever you use must be waterproof.

If the plants have been ordered early enough they will arrive some time in the autumn. Do not unpack them until you are ready to plant, and if there is frost, or if the ground has been swamped by heavy rain, leave them unpacked in a cool shed but never in a heated building. They will remain in good condition for several days because the roots are packed in moss or some other moisture-retentive material. Never leave the roots exposed to drying winds while planting. Take one plant at a time, settle it in, and leave the remainder with their roots covered by sacking or other material.

Lay out the packages close at hand but not on the planting site; they would be in the way there and hamper planting. Do not get the varieties mixed, keep the nurseryman's labels on them until you have completed your own labelling. Begin planting according to your plan, by starting at the top left-hand corner of the border and planting the whole of the back row first.

The best tool to use for planting is a good trowel. Make the planting holes large enough for the roots of each plant to be spread out according to the nature of the root growth. When the planting of an individual item has been completed, the crown of the plant with its dormant buds should be just below the surface.

Some plants will have retained a little foliage. Have this just above the surface of the ground. Scatter the fine soil carefully over the roots by hand, then firm with the hands, finally pressing the soil around the plant very firmly indeed. Leave an indentation in the soil around each plant, so that water will run into the centre of the plants and not away from them. Give all plants a thorough soaking when all planting has been completed. Erase footmarks with a small rake or the Dutch hoe.

Some perennial plants do not like being disturbed for several years; some will not flower the first year and perhaps not even during the second year. Among these are the paeonies and irises. Most of the other perennials can be divided about every four years.

Not a lot of attention will be needed for the herbaceous border during the first year. Constant hoeing with the Dutch hoe will be necessary in order to destroy annual weeds and to loosen the soil for the air to enter. Watering will be required during any prolonged dry periods. One of the main tasks during the growing season, as with any other border, will be the supporting and tying of tall and intermediate plants. Keep the supports as inconspicuous as possible. Natural twigs and branches, picked up in a forest or copse, are the best if they can be obtained. If other wooden stakes are used see that they are painted or dyed some unobtrusive moss- or pastel-green. Do not use a brilliant glaring green or a prominent white. Always tie plants with green twist or soft fillis string. Do not tie too tightly, allow enough room for the shoots to grow and swell.

When the plants are in flower, remove all dead flower heads in order to prolong the flowering season. When there are no more blooms to come, do not be in too much of a hurry to cut down the stems; leave them until they have become brown and withered. It is a good plan to provide a mulch for the plants during autumn after the first flowering season. Let it remain on the surface all winter and dig it in carefully during early spring. Be careful not to thrust the garden fork deeply into the roots, and keep a little distance away from any shallow rooting plants.

Plenty of slug-killer pellets will be required around the plants during spring and early summer, especially after rainy periods. Slugs particularly like the young shoots of delphinium and lupins. Well-weathered soot can be put around the plants as a deterrent.

Unlike the annual border, the herbaceous border cannot be deeply dug and manured with compost annually, so I emphasize the importance of thorough preparation of the plot at the onset. Any manure given once the border has been planted and has become established will consist of top-dressings, and these can be applied during spring and autumn. If any additional manure is needed, a sprinkling of four ounces of bonemeal to each square yard may be given during early spring.

When the plants begin to grow vigorously during the second spring, and if they are producing a good many over-crowded shoots, some may be removed gradually, leaving five or six per plant. This treatment will produce much finer flowers and will give the shoots growing space.

PERENNIALS FOR THOSE WITH LIMITED SPACE

There will be many people who only have limited space and can only grow a few of the perennials but nothing like a full herbaceous border. What shall they grow?

First, all the perennials chosen must grow in company on the same site. Some of the most colourful, satisfying and easily grown perennials are aquilegias, delphiniums, Russell lupins, paeonies, irises, Michaelmas daisies, and phlox. Russell lupins can only be grown on a lime-free soil unless they are raised from seed annually.

The delphiniums, lupins and tall Michaelmas daisies can be planted at the back of this site, the irises, paeonies and phlox can be brought towards the centre, with the dwarf Michaelmas daisies in the front.

One could hardly find a more showy or more easily grown perennial than the paeony. Although many of the newer varieties of certain plants are an improvement on the older ones, one could hardly say this about the paeony. The old-fashioned double crimson paeony, *P. rubra plena,* is still a most magnificent plant. We have seen this colourful flower in almost every country cottage garden for a great number of years.

Once planted, paeonies do not like to be disturbed for some years; and as they grow best in a rich deep soil, deep digging and plenty of garden compost should be the rule during the preparation of the flowering site. Paeonies will flower well in full sun or in partial shade. They are best planted in autumn but can be planted in spring. A top dressing of well-rotted garden compost should be given annually in the autumn. Remove all flower heads as they fade, but leave on the stems and leaves until spring. Cut them from the plant in early spring, for during the winter they will have offered good protection against frost.

Besides the well-known border paeonies, there are the so-called Chinese paeonies. If some of these are planted, they extend the flowering season, as most of them bloom from early June onwards. The colour range of the Chinese paeonies is greater. There are light and dark reds, white, pinks, and many intermediate shades, including lilac. All of these are fragrant, and there are double and single kinds.

The Tree Paeonies are really small shrubs which flower in April and May; these are best grown where they are sheltered from the morning sun. No pruning is necessary.

Here is a list of varieties of Paeonies to choose from:

Single Paeonies

'Torpileur'	Large purplish-carmine
'Bowl of Beauty'	Outer petals bright rose, inner petals small-toothed and a lemon-yellow
'White Wings'	White, masses of golden stamens

Double Paeonies

'Albert Crousse'	Bright pink, crimson centre
'Auguste Dessert'	Semi-double salmon, edged white
'Lady Alexander Duff'	Delicate pink, golden anthers
'Reine Hortense'	Lavender-pink, flecked salmon centre
'Sarah Bernhardt'	Apple-blossom pink
'Felix Crousse'	Brilliant crimson
rubra plena	The old double red
'Duchesse de Nemours'	Sulphur-white
'Emilie Lemoine'	Ivory-white
'Festive Maxima'	Pure white, red blotch
'Solange'	Creamy-white, suffused buff and salmon-pink

Aquilegias (Columbines) are fairly easily grown from seed, although they sometimes take a long time to germinate. Some seed may lie dormant for several months until the seeds have been subjected to frost. Producing the plants from seed is the cheapest way to secure a collection of these delightful spring-flowering plants, so useful as cut flowers.

Prepare a seed bed by producing a good tilth, and sow the seeds during April; when large enough, transfer them to a nursery bed and let them grow on and develop until September when they can be planted into their flowering positions. Sow thinly and put a good label at the ends of the rows, so that their position can be seen if germination is slow. Put down slug-killer pellets when the seedlings appear above the surface.

The following types can be grown from seed. 'McKana's Giant Hybrids' have flowers that average four inches across, with spurs three or four inches long. There are shades of blue, purple, pink, maroon, red and yellow with many attractive bi-colours. 'Hensol Harebell' is a lovely dwarf form only growing to a height of a foot, with blue and white flowers. 'Toy Town' is a miniature race of aquilegias with either double or single flowers in a wide range of colours. All of the varieties can be purchased from nurserymen as plants in the autumn, together with the following popular varieties:

'Crimson Star' has a rich colouring of crimson with a conspicuous white centre. It grows to eighteen inches. 'Blue Bonnet', twenty-four inches, has large delightful mid-blue flowers; 'Pink Bonnet', its companion, grows to a foot and a half.

The delphinium is happy in most soils but it will benefit from a little garden lime worked into the surface soil during the spring, some time after its autumn planting. Remember not to apply lime at the same time as garden compost or farmyard manure is being put into the soil.

The delphinium needs plenty of organic material and deeply dug soil if fine spikes of flowers are to be produced. There is nothing quite like the blue of a delphinium, and it has a place in all gardens. The owner of the small garden should aim at medium-sized spikes of flower, and in very small gardens perhaps the 'Belladonna' types would be more suitable. These grow to a height of three feet and are dainty and well branched.

There has recently been a new introduction from America called Delphinium 'Connecticut Yankees'. These are bushy plants growing to a height of two and a half to three feet. They are excellent for cutting. The colours range through light and dark blues, purples, lilacs and lavenders. If the seed of these plants is sown under glass in February or March, they will bloom during the same year.

All delphiniums may be grown from seed, although they do not breed true, as modern delphiniums are hybrids. Seed may be sown in the same way as for aquilegias, but more space must be given between each plant in the nursery bed and when transplanting to their final flowering quarters. Two feet of space between each plant should be allowed at the final planting, but six inches more would be better if space permits.

If the gardener, after delphiniums have been grown, would like to propagate some of the varieties he specially likes, then he can take some cuttings. When the plants are growing away in early spring, and some nice thick shoots have grown from the old plants, remove a few of these with a heel of the old plant attached. The stems of delphiniums are tubular and roots are formed much more easily on the woody sealed-up heel. Some of the soil will have to be removed from around the crown of the plant in order to take the cuttings. Insert the cuttings into small pots or seed boxes and place them in a cold frame away from direct sunshine. Delphinium cuttings are not quick rooting and it is generally about six weeks before they are ready to be potted up into individual pots and allowed to grow on. They should be planted out into the open ground in early summer. When roots have formed, and at all times afterwards, delphiniums should be given plenty of air, as like the sweet pea they are quite hardy. When inserting the cuttings in the pots, and when potting on, make the soil firm with the hands around the cuttings, and keep moist at all times. If any flower spikes appear while the rooted cuttings are in pots, nip these out, because at this stage the plant will need all its energy to build up a good root system.

During the second year of growth the delphinium will throw up many shoots; and if good flowering spikes are required, some of these should be thinned out. Put plenty of slug-killer pellets around the delphiniums as soon as shoots are seen, and perhaps a week or so before.

Staking will have to be attended to as soon as the delphiniums have reached about a couple of feet in height, as the tubular and brittle stems are very easily broken by winds. One of the best methods of staking is to thrust thin bamboo canes, one in front and two behind the plant, to form a triangular shape and then to contain the plants and flowering spikes within this area, by tying soft green string at intervals around the canes.

The plants must never be allowed to become dry during a hot summer. Give plenty of water. Delphiniums usually send up a second lot of flowering spikes during August and September. If the gardener requires established named plants from the nurseryman for his initial planting, here is a list from which a selection can be made.

Tall Varieties of Delphiniums

'Bermuda'	Cobalt, suffused violet-black with gold eye
'Blue Pearl'	Deep sky-blue
'Sidney'	Mediterranean blue, white-striped eye
'Swan Lake'	White, black eye
'William Richards'	Electric blue
'Lady Guinivere'	Semi-double mauve, white eye
'Etonian'	Cobalt-blue
'Father Thames'	Rosy-violet and gentian blue
'Duchess of Portland'	Ultramarine, white eye
'Lorna'	Deep blue, dark brown eye
'Merry England'	Deep blue, suffused pale rosy-purple, white and rose eye
'Garter Knight'	Heliotrope merging with cobalt-blue, black eye
'Blackmore's Blue'	Sky-blue, white eye
'Beau Nash'	Deep purple and dark mauve, black and gold eye

Belladonna Delphiniums

'Blue Bees'	Clear sky-blue
'Isis'	Rich gentian blue, shaded plum
'Persimmon'	Sky-blue
'Pink Sensation'	Pure pink
'Wendy'	Deep gentian blue
'Lamartine'	Deep violet-blue

Anyone with a very chalky sub-soil will not be able to grow lupins to perfection, but with the addition of plenty of good top soil containing plenty of garden compost and garden peat, some reasonable flowering plants can be cultivated. The best way to achieve this is to sow frequently and produce new flowering plants almost annually. The lupin does not have a very long life on the chalk.

The modern lupin is now one of the best and easiest herbaceous plants to grow on soil that suits it. For the modern Russell lupin, our thanks are due to old Mr. George Russell, the Yorkshireman who grew lupins for years in his garden and on his allotment. He kept on selecting, discarding and crossing lupins until at last he produced the new race of lupins which bears his name.

Russell lupins are quite easy to grow from seed, and as so many beautiful colours and bi-colours are represented, they will fit into most gardens. If the seeds are sown in boxes, in the cold frame in early spring, they can be brought into flower during the first season. They can be sown in the open ground during April. Prepare a seed bed in the usual manner and sow thinly, keep the seed bed free of weeds. If the seedlings are kept moist, lupins usually make fairly quick growth, producing some good plants ready for planting into their flowering positions during September. As the seeds have very hard outer skins, it is sometimes advisable to nick them slightly with a sharp knife, away from the mark which shows where they were adjoining the pod. Be careful with this operation, as the seeds are glossy and the knife or razor-blade will easily slip.

The bed for lupins needs to be deeply dug and plenty of garden compost or farmyard manure should be put in. Lupins will need staking and plenty of water during dry spells. They can be propagated from root cuttings and by division in March and April, if special colours and varieties are required.

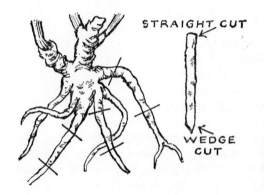

Root cuttings from Lupins. Root cuttings can also be made from anchusas, verbascums, hollyhocks, perennial statice, romneyas, phlox haniculata, gaillardias and seakale.

For root cuttings, a section of thong—as the fleshy roots of the lupin are termed—is cut away from the lupin root system and then cut into further lengths of about three inches. The end of the cutting farthest away from the crown of the plant is cut into a wedge-shape and the end nearest the crown is cut square across the top. They are put into pots, the cuttings being put into position with the wedge-shape end inserted into the soil. The root cuttings are placed around the edge of the pot and soil is pressed around them firmly. The square-cut end of the cutting should be just covered with soil. These will root in a cold frame, but are better if a cool greenhouse is available where advantage can be taken of a little heat, with a night temperature of 50°F. sufficing. If some named varieties of Russell lupins are wanted, here is a list from which a choice can be made:

Russell Lupins

NAME	COLOUR OF BELLS	COLOUR OF STANDARDS
'Day Dream'	Peach-pink	Golden-yellow
'Jane Eyre'	Violet-blue	White, blue base
'Lady Fayre'	Rose	Rose, shaded coral
'Lilac Time'	Rosy-lilac	Cream and mauve
'Comet'	Cerise	Ivory, flushed cerise
'Lady W. Thompson'	Pale pink	Yellow turning white and pink
'Rhapsody'	Deep rose	Crimson
'Serenade'	Orange-red	Crimson, flecked gold
'Thundercloud'	Violet-blue	Violet flushed rosy-mauve
'Wheatsheaf'	Golden	Deep yellow

Self-coloured Russell Lupins

'Lady Gay'	Pale yellow
'Cherry Pie'	Cherry red
'Fireglow'	Orange-flame
'Joy'	Reddish-orange
'Masterpiece'	Deep purplish-red

There is nothing difficult about the growing of irises. The two essentials for success are a well-drained soil and a sunny situation. They are fond of lime, and when they are being planted the bulbous rootstock (called a rhizome) should be set on the surface of the soil, with the roots firmly held under the soil. They are propagated by

DIVISION PREPARED   KEEP RHIZOME NEAR SURFACE

The propagation and planting of Irises

division, usually soon after flowering, if conditions are damp enough. They can also be divided in the autumn. The *Iris germanica*, or bearded Iris, which is the one usually grown in the herbaceous border and sometimes in special iris borders, has flowers of two distinct parts—standards and falls. These are very often of different colours but where both standards and falls are of the same colour, the term 'self' is used to describe this.

Good well-dug soil, with plenty of decayed garden compost with a little garden lime, if not on chalky soil, will suit the irises. One will have to purchase from a good nurseryman for the start of a collection, unless friends have some good varieties which they are dividing.

Here are some good varieties:

Iris Germanica or Bearded Iris

'Maréchal Ney'	Chestnut-red self
'Lambent'	Gold standards, maroon falls
'Sandia'	Deep pink, suffused yellow self
'Aline'	Azure-blue self
'Député Nomblot'	Coppery-bronze standards, claret-crimson falls
'Benton Baggage'	Rose standards, red-lilac falls
'California Gold'	Deep golden-yellow self
'Cheerio'	Red flushed old gold, self
'Lilias'	Strawberry-pink and gold self
'Senlac'	Mulberry red self
'White City'	White self
'Alfred Edwin'	Primrose standards, white falls
'Amandine'	Pale cream, flushed lemon ruffled self
'Benton Evora'	Orchid purple self
'Black Hills'	Blue-black self
'Blue Rhythm'	Cornflower blue self, silvery overtone
'Great Lakes'	Pure blue self
'Lady Mohr'	Oyster standards, greenish-yellow falls with red-violet patch
'Ola Kala'	Orange-yellow standards, flame falls
'Ranger'	Crimson self
'Rocket'	Chrome standards, orange-chrome falls
'Solid Mahogany'	Mahogany-red self
'Starshine'	Deep cream, blue and white self
'Wabash'	White standards, deep violet falls bordered white

There are two other irises grown as herbaceous plants; these are

Iris sibirica and *Iris stylosa*. *Iris sibirica* has grassy foliage and it is an ideal plant for damp situations, but it will flourish in any soil that does not dry out. Therefore plenty of garden compost for moisture retention is essential. 'Emperor' is cornflower blue, 'Perry's Blue' is sky blue, and 'Snow Queen', milk white.

Iris stylosa has large and lovely scented flowers of lavender-blue which are produced during the winter. To encourage this iris to produce flowers instead of foliage, plant in full sun and in poorish soil. This plant is now known as *Iris unguicularis*.

If you are one of those gardeners who have recently taken over an established garden filled with clumps of those weedy old varieties of Michaelmas daisy with such tiny insignificant flowers, then take them out immediately. They should have been discarded years ago and they have been occupying valuable space without contributing anything of value to the beauty of the garden. The handsome newer varieties are just as easy to grow as the old ones and they will give a brilliant splash of colour and provide sprays of lovely flowers for cutting. Many people have little knowledge of the possibilities of the Michaelmas daisy, so long have these been neglected and planted anywhere, often without water, and certainly deprived of adequate plant food.

The Michaelmas daisy will respond well to liberal treatment and provide a magnificent show of blossom. Many of the new sorts have a wonderful range of colour. Dig the site deeply and put in plenty of good garden compost. An additional manure of a sprinkling of bone meal or hoof and horn meal raked into the surface soil is also excellent, as there is a long growing period from very early spring, until the frosts come to spoil their autumn flowers.

The best time to plant established plants from the nursery or elsewhere is during autumn. When a group of plants has become well grown and reached a sizeable clump—this usually takes about four years—they can be divided in order to increase stock. The best way to do this is to employ two hand forks, inserting them into the clumps, after they have been lifted entirely from the soil; put them back to back, and lever the clumps apart. This action will force away pieces with roots attached, ready for planting in the bed or elsewhere. The best plants come from healthy, strong portions which have been taken from the outside of the old plants. Plant out the rooted portions by using a trowel, making firm, and watering in.

The perennial Aster (which is what the Michaelmas daisy is) will throw up many more shoots than are required for good-quality flowering sprays, so thinning of the shoots will become necessary. Leave about five strong ones to each plant. Staking will be necessary for the tall varieties. Similar staking to that recommended for the delphinium will be suitable. Use well-camouflaged stakes, with no glaring colours. Do not think that very thick, heavy stakes will be required, for the stems of Michaelmas daisies are rather thin. In addition to the tall and medium Michaelmas daisies there are some very beautiful dwarf kinds which are bushy and very useful for the front of the border. The following varieties will offer a good selection:

Tall large-flowering Hybrid Michaelmas Daisies

NAME	COLOUR	HEIGHT
'Blandie'	White	5 ft
'The Dean'	Carmine-pink	4 ft
'Eventide'	Deep violet-blue	3 ft
'Fellowship'	Clear pink	3 ft
'Festival'	Rosy-lilac	$3\frac{1}{2}$ ft
'F. M. Simpson'	Purplish-blue	$3\frac{1}{2}$ ft
'Harrington's Pink'	Salmon-pink	4 ft
'Marie Ballard'	Powder blue	3 ft
'Picture'	Reddish-carmine	3 ft
'Plenty'	Lavender-blue	4 ft
'Red Sunset'	Rich red	3 ft
'Sweet Seventeen'	Pinkish-lavender	$3\frac{1}{2}$ ft
'Treasure'	Deep lavender	4 ft
'Apple Blossom'	Cream, overlaid pink	3 ft
'Crimson Brocade'	Ruby-red	3 ft
'Destiny'	Rosy-violet	3 ft
'Little Pink Lady'	Pink	$2\frac{1}{2}$ ft
'Moderator'	Deep violet-purple	$3\frac{1}{2}$ ft
'Peerless'	Heliotrope	4 ft

Dwarf Hybrid Michaelmas Daisies

'Sonia'	Bright pink	2 ft
'Audrey'	Lavender-blue	1 ft
'Autumn Princess'	Lavender-blue	15 ins
'Blue Lagoon'	Deep blue	$1\frac{1}{2}$ ft
'Jean'	Violet-mauve	15 ins
'Lady in Blue'	Rich blue	10 ins
'Peter Harrison'	Rose-pink	1 ft
'Rose Bonnet'	Pink	10 ins

The Phlox is one of the gayest of the summer flowers and is most striking when planted in groups of three or more of the same variety. As they usually bloom during the driest part of the summer, and are surface rooting, they require rather more water than other border plants. Hand weeding will have to be carried out, as the roots are too near the surface for the hoe to be used.

A sunny position or partial shade and a well-dug soil with plenty of garden compost will suit the phlox. A good top dressing of well-rotted compost or very well decayed farmyard manure should be applied annually in the spring. Thin out any weak shoots. The phlox is best propagated by root cuttings or by using the thinned shoots as ordinary cuttings and potting them up in April. The phlox must be given adequate staking and tying before they become too tall, as they easily become bedraggled and are laid low by strong winds.

A selection can be made from the following good varieties. All are three feet in height:

'A. E. Amos'	Fiery scarlet
'Aida'	Crimson-purple
'Balmoral'	Soft rosy-purple
'Blue Lagoon'	Lavender-blue
'Brigadier'	Crimson, shaded carmine
'Fanal'	Flame-red
'Europe'	White, crimson centre
'Frau A. Buchner'	Pure white
'Lady Mowbray'	Carmine-red
'Marlborough'	Purple
'Sir John Falstaff'	Rich salmon-pink
'Undine'	Delicate lilac
'Border Gem'	Deep violet
'San Antonio'	Deep purple-red
'Vintage Wine'	Rich claret
'Eventide'	Mauve-blue, flushed lilac
'Norah Leigh'	Pale lilac
'P. D. Williams'	Apple-blossom pink
'Mother-of-Pearl'	White, flushed rose

SWEET PEAS

The sweet pea has been called the Queen of Annuals and I know of no better title for it. There is no flower which will respond more rewardingly to good treatment and give a greater return for the work and care lavished on it than the sweet pea. Nor is it possible to find another annual which will give flowers from the end of May until the end of October, which is possible in the south and in sheltered parts in the south-west of England.

To grow sweet peas successfully it is important to obtain the best seed, which should always be purchased from a well-known seedsman who specializes in growing sweet pea seed.

To obtain exhibition blooms the plants must have a long period of growth. Autumn sowing is always best. Some gardeners and nursery-men sow in slight heat in January, in a cool greenhouse, but the plants and blooms produced from this method are never as fine as are those grown from autumn-sown seed. Seed should be sown during mid-September in the Midlands and north and during early October in the south of England.

Send for a sweet pea catalogue in July and according to the space available for sweet peas (they are best grown in the cut-flower depart-ment) order a few varieties. Sweet peas are usually sold in packets containing twenty seeds, and half-packets are supplied. It is difficult for a beginner to judge how many seeds he will need. It is best to order a few more than are needed to make up for any losses. These losses can be due to failure to germinate, severe frost, the drying-out of pots, depredations of field mice, birds and slugs.

As a rough guide for ordering, a plot which is fifty feet long and six feet wide and is intended for sweet peas only can accommodate three rows with a foot between each plant. So this would be 150 plants. At this rate 16 half-packets would give 160 plants or 10 spare seeds to cover losses. Usually there are more than ten seeds in packets so marked. This quantity of plants which I have mentioned would probably be too many for most gardens. Fifty plants would be an average number, or five half-packets.

I shall now give a list of modern varieties which I have grown and found the best for decoration and all-round purposes.

'Gypsy Queen' was put on to the market during 1965 and it is a large one with grand texture and of an unusual colour of ruby-red; it is just about the best red variety. 'Elizabeth Taylor' is a large beautiful flower of clear mauve, a warm and rich colour; the blooms are frilly and it is a vigorous grower. 'Gertrude Tingay' is a flower of deep self lavender and it gives a large perfect flower of solid texture. 'Harrow' has large crimson flowers with a touch of mahogany. 'Jupiter' is undoubtedly the best sweet pea I have ever grown. It is vigorous, has a very large bloom, and is of a striking colour, a bright mahogany enlivened by a lustrous sheen of purple, reminding one of a beautiful ripe plum. When growing among other sweet peas its form and colour are really outstanding, compelling attention from all who see it. It is also wonderful to look upon when arranged with other sweet peas in a bowl in the house. 'Mrs. C. Kay' is a bright, clear lavender with large flowers and plenty on each stem. 'Pearl' is well named, for this beauty really does resemble a pearl in colour. It is large and of a different shape to other varieties mentioned, of a delicate cream pink, soft and opalescent. It is also a vigorous grower. 'Princess Elizabeth' caused something of a sensation when it was first exhibited at the Chelsea Flower Show. It is one of the loveliest of all sweet peas. The flowers are beautifully formed and are quite unlike any other sweet peas in colour. It is salmon-pink on creamy buff and the colour continues to the base of the flower. 'Reconnaissance' is a two-colour sweet pea (these are called picotees). It has a pink edging to the cream-ground flowers. 'Swan Lake' is the best white sweet pea I know, with flowers of perfect form and texture and nice strong stems. 'Stylish' has ousted many of the old blue sweet peas. It produces flowers of mid-blue of enormous size and they are well placed on the stems. This blue is another beautiful colour which gives pleasure to all. Often a dark colour is required in a flower arrangement and for this purpose I have always grown an older variety called 'Maroon King'. Seeds of this variety have to be ordered early if required. It is about the darkest variety which can be found, a dark maroon, and is not often seen in a florist's shop. 'Mandy' is a silvery lavender, one of those lovely pastel shades so much sought after for flower arrangements.

The black, hard-coated seeds of some varieties will have to be chipped on the opposite side to where the pea was joined to the pod. Just cut a little of the outer husk with a sharp knife or razor-blade; this usually chips off quite easily. As with chipping lupin seeds, be careful with sharp instruments, and cut away from the hands rather than towards them. It is usually indicated on the seed packets which seeds need chipping. On the other hand some of the softer-skinned peas such as 'Princess Elizabeth' sometimes rot if put into ordinary John Innes compost. The seed soil mixture which is put into the pots or boxes for these varieties will therefore need a larger proportion of silver sand.

Sweet pea seeds are best sown in 3-inch pots which are a little deeper than the usual pots. They need to be at least four inches in depth. The plants will make a lot of root before being planted out and so are best sown individually, one seed per pot. The potting soil must contain plenty of moisture-retaining material, as more losses among sweet pea plants are caused through pots drying out during winter, when there is prolonged frost (with no watering possible) than are caused through actual frost. Some good medium loam with a little silver sand and plenty of rotted leaf mould I have found to be the best sowing medium, although John Innes Compost No. 2 can be used.

Put good drainage in the form of crocks into the bottom of the pots, and fill the pots with the sowing medium. Leave a little room at the top for easy watering. Make a hole in the centre of the soil with a pencil about three-quarters of an inch deep, put in the seed and cover with soil. Then give the pots a good watering with water which has had the chill taken off. The name of the variety can be written in black pencil on the side of the pots, or a label may be put in the pots.

The cold frame will have been made ready to receive the plants. Have the glass clean, as light is important during the short winter days. Spread a covering of ashes on to the floor of the frame to discourage slugs and to help drain any water which may be spilled during watering.

Try to space the pots so that they do not touch each other. They will need covering with brown paper until germination takes place, and the glass lid or light of the frame should remain closed. When the shoots can be seen pushing their way through the soil, remove the brown paper and open the light a little to let in some air.

If there are not enough pots available at seed sowing time, fairly deep seed boxes can be used, spacing the seeds about two inches apart each way. Put in some broken pieces of pot at the bottom of the box to ensure good drainage.

After the seeds have been sown and the pots or boxes watered, and the brown paper put on, no watering must be done until the shoots are showing above the soil. Do not use builders' sand in the seed-sowing compost as this will dry out too quickly and it will cake hard, preventing air from reaching the seeds.

A close watch will now have to be kept for mice, especially for field mice if you live in the country. Let the cat wander around the garden freely if you have one; if not, when the lights are open set several mouse traps inside the cold frame.

Leave as much space as possible around each pot so that each seedling has abundant air, light, and room for development. Space around the pots also makes it easier to water, and for fixing in twiggy small branches for supporting the seedlings until transplanting into the open ground takes place. As soon as the seedlings have made three pairs of leaves, their tips need to be nipped out to encourage the seedlings to produce basal growth. The sweet pea does not build a good flowering plant from the original leader and it dies away eventually as developing lateral shoots take its place.

When the shoots are well above the soil, leave off the light of the cold frame entirely to expose the seedlings to the air freely at all times. Replace the light at night but leave it open a few inches during mild weather.

During times of very hard frost, during January and February probably, leave the light on day and night and cover up the frames at night with old sacking, old carpets, or straw. Remove the covering at about 9 a.m. and replace at about 4.30 p.m. When frost has gone

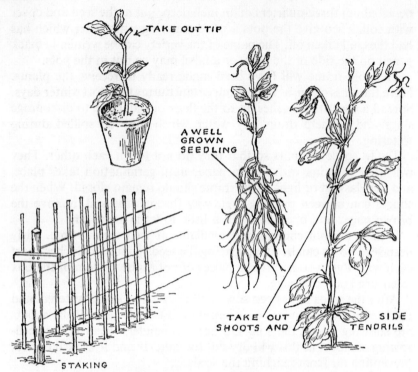

TAKE OUT TIP

A WELL
GROWN
SEEDLING

TAKE OUT
SHOOTS AND

SIDE
TENDRILS

STAKING

The growing of Sweet Peas by the cordon method

and a thaw has set in, carry on as before, allowing as much air as possible to reach the seedlings, only closing the lights during heavy downpours of rain. During mild days in winter, the lights can be taken off entirely during the day.

While the plants are in the seedling stage in the cold frame, and as soon as shoots appear, put around the pots, and on the floor of the cold frame, a number of slug-killer pellets. These will have to be renewed from time to time. If the plants are attacked by any insects such as greenfly, dust the plants with derris dust.

The seedlings must be kept moist during winter but they do not usually need much watering. There is usually enough gentle rain from time to time which can be taken advantage of. Do not let the pots dry out at any time as this is usually the cause of many casualties during the time the plants are the occupants of the cold frame. Keep twiggy branches of brushwood among the seedlings throughout the whole of the period they are in the cold frames; do not let the stems spill over the pots and trail along the floor of the frame.

During early March, or a week or two before the plants are put into their flowering quarters, the pots need to be stood outside the frame day and night for a final hardening off before being planted out some time in March or early April, according to the weather and suitable planting conditions.

The site for the growing of good sweet peas should be sunny but sheltered from high winds. The soil must be thoroughly prepared during autumn or early winter. Some gardeners have said that there is no need to dig a trench for sweet peas, that ordinary digging one spit deep, and incorporating manure as you go along, is sufficient for the growing of good sweet peas as it certainly is for many other plants. I have tried this method together with others, and I have found no method which is equal to the old method of trenching.

The depth you dig your trench depends on the depth of good soil you possess in your garden. Some people can dig a trench three spits deep before coming to poor sub-soil or clay. However deep you dig your trench, remember to put the good top soil on one side of the trench and the sub-soil on the other; be sure not to mix the two. I usually dig my trench for sweet peas at least three spits deep, and I put a layer of well-rotted, good garden compost on the bottom of the trench about nine inches in thickness. Well-rotted compost is the best of all organic manures for sweet peas.

Mark out your trench to two or three feet in width, according to how many rows you are growing. Dig out the soil with a spade, dig over the bottom of the trench with the garden fork and put in a good thick layer of well-decayed garden compost. Sometimes it will be necessary to tread this in. Put back the sub-soil first and then the good top soil, firming it now and again. When the whole of the soil has been put back leave the surface soil as rough as possible so that it can take advantage of the winter frosts and snow.

Some time in early spring, the stakes for supporting the climbing sweet peas must be erected. There will need to be a stout post at each end of the rows, sunk firmly into the ground to a depth of three feet. To each post will be attached a spreader which will extend to the width of the rows. At each end of these spreaders wires are stretched tightly from post to post. To the wires, firmly fixed by winding round the wire a couple of times, are bamboo canes or better still, hazel or other coppice stakes. The stakes will be thrust firmly into the ground and will be a foot apart. They should be about ten feet high. It is always better to have two strands of thin wire running the length of the rows between the supports, one about eighteen inches from the ground and the other about three feet six inches from ground level.

Under good cultivation methods, sweet peas will reach a great height, with a large leaf area. During the strong winds of July and August they are easily swept away unless strong supports are provided. The middle of March is early enough for the planting out of sweet peas, but the gardener may have to wait until April. Never plant out or sow any garden subject by date; wait for the right conditions. Plant when there is a good tilth, with the soil just moist, not too wet and not too dry.

Use a trowel for planting, make a hole deep enough and wide enough to accommodate the ball of soil and roots. Make the planting hole up close to the supporting stake. Knock out the plant from the pot carefully, take away the crocks from the base and plant carefully but firmly. There has been a lot of discussion among professional gardeners as to whether it is best to unravel the long white roots which fill the pots, or whether to plant the ball of soil intact. I have found it best to plant each one just as the soil and roots come from the pots. I give the pots a small amount of water just before planting out and I find that then the soil will come away quite easily from the pots. Often some of the roots are partially unravelled too.

Let any unravelled roots sink carefully to the bottom of the planting hole and then firm some fine soil around them. Let the rest of the ball of soil rest firmly against the sides of the hole and firm around this some fine soil with the hands. Leave an indentation in the soil around the finished planting to enable water and moisture to flow through to the roots. Leave all basal and lateral shoots intact at the time of planting. I let all these stay for a while until the plants start to make strong growth. This is so as to have a reserve in case some of the shoots are broken or eaten by slugs or snails. Later on remove all shoots except the healthiest and strongest-looking one. Train the shoot up the corresponding support. At the time of planting, put the short twiggy supports from the pots around each plant. This will support them until they have grown tall enough to be tied to the stakes; it will also give some protection from cold winds or a late frost.

When all the plants have been transplanted finish the work by watering well in. One label at the start of a group of varieties, clearly printed, should be inserted into the soil or fixed on to one of the supporting canes. Scatter slug-killer pellets freely along the rows, and renew at intervals. The plants will now appear to be lying dormant for three to four weeks and hardly any top growth will be observed, but they are extending their root system during this time. Top growth will soon spread rapidly and during May you will be kept very busy tying to the stakes, and removing all tendrils. All ties must be made loosely enough to allow for expansion as the main shoot gradually thickens up to about half an inch in diameter.

The selected shoot should be tied loosely but firmly with raffia, soft fillis string or soft green twist. Sweet pea rings made specially for the purpose are handy for very busy people or at odd times when one has run out of other tying material. They have to be used carefully or the stems are very easily split by the wire from which they are made.

The main stem, as it grows, should be treated as a single cordon and all lateral or side shoots taken out as soon as they appear. All tendrils should be removed at an early stage in their growth. During June, growth goes on at great speed, and tying and removal of laterals and tendrils will need to be carried out twice weekly. Use the Dutch hoe between the rows to remove surface weeds and to let in air to the soil.

If plenty of compost has been put into the bottom of the trench during the autumn preparation, not a lot of watering will be required. If watering is needed during a long drought, always give a good soaking. A small amount of water will do more harm than good.

Never feed sweet peas by the application of top dressings of artificial manures. If plenty of compost is lying down below in the bottom of the trench this will be sufficient manure for the plants throughout the whole of the season. The roots will reach and feed on this compost at just about the time when they most need it, as they start producing flowers. Frequent applications of nitrogenous artificial manures will soon bring disease to any plant and even kill a sweet pea plant. When watering, be careful not to splash the lower leaves during hot sunny periods; they can easily become scorched if the leaves get wet. The leaves turn white and then yellow and the gardener will be mystified by the happening.

The gardener will have to go over his plants very frequently during the height of the summer, tying, removing side shoots, tendrils and spent flowers. Never let dead flowers stay to produce seed pods. He will also have the very pleasant task of cutting very many choice blooms for house decoration.

The only pest which may trouble him during the growing season is the greenfly. These are not usually much in evidence on sweet peas, but they do occasionally arrive. They are quite easily controlled by dusting with derris powder. Sometimes the colourful bullfinch will attack a few buds just as they are showing colour, but if the cat is encouraged to wander around the garden, and plenty of water is put down for birds, there is not usually a lot of trouble.

When the plants have reached the top of the supporting stakes they can be detached, brought down, taken along the ground to a different support, and trained up again to produce many more flowers until the frosts arrive. With this procedure great care must be taken, as at this period of the summer the main stem is quite brittle and very easily broken. First, select a plant at the end of a row, and another one about eight feet away. Cut the tying string from the first plant, and lay the haulm along the ground to the stake which is eight feet

16

away. Carry out the same procedure with the other plant and then train up the haulms by tying them to their new supports. This is done until all the plants are trailing up a fresh support. Some will be going in one direction along the rows and some will be travelling in the opposite direction When all the haulms have been trained to a new support in this way, the parts which are trailing along the ground can be raised from the ground a little, by tying raffia around several haulms and then tying them to the bottom of stakes at intervals. When this work has been completed the growing main stems should be tied to their supports with the growing tip about nine inches from ground level.

Sweet peas flowers for the house should be cut with the bottom flower fully open and with the next one above it in bud. It is best to gather the flowers first thing in the morning rather than when the blooms have been in full hot sunshine. Cut with scissors as the tugging by hand from the leaf axil often causes damage to the plant.

After the frosts have arrived and the haulms have withered, remove them from the supports and take the supports from the ground. Clean the supports and stack them under cover or in as dry a place as possible. Fresh stakes will, if looked after, last about three years. Dig over the vacant ground and put in compost as you go and use the ground for another crop the following year. If possible grow sweet peas on a different site each year.

There are other ways of growing sweet peas as well as on the single cordon system. The other methods will not produce such large exhibition blooms. A piece of ground can be manured in the autumn with garden compost, left rough for the winter weather, and raked down to a fine tilth during early spring. A seed drill can be drawn, and after the seeds that require chipping have been attended to, they can be sown about half an inch deep in the open ground. Pea sticks are then inserted when the plants appear above ground. The sweet peas are allowed to wander up among the pea sticks, and no side shoots or tendrils are removed. In this way very many flowers are produced for garden decoration and for cutting. They are usually much smaller than those grown on the single cordon system.

Another method of growing sweet peas is to carry out the above method, but to sow the seeds in the open ground during autumn. Some losses are bound to occur through severe frost and field mice. The plants can be protected by glass cloches until early spring, then little damage will be experienced. The plants can be also protected by bracken or straw, removing this material during the day or during mild periods.

With both of these systems of growing sweet peas, attention will have to be given to the control of slugs, birds, and mice. I have seen magnificent masses of bloom from autumn sowings in the open ground in Norfolk, in sheltered spots near tall hedges.

For the person who has not the time to spare for all the tying and the removal of side shoots and tendrils, a further method is available. Make an autumn sowing in the cold frame and grow on in the same method as for exhibition blooms. Plant out in early spring and let the plants ramble among pea sticks in a natural manner without removal of tendrils or side shoots. Reasonable-sized flowers are produced in this way and it obviates the risk of losing expensive seed in the open ground by an autumn sowing outside.

An exciting way of growing sweet peas is to purchase a packet of mixed seed from a sweet pea specialist, instead of the usual named varieties. You will not know what colours or varieties are going to appear until they start to come into flower. The mixed packets usually contain some of the best named sorts as well as some unnamed seedlings. Whichever method of growing sweet peas is favoured, do not forget to pinch out the tops of the young seedlings when they have made three pairs of leaves.

There are several other kinds of sweet peas which can be grown but none of them are so fine as the ordinary sweet peas which have been described. None of them are suitable for exhibition or for growing on the single cordon system.

Seeds can be obtained of some of the very old varieties and these are known as the 'Old-fashioned Sweet Peas'. They have small plain flowers but these give out a very strong perfume. The new Multiflora Sweet Pea called 'Galaxy' is an unusual new type producing long sprays of five to seven fragrant flowers, and it is very vigorous. It is only really suitable for bush growing. Cuthbertson 'Floribunda' Sweet Peas are fairly new and they come into flower earlier than the ordinary varieties. They are useful for early flowering under glass. 'Dwarf Mixed Colour Carpet' is a mixture of dwarf carpeting sweet peas which are suitable for the front of borders. 'Zvolanek's Plenti-flora Sweet Peas' are an American type having five to eight blooms per stem, but are not suitable for exhibition blooms. Sweet Pea 'Dwarf Bijou Mixed' are from America and can be grown without supports. Their height is twelve to fifteen inches and the flowers are large and frilly. Unwin's 'Mixed Stripes' are a mixture of unique striped sweet peas.

If the gardener has no facilities for raising his own plants from seed, strong plants can be purchased from nurserymen in spring. These have usually been sown in January in heat and are not so fine as autumn-sown ones. The very best plants are obtained by the gardener himself when they are raised and grown in the manner which has been described. Keep all sweet pea plants growing along as hardy as possible, allow as much air as you can into the cold frame at all times. Leave the light off on all mild days in winter, only keeping it completely closed during very severe weather.

The perennial *Gypsophila* is about the best flower to mix with sweet peas in vases. 'Bristol Fairy' provides billowing masses of small white double flowers on wiry stems. 'Flamingo' is similar in habit but the flowers are lilac-pink. 'Rosy Veil' has delicate pink double flowers. *G. paniculata* produces clouds of small white blossoms.

The annual Gypsophila is also very lovely when mixed with sweet peas. It is called *Gypsophila elegans* and there are white, pink and crimson forms. The seeds need to be sown at fortnightly intervals during spring and summer, as they finish flowering rather quickly.

ROSES

No garden is really complete without the addition of some roses, either bush, standard, climber or rambler. Good roses can be grown on almost any kind of soil except in poor sand or gravel, or where there is only a very thin covering of soil over solid chalk. Some ramblers, notably 'American Pillar', will even grow here.

During recent years very many new roses have been raised. Some of them are an improvement on the old varieties and there is certainly a wider range of colour among them, but many are not nearly so vigorous or so long-living as the older sorts. One must be prepared to replace rose bushes from time to time.

An exception can be made with the variety called 'Peace', which is one of the most vigorous of roses and more disease-resistant than almost any other variety.

Before purchasing an initial stock of roses, have a good look at some growing and flowering during June and July in a good nursery. Note the more vigorous ones and make a choice of colour and formation of bud and flower. Many of the newer red varieties are very similar in colour.

It is very unwise to buy roses from a market stall or street vendor unless the seller is a well-known rose grower.

It would be useful to know the meaning of the different descriptions of the various types of rose. Hybrid Perpetuals are so called because they come from crosses between a number of types (hence 'hybrid'). In actual fact they are not so 'perpetual' as they only usually produce one good show of blossom per year. They are still grown by many rose enthusiasts.

Hybrid Tea roses have been obtained by crossing Hybrid Perpetuals with Tea Roses. They are, at present, still the predominating class of bush roses although the Floribundas are becoming more and more popular each year. The Hybrid Tea roses flower freely over a long period, often from early June until Christmas. This is especially so if all dead flowers are removed; and if, after their removal, the stalk is cut down to just above a shoot bud in the same manner as when the bush rose is pruned. The introduction of the Hybrid Tea roses greatly increased the range of colours.

Tea roses are so called because their perfume has been likened to that of fresh-made tea. They are free flowering, with many lovely shades of colour, but they are not too hardy and are often killed during a severe winter. For this reason they are not extensively planted in this country, although they are still grown in France.

Multiflora roses are climbing roses which have large clusters of blooms. Pernetiana roses are a cross between the Austrian Briar and the Hybrid Tea. This cross produced many shades of yellow and orange. They are named after their producer, M. Pernet Ducher.

Polyantha roses are crosses between Multiflora roses and Hybrid Teas. They are dwarf rose bushes producing clusters of flowers in a variety of colours.

Floribunda roses are hybrid polyantha roses or polyantha roses crossed with other species. They are very similar to polyantha roses but have larger flowers, freely borne in trusses and useful for many purposes. They are suitable for rose beds, borders, edging, low hedges if lightly pruned, and to bring brightness to the front of the shrubbery.

Climbing roses are mainly climbing varieties of the Hybrid Teas, and very beautiful they look against the background of a light wall of the house. They should be planted against a south or south-west wall.

Wichuraiana roses include most of the popular rambler roses. They are the roses which produce very long new shoots from the base each year and long lateral growths from old shoots. They are very vigorous-growing roses and will quickly cover walls, archways, pergolas, pillars, old tree stumps or trellis work.

The Noisette roses have similar characteristics to the Wichuraianas and most varieties are strongly scented.

Shrub roses include the old Hybrid Musk roses and there are also some new roses in this section named after their raiser Wilhelm Kordes, and called Kordesii. The Musk roses are perpetual flowering and brightly coloured, between four and six feet in height. The richly scented flowers vary in size and are borne in clusters. The new Kordesii race have great vigour and hardiness and are continuous-flowering. Here, too, the flowers are in large clusters.

Moss roses are so called because of the lacy moss upon the stems and sepals. When in bud they are most exquisite and they open into wonderfully fragrant blooms of the old-fashioned cabbage form.

Standard roses are usually Hybrid Teas which have been budded near the top of a tall-stemmed wild briar or other stock. They bloom at eye level and are sometimes used when there are large beds of roses to relieve the general flatness of the beds. When growing standards, very good specimens must be obtained, otherwise they are best left out of garden schemes. A badly-grown standard rose at eye level can provide a somewhat discordant note when it is growing among other choice bush roses.

Weeping standards are rambler roses which have been budded to the top of the stock, so they are really rambler roses growing from the top of a stout stem. As the shoots and lateral growths are unable to climb or ramble they grow downwards like a weeping willow. As specimen trees in the centre of a lawn, or to one side, or at some other focal point of interest, they can look really lovely, but they, too, must be well-grown trees. They must be well staked or they will soon be carried away or broken by winds. The safest way to grow them is to train them over a specially built umbrella-shaped trainer. The Fancy or Miniature Roses have been described in the chapter on rockery plants.

Although roses will grow on almost any soil the deep, heavier soils seem to suit them best if the site is well drained. The best time for planting roses is in November, so the rose bed should have been well prepared and have settled down before this time. Roses are best grown in beds of their own. Dig the bed or border reserved for the roses deeply and put some well-decayed garden compost at the bottom of the trench. Do not have any garden compost in the top soil, as no organic manure must come into contact with the roots of new young roses. Farmyard manure is too strong for them. When the roses have become well established, top dressings of garden compost or well-rotted farmyard manure can be applied annually. If the soil is deficient in lime, a little garden lime should be sprinkled on to the surface soil and lightly forked in before planting. Although November is the best planting time, roses can be planted at any time from October to early March if soil conditions and weather are suitable.

Before ordering roses, work out how many you will require for the allotted space. When they are planted, bush roses will need at least two and a half feet of space each way between the most spreading shoots after pruning. More space can be given if plenty of room is available. Never cramp roses; give them enough space at the start, as it is more difficult to move them later on.

As soon as the bushes arrive from the nurseryman unpack them carefully, trying to avoid breaking any small branches or roots. Put the roots into buckets of water immediately, for they must never be allowed to become dry. Make a large planting hole and spread out the roots from the centre. Work in fine soil around the small roots and pack soil under large main roots and make firm with the hands. Plant at the same depth as they were planted in the nursery; it is usually quite easy to see the original soil mark. Fix a metal label to one of the main stems with the name of the variety clearly indicated. Before planting, sever with a sharp pair of secateurs any broken roots. After firming the roots by hand, finish the operation by treading the soil firmly. When the planting of the roses has been completed for the day, give them all a good soaking of water.

There has recently been much new thinking among gardeners about the most suitable times for pruning bush roses. Until a year or so ago, the pruning of bush roses was always carried out in April. Some gardeners now prune in January or February. It seems quite a sensible

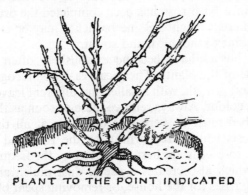

PLANT TO THE POINT INDICATED

The correct method of planting a rose bush

thing to do, to prune most trees or bushes during the dormant period. Provided that there is no severe frost to kill the bud below the pruning, roses will generally be in flower earlier, with earlier pruning. I think that the safest time to prune is at the beginning of March or just before the sap starts to rise. Growth begins rapidly after pruning and if shoots are too far forward they may be damaged by frost; although if this does happen, there are other buds to take their place.

Many people think that you must prune bush roses in order to get flowers. When we say 'bush roses' we are mainly thinking of the Hybrid Teas. If a rose is growing in good soil, it will flourish and produce flowers even if you have forgotten the pruning. It is best to prune annually for several reasons. When you prune it is done to remove dead and diseased wood, twisted and crossing branches and weak stems; to let light and air into the centre of the bush, to give it a good shape, to encourage healthy growth and to produce large flowers.

Begin the pruning of bush roses by removing any diseased or dead wood. Then cut away any very thin weak-looking stems, or twisted and crossing branches. Next take the branches arising from the

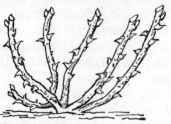

bottom of the bush one at a time and select a shoot bud which is pointing outwards away from the centre of the bush. On strong branches this bud should be the fourth one up from the base of the bush. Cut off the remainder of the branch above this bud, by making a sloping cut with the secateurs about a quarter of an inch above the bud. With weaker-growing branches

A rose correctly pruned

cut above a bud which is nearer the base of the rose bush. So when the pruning of a bush rose has been completed the pruned branches will be at different heights. Some branches may be cut back to the fourth bud, some to the third, and so on.

When the bushes have become established, often suckers arise from the base of the plants. These can easily be recognized, as they are of long, soft growth, with smaller and different leaves and usually of a different colour. Always remove these as soon as they are seen.

The rose bed must be kept free of weeds at all times as weeds encourage pests which are harmful to the rose and other plants. Weeds in the rose beds are best destroyed by the frequent use of the Dutch hoe which also creates a useful dust mulch and lets in air. When cutting roses for the house, or removing spent blooms, always cut a stem of about eight inches in length and cut to an outward-pointing bud; in this way many more flowers will be produced. If a top dressing of manure is required, this can be given in autumn or in very early spring. Two of the best materials for a top dressing are old leaf-mould or well-decayed horse manure.

The greatest enemy of the rose in this country is the disease called black spot. This is a fungus and consequently is more prevalent during a wet summer, and it is seen in country districts more than in town areas. It comes in the form of brownish black spots on the leaves which spread rapidly, until the leaves shrivel and drop, leaving the plant bare. It must be dealt with early, otherwise it often spreads to the branches. To control black spot a good copper spray should be applied every ten days. The powder for making the fungicide can be obtained from any shop which sells seeds or garden materials. Collect all prunings and any diseased leaves which have fallen on to the bed and burn them to prevent the spread of the disease. If good culture and good garden hygiene are practised in every part of the garden, the risk of disease is considerably lessened.

Other nuisances which rose growers are likely to experience are aphides or greenfly, some caterpillars and mildew. All three are fairly easily combated. Attack the greenfly early; use a fine-nozzled sprayer, and ordinary soapy water can be sprayed on. This will deal with a small number effectively but if the bushes become heavily infested, liquid derris spray may be used. Never discourage or destroy the ladybird beetle or its larvae, as they are the natural enemies of the aphis, destroying thousands in a season. Caterpillars can be hand picked as there are usually only one or two. These are usually located where a leaf is curled and are nearly always found during early spring when the first young tender leaves are formed. The fungus disease of mildew is quite easily controlled with flowers of sulphur as soon as it is seen.

Rambler roses are easy to grow and maintain. If they are being grown for the first time, and the intention is to train them to a wall, the soil needs to be very well prepared and plenty of good garden compost put into the soil near the wall. Soil under walls soon dries out and the compost retains moisture as well as supplying plant food.

Ramblers look well when they are growing over the porch of a house, along trellis work, on pillars or pergolas. 'Dorothy Perkins' is a variety which must not be trained to a wall, otherwise it is usually heavily attacked by mildew. It needs a place in the garden where it can receive plenty of light and air. Rambler roses are most vigorous, and once established they grow very strongly and in a few years they will cover a fence, trellis work or porch.

New growths arise from the base of the plant and many new lateral growths are also produced from the old shoots. These need to be secured temporarily until pruning is undertaken. The pruning of ramblers is best done when flowering has finished. September is a good time for this work. Begin by cutting out some of the oldest rambling shoots and branches. Keep some of the old branches from which strong lateral shoots are emerging. Tie in the young growths which are coming from the base, these are usually a light green in colour. Then retain and tie in some of the young lateral or side-growing shoots, from the old branches. Always remove dead flowers.

Rambler roses are very useful for covering objects quickly and giving a lavish display of blossom. They do not flower quite so continuously as other types of roses.

Climbing roses are nearly always climbing varieties of Hybrid Tea Roses. They are trained to the walls of houses and for this purpose some form of attachment to the wall must be provided. As with all subjects growing near walls they will need copious amounts of water during dry spells. The cultural requirements are much the same as for other roses. Climbing Hybrid Tea Roses require very little pruning, except to keep them within the limits of the spaces allotted to them. Newly planted climbers should be pruned to within five or six buds from the base. On established trees prune most of the oldest wood in autumn and tie in the new growths. In March the new growths should be tipped to encourage laterals.

The Floribunda or Hybrid Polyantha roses need the same general culture as the Hybrid Teas. They are very vigorous growers and of a free-flowering habit. Newly-planted floribunda roses should be pruned in March to within six inches of the base and as with the Hybrid Teas by cutting just above an outward-pointing bud. During the second year lightly prune all healthy growth made during the previous summer. For the third and subsequent seasons, prune all older wood hard to one or two buds from the base, and all new basal shoots lightly. Always remove dead flowers to encourage perpetual flowering.

Standard roses are pruned in the same way as the Hybrid Tea bush roses, and culture is the same, except that strong stakes have to be provided and firm tying attended to.

All types of rose need to be carefully examined in early spring, as many will need to have the soil firmed by treading around them. The winter weather conditions, in particular the frosts, often make the soil quite loose around the roots. A few gardeners like to enjoy

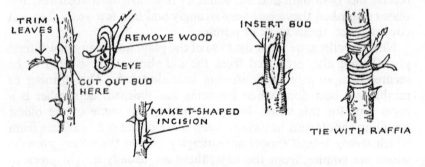

The propagation of roses by budding

themselves by attempting to propagate bush and standard roses by the method known as budding. This is how most of the nurserymen's roses are increased. First some good briars (one of the wild roses) must be obtained, either from a nurseryman or from the hedgerow. The Sweet Briar or *Rosa rubiginosa* will do. *R. rugosa, laxa* and *multiflora* are also used by the nurserymen. This plant can be found chiefly in the south of England. It forms a small bush with erect or arching branches which are set with hooked prickles mixed with glandular hairs and bristles. The leaflets are aromatic and the flowers are small and pink. The fruit produced is globular in shape. I have described this wild flower so that you will know which one to look for. Before looking for briars ascertain, if not on your own land, whether there are any local bye-laws relating to the removal of wild plants in your district. I do not think the owners of waste land would object to the removal of one or two briars, but I would not like to hear of any other wild flowers being taken from their natural surroundings.

Dig out the briars during autumn and plant them on a spare piece of land. Do not use any which show the slightest sign of disease. Take some shoot buds from the roses to be propagated, usually Hybrid Teas, during July and August. Choose buds from the current year's growth. The buds are removed by taking a shield-shaped piece of the bark with the bud on it, together with the stem and leaves immediately adjoining the bud. Remove the leaves, but leave a portion of the stem. Remove the thin sliver of wood at the base of the bud.

The stock or wild briar is prepared to receive the bud by making a T-shaped cut through the bark of the briar-stem. Do not cut deeper than just through the bark or rind. Slip the bud shield into this T-cut so that it fits snugly against the interior of the wild briar stem. Then tie firmly around with raffia, leaving only the bud exposed. In the following spring the stock should be cut back to just above the bud. Several buds may be inserted in this way on different sections of the stock in case some do not take.

For bush roses, place the buds near to the ground. For standards place the buds on a lateral growth at the top of the briar stem. Budding roses in this way is often very successful, and the gardener can increase his favourite roses and at the same time, gain a measure of satisfaction from the knowledge that he has achieved this by his own efforts and skill.

Some bush roses, and certainly many of the ramblers, can be grown from cuttings. The cuttings should be taken in autumn. Select ripened young shoots which have not flowered, of about ten inches in length. Cut just below a bud and remove the bottom foliage. Make a narrow trench with a spade or trowel in a partially shaded border, about six inches deep, and insert the cuttings six inches apart. Make the soil very firm around them and well water them in. Leave them in position until the following autumn, then those which have rooted can be planted either into their flowering position or into a nursery bed temporarily.

There are a very great number of old-fashioned roses and species roses, many of them very attractive and with climbing sorts among them. Some are grown on walls and many make magnificent subjects for the shrub border, or as specimen shrubs. Others make delightful informal hedges and some bear striking ornamental fruit as well as

prolific blossom. There are plenty of large books on roses only,
describing them all and the best ways of growing them. Gardeners
who want more information about members of the large rose family
can obtain catalogues from well-known nurserymen who grow them.
Here is a short list of the kinds of roses which I have been discussing,
with their colours. These will generally grow well under ordinary
garden conditions.

Hybrid Tea Roses

NAME	COLOUR	REMARKS
'Crimson Glory'	Velvety crimson	Lovely perfume
'Josephine Bruce'	Rich blood-red	Well-shaped blooms
'Etoile de Hollande'	Dark red	Sweetly scented
'Wendy Cussons'	Rosy-red	Nice scent
'Lucy Cramphorn'	Geranium-red	Scented
'Eden Rose'	Carmine and pink	One of the most vigorous I have grown
'Grace de Monaco'	Silvery-pink	Vigorous
'Opera'	Carmine and flame	Delicate scent
'Perfecta'	Cream, deep pink-veined	Free flowering
'Picture'	Clear bright pink	3 ft high
'Silver Lining'	Silvery-pink, paling at base	Fragrant
'Montezuma'	Orange-salmon	Free flowering
'President Hoover'	Apricot and rich rose	Light pruning
'Super Star'	Pure vermilion	Bronze leaves
'Beauté'	Apricot-orange	Nice scent
'Grandmère Jenny'	Pale gold, flushed carmine	Free flowering
'McGredy's Yellow'	Bright yellow	A good yellow
'Peace'	Deep yellow, pink edging	Very vigorous
'Spek's Yellow'	Bright golden-yellow	Free flowering
'Sutter's Gold'	Yellow, with Indian red shading	Beautiful buds
'Sterling Silver'	Silvery-lavender	For those who like this shade
'Rose Gaujard'	Pink, white reverse	Bronze leaves
'Tzigane'	Scarlet, with chrome reverse	Fragrant
'Virgo'	White	The best white

Floribunda Roses

'Frensham'	Deep crimson
'Lili Marlene'	Bright red
'Rosemary Rose'	Bright carmine
'Sarabande'	Dazzling scarlet
'Dearest'	Rosy-salmon
'Plentiful'	Deep pink
'Queen Elizabeth'	Clear pink
'Highlight'	Orange-scarlet
'Jiminy Cricket'	Tangerine-red
'Orangeade'	Bright orange
'Allgold'	Golden-yellow
'Iceberg'	Snow-white, pink buds
'Circus'	Bright yellow and orange buds changing to pink and salmon
'Masquerade'	Yellow turning to salmon then red
'Shepherd's Delight'	Yellow, orange and red shades

Climbing Roses

'Etoile de Hollande'	Dark red
'Guinée'	Dark scarlet
'Madame Grégoire Staechelin'	Pearl-pink with carmine
'Ophelia'	Pale pink, deeper centre
'Shot Silk'	Cerise-pink, overlaid orange-gold
'Masquerade'	Yellow, turning salmon, then dark red
'Mrs. Sam McGredy'	Scarlet coppery-orange
'Allgold'	Semi-double golden-yellow
'Gloire de Dijon'	Buff-orange centre, yellow-apricot tints
'Golden Showers'	Golden-yellow
'Spek's Yellow'	Bright golden-yellow
'City of York'	Creamy-white
'Madame Alfred Carrière'	Old, but one of the best whites

Rambler Roses

'Alberic Barbier'	Buds yellow, cream flowers	Thick foliage
'Albertine'	Coppery-chamois, fading rich salmon-pink	Early, scented

'American Pillar'	Single large flowers of clear rose with white eye	Vigorous, even on chalk
'Emily Gray'	Semi-double golden-yellow	Early, long flowering
'Paul's Scarlet Climber'	Vivid scarlet	Free flowering
'Wedding Day'	Cream, golden stamens	Scented

Hybrid Perpetual Roses

Many of these varieties were raised in Victorian times when they became very popular. They are best used as shrubs, being rather tall for mixing with the Hybrid Teas. Their height is usually about 6 feet.

'Frau Karl Druschki'	Pure white	One of the few white bush roses
'Hugh Dickson'	Bright crimson	Scented
'Reine des Violettes'	Rich lilac-purple	Grey leaves
'Roger Lambelin'	Blood-red, edged white	Lovely scent
'Ulrich Brunner'	Bright red to lilac-pink	

DAHLIAS

The dahlia is one of our most easily grown plants. It is most floriferous; it will give a long flowering period. If the tall varieties are adequately staked and all dead flowers are removed from all varieties, many hundreds of blooms will be produced for cutting and for garden decoration. There is also a very wide range of form and colour.

Many people are realizing today that there is really no need to save Dahlia tubers as they are so easily grown from seed to flower during the same year. Dahlias are one of the best flowers for the busy man to grow. It is doubtful if there is another garden flower which is so trouble-free and which will give such a good return of so many different coloured blossoms if grown in fairly rich soil.

Dahlias are divided into several classes and the grower will choose those he admires the most. Some gardeners will only grow the giant decorative dahlias. These are splendid for a bold garden display, but are too large for cut flowers. The owner of a small garden would probably be best advised to grow some of Unwin's 'Dwarf Hybrids', a few small cactus dahlias and some small pompoms. All of these are very easily grown from seed each year and if the gardener has no cool, moist shed which is frost-proof for storing the tubers during winter, he need not worry about saving tubers. Simply sow fresh seed each spring.

The various classes of dahlias which have been classified by the National Dahlia Society, are as follows: Single Dahlias, Star Dahlias, Anemone-flowered, Collarette, Paeony-flowered, Giant Decorative, Large Decorative, Medium Decorative, Small Pompom, Giant Cactus, Medium Cactus, Small Cactus and Dwarf Bedders.

Growing dahlias from seed can be a very pleasurable occupation and a wonderful range of rich colours can be produced by this method. Purchase packets of mixed seed of the classes of dahlias desired, from a reputable seedsman. Dahlia seedlings can be raised in an ordinary living-room where there is a constant temperature of 60°F. The cool greenhouse is the best place for seed raising if a constant temperature cannot be kept elsewhere. They can be sown about the second week in March.

Obtain clean seed boxes, put a few crocks in the bottom for drainage, cover with a layer of old leaf-mould and then fill with John Innes Compost No. 1. Water the boxes well and leave to drain for a while. Draw drills in the soil in the boxes about a quarter of an inch deep and place the seeds in the drills, spacing them to about an inch apart. This is easily done as the seeds are large enough to handle. Place a sheet of brown paper over the seed box and remove this as soon as germination has taken place. Do not water until all the seedlings are above the soil. Then water for a while with Cheshunt Compound for control of damping-off disease. Seedlings will soon dry out in seed boxes.

As the safe time for planting out dahlias is about May 20th in the south and a little later in the north and Midlands, the seedlings may grow too rapidly in the seed boxes. They may need planting into deeper boxes and given more space, or better still, if plenty of pots are available, they could be potted into 3½-inch pots. Crock all pots well for drainage.

When the seedlings have reached a certain stage of growth, they need to be put into the cold frame, and gradually hardened off, preparatory to planting into their final flowering positions. Dahlias grown from seed are usually more vigorous and quicker growing than those grown in other ways.

Dahlias can be propagated in various ways. When fully grown the dahlia produces a number of thick tuberous roots, which are not attached to underground stems, as with the potato, but all converge on to a central stem. When the first frost is imminent, these tubers, with the stems cut near to the tubers, should be lifted intact. They can be stored during the winter. This is the way in which special named varieties or colours can be saved to be grown the following year. Always tie a label with the name of the variety printed on it, to the tubers which are being saved. The tubers must be kept in a cool, frost-proof place but where there is a certain amount of dampness. They must not be where there is any artificial heat or where it is too dry, for this will lead to a continuous loss of moisture until very little growing-power is left in the tuber.

There are several methods of growing dahlias from the saved tubers. One way is to plant the stools intact, just as they were lifted in the autumn. Put them into the open ground about the middle of April. A large collection of tubers will give a plentiful supply of growing shoots and these will have to be reduced to one or two per plant. If the varieties of dahlias grown are tall ones, staking will be required. The stakes must be inserted before the dahlia tubers are planted out, otherwise they will be driven into the fleshy roots. The dahlias grown from the old tubers in this way generally flower earlier than others.

Another method of growing from the old tubers is to cut the tubers carefully from the central stem, and to plant each one separately. When dividing these tubers, there must be a piece of the central part or crown of the plant attached to the tubers to obtain any growth. There is no actual growth from the tubers alone. It is no use pulling one from the bottom of the clump, putting it in the soil and expecting it to grow. They can be planted out from the middle of April onwards and they must be planted about six inches below ground level.

Some losses will be experienced from this method, so it is not suitable if a bedding scheme is envisaged. It is a method that suits the cut-flower border. For propagation by cuttings, stools of the previous year are placed in the cool greenhouse in gentle heat in February. The stools are put into fairly deep boxes on top of about three inches of soil which has plenty of old leaf-mould and peat mixed with it. Then some of the same mixture is put on to the top of the tubers and worked in between them to a depth of about an inch. A temperature of 60°F. is needed and this should not be exceeded. Shoots are taken from the stools for cuttings when they are about three inches in length. Cut the shoots square just above a node and remove the lower leaves. Plant the cuttings firmly into small pots filled with the same mixture but with some silver sand added. Make the planting hole square so that the base of the cutting rests firmly on the bottom of the soil. Well water the pots after putting in the cuttings. Do not water again until they have rooted, unless they are really dry. Dahlia cuttings take about ten days to form roots. If the weather is sunny before the roots have formed, some covering with newspaper will be necessary to act as shading to prevent too much flagging. After they have rooted, it is a good idea to place them on the floor of the greenhouse where it is cooler. They can be put into larger pots as they grow on, and then John Innes Compost No. 2 should be used. After a while, the rooted cuttings can be moved to the cold frame and gradually hardened off. Put plenty of slug-killer pellets around the pots and space the pots out in the frame, to give them growing room and light and air.

Dahlias like an open site in the garden. The ground should be well prepared in the autumn by deep digging and by putting into the bottom trench a liberal amount of good garden compost or farmyard manure. The spacing of the plants will vary with the types grown and their mode of growth. As a general rule, the giant decorative and giant cactus types will need about four and a half feet of space between plants. The smaller decoratives, collarettes and paeony-flowered kinds will require three feet and dwarf bedding sorts about eighteen inches of space.

Most of the varieties, excepting the dwarf bedding, will need adequate staking. The stakes must be put into position first, and the dahlias are planted closely to the stakes. There are various ways of supporting them. One stout central stake can be put in and the three or four main stems tied in separately with soft string or raffia. For tall, bushy plants four stakes can be used, one at each corner, and the soft tying string is brought round the outside of the stakes. If planting out from pots and boxes, give them a good soaking of water about half an hour before planting. If planting various types in a dahlia bed of their own, plant the taller ones at the back first and then the short varieties in front. Plant with a trowel and make firm with the hands. Well water all plants finally. During the growing and flowering season always water well if there is a dry spell. Dahlias need rather more water than most other garden subjects.

If good blooms are to be grown some dahlias will need stopping and disbudding. This is especially so with large decoratives. The dwarf bedding types are never stopped or disbudded. Stopping is done by nipping out the tip of the central stem when it is about twelve inches high. If a display of blossom for the garden only is required, about six of the resulting lateral shoots may be left. All side flower buds should be removed, leaving the terminal one.

Types of dahlias which can be grown from seed easily are 'Autumn Festival' which has dark glossy foliage the colour of copper beech and flowers in shades of crimson, red, orange, yellow, apricot and purple. Cactus-flowered hybrids with various colours, decorative double mixed, Coltness hybrids, Unwin's dwarf hybrids and pompom double mixed are others.

17

It would be difficult to give a list of recommended varieties, as one would have to include most of them. I do not remember ever seeing a bad dahlia, or one I did not care for. The best way to make a choice of named varieties, that is if they are not being grown from seed, is to attend a good autumn or late summer flower show. There you can see all the best varieties in flower and make a note of those you most admire, and very often you can make your order for plants from any nursery showing at any particular show.

OUTDOOR CHRYSANTHEMUMS

Early-flowering outdoor chrysanthemums are other easily grown subjects which are admirable for any garden. They will thrive on almost any type of soil as long as it has been deeply dug and well enriched with garden compost or farmyard manure. Carry out the preparation of the soil in the autumn as for dahlias.

For starting a collection of chrysanthemums first obtain a catalogue from a specialist chrysanthemum grower. Study it and pick out the sorts you would like to have growing in your garden. About a dozen plants, each one a different colour, would perhaps do for a start in a small or medium-sized garden. The newer introductions are always much more expensive than the older sorts, and there are new introductions every year. If the rooted cuttings are purchased from a reputable chrysanthemum grower, all the varieties listed will give a splendid show of bloom. Rooted cuttings of early-flowering chrysanthemums are normally dispatched in April for those with a cold frame, and in May for those who do not have glass. Cuttings obtained from the specialist grower should be planted out in May in the open ground when all danger of frost has passed. They are usually rather small and the stems are tender and sometimes brittle. They are therefore very easily broken, and once the stem has been severed from the root near to the base of the plant, and that is what usually happens, the plant is of no more use. So unpack the cuttings carefully and keep the roots covered with a piece of sacking or paper until you are ready to put them into the planting hole. The roots must never be allowed to become dry.

Put in supporting stakes of about four feet in height above the ground and space them about sixteen inches apart. Plant the cuttings by making a planting hole with the trowel large enough to accommodate the roots without any cramping. Chrysanthemums are fairly shallow rooting and it is most important not to bury any part of the stem when planting. Firm the soil around the plants and then finish with a good watering. Label all plants with the name of the variety clearly printed.

It is not difficult to grow good early-flowering outdoor chrysanthemums. The elaborate stopping and hardening practices of old were unnecessary, in fact they actually impeded growth and the production of good blooms. Nearly every early-flowered variety should be encouraged to make good growth, and the only stopping that should be done is when the break bud, which is the first one to appear, is removed. By this time, many side branches have grown out from the main stem. If any other stopping is necessary, apart from the removal of this first bud, then the raisers will indicate this when sending the cuttings.

Chrysanthemums need water when very dry conditions persist, but make sure that the need is real. They must never be over-watered. During the growing season, a number of side growths will come from the main flowering stems. Remove these as soon as they become large enough to handle. 'Taking the bud' means allowing the bud you wish to flower to remain on the stem, and removing all other buds and sideshoots on the same stem. Make sure that the bud which you leave is the best one and that it is undamaged. Begin to disbud from the top of the stem downwards. Break out side shoots rather than pinch them out. Do not scar the stems with long sharp fingernails as this can cause distorted flowers. No disbudding or stopping is needed for the spray varieties.

When all flowering has ceased, remove the supports, clean them, and stack them under cover for future use. Cut down the stems of the chrysanthemums to within six inches of the ground. Lift the plants from the ground carefully with a garden fork, reducing the ball of earth and roots in size by shaking some of the soil away on to the garden. The cut-down plants are now known as 'stools'. Take them to the cold frame and place them on to the bottom, working some finely sifted soil between the roots, and covering them with about two inches of sifted soil. Give them light and air in mild days during winter, but cover the frame with thick sacking, straw or bracken during severe frost.

Outdoor chrysanthemums, like their greenhouse counterparts, are propagated by the taking and rooting of cuttings. The best cuttings to take are the fresh shoots which spring up together. A good cutting is short-jointed, firm and turgid and about three inches long. The cutting should be trimmed directly below a joint, and the lower leaves carefully removed. Use a thin, sharp knife for this purpose, or a razor-blade. Dip the cut end lightly in a hormone rooting powder and insert into the rooting compost. The rooting compost should be a mixture of half loam and half silver sand. The cuttings can be inserted into 3-inch pots, with three cuttings around the edge of the pot, or they can be put into fairly deep seed boxes. Cuttings should be put into the rooting compost about half an inch deep, with the cut end resting firmly on some silver sand. The rooting compost must be made firm before putting in the cuttings, and after planting all cuttings must be well watered. They may be placed in a propagating frame in the cool greenhouse or into the cold frame. Do not water again until they have begun to root, which is usually in about fourteen days.

As soon as the rooting process is complete, the plants should be lifted carefully with a wooden plant label and potted singly into 3-inch pots using a compost of 2 parts loam, 1 part decayed leaf-mould, and 1 part silver sand; or John Innes Compost No. 2 will do quite well. Place the plants into the cold frame and water them well. Give plenty of light and air, except during frost, and gradually harden off. Early-flowering outdoor chrysanthemum cuttings are usually taken during March and April. Never allow the pots to dry out, and pot on to larger pots as necessary. Do not break the ball of soil when repotting.

Plant out towards the end of May, and until the plants get fairly tall and sturdy, scatter plenty of slug-killer pellets around. Do this also when the plants are occupying the cold frame, or when they are standing outside undergoing the hardening-off process.

OUTDOOR SPRAY VARIETIES

These are trouble-free plants, and they provide a wonderful show of colour from August until late autumn. They can be planted into the herbaceous border if desired, to give a contrast of colour with the Michaelmas daisies. This is especially so if white, yellow and cream varieties are put near the Michaelmas daisies. They make good cut flowers. Pinch out the growing point three weeks after planting out, and no other attention apart from watering is needed, if the soil was well prepared during the previous autumn. They nearly all grow to a height of about two feet. Here is a list of good spray varieties:

Outdoor Spray Chrysanthemums

NAME	COLOUR	REMARKS
'Aphrodite'	Single pink	1 ft high
'Coral Mist'	Single coral-pink	Long stems
'Fairy Wedding'	Single pure white	1 ft high
'Merstham Cheer'	Single golden	Bush-like
'Vulcan'	Cardinal-red	Showy
'Amber Glory'	Bronze-yellow	1 ft high
'Apache'	Fiery-purple	Tapered petals
'Golden Wedding'	Golden-yellow	Semi-double
'Ivory Glow'	Ivory-white	Incurved
'Scarlet Glow'	Fiery-scarlet	New, expensive

Early-flowering Outdoor Chrysanthemums

These are very suitable for cutting, garden decoration or for exhibiting, if required. They will need to be staked, but there are no very tall ones in this list.

'Appeal'	Intense red	Fadeless
'Bessie Rowe'	White	Incurving
'Brenda Talbot'	Carnation-pink	Large
'Charles Horwood'	Yellow	Large incurving
'Contessa'	Shell-pink	New
'Congress'	Old rose, flushed gold	Unusual colour
'Delightful'	Primrose	Early
'Escort'	Deep crimson	Weather resistant
'Gazelle'	White	Tightly incurved
'Glenavon'	Flame	Vivid colour
'Hamburg'	Yellow	Late September
'Harry James'	Bronze	Large, incurving
'Jim Plummer'	Scarlet	Spiky, reflexing
'Kathleen Howard'	Apple-blossom pink, cream reverse	Large
'Lilac Moon'	Soft lilac	Incurving
'Misty Night'	Purple, silver sheen	A lovely colour
'Orange Good Taste'	Orange sheen	A bright colour
'Prairie Sunset'	Bronze, gold reverse	Large
'Primrose Pride'	Primrose	Soft colour
'Satin Dawn'	Pink and beige	Reflexing
'Snowdance'	White	New
'Touchdown'	Persian rose	Early
'Yellow Snowdance'	Yellow	A lovely colour

Outdoor Pompom Varieties

These give several small round flowers to each plant, and are particularly trouble-free. After planting out into the open garden in May, the only attention needed is the pinching out of the growing point, three weeks after planting. Only small stakes will be required and sometimes no staking at all, as many sorts only grow to a height of two feet. They will produce a mass of flowers with a long season.

'Beeswing'	Crimson and gold	Changing to bronze
'Cameo'	White	Good shape
'Eve'	Purple	Medium size
'Fairie'	Strawberry-pink	1 ft high

'Imp'	Deep crimson	Unique colour
'Janet Wells'	Yellow	Long-flowering blooms
'Joy'	Primrose	Large
'Mitzi'	Creamy-white	Soft green centre
'Piccolino'	Golden-bronze and yellow	Vigorous

GERANIUMS

The old-fashioned geranium or pelargonium is still a wonderful garden plant. There are not many flowers to compare with it for giving a massed display of colour and a continuation of flowering during our short summers. Geraniums are easily rooted from cuttings from May until the end of September. Although it has been the usual custom to take geranium cuttings during August and September, I have found that cuttings taken during June and July from strong-growing plants, which have been bedded out into the open garden, make much finer plants.

These rooted cuttings, potted into 3-inch pots, can be wintered in the cool greenhouse, cold frame or even in the living-room, if no other accommodation is available. The important point to remember is that frost must be excluded from them at all times, and during the winter they must be watered very sparingly, if at all.

At the end of May, the geraniums which have been wintered in the cool greenhouse or elsewhere should be moved to the cold frame. Again water carefully. Pinch out the tops of the plants at this stage to induce bushy growth. Leave a space of several inches between each pot to allow for the spread of the foliage and shoots. Never over-water geraniums; tap each pot individually to see when water is needed.

When all danger of frost has passed, stand the geraniums outside on a bed of ashes in full sunshine. When thoroughly hardened off, plant them into their flowering position by using a trowel and by knocking the plants from their pots carefully. Try to keep the ball of soil intact when planting out.

The geranium in the open garden must be sited carefully. It must be in a bed where there are geraniums only. Do not plant a bed of vivid geraniums near other flowers so that their brilliant hues clash with them. They are perhaps best used in formal gardens in association with stonework or on terraces of Italian style and in similar locations. They are admirable for planting in tubs, old urns or earthenware receptacles on a weathered brick or paved surround. Keep removing dead clusters of flowers for a long display of colour.

Besides propagating the geranium by taking cuttings, the flowering plants themselves can be taken from the open ground during September or October. If they have made a lot of growth, which is usual during a wet summer, rather large pots or deep boxes will have to be found for them. If the rooted cuttings and the old plants are to be housed in the cold frame during the winter, the lights must be closed on cold days and nights. During frosty nights, adequate thick coverings will have to be added to the lights; and straw should be banked up at the sides of the frames, or thick layers of bracken, sacking, or old matting may hang over the sides of the frames down to ground level.

If the plants are being kept in an unheated room in the dwelling-house, bring them away from the windows during cold nights and cover them with newspaper. As well as making a good bedding plant, the geranium is a good subject for pot culture in the cool greenhouse

PREPARED GERANIUM CUTTING   INSERTED ROUND EDGE OF POT

Preparing and planting geranium cuttings

or as a house plant. It is also very suitable for hanging baskets and window boxes.

It is possible to root geranium cuttings by inserting them round the edge of a large pot in the open garden, in a partially shaded spot. For convenience, geranium cuttings are generally propagated during August and early September in a cool greenhouse in a cold frame. Well-ripened non-flowering shoots should be cut from the parent plant. These should be about five inches long and have several leaves. Immediately below a joint, cut the stem across squarely and remove the lower leaves. Dip the cutting lightly in hormone rooting powder and insert the cutting in a compost of 2 parts loam, 1 part well-decayed leaf mould, and ½ part silver sand. Rest the cutting squarely on a bed of silver sand and make it quite firm.

If pots are used, crock them well for drainage and firm the soil a little at a time when filling the pots, so that the whole of the soil in the pot is firm. Large wooden boxes may be used in the same manner. Place the cuttings around the edge of the pot; 4-inch pots are best, and these will accommodate four cuttings. Press the soil in firmly around the cuttings. After the cuttings have been inserted, give the pots or boxes a good watering. No further water should be needed until they have rooted. Do not worry about the cuttings flagging, as they always will unless they are put in a small propagating case, a box with a glass covering over the top, and placed on the cool greenhouse bench. Although geranium cuttings strike best in gentle warmth, they will also strike in lower temperatures, but the rooting process is then slower.

Geraniums can now be grown from seed, and a bed of plants produced from a packet of mixed seed is a glorious sight. A packet of 'Large-flowered Hybrids' will provide huge flower heads in unusual shades of pink, rose, salmon, scarlet, crimson and white. A new variety called 'Nittany Lion' produces plants true to type from seed. Strong compact plants bear large flower heads of bright scarlet. The folage is zoned with red.

The seeds need to be sown in John Innes Compost No. 1 in well-crocked seed boxes in a temperature of 60°F. Sow in January or February in the cool greenhouse or in September, shallowly and thinly. Prick off into larger pots or boxes as necessary. Move to the cold frame and harden off in the usual manner. The seedlings will flower within six months of sowing, if well managed.

HARDY LILIES

Hardy lilies are among the most beautiful of flowers, real aristocrats of the plant world. They cannot be grown to perfection in every garden and are expensive to buy when starting a collection, so the requirements of the lily must be studied well before you attempt to grow them.

Most varieties require protection from north and east winds, their roots need to be in the shade, the flowers must be partially shaded during part of the day, good drainage is essential, much moisture is needed at the roots, and good soil is necessary, containing an abundance of humus. The owners of gardens without these conditions can still grow such lilies as are content in most soils.

An ideal situation for lilies demanding the conditions set out above is on the edge of a woodland or coppice, where they can take advantage of years of accumulated leaf mould and the partial shade offered by the trees. They do not want to be in thick shade in the centre of woodland. Having chosen such a site, prepare the soil by digging in plenty of old leaf-mould, some garden peat, and a quantity of well-decayed garden compost. Never apply fresh farmyard manure for lilies, or fresh manure of any kind.

Lilies can be planted towards the front of a shrub border, where the shrubs provide shade for the roots and protection from cutting winds. Lilies are bulbous-like plants with loose scales. Having purchased your lilies, be careful not to leave them exposed to the air; the scales are brittle and soon become lifeless if they are left to become too dry.

Plant the lily bulbs as soon as they are received from the nursery-man; have the site ready well beforehand. Plant the bulbs about six inches deep, as lilies appreciate a little more depth than most other bulbs. It is important with lilies that the ground should be well drained. Although the lily appreciates much moisture, it must not be left in stagnant waterlogged ground. Lilies once planted should be left alone, to become a more or less permanent feature. As they remain in the same flowering position for a good number of years, they must be given room in which to multiply, so the initial planting should allow at least eighteen inches from bulb to bulb.

The grower of lilies must not be disappointed if he does not see much growth during the first year, as some lilies remain dormant until the second season. Do not disturb them or dig them up to see what has happened. When planting, mark the spot with a clearly printed label. Often, during the second and third season, blooms are fewer and spikes smaller, while bulb splitting is taking place beneath the soil. Eventually a colony of flowering-sized bulbs will become established.

Wait until a good number of flowers have been produced before cutting long stems for the house. Lilies are very much in demand in the professional florists' trade, and growers here purchase flowering-sized bulbs annually and plant them in a cut-flower plot. If lilies are required for the house in any numbers, then this procedure would have to be carried out.

Some protection from frost will have to be given in early spring if the garden is in a position where damaging frosts can be expected. Where obtainable, bracken makes a good covering for this purpose; straw may also be used.

Mention must be made of some lilies which are stem rooting—that is, they produce roots above the bulb and on the stem. This habit must be allowed for if lilies are being planted in tubs or pots or for open garden culture, by placing them deep enough in the soil for the stem roots to enter. The stem-rooting lilies generally grown are *Lilium auratum* and varieties, *longiflorum* and varieties, *tigrinum* and varieties, *speciosum* (*lancifolium* varieties) and *hansonii*.

As there are about 400 so-called species of lily, it would be impossible to mention most of them here. This is a list from which a good selection can be made for most purposes. Most dormant bulbs are planted in November, but they should be planted as soon as they arrive, which will probably be some time during autumn.

NAME	COLOUR	FLOWERING TIME
L. auratum	White, crimson and gold	August
L. candidum	White	June
L. dauricum	Yellow	May–June
L. hansonii	Yellow, spotted brown	June
L. henryi	Orange, spotted bronze	July–August
L. martagon	Purple	June
L. pardalinum	Orange-red, purple spots	June–July
L. pyrenaicum	Yellow	May
L. regale	White, yellow markings	June–July
L. regale 'Creelman Hybrid'	White, tinged purple	June–July
L. speciosum rubrum	White, carmine spots	August
L. maculatum	Orange	June
L. tigrinum fortunei	Red, orange and black	August
L. umbellatum	Orange-red	June

BORDER CARNATIONS

Border carnations should be near the dwelling-house, so that their lovely perfume, beautiful markings, grey-green foliage and symmetry of growth can be fully appreciated. They like a position in full sun. Although the border carnation is not a heavy feeder, deep cultivation is important because good drainage is absolutely essential. If the garden soil is on the acid side, some garden lime worked into the surface will be beneficial. Work in some good well-decayed garden compost while preparing the soil. If the carnations are to be grown on naturally wet soil or on very heavy clay, then drainage will have to be attended to.

If the clay or any other badly drained soil is of some considerable depth, then it will have to be trenched, that is, the plot must be dug to a depth of two spits. Break up the sub-soil at the bottom with a fork and put on a layer of clinkers, rubble or stones. Into the top soil work some coarse grit (not sand), old crushed mortar rubble, if obtainable, and chopped straw together with the garden compost. Be careful not to bring the sub-soil to the surface.

The site for the carnations, if on this kind of soil which needs draining, besides being in full sun will have to be so positioned that the surplus water can flow away into a ditch or sump. Carnations rarely succeed on an acid soil and they always give of their best where there is some chalk in the sub-soil. As they are not great feeders they are something which people who are on the chalk can grow well if they add some garden compost to the site. Those who are not on a chalky sub-soil should add some garden lime to the top soil, but should not apply the lime at the same time as garden compost or farmyard manure.

Border carnations can be increased by sowing seed or by layering. For layering, a growth of carnation which has not flowered is selected from near the base of the plant. These shoots are stripped of their leaves until only a tuft is left at the top. On the stem chosen, a long tongue starting from a joint should be cut on the underside and the stem bent at this point. The stem is then secured to the ground by a wire peg. Over this tongue and layered stem a couple of handfuls

SANDY LOAM

The layering of border carnations showing suitable shoots

of fine sandy soil are placed, and the whole is well moistened with water. In a few weeks roots will have sprung from the tongue and the new plant can then be severed from its parent plant. These young plants should be lifted carefully with a trowel and planted into their flowering positions. Put them about eighteen inches apart. Layering is done during July and August.

Stakes are needed for the carnations in spring, but they should not be more than eighteen inches above ground. Try to make them as unobtrusive as possible. Some disbudding is necessary with border carnations. Remove the lateral buds and retain the terminal bud or the one in the centre of the stem. Keep the carnation beds free of weeds at all times. Many named varieties of Border carnations can be obtained from well-known nurserymen in all the beautiful carnation colours.

Border carnations, like the annual carnations, can easily be raised from seed in the cold frame or cool greenhouse. Sow in the cold frame in June and in the cool greenhouse during April. Attend to drainage in the seed boxes, then fill with John Innes Compost No. 1. Water the boxes with Cheshunt Compound prior to sowing, and sow very thinly. The carnation seeds are large enough to enable this to be done. Do not discard the smaller seedlings when pricking off or transplanting, as these often make the finest plants. Cover the boxes with brown paper until germination has taken place and close the lights if using the cold frame. When watering is required after germination, use Cheshunt Compound until the seedlings have become well established. Give plenty of air and light while the seedlings are in the cold frame or cool greenhouse. Gradually harden off in the usual manner.

Prick out the seedlings as soon as large enough to handle, and as carnations should be grown with as little check as possible, they should be planted out into their flowering positions as soon as the weather is suitable. They should be ready for planting out when about four inches high.

Obtain border carnation seed from a good seedsman, a carnation specialist if possible. Douglas's Border Strain are hand hybridized and they include 'Bizarre', 'Fancy' and 'Self' types. Grenadin Dwarf Strain is a miniature race flowering from July and carrying masses of double flowers in a fine range of attractive colours. Grenadin 'Special Mixed' grow to a height of two and a half feet and flower from July to September. They have long stiff stems and the colours range through shades of pink, salmon, scarlet, crimson, yellow and white. Grenadin 'Mother's Day' is a fairly new variety of compact habit, and includes colours of pink, salmon, scarlet, crimson, yellow and white.

GARDEN PINKS

The garden pink is still a charming and very fragrant flower for any garden which suits it. It needs to be planted and left undisturbed for a good number of years. A garden with a chalky sub-soil and in full sun suits them best.

Pinks root readily from cuttings and these should be taken just after the flowering period has ended. They are easily rooted in a cold frame, or in an improvised one—a wooden box covered with glass. Attend to ventilation carefully and grow on in a similar manner to border carnations. Plant them out into a well-drained position in full sun.

They make splendid subjects for a large dry wall or between crazy paving, where they will not be walked over. They can also be planted in a border and left to themselves. Some of the lovely sweet-scented, old-fashioned varieties are now unobtainable, unless one is fortunate enough to come across some growing in a cottage garden somewhere in the Dorset or Hampshire countryside, where they have been left undisturbed for fifty years or so. There are still a few good ones, not so old, to be obtained in many colours from some nurserymen.

Pinks can also be grown from seed. Use the same seed-sowing method as for the carnations, and the same after-culture. Seeds are usually sold in packets of mixed colours.

THE SWEET VIOLET

Another old-fashioned beautiful flower is the sweet violet. The small wild sweet violet from which it is descended, or to which it is closely related, looks so charming growing in the New Forest area, on the edge of the woods. It is indeed found in most parts of England. To grow good sweet violets we must try to reproduce the conditions they enjoy in their wild state as nearly as possible. The position for the sweet violet must be partially shaded and sheltered. Also the soil must contain plenty of leaf mould, well-decayed garden compost, and some garden peat if available.

Prepare the site in autumn and mix the ingredients well into the soil by frequent forking. The sweet violet is a perennial and it reproduces itself in much the same way as the strawberry does, by runners. Spring is the best time to propagate the violet. Some runners may be obtained from a friend who has some good plants, or perhaps from a nurseryman. If the gardener already has a few violets, then the clump should be lifted in spring and a few runners detached from those which surround the central crown. Some runners will already have formed roots but some will not have done so, and these can be induced to produce roots.

The stems of runners which have not rooted, and which have a head of foliage, should be cut to form cuttings of about three inches in length. Any small leaves at the bottom of the stem should be removed. The cuttings can be propagated in the open ground but more quickly in the cold frame. John Innes Compound No. 1 will do for this. Some finely sifted soil containing plenty of leaf-mould and a little silver sand would also be suitable. Press the cuttings firmly into boxes of this soil after drainage material has been placed at the bottom, and water in well. After the insertion of the cuttings place the glass lights on and leave them for about three weeks, when rooting should have been effected. Give ventilation gradually, finally leaving the lights off completely. Protect from slugs with slug-killer pellets at all times and shade the frame on very bright sunny days while rooting is taking place.

Remove the rooted cuttings carefully from the boxes and plant into their flowering positions by using a trowel, and space them about sixteen inches apart. Water well and keep the violets moist at all times. Success with violets depends upon plenty of humus, much moisture, some shade and shelter. Under good conditions growth will flourish and plenty of side shoots which would become runners soon emerge. Remove these as soon as they appear and so let the violet devote all its energy to building up a plant with plenty of good flowers.

The violets can be left in the open ground for the winter, but in very cold districts it would be advisable to protect them with cloches. For those who require winter blooms, the crowns should be lifted in mid-September and placed in the cold frame. When lifting from the open ground, use a small spade and leave as much as possible of the garden soil adhering to the roots. Deep wide boxes will have to be used, or the violets can be planted straight on to the floor of the frame using good soil with plenty of well-decayed leaf-mould, some garden compost and a little garden peat mixed with it. Remove the lights on mild days and water well until colder days come along. Close the lights at night and cover up the frame in the usual way during severe weather. Never leave any covering on longer than is necessary; ventilate well when possible and remove all dead foliage.

Violets can be grown in a similar way in the cool greenhouse, using the same methods. Sweet violets can also be grown from seed by making a sowing in the open ground during April. Mark and label the spot well because germination is often slow and erratic and will not take place until the seeds have been subjected to frost. These plants usually flower from March to May.

Violet plants can be purchased in colours of purple-blue, purple-blue with a pink centre, bright mauve-blue and reddish-purple. There is another class of violet called the 'Parma Violet'. Some of the sweet violets may have single, semi-double or double flowers but the Parma violets are all double. Propagation and treatment of the Parma violet is similar to that of the sweet violet, except that it is not a woodland plant and therefore does not object to full sun. The Parma violets are all sweetly scented and there is a white variety.

ORCHIDS

I well remember admiring a very beautiful orchid when attending the first Chelsea Flower Show that was held after the last war. When I asked the price I was told it was for sale at £45.

Fortunately many people with a heated greenhouse could gather together a collection of orchids and grow them for much less than £45. There are a great many species of orchid which can be grown here, some wanting only gentle heat and some needing a temperature of 70°F. during the night.

A cool greenhouse with a night temperature of not less than 50°F. in the winter will grow quite a large variety of orchids. Genera named *Cymbidium* and *Odontoglossum* and some of the *Cypripedium*, *Coelogyne, Miltonia* and *Dendrobium* will grow in this kind of house.

The special compost for these orchids must consist of Osmunda fibre and sphagnum moss. For the *Cypripedium* a proportion of fibrous loam and good clean leaf-mould is added.

Annual potting is not necessary, for the orchids remain in the same pots for some time. No feeding is given to the actual pots but sometimes liquid manure is poured on to the floor of a warm greenhouse and the plants absorb this. All orchids need plenty of ventilation but no draughts. Rainwater should be used for watering, and plenty is given during the growing season but very little during the dormant period. Light syringings may be given in the morning during hot weather and the greenhouse should be damped down three or four times during summer and once or twice at other times. Orchids will last a very long time as cut flowers in water. That is why they are also worn as buttonholes.

8

Flowers for Display

Supplying cut flowers for the house — everlasting flowers — flower arrangements for each month — stage shows and concerts — new introductions

One of the nicest spare-time occupations to become popular with both women and men during the past ten years or so, is that of flower arranging. People with real artistic ability and a sense of form and colour can create works of art which are really living. If the flower arrangers grow their own flowers and foliage, then there is even more satisfaction for them from this creative pursuit.

In this chapter we shall see that lovely flower arrangements can be made from flowers which are easily grown in almost everyone's garden, without having recourse to expensive flowers and foliage from the florist's shop. Before going further with the actual flower arranging, which we shall be concerned with later on in this chapter, we must see what can be grown to provide a continuous supply of cut flowers for the house. The size of the garden will largely decide the variety and quantity of flowers grown. A good selection can be made from the flowers and foliage mentioned here.

Flowers can be exchanged between neighbours and friends. If there is not enough room for a special cut-flower border, flowers can be cut sparingly from the annual and herbaceous borders. Some flowers, by the nature of their growth, colour and shape, and through being more floriferous than others, are highly suitable for cutting. Many also have the quality of lasting for some time when cut and put into a container of water.

Then there are flowers and leaves which as well as being used in the normal manner can also be dried and preserved for winter decoration. We must not forget, too, that there are many suitable wild flowers, seed heads, berries, grasses and ornamental fruits, which can be easily gathered from the countryside. All flowers can be intermixed when well arranged in a suitable and attractive container. Annuals, perennials, berries and grasses can all be put together if the colours harmonize or offer suitable contrasts.

If there is a large enough garden, with some space to spare at the bottom of the plot, then the ideal method for cut-flower producing is to create a special border here. It would need to be well sheltered, but at the same time so located as to receive plenty of sunshine. It would have to be divided into sections with a place for autumn-sown annuals, sown outside and over-wintered, and another for spring-sown annuals. Room must be found for a few half-hardy annuals, which would include some of the everlastings, biennials, perennials, bulbs and corms.

Late summer would appear to be about the best time to prepare such a border. Then it could be completed in time for the planting of perennials, the sowing of autumn-sown annuals, and the planting of bulbs. The following spring would see the sowing of hardy annuals and the planting of half-hardy annuals which have been raised in the cool greenhouse and cold frame. Rooted early-flowering chrys-anthemum cuttings, dahlias, sweet pea plants and gladioli corms would also be planted at this time, with a sowing of biennials during April and May.

The best hardy annuals to grow from seed for cutting are annual chrysanthemums, annual sunflowers, annual sweet scabious, candy-tuft, cornflowers (all colours, but especially blue), calendula, gyp-sophila, larkspur, *Nigella* (love-in-the-mist), nasturtium, salvia (clary), sweet sultan and sweet peas.

The most suitable perennials for cutting are *Achillea, Aquilegia, Anthemis, Chrysanthemum maximum* (sometimes called Marguerite or Shasta Daisy)—both single and double kinds—*Delphinium, Doronicum, Echinops, Erigeron, Eryngium, Gaillardia, Geum, Heleni-um, Helleborous niger* ('Christmas Rose'), Michaelmas Daisy, *Nepeta* (Catmint), *Pyrethrum*, Scabious and *Solidago*.

There are some other perennials which can be used for decoration in large houses, perhaps in the hall or near the front door, such as paeonies, the flowers of the globe artichoke, tall foxgloves, astilbe, bearded iris, *Kniphofia* (red hot poker), and *Sidalcea*. As these all have very large flowers or tall stems, I have not included them in the first list, but they can all be used to make very imposing displays.

The half-hardy annuals for our purpose are antirrhinums, asters (especially single types), Unwin's Dwarf Hybrid dahlias, pompom dahlias, Coltness hybrid dahlias, Mignon dahlias, *Kochia* (burning bush), African marigold, and rudbeckia, stocks, tagetes and zinnias.

The flowers grown for drying and preserving for winter decoration are acrocliniums, achilleas ('Gold Plate' types), ammobiums, catananches, cornflowers, delphiniums, *Echinops* (globe thistle),

Eryngium (sea holly), *Gypsophila paniculata, Helichrysum,* larkspur, *Molucella* (Bells of Ireland), *Physalis* (Chinese lantern), *Rhodanthe, Statice* (Sea lavender) and *Xeranthemum.* Honesty (for its attractive seed vessels) and ornamental grasses can also be included in this list.

Many wild flowers can be used for their unusual seed heads and useful blossoms when dried. Among these are teasels, wild clematis (or old man's beard), pine cones and various wild grasses, including the giant reed mace. A few culinary onion seed heads make charming floral material and then there are the ornamental kales and cabbages. If anyone should be forcing his own rhubarb then the young yellow-green leaves are admirable material for arrangements, with their unusual colour and form. Heads of hydrangea flowers left on the plants during winter until required are another addition to the preserved material which can be used.

The flowers from most bulbs are wonderful for spring flower displays in the house. Daffodils and narcissi of mixed varieties, anemones and irises are the most suitable. Tulips can be used, but they tend to open up quickly in warm rooms and do not then look nearly so attractive as when they are closed. Other good spring-flowering perennials are polyanthus, primulas and primroses of various colours.

The best types of gladioli to grow for flower arranging are the *primulinus* hybrids, the butterfly kind, the ruffled miniature and the small-flowered sorts. Some of the large-flowered, plain-petalled types can be used in large displays, in suitable containers, with a background of foliage such as copper beech. These are also very effective for arrangements at stage shows, concerts, receptions and other public functions, where bold groups of colour must be used.

There are very many ornamental grasses, both annual and perennial, and these are just the right plant material for adding elegance and distinction to many flower arrangements. They are most graceful and charming and can be used directly after cutting for lightening a display of heavy or stiff blossom, or for drying and preserving for numerous winter decorations. In addition to the ornamental grasses grown as such for flower decoration, there is the ordinary barley grown as 'corn', which can be dried and used in the same way.

Very much varied foliage for intermixing and providing backgrounds for flower displays can be provided by the many trees and shrubs mentioned in Chapter 6. Especially valuable are those which give splendid autumn tints such as the maples and many of the *Berberis* family. The foliage shrub which I must mention above all others is *Elaeagnus pungens aurea variegata* or 'wood olive'; this shrub is almost an indispensable for keen flower arrangers. As well as providing striking foliage many of these trees and shrubs produce colourful berries. All can be used to create inspiring floral designs.

When cutting foliage or detaching sprays of berries, care must be taken not to denude the tree or shrub of too many branches. The shape of the trees must not be spoilt, neither must their growing power be weakened by the removal of a large amount of foliage, which amounts to stopping a part of their food supply. A few twigs taken here and there will do no harm to a large bush, and if this is done judiciously, it will act as a part of the pruning programme.

There are one or two special classes of cut flowers which will have to be put on their own in the cut-flower border or elsewhere. These are the early-flowering outdoor chrysanthemums, other classes of dahlias beside those mentioned, and border carnations. All are valuable acquisitions to the cut-flower department.

Of the biennials, double daisies, pansies grown as biennials, and *Cheiranthus* or Siberian wallflower are all lovely for small arrangements. Canterbury bells make a beautiful decoration, and all their colours harmonize so well together. Brompton and East Lothian stocks are admired for their colours, their enchanting perfume and their habit of being available when there is little else flowering outdoors. Two old-fashioned biennials, wallflowers and sweet williams, will fit in almost anywhere.

When preparing the soil in the cut-flower border in summer, dig deeply and put in plenty of well-decayed good garden compost. This is even better than farmyard manure which contains more nitrogen and tends to produce a large quantity of foliage rather than a profusion of blossom. The flowers grown for cutting are more easily managed if they are grown in long straight rows in much the same way as vegetables. In this way flowers can be easily seen and selected, and are more accessible.

The best arrangement is perhaps to have about four long rows of plants with a two-foot-wide path in between. Staking and tying will be very necessary and this should be attended to early. If we are going to begin our planting and sowing in early autumn, the ground must be left as long as possible after digging to weather a little in spite of its being summer, and to settle down.

At the beginning of September the border must be ready for the sowing of the autumn-sown annuals. Tread the ground well and rake down to a fine tilth. Choose the most sheltered position for these annuals. Draw the drills with rake or hoe and sow thinly. Cover the drills with soil, rake in carefully, and press down lightly with the rake head. Label each row with clearly printed waterproof lettering. Hardy annuals for September sowing in the cut-flower border are calendulas, candytuft, cornflower, *Gypsophila*, larkspur, *Nigella* and

Salvia horminum (clary). If cloches are available for these plants, then they can be covered with them on the approach of winter. Bracken and straw can be used as frost protectors if there are no cloches. Most of these plants will come through a normal winter without protection, especially larkspurs and cornflowers.

Some thinning out can be done if there is a very mild autumn and the plants make a lot of growth. Transplant to about nine inches apart and then the plants can be spaced further apart in the spring when warmer weather appears. When transplanting autumn-sown annuals do not disturb the roots unduly; plant firmly and water in. Keep the cut-flower border free of weeds at all times by making frequent use of the Dutch hoe. Autumn-sown annuals and other flowers which are in the open ground during winter often have the soil loosened around the base by frost. After a thaw, and when the ground is not too wet, examine the plants and if necessary firm the soil around them with a trowel handle or by treading. Slugs are very active during a damp, warm autumn, so put down plenty of slug-killer pellets when the small seedlings first appear.

When sowing and planting out the autumn-sown annuals, the larkspurs and cornflowers can be put in the back rows, the calendulas and *Nigella* in the middle rows and the gypsophilas, salvias and candytufts in front. For cutting purposes, it would be best to put flowers of the same kind together. Buy packets of mixed colours where possible. Put in bushy twigs or brushwood for protection and for early support. When the plants are in flower, continuously remove all dead flower heads.

After the autumn-sown annuals are in, it will be time to think about planting the perennials. If the grower is getting these from a nurseryman, it is important to order early, at least six weeks before requirement, to be certain of getting the right variety. Having prepared the site for the perennials by adding plenty of garden compost while digging the plot, unpack and plant in the way suggested for the herbaceous border.

Tall Michaelmas daisies, delphiniums, *Echinops*, *Achillea*, tall *Solidago* and *Helenium* will be in the back row; *Aquilegia*, *Doronicum*, *Gaillardia*, *Eryngium*, *Chrysanthemum maximum*, *Anthemis*, *Erigeron*, *Scabiosa* and *Pyrethrum* will make up the centre rows while *Geum*, Christmas Rose and *Nepeta* will occupy the front row. Staking will be required for the whole of the back row subjects and for most of the middle row. These supports should be put in during early spring. Many of these perennial plants will put out more shoots than are required for the production of good-class blooms, so thin them out. On average about six shoots per plant should be left. More might be allowed to remain on extra-vigorous plants and fewer on smaller ones.

Slug-killer pellets will be needed when the plants come into growth during early spring. There are several named varieties of each perennial for the cut-flower border. For some of the flowers, varieties can be selected from the lists given in Chapter 7. Here is a further list for the flowers which remain:

NAME	COLOUR	HEIGHT IN FEET
Achillea 'Coronation Gold'	Rich yellow	3
Achillea 'Gold Plate'	Rich gold	4
Achillea 'Ptarmica'	Double white	2
Anthemis 'Grallagh Gold'	Yellow	3
Anthemis 'Mrs. E. O. Buxton'	Pale lemon	$2\frac{1}{2}$
Chrysanthemum maximum 'Cobham Gold'	Lemon	$2\frac{1}{2}$
C.m. 'T. Killin'	White, lemon centre	3
C.m. 'Esther Read'	Double white	2
C.m. 'Everest'	Single white	3
C.m. 'Wirral Pride'	White	$3\frac{1}{2}$
C.m. 'Wirral Supreme'	Double white	$3\frac{1}{2}$
C.m. 'Clara Curtis'	Pink (autumn)	$2\frac{1}{2}$
Doronicum 'Mme Masson'	Yellow	2
Doronicum plantagineum	Butter-yellow	2
Echinops ritro	Steel-blue	3
„ 'Taplow Blue'	Powder-blue	5
Erigeron 'Forster's Darling'	Rose-pink	2
„ 'Quakeress'	Silver-lilac	2
„ 'Sincerity'	Deep mauve	$2\frac{1}{2}$
„ 'Vanity'	Clear pink	3
„ 'Darkest of all'	Dark violet	2
„ 'Festivity'	Delicate violet	2
„ 'Frivolity'	Rose-lavender	2
„ 'Mesa Grande'	Violet-mauve	2
„ 'Violetta'	Violet-blue	$1\frac{1}{2}$
Eryngium oliverianum	Rich blue	3
„ *tripatitum*	Blue	$2\frac{1}{2}$
Gaillardia 'Dazzler'	Crimson and gold	$2\frac{1}{2}$
„ 'Wirral Flame'	Coppery-red	$2\frac{1}{2}$
„ 'Ipswich Beauty'	Yellow and crimson	$2\frac{1}{2}$
„ 'Mandarin'	Orange	$2\frac{1}{2}$
Geum borisii	Orange-scarlet	1
„ 'Fine Opal'	Orange-flame	2
„ 'Lady Stratheden'	Golden	$1\frac{1}{2}$
„ 'Mrs. Bradshaw'	Scarlet	$1\frac{1}{2}$

NAME	COLOUR	HEIGHT IN FEET
Helenium pumilum	Pale gold	2
,, *bigelovi aurantica*	Orange-yellow	2
,, 'Chipperfield Orange'	Orange	$4\frac{1}{2}$
,, 'July Sun'	Yellow, flaked crimson	3
,, 'Moerheim Beauty'	Rich crimson	3
,, 'Riverton Gem'	Terra cotta	4
,, 'Copper Spray'	Coppery-orange	2
,, 'The Bishop'	Yellow	$1\frac{1}{2}$
,, 'Waltraud'	Golden-brown	$3\frac{1}{2}$
,, 'Wyndley'	Brown and yellow	3
Helleborus niger	White	1
,, *orientalis*	White to plum	$1\frac{1}{2}$
Nepeta macrantha	Lilac-blue	$1\frac{1}{2}$
,, *mussinii*	Lavender-blue	1
,, 'Six Hills Giant'	Deep blue	$2\frac{1}{2}$
Pyrethrum 'Brenda'	Cerise	2
,, 'E. M. Robinson'	Salmon	2
,, 'Evenglow'	Red-salmon	$3\frac{1}{2}$
,, 'Harold Robinson'	Crimson	2
,, 'J. R. Twerdy'	Double crimson	2
,, 'Margaret Deed'	Red	2
,, 'M. Robinson'	Rose-pink	2
,, 'Progression'	Double clear rose	2
,, 'Radiant'	Crimson-scarlet	2
,, 'Salmon Beauty'	Bright salmon	2
,, 'Scarlet Gown'	Scarlet-crimson	2
,, 'White Madeline'	Double White	2
Scabiosa 'Moerheim Blue'	Violet-blue	$2\frac{1}{2}$
,, 'Miss Wilmot'	White	$2\frac{1}{2}$
,, 'Clive Greaves'	Lavender	$2\frac{1}{2}$
Solidago 'Golden Gates'	Rich yellow	2
,, 'Goldenmosa'	Golden	2
,, 'Golden Showers'	Deep yellow	$2\frac{1}{2}$
,, 'Golden Wings'	Deep yellow	6
,, 'Lenmore'	Primrose	2
,, 'Ledsham'	Lemon	2

Many of the perennial flowers for the cut-flower border can be raised from seed. A seed bed can be made on a spare plot in the garden. This piece of land should be dug in autumn and it will not need manure or garden compost. Some garden peat and well-decayed leaf mould could be worked into the top layer for moisture retention.

Some of the plants can be raised from outdoor sowings made in April, but others, with very fine seeds, should be sown in boxes and put into the cold frame.

Leave the ground as rough as possible after digging has been completed, for weathering during the winter. Remove weeds during early spring and rake down to a fine tilth. Select a suitable day in April and sow the seeds shallowly and very thinly. Mark the rows by putting in clearly printed waterproof labels; this is very important. You must be able to see where your plants are, and not hoe them out in mistake for weeds. Some perennial plants are often slow to germinate, and these include *Aquilegia* and *Helleborous*. In some years aquilegias germinate quite easily, but great care must be taken when weeding between the rows and plants, because nature has the remarkable ability of throwing up weeds near to the seedlings, with foliage which is very similar to the flower plants. Put down plenty of slug-killer pellets when the seedlings are appearing above the soil. Sometimes *Helleborus* and the aquilegias lie dormant in the soil for six months or more until the seeds have been subjected to frost. This does not happen every year.

When the seedlings have become established, prick them out into nursery beds and grow on until they are large enough to plant into the cut-flower border, which can be during the autumn. Well water the seedlings, using a fine rose, if conditions become very dry during the summer. The perennials which can be sown in the open ground are *Achillea, Aquilegia, Anthemis, Chrysanthemum maximum, Delphinium, Echinops, Eryngium, Gaillardia, Geum, Helleborus, Nepeta* and *Pyrethrum.* Many gardeners would not like to risk some of these valuable seeds in the open ground; in this case all of them may be sown in boxes and put in the cold frame, or they could be sown under cloches. *Scabiosa*, as the perennial scabious is sometimes listed, would do better if it were given the protection of a cold frame and then hardened off in the usual way. Delphiniums are also sometimes better grown if treated in this way. By putting seeds into boxes in cold frames there is more control over pests and weather conditions.

In addition to the perennials mentioned, there is a perennial rudbeckia called *purpurea echinacea* which has large flowers of shades of rosy-mauve and a large black central cone. This variety does well on dry soils. It should be started under cold frame conditions and thoroughly hardened off. Keep all seed beds moist after germination and well weeded at all times. Weeds can soon smother tiny seedlings.

After the perennials have been planted into the cut-flower border the next task which confronts us is the planting of the bulbs. The site for these will have been well prepared in the manner described for the growing of bulbs in Chapter 7. Prepare the plot either in the spring or early summer. Named bulbs are expensive, so for the cut-flower border the gardener would be best advised to purchase some of the cheaper lots offered as bulbs for naturalizing (see page 203). These are always very good value for the money.

Daffodils and narcissi need to be in the ground by the middle of September. They should be planted about four inches deep and for the cut-flower border can be planted closer than usual, about six inches apart. A cool, sheltered part of the border would be the best position, where they are not likely to be beaten down by the winds and rains of March and April.

The best tulips for cut flowers are the early single, lily-flowered, Darwin, parrot and the cottage types (see pages 208–11). The same soil and growing conditions will suit tulips and daffodils. Plant tulips during October. Parcels of mixed tulips for naturalizing can also be purchased at reduced rates.

Anemones make good cut flowers and look very attractive when arranged in suitable small containers. They are very free-flowering and appreciate a good soil with plenty of well-decayed garden compost. The corms should be planted from September until October, placing them three inches deep and about six inches apart in a sheltered position. For a succession of bloom planting is carried out at fortnightly intervals. To obtain early flowers, cloches may be placed over the plants.

The irises which are grown from bulbs make excellent cut flowers. They have easily managed stems which suit all kinds of containers, they last well in water, and the colours fit in well with most floral schemes.

Having sown our autumn-sown annuals, planted the perennials and bulbs, we must now turn our attention to preparing the ground for the sweet peas. The selection of varieties and colours given in Chapter 7 under 'Sweet Peas' are also the best varieties for cutting. The land should be prepared and autumn sowing in a cold frame carried out as suggested in Chapter 7. If exhibition blooms are not required, sweet peas may be grown in the cut-flower border by planting out in spring and letting the plants ramble up pea sticks, without removing side shoots or tendrils. Keep the Dutch hoe employed frequently between the rows of plants and give a good soaking of water during long dry spells. Put down plenty of slug-killer pellets when the plants are small.

The position for the hardy annuals (spring sown) will have to be thoroughly prepared by deep digging and the addition of plenty of good garden compost in the previous autumn. Sow the seeds thinly and shallowly some time in April, when the right sowing conditions prevail. The cornflowers, sweet scabious, larkspurs and sunflowers should be sown in the back rows. The annual chrysanthemums, sweet sultans and love-in-the-mist in the centre with the nasturtiums, salvias, calendulas, gypsophilas and candytufts in front. Put in supporting twigs early and protect from slugs. Remove dead flower heads to prolong the flowering period.

The half-hardy annuals will have been raised and hardened off in the correct manner and be ready for planting out during May. Prepare the site as for other annuals and grow on in the same way. This time rudbeckia and African marigolds will occupy the back positions, the kochias, stocks, zinnias, dahlias, antirrhinums and asters will take up a middle section with only one applicant for the front row, which will be the *Tagetes*. The arrangement of these plantings can be left to individual ideas and according to how many, and which, varieties are being grown.

While suggesting single asters as the best asters for cut-flower purposes, all gardeners can grow any sort of aster, according to their gardens' position, the asters they particularly like, and the sort needed for any special kind of flower decoration. There are a great many different types of aster grown today and many people like the 'Ostrich Plume' type or the asters with the thin spiky petals called 'needle-flowered'. Any type of aster will fit in and make a lovely flower arrangement. Just asters alone, using several types, make beautiful displays and they always look well in churches, halls and restaurants. The new single asters called 'Madeleine' are magnificent for floral displays, producing many long-stemmed flowers which are much larger than the older single types. There is also a wonderful colour range among them, bringing in bright blue, cherry-red, fuchsia-pink, lavender, cerise, salmon-pink, and white—enough to delight the heart of any flower arranger.

At about the same time as we plant out the half-hardy annuals we shall think about planting the gladioli corms. Plant the corms and cultivate as explained in Chapter 7. Have plenty of stakes for support close at hand. When growing gladioli for cut flowers only, it would be best to plant mainly *primulinus* Hybrids the miniature and butterfly types. Two or three corms of several varieties will be required and a collection can be built up within a few years, or as many as can be accommodated in the space reserved for them. A good selection can be made from the list in Chapter 7 or from a seedsman's catalogue.

After the planting of the gladioli corms, it will be time to plant out the rooted cuttings of early-flowering chrysanthemums. Several different colours and varieties of these lovely long-lasting flowers, will be needed to provide cut flowers for the house, when many of the others have finished flowering. A selection of varieties can be made from the list set out in Chapter 7. Those with a cool greenhouse can further extend the flowering period of chrysanthemums by growing some which need protection from October to December.

Some of the biennials which we are using for the cut-flower garden may be sown outdoors, and some are best sown in the cold frame. Prepare the seed bed for the outdoor sowings in early autumn and leave the surface rough for the winter weathering. No compost or manure will be needed, as the seedlings will be transplanted to their flowering quarters in the cut-flower border.

Canterbury bells can be sown outdoors during April when sowing conditions are suitable. It would be best to sow a few seeds of mixed colours of the cup and saucer, double and single, and single varieties. Thin out when large enough and grow on until they are ready for their permanent flowering position. Transplant during showery weather.

The double daisies can be sown during April and May either in a cold frame or in the open ground. Move to their final positions in autumn. These plants should be grown under cool, moist conditions.

For pansies treated as biennials, sow in boxes in the cold frame from May onwards. Prick out and plant into their flowering position during September and October.

Brompton stocks are sown in the cold frame from June onwards and the dark green seedlings are removed, for, as already pointed out, these are the single-flowered plants. Transplant the light green seedlings and grow on in the usual manner. In the south these plants can be planted into their flowering positions during autumn but they are best over-wintered in cold frame in other districts. East Lothian stocks are sown in February and March, when they flower from July onwards. They are sown in the cold frame, hardened off and planted out in the usual way.

Sweet Williams are very easily grown from seed. Sow in shallow drills outdoors during April. Transplant early, as they want plenty of growing room. A little garden lime worked into the surface soil of their flowering position would be beneficial. Wallflowers of mixed colours, and the Siberian wallflower, can be sown in the open ground during April and May. Prick off and transplant to their flowering quarters during showery weather. Plant firmly.

Many people are not aware of the beauty of ornamental grasses. There are hardy and half-hardy types, annual and perennial. The hardy annuals are grown in the same way as the hardy annual flowers but should be sown extra thinly preferably where they are to flower, and then thinned out early. They can be sown in April but in the south they can be put in during August and the plants are over-wintered, giving early summer flowers.

The half-hardy varieties are sown under cloches or in the cold frame in April and after hardening off the plants can be put out during late May. The perennial grasses can be propagated from seed sown during May in the open ground, or grown from the division of roots in April or October. Perennial grasses grow best on well-drained, sunny, open positions. Ornamental grasses are, I repeat, wonderful subjects for the flower arranger. They can be used in their fresh green state or dried and preserved for winter use. They are charming when used for making up bouquets. Here is a list of annual and perennial grasses:

Annual Grasses

NAME	REMARKS	HEIGHT
Agrostis nebulosa	The cloud grass, delicate spikelets	18 ins
Agrostis laxiflora	A cloud grass	3 ft
Avena sterilis	Oat grass, large drooping spikelets	2 ft
Briza maxima	Quaking grass, green and white nodding spikelets	15 ins
Coix lachryma-jobi	Job's tears, half hardy	2 ft
Eragrotis elegans	The love grass	2 ft
Hordeum jubatum	Crested barley, graceful spikes	2 ft
Lagurus ovatus	Hare's tail grass	1 ft
Milium effusum	A pretty millet grass	2 ft
Panicum 'Teneriffe'	The Teneriffe grass	4 ft
Setaria italica	Foxtail millet	2 ft
Zea mays variegata	Red and golden striped leaves	3–12 ft

Perennial Grasses

Elymus arenarius	The lime grass	4 ft
Festuca glauca	Silver feather grass	6 ins
Holcus mollis variegatus	Silvery buff-striped	8 ins
Molinia caerulea	Green and cream striped	1 ft

A very useful material which can be gathered in the country is bracken; it can be cut while green or collected when it has assumed its golden autumn colour. This gives splendid protection to all kinds of plants and it is easily removed from them when not required. When severe frost threatens, the golden bracken can be placed over the rows of autumn-sown annual flowers, to be left on them for a while but removed as soon as the weather improves. It can be left stacked along the rows in position for further use. It can be used for the protection of very early potatoes, appearing above the soil; it can be placed, in thick layers, over the cold frames which are housing sweet peas or other over-wintering plants. It can be put over and around the roots of tender flowering shrubs. When it has partially disintegrated through much use it makes splendid manure when rotted down on the compost heap. When burnt it yields much natural potash.

EVERLASTING FLOWERS

Many people have grown, or heard of, helichrysum and statice and know that they are grown not only for garden decoration but also for winter flower arrangements when preserved for this purpose. There are very many others which are not so well known or used. Some are grown as 'everlastings' and some are well-known border flowers which can be dried. We will first take the 'everlastings' grown as such, and describe their culture and method of preserving.

Acroclinium is a hardy annual everlasting flower and should be grown in the same way as the ordinary annual flowers. It is showy, with large semi-double flowers of rose, pink, white and cerise red. The stems of about twelve inches in length should be cut when the flowers are just fully open, and should be hung upside down in the dark and where it is fairly warm.

Ammobium is a half-hardy annual which is sown in the cold frame or cool greenhouse during February, hardened off, and planted out in April. The flowers are white with a bold yellow centre; they are cut and preserved in the same way as *Acroclinium*.

Anaphalis triplinervis is a hardy perennial plant which flourishes in a light soil. It has many greyish woolly leaves which make a dome of foliage, and this is covered with white starry flowers in September. It will grow in full sun or partial shade. The stems are eighteen inches long and should be cut when the flowers are at their best. They should be preserved in the same way as the first two 'everlastings' mentioned above. These are very useful because they are white and will mix well with any of the coloured preserved flowers.

Helichrysum monstrosum or strawflower can be grown as a hardy annual in southern districts; in other areas it is usually treated as a half-hardy annual. It can be used in flower decorations when cut in the ordinary way, but its main use is as an 'everlasting' and it is one of the best for this purpose, usually keeping its colours well. It should be cut when only just out, tied into bunches, and hung upside down in a shed. *Helichrysum* will dry and keep its colour well when hung in a brick shed or garage without any artificial heat, and in semi-darkness.

Molucella (Bells of Ireland) can be grown as a half-hardy annual or treated as a hardy annual when sown in the open ground during mid-May. Germination is often erratic and when treated as a half-hardy annual, the seed should be sown in a temperature of 65° to 70°F. When it is sown in the open ground, the soil should be fairly warm and moist. This is an attractive 'everlasting' with apple-green bell-like flowers, very striking when used in winter arrangements and making a pleasing harmony with the other flowers. The plants grow to two feet; they should be cut and dried in the same way as *Helichrysum*.

Rhodanthe has attractive 'everlasting' nodding heads of rose or white flowers, and is usually grown as a half-hardy annual, growing to a height of one foot. Treat in the same way as *Helichrysum* for preserving.

There are three kinds of *Statice* (Sea Lavender) which can be used as 'everlastings'. Two are usually grown as half-hardy annuals and one is perennial. *Statice sinuata* can be grown as a half-hardy annual, or seeds can be sown in the open ground at the end of April or during early May. The seeds can be obtained in separate colours or mixed shades. The varieties sold as 'art shades' offer a blend of pastel shades, then there are 'Golden Yellow', 'Market Growers' Blue' and 'Market Rose'. They all grow to one and a half feet. All *Statice* should be cut for drying when not fully open, and hung, head downwards, in a dry, semi-dark shed. *Statice suworowi* is a half-hardy annual often grown as a pot plant in the cool greenhouse. Seed can be sown in boxes, and the plants are treated as half-hardy annuals and planted out in the garden. This *Statice* has long tail-like spikes of rosy-pink flowers. The perennial *Statice*, *Statice latifolia*, produces large panicles of lavender-blue flowers from July to September, growing to two feet, and it has tiny flowers admirable for small arrangements.

Xeranthemum is a hardy annual flower not often seen today. It is easy to grow in the same way as other hardy annual flowers, and makes an excellent 'everlasting' as it usually retains its colour well. *Xeranthemum imperiale* has flowers of rosy-violet and *Xeranthemum superbissimum* globular flowers of a rich purple. Dry and preserve in the same manner as for *Helichrysum*. All 'everlasting' flowers must be gathered when quite dry.

These are the true 'everlastings', but there are many other perennial and annual flowers which can be dried for winter arrangements. Annual flowers which can be used in this way are *Nigella* (love-in-the-mist), valuable for the unusual seed heads, larkspur and cornflowers. Honesty, grown for its silvery seed heads, is a biennial. All of these can be grown like hardy annuals in the open garden but they require slightly different treatments when being dried for winter.

Larkspurs should be gathered on a dry, sunny day when not fully out, but when the first flowers at the base of the spike are in perfect condition. They should then be stood in jars of water each containing about a pint. These containers should be stood in a room or shed facing north or in a shaded place where sunshine cannot reach them. When the water has entered the stems and has fully evaporated, the leaves will droop and wither; the flowers will become slightly papery, but will keep much of their colour and will be firmly held to the stem.

Love-in-the-mist will provide good globular-shaped seed heads of a grey-brown, and several will be on one flower spike, making for effective arrangements during the winter. These should be hung in a semi-dark shed in the same way as *Helichrysum*.

Cornflowers of mixed colours can be dried in the same way. A whole plant can be cut and hung, heads downwards. When dry and ready for use, the withered leaves and buds can be removed. Cut the cornflowers on a dry day when most of the flowers are just out and in perfect condition.

Honesty, grown as a hardy biennial, is popular with many people for winter floral schemes because of the aforementioned silvery seed heads. These are flat, transparent and oval-shapped, and the 'silvery' disc appears when the outer teguments are slipped off between finger and thumb. They have to be used with caution, however, as too many would rather dominate the arrangement and dwarf the other colourful 'everlastings'. Just one or two spikes are useful for lightening up fairly large displays of dried flowers and ornamental fruits. The seed is sown in June and the plants transplanted to flowering positions during autumn. They will flower during the following May to July. The stems should be cut when green, when the flat capsules are complete, and when no flowers, which are a bright pinky-purple, remain. They should be hung upside down in a dry, sunless shed. The shiny, transparent seed heads will be discovered when the green coverings have become brown. Most of these coverings can be shaken from the plants but some will need peeling, as described a few lines back.

We have several perennial plants which can be preserved for winter use. Achilleas, of the 'Gold Plate' varieties, are excellent for drying. They take on a mustard-yellow colour and the flat flower heads stand out well when mixed with other blue and white 'everlastings'. If there are several Achilleas in the herbaceous border, enough flowers for preserving can probably be gathered from here. If not, some plants can be grown in the cut-flower border along with the other perennials. Cut the flower heads on a dry day and when they are in perfect condition. They should be hung upside down in a dry, semi-dark place.

Catananches, growing to three feet high, are sometimes called

Cupid's darts. The blooms of the best-known variety, *coerulea,* are very blue indeed. There is also a white and blue variety, *coerulea bicolor*, only a foot high. They can be grown from seed sown in the open ground during May and flower in July and August. Cantananches are cut when in a perfect state, on a dry day, and dried in the same way as the Helichrysums. Delphiniums are cut and preserved in exactly the same way as the larkspurs.

The *Echinops* (Globe Thistles) are wonderful for flower decoration, whether in their fresh state or preserved for winter displays. These must be cut on dry days and when the flowers are only just out. They too are hung in a shed. These lovely flowers can be grown from seed sown in the open ground in June. They are of a beautiful deep blue and although they lose a little of their colour while drying, they are still splendid subjects for winter floral displays.

Eryngium or Sea holly is another ideal flower for drying and using in the same way. An added attraction are the steely-blue and purple stems of this lovely plant. There are two varieties in general use: *E. alpinum* has large silvery-blue flower heads and blue-tinted stems growing to a height of two feet and flowering from July to September; *E. giganteum,* the giant sea-holly with grey-green foliage and large oval heads of bluish-grey, could be four feet tall. The flowering time is July to September. Both sorts can be grown from seed in the same way as the globe thistles, and need the same drying treatment.

Gypsophila paniculata, the well-known perennial plant used for mixing with sweet peas and for bouquets, can also be preserved for winter floral work. It can be grown from seed, by sowing the seed in boxes for greater control of weeds and pests, particularly slugs. Stems should be cut to their full length and hung in a dry atmosphere.

Physalis (Chinese Lantern) is well worth growing in the garden, if room can be found for it. These reddish-orange lanterns or seed heads are expensive to buy for Christmas decorations. *Physalis bunyardii* has stems three feet tall with lanterns of deep red-orange. It needs a mildly warm, darkish place for drying. Another variety is *Physalis franchetti* which is of a more dwarf habit, growing to about a foot and a half. These can be grown from seed.

The flower heads of hydrangeas can be preserved for winter decoration in two ways. They can be left on their stalks in the garden, where they die and dry off naturally, assuming various shades of blue, grey and pink; or they can be cut and treated by putting them in water just as was done with the larkspurs and delphiniums.

Another useful addition to the winter floral display is the preserved rose. Many nice buds or flowers can be cut from the rose bushes late in the year, sometimes up to December during a mild autumn. When there are some well-shaped flowers in the semi-bud stage but not fully open on the bushes during autumn, cut them and seal the ends of the stalks with sealing wax or melted candle grease. Wrap them up in waxed paper and shut them in an airtight tin. They can be preserved in this way for some weeks and are often in a very good condition for Christmas flower arrangements. When you take the roses from the tins, remove the wax, cut across the base of the stems, and place the roses in water at once.

There are one or two important points to be borne in mind when you grow and preserve flowers for winter decoration. First, enough must be grown to enable one to replace arrangements when they become dusty and tired-looking, or when you and others would like a change. The flowers need to be tied in small bundles, as large bunches do not dry satisfactorily. Then the flowers must be cut on dry days and when they are just out, otherwise they will soon disintegrate.

Ornamental gourds are colourful and useful for many winter displays. They are climbing plants, so need supports: ordinary pea sticks with two rows of sticks sloping in towards each other would be suitable, or bean rods could be used in the same way. The seeds are sown in 3-inch pots at the end of April in a temperature of about 65°F. They are put into the cold frame, hardened off in the usual way, and planted out in June. When the gourds have assumed their bright colours, they are detached from the plants and dried. They can be left out in the sun for a day or two, then put on shelves in an airy shed, not touching each other, and used as required.

When thus ripened and dried the gourds can be used over and over again, as they are very tough. There are very many colours, and shapes resembling those of apples, pears, oranges, eggs, bottles and spoons. These are the small-fruited varieties. With the large-fruited, kinds, shapes have such names as 'Calabash', 'Caveman's Club', 'Powder-horn', 'Siphon', 'Turk's Turban' and 'Bottle'.

One could easily go into too much detail about the many wild berries and flowers from the hedgerow which can be used in flower decorations, but these are all suitably described in specialist books.

As well as the wild flowers, seed heads and berries, there is a wide choice of ornamental twigs and foliage. By degrees the flower arranger becomes more proficient in this art and will not overlook any possibility. Every autumn he or she will make some new discovery.

FLOWER ARRANGING FOR EACH MONTH

We must now discuss the best ways in which our flowers from the cut-flower border can be used for pleasing arrangements for the house. Of course we begin by collecting suitable containers. The tall, narrow vases which were once seen everywhere are not very suitable for only a few flowers can be put into them and these cannot be arranged gracefully. Never give the impression that flowers are cramped in a narrow vase. The best containers for general use are those which are not very tall but are fairly wide, for plenty of water and space for the flowers are the chief requirements.

Containers can be made of many materials, and various sizes will be wanted. A few smaller ones will be needed for the dinner table. The colour of the containers should be neutral, generally speaking, and some should be crystal-clear. There must be harmony with the flowers, or possibly a pleasing contrast. Where possible, the container should be in keeping in more subtle ways with the kind of flowers used. Delicate china vases could contain sweet peas and gypsophila, zinnias would look at home with ornamental grasses in a brass or copper holder, while such large strong subjects as African marigolds or border chrysanthemums need a sturdy-looking piece of pottery. Transparent glass vases are for thin-stemmed flowers.

Most people inherit or are given containers with large colourful patterns on them. These are unsuitable, for the attention of the beholder needs to be focused on the flowers and must not be distracted by the receptacle. Some exquisitely patterned pieces, how-ever, seem to invite certain flowers. If you are using a choice piece of china for some special occasion, it is advisable to put in an inner container to prevent scratching or other damage to the prized piece.

When making table arrangements for meals taken in artificial light, it must be remembered that several colours alter considerably under lighting. Try out the colours under the light beforehand. Let the table display accord with the colour of the lampshades, china and tablecloths, even with the background of the furniture and wallpaper.

A flower holder is the material which is put inside the vase to keep the flowers in position. The best possible holder is that which is fashioned from wire netting. Cut a piece of wire netting with wire cutters about twice as long as the base of the container and a little wider. Screw it up into a ball which just fits the container and nestles very firmly against all sides. In very shallow containers, the wire netting can be held firmly in place if a small piece of plasticine is placed at each end inside the container. Press the netting on to the plasticine.

Now we come to the use of colour and the colour relationship between the flowers in the arrangement and the containers. Black and white can be used in any floral display. When we speak of black

19

and white, we mean white flowers and black berries and white and black vases. The flower arranger has to learn which colours will go with one another. This will gradually come with experience and by trial and error. The skilful flower arranger must become colour-conscious.

Everyone knows the primary colours of red, blue and yellow. Colours which are opposite each other when we look at the spectrum are known as complementary colours. Green is the complementary of red, orange of blue and violet of yellow. Flowers of complementary colours can be arranged together easily in harmony, and white can be added. We can think of mauve pansies in a yellow jug or blue cornflowers with yellow marigolds or red roses in a green rose bowl. Although these arrangements are fairly simple once this colour relationship has been understood, many people will still want bowls of mixed flowers, using many varieties and leaves of several shapes and colours.

Bearing in mind the primary and complementary colours, many variations can be made. We need not have a bright red with a strong green. Some soft pastel red or pink would serve with a pale green vase, or flowers of these colours could be mixed with many of the pale and subtle shades of green found in many of the grasses. Mauves can be mixed with primrose or cream; apricots, golden-yellows, lemon, cream and white can go with dark blue and light blue.

Other colour blends can be made without reference to complementary harmony. Many colours can be used which merge into each other, with only slight variations, and they are known as analogous colours. Examples are tints and shades which run through red, violet and blue or through blue, green and yellow. There are many natural flower analogies. Nasturtiums, for instance, with their reds, yellows, creams and shades of brown and orange can be arranged together to give a pleasing effect where nothing looks out of place. The same can be said for zinnias, wallflowers, delphiniums, marigolds, daffodils, narcissi and Michaelmas daisies.

Many flower arrangers will study these natural examples and learn much from them. Many wild flowers and berries show this colour analogy as well. How often on a country walk have we seen a grassy bank spread with flowers, and have thought that they might have been a well-thought-out colour scheme?

Besides the colour harmonies we have discussed, there are also the contrasting colours. Here one must use care. Too glaring a contrast is disturbing, yet one bold departure from all the rules could be stimulating. In an arrangement of mauve, blue and white cornflowers with lemon marigolds, one single bright orange marigold as a contrasting flower would be sufficient. Even then it might have to be partially hidden somewhere in the centre of the container.

Fruits and berries can provide extra unusual colour when required. They can be used at any stage: berries may be green, yellow, orange, red or black as long as they harmonize or contrast with the flowers or container. When using foliage, the kind and colour to blend well with the flowers must be chosen. Maidenhair fern would go well with sweet peas or carnations, golden privet with forsythia and daffodils, and copper beech would make a good background for red gladioli in a large display.

One of the rewarding things about flower arranging is that once a knowledge of colour and some skill in the placing of flowers have been acquired, there is no limit to the variety of flowers and designs which can be used. There is no need for someone with room to grow flowers in his garden ever to purchase expensive florist's flowers. Recherché arrangements as pleasing and satisfying as any can be made from flowers grown in one's own garden.

The best time for cutting flowers from the cut-flower border is about ten in the morning. Most of the flowers will be fully out by this time, but the sun's heat will not have been strong enough to make some of the flowers flag. If you cut flowers in the evening, remember that some flowers start to close up early, for example annual chrysanthemums. It is then difficult to arrange them properly or to see their true colours and the shapes they will assume next day.

Having thought out the colour scheme, cut the flowers and lay them in separate colours on the table, which should be covered with a soft cloth. Fix the wire netting holder, and partly fill the receptacle with water until it nearly reaches the top. A pair of scissors will be needed as flower stems will have to be cut to different lengths.

The semi-circular design is a fairly easy one for beginners to attempt. Start the arrangement by inserting flowers all of one colour. The first one to be placed is the central stem. Put this as near the centre of the receptacle as possible. This will be the tallest flower. It might be difficult at first to keep it there in an upright position, but other flowers can be wedged against it to hold it firm as the arrangement proceeds. These will be flowers on shorter stems.

After fixing the central stem, put one at each side, of the same length, at right angles or near to right angles. Then fill in to make a pleasing design with all of the flowers of one particular colour which you are using. Stems will be shortened as necessary. Fill in with the next colour, and so on. Complete the picture by putting some short stems around the edge of the bowl and one or two in the centre of the bowl, or anywhere where wire netting or stalks need to be hidden. Some flowers should slightly hang over the edge of the receptacle and partly hide it here and there. Many flowers in the arrangement will be partly hidden, others showing up boldly, and the whole arrangement should be effective when viewed from any angle.

So far we have considered an arrangement which relies on a massed display of colour. There are many other designs which can be used as basic ideas and then adapted, improved upon, or altered in some way to make your own original displays.

The 'Hogarth Curve', used so much by professional flower arrangers and makers of florists' bouquets, can be used as a base and then altered to suit individual taste. It is roughly an S shape, used vertically or horizontally, or in any way between an upright or horizontal position. When we are using the 'Hogarth Curve' or a crescent shape, or a combination of the two, we are making the accent on line instead of on massing. When an arrangement is used thus with line as the accent, there should be a centre of interest which is called the 'focal point'. This is achieved by placing one, or sometimes several, brightly coloured or contrasting flowers at the point where the stems radiate from the rim of the receptacle. The focal point could consist of a single flower which is much larger than the rest of the arrangement. Usually rounded flowers are best for the focal point in a vase of mixed flowers, leaving some flowers partly open at each side of the focal point flower, and next to these, some in bud and then spiky flowers to continue the line.

Every flower display indoors, large or small, should be carefully planned. Several small arrangements dotted about a room are rarely satisfying; one larger, well-designed one is generally more in keeping. It is important to have good balance in all displays and to maintain harmony of design throughout.

FLOWER ARRANGEMENTS FOR EACH MONTH

Here is a list of flowers for arranging each month. Every one of these flowers may be grown in most people's gardens and there will be no need for costly purchases. They may be arranged by one of the methods described and if some of the flowers are not grown in the cut-flower border or elsewhere, other flowers of equal merit may be substituted.

January Laurustinus for foliage and flowers to give body to the arrangement. Winter Jasmine, and then some of the preserved everlasting flowers added to the bowl. These could be yellow *Achillea*, yellow and white *Helichrysum*, yellow and blue *Statice*, love-in-the-mist seed heads, and any well-shaped ivy foliage with green and yellow berries.

February Enough Christmas roses might be found in flower, and some snowdrops. Laurustinus can still be used, as it will still be in flower. The rest of the bowl will again have to be the preserved flowers. Green-blue hydrangea heads will harmonize with this arrangement, and sea holly, catananche, and the seed heads of old man's beard or the wild clematis. If quite a lot of snowdrops are to be seen, these are attractive on their own, in medium-sized containers, with some suitable foliage or just their own leaves.

March An arrangement consisting of early daffodils, *Elaeagnus variegatum*, forsythias and golden privet, where just greens and yellows are used, really looks superb.

April More daffodils and jonquils will form the basis of an April arrangement, with primroses, yellow polyanthus and primulas, doronicums and white arabis. For blue flowers with this arrangement, some grape hyacinths and aquilegias may be out in sheltered spots. Forget-me-nots may be used, but they soon fade when cut and put into water. They would have to be frequently replaced. Some blue anemones, blue primroses or early blue aubrietia might also be available.

May For a May floral design, late-flowering narcissi, such as 'Pheasant's Eye', golden alyssum, aubrietia in variety, doronicums and catmint may be put together. A combination of pyrethrums in variety, with many of the flowering shrubs now in bloom, will make pleasing displays, if one is careful to combine harmonizing colours.

June There are innumerable displays which can be made in June, because there is such a variety of flowers available. Roses can be tastefully arranged, with some of the flowers in bud and some just past the bud stage, but none fully out, or they will only last a couple of days. The English irises, grown from bulbs, will now provide lovely material for cutting, and arranging. Aquilegias in many combinations of colours mix beautifully with other suitable flowers, grasses or foliage. Many sweet peas will now be in bloom, if they were autumn sown. The varieties of sweet peas mentioned earlier will all look very attractive arranged in a bowl together, or with gypsophila if there is some available.

July We now come into a month when many of the autumn- and spring-sown annual flowers are in their full glory. A pleasing combination of flowers can be made from red shades of the annual chrysanthemums, white, pink and red cornflowers, pink annual salvias (clary), red nasturtiums, and white 'Esther Read' *Chrysanthemum maximum*.

From the perennials endless displays can be made from delphiniums, erigerons, purple loosestrife, nepetas, rudbeckias, sidalceas and heliopsis. Lovely designs with mixed zinnias and ornamental grasses in copper or brass containers are now possible. For another arrangement for July, using the blue and yellow complementary scheme, the following can be used: blue and white cornflowers, 'Esther Read' or single *Chrysanthemum maximum*, yellow and cream calendulas, yellow and white annual chrysanthemums, purple salvias (clary), and violet, mauve and white candytuft.

August August will bring us plenty of gladioli which can be arranged with suitable foliage and gypsophila. *Sedum spectabile* and many red shades of dahlias can be incorporated in schemes where red will predominate. Another good floral design uses red dahlias, red shades of annual chrysanthemums, red nasturtiums, pink and white cornflowers, pink salvias (clary) and spiraeas. We must not forget the beautiful globe thistles, for these wonderful flowers are now at their best and they add a touch of quality and originality to any blue and yellow scheme. If the annual gypsophila is sown at frequent intervals, sweet peas may be arranged with it and with ornamental grasses. This combination can be in the house from June until October.

September A lovely arrangement for September consists of mauve, purple and blue Michaelmas daisies, purple, maroon and blue cornflowers, lemon and gold calendulas, yellow and white annual chrysanthemums, yellow heleniums, yellow nasturtiums, purple larkspurs, violet salvias (clary) and tall lavender and mauve shades of sweet scabious. These scabious can be in the centre and fanning out at right angles. Many displays of the single and double asters may be made now, and many early-flowering outdoor chrysanthemums can also be used.

October Michaelmas daisies of all varieties and out door chrysanthemums will form the background for most arrangements during this month. Annual sweet scabious will be also a very useful subject for autumn displays. Ideal for foliage effect are the bright yellow lower leaves of curly kale from the vegetable garden, and the variegated kales, if these are grown. *Solidago* (golden rod) will be a beautiful partner for the blue shades of Michaelmas daisies and asters. Some yellow calendulas, nigellas, larkspurs and annual chrysanthemums can still be gathered, if dead flowers have been removed regularly.

November This is a month when the Korean chrysanthemums can be used in conjunction with much autumn foliage now available in a rich variety of colouring. The coloured barks of *Cornus alba* and *Cornus stolonifera*, together with many seed heads and berries, can also be utilized. Some winter jasmine may also be coming into flower. It must be remembered that in order to produce richly-coloured winter wood, the *Cornus* must be pruned back hard every spring.

December The Christmas wreath, to hang on the front door, seems to come into fashion in some parts, stay a while, and then go out for a few years. In case they come in again soon, I will show how they can be made. They are not difficult, and can be made in any shape you choose, and not only in circles. Oval and heart-shaped or some other design are just as easy to make.

A wire frame is constructed first, to the shape wanted; this can be done by any handyman. Take two pieces of stout galvanized wire and bend them to shape and finish with two wire rims running parallel to each other. Squeeze in plenty of ordinary moss between the two rims. Then bind it in firmly with green string, by passing the string over and over the moss and round under the wire frame. Then cover the mossed framework with foliage; this can be thrust into the moss, or it can be wired in.

Next, wire in the holly; this can be variegated holly which looks more colourful, and it can have berries the whole way round or congregated in the right-hand corner or at some other focal point. *Pyracantha* berries can be used with the red holly berries, either the red or yellow variety. More colour can be added with the use of orange *Physalis* and one or two showy candles, either red or yellow. Other material which can be used effectively in the making of one of these wreaths is golden privet, variegated box, white snowberries, ivy foliage, flowers and berries, dried hydrangea heads or any of the preserved flowers. Any suitable coniferous evergreen foliage can be utilized, and colourful green, red or yellow ribbon may be used.

For the Christmas lunch-table decoration, have a low container that will not easily be knocked over. Family and guests must be able to see over the top of the flowers and not have to look through them or peer round them. Avoid too much artificial decoration such as silvered or gilded leaves or imitation snow. A couple of the coloured glass spheres, generally used on Christmas trees, and which will catch and reflect the light in a continuous mauve, white or yellow sparkle, are suitable. A satisfying Christmas table decoration can be made with variegated holly with red berries, mistletoe, the red bark of *Cornus*, *Elaeagnus variegatum*, *Physalis*, a little honesty and red helichrysums.

Many people dig a Christmas tree from the garden or copse, often damaging the roots, put it into a cardboard container, leave it in a hot stuffy room for about two weeks, without water, then wonder why it dies away when they plant it again outside, often in freezing conditions.

If you want your Christmas tree year after year, then you must give it the right treatment. Dig it from the garden carefully, do not damage the roots, and have a ball of soil adhering to it. Select a large pot or large wooden box. Put in drainage material and some ordinary garden soil. Plant the tree into the pot or box, and make quite firm. Give a good watering. Stand the tree on some waterproof material or in a large tray so that it does not damage valuable furniture by dampness. When Christmas is over gradually harden the tree off, before planting on a mild day. Give the pot or box some water over Christmas, if the soil becomes very dry. Do not select a Christmas tree which is too large for the room it will occupy.

FLOWERS FOR STAGE SHOWS AND CONCERTS

Flowers bedecking a village or town concert hall on the occasion of a play or concert by the local dramatic society, not only add to the enjoyment of the audience, but also creates the good impression that the surroundings matter, as well as the stage. Such good impressions are needed in these days of thin support for local shows, and a good display of flowers will perhaps attract to subsequent productions people who would have been put off by a neglected auditorium. It is difficult enough to attract large crowds to local shows these days, and a nice setting with floral displays is one of the inducements to come again.

A good dramatic society usually has several members who have good gardens with plenty of flowers, who can help. This is sometimes difficult, because often plays are produced from November until about May, when flowers are in short supply. Some members may possess greenhouses, however, and may be able to lend colourful pot plants.

If flowers cannot be obtained in this way, then it is a good idea to approach a local nurseryman who will often provide flowers free of charge as a form of advertising. A note to this effect, stating the nurseryman's name, and the fact that he supplied the flowers, is then printed on the programme. Some nurserymen will make just a small charge for the flowers, the prices being very much below the usual ones. Others will lend free of charge such items as hanging baskets and suitable receptacles, and some will provide flowers and equipment.

Perhaps the nurseryman will supply basic material in this way and members or other helpers may be able to provide or collect suitable foliage. Members might also bring along some large containers for the flowers.

The flowers provided might as an extra amenity be ones which suit the particular play or concert: plenty of gay colour and lightness of blossom for a musical; for a play where the scene is set in a middle-class drawing-room, perhaps gladioli and perennial scabious; an unusual or weird arrangement for a mystery; roses or sweet peas for a romantic setting; cottage garden flowers for a play about the country; and old-fashioned flowers like sweet williams, the old rose species, and lavender for historical plays. The thought behind such choices will be wasted on many but not on all.

A large number of flowers can be used in concert halls because they will in no way detract from the performance; for the flowers will be in darkness once the play or concert begins. The best way to display the flowers is to put them in hanging baskets, with plenty of foliage, along each side of the hall. Some way of fixing them very securely to the walls must be found, for we must not have them crashing down during the performance or before. Flowers should also be banked up at each side of the stage; there is usually plenty of room for them here. In the foyer also there should be an attractive and welcoming bowl of flowers.

Inside the hanging baskets there must be a container with a flower holder of wire netting. The flowers should be arranged during the morning of the first day's performance. It is advisable to start early, as it is surprising how long an attractive display for a large hall takes to prepare. Several keen flower arrangers could take part in this. Before each night's performance the containers will need to be topped up with water. In the heat of the theatre a very great amount of water is absorbed by the flowers, and some dead ones will have to be replaced with fresh ones as the nights go by.

Flowers to suit types of plays have been mentioned, but here again the flowers which are available and in season will have to be used. Some of the 'everlastings' and preserved flowers might have to be used, unless some members have large greenhouses and can supply enough flowers to suit the occasion. Berries and grasses can be brought into service.

Even nurserymen who will not bother with cut flowers might lend as a form of advertising, such pot plants as cinerarias, coleus, geraniums, primulas, and schizanthus. Some stages have one or two steps at the front leading up to the acting platform and cinerarias look well here, if one or two are put together on each step, so that they show one above the other. Watering will have to be done carefully so that none is spilled on to the steps.

If hanging baskets are impractical, special wall flower containers may be used. When making flower displays for concert halls, it will be realized that they have to be on a much larger scale than home decoration if they are to be effective. They have to be viewed by a large number of people from a distance, therefore a fairly large number of flowers with plenty of foliage will be employed. A few bright flowers must certainly be used. They have to be seen from behind other people so they have to be placed high enough. Ever-greens, ivy and ferns, which are nearly always easily obtainable in country towns, together with any decorative shrub foliage, are the best materials to use as backgrounds to the flowers.

Colours should be grouped and not dispersed or dotted about the foliage. Bold groups of colour are most desirable. The faces of most of the flowers should show towards the audience. When making these flower arrangements for concert halls, always remember colour harmony or contrasts, and have these correct, for errors of judgment will show up very forcibly here.

In many plays, where the action takes place in the rooms of a house, vases of flowers are needed on a table or mantelpiece. Here are the flowers which could match those in the hall, unless specific flowers are mentioned in the script, or if the action takes place at an inappropriate time of the year. In this connection there is further scope for the flower arranger. Very often the flowers on stage will need to be suited to the furniture or the actresses' dresses.

Flowers for the concert hall display will have to be cut and put together ready for transport to the hall the evening before the day of arranging. This will take some time because there will probably be a large number. Leave them overnight in large containers of water in a cool place. All flowers need a long cool drink before being arranged.

There is no reason why members of dramatic societies should possess a set of show equipment like the professional exhibitors for displaying their flowers. Many kinds of containers which are readily available can be adapted to unusual purposes. For instance, those tin wastepaper baskets which can be purchased cheaply in some of the large stores make admirable large receptacles for displays of flowers in large halls. Just press some wire netting into shape to fit the container and partly fill with water. Plain bins can be obtained, or patterns on them can be obscured by overhanging foliage or flowers. Ordinary enamel buckets can also be used, with handles similarly concealed by greenery and blooms.

Transport the flowers and foliage to the hall in a van with just a little water in the containers, or lay them carefully on the back seat of a car. A trestle table or a large unpolished table which can be used without worrying about spilt water, is the best sort of table for arranging the flowers on. If this is not available then use a thick old coloured tablecloth over another kind of table. Containers to fit the hanging baskets for the walls will be fitted into the baskets, and it is very important to hang these baskets on the walls all in a perfectly straight line. Have the same space between baskets on both walls.

Be careful not to place any pot plants or flowers in such a position as to hamper the entry and exit of actors. These precautions also apply to emergency exits, doors and passages used by the general public. This will generally be pointed out by the producer. If the leading lady or the producer is to be presented with a bouquet at the end of the performance, there is further scope here for the good floral artist. A good amateur flower arranger can make a fully acceptable bouquet, if she or he has the requisite flowers available.

The very best blooms that one possesses must be used for this work, and they must be ones which are just out. For the presentation bouquet it is best to use what I call top-class flowers, and these include (according to the time of year) roses, daffodils, narcissi, tulips, carnations, lilies of all types, delphiniums, irises, pyrethrums, sweet peas (with the bottom flower only just out), gladioli (primulus and butterfly type only), dahlias (dwarf), hydrangeas, chrysanthemums, scabious (perennial and annual), stocks of all kinds, and Christmas roses.

Other flowers can be used in conjunction with these to lighten up the bouquet. Good specimens of cornflowers, gypsophila (perennial and annual), larkspurs, love-in-the-mist and ornamental grasses will be suitable for this work. Sweet peas have been included because they are so lovely and are ideal for bouquets, being everyone's favourite. However, one must be careful when using sweet peas, as they soon flag. Cut them in the early morning with the bottom flower just open on each stalk and the rest in bud. Place them immediately in water, and put the receptacle in a cool, shady place. Sweet peas for this work or for showing, need a few hours in water before arrangement.

Where and when possible, the bouquet should stand in a bucket of water somewhere out of view of the recipient. A few minutes before the presentation the bouquet can be taken out of the water and the stalks are wiped to remove excessive moisture; the whole can then be carefully inserted in a cellophane wrapper.

To make the bouquet, gather some suitable light foliage. Although not a lot of foliage will be required, we need a background to lay the flowers on. Having selected several pieces of foliage, we need to place this flat in the shape of a half-open fan. Any suitable leafage will do but it must be light in character. Any heavy-looking stems can be hidden by the use of dainty pieces of fern. About six inches from the bottom of the stalks, the foliage is bound with green soft string to keep it in place while the flowers are being placed on it. An average length for a presentation bouquet would be about eighteen inches. They can be longer, but not much shorter.

Take the longest flower to be used and place it in the centre on the foliage with the bloom facing the front. Next, select two shorter ones and place them by the side of the first one. Then build around these with shorter stems until flowers are showing all the way down and out in a half-open fan-shape to about three-quarters of the way down to the ends of the stalks. Do not cut the stalks at the end in a straight line across, as this looks rather unnatural; have them of varying lengths.

Think of colour harmony or contrast all the time, and if you are using heavy-type flowers, lighten the look of the bouquet by putting in gypsophila, ornamental grasses or other very delicate flowers. When all the flowers have been placed in position, bind round again with green string and fasten the flowers to the foliage. Florists' wire can be used if you prefer. A piece of ribbon of a suitable colour can finally be tied round, ending in a bow to hide the green string. If ribbon is not used, the string can be hidden with fine-textured fern.

A person who can fashion good bouquets of this nature can make them for many occasions, for swimming galas, fêtes, garden parties and for presentation to well-known personalities who may visit a town or village for some special function.

When choosing flowers for presentation bouquets, try to avoid those which are commonly used for wreaths and funereal tributes. Dark-coloured asters or chrysanthemums and the arum lilies are best left out.

Most of the foregoing recommendations apply equally to flower arranging in churches. It is noticeable in some churches that while most of the flowers are tastefully arranged, they often cannot be seen when the congregation stands up. They need to be seen at all times. In all windows they should be put into some special wall container if the window ledges are not wide enough to accommodate flower receptacles. A hanging basket of flowers in the porch is a very welcoming sight.

Almost all flowers can be used in church, and for very many different occasions. In flower arranging for the home or for church, I do not think there is any need for the elaborate hammering and crushing of stems, or boiling water treatment, as advocated by some professionals. Churches in particular are usually cool in summer and very cold in winter. This means that flowers displayed in church will last longer in water than they do in other places, especially if the water is frequently topped up. The flowers look well and last well, because stained-glass windows offer shade and subdued lighting. Yew and other large coniferous trees in the churchyard also give some shade. This, together with the stone construction of the church, ensures that the interior is always cool. In winter it is usually indeed very cold, except on Sunday when the heating is switched on. This does not matter a great deal because chrysanthemums are nearly always used in winter, and these can withstand cold conditions.

As with concert halls, so with churches; we have to contend with vast spaces, so that simple, bold effects are best, and there is no need for a tremendous number of different varieties at any one time. Good brilliant colour in dark corners, light-coloured flowers against or near stained-glass windows, and in all cases as much light as possible shining on to the flowers: these are the principal rules to follow.

Do not use the unsuitable tall thin glass vases found in many churches. Acquire and use some which are more in keeping with the surroundings, such as stone urns, robust vessels of many shapes and sizes, or old weathered earthenware mixing bowls. They need to have considerable capacity for holding plenty of water. Pottery and china containers in good clean chapes, and anything suitable made of copper, always look well. Brass, bronze and pewter reflect lights and flatter flowers of the right colours. Silver is not very suitable on account of the endless cleaning involved.

To achieve the right height for the flowers so that everyone can see them, they should be placed on high tables or pedestals as well as on window sills, and in hanging baskets or wall holders. Pedestals can be acquired or made by local craftsmen who are friends of the church. Pedestals can be found, made of stone, wood or wrought iron. Wooden ones can be plain or carved. They should blend in well with their surroundings and for this purpose they may be painted in some soft pastel shade. Gold or silver paint in a church, or anywhere else, nearly always has an artificial look about it.

Arrange the flowers in church as advised, but when doing so be careful not to drop wet foliage on to the stone floor and cause accidents: one can all too easily slip on wet leaves when lifting a heavy urn up to a fairly high pedestal. If you are arranging a pair of vases for any position in the church, first divide the flowers and foliage into two equal lots. This seems obvious enough, yet not all flower arrangers think of it.

Weddings and harvest festivals are the occasions offering plenty of scope when keen flower arrangers can exhibit their skill and art to the fullest extent. The bright vegetables, berries, flowers, fruit, corn and other grasses provide a great amount of material for tasteful display when the Harvest Festival service arrives.

It will not be possible to include in special decorative arrangements all the masses of vegetables and fruit brought in. Make one or two well-planned and artistic arrangements in special positions, using a combination of fruit, flowers, foliage and vegetables, bearing in mind the need for good colour schemes, shape and line. There are so many harmonious colours to play with, using red apples, orange carrots, purple cabbage, the red and purple lower leaves of cottager's kale, autumn foliage, red shades of dahlias and chrysanthemums with perhaps some large white chrysanthemums at a focal point. Blues and yellows are found in the marrows, swedes, apples, grapes, yellow dahlias and chrysanthemums, Michaelmas daisies, asters and cornflowers.

When the special show-pieces have been completed, try to arrange the rest of the produce as artistically as possible.

For weddings, the church can be tastefully decorated, but it must not be overdone. A couple of good displays of flowers would be ample, and not distract too much attention from the bride and central figures. Flowers will be chosen from whatever is available at the time of the year. The bride will be consulted about which flowers she would like used, but she usually leaves it to the skilled arranger. Flowers should be chosen to match or make pleasant contrast with the bridesmaids' dresses. Plenty of white flowers can be used at all weddings; other colours could perhaps be pastel shades of blue or pink, according to the colour of the dresses worn.

Some very artistic amateur flower arrangers, who have deft fingers, might be able to make a good job of the bride's bouquet and guests' buttonhole flowers. Although most practised flower arrangers can quite well manage the floral displays in church, they might not think themselves competent to make a bride's bouquet or buttonhole flowers. If the date of the wedding is known some months beforehand, flower arrangers may be able to practise the art of making a bride's flower sheaf and guests' buttonhole assemblage. They may use any flowers for practice but not the choice lilies or other flowers which may have been chosen for the wedding day.

The bride's sheaf must be wired with florist's wire. The principal function of a wire is to give additional strength to the stem of a flower and to make sure that the blooms do not break away from the stems. It is most important that a bride's bouquet remain in perfect condition during the ceremony and afterwards when photographs are being taken. Florist's wires are supplied in several gauges or thicknesses and are generally ten inches and fourteen inches long. The higher the number of the gauge the thinner the wire. As a general rule, light-weight blooms need light-weight wire, and vice versa.

When making up a bride's bouquet, each flower stem will have to be wired separately. It must be stressed that only perfect flowers should be used. Holding one of the chosen flowers in the left hand, and the wire in the right between the forefinger and thumb, thrust the end of the wire into the seed box of the flower from underneath and close to the stem. Then bring the wire down and twist around the stem in a corkscrew fashion, moving round the stem in an anti-clockwise direction. Do not twist the flower in any way. The wire should be wound round closely to the stem and be as inconspicuous as possible.

There are one or two other forms of wiring which may need to be employed in the making of a bouquet. Some flowers lack stem foliage to hide the wiring. Then invisible wiring is employed. This is used with hollow-stemmed flowers such as zinnias, daffodils and narcissi. In this case, the wire is forced up the hollow stem from below, until it reaches and fixes itself into the flower, but without protruding through the bloom and becoming visible or dangerous. Care must be taken when wiring to see that no foliage is bound into the stem so that it looks unnatural.

After each flower has been given its supporting wire, a further wire for mounting each flower on to the foliage at the back of the design will have to be attached to each flower stem. Holding the stem in the left hand between forefinger and thumb, thrust the end of the mounting wire through the stem at a point which is about one inch from the bottom of the stem. The mounting wire will now protrude on either side of the stem, but on the right-hand side we need the wire to be about an inch and a half longer than it is on the other side. This can be achieved while thrusting through, or it can be drawn back a little to allow for the difference in length. We now pull down the left-hand wire close to the stem, and then the right, to make a hairpin shape. Then, taking the tip of the longer wire, on the right, and holding the whole in the left hand, we go round the bottom of the stem in an anti-clockwise fashion, binding in the left leg of our mounting wire. We complete this wiring by having two legs running parallel and protruding from the bottom of the stem.

When making the bride's sheaf of flowers, the height of the bride must be taken into consideration. A short bride will need a shorter bouquet than a tall bride. To begin making the bouquet, select the longest flower, which will be the centrepiece. Take a long piece of asparagus fern, or other light suitable foliage, and attach it to the back of the flower firmly with green thread. Take the two next longest flowers and lay them on each side of the central stem. Bind these three stems and foliage together with green wire or soft green string. This part of the bouquet will be the part which the bride will grasp. The fourth flower is now applied and it should be placed over the stem of the central flower. Now begin to widen the sheaf a little by placing other flowers further out to the right and left of the central stem. Fill in any obvious spaces with some delicate foliage as the work proceeds.

The sheaf can be short and squat or long and slender. It can remain as one piece made as already described, or another one, exactly the same, can be made and the two are joined together by means of the mounting wires. When the second piece has been made, it will be placed in a position opposite to the first one, so that the end stalks of each are joined together. Where the return ends join, some fern will be added, or perhaps some small flowers to the front, to hide the ends of the stalks and the wiring. This is where the bride will hold the bouquet.

The sheaf must now be turned over carefully and any protruding wires are cut or bound into the stems and foliage, so that none can damage hands or material. Ribbon can be put round the carrying part of the bouquet if you like.

Carnations are still the most popular flowers for buttonhole wear at weddings. These can be wired in a similar manner to that described but most people prefer them not wired. More than one carnation may be used for a buttonhole and other foliage besides fern may be employed. Green and variegated ivy leaves, autumn leaves suiting the colour of the carnations, gypsophila, carnation foliage, love-in-the-mist foliage and other delicate leaves might be used.

COLLECTING FLOWER HOLDERS

We have discussed at some length in this chapter the arrangement of flowers in the home and elsewhere. One of the problems which arises with this delightful occupation is how to acquire a number of suitable flower receptacles. There is a way of collecting these flower containers without going to the great expense of purchasing them from florists' shops.

One way is to visit all local jumble sales. Here, for a few coppers, you will find many odd pieces of old china, glassware, pewter and brass; often many of them have graceful and suitable shapes. Capacious old water jugs, which used to be a familiar sight in Victorian bedrooms, are just the thing for large displays of colourful flowers in a hall or large room. Various ancient soap dishes, tureens, teapots, jugs of all kinds, sugar basins, butter dishes, vases, fruit bowls, meat and vegetable dishes, mugs, saucers and large deep plates can all be obtained at very little cost and all can make wonderful containers for floral displays.

Store these treasures in a safe cupboard where they will not easily be knocked over and broken, or put them on a high shelf. Perhaps some elderly relations have some of these kinds of flower container tucked away somewhere, for which they have no further use, and they might be willing to let keen flower arrangers have them.

There are two other ways of obtaining these materials at a reasonable price. One is to visit market stalls. On market day, there is

nearly always more than one stall which has for sale a selection display
of the articles we have been looking for. These can usually be purchased for a reasonable sum, but do not invariably give the price
marked. On occasions, some of these pieces are marked at a sum
far above their real value; in these cases, if you see something you
really want just make an offer of what you think it is worth.

The other method of collecting these containers is to go to an
antique or junk shop. Here you can have an unhurried look round
and make offers for what you see. At the same time any little figures
which will look well beside a bowl of flowers can be obtained, also
any suitable garden ornaments or garden furniture. Many useful
acquisitions can be made at furniture sales. It is as well, too, to make
a collection of any odd wire netting which is lying around, or of
florists' wire, and store this with the containers in the cupboard.
Many an unusual flower receptacle acquired in one of the ways
suggested has won prizes at important flower shows.

WINDOW BOXES

How can the people of London and other large cities practise the
art of gardening, when they live in confined spaces with their smoke-
laden atmospheres and where there is no spare land? House plants
in pots are immediately thought of as the solution. There is also
another form of garden which can bring much permanent joy to its
creator, an attractively planned and colourful window box. The
popularity of window boxes is increasing in this country, and they
have been a colourful feature of many Continental cities for years.

The boxes are constructed of pine, oak, teak and deal. A box made
of teak will last for many years, but a deal box only has a life of about
three years. It will have to be painted on the outside with an under-
coating and a couple of coats of hard gloss paint on top. Never use
creosote for window boxes, for it is detrimental to plant life. The box
should be at least eight inches deep and about ten inches wide or wide
enough to fit the sill. The length will, of course, depend upon the
length of the window sill. If the sill is sloping in any direction it must
be made level by inserting wedges underneath the box. If the boxes
are not level water will run in one direction, and maybe some corner
of the box will be saturated and other parts very dry.

Window boxes should have one or two drainage holes cut into the
bottom of the box. Over these, place some crocks and then a little
well-rotted compost and some leaf mould. The rest of the box can
be filled with John Innes potting compost. It is important, especially
with boxes which are well above ground level, for them to be fixed
firmly by some means to the wall of the house. It would be very

20

A WINDOW BOX FIXED TO WALL AND WEDGED

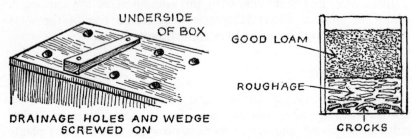

UNDERSIDE OF BOX

GOOD LOAM

ROUGHAGE

DRAINAGE HOLES AND WEDGE
SCREWED ON

CROCKS

Window boxes and their construction

dangerous to have a heavy box in position which is liable to go crashing down into the street below.

The watering programme for window boxes must be carefully carried out. Many plants in window boxes are killed by over-watering. Water only enough to keep the soil moist. Some boxes will be able to receive the natural rainfall, others will be under over-hanging eaves and liable to dry out, unless watering is attended to. In winter, a weekly watering will be ample in most cases.

Flower seeds sown directly into window boxes in large towns rarely give satisfactory results. Pot-grown plants transplanted into the window boxes at various times throughout the year will enable you to enjoy a continuous display of colour. Suitable plants must be selected, as not all flowers will grow well under these conditions.

For the first display in spring, a filling of mixed bulbs is suitable. Crocuses are best omitted, especially in boxes above ground level. They are too often attacked by house sparrows, and so are primulas and primroses. Hyacinths are very attractive subjects for the window box, either in one variety or in mixed colours, and they have a long flowering period. It is not absolutely essential to plant the bulbs in autumn directly into the window box. Bulbs which are growing in the

open garden from an autumn planting can be dug up and transferred
to the window box during late February or March. This only applies
where there is a garden as well as window boxes. Those who live in the
city with only a window box will have to plant their bulbs into the
box during autumn.

A good flower to follow the bulbs are ten weeks' stocks and then
geraniums. The stocks will probably be purchased in boxes. Water the
box of stocks and when transferring them to the window box keep
some soil pressed around the roots. Well water in and plant firmly.
Geraniums will be in pots and this will promote ease of planting. Do
not plant out geraniums into window boxes before the third week in
May, otherwise they may be damaged by frost and take some time
to recover. The whole object of window box planting is to provide a
continuous display of colour without any check. Some geraniums
refuse to flower well where there is a lot of traffic, with the resultant
smoke and petrol fumes. Ascertain from your local nurseryman the
best varieties to plant in your particular district.

Ageratum and Heliotrope grow very well in city areas, and so do
many kinds of fuchsia. Petunias and lobelia are other suitable
window box plants. It must be remembered that window box flowers,
unlike those in the open garden, do not have unlimited root run
and plant food supplies, so their full flowering period is somewhat
shorter. Therefore it is usually advisable to make another planting
towards the end of May.

Coleus look well at this time of the year and plenty are usually
obtainable in pots. Some short varieties of early outdoor flowering
chrysanthemums are also suitable for planting now. For a winter
filling a shrub called *Skimmia japonica* is about the best subject. It has
bright red holly-like berries which are retained on the shrub from
November until May. Male and female forms are necessary for
berrying, so make sure that the right form is obtained from the
nurseryman. There must not be any lime in the soil for this shrub.

Throughout the year, the surface soil of the window box needs to
be pricked over or stirred. An old kitchen fork is useful for this
purpose. After planting, it is a good idea to cover the surface soil
with about an inch of granulated peat; this will help to conserve
moisture and discourage weeds. During the summer it is advisable to
add a very small amount of bonemeal between plantings. It will be
necessary to change the soil every other year.

As well as growing flowers, some people will like to try a few
vegetables or herbs. If a number of window boxes are being planted,
a flower display can be in those which face the street and there could
be a box near the kitchen containing herbs and another with
vegetables growing in it. Lettuce, stump-rooted carrots, radishes and

spring onions can all be grown in window boxes. The best variety of lettuce to grow is 'All-the-year-round', but if this is thought to be too large, 'Tom Thumb' could be grown instead. The first sowing could be made in March, with continuous sowings throughout the summer and early autumn, keeping the soil moist. Carrots can be sown in March, using 'Chantenay Red-Cored' or 'Tip Top'. Radishes are easy to grow; thin them out by using the largest first. Suitable varieties for window box culture are 'Cherry Belle', 'French Breakfast', 'Scarlet Globe' and 'Sparkler'. Sow in March. Also make a sowing in March of white Lisbon Onion for pulling green for salads. Sow all of these vegetable seeds shallowly and thinly. Thin out the lettuce early.

Many kinds of herb may be grown in window boxes. The most useful are mint, sage, parsley and thyme. A sowing of parsley may be made in March. It takes longer than most seeds to germinate, so it must be kept moist. It is usual to thin the plants to six inches apart, but in a window box three inches would have to be sufficient. It would be best to obtain from a friend a piece of rooted mint. This is quite easy to grow if the soil is kept moist. The sage is a perennial and as only about four plants would be required it would be best to purchase these. Thyme can be obtained and planted similarly.

HANGING BASKETS

Hanging baskets of flowers add distinction to any garden and are very valuable in a small garden of formal character, where they fit in well with the surroundings. Two wire baskets filled with colourful flowers hanging above the back door porch, one at each side with the lawns and flower borders stretching out ahead, is a very attractive garden feature. They can also hang at the front door and sometimes they are used as extra decoration in the cool greenhouse.

Fairly large wire baskets are best for a good display and the only problem is watering and how to keep the soil moist without it running away through the wire. To cover the soil on the exterior side, moss is used. Sphagnum moss is the best moss for this purpose. A thin plastic lining can be put between the moss and the soil, but a few drainage holes would need to be pierced through it.

Put in the moss first, and pack it tightly around the wire frame with the green part of the moss showing through the wire. If using a plastic lining, put a layer of moist soil next to the moss before fitting in the lining. This is for the moss to root in and feed upon. At the bottom of the wire frame and around the sides put some rotted garden compost and coarse leaf-mould, to prevent the finer soil running away through the wire frame, after watering. Fill the remainder of the basket with a mixture of John Innes No. 2 compost or a similar soil.

Hanging baskets look much more attractive if they are suspended from a well-made bracket, rather than hanging from an ordinary nail. Before planting the basket, water the soil well while the basket is on the garden and before hanging in its appointed place. Plant with a trowel and firm and water in well.

There are many plants which are suitable for hanging baskets and as in all flower gardening the colour scheme needs to be thought out. Tall, strong-growing flowers cannot be grown but there are a lot of satisfactory dwarf, semi-dwarf and trailing plants available. The shorter pink antirrhinums could be planted in conjunction with a

LINE WITH MOSS.

TRAILING PLANTS MAY BE PUSHED BETWEEN WIRES

Hanging baskets: preparation and planting

trailing variety of lobelia, either 'Blue Cascade' or 'Sapphire'. Geraniums make good plants for baskets and these can be used with petunias and trailing lobelia. Another good combination is the shrubby trailing periwinkle with its delightful blue flowers, inter-planted with yellow, cream and orange nasturtiums.

Never let hanging baskets dry out, and water them regularly. This can be done in two ways, either by taking them down and immersing them in a water tub, or by watering them with a watering-can while they are lying on the ground. It is never quite satisfactory to stand on a chair and water from above. One can easily fall from a chair while holding a heavy watering-can, and then there is the dripping of the water on the paved courtyard, or elsewhere. Always remove dead flower heads as they appear to keep up a continuous show of colour.

SOME NEW FLOWER INTRODUCTIONS

Many flowering plants are appearing as new introductions each year;

some are great improvements and some prove popular only for a year or so, and then sink into obscurity.

The best plan for the gardener is to try out a few of the new plants each year and then to grow those which are especially to his liking during other years. In this way something new will be in the garden each year.

If the gardener is contemplating planting some of the new roses advertised, he should have a good long look at them when they are in flower in a good nursery. Many of the new roses so colourfully displayed in catalogues are of doubtful vigour or disease resistance, and many are not an improvement on existing varieties.

A fairly new Cosmos called 'Goldcrest' appears to be a good cut flower, for it begins to flower in early summer and is semi-double. It is also a rich glowing orange-yellow. This would be a good flower to use in an arrangement with blue and white flowers.

There is now a green variety of the old-fashioned *Amaranthus caudatus* or love-lies-bleeding. This will probably be grown by many flower arrangers as the greenish-yellow tassels are of a colour not easily come by. It will be much more suitable for flower arranging than its old crimson counterpart, which is rather a dull colour and difficult to fit into colour schemes.

There are many new introductions of petunias of the F1 Hybrid Types and they are rather too numerous to mention here. 'Blue Lagoon' is a bright mid-blue, 'Gypsy' has large bright coral-cerise flowers, 'Pacesetter' is a brilliant carmine-rose, 'Pink Bountiful', a new shade in petunias, is a glistening salmon-pink, 'Tivoli' has white flowers boldly striped with cerise-scarlet, 'Starfire' is scarlet and white striped, and 'Red Cap' is an intense crimson-scarlet

There is a new race of Russell lupins which are dwarf, growing to a height of two and a half feet. The spikes and flowers are not quite so large as the well-known tall-growing varieties, but the flowers are early and there are plenty of them. There is a wide colour range, and if seed is sown early in the year in the cool greenhouse or cold frame they will flower the same year. Summer-sown seed will produce plants to be over-wintered and to flower during the following summer.

A dwarf French marigold, 'Yellow Nugget', is of a very useful bright yellow and the petals are attractively frilled. This is an F.1 Hybrid and the work involved in producing the seed makes it more expensive than other kinds.

There is an annual sweet william called 'Red Monarch'. If it is sown early under glass, the plants will flower in the same year from August onwards. The plants are fairly dwarf and compact, growing to a height of fifteen inches. It can also be used as a biennial like the other sweet williams.

Many new asters and antirrhinums are introduced nearly every year and there is not enough space to describe them all or even to describe each one mentioned in full detail. Of the asters, 'Super Princess Goldstrike' is a very deep yellow. The petals are at first broad and then they become quilled; this one seems to be an improvement on other yellow asters. 'Waltztime' is an aster which has very pretty twisted petals of a brilliant rose colour. The flowers are often five inches wide with eighteen-inch stems.

There is now a new antirrhinum which is really different from all others. It is called 'Bright Butterflies' and the flowers are most unusual, resembling those of the pentstemon. The flowers are much more open and there is a fine range of colours.

Of the flowers for the cool greenhouse, two of the most interesting are the double-flowered cyclamens and the *Lithops* which are known as 'Living stones'. The double cyclamens are vigorous and free-flowering but very shy of producing seed, thus making the seed rather expensive. The 'living stones' are succulents, belonging mainly to the *Mesembryanthemum* group. They have thick oval leaves, and bear a great resemblance to stones or pebbles. They can be grown in the cool greenhouse in pots and they need a sunny position and plenty of ventilation. They have resting periods when no watering is needed and will begin to grow again after the rest period.

The following flowers are new or of recent introduction and all can be used in floral displays. Some are annuals, others perennials, and they are in alphabetical order.

Achillea 'Cerise Queen' has flower heads of deep cherry-red and they can be treated as half-hardy annuals, flowering during the same summer from an April sowing. *Aquilegia* 'Dragonfly Hybrids' are a new variety offering a delightful range of colours. The maximum height is only eighteen inches. Grow from seed. Annual Chrysanthemum *spectabile becilia* is a flower with large single white blooms, and gold zones and centres. It is a very attractive flower for cutting.

An improved form of Unwin's 'Dwarf Hybrid Dahlias' has been produced, known as 'Dwarf Double Hybrids'. These have double or semi-double flowers in a glorious range of colour, including shades of apricot, salmon, orange, scarlet, crimson, bronze, yellow, white, cream and lavender. These are wonderfully free-flowering plants, one of the best flowers that any gardener can grow. They will fit in with any flower arrangement, and are easily grown from seed.

An annual delphinium, *chinensis* 'Blue Mirror', is a delightful low-growing annual with vivid gentian blue blossoms. *Delphinium* 'Connecticut Yankees' are single-flowered hardy perennials, growing to a height of three feet. Treated as half-hardy annuals and sown under glass in March, they can be in flower by August of the same year.

Impatiens 'Baby Varieties' are a fairly new dwarf strain of the ever-popular house plant known as Busy Lizzie. The plants are only six inches tall and from a mixed packet of seed plants with a colour range of shades of orange, pink, scarlet and white can be obtained. Treat as a half-hardy annual.

Layia elegans 'Cutting Gold' are easily grown hardy annuals, with single flowers like annual chrysanthemums. They have lovely gold centres with a prominent white edging. *Nigella* 'Persian Jewels' are a new colour breakthrough. Previously there was only a blue love-in-the-mist, but now we can obtain a wonderful array of new colours, including shades of rose, pink, mauve, purple, blue and white.

The dwarf compact 'Jewel' are a new race of nasturtiums. In most years the flowers of the old varieties of nasturtiums have been hidden by an excess of foliage. In this new type, the flowers are held well above the leaves. They produce a glorious mass of colour in all the nasturtium shades, are easily grown, and are good plants for flower arranging.

Polyanthus 'Pacific Giants' produce blooms of incredible size compared with other varieties. Shades of yellow, blue, red and white all have a long flowering period.

Rudbeckia gloriosa 'Double Daisies' are a lovely development. Rich golden-yellow, double and semi-double flowers up to four and a half inches across, often with a contrasting dark velvety centre on good stems, are freely produced. *Solidago* 'Baby Gold', when treated as a half-hardy annual, will produce in the first season large flower heads of a deep rich golden-yellow. It is only two feet in height.

Salvia 'Pink Rouge' gives us a new colour in salvias, a charming salmon-rose. *Salvia* 'Violet Crown' is another interesting colour break. Long violet-purple spikes are borne very freely on compact bushy plants. I grew the large-flowering gladiolus called 'Green Woodpecker' when it was first introduced, and I found that some of the lighter colours of the plumage of this colourful bird really were represented. It is a most unusual subject and a very valuable acquisition for flower arrangers.

9

Lawns and Grassland

Making a lawn — maintenance — tools for the lawn — managing other grassland

Lawns can be made in two ways, by seed sowing in autumn or spring, or by laying turf. Whichever method is used, thorough preparation of the site is essential. If a lawn is being made for the first time on a new site, where a house has been recently built, the land will first have to be cleared of builders' debris.

All the heaps of coarse builders' sand must be taken away as this is useless for any garden purpose, except for bedding down crazy paving or for mixing with cement for concrete paths or other stonework. Dig over the plot carefully to remove all bricks, glass, odd piping and timber which may have been left by the builder. A medium-sized garden fork is the best tool to use for this job.

Having disposed of all rubbish of this nature, the next stage is to consider levels. The natural run of the lawn with the rest of the garden need not be altered. Gradual slopes are in order. A lawn does not look right if it is high in one part and low in another.

Having decided the shape of the lawn, its levelling and size, we then have to dig the site over. It is best to clear the ground and to dig it if possible in early spring. This will allow for the settling down and the continuous removal of weeds, which must be done throughout the summer. It will then be ready for seed sowing in September. We must remember that once the seed has been sown the lawn will not be dug and manured for a great number of years except for top dressings of a suitable fertilizer. Therefore it is absolutely essential that liberal amounts of good well-rotted garden compost or decayed farmyard manure be dug into the soil initially. Dig one spit deep with a spade, and put in a good thickness of manure or compost into the bottom of the trench. Remove all perennial weeds as the digging proceeds, a rough level can be achieved at this time. The final levelling is done just before seed sowing.

When the digging has been completed, leave the surface rough for a month or so; in this way the soil will become weathered and well aerated. On several occasions during summer, after raking tread the soil gradually. Keep on raking and treading but be sure not to create an impenetrable solid mass. The soil needs to be gradually firmed so that it will not sink in any part after the grass has been sown. Do not rake away or remove every little stone which appears, only remove the larger ones. The stones will help later on with drainage, and will eventually be rolled into the ground with the regular mowing.

Have some soil put to one side, of the same kind as that which makes up the rest of the lawn, for filling in any cavities caused by the ground sinking from time to time. The same sort of soil is required, otherwise the grass may not be of the same colour and may also be of a different texture and give odd patches.

Throughout the summer, let the site lie fallow, hoeing out annual weeds and digging out perennial weeds with a small handfork. Towards the end of August rake the area absolutely level by using a straight-edged board and a spirit level. A steel-toothed rake can be used for this work but sometimes a wooden hay rake proves useful, especially for removing any large stones or other rubbish.

If there has been any heavy rain during the summer it may have been noticed that some parts of the lawn site have become rather waterlogged. In these cases it would be best to arrange some form of drainage for these areas before sowing the seed. Drainage has been discussed in a previous chapter and the same instructions should be followed in this case. In most cases it might be sufficient to dig out the wet patch and put some broken bricks, clinkers or gravel over the sub-soil after forking it, and then replacing the good top soil.

If sufficient treading has taken place during the spring and summer, it will not be necessary to use a roller. If the site is not very firm, then a light roller could be employed. There are very few occasions when a roller is needed for a lawn, therefore do not go to the expense of buying one. Usually one can be borrowed. The only place where a roller is needed is on the batting area of a cricket pitch, on a bowling green and a putting course.

When the site has received its final raking and levelling, some bone-meal should be well raked into the surface soil. This should be done about a week before seed sowing. The seed should be sown at the end of August in the north and during the first week of September in the south. The bonemeal should be raked in at the rate of two ounces to the square yard. At seed sowing time choose a calm day and mark out six-foot-wide strips both ways. Sow one strip at a time. Give a very light raking and then sow the seed at the rate of one ounce to the square yard. Broadcast the seed and divide it into separate ounces and in this way the correct amount of seed will be sown. Lightly rake over the seed to give a covering of soil not more than a quarter of an inch deep.

If the owner of the lawn has any pet that may cause trouble, such as a badly trained dog (cats rarely do much damage), then it must be kept away from the seeded area. A cat may even do good, by keeping the birds from the site. In the case of dogs, it might be necessary to erect a fencework of wire netting about two feet high around the whole area. Brushwood of the same height, thrust in at an angle, will usually do much towards keeping a dog away. Any free-range poultry must be excluded, otherwise the whole of the seed would soon vanish.

The next problem is birds. Allow the cat to roam freely. Erect a scarecrow with loose jacket sleeves fluttering in the breeze. If it is to be a fairly small lawn, then black thread, which the birds cannot see, is usually effective. Insert sticks here and there and fix the thread to these, so that the whole seeded area is covered with criss-crossed black thread. Silver foil on strings attached to several pea sticks is another bird-scarer.

Germination is usually quicker from a September sowing than from a spring sowing. The earth has been warmed by the summer sun and there is usually some gentle rain from time to time and at least some heavy dew. The seed will generally germinate in about ten days. Do not be in too much of a hurry to cut the new grass. It should be at least two inches high before cutting is attempted. If the weather is dry before cutting, a very light rolling will be beneficial. Those gardens which have rollers generally have one which is much too heavy. Borrow a light roller and use it on the young grass at this time just prior to the first cut. It is very important for rolling and cutting that the site should be in a dry condition. If it is wet, the roller will sink in and cause depressions and drag out some of the young grass plants. Similarly, in wet conditions the lawn mower will damage the young grass. The rolling at this stage is done for three purposes: to compress the soil, to push in stones that would otherwise obstruct and damage the blades of the mower, and to assist the young grasses to spread out. A day or so after rolling, a light lawn mower should be put over the grass. If it is at all moist, so that there is danger of dragging the young grass out by mowing, then sharp garden shears will have to be used.

For the first cut, the blades of the lawn mower must be adjusted to cut the grass about an inch from the surface. The cutting cylinder must be sharp for the first cut and the whole machine should be in first-class condition. Before mowing the grass for the first time, oil all parts of the mower thoroughly. The knife cylinder and the bottom cutting plate, against which the cylinder knives grind, should both have been sharpened. The knives should be adjusted so that when revolving, they rub gently against the bottom plate. The adjustment can be tested by holding a piece of paper between the knives and the plate. If the paper cuts easily and cleanly when the knives are gently turned, then the mower is ready to be used on the young grass. When making this test great care must be taken to see that the fingers are not damaged by the sharp cutting cylinder. Turn the cylinder by hand very gently and slowly.

Mowing will need to take place twice a week during this period, up to November if there is a mild autumn. Better to do a little late cutting than be faced by a difficult piece of grass in the spring. It is best, as said already, to make the first cut when the grass is about two inches high, because if left longer, and humid conditions ensue, young grass can be attacked by a fungus disease, which can quickly sweep through a whole lawn. Sometimes this fungus will attack young grass, although it has been mown, if there are damp, muggy conditions during the early growing period. Watch for signs of fungus disease. Brownish-yellow round patches of collapsed grass from about one inch to one foot across may be symptoms of Fusarium patch disease, *Fusarium nivale*. Place a glass cloche or jam jar over the affected grass and if a pinkish-white fungus growth develops, it confirms the diagnosis. For treatment of this disease apply a Bordeaux Mixture turf fungicide to the whole of the lawn and repeat after three weeks. Another fungus which may attack the young grass is *Corticum fuciforme*. Symptoms of this disease are bleached grass covered with a reddish thread-like fungus in the form of pink needles on the tips of the grass. Treat with a mercury turf fungicide or Bordeaux Mixture. Fairy ring fungus can be first watered with a turf fungicide and then, to complete the treatment, a few days later water with a solution of potassium permanganate at the rate of half an ounce per gallon of water to two square yards of lawn. If this treatment does not bring results, then cut out the patch affected, burn the turf, fork over the soil, sterilize and then returf or resow.

Although great efforts may have been made to eradicate all perennial and annual weeds, they will still make their appearance from time to time. The perennials must be carefully removed with a small hand fork and the larger annual weeds may be pulled up by hand. The continuous use of the lawn mower will gradually dispose of most annual weeds. An autumn-sown lawn which has been well prepared, rolled and cut should survive the winter well and be in quite good condition in the following spring.

As well as autumn seed sowing, grass seed for a new lawn may be sown in the spring. For a spring sowing, the site must be prepared in the autumn. Dig one spade's depth and into the bottom trench put a liberal supply of well-rotted garden compost or decayed farmyard manure. Try to spread this to an even thickness to allow for even settling of the soil. In an autumn preparation for spring sowing, it is better to leave the surface soil rough so that the frost and winds of winter may pulverize the soil and destroy weeds and pests. Hoe through any weeds which may appear.

Some time in March, tread the soil as evenly as possible and then a light rolling could be given. Rake down the soil to a fine tilth and then make it perfectly level. Wait until conditions are just right for sowing; this is usually some time in April. When the garden is fit for sowing annual flower seeds, it is suitable for sowing grass seed. Sow in the same manner as for an autumn sowing and take the same precautions against birds. Protect the seed bed from any animals. The spring-sown grass will grow rapidly during mild conditions and when the whole of the seed has germinated, a light roller should be passed over it. The rolling must only take place when the soil is dry. Be careful with the first cutting, cut when two inches high during dry conditions. Set the knives of the mower fairly high for the first attempt. Remove weeds as they are seen. Sometimes a spring drought is experienced with drying winds. In this case it is sometimes advisable to water the new lawn, using a fine rose. Light sandy soils will need special watering attention.

Do not contemplate a close cut on a newly sown lawn for at least three months after the first cut. Grass-seed sowing can take place in the spring from the third week of March until the end of May, whenever the ground is ready and sowing conditions are right. Where there are worn areas of lawn which need patching, the surface must be raked vigorously and on the loosened surface spread a small quantity of fine soil of the same nature as that of the rest of the lawn. Rake in a small amount of bone meal and allow to settle for a few days. When renovating a lawn in this way from one to one and a half ounces should be a sufficient rate of sowing to the square yard.

There are many mixtures of lawn grass seed to suit many different areas and purposes. It is best to ascertain from local people who have made good lawns in your district the kind of seed mixture which they used. Also the local seedsman can be consulted. Those who need a hard-wearing lawn on which the children can play games or where sticks are thrown to the dog will need a mixture containing the hard-wearing rye grass. A mixture of this kind is also suitable for football pitches and cricket outfields. It is made up as follows: 40 per cent perennial rye grass, $22\frac{1}{2}$ per cent Chewing's Fescue, $22\frac{1}{2}$ per cent Creeping Red Fescue, 10 per cent 5.23 Perennial Rye grass and 5 per cent Crested Dogstail.

For those who want a perfect piece of turf with fine dwarf grasses, but which will not stand up to rough use, the following mixture will provide it: 65 per cent Chewing's Fescue, 20 per cent Creeping Red Fescue and 15 per cent Brown Top Bent. For a fairly hard-wearing lawn of good quality, the following mixture of dwarf grasses, together with a small proportion of 5.23 perennial rye grass, will be suitable. This is a mixture for a lawn which looks good but will also allow for a certain amount of walking on while hanging out the laundry and for putting out the deck chairs and garden tables. The mixture consists of 36 per cent 5.23 Perennial Rye grass, 20 per cent Chewing's Fescue, 20 per cent 5.59 Creeping Red Fescue, 12 per cent Crested Dogstail, 6 per cent Rough-stalked Meadow Grass and 6 per cent Brown Top Bent.

For bowling greens and putting courses only two of the best dwarf grasses are needed. This turf is suitable where a fine lawn which will be closely cut and occasionally rolled is required. The specification is 80 per cent Chewing's Fescue and 20 per cent Brown Top Bent.

Before we go on to the maintenance of an established lawn we must talk about a further method of constructing a lawn, that of laying turf.

LAYING TURF AND TURF BEATER

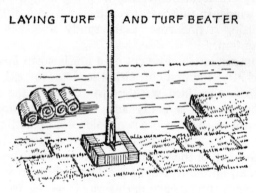

The laying of turf

Turf laying is a much more expensive way of making a lawn and it does not always give as good results as seed sowing. It is not easy to buy good turf. It is no use purchasing expensive turf which is sometimes advertised, and which is cut many miles from one's home. Many people have heard of Cumberland turf, and very fine turf it is, but only when it is growing in Cumberland. Certain grasses grow well in certain districts, where the soil and climatic conditions suit them, just as certain wild flowers grow well in certain areas. Anyone who has cycled through several counties of England will have noticed how the varieties of wild flowers and grasses change rapidly from county to county. Therefore turf will only usually be successful if it is taken from a meadow or other suitable spot near one's own district.

If it is decided that the lawn shall be made from turf, and some good turf is obtainable, it is best to lay it during October, November or December, if there is no frost. It is difficult to lay turf during the summer as it does not knit well with the soil below if the weather is very dry. Turf usually arrives rolled, and the sizes vary, some turves being 3 feet long, 1 foot broad and $1\frac{1}{2}$ inches thick, others 2 feet long. When ordering turf ask for it to be all of the same thickness, otherwise a lot of extra work will be caused and it will be difficult to set all the turves level. Turf from a meadow generally has some weeds in it, very often buttercup. It is easier to remove these weeds while the turf is upside down on the pile than after the lawn has been laid.

The preparation of the site for turf laying is similar to that described for seed sowing, except that the soil below the turf needs to be fairly solid. Any turf which has been incorrectly cut and is not deep enough will have to have the thickness made up by putting fine soil underneath by hand; or some of the thickness may have to be sliced away to make it correspond with the remainder of the turf. Lay the turf firmly and press the joints together well. Not too much heavy beating with a turf beater or spade is required, neither should a heavy roller be employed. If rolling is necessary, use a light roller. Brush a fine sandy soil into the crevices with a birch broom or yard broom. Do not mow newly laid turf too quickly; give it a chance to knit together and then mow when there is a reasonable growth. When preparing land for grass sowing in autumn or spring, or for turf laying, improve it according to the type of soil, as suggested in Chapter 1.

MAINTENANCE OF THE LAWN

The owner of a lawn can decide whether he requires a perfect lawn of the bowling-green type, a general purpose lawn, or just something which looks green and on which the children can play; in the last case, he need not worry too much about weed control. The important point to remember is that with a lawn we are growing a crop just like any other crop in the garden. The land on which the crop of grass, in this case, is growing, must be especially well-drained. Good drainage is important to a lawn for several reasons: for grass will not grow well in a waterlogged soil, it cannot be cut with a lawn mower, and the lawn cannot be used if too wet.

On badly drained land a proper system of drainage must be carried out as described in Chapter 1. For damp patches cut the turf carefully, remove it and lay it to one side. Dig out the soil to a spade's depth, fork over the sub-soil, put in clinkers, cinders, stones or broken brick and cover with a layer of sharp sand. Replace the good top soil, tread it and relay the turf firmly. Always remembering that we are growing a crop, prepare the site for a new lawn in the best way possible. Just as with preparing the land for the herbaceous border, we shall require plenty of good garden compost or well-decayed farmyard manure. Then as we cannot dig in further manure once the lawn has become established, we must feed the crop of grass with top dressings of suitable fertilizers.

Lawns must be watered during long drought periods just like any other part of the garden. Do not wait until the lawn is parched and brown; give it a good soaking before a dry period is expected. When we use the Dutch hoe in the garden we are not only disposing of annual weeds, we are letting air into the soil at the same time. Lawns

Various lawn aerators

need air for the grasses to grow and they are seeking air under difficult conditions. The lawn is being continuously mown, rolled and walked upon, compressing it solid and flat. Aerate the lawn frequently by pushing the garden fork in all over the lawn to a depth of a few inches, or use one of the special tools for the job called a 'lawn aerator'.

Pulling a heavy roller over the lawn is far too frequent an exercise. An established lawn does not need rolling. The small roller attached to the lawn mower is quite sufficient for any lawn. The only rolling that is essential is that given when making a new lawn. Even then, only a very light roller must be used. Do not use worm killer on a lawn, as the worms help to aerate it.

As we weed the garden, so we must weed the lawn, otherwise plant food needed for the grass is used up by weeds. They will also soon smother the grass, especially the fine dwarf grasses and take over from them. Many weeds on the lawn can be hand-weeded. Most of the common weeds can be controlled by the application of three parts of sulphate of ammonia and one part calcined sulphate of iron at the rate of two ounces to the square yard. If the applicator does not feel confident enough to spread this mixture evenly, and some scorching may result if it is not so done, he may reduce the amount to an ounce per square yard and then make more frequent applications. Mix the chemicals well and make sure that they are perfectly dry before distributing so that they fall in dust-like form. Mark the lawn into sections of one square yard and place two ounces of the chemical into a tin with a perforated lid, and distribute evenly over the square yard. This mixture is a fertilizer for the grass as well as a weed-killer.

Some people may want to use some of the selective weed-killers, those which kill weeds but do not harm the grass. When using one of these, make sure that it is not harmful to animals, birds or bees. Bees come to wet grass in the spring to obtain moisture and birds are always on the lawn looking for worms, slugs and snails. One word of warning if you do use a selective weed-killer: you must not put the lawn mowings which follow on to the compost heap. Dry them by spreading on a waste piece of land, where less harm will be done, and then burn them on the bonfire. Wash all watering-cans and other utensils thoroughly after they have been used for weed-killer. If you use the sulphate of ammonia and iron the future mowings can be put on to the compost heap with safety.

Regular mowing of the established lawn makes the work easier, whether a mower which is pushed by hand is used, or one with a motor. It is when the lawn has been left for the grass to get long that the work becomes hard. Twice weekly is the amount of mowing required to keep a lawn in good order and for making the task of mowing reasonably easy. The mower must be regularly overhauled and the blades kept sharp. Always give the mower a good oiling before starting work with it. When the mowing of the lawn has been completed for the day, brush all grass and dirt from the machine and clean it well before putting it away.

There are the right seasons for carrying out work on the lawn just as there are for other parts of the garden. In January any poorly drained areas can be discerned and marked for future attention when drier conditions occur. On very exposed parts of a lawn the drying winds and frosts of winter can do damage to the grass. Some form of shelter can be erected to deflect the wind and a top dressing of sifted loam can be put over the area.

In February, the raking and levelling of the seed bed where grass seed is to be sown should be done. During this month aerating of the lawn can take place by inserting the garden fork into the lawn a few inches. Brush away worm casts. Where moss is prevalent rake it out with a steel garden rake. This will destroy most of it but not all, and it can be raked out again when any quantity is seen. Another way of destroying moss is to apply a moss eradicant. Make sure that this chemical is non-poisonous to animals, birds, bees and other helpful insects. Find out the underlying causes of the moss growth. The area where the moss is growing may be too shaded, there may be poor drainage, poor soil fertility or weak-growing grasses which allow the moss to take over. Towards the end of February the first application of weed-killer and fertilizer (sulphate of ammonia and iron) can be made. Complete any levelling of the established lawn that may be needed.

Towards the end of March, if growth has begun the first mowing can take place on established lawns, but take a fairly high cut. Leave the grass box off the mower and let the mowings return to the lawn. Keep a watch for leather-jackets; they are greyish-brown or black and are the tough-skinned grubs of the crane fly or daddy-long-legs. They may be present where there are any loose patches of brown grass. Treat the lawn very heavily with water towards evening and cover the turf closely with tarpaulins or boards to exclude air. Remove the coverings in the morning and sweep up and destroy the leather-jackets lying on the surface.

In April, if there is mild weather and showers, regular mowing can take place on well-established lawns. Before beginning to mow, take a birch broom or other broom and brush vigorously all round the edge of the lawn. Brush towards the gravel path if one is present to remove any stones, otherwise the cutting blades of the mower may be damaged. Similarly brush away from the lawn, on to the garden where the lawn borders it. Look over the lawn and remove any twigs or other objects that may have appeared. Now is the time to sow the grass seed for a spring-sown lawn. Water with a sprinkler after ten days, if no rain falls. When the grass is two inches high, mow lightly. From this time onwards, plenty of lawn cuttings will become available. Put them on to the compost heap in light layers so that they mix well with the other substances. Do not put on a large quantity at a time, or it will not rot down well. After putting on a light layer, add other suitable material on to the compost heap before adding another layer of lawn mowings. A heap of lawn mowings can be kept separate and put on to the compost heap gradually. Never waste any lawn mowings, for they make very valuable plant food when composted. Any parts of the lawn which need renovating can be seen to at this time of the year.

During May it is likely that the newly-sown lawn will need cutting. Have the blades of the mower high and as sharp as possible. Test the mower for the correct adjustment carefully. No selective weed-killers should be used on a newly-made lawn until it is at least three months old. Full mowing can take place on established lawns and twice-a-week cutting may be needed. Keep the edges neatly cut with edging shears and run the Dutch hoe through the garden, close to the edge of the lawn, to help prevent weeds spreading to the lawn.

June work on the lawn consists of mowing twice weekly if the weather is not too dry. If there is a continuance of very dry weather once a week would probably be sufficient. If there is any likelihood of browning of the grass, adjust the height of the cut to avoid very close cutting. Watering might be needed on light dry soils. If watering is undertaken, water copiously. No lawn sand or selective weed-killers must be used during dry spells. A newly-made lawn may need some shading from very hot sun.

July is the time to remove the grass box and to water really well by saturating the lawn with hose pipe or sprinkler. A start can be made on raking down and levelling any new lawn site contemplated, which was dug in spring for an autumn sowing.

During the latter part of August seed can be sown for a new lawn in the north of England. In the south the fertilizer chosen can be raked into the top soil on the new lawn site. When sowing seed, choose the right mixture for the purpose in view, bearing in mind the soil and neighbourhood.

September is the best month for grass seed sowing in the south of England. Worn patches on established lawns can be returfed. Brush away worm casts which often appear in number during a mild September. This is a good period to aerate the lawn with fork or aerating tool. A September-sown lawn will probably need cutting during October with the knives raised.

In October an autumnal top dressing can be given to the lawn. Well-rotted and well-sifted garden compost can be used, which should be a layer of about an eighth of an inch in thickness but not more. Some good sifted soil can be mixed with the compost. An autumn fertilizer consisting of bonemeal at two ounces to the square yard should be given at the same time as the top dressing of compost. Most lawns will need mowing during October, especially if the autumn has been wet and mild. This often presents a problem, for the lawn is seldom dry enough for mowing when the owner is at home to do it. During most of the morning heavy dews persist and then the lawn begins to get damp again by about 5 p.m. Try to wait for some sun and drying winds during the day, but avoid too long a waiting period, or the grass will get beyond easy cutting conditions. Between 3 and 6 p.m. seems to be the best time for mowing in October, but put on some insect repellent.

Turf laying can take place in November, provided that there is no frost. Fertilize the soil before laying the turf, with two ounces of bonemeal to the square yard. This is in addition to the liberal amount of garden compost dug into the soil during the initial preparation of the site. An occasional mowing of established lawns may be necessary if the month is mild. This is a good time to undertake any edging of lawns which may be required. Use a stout garden line and a half-moon-shaped lawn edging tool. The special action required when using this tool is to move it up and down and along the garden line in a slicing movement as though using a knife. Do not use it like a spade by pressing on the blade with the foot; in this way it is soon broken.

December is the time to overhaul all lawn tools. Have the lawn mower sharpened, repaired and set. Give the mower a thorough clean, oil it well and run a smear of grease or oil over all shiny parts. Be careful when oiling, cleaning or greasing sharp parts, hands are easily injured. Store the mower in a damp-proof shed for the winter. Sharpen the half-moon cutter and have all shears adjusted, sharpened and oiled. Store them in a dry place.

This completes the month-by-month maintenance work on the lawn. Keep dogs from lawns at all times unless you want to be constantly renovating the turf. On no account overfeed a lawn with top dressings of fertilizers; regular light applications are better. Do not practise constant close mowing; this will cause browning of the grass in summer and bare patches. Give the grass a chance to grow and breathe. Keep the grass box on in order to collect valuable material for the compost heap, except in drought conditions.

Always keep the edges well trimmed with edging shears and clear up the cut grass from borders and paths when the job has been completed. Grass trimmings left at the edge of a border only encourage slugs. Use a special wire lawn rake for raking leaves and other debris from the lawn. These rakes are springy and they will not tear out the grass. Give the lawn an occasional good vigorous brushing with a birch broom or yard broom during the winter. Use non-poisonous weed-killers at all times. No heavy rolling is required. Remember that a lawn, which is often one of the most important features of a garden, needs an adequate supply of plant foods. It is often the most neglected part of the garden; in spite of this, many people expect to have a beautiful green springy carpet, weedless, and a joy to behold. This can be the case only if the simple rules outlined are carried out.

TOOLS FOR THE LAWN

When choosing a lawn mower several points have to be considered. If it is only a small lawn then a mower which is pushed by hand will be suitable. Using a hand-propelled lawn mower is not laborious work if the lawn is cut regularly and the cylinder cutting blades of the machine are kept sharp, and if the working parts are oiled before starting the work. The choice of mower, and whether it is to be a hand-propelled one or a mechanically-powered one, will also depend on what can be afforded by the owner. On a very large lawn, mowing twice a week with a hand mower would take up some considerable time which might be better spent in other parts of the garden where important food crops are being grown.

There are many types of hand mower to choose from and any garden machinery catalogue will show a bewildering list. As with all other gardening tools, choose one of the right weight and balance. It is important to find the correct length of handle for the user, the one most manoeuvrable for the particular lawn, and the right width of blades. Often a greater width of blade means a heavy machine and instead of getting over the task more quickly, by taking in a wider width of lawn, the gardener has to rest frequently, so that the job is slower in the end.

A mower with side wheels is the easiest to push and is the best machine for lawns where the grass is fairly rough and where the owner is not too fussy about producing a perfect, closely cut lawn. The only disadvantage which this machine possesses is the fact that it is difficult to cut right up to the extreme edges of the lawn. After some practice, this can be achieved by tilting the machine towards the edge to be cut, holding the handle firmly, and having only one side wheel on the lawn. The other one will project over the edge of the lawn being cut. During this operation, for some time neither of the side wheels is in action. Often when cutting the edge in this way, especially if the lawn is damp, the lawn mower will slip, producing indentations in the lawn, and will also sometimes shave parts of the lawn bare, exposing the soil. This does not very often constitute any serious damage to the lawn. The indentations can be rolled level or flattened out by the use of the garden spade. A mower with a 12-inch width of cut would be suitable for most small or average-sized lawns. There is now a mower with side wheels which, the makers claim, will cut to the edge of the lawn without difficulty.

Most side-wheel mowers have a small wooden roller at the rear of the machine and some have rubber-tyred side wheels; these lessen any marks made by the mower slipping on wet patches. It is more convenient to have a mower with hand-wheel adjustment to alter the height of the cutting blades or front rollers. This is better than having to use a spanner each time. Where a spanner has to be frequently used, the nuts become worn and have to be replaced, and often it is difficult to move them at all.

The other main type of hand mower, apart from the side-wheel machine, is the one with an iron roller at the back of the machine. This type provides all the rolling necessary on an established lawn. Sometimes these rollers are two-piece rollers and cutting cylinders in these types of machine are fitted with ball-bearings. There are roller-type hand mowers with five-, six- or eight-cylinder blades. The higher the number of blades, the shorter the grass can be cut. Where one has a lot of rough long grass, such as might be found in the wild garden or orchard, use can be made of the mechanical cultivator fitted with a cutter bar.

Of the two main types of motor mower, the cheapest and simplest is the rotary grass cutter. It does not collect the grass and there is no grass box. It is light and speedy to operate. It will cut long wet grass and it can be used on awkward and difficult pieces of lawn where a cylinder mower could not be used. For first-class work on first-class lawns, a revolving cylinder motor mower, with six or eight blades, is the best machine to use. For small lawns a 12-inch width of machine can be obtained.

The machine can be driven by either a petrol engine or an electric motor, and the engine may be two- or four-stroke. Some machines are non-self-propelled; that is, the engine will only drive the cutting cylinder. In others, both mower and cylinder are power driven and some are fitted with dual-drive where the mower or cutting cylinder may be disengaged at will. With an electric mower, a cable can be attached of almost any length, but they are often supplied in lengths of 25, 50 and 100 yards. There should be an attachment on all electric mowers that will hold the cable well away from the cutting cylinder. Some accidents have occurred where the mower has cut through the cable.

For the gardener who needs to keep his lawn under reasonable control, but has not the time for frequent mowing and is not too fastidious, there is the Rotoscythe which is the only rotary mower with a grass box. This machine will do almost anything that a rotary cutter will do and it will work on slopes, under and between trees, and on long wet grass. It will also cut a lawn fairly short, but will not give it a close-cut 'bowling-green' finish. It will cut the lawn short enough for most people and is a real all-purpose machine. There are powered machines which are specially designed for cutting lawn edges but these may only be required for very large lawns.

The hand shears needed for lawn maintenance should be of a light weight and very sharp. The blades should meet closely otherwise a clean cut cannot be made and the grass will be merely tugged away. There is hardly anything met with in the gardening world which gives more irritation than a blunt pair of hand shears. Edging shears with

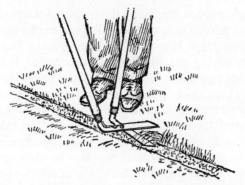

Trimming lawn edges with long-handled shears

long handles are needed for almost every lawn, in order to avoid a lot of unnecessary stooping and laborious work with hand shears. These should also be kept very sharp and with close-fitting blades. Before edging a lawn with shears, move the earth and stones towards the garden and away from the lawn edge, to avoid cutting into stones and soil and so damaging the blades (see page 322).

When a lawn needs to be edged with the half-moon edging tool,

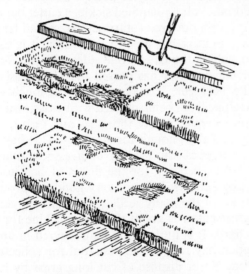

TO REPAIR WORN EDGE OF
LAWN, CUT ROUND AND
REVERSE THE PATCH
SOW WORN PARTS WITH GRASS
SEED

A method of repairing the worn edges of a lawn

put down a tight garden line along the length of the lawn to be edged. There are other garden aids and tools for use on the lawn and among these is the lawn rake. It is used for raking away leaves and debris from the lawn during autumn and at other times. It has wire teeth which have a springy action when used and it rakes the lawn without damaging it. These rakes possess a varying amount of teeth, some with up to thirty teeth and others with eight. There are others with rubber teeth and these are easy to use and they rake everything, leaving the lawn looking really clean and tidy. Special lawn rakes for attaching to garden cultivators can also be obtained.

Other aids for lawns are lawn aerators, of which there are several kinds, fertilizer spreaders and lawn sweepers. Lawn sweepers can be used on other parts of the garden such as paths and drives which are fairly smooth. They have revolving brushes which sweep leaves, lawn clippings, twigs and other debris into large capacity catches and they are light and easy to use.

MANAGING OTHER GRASSLAND

Rough, long grassland can be left to grow and then scythed for hay. Not many people can use a scythe today, but grass can be cut by many other methods. A long-handled sickle, a cutter bar attached to a garden cultivator, or a powered rotary scythe, can all be brought into use. When using a cutter bar type of cultivator, it is useful to have another person pulling the hay to one side, with a rake or hay fork after the cutter bar operator has passed by. The grassland will then be clear for the next cut; it makes the work much easier and it prevents the machine from being choked with grass, which sometimes stops the machine engine. Leave the grass and turn it several times until it is ready and dry enough for stacking. This hay can be used for very many purposes, the feeding of livestock, material for the lining of nest boxes, bedding for the floors of hen houses and pig houses, or for dog kennels. It is not very good for protecting plants from frost because of the many seeds which fall and germinate.

The rotary grass cutter is about the best machine for cutting long grass in an orchard. It is quite easily manoeuvred in and out of the trees. The wooden hay rake is the best tool for collecting the grass after it has dried. Never dispose of cut long grass by burning it, as I have seen many people do. This is a great waste of useful material. If it cannot be used as hay for fodder or bedding purposes, then put thin layers of the green grass on to the compost heap; mixed with other compost heap material it will rot down into valuable plant food. Neighbours with livestock will be glad of the surplus hay if it is not wanted for any other purpose.

With rough, long grass the work entailed is not heavy, as only about three cuts per year are required. It is often possible in country districts to borrow a motor scythe of some kind from a neighbour. When borrowing a machine, always go over it thoroughly before starting work. Borrowed machines usually need topping up with oil for the engine and gear box. Also check all nuts and see that they are tight. Cutter-bars shake a machine considerably and nearly always loosen nuts and other parts of the machine.

Another way of keeping down rough grass or even lawns is to employ one or two geese. Geese are natives of Britain and they are the most hardy of our poultry. Compared with other domestic birds, they live to a great age, twenty years being quite common. Although geese are water birds, they will live quite happily without a pond to swim in. They are very easy to keep, needing only a simply erected shed for shelter. Except when hard frost covers the lawn or grassland, or during a very dry period when all grass has withered, they can live entirely on grass. Five or six geese will eat as much grass as a sheep. Their grazing and droppings actually improve pasture.

When there is no grass they can be given root crops, consisting of cooked potato, cut-up cabbage, swedes and turnips. Always leave geese with a container of water. Most breeds of geese lay about thirty eggs a year, the exception being the Chinese goose, which can lay up to a hundred and forty. I have seen several lawns and grasslands which have never required mowing with a lawn mower; the grass has been kept permanently short by geese. If geese are going to be kept to keep down the grass, then a wire netting fence will be needed to enclose the vegetable patch, otherwise they may start eating the green vegetables. The keeping of a few geese is a good proposition for someone with a considerable amount of grassland who has not the time to spare for mowing. They make excellent table birds and the eggs are rich, large and tasty. They also take the place of a watchdog in the country, or wherever such an animal is needed. Geese will give the alarm much more quickly than a dog when a stranger approaches the house. They make a tremendous noise and their cackling is loud. They are far easier to look after than a dog and cost much less to keep, and are also productive.

There are a number of excellent breeds of geese. Some of the best known are the Toulouse, a very large grey bird, the Embden, a large white bird with sky-blue eyes, and the Chinese goose, which is a smaller bird with a long, swanlike neck. There are fawn and also white varieties of this bird. The Roman goose is a small white goose and the Sebastopol is white with curly feathers. Most of the eggs of the goose are reserved for hatching. A goose will cover about fifteen eggs and they take thirty-one days to hatch. The gander is the only male bird of domestic poultry that is concerned with the welfare of his family. He will protect the eggs and young goslings fiercely.

If one has a paddock or field and is in possession of enough garden to supply the need for vegetables and flowers, without the necessity of ploughing and cultivating any of the grassland, then the problem of using the grassland to the best advantage often presents itself. Apart from turning part of it into an orchard, it is often a good idea to let it to someone who has a pony or two. As well as collecting a small rent, there would not be the work or expense of cutting the grass and the horse manure could be a valuable contribution to the manuring programme of the garden.

Goats are another good form of livestock for anyone with the problem of how to use a quantity of rough grassland. It is better not to keep male goats owing to their rather strong odour. Goats will live on almost any kind of herbage so they must not be given access to other parts of the garden. Goats' milk is comparable to that of cows, although somewhat more variable. On the average it is rather richer in fat and poorer in other solids. It is often more easily digested by delicate people and invalids, and has the great advantage over cow's milk of being free from tubercle bacilli, which are the commonest of the more dangerous organisms which can sometimes be found in cow's milk. Goats of a good type can produce from six to ten pints of milk per day.

One more way of using grassland is to stock it with poultry. There are several systems whereby grassland can be used for poultry-keeping. The Free Range System consists of running the fowls on unfenced fields. Houses are provided to accommodate the birds at night and for egg-laying. Movable general purpose houses are suitable for this system, as they can be pulled on to other land, if some is to be used for cropping. The Folding System consists of keeping a few hens in several small portable houses with attached wire-netting runs. These houses have slatted floors and are provided with nest boxes and eating and drinking vessels. They hold about twenty-four hens. These units are moved daily to fresh ground so that the grass is used up by the hens every day. The droppings spread evenly and are valuable for improving the soil.

The Semi-intensive System is one where there are fixed houses and semi-permanent runs. Wire netting is used to make the enclosures and several out-runs are made, so that when one is being rested the hens can run on to others. The floors of these houses are littered with straw or hay, which the owner of plenty of grassland can provide at little cost. In all of these systems the grassland is used to good advantage. As well as providing plenty of eggs and table meat, poultry do inestimable good for the gardener. They help fertilize the soil and grassland by their droppings. They cultivate it with their continual scratching and foraging. They keep down weeds and they feed on innumerable pests. Fresh eggs are also useful to the gardener and his family and they are very nutritious.

Although one can see plenty of poultry throughout the country, geese or goats are seldom seen. This is rather surprising, when we consider how valuable they are, are not expensive to keep, and are so easily managed.

10

Growing your own Vegetables

Peas and beans — root crops — potatoes — cabbages and cauliflowers — salads — the Onion Family — which herbs to grow — storing vegetables — unusual vegetables

This is perhaps the most important chapter in this book. A man with a good vegetable plot will never be short of food. In times of plenty there is still nothing quite so good as vegetables grown by oneself, taken straight from the garden and put straight into the saucepan. A man can keep himself and his family in good health if he has a plentiful supply of fresh vegetables throughout the year. During hard times, the man with the vegetable plot will survive, no matter if other foods are in short supply. Fresh vegetables in variety can supply carbohydrates, proteins, fats, minerals and vitamins.

Vegetable growing is not difficult once you have studied and learnt each vegetable's soil and food requirements, the correct sowing time, planting distances, and the few cultivation methods needed for individual varieties.

The vegetable garden should be in an open position, but for very early crops some shelter from north and east winds is desirable. Crop rotation means growing a different crop on a particular part of the vegetable garden each year. If the same crop is grown on the same patch of ground year after year, it will in due course upset the balance of soil fertility. This can be avoided by growing different crops in rotation. It simply means, do not grow the same kind of vegetable in exactly the same spot each year. Not only are the balance of soil and the fertility maintained by practising rotation of crops, but also pests and diseases are discouraged.

There is no need to worry too much about crop rotation as practised by farmers on a large scale. Just remember to grow a different crop to the last one grown on a particular spot of ground. A good way to ensure this, and also to make an even distribution of manure, is to grow the potatoes at one end of the allotment or vegetable plot one year, and to plant them at the opposite end the following year. The next year they could be grown in the centre of the plot. If good farmyard manure or garden compost is put under the potatoes each year, this will ensure that every part of the plot is receiving sufficient plant foods. Some vegetables grow better on ground which has been well manured for a previous crop.

If a liberal amount of manure has been used for the potatoes in early spring, it will enable the brassicas or cabbage family to be planted here during the following year, in early summer. In this way the area can be limed after the potatoes have been lifted in the autumn. The brassicas will need the lime, and the time of liming will not interfere or intermix with the compost or farmyard manure (see page 14).

The amount and variety of vegetables grown will depend on the size of the plot, the nature of the soil and the kind of produce liked by the gardener and his family. A man with twenty rods of land can supply a family of four with fresh vegetables throughout the whole of the year. This means fertile soil, a good system of manuring, good planning for successional crops, and good cultivation.

Only grow those vegetables which are liked by the grower and his family. Grow more of the crop which is particularly enjoyed. Even with the most expert planning, there is often a surplus of some particular vegetable. Never waste any vegetables, never let them remain on the plot to mature and decay. Surplus vegetables can be disposed of by the gardener exchanging for something else which he does not grow; they can be sold, they can be given to people who have no garden, to old-age pensioners and the like, and they can be fed to poultry or pigs.

If the gardener has room, it always pays dividends to keep a few laying hens. All the very small potatoes can be fed to them, the outside leaves of cabbages, lettuce which may have bolted, and other green stuff can be thrown to them to provide their daily intake of calcium and vitamins for eggshell formation.

The allotment holder without a family would do well to consider what he is likely to have a surplus of, and plan accordingly. It would be much better for him to have a surfeit of early potatoes, spring cabbage, radishes, spring onions, early peas, tomatoes, lettuce and cauliflowers, for these are generally very saleable. Maincrop potatoes, turnips, swede, main crop carrots, parsnips and vegetable marrows would be more difficult to dispose of.

The owner of a small garden for vegetables will have to practise the principle of intensive cultivation to produce the amounts and varieties required. The largest possible number of crops must be produced and this means well manured soil and that no part of the garden must be left lying fallow for any long period. On a small vegetable plot, the owner would be best advised to leave out main-crop potatoes and any other crop which is easily obtained and cheap to buy. It is best in very small gardens to concentrate on a few lettuce in succession, especially early ones, a few early potatoes, runner beans, which do not take up much room and are very prolific, early peas, broad beans, early stump-rooted carrots, radishes, spring onions and a couple of rows of bush tomatoes.

Have a good look at the proposed site for vegetable growing, before ordering the seed. Allot a certain amount of space and make sure you have left enough room for all of the vegetables you intend to grow. Leave an area for a load of farmyard manure to be delivered and unloaded, if it is being used. Similarly, space for a compost heap and for storing pea and bean sticks will be required. Work out where the seed beds are to be made for transplanting from, and what you are going to grow on this space when all transplanting has been completed.

Order your seed early from a well-known seedsman, after having a careful look at the seed catalogues. Beware of cheap offers of seeds or plants from unknown advertisers. This is particularly important with seed potatoes; very often cheap lots offered are suffering from dry rot disease which is not easily discernible to the untrained eye.

The average allotment or kitchen garden will only need a small packet of seed of each variety of vegetable being grown. Frequently too much seed is purchased with the result that it is saved for the following year. When sown during the following season germination is often poor, the seed having deteriorated when in store. To help estimate the amount of seed required, it should be borne in mind that half a pint of broad or runner beans will sow a fifty-foot row and a quarter-pint of French beans will sow the same distance. About seven pounds of seed potatoes are needed for a fifty-foot row and half a pint of garden peas sown at one time would be enough for most people.

The nature and weight of crops finally produced from these sowings depend on many things. The weather, the quality of the seed when sown, the skill of the cultivator, the fertility of the ground, and the existence of pests and diseases are some of the factors making for good or mediocre or poor quality. If fairly good growing conditions are experienced, half a pint of peas will produce about thirty pounds of crop, and a stone of early potatoes about eighty pounds. Runner beans will go on producing as long as weather conditions are suitable, only ceasing when frosts or cold east winds appear. It will generally be found that half of a packet of seed of any variety of brassica will be sufficient seed to sow, and even then there will be plenty of plants to spare. To help the seeds keep their germinating power, so that you can sow the half packet of seed left over, seal the packet at once with adhesive tape. Never put seeds in an airtight container because they need to breathe.

We have discussed the preparation and improvement of all kinds of soil in Chapter 1. It may be emphasized here that with all vegetable growing the soil needs to be deeply worked and to have a liberal amount of farmyard manure or garden compost added to the bottom trench when digging the site.

Good garden hygiene must be practised and there must, I repeat, be crop rotation. There are many old ideas adhered to today which have been passed on by generations of gardeners, and this is especially the case in the vegetable section. There are also some new ideas, some of them designed for lazy gardeners. Of the old ideas, one which we can dismiss is that the onion crop can grow in the same place year after year. It is common sense to move this crop to fresh land annually, for onions are gross feeders and they extract a lot of plant foods from the soil; and the onion fly is more likely to be kept in check if the crop is moved to fresh quarters. The fungus disease called White Rot rarely attacks onions which are grown in fresh positions from year to year. Runner beans are grown in the same position year after year by some growers, but this also is not good gardening. All pod-producing vegetables should be followed by leafy plants such as lettuce and brassicas, so that they can take advantage of the extra nitrogen left in the soil by the peas and beans.

Of the new advocacy of no hoeing and no digging, there is nothing to be said in the vegetable garden. All vegetables need to breathe, and hard, compacted soil around them must be broken up by the use of the hoe, to let the air in. Hoeing also lets in moisture and destroys weeds. The only place in the garden where hardly any hoeing is required is where surface-rooting plants like rhododendrons are growing.

We have already talked about the advantages to be gained from an under-glass start for some vegetables, and the uses of cloches; glass should be utilized wherever possible. We have discussed at some length in other parts of this book the best way to prepare a seed bed and how to transplant. These important operations will be referred to briefly when each vegetable is mentioned.

The man with an allotment or vegetable garden in the country can generally obtain some farmyard manure, pig manure or deep litter poultry droppings. It seems the best plan for an allotment holder to obtain either one of these. For the man with an allotment which is some distance from his home it is difficult to obtain sufficient material for compost-making. This is more easily made where the vegetable garden is attached to the dwelling-house with a flower garden and lawns. Then there is plenty of material, with the addition of the kitchen waste. Make a compost heap on the allotment if there is sufficient material. The allotment holder will find it better to manure half his plot with organic manure each year. Not all crops can take advantage of freshly manured land, many of them grow better on ground which has been previously manured for another crop. The cost of manure will be halved in this way.

The town and city dwellers who find it impossible to obtain farm-yard manure or similar plant food will have to rely on any organic manures they can get. These will be from the compost heap, poultry and pigeon manure, rabbit droppings, wool shoddy, fish manure, bonemeal, soot and wood ashes.

There are a few general rules for the vegetable garden. Good garden hygiene is most important at all times. Burn all plants which are obviously diseased. Do not throw them down anywhere on the plot or put them on to the compost heap. Collect all refuse which is disease-free and put it on the compost heap immediately. Do not leave any refuse lying about on the plot. Heaps of rubbish provide ideal homes for all sorts of garden pests. Field mice have been known to make nests in piles of grass which have been left about all winter. If these pests are left unmolested, the gardener can give up all idea of growing peas during the following spring.

Keep the plot tidy and weed free at all times. Collect all pea sticks, bean rods and other supporting stakes, when the last crops have been gathered. Clean them and store them under cover. Keep grass verges and paths cut short. Wherever possible, dig your vegetable plot during autumn and early winter. In this way many pests will be exposed to the birds, the frost will enter the ground to pulverize it and help destroy pests and diseases.

Keep any hedges well trimmed, do not let them keep out the sunshine and air from the vegetables. Destroy slugs and snails which may be lurking in hedge bottoms. When the main gardening operations have finished for the year, clean all tools and oil them. Keep tools clean at all times, for dirty tools spread disease and hamper work. Keep them well sharpened too. Have a first-aid outfit handy, in case of accidents when constantly using sharp tools. Good use can be found for a soil-testing outfit in the vegetable garden. Brassicas do not grow well on an acid soil, so add lime when necessary.

PEAS AND BEANS

Good crops of garden peas can be grown if the gardener commands plenty of patience and is prepared to undertake all the many cultiva-

A well-designed
heath garden

A good hedge of
*Chamaecyparis
Lawsoniana*

A fine example of a
herbaceous border
with the right view
from the house

A window box planted with geraniums and asparagus fern

Well-staked peas growing in succession and interplanted with lettuce

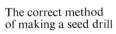

The correct method of making a seed drill

tion tasks at the right time. Peas like a good medium loam with some chalk content, but peas will grow on most fertile soils except those which have only a thin covering of soil over solid chalk. These soils lack the iron which is necessary for good growth and maturity. All pea plants develop an extensive root system, so this suggests at once that the soils need to be dug deeply and that plenty of plant food must be provided. If early peas are to be tried, a sheltered spot in the garden or allotment needs to be chosen.

It is best to dig the plot chosen for all peas in the autumn. For the best results, the plot should be dug two spade depths deep, being careful not to bring the sub-soil to the surface. Into the bottom of the trench goes a good six-inch layer of well rotted garden compost, well trodden in; it will perform two important functions. The first is the conservation of moisture, so important in the growing of good peas. Second, the compost provides essential plant foods. The roots of the pea plant will have spread well into the compost at just the right time, when the plant is coming into blossom and producing the first young pods.

After the autumn preparation of the pea site has been concluded the surface needs to be left as rough as possible. This will enable the soil to take advantage of the effects of rain, frost and snow. Frost and snow will break up the hard lumps underneath (especially clay) and also destroy pests and help to eradicate diseases. The rain will penetrate rough soil more easily and reach the compost, to build up a better moisture content for any possible drought during June and July. If no rotted garden compost is available, half-decayed but not fresh manure may be incorporated into the bottom of the trench.

Most soils already have enough chalk or lime available for the peas. If a soil test is made and the land is found to be too deficient in chalk, a little garden lime may be raked into the surface, a few weeks before sowing time. It must be remembered, however, that lime must not be mixed with farmyard manure or any nitrogenous or phosphatic manures. Lime will cause the valuable nitrogen in the manure to break up and the plant food will vanish into the air.

Successional crops of peas can be grown by using the four classes. These are: early; second early; maincrop and late. The growing of early peas is always a gamble; it depends so much on the weather. If plenty of humus (compost or farmyard manure) has been worked into the soil, the problem of retaining enough moisture until the peas have germinated is largely overcome. Peas cannot withstand much frost however, and a hard frost may occur just as the peas have pushed themselves through the soil. Again after the seeds have been sown, several weeks of low temperatures may persist and instead of germinating, the seeds may rot in the ground. This often happens,

22

especially if there has been a considerable amount of rain. Many growers are prepared to take a risk, for the sake of enjoying some succulent early peas after many weeks of eating cabbages and stored carrots.

It is seldom worth sowing early peas out of doors, before February. Two good varieties are 'Little Marvel' and 'Kelvedon Wonder', both a foot and a half in height. Dwarf varieties are best for early work as they present less foliage to the wind. Select a sheltered spot and aim at having your seed drills running north to south. In the north-south direction, the sunlight will shine on one side of the rows in the morning, on the other side in the afternoon, while at midday the sunlight will pour down the rows, shining upon all the plants. So that all the crop will get more light when the north-south line is selected; this is most important in the early part of the year when the hours of daylight are fewer than at other times. We also need as much conservation of warmth from any sunshine that we may get if we are to obtain early crops. Put down the garden line and make a trench about a foot wide and six inches deep. This can best be done by putting the draw-hoe against the line and drawing the soil forward to the feet of the gardener. Afterwards the whole of the trench can be made level with a garden rake.

Now at this stage we have to think of the troublesome pest that is particularly fond of early peas. This is the field mouse. Later on in the year, when this animal can find an abundance of other foods, peas and beans are not so liable to attack. The old method of shaking the seed before sowing in some paraffin and red lead powder is effective in some districts. If the site for early peas is on land adjoining your house, then the best safeguard against mice is to get a good cat and encourage it to spend its days and nights in the garden or nearby. It will also discourage birds. If you are growing early peas on an allotment or land which is some distance from your house, the most effective way of preventing mice from taking the seed is to use sprigs of gorse with plenty of prickly spines along the drills, covering every pea. The mice smell the peas and burrow into the rows, consequently they are pricked on the nose by the sharp needle-like points of the gorse. After a few attempts, they give up and the peas survive. If no gorse is to hand, other prickly plants may be used. The setting of several mousetraps along the rows is another method of control. Unfortunately sometimes harmless birds who help the gardener by keeping down harmful grubs are caught in the traps instead of mice.

When you have drawn the drills and made them level, put in the peas by spacing them singly in three rows with about three inches between peas. After putting on the gorse, cover the seeds with two inches of soil and press down lightly with the head of the rake. Do not attempt to fill the trench completely, for the earth at the sides will offer protection and the shallow trench that is left will catch the rain.

We now have certain kinds of birds to deal with, who will pull out the young seedlings. These are usually rooks, crows and sparrows. Special pea protectors, made of wire netting, are effective if one remembers to block each end. An easy and cheap method of protection is to put in several short sticks here and there throughout the seed bed, and to connect them up with black thread or cotton. The birds cannot see this very easily and alighting once and feeling the cotton against their wings they become frightened and keep away. When the pea seedlings show above the ground, a watch has to be made for slugs and snails and control measures taken. Old soot or lime sprinkled around the edges of the rows will discourage them. Slug killer pellets will have to be put at intervals along the rows.

With the seedlings about one inch high, the pea and bean weevil is likely to put in an appearance. This is a small beetle about a quarter of an inch in length, of a brownish-grey colour above and light underneath. It is almost invisible if it falls to the ground. This weevil is hardly seen during some years but is most prolific at other times. During the spring of 1964, peas and broad beans were heavily infested in the south of England. As the beetle eats the young leaves, everything possible must be done to encourage rapid growth. This will include hoeing and watering if very dry. These weevils eat out rounded notches in the margins of the young leaves. The damage may be mistaken for that of slugs, but is more regular and confined to the leaf edges. The treatment is to dust all the foliage with derris powder or old well-weathered soot. This will need to be done at intervals until the damage has ceased and no weevils are seen.

It is best to provide pea sticks for all varieties of peas, including dwarfs. Peas should always have their supports firmly fixed in the ground. These should be inserted after a shower of rain when the ground is soft, before the tendrils appear and before the wind has laid the seedlings flat on the ground. If one lives near a wood or forest, suitable brushwood is easily obtainable, and usually free of charge. The brushwood of hazel is best, although larch, chestnut, maple and many others can be used. Put in two rows of stakes either side of the trench and tilt them at an angle of 45°. Pieces of thin branching brushwood need to be thrust in at the bottom of the stakes to provide the young tendrils with something to cling to, until they reach more solid support. Of course, the stakes need to be cut to the height which suits the variety being grown. Another method of supporting peas is to erect a row of wire netting of three-inch mesh along the centre of the row of peas. Firm posts need to be implanted at each end and also one or two at intervals along the row. A double row of netting, erected on either side of the trench, may be used to give greater support and a certain amount of protection from bad weather.

There is now not a lot of work to do before the gathering of the crop. The few odd greenfly sometimes appear, but these are easily dealt with by spraying with weak, waste soapy water or with clear water. Just syringe them away. If plenty of compost was put into the bottom of the trench, no watering for early peas should be necessary. In some districts, birds are troublesome when the pods are ready for gathering. In a very dry season they seem to come for the moisture which is present in the succulent outer husk of the pea pod. If the peas are grown where plenty of water is to hand, it is a good plan to put pots or buckets or other containers filled with water in various places in the garden. The birds are then more likely to leave the peas alone. Bird-scarers of tinfoil, which shine brightly in the sunlight and crackle in the breeze, can be dangled from the pea sticks as a deterrent. I have found a scarecrow to be very effective for keeping birds away from all crops. You must move the scarecrow around from place to place and have a loose sleeve preferably of light-weight fabric which moves in the breeze.

Peas should be gathered regularly, testing a pod here and there. They should be gathered carefully and not by tugging at the pods so that the haulm is damaged. Pea plants are very easily pulled from the ground. The same preparations of the ground is necessary for second early, maincrop and late peas. It is even more important to put into the bottom of the trench plenty of moisture-retaining material for the remainder of the season's sowings. As the year advances, the peas will need more and more moisture. It is best to withhold watering as long as possible, but it sometimes becomes necessary in order to save the crop. It is better to have tanks of water warming in the sun for some days before applying the water to the pea trench. Peas dislike cold water coming through the hosepipe direct from the tap. It is important to remember with all watering that a little watering is worse than no watering at all. The tiny fibrous roots are made to grow upwards to seek the wet soil if you give only a sprinkling. Roots must be encouraged to go down and not up. Therefore with all watering the whole area to be watered must be thoroughly soaked. Also keep the water away from the foliage as much as possible or the leaves may become scorched by the sun. Water during the early evening.

Good second-early varieties are 'Progress', 1½ft.; 'Onward', 2¼ft.; and 'Lincoln', 2ft. These can be sown in March and early April. One of the best maincrop peas, which is a very heavy cropper, producing an enormous weight of large pods, is 'Alderman'. It is worth obtaining good pea sticks for this pea as it grows to a height of five feet.

A dwarf maincrop pea with very large pods is 'Giant Stride', 2ft. For late peas, the early varieties sown again in late June will provide a good crop in September. Late peas sometimes suffer from mildew but this is easily controlled by dusting the plants with flowers of sulphur, obtained from any chemist quite cheaply. If the gardener lives in a district where it is almost impossible to obtain pea sticks then he would do well to use the wire netting method or grow dwarf varieties. To obtain successional crops of peas it is a good idea to sow more peas when the previous sowing is well above the ground.

If the roots of pea plants are examined, little swellings, called nodules, will be found on them. These are caused by special bacteria which live in the soil, and have the power to fix nitrogen from the air and cause the gas to form part of a solid substance. These bacteria provide the pea plant with plenty of nitrogen, and extra nitrogen is ready in the nodules for any following crop. So it is essential not to destroy the pea roots when the crop is finished, but to dig them back into the soil. Plants which make plenty of leaf like lettuce or cabbage should always follow peas. These plants will then be able to take advantage of the extra nitrogen. Nitrogen is a leaf-forming plant food. This practice also forms part of a proper crop-rotation scheme.

If the gardener has some large cold frames and has the time to spare and does not mind the extra work involved, early varieties of peas may be sown in pots in January. These pots are placed in the cold frame and should be ready for planting out about mid-May. For this cold frame work, some good garden soil containing plenty of leaf mould and a little sand should be made ready. It is best to use pots that measure three inches across the top and are about three and a half inches deep. For sowing, make a hole with a pencil about half an inch deep in the centre of the soil in the pot. After all sowing has been completed, water well all the pots and place them in the cold frame, leaving a little space between each pot for the free circulation of air. They must not be watered again until germination has taken place. Cover the pots with some sheets of newspaper or brown paper to keep out the light, and to conserve the moisture while germination is taking place. In about five days, the peas will have germinated and the paper must be removed immediately. If severe frosts appear the frames will need a thick covering of sacks or old carpets at night. Allow as much air as possible to penetrate the frames during the time that the peas are the occupants. On mild days remove the frame lids altogether. Gradually harden off as planting time approaches, finally standing the pots outside the frames prior to planting out, for a few days. The plants will need a lot of watering during the early months but at no time must the pots be allowed to dry out. More losses are caused in this way than by the effects of severe weather.

Slug killer will need to be scattered here and there and around the frames and precautions must be taken against mice and birds. Plant out with a trowel on the prepared site and firm the soil around the plants and water them in. Again put down slug killer and provide the supports. They will probably have grown large enough to be able to dispense with the black thread. A watch will have to be kept for the pea and bean weevil. Early peas can also be sown early in November in the garden and the use of glass cloches is indicated. After preparing the ground in the usual manner and sowing the seed, the cloches are put over the rows. Each end must be blocked with glass. The cloches can be taken off when the weather is suitable, usually in April. After they are off, the plants will need supporting.

Other good varieties of peas not mentioned so far are as follows. Early Peas: 'The Pilot', 3ft. This is a round-seeded variety. The pods are carried in pairs and are of a very good flavour. 'Gradus', 4ft.: an old variety which is a quick grower. 'Laxton's Superb', 2ft. This is a very early variety. Maincrop Peas: 'Phenomenon', 2ft. This is one of the largest-podded dwarf peas. The pods are slightly curved.

If the gardener wishes to grow peas for exhibition he will first of all need to choose a variety which will mature by the time of the show. Exhibition peas are planted out from pots just like the first earlies, in a double row with the plants about a foot apart. When large enough, they are tied to stakes of the required height. All lateral or side growing shoots are removed, leaving a single main stem. This stem will provide very large leaves and produce pods from five to seven inches long. The stem bearing the pods is additionally supported and is tied to the stake with raffia or very soft tying string. All lateral shoots must be removed continually for they grow very thickly. Remember on the day of the show to exhibit only the number of pods asked for, and choose them of uniform size and shape.

People may well ask, 'Why go to the trouble of producing first-class peas, when packets of frozen peas are so easily obtainable?' The answer is, of course, that there are no peas to compare with those you have grown yourself, freshly gathered and cooked almost at once. The pleasure and satisfaction gained by the gardener who grows his own produce is also a rich compensation. Fresh peas have also much more nutritive value. It is well worth supplementing the dietary with plenty of peas because of their high protein content, especially in these days of costly meat. The high nutritive value of peas is due to the large percentage of nitrogen and of salts of calcium and potassium which they contain. Dried peas actually contain more protein than lean meat. Lean meat and peas and beans, however, supply the body with about the same amount of protein. This is because some of the protein contained in peas is undigested by the human stomach. Two factors account for this: the first one is that the protein is enclosed within a casing of indigestible cellulose, so that it is not entirely acted upon by the digestive juices. Secondly, vegetable foods in general are passed more quickly through the digestive tract than animal foods.

When the peas begin to show above the surface, many gardeners have found that pea sticks are in short supply and expensive. The gardener with a copse bordering his land is, of course, very fortunate; as I have said before, he can cut his own hazel or other suitable sticks. People living near forest land or woods can obtain plenty of sticks suitable for peas, and the time to collect them is during winter, when the gardener is not so busy in the garden; it is no good leaving this task until the peas are up above the ground.

During the winter, over much of the forest land are strewn tons of dead branches, very suitable material indeed. Branching larchwood there is in abundance, so much that after one has gathered about four large bundles from one area, it is impossible to see that any has been taken. Four large bundles would be plenty for most vegetable gardens. When gathering pea sticks in this fashion always take with you plenty of thick cord. Select good branching pieces and lay them one by one on good lengths of cord, one at the top of the bundle and one at the bottom. When you have gathered sufficient for a bundle, tie them in tightly with the cord. The bundle of pea sticks can be drawn up together neatly and the branches will not break, as they are very resilient. A bundle can be light enough to carry on the shoulder. This sort of work might mean three or four trips, but it is very pleasant work and well worth the trouble because, if looked after, the pea sticks will last for several years.

Some long, thicker, straight pieces of dead wood may be searched for and tied into bundles in the same way and used for runner bean poles. Those who live near forest land and have the Rights of Commoners may take as much dead wood at one time as they can carry on their shoulder. No one must ever cut down new wood or take any wood already cut for a specific purpose. Although the wood which may be used has been described, I would hasten to say, 'Always ask permission first, either from the Forestry Commission or the owner of the copse, and state what you require the wood for.' Most people, I think, would be pleased to have a bit of cleaning up of dead wood done free of charge. In the New Forest, official permits can be obtained from the Forestry Commission for a small charge.

While gathering pea sticks or bean rods, it is better not to take children or dogs with you; they will almost certainly frighten rare birds or deer. Close all gates and be very careful not to cause any damage; and above all, never smoke in the forest or woods, there is too much danger of fire. Small twigs or brushwood may also be gathered for staking flowering plants.

BROAD BEANS

Broad beans are a delightful vegetable with a wonderful flavour for most people. Those of us who really like broad beans, enjoy them as young beans or when they are old. We like them at any meal and served with any savoury dish, hot or cold. They are wonderful, too, in cold salads, and are a most satisfying vegetable dish, and with their protein and iron content, are one of the most valuable vegetables to grow. They are very hardy and easy to cultivate. Broad beans, like peas, are able to take up the free nitrogen of the air and assimilate it, so by growing broad beans we are adding extra nitrogen to the soil, if we dig in the roots. Follow the broad bean crop with leafy vegetables.

TOP SHOOTS PINCHED OUT

A Broad bean plant with top re-moved to prevent an attack by Black Fly

So many amateur gardeners say that they cannot grow broad beans, that the crop failed through the ravages of the black fly or aphis. If the growing tip of every broad bean plant is pinched out when the plants are well in flower, or as soon as a single aphis is seen, then the danger will be dispelled and the gardener can be almost certain of a crop. By pinching out the tips, the gardener also ensures an earlier crop and better-filled pods.

One of the many good points about the broad bean is the fact that the seeds retain their germination ability well, much better than most other vegetable seeds. Almost every seed sown will come to maturity, unless ruined by aphides, mice or birds. Broad beans, for early crops, can be sown in the open ground in late October and early November and again in January. Maincrop sowings can be made from mid-February to mid-April.

The soil for broad beans should be deeply dug with plenty of well rotted garden compost or farmyard manure put into the bottom trench. If autumn sowings are going to follow previously well manured crops, such as potatoes, then ordinary plain digging with a fork will be sufficient. If only maincrop beans are to be grown, with a sowing in February or March, then the ground should be well dug with a spade in autumn. Leave this ground as rough as possible during the winter.

Some gardeners believe that autumn sowings of broad beans are a waste of seed. This is not the case, however, during most winters, and the beans sown during autumn will produce a good crop about a fortnight before the spring-sown varieties. If glass cloches are available to put over the beans from November onwards, failure of the crop is rare. Most autumn-sown broad beans come through the winter without protection as they are very hardy. By sowing in a sheltered position, the gardener helps his beans to mature earlier.

For the November sowing, fork over the soil if the beans are following a well-manured previous crop, about three weeks before sowing time. At sowing time, in late October or some time in November when conditions are good, tread the soil fairly firmly, rake to a tilth and level the site. Where not a lot of manure has been used, the beans will benefit from an application of bonemeal or fish fertilizer raked into the soil at sowing time. Use this at the rate of

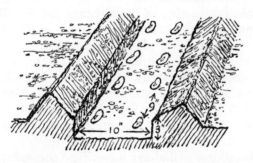

The correct way to sow Broad beans

three ounces to the square yard, plus wood ashes, if available, at five ounces per square yard.

When the soil has been prepared in this way, put down the garden line and draw a drill with the draw hoe or the end of the rake. Have the drill running from north to south wherever possible. Draw two parallel drills ten inches apart and insert single seeds three inches deep and nine inches apart. If more drills are needed leave a two-and-a-half-foot space before drawing the next two drills in the same manner. Cover the seed with soil by using the rake and press down lightly with the head of the rake. In districts where field mice are prevalent the same precautions as those used for garden peas must be taken. Cover each seed with a sprig of spiny gorse or other prickly material such as rose thorns, hawthorn or berberis.

Methods of protection from birds are very necessary with autumn sowings of broad beans. Crows, rooks and pigeons will pull up the young seedlings during autumn and winter, when they cannot find much variety of food. Put down a barrier of black thread or black cotton as recommended for the growing of peas. Encourage the cat to stalk around. The pea and bean weevil is unlikely to be seen attacking the foliage during autumn although it will still be present close at hand. These pests may attack the autumn-sown beans during early spring, and will attack the maincrop sowings as well. Dust with derris when their presence is detected or damage noted.

Keep the beans growing along strongly at all times. Even in winter, if the weather is mild, weeds will grow, so that an occasional hoeing between the rows is desirable. When hoeing during winter, be careful not to break the black thread which has been put down. This will be wanted all winter, as the beans will not have grown large enough or strong enough to deter the birds. January sowings of beans in the open ground are usually only undertaken if continuous glass cloches are available to put over them at sowing time. Cultivate in the same way as for the November-sown.

For the maincrop sowing of broad beans the site should be well prepared in autumn with plenty of compost or farmyard manure dug into the soil. This is for plant food and for moisture retention. Sow in the same way as for autumn sowing and put down the black thread for protection from birds. In some areas, the mice protection measures might be dispensed with for the spring sowing, as in spring the mice can find other plentiful food. If the district is well populated with this pest, recommended measures for their control must be taken.

When the beans are well above the soil, go through the rows with the Dutch hoe to break up the soil. This is to kill the weeds and to let in air. Be careful not to break the black thread until the beans are about five inches high. After the Dutch hoe has been used one can almost see the beans growing. At about this time keep a good look for the pea and bean weevil. Dust the plants with derris dust if the weevil is present, also put down slug killer as soon as the beans are above ground. When the beans are well in flower, and this applies to the November- and January-sown as well, nip out the growing point. Sometimes in open areas, where there are likely to be strong winds, the beans will need staking. Some varieties grow to a height of nearly five feet in the south on good land.

It is a good plan to draw some soil around the bottom of the plants with the hoe, to help support the stems. In exposed areas, where the tall varieties are grown, put in some stout wooden stakes at the ends of the rows and at intervals along the rows. Connect all the stakes with about three rows of strong cord. This will usually prevent the beans being broken by high winds. When the pods are forming they are sometimes attacked by two kinds of birds, the jay and the hawfinch. The hawfinch, which is a shy bird and rarely seen, also attacks garden peas. For prevention measures, erect bird-scarers, again encourage the cat or make a scarecrow and keep moving it to different positions.

If one is a great lover of broad beans, it is well to try and grow successional crops. This means, in fact, being able to pick broad beans from early June through to September. It is even possible to pick beans in October in the south. To do this we must have a November sowing and then one about every three weeks through February to April.

It is quite easy to save one's own broad bean seed. Leave one or two pods on good plants here and there and gather them when the pods are black and brittle, and when the seeds are perfectly dry. This is usually some time in October. If the seeds are of a suitable hardy variety, the seeds which have been gathered in October can be used for the November sowing.

Gather broad beans while young, but not too young; it is no good picking them when the beans are only the size of a pea. This is a waste of good food. On the other hand, do not let them get too old and leathery. Young beans of cookable size are richer in protein than old tough beans. There are one or two ways of dealing with the bean haulms when the crop has been finally gathered. You can leave one row, or part of a row, for seed, and cut *down to ground level* the remainder of the haulms and put them on to the compost heap. On no account dig them out; we went into the reasons for that earlier; we want the roots with their nitrogen content left in the soil. If the gardener is keeping some livestock, the bean haulms, if they are green and succulent, may be fed to cattle, ponies, pigs and poultry. In the green state the bean straw is little inferior to good hay. If the haulms are allowed to become dry and brown they are no good for livestock, being then unpalatable, fibrous and not at all nutritious. On acid soils, broad beans will grow better if a little garden lime is raked into the top soil, but not at the same time as an organic manure. This has been said many times, but bears repetition (see page 14).

Broad beans are a good crop for newly-broken grassland. They are not much liked by wireworm and so would do better on this kind of land than would potatoes, which are very liable to be attacked by this pest. In addition to the sowing times and methods mentioned for growing broad beans, they can also be sown in deep boxes and put into the cold frame during January, being hardened off and transplanted into the open ground during March.

There are three main types of broad bean, the long-pod, the Windsor and the dwarf. All of these types may have green or white seeds. If you are growing broad beans for the first time, or after a lapse of several years, it is best to grow a few of each type and see which you prefer. Some people say that the green-seeded varieties are more tender and palatable than the white. This, as in many other aspects of gardening, is entirely a matter of personal opinion. Long-pod beans are hardier and yield more heavily than the Windsor types. They are therefore, on account of hardiness, the right sort to sow in November and for very early spring sowings.

A new dwarf variety called 'The Midget' is the one to grow in a very small vegetable plot. It grows to a height of twelve to fifteen inches and therefore needs no staking or tying. Each plant produces three or four stems each bearing a cluster of five-inch pods. This variety is best sown in single rows as each plant will spread to about eighteen inches across. There are many different varieties listed by different seedsmen. Any good seedsman's strain of long-pod bean can be chosen, and since all long-pods are hardy, they can be sown in the autumn or in spring.

The gardener would not be disappointed if he grew some of the following varieties. For autumn sowing: 'Dreadnought', 'Rentpayer', 'Giant Seville', 'Super Aquadulce' and 'Johnson's Early Long-Pod'. For spring sowing, any of the above, and 'Giant Green Windsor', 'Giant White Windsor', 'The Midget' and 'Express'. Although some of the new varieties are an improvement on some of the older ones, this is not always the case. I am growing a broad bean, the seed of which has been saved for the past thirty years in Norfolk. No one knows the name of the variety but they are one of the finest varieties of broad bean I have ever grown. This opinion is shared by many other gardeners who have grown broad beans from the same seed.

DWARF FRENCH BEANS

There are climbing French beans as well as the well-known bush varieties. The bush varieties are the ones most usually grown. Although most people with a vegetable plot will always grow a few runner beans, not so many people grow the dwarf French beans. This is rather surprising, for there could hardly be a vegetable more easily grown or one so productive over a long period. There are very many ways of growing French beans. Very early crops can be obtained by the use of glass, and September crops can be gathered with a July sowing in the open garden. Some people think that the French bean possesses a superior flavour to the runner bean. The flavour of runner beans or French beans depends a lot on the way they are cooked. If French beans are sliced into minute pieces, much of the flavour is extracted by the boiling water.

Dwarf French beans can be sown in pots in the cool greenhouse, in pots in cold frames, under cloches in late March and in the open ground from April until early July. It will be seen that a long succession of crops can be ensured by these growing methods. Most people are very fond of runner beans but gardeners should always grow some dwarf French beans in addition to runner beans. The reason for this is that much earlier crops can be obtained from French beans. As they do not grow very high they produce flowers and pods more quickly than runner beans. They make a welcome change of vegetable while we are waiting for the runner beans.

On an acid soil, lime is necessary for all peas and beans. Rake in from four to seven ounces per square yard but do not apply the lime at the same time as the organic manure. If the land is being prepared in autumn and receiving farmyard manure or garden compost at this time, rake in the lime during early spring. French beans grown in the open garden are tender subjects and generally should not be sown until mid-April, although in the south of England they can be sown during the first week of April.

Prepare the ground in autumn in the usual way and incorporate with it in the bottom of the trench plenty of farmyard manure, or garden compost. Most seedsmen supply French beans in half-pint packets and this is usually enough seed for the average vegetable plot. In any case, if more are required they are usually easily obtainable throughout the spring and summer. Tread and rake down the soil to a fine tilth in early spring. Put down the garden line and draw two drills two feet apart. Two rows of plants will be ample for an average width of kitchen garden or allotment; in many cases one row would be enough for the first sowing, as French beans are very prolific. They will keep bearing as long as no pods are left on the plants to mature. Sow the beans two inches deep and nine inches apart. Cover with soil and press down with the head of the rake.

When the plants begin to appear above the soil put down slug killer pellets, as there is nothing slugs like better than the young fleshy leaves of the French bean. French beans do not require much other attention during the growing season. They will need watering if some very dry weather appears, but this will not be often, if plenty of moisture-retaining material like garden compost has been put into the bottom trench during autumn preparations. Keep the rows weed-free by using the Dutch hoe; this will also let air into the soil.

The dwarf French beans will need supporting with bushy twigs, otherwise they may be blown over by heavy winds and rain. During rough weather the beans get muddy and often unfit to eat. The supporting of French beans is not a difficult task, as only one or two twigs per plant are needed. If climbing French beans are being grown, they will need supporting with bushy pea sticks in the same manner as for tall varieties of garden peas. They will not climb a bean pole as a runner bean will.

The grower of French beans is rarely troubled by birds or mice, as by the time April comes along the mice have gradually found other foods. Birds rarely attack the pods of French beans and the plants are not subject to attack by the pea and bean weevil. In fact, it is about the easiest vegetable to grow. The important point about their culture is one must make frequent gatherings of the fresh young beans before they become old, tough and stringy, which very quickly happens. French beans can be gathered, suitable for cooking, when only about three and a half inches in length.

Successional sowings can be made in the open ground at the end of April and during May and June, also during the first week of July. The gardener will decide for himself whether he will want to sow after the first sowing in April. This first sowing will produce beans while one is waiting for the runner beans. The other sowings will provide beans while one is still picking plenty of runners. Some gardeners may decide to grow French beans only and so dispense with bean poles or wire netting to support runner beans. If runners are being grown as well as French beans, then perhaps the first sowing and the last one in early July will suffice for most people.

If the grower can maintain a steady temperature of 60°F. by day and night, French beans can be grown in the greenhouse, if it is large enough and if it is thought desirable to use the greenhouse for this purpose. If the greenhouse is being used for other purposes, then perhaps the grower can grow a few pots of French beans if he thinks it worth while. It is possible to have a continuous supply of French beans from late November until May, but this means a very efficient heating apparatus because the temperature must not vary. The first sowing can be made in the third week in September, and these will mature in about ten weeks. Successional sowings should be made every three weeks until March.

One of the best methods of sowing French beans for greenhouse work is to put single seeds into a sweet pea pot, then transfer three matched plants of the same height to a ten-inch pot. The pot should be half filled with John Innes Compost No. 2. You add another two-inch layer when the plants are about eight inches high and then gradually add the same compost as surface roots appear until the pot has been filled to within an inch of the top. Stand the pots on shingle and water frequently, never letting the pots dry out. Never over-water and the water should never be ice-cold direct from the tap; use water with the chill taken off it. Keep a fairly humid atmosphere by spraying the foliage overhead and damping the floor. Do not overdo this; try to keep the atmosphere slightly humid, only damping down on very sunny days. Support the plants in some way, either with twigs or split bamboos. Remove any runners which may be thrown out.

French beans, growing in pots in a greenhouse, can be fed but great care must be taken not to overdo this. Liquid manure made from animal dung, diluted to the colour of light straw, can be used. Fortnightly light applications would be sufficient. Dried blood can also be used, but extra care must be taken when using this. Follow exactly the makers' instructions on the packet. Climbing French beans can be grown in the greenhouse and allowed to climb up strings attached to the roof. They can grow right up to the greenhouse roof.

For growing French beans in cold frames, the same method, using the sweet pea pots first, can be used. They can also be grown in John Innes Compost No. 2 without pots. Fork over the ground at the base of the cold frame and fill in with John Innes Compost No. 2 to a depth of about twelve inches. Some well rotted garden compost can be put at the bottom of the cold frame on to the soil that has been forked over. Make the first sowing in the frames during the middle of March. Place the seeds two inches deep and three inches apart in rows a foot apart. When the plants are through the soil, thin out to six inches apart and transplant the thinnings to other cold frames or into the open ground under cloches.

As in the case of sweet peas, do not give air until the seeds have germinated. When frost is about, cover the frames with straw, sacking or mats. As the plants grow give more air, but close the lights during very heavy storms or during late frosts. By mid-May it should be possible to remove the lights entirely during the day, only closing them at night. Water the plants during dry spells but do not overwater. Use water with the chill removed. Picking should begin about the second week of June. Protect against slugs at all times. A further sowing of the beans can be made in early April in the cold frames for growing on, hardening off, and transplanting in the open ground. Transplant about the third week in May. Lift the plants very carefully from the cold frame when transplanting and squeeze the soil gently around the roots when doing so. Soil very easily falls from French bean seedlings, exposing the roots. It is a help if the seedlings are gently watered just prior to lifting from the cold frame. These transplanted seedlings can be grown on without protection or they may be grown under continuous cloches until the end of May.

For growing French beans under continuous cloches the site should be well prepared in autumn by digging in plenty of good garden compost or well rotted farmyard manure. The cloches should be put over the site about three weeks before the sowing date to warm the soil. The seeds should be sown in the same way as for the open ground sowing. Choose a day for sowing some time in late March when the ground is moist enough to allow for germination. Sow the seeds and then cover the rows with continuous cloches of the barn type. The cloches can be taken from the rows at the end of May. The seeds sown in late July can also be covered with cloches to allow the picking of beans to go on into October. Do not forget to close the ends of the rows of cloches with panes of glass.

There are many varieties of French beans under different names in various catalogues. If a selection is made from the following, and they are purchased from a well-known seedsman, satisfactory results should be obtained. 'Duplex', 'Masterpiece Stringless', 'The Prince' and 'Golden Butter' (pods of golden-yellow) are good bush varieties. 'Veitch's Climbing' is naturally a climbing sort.

RUNNER BEANS

One could hardly find an allotment in England without some runner beans growing upon it during the summer. This is not surprising when one considers the number of succulent pods that can be pro-duced from one seed. Runner beans are very productive and they will keep on bearing pods until the frosts arrive in November. They must be frequently gathered, and none of the pods must be allowed to mature. It is quite usual for many gardeners to save their own seed from year to year. This can be done by allowing one or two pods to remain for seed production.

If one has only a small garden and can only grow a few varieties of vegetables, it would be wise to include the runner bean or French bean in the selected list. Runners are easy to grow and they can provide a supply of fresh vegetables from July to October almost every day. If there is really not enough room for the erection of bean poles, then runner beans can be grown on the flat, or the variety called 'Hammond's Dwarf Scarlet' can be used. This kind does not need bean sticks.

Runner beans will grow well on most well-manured soils. They will not grow and bear well on soils which have only a thin layer of soil over solid chalk. They *could* grow here if the solid chalk could be excavated to a depth of about three feet and plenty of garden compost were put into the bottom of the trench and the remainder filled with good soil. If the grower has only a small amount of garden compost or farmyard manure, then he would do well to use some of it for his runner beans. In the ordinary way the site for the runner beans would be trenched and liberally manured in the autumn with garden com-post or farmyard manure. This work can be done in early spring but autumn is a better time. Garden compost is a particularly good

A row of Hammond's Dwarf
Runner Bean showing its compact
and floriferous form

Home Guard potatoes. The
sort of crop to expect from
good, well-sprouted seed
growing on good land

Some well-grown Celeriac

A basket of first-class Endive. Variety: Green Curled

Melons, growing in the most suitable type of greenhouse, well trained and supported
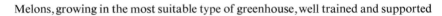

manure for runner beans, which need plenty of good garden compost in the bottom of the trench at soil preparation time. They are good feeders and require plenty of moisture-retaining material, for they are producing pods during the height of the summer and early autumn, when conditions are usually particularly dry.

If the whole of the vegetable garden has not been dug and liberally manured during autumn, then the site for the runner beans must be specially prepared. This is best done in autumn. A similar trench to that prepared for sweet peas is taken out. Dig out the soil to a depth of two feet, keeping the good top soil on one side and the sub-soil on the other. Fork over the bottom of the trench and put in a thick layer of good garden compost and tread this firmly. Put back the sub-soil, then the good soil, and tread as you go along. Make the soil fairly firm but not rammed to an impenetrable mass. Leave a small depression along the length of the trench when the soil has been returned. Leave the surface as rough as possible for the action of winter weather. Rake the soil down to a fine tilth during early spring. Sow the beans during early May.

Put down the garden line and draw a wide drill with a draw hoe. Have the drill wide enough to enable the beans to be sown in two rows, which are two feet apart. Space single beans nine inches apart and two inches deep. Have bean poles ready and insert them into the soil on the outside of the beans, when they are well above the soil, being careful not to thrust the points into the roots of the plants. Many kinds of branches can be used for bean poles. Generally beans will climb more easily the rougher-barked wood. Larch poles are quite good, so are hazel and many other kinds of wood. If the base of the bean rod is about three-quarters of an inch to an inch in diameter and tapers thinly towards the top it should prove suitable. The bean sticks should be about eight feet above the ground. They are best thrust in at an angle. Tilt the poles in each row, so that they

RUNNER BEANS. ONE POLE PER PLANT

The staking of runner beans

cross the poles in the opposite row and so that they make a V-shape along the whole of the row about two feet deep. Then lay poles horizontally along the trough so created, and fix firmly together with strong twine. The poles must be very firmly fixed in the ground and it is advisable in windy areas to run wire or strong twine along the entire length of the rows of bean rods. Fix the wire or string to each pole and connect them firmly. Have this support running along about two feet six inches from ground level.

When the plants appear above the soil, put well-weathered soot along the outside of the rows to discourage slugs. Put down slug-killer pellets as well. When the plants start to throw out long tendrils it will be frequently seen that they are making a lot of growth without being inclined to start climbing the poles put ready for them. In these cases they can be assisted by the gardener if he takes the long tendril and carefully winds it around the support, always remembering that a runner bean climbs anti-clockwise. If more than one double row of runners are being grown, then the next double row needs to be at least five feet away. This is to allow room for cultivation during the growing season, for gathering the crops, and to allow enough light and air into the plants. Runner bean plants will need to be well watered during prolonged dry spells of weather. Overhead spraying with water, using a fine rose, will help to set the blossom. Carry out this operation during warm summer evenings. Do not let runners grow on beyond the tops of the poles so that they wave about wildly in the air. Pinch out the tips when they reach the top.

For people who live in towns and cities and who cannot obtain bean poles at all easily, there are other ways of supporting runner beans. Two stout wooden supports rising eight feet above the ground can be erected at either end of the rows. A wire can be run from the top of each support to the one at the other end. Then a stout wire can be run through the centre and another one along the bottom a few inches from the ground. To these can be tied vertical lengths of string and the plants can climb these. Wire netting can also be erected and stretched between two firm supports. Beans can then be staggered each side of the wire netting and allowed to climb this.

There is another way of growing runner beans, which method does not need supports. Prepare the land in the same manner and sow the seeds in the same way. Allow the plants to grow about a foot high and then pinch out the tops of the resultant tendrils as they appear. The crop is not so heavy when grown in this way and the pods are often distorted. Slugs cause more damage to the pods as they are nearer the ground, so put down plenty of slug-killer pellets. This method is used by commercial growers to save the time and cost of erecting bean poles.

There is now a comparatively new variety of non-trailing or non-climbing runner bean named 'Hammond's Dwarf Scarlet'. This is a dwarf variety growing to about sixteen inches in height. It is very useful for early crops and for growing under large barn-type cloches. It does not bear so heavy a crop as the climbing varieties.

Many people sow runner beans in deep boxes in early April and put them into the cold frame. They are then grown on carefully, hardened off, and transplanted to the open ground during the second week in May. They can then be grown on in the ordinary way or have cloches put over them for a time, in order to obtain very early crops. Runner bean roots can be saved to replant the following May. Those who would like to do this will find it quite simple. Just remove the haulm three inches above the soil when the plants have finished bearing, lift the roots with a fork, wash away every trace of soil and, when dry, store in boxes of just-moist sand in a frost-proof shed. There are many varieties of runner beans and there is no need to bother about the length of bean. They are just as good food value whether the bean is three inches or a yard long. The variety 'Princeps' is usually about fourteen days earlier than other varieties and is dwarfer in growth. A selection from the following will be found suitable for most purposes: 'Scarlet Emperor', 'Prizewinner', 'Streamline', 'White Wonder', 'Princeps', 'Kelvedon Wonder', 'Crusader' and 'Hammond's Dwarf Scarlet'. A lightish, good soil in a sunny position with a deep, cool root-run, will suit the runner bean best. One pint of runner bean seed will sow a row of about fifty feet in length.

ROOT CROPS

All root crops grow well on ground which has been previously well manured for other crops. When we speak of root crops, we usually exclude potatoes which are put into a class of their own. In any case, they are not roots but are swollen underground stems.

It is useless to attempt to grow vegetables with long roots on anything but fairly light, deeply cultivated soils. For those who wish to grow long carrots, long beet or parsnips, deep digging is essential. The roots of these crops penetrate deeply into the ground. The soil should be friable and even-textured, therefore it must be broken up with the garden fork or rake. Good root crops cannot be grown on thick, lumpy, stiff clay soil. A sandy loam is the ideal soil.

If the gardener who wishes to grow root crops does not have a suitable soil, he must try to make it as suitable as possible for root crops. A heavy soil must be lightened by the addition of a little silver sand, plenty of garden peat, leaf-mould and good well-decayed garden compost. Fork these ingredients in and keep on forking and hoeing until a good texture of soil has been achieved. For a person who finds this work too laborious, especially in one of these intractable clay soils, it would be best for him to try and grow some of the short and intermediate types of root vegetable. Even then a certain amount of lightening of the soil would have to be done, but the soil would not have to be cultivated too deeply. Although root crops grow best on land which has been well manured for another crop, some well-rotted garden compost can be used but not fresh farmyard manure. A small amount of bonemeal can be raked into the surface soil a few weeks before sowing time.

CARROTS

There are three classes of carrots, stump-rooted, intermediate-rooted and long-rooted. The stump-rooted sorts are usually used for early work, for growing in cold frames, under cloches or for early crops in the open ground. The intermediate and long-rooted kinds can be used as a main crop at any time during the summer or early autumn, and also for storage for the winter. Stump-rooted varieties can also be used to provide a succession of quick-maturing, succulent young carrots for use in the kitchen at any time during the summer.

Carrots grow best on a deep, medium-to-light loam. Prepare the site for the carrots by deep digging during the autumn. If the carrots are to be grown on land which has been already liberally manured for a previous crop, like spring cabbage or potatoes, then there is no need to add more. If carrots are grown on freshly manured land the roots tend to fork, reducing their value. If the carrots are being grown on land which has not received manure for a previous crop, then the best possible manure for them is good well-rotted garden compost. Dig the land deeply with a spade and break up the sub-soil, add a good dressing of garden compost to the bottom trench and leave the surface soil rough for the winter frosts and snow to improve the texture.

It is very important to move carrots to a fresh spot each year in order to discourage their worst enemy, the carrot fly. There are two generations of the carrot fly each year. Most of the first generation emerge at the end of May; they find sheltered places in the garden and then lay their eggs in the soil very near to the carrots, which may be attacked during any stage of their growth. The grubs burrow into the roots, destroying many plants and damaging others. The larvae pupate after feeding on the carrots and a second generation of flies are produced during August to October. These in turn produce further maggots which tunnel into the roots, even after they have been lifted and stored.

There are several methods of control for the carrot fly. The old-time gardeners used to soak sand with paraffin and run a row of sand on either side of each row of carrots at sowing time. This was, and still is, fairly effective, as all the measures of control taken are aimed at masking the smell of the carrots (the flies are attracted to the bed by the strong scent of the carrot). One can also run some creosoted string fixed to stakes along each row. Have the string fairly close to the ground. Naphthalene can also be scattered along the rows. Fortnightly applications of derris dust from the time of sowing onwards would also be a good deterrent. D.D.T. was found to be effective but as there are now doubts as to its degree of poison and its effect on humans and wild life, it would seem to be much safer to use derris dust. If you well firm the soil after thinning, and bank up the soil a little around the roots, it will make it more difficult for egg-laying.

Carrots must be kept free of weeds at all times. The seedlings are slow growing at first during the early days of spring, but later sowings during the warm weather make quicker progress. During the slow growing period the carrots cannot compete with weeds, their foliage is delicate and is soon crowded out with stronger-growing weeds.

During February, tread down the soil which has been prepared during autumn and rake to a fine tilth. If necessary some good fish manure can be raked into the surface soil at the rate of four ounces to the square yard. Carrot seed will not germinate if conditions are too dry and gardeners often wonder why their carrots have not appeared above the soil. During dry conditions at sowing time, the drills may be watered by using the fine rose on the watering-can. Do this before sowing the seed.

Choose a stump-rooted variety for an early crop by sowing in the open ground during March. Put down a garden line and draw drills with the end of the rake. They should be no more than three-quarters of an inch deep; it is a great mistake to sow any seed too deep. The smaller the seed the shallower should be the drills, and carrot seed is small and light in weight and colour. If watering the drills, leave them open to drain a little before sowing the seed. Many people will find the sowing of carrot seed a difficult task. It is very easy to sow the seed too thickly. Take a pinch of seed into the right hand and walk along the side of the drills fairly quickly, shaking some seed into the drills as you go along. Hold the hand down low into the drill, for the slightest breeze will blow the seed away. If there is a strong breeze or wind the seed will have to be covered with soil quickly, sowing and covering one row at a time. Another method of thin sowing is to sow three seeds every three inches along the drill and thin out to one per station, when large enough, usually about three weeks later. This

thinning might not always be necessary, as some of the seeds may not
have germinated.

Do not worry if the first early crop of carrots fails to mature. This
often happens if there is a dry, cold spring. Subsequent sowings
nearly always grow well and produce a good crop during the warmer
days. Choose a warm, sheltered spot, if possible, for the earlier
sowings. Put the drills six inches apart and cover the seed carefully
with the rake; press down the soil gently with the head of the rake—
no need to worry much about birds as they rarely do any damage to
the carrot seed sowings.

Early carrots can be pulled when they are thought to be of usable
size. Try to pull them when the soil is moist, otherwise the foliage
easily comes away in the hand, leaving the root firmly fixed in the
ground. Carrots are more easily removed from the ground with the
aid of a trowel or old kitchen fork. Firm all soil after thinning, to
make sure you give no assistance to the carrot fly.

Carrots for immediate consumption can be sown at any time from
March to the end of July. The seed of the main crop should be sown
in April and if these are to be stored for winter use, a long-rooted
variety should be chosen. Intermediate rooting varieties can be sown
throughout the spring and summer for immediate use in the kitchen,
but an early stump-rooted variety should be chosen for the July
sowing. These only take about ten weeks to mature so they make nice
young roots for use during the autumn. Sow the seed of the main crop
in April and make the drills from twelve to eighteen inches apart,
according to the size of the variety. All carrots should be sown thinly
and any subsequent thinnings can be used immediately in the kitchen.
Keep the rows free of weeds at all times by using the Dutch hoe. This
is the best tool to use because it does not disturb the soil so much as
would the draw hoe.

Stump-rooted carrots are good subjects for cold frames, very useful
for providing early vegetables. Have the frame facing south and sow
the seeds in mid-February. Prepare the base of the frame in the same
way as for French beans, but fill it with a good sandy light loam,
with plenty of good well-decayed garden compost mixed with the soil.
Sow the seed thinly and leave the lights on until germination takes
place. Then allow air during the growing season according to the
weather conditions. Grown in this way carrots can be ready for
pulling in April. Some gardeners like to mix radish seed with the
carrot seed in order to take a catch crop of radishes which mature
very quickly in a cold frame and are ready in about four weeks from
sowing. This kind of cropping is only possible in a warm spring and
in a sheltered, warm neighbourhood. These crops will usually take a
little longer to mature in other districts.

Cloches can be employed for early carrot growing. Put the cloches over the prepared site about three weeks before the sowing date. Sow an early variety at the beginning of March, put the cloches over the drills and remember to block the ends of the rows of cloches with a pane of glass held securely. For these early crops in frames and under cloches about the best variety to use is 'Amsterdam Forcing'. It does not grow to a large size but it matures early. For main crop work, for winter storage, and for large roots, the best kind is 'Long Red Surrey'. Good varieties of carrots are 'St. Valery' and 'James Intermediate (Selected)'; long-rooted main crop are 'Long Red Surrey', 'Autumn King' and 'Prizewinner'.

Some nurserymen are now offering carrot seed which has been treated against carrot fly. It is stated that protection will last from four to five months with early-sown crops and from two to three months with late-sown ones.

GARDEN BEET

There are three types of beet, the round globe, the intermediate and the long-rooted. The most popular is the globe beet; it can be grown where the garden does not have a great depth of soil. It is suitable for a small garden and it is easier to get into saucepans in the kitchen. The intermediate type can be grown by most people and very many of these have the quality of the round beet with a much heavier yield. These are very suitable for people with a large pressure cooker. The long-rooted kinds are not very suitable for ordinary kitchen utensils. They give a very heavy yield and are a good sort to grow for use in hotels and boarding-houses where they may have very large cooking urns in operation.

The best soil for beet is one which has been well manured for a previous crop. They prefer a light loam, of good depth, but the globe variety can be grown on a fairly shallow soil, if it has been previously enriched with farmyard manure or good garden compost. The sowing of beet can begin about the end of March with sowings succeeding one another up to August. Although it is possible to harvest beet in November from an August or late-July sowing, very much depends on the weather. Warmth is needed for the roots to attain any 'cookable' size.

For the March sowing a south warm border must be selected and cloches used if available. The end of April or the beginning of May is the best time to sow beet in the open ground. They are one of the easiest vegetable crops to grow and are practically pest free. If the ground has been deeply dug in the autumn, make firm and rake down to a fine tilth. If it is thought necessary, and be guided by the richness of the soil, add some fish manure at the rate of four ounces to the square yard, which can be raked into the surface soil about a fortnight before the sowing of the seed.

Put down the garden line and draw the seed drills with the rake head. Make the drills two inches deep and fifteen inches apart. There is no difficulty with the sowing of beet seed. It is of a light colour and large. It is very easily handled. Each seed of beet is really a capsule containing a number of seeds. Sow one seed along the rows every four inches and cover the drills with fine soil. If several seedlings appear later, thin them to one per station, finally thinning the younger plants to about eight inches or so apart according to how large you require your roots.

During the growing season the crop will appreciate an application of agricultural salt at the rate of one ounce per yard run and hoed in. The wild beet grows on or near the seashore. Apart from keeping down weeds, no other attention will be necessary except for putting down a few slug-killer pellets when the seedlings are small. Beet for winter storage is best sown in May and harvested in early October. Although beetroot will stand some frost, it is best to store roots which are undamaged. Roots for storage must be lifted very carefully with a garden fork; do not rush this task. Beet must not be pierced with the fork and they must be handled very carefully. It is fairly common knowledge that beet will bleed if damaged in any way, and if a beet bleeds it is of no use for cooking as it loses all its colour and goodness. The foliage should always be twisted away by hand, but not too near the crown, and must never be cut from the root.

Beets for salads can be sown at any time from April until July. Pull them when they are young and tender and of any cookable size. Twist off the foliage. Sugar beet can be grown in the garden; it is a good vegetable with a high sugar content, which can be cooked and eaten like beetroot. The gardener may not think sugar beet worth growing because of the expense of fuel for cooking them, as they take rather a lot of boiling. They are useful for soup making.

A very useful tip for the vegetable grower is that with sown beet he can thin some of the rows in the usual manner, but leave some others unthinned. The thinned rows will produce early beetroot and the unthinned rows nice small to medium-sized roots throughout the season. The cook does not require huge, tough beetroot which take hours to cook and use up so much fuel. This is what happens if all beet are thinned; those which cannot be used within a few weeks go on growing and become large and coarse. This does not happen if rows remain unthinned. This practice can be followed with other crops if you like.

Good varieties of globe beet are 'Crimson Globe', 'Detroit',

'Egyptian Turnip-rooted' and 'Feltham Globe'. Intermediate roots are 'Sultan' and 'Cylindra'. Long-rooted sorts: 'Cheltenham Green Top' and 'Crimson King'.

CELERIAC

This is really a turnip-rooted celery, and is often grown instead of celery because it is much easier to cultivate. It does not produce stems alone like celery but the plant forms a swollen turnip-like root which can be eaten in slices raw, as a substitute for celery, or boiled like potatoes, or used for flavouring soups. The leaf stalks may also be eaten, so it is a plant without any waste whatsoever, as every part of any surplus plants can be used to feed poultry. It can be cut and fed raw to poultry or cooked and mixed with the mash.

Celeriac is a half-hardy plant, so it can only be grown from seed in a cool greenhouse. One seldom hears of a nurseryman offering plants for sale in the same way as they do celery plants. Crock some seed boxes, fill them with John Innes seed compost, water the soil and allow to drain. Sow the seeds thinly during March in a temperature of from 60° to 65°F. Prick out the seedlings when large enough to handle and harden off in the usual way. Plant out in May, twelve to fifteen inches apart in rows two feet apart, in the same kind of soil as that prepared for beetroot. Celeriac grows well on land which has received plenty of good garden compost. Do not plant too deeply and water well during dry periods. Remove all side shoots during the growing period, keeping the plants to a single stem. Remove all lateral growth, suckers and fibrous roots from the swollen root, so that it stands out of the ground looking very bare. When growth has been completed, any plant not used may be left in the ground and lightly earthed up as a protection against frost. Do not do this before November or the side growths may be produced again.

Celeriac is generally lifted during October but it can be used at any time when ready. If celeriac is being stored for winter use, remove all leaves except the small tuft in the centre. If this is removed the root will produce another set of foliage, making the root rather unfit for eating. The variety listed today is 'Globus', and it has large solid globe-shaped roots, with very much more edible flesh than the old kind called 'Giant Prague'.

PARSNIPS

There are intermediate and long-rooted varieties of parsnips, as there are of carrots. Parsnips can be sown in the open ground during February, March and April. The soil is seldom ready for seed sowing in February, so wait until conditions are suitable. The parsnip needs a long period of growth, so put it on a plot where the ground will not be needed for other purposes. It grows best on a soil which has previously been well manured for a preceding crop. Parsnips are left in the ground until the frosts have arrived to sweeten the roots. As with celery and Brussels sprouts, frost improves the flavour. If you want to harvest long, straight roots, the soil for parsnips must be very deeply dug. They require very little attention during the growing season and are a very easy vegetable to grow. Parsnip seeds germinate very slowly, so mark the end of each row with a clear label.

Prepare the ground in autumn, if not following a previously well-manured crop, by digging quite deeply, at least two feet deep, and work in plenty of well-decayed garden compost. Leave the surface rough during the winter and tread and rake down to a fine tilth in early spring. Put down the garden line and draw drills about half an inch deep and fifteen inches apart. Parsnip seed is quite large enough to see clearly, so it can be sown very thinly. Cover with soil and press down fairly firmly with the rake head. When the seedlings are large enough, thin them out to eight inches apart. Keep well weeded and lift the roots with a fork as required after frost.

Some parsnip growers go to the trouble of making deep holes with a crowbar a foot apart, and then fill these holes with a prepared soil like John Innes Compost No. 2. Two or three seeds are sown on top of each prepared hole after making the whole of the soil firm. When the seeds germinate, the strongest specimen is left to grow on and the rest are pulled out and discarded. Varieties of parsnip are 'Selected Offenham', a half-long variety, 'Tender and True', 'Hollow Crown', 'The Student', medium-size, and 'Improved Marrow'.

SWEDE

Once garden swedes have been grown, and it is found that the flavour pleases the family, they will find a place in the vegetable garden every year. They deserve to be a much more popular vegetable, for the flavour is delightful. There is hardly a better vegetable dish than a portion of garden swede mashed with butter and pepper. They are easy to grow and hardier than turnips. They take a little longer to mature than turnips, so if both are sown at the same time the gardener will have a good vegetable to follow the turnips.

Two kinds of swede can be grown, the garden swede and the field swede. If there is room for a few rows of each, so much the better, but grow the garden swede in any case. It has a wonderfully delicate flavour, but it is a little less hardy than the field swede. If both are grown the gardener will have three good root crops for succession, turnips, garden swedes and field swedes. Field swedes mature later and grow larger than garden swedes. There are no storage problems with field swedes because they can be left in the open ground until after Christmas. Land which has been well manured for a previous crop is the best kind for swedes. Good garden compost suits them well.

Swedes need moist conditions, as turnips do, and they succeed well during a wet summer. Some of the essentials for good swede growing are plenty of moisture-retentive material in the soil, and not too far down, as the swede sits on top of the soil and does not send down a mass of roots into the sub-soil. Prepare the site in autumn if the swedes are not following a previously well-manured crop, by digging in plenty of good garden compost. Leave the surface soil as rough as possible during the winter. Tread and rake down the soil to a fine tilth in early spring. A first sowing may be made at the end of March, followed by sowings in April, May and June to provide a succession of young tender roots for either a second vegetable or for stews. The field swedes may be sown during May and left in the ground until after Christmas, and used as required. Garden swedes may also be sown in May and lifted for storage during October.

Put down a garden line and draw drills with the rake three-quarters of an inch deep and a foot and a half apart. Sow thinly and cover the seeds by raking over the soil carefully and firming with the rake head. The swede and turnip have one great enemy, the flea beetle, a minute black beetle which attacks the seedlings just as they come through the surface soil. During dry periods, the seedlings will be covered with these pests, and if they are left unmolested the rows of seedling swedes will soon disappear from view. After sowing the seed, sprinkle the rows with old well-weathered soot; this will act as a deterrent. As soon as the seedlings appear above the soil, dust them with flea-beetle dust or derris dust. Repeat the application every week until the seedlings are growing away well. If the gardener attends scrupulously to this dusting, he will be practically assured of a good crop.

When the plants are growing away strongly they will have to be thinned. Thin them to one foot apart during showery weather. When the swedes grow larger and produce plenty of foliage they are sometimes attacked by small snails and slugs; this happens during a wet summer. Put down slug-killer pellets if it does occur. The swedes will not require further attention apart from keeping the weeds down with the Dutch hoe. Good varieties of swede are 'Laing's Garden', 'Purple-Top Garden', 'Improved Garden Swede', 'Yellow, Improved Garden Swede', 'White'; and the field swedes are 'Champion Purple Top' or 'Improved Purple Top'.

TURNIPS

There are white-fleshed and yellow-fleshed turnips. They need the same treatment as swedes except that they can be grown on slightly richer soil, and to ensure the production of large tender roots that have not become woody, quick growing is essential. If grown well, turnips will mature in about ten weeks from the date of sowing. They need cool, moist conditions and must be grown without check. Early turnips do not keep well and they are used as they mature. The yellow-fleshed turnips are better keepers than the white ones and they can be left in the ground later as they are more hardy.

There are three main sowings of turnips. One is made in mid-April, the second in May, and the third at the end of July for winter turnips. Turnips can also be sown in August and September to provide turnip tops in winter and spring. These tops are the foliage which is cut from the plants and cooked like cabbage. Winter turnips can be left in the ground and pulled as required in the south and other warm areas.

Prepare the soil in the same manner as for swedes but a richer soil can be used. Put down the garden line and draw the drills three-quarters of an inch deep and fifteen inches apart for the early crops. Dust with flea-beetle dust as the seedlings appear, after a previous application of old soot. Thin out to nine inches apart. Turnips are best for cooking when they are about the size of a tennis ball. To keep the moist conditions essential for the quick growing required, plenty of garden compost needs to be worked into the soil, but not too deeply. Old leaf mould is another valuable ingredient for the top soil.

Turnips are a good early crop for growing in cold frames, but the frames must be situated in a warm, sheltered position where they will get plenty of sun, and where warmth can be trapped and maintained. Heated frames can be utilized for turnip growing; for sowing in cold frames, make drills three-quarters of an inch deep at the end of February or the beginning of March and thin the seedlings to six inches apart. Keep the frames closed after sowing and ventilate and water as required during the growing season. About a ten-inch depth of good, rich light soil is required in the frame. This soil needs to be well prepared some weeks before sowing, and the lights are left on in order to warm the soil should there be a spell of warm sunshine. Do not sow until the soil is fairly warm and good conditions for germination and growing are present. Under good growing conditions, which means warmth, the crop can mature in about two months.

Turnips can be started under cloches. The first sowings are made in March and thinned to six inches apart. The rows should be about two feet apart to allow for the use of tent cloches, which can be removed during April. The cloches can be put on again for crops growing in the open ground during September. The varieties for early cloche work are 'White Milan', 'Red Milan' and 'Early Snowball'. Turnips grown for turnip tops can be left in the rows unthinned. The best varieties are: 'Model White, a fine pure white, round sort, the best kind for general purposes; 'Golden Ball', a round deep-yellow variety which keeps well; 'Early White Milan', the best for early work; 'Red Top Milan', also early; 'Manchester Market' for late sowing and for winter use; 'Early Snowball', 'Green-top Six Weeks' and 'Veitch's Red Globe'.

POTATOES

Before ordering potato seed it is best to try and estimate how many will be needed for the home. As a rough guide, fourteen pounds of early potatoes will yield about eighty pounds of potatoes during early July; and twenty-eight pounds of maincrop seed will produce about three and a half hundredweight of potatoes during September and throughout the winter from storage. These figures can only be approximate because so many factors have a bearing on the ultimate crop. A much heavier crop is produced if there is a wet late spring and summer; that is if, the plants are not attacked by potato blight. Also the crop is greatly affected by the quantity, or quality, of manure used and the quality of the seed, and whether it has been well sprouted or not. Much also depends upon the skill of the cultivator. Two tea chests filled with maincrop potatoes will generally keep a family of four supplied with enough potatoes throughout the year. Try to work out how many potatoes will be wanted in the kitchen and then order the seed as early as possible in the year.

'Certified' Scotch or Irish seed implies that the seed is free from any virus-borne disease. Potatoes grown from seed in the cooler regions of Scotland and Ireland are more disease resistant. The seed does not deteriorate in the same way as that grown in England on the same land from year to year. This is largely due to the absence of greenfly, which is one of the principal sources of infection of virus diseases. It is wise to purchase only this certified seed initially; some of your own seed can be saved each year, if the plants have not suffered from any potato blight infection during the growing period or while in store. You can save some of your own seed as well as introducing some certified Scotch or Irish seed every year. Very many gardeners like to purchase only Scotch or Irish certified seed and do not save any of their own seed.

One cannot recommend certain varieties of potatoes for every district. A kind which does well in one district may be a failure in another. In my own particular district of the New Forest there is some good potato-growing land because of the acid present in the good medium loam. Here the varieties which grow and yield best are 'Sharpe's Express' and 'Arran Pilot' for the early crops, 'Craig's Royal' as a second early, and 'Majestic' for the main crop. These grow well with the addition of well-decayed strawy pig manure in the bottom trench. Although the soil is acid here, strangely enough 'Arran Pilot' and 'Majestic' will also grow fairly well on a chalky soil. These varieties would not suit every district and it is best for the newcomer to a neighbourhood who is growing potatoes there for the first time to consult an old hand as to the best varieties to grow. He could also carry out some interesting experiments by growing several varieties until the most suitable were found.

Most people like to grow a few early potatoes, and fresh-dug potatoes from one's own garden are definitely superior in flavour to any which can be bought from a shop, especially if the mint is not forgotten. Early potatoes start to lose their flavour as soon as they are removed from the soil, just as tomatoes start to lose their flavour when they travel from producer to market, and then remain in the greengrocer's shop for several days before they are taken home and eaten. So only dig enough early potatoes at one time for immediate use.

The cause of maincrop potatoes taking on a black colour after cooking is careless handling of the crop during harvesting and transporting. Always handle your own potatoes carefully; do not let them become bruised and then they will not become discoloured in the cooking. Order your seed potatoes from a well-known seedsman early in the year. Try to have them in your sprouting trays by late January or February. Order some early, second early and maincrop varieties. Sprouting before planting is an essential part of the culture of potatoes. If possible, put the potatoes into a wooden potato tray (they are about 2ft. 6ins. long, 1ft. 6 ins. wide and 3½ins. deep). In the

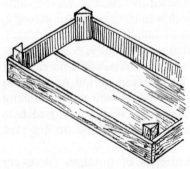

An ideal box for sprouting potatoes

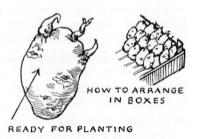

HOW TO ARRANGE IN BOXES

READY FOR PLANTING

Potato sprouting

corners of these boxes there are small triangular posts standing about two inches above the sides. With these, trays may be placed one on top of the other during the sprouting process. This makes for ease of storage when there is not much room available. If these special boxes are not obtainable, ordinary seed boxes will do. Any container which is shallow and large enough to hold about two dozen potatoes can be used.

We sprout potatoes in order to make sure that we are planting good seed with a reasonable expectation of a successful crop. With sprouting we can regulate the number of shoots per plant, for with a haulm composed of a forest of shoots, only a light crop of small potatoes would be produced. We can detect any diseased or frosted specimens before we plant. We give ourselves more latitude for planting, for we can wait for good planting conditions; the sprouted potatoes may already have produced small leaves, and will soon push themselves above the soil. We also get a stronger plant.

Unpack the bag of seed potatoes as soon as possible and place them rose end upwards into the sprouting trays. By the 'rose end' we mean the most rounded end of the potato where there are the greatest number of eyes. The potatoes will be touching each other and holding each other up in the trays. The tubers may be disbudded as they grow, leaving only two or sometimes three of the strongest shoots. Most people leave all the shoots on until planting them and then rub off the surplus ones as they put the potato into the planting hole or trench. This is done in case of any shoots being damaged in transit from house to allotment or garden. The trays of sprouting potatoes must be put in a light, dry, frost-proof place. Sprouting potatoes need a temperature of about 40°F., not any higher, and so a greenhouse is entirely unsuitable. Too much heat produces spindly shoots and shrivelled tubers, leaving no food for the plant to live on when planted, before it has produced foliage above the soil. Many people find it difficult to hit on a suitable place for sprouting potatoes, especially if they have a fairly large number to sprout. A spare bedroom facing south on the ground floor is a good place, if there is such a room where the potatoes will not be in the way. Cover them up with newspaper should there be any severe frost. Remove any diseased or non-sprouting potatoes, as sprouting continues. Apart from frost, not much harm can come to the sprouting potatoes, unless rats get in. Keep a look out for greenfly and if some are discovered spray the tubers with a solution of soft soap.

It is often said that potatoes are a cleansing crop. This is a very misleading statement. The potatoes do not clean land, it is thanks to the many operations needed for the growing of a good crop of potatoes that the land is automatically cleaned by the gardener.

Although potatoes will grow on almost any kind of land, it is no use planting them on impoverished soil which has been inadequately dug and which is infested with perennial weeds. Usually potatoes grow well on a deep, well-drained medium loam.

The soil on which you intend to grow potatoes must be deeply dug and made friable. It must be broken down to a fine texture so that the underground stems can run along and produce the swellings which are the potatoes. The young potatoes must be able to expand, and if they are pushing against hard lumps of clay or large stones their growth is greatly restricted and only small potatoes are produced. So break down your soil as finely as you can.

If potatoes are to be a first crop on newly broken grassland, then the plot should be double dug with the turf buried upside down in the bottom of the trench. This will allow weathering and the exposure of wireworm and other pests to the birds. If the grassland can be dug and used for another crop such as broad beans before planting potatoes, so much the better; for in this way the wireworms will be discouraged. In any case good potato crops can be grown on grassland which has been dug in autumn. The turf is fairly well rotted by the time the roots reach it and they can then take advantage of the plant food.

After leaving the surface soil rough during the winter, tread it in spring if necessary, and rake down fine. Have some good well-lettered wooden labels ready for marking the rows, so that you will know which varieties grow well, produce well, and suit your district. There are several ways of planting potatoes. Whichever method is used, never plant with a dibber. The dibber method of planting consolidates the soil at the bottom of the planting hole and often leaves the potato suspended with an empty space below it.

Do not undertake potato planting when the ground is wet and sticky. Wait for good planting weather, when the ground is soft and friable. The gardener who has sprouted his potato seed can afford to wait for the best planting period. Potato seed which is too large can be cut. The ideal size for seed potatoes is about the size of a hen's egg. Cut any large potatoes at the time of planting, leaving at least two good strong shoots on each cut portion. Do not dip the cut portions in lime, as this will withdraw moisture, and the cut portions of the tuber need to be kept moist at planting time so that the potato can draw on this plant food until it is well above ground and can manufacture other food. This is done through the agency of the chlorophyll in its foliage combined with sunlight.

The best planting times for early potatoes come during the middle of March. Some people can plant earlier in sheltered, frost-exempt areas like the south coast. Some will have to plant later, and all planting should be done according to weather conditions. The only drawback to early potato planting is frost. If the shoots of early potatoes show up well above the ground when there is still danger of them being injured by late frosts, there are one or two methods of protection. Soil can be drawn up over the shoots lightly with a hoe, or the shoots can be covered with sheets of newspaper weighted down with large stones. Bracken or straw can also be used to cover the young shoots. These methods of frost protection can be carried out if the potato plot is near the dwelling-house. It is difficult if one has some distance to travel to an allotment. Not many gardeners are enthusiastic enough to travel to their allotment after returning from their place of employment and then to cover up the whole of their early potatoes. For then they would have to journey to their potato patch again early next morning to remove the coverings. The safest thing to do in these circumstances is to cover the whole rows with cloches if they are available and leave them on until the danger of frost has passed. The only other method would be to keep on drawing soil up over the shoots. Usually potatoes recover after being touched by light frost, although the resultant crop is ready a little later.

Old-time gardeners always planted their early potatoes on Good Friday irrespective of the weather conditions. This was a tradition which happily seems to be dying away a little. This adhering to tradition was probably due in some ways to the fact that only a few years ago the working man did not get many paid holidays, and he had to plant his allotment whenever he could get an odd day away from his employment. The times for sowing usually printed on all seed packets are only intended as a rough guide. Always sow according to the weather and soil conditions and remember that if you live in the north you should be a little later with your sowing and planting.

When the soil has been broken down in the spring and raked to a tilth, and weather conditions are right, and the potatoes well sprouted, planting can begin. This can be done in several ways. First prepare two measuring sticks, one twelve inches long for obtaining the correct spacing between each potato, and one double that length for measuring the distance between each row. Use a good garden line, one that does not break easily. When planting sprouted tubers take great care not to break the shoots. Care must be taken at all times when handling sprouted tubers, when taking them from the sprouting trays, and when putting them into bags for transporting to the allotment, as well as during planting.

One planting method is to put down the garden line and draw flat-bottomed drills with a draw hoe about four inches deep across

24

the plot. Avoid planting potatoes too deeply. Put the potatoes with shoots upwards along the drills a foot apart, by using the twelve-inch measuring stick. Remove all shoots except two, or at the most three of the strongest ones. Cut any very large potatoes and leave the same number of shoots on each cut portion. Cover each potato with crumbly soil first before raking over the entire soil which was moved to one side when the drill was drawn. Mark the first row clearly with a wooden label. Next measure the space between the rows with the two-foot measuring stick and mark clearly at each end, for early potatoes should be planted a foot apart with two feet between the rows. Put the line down firmly at the new position and draw another drill and proceed as with the first row.

Another method is to put down the line and dig out holes four inches deep and a foot apart along the line, by using a small spade or trowel. Cover the potatoes in the same way as in the first method, by using the garden rake. Rake level and lightly rake out all foot-marks when planting has been completed. Label each variety clearly. Some gardeners who are hard pressed for time, or who have just taken over an allotment or vegetable garden at potato-planting time, may have to dig, manure and plant all in the one operation. If this method is used, be sure to use the garden line and measuring sticks accurately. When digging and planting at the same time, manure can be put into each planting trench. This should be very well decayed manure and a thin layer of soil must be put on to the top of the manure before depositing the seed potato. Well-rotted pig manure which has a portion of rotted bedding straw well mixed with it is ideal for this form of planting in early spring. Or good garden compost could be used.

When planting the second earlies and maincrop varieties, two more measuring sticks are required. These potatoes should be planted fifteen inches apart in rows thirty inches apart. Potatoes have to be earthed up or bank-hoed for two reasons. 'Earthing up' means using a draw hoe or mattock hoe and drawing soil up to the base of the haulms to form a bank of soil on each side of each row of growing potatoes. This is done to support the haulms and to cover with soil the young potatoes which form near the surface. If earthing up is not done, the haulms may become flattened by wind and rain. Young potatoes push through the surface soil and will soon become exposed and turn green. Green potatoes contain a poison and are unfit for eating or giving to livestock. They also have a very bitter taste. Before earthing up the potatoes, the land should be made friable between the rows for ease of banking the soil. Run the draw hoe or Dutch hoe through between the rows to loosen the soil and to remove surface weeds. Begin earthing up at the end of a row when

Potatoes bank hoed

the haulm is about nine inches high. Draw up the soil to the stems by standing on one side of the row. Sometimes it will be found necessary to hold the haulms towards you while drawing up the soil, holding the hoe in one hand. Be careful not to miss a stem and so bury it under a mound of soil. Further soil may be drawn up about ten days later until there are about six inches of haulm exposed. Leave the ridges with sloping sides. Do not delay earthing up until the haulms have got so large that you cannot walk between the rows.

Potatoes are liable to become infected with several diseases. Scab disease is not very likely to appear unless the plot has been fairly heavily limed, so do not lime the soil for potatoes. Potato blight, a fungus disease, is likely to be seen, especially during a wet spring and summer. As potato blight attacks any variety of potato or outdoor tomato, it is advisable to take precautions against it. Potato blight begins with yellow blotches on the leaves; the haulm turns brown, then black, and finally dies away. The disease spreads to the tubers and these will either rot in the ground or in store. For control of this disease, spray with Bordeaux or Burgundy Mixture. There is seldom need to spray the early varieties. Spray the main crop in the southwest at the end of June, in the south during the first week in July, and in the Midlands and on the east coast during the second week in July. If the weather is wet and muggy, give a second spraying a fortnight after the first.

Early potatoes can be lifted as soon as they are large enough to cook. Many people do not mind if they are very small, so long as they can enjoy some new potatoes early in the season and when they are very expensive in the shops. After a few have been lifted, a shower of rain usually comes and then the potatoes very quickly increase in size. Do not forget to put a sprig of mint with them when cooking; it makes all the difference and greatly improves the flavour. When lifting potatoes, be careful not to spear them with the garden fork. A special potato fork with flat tines may be acquired for use where a great number of potatoes have been grown. Any speared or damaged potatoes should be used at once in the kitchen.

Second-early potatoes serve their main purpose of providing potatoes from the time the early ones have all been dug. So if not too many rows of earlies have been planted, and enough second earlies have been sown, well-flavoured new potatoes can be dug from the end of June until the frosts come. While the second-early varieties are being harvested, the main crop for winter storage will be growing along nicely after having been sprayed with a fungicide to control potato blight. Maincrop potatoes are lifted when the foliage has died after turning a healthy yellow. If spraying against blight has been omitted, and the haulms of the maincrop potatoes are blighted, but the tubers have not become infected, remove the haulms carefully on a dry, windless day with a sickle; carry these diseased haulms very carefully to the bonfire and burn them. After lifting, burn any diseased tubers also.

Lift the maincrop potatoes on a dry day, some time at the end of September or during October. Leave them on the ground for a few hours for them to dry and see that they are thoroughly dry before storing them. Do not waste the very small ones; cook them for the poultry if you have any, or give them to someone who does keep poultry. Before storing examine the potatoes carefully, putting to one side for immediate use any which are damaged.

There are very many varieties of potatoes now listed in the seedsmen's catalogues. Find out which are the best sorts for your district and soil (see page 366). Potato varieties are fairly shortlived. Some varieties which are very successful for a few years tend to be superseded by newer and more promising sorts. Some of the very old varieties are still going strong. Degeneration of some of the older varieties has been due to the accumulation of virus diseases in the stock. Selected stocks of other quite old varieties have been built up and these do not seem to be any less vigorous than the original plants. Examples of these old varieties which are still very popular today are 'Duke of York', 'Sharpe's Express', 'British Queen', 'Epicure' and 'Eclipse'. A selection of seed potatoes may be made from the following list. The word 'Immune' after a variety implies that it is immune to wart disease.

Early Potatoes

NAME	COLOUR	SHAPE	REMARKS
'Arran Comet', immune	White	Oval	New, heavy cropper
'Arran Pilot', immune	White	Kidney	Heavy yield, poor keeper

NAME	COLOUR	SHAPE	REMARKS
'Duke of York'	Yellow	Kidney	Yellow flesh
'Epicure'	White	Round	Hardy, deep eyes
'Eclipse'	White	Kidney	Good keeper
'Home Guard', immune	White	Oval	Good cooker
'Pentland Beauty', immune	Cream	Oval	Red marks
'Red Duke of York'	Red	Kidney	Same as 'Duke of York'
'Sharpe's Express'	White	Kidney	Good flavour
'Ulster Chieftain', immune	White	Oval	Low haulm
'Ulster Premier', immune	White	Kidney	Splashed pink
'Ulster Prince', immune	White	Kidney	Very early

Second-Early Potatoes

'Catriona', immune	Yellow	Long kidney	Purple eyes
'Craig's Royal', immune	White	Long oval	Pink eyes
'Great Scot', immune	White	Round	Good quality
'Manis Peer'	White	Oval	New, good cropper
'Ulster Dale', immune	White	Thick oval	Long, smooth skin

Maincrop Potatoes

'Arran Banner', immune	White	Round	Early maincrop
'Arran Comrade', immune	White	Round	Keeps well
'Arran Consul', immune	White	Oval	Vigorous
'Arran Peak', immune	White	Oval	Late, good keeper
'Desirée', immune	Cream	Oval	New, from Isle of Man
'Dr. McIntosh', immune	White	Kidney	Early maincrop
'Dunbar Standard'	White	Oval	Good shape
'Gladstone', immune	Coloured	Kidney	Like K. Edward
'Golden Wonder', immune	White	Kidney	Good cooker

'King Edward'	White	Oval	Splashed pink, good table quality
'Majestic', immune	White	Large, oval	Good yield
'Pentland Crown'	White	Oval	Heavy cropper
'Red King'	Coloured	Oval	Pink skin
'Stormont Dawn', immune	White	Oval	Good cooker
'Ulster Ranger', immune	White	Oval	Cream flesh
'Ulster Supreme', immune	White	Oval	Late
'Ulster Torch'	White	Oval	Blight resistant

CABBAGES AND CAULIFLOWERS

The whole of the brassica family needs a fairly alkaline soil, so although there is no need to lime the soil for potatoes, you must lime for brassicas, especially if your soil is on the acid side. If the gardener is compelled to be economical with his farmyard manure or garden compost for his green vegetables, owing to short supply, then it would be best to adopt the following system.

Plant the 'Curley Kale', 'Hungry Gap Kale', 'Cottager's Kale', 'Purple Sprouting' and 'White Sprouting' Broccoli, 'Savoys' and 'Spring Cabbage' on ground which has been manured for a previous crop. Plant all other cabbages where you can put in some manure, but plant Brussels sprouts and all cauliflowers in fairly heavily manured land. It will be seen from these recommendations that different brassicas require varying amounts of manure. It is quite useless to plant Brussels sprouts and cauliflower on poor land.

For all the brassicas, good strains from reputable seedsmen must be obtained. By choosing the sowing date carefully, and by using the right varieties, it is possible to cut cabbages and cauliflowers almost all the year round. Brassicas need very firm soil, but this does not mean that the soil must be consolidated into a concrete-like mass. If the soil is dug deeply and then left to settle, well trodden and raked level, it should be suitable for growing good crops of brassicas.

The gardener will have to decide when he wants plenty of cabbage. For example, a large number of hearting cabbages would not be required in July, if he hoped to have plenty of broad beans and peas at this period. If a few seeds of the early-maturing varieties such as 'Primo' or 'Greyhound' are sown in a cold frame in February, and subsequently planted out, they can be cut during June. For a succession of cabbage to cut all the year round the following list in order of cutting and sowing is given. The dates are all for seeds sown in the open ground.

NAME	SOWING DATE	WHEN MATURE	REMARKS
'Dainty'	March	July	Medium
'June Giant'	,,	End of June	Stands well
'Golden Acre'	,,	August	Large
'Primo'	,,	July	Dwarf medium
'Greyhound'	,,	End of June	Medium size
'Velocity'	,,	June	Medium
'Enfield Market'	,,	Late August	Medium
'Winningstadt'	,,	September	One of the best in cultivation
'Christmas Drumhead'	April	November	Large, dwarf-growing
'January King'	May	Nov.–Jan.	Flat round heads

SPRING CABBAGE

For spring cabbage, sowings are made in July and August for cutting during the late spring of the following year. Find out which are the most suitable varieties for your district. Spring cabbages have to be hardy in the district in which they are grown, and they have to be free from any tendency to run to seed prematurely instead of forming good hearts. 'Early Evesham' is a good variety for the Midlands and 'Early Durham' is grown in the north of England. Most of the others listed will grow in most parts of England and Wales.

NAME	REMARKS
'Covent Garden'	Early, medium size, conical
'Market Gardener'	Very early, medium size
'Durham Early'	Early, pointed, medium size
'First Early Market'	Early, conical
'Flower of Spring'	Largest of spring cabbage
'Wheeler's Imperial Selected'	Dwarf and compact
'Early Offenham Selected'	Pointed heads
'Early Evesham'	Large heads, dark foliage
'Harbinger'	Small and compact

The last-named is also very suitable for sowing in early July and for cutting from the third week in December onwards.

On new land, or on a plot reserved for cabbages, dig the land deeply and incorporate farmyard manure or plenty of good garden compost during early autumn. Leave the surface soil rough during winter. Tread the soil well and make the plot firm during early spring. Rake it level. The cabbage plants for transplanting will be grown on a special seed bed or nursery plot. Prepare this seed bed or nursery plot during early spring. One of the most important tasks at this stage is to prepare clearly printed and waterproof labels of some kind for marking the position where the different varieties of brassicas are sown. It is very difficult for a beginner to distinguish one brassica from another when it is in the small seedling stage. He must be certain of knowing which variety he is planting out, as you would not require a large amount of one variety and only one or two of another sort. Plants can very easily become mixed if they are not clearly labelled.

Another difficulty is that of finding you have far too many cabbage plants for your garden. Any extra plants can be sold or given away before they become too large for transplanting; this happens very quickly if there are a few showers during April. Extra plants can also be thrown to the poultry if no other use can be found for them. It is much better to only sow quarter-packets of seed than to have a great many surplus plants each year.

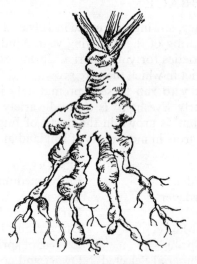

Club Root disease of Brassicas

Put down the garden line and draw drills half an inch deep and six inches apart. Along the drills sprinkle some calomel dust for the control of club root disease and the cabbage root fly. Sow the seeds thinly and cover with soil by using the garden rake. Press down lightly with the rake head. Rake out footmarks lightly. When the seedlings begin to show through the soil they must be dusted with derris dust for the control of flea beetle. The application must be repeated after about a week until the plants are growing away well. Sometimes a fungus disease called leaf spot appears when the plants are in the seed beds. The older leaves become yellowish with many circular brown spots. This disease is soon disposed of by dusting with flowers of sulphur.

Always plant out in showery weather or when rain is imminent. Make a planting hole large enough to receive the plant. Planting can in this case be done with a dibber or a trowel. To protect the plants further against club root and cabbage root fly dip the roots of each plant into calomel dust before putting into the planting hole. Some larger market growers dip the roots into garden lime before planting. This seems to be successful so long as only a very little is used. An excess of lime would burn the small roots. Cabbage should be planted out to about two feet apart and in rows two feet apart. If there is no rain after planting, water well until the cabbage are growing away well. Plant very firmly by pressing the trowel handle or dibber tightly around the roots.

The further cultivation of the cabbage consists of regular hoeing and destroying of weeds, removing dead foliage and conducting a war on the small and large white butterflies. Their caterpillars are active from June to October. Keep a close watch on the cabbage crop and destroy the eggs which are usually on the underside of the leaves. Crush the eggs with your fingers and hand pick the caterpillars. A weekly dusting of derris dust will be an effective control. Cabbage aphides are a nuisance in some seasons. Do not leave old cabbage stumps in the ground throughout early spring and summer. Remove the aphides by spraying with water, or dust with derris.

When cabbages are cut in summer or autumn, if a cross-cut is made with a knife on the top of the stump which is left, often some nice spring growth is made, suitable for cooking as spring greens. After these have been cut, dig out the stumps, cut them up and put them on to the compost heap. Presence of cabbage root fly can be diagnosed if some of the plants are looking sick and lifeless. The healthy green colour disappears and growth ceases, with the foliage becoming grey-green and distorted. Pull up a plant, and white maggots can easily be seen in the roots and partway up. Pull up all infected plants and burn immediately on the bonfire. Club root gives a similar appearance to the plants, and infected plants should be dealt with in the same way. This disease is soon apparent as it leads to misshapen and swollen roots.

For the growing of spring cabbages it is best to choose land which has been manured for early potatoes. Tread the soil and rake level. Plant out and give plenty of water if dry conditions are encountered. Plant in rows eighteen inches apart and with one foot between the plants. Dip each root in calomel dust or garden lime. Plant firmly. Choose two varieties of spring cabbage which suit your district and sow about a quarter-packet, some seeds in July and some in August. There is then a better chance of getting enough cabbages without their bolting or refusing to grow good solid hearts. Sow the seed in the same way as for summer and autumn cabbage. As cabbages grow better on land which is on the heavy side, a very light soil can be improved by the addition of plenty of farmyard manure and garden compost. Spring cabbage will not need such a heavy soil as the summer, autumn and winter types.

Red cabbage, grown for pickling, is sown in March. Plant out when large enough and take precautions against the usual cabbage pests and diseases. The red cabbage sown in March will come into use during the autumn. In the north of England, red cabbage sometimes makes huge heads. These are obtained by sowing the seed in August, planting out in October, and cutting the following August. As the red cabbage occupy land for a whole year, this would not be an economical way of growing them, unless one was particularly fond of pickled cabbage.

For people who like plenty of cabbage there is a useful way of bridging the gap between the cutting of the spring and the autumn cabbage. Sow during August an autumn-maturing variety such as 'Winningstadt' and leave in the seed bed to over-winter. Transplant these in April and they will be ready for cutting in July instead of September.

Savoys are hardy winter cabbage with crinkly leaves. It is always advisable to include a row or two in case there are severe frosts or very hard weather during early winter. These cabbage will nearly always come through hard winters and will stand in the ground for a long time. They fill the gap until the Kales are ready for cutting in early spring. Savoys are best grown on land which has been well manured for a previous crop. Sow the seed during April and May on a prepared seed bed in the same way as for other cabbage. Plant out two feet apart each way in July and August, choosing showery weather or watering well. Savoys may be sown in late July and treated as spring cabbage. Should there be a very severe winter, the spring cabbage might not survive, but there would be more chance of the savoys doing so, if precautions were taken against wood pigeons, rabbits and hares.

Broccoli is the name given to spring and winter cauliflowers. It is the same as a cauliflower but much hardier, and it frequently produces a larger curd. Broccoli grow well on a soil which has been well manured for a previous crop. It prefers a fairly heavy loam but it must have a very firm soil. It is possible to grow broccoli so that one may be cut every day of the year. The ordinary gardener will not want this, neither will he be able to grow all the different varieties needed. It would not pay him to purchase packets of seed of the very many different varieties, for he only needs a pinch of seed to get enough plants for his own use. It would perhaps be best for him to grow two varieties, one to cut in late March before the spring cabbage come into use, and another for cutting in late May and June.

If the ground is too dry and hot for summer cauliflowers, and they certainly need plenty of moisture, a third broccoli might be tried which can be cut in autumn or early winter. Sprouting broccoli may also be grown to provide crops for February and March. Sow broccoli seed in a prepared seed bed from March to May and treat in the same way as for cabbage seedlings. Plant firmly into very close-textured soil which should be trodden and made level. Plant out two feet apart each way. Varieties of broccoli are:

NAME	DATE OF MATURING
'Walcheren'	September
'Veitch's Self-Protecting'	October and November
'Yuletide'	December
'Christmas'	December
'Snow's Winter White'	January
'Adam's Early White'	February
'Roscoff'	March
'Leamington'	April
'Purity'	April
'Late Queen Selected'	May to June

Sprouting broccoli are very popular and rightly so. They are easy to grow, hardy, very prolific in bearing, and of delicious flavour. Sprouting broccoli is sown in a seed bed in the same way as cabbage. The same protection measures are needed against the same pests and diseases. Sow the seed three-quarters of an inch deep on a prepared seed bed during June and July, and water in well if no rain is likely. Most people grow the purple variety but the white can be grown in the same way, although it is slightly less hardy. These do not produce one large curd like the cauliflower but send out very many elongated small ones during early spring. These are cut when they are growing out from between the axils of the leaves. After cutting, more are produced, and one can keep on cutting until the shoots start to get hard and woody, and the plants are anxious to run to seed. Varieties are: 'Calabrese', with many green shoots and a delicious, delicate flavour; 'Early Purple Sprouting', ready in March; 'Late Purple Sprouting', for use in April and May; 'White Sprouting', ready in March; and 'Nine Star Perennial' which produces many heads to each plant continuously, and is ready for use during April to June.

To grow Brussels sprouts well you must give them good, rich, deeply-dug and firm soil. They need a long period of growth. Brussels sprouts will not produce firm, hard buttons unless there is plenty of farmyard manure or good garden compost in the bottom spit. There are early, mid-season, and late varieties. Early or mid-season sorts are grown if sprouts are wanted for Christmas. Again, find out which varieties produce the best sprouts in your district, and grow these. If no particular kinds are better than others in a certain district, then the gardener would do well to grow those which have been bred and tested at the Horticultural Research Station at Cambridge. These are listed in catalogues as 'Cambridge Early No. 1', a medium-sized early producer; 'Cambridge No. 3' for the main crop; and 'Cambridge No. 5' for a late crop.

Tall varieties of Brussels sprouts need staking in exposed positions; this will need to be taken into consideration when ordering seed. To get good sprouts, a long period of growth is needed. This is achieved in different ways. A sowing can be made in autumn and seedlings will have to be given some protection such as glass cloches and over-wintered, to be planted out in early spring. Seeds can be sown under glass during January and February and grown on in cold frames, hardened off, and planted out early in spring. If seeds are to be sown in the open ground, get them in early, at the beginning of March if possible, and use for this purpose a quick-maturing dwarf variety. Other kinds can be sown in the open ground but they will mature late and will not produce good buttons. Seeds can be sown during February and March in a cold frame, hardened off and planted out as soon as they are large enough.

To get those fine plants which are covered from top to bottom with large, closely-set sprouts (so frequently displayed in picture form in all seed catalogues), we must have deeply-dug, heavily manured soil, firm, and on an open site. They must also have enjoyed a long period of growth. So this means sowing the seed according to one of the methods for obtaining early plants described above. They need to be planted into their final positions before the end of May. Many gardeners plant their Brussels sprouts plants too closely. Tall large varieties need to be spaced three feet apart and other kinds at least two and a half feet apart each way.

They need the same cultivation methods as cabbage, but must be examined from time to time to see that none of the plants have become loosened in the soil. This frequently happens during strong winds and storms. Go round the plants from time to time and draw up some soil with the draw hoe around the base of the stems. Tread the soil around the plants when it has become loosened. Stakes may be required for tall varieties. A top dressing of old soot is beneficial to the plants during August and it acts as a deterrent to pests also. The soot should be hoed in. The cabbage-like head at the top of the sprout plant should be left on until all sprouts have been gathered. Then it will make a tasty dish itself. Remove all decayed basal leaves as they appear.

So the rules for good sprout growing are: selection of seed suitable for the district; early sowing; rich and firm land; and the retention of the plant tops until all sprouts have been gathered. A selection can be made from the following varieties: 'Early Dwarf', only a foot and a half in height and ready from October; 'Exhibition', a maincrop sort of medium height; 'Cambridge Special', early maturing from September to November; 'Jade Cross' (F.1 Hybrid), an early variety two feet in height (this variety should not be sown under glass); 'Cambridgeshire No. 1', 'Cambridgeshire No. 3', 'Cambridgeshire No. 5', the 'Wroxton', an old variety, 'Evesham Special' and 'Irish Glacier'.

Every gardener should try to include some of the kales or broccoli in his kitchen garden. They all provide appetizing dishes of spring and early summer green vegetables, and contain much iron and vitamins; and as all of the foliage is exposed to the life-giving sun and fresh air, their food value is great. Plant kales on ground manured for a previous crop. They can follow early potatoes or peas. Prepare the seed bed, attack the flea beetle, and take control measures against club root, cabbage root fly and aphides in the same way as for all brassicas.

Sow the seed at the end of April and plant out two feet apart each way when large enough. Sow 'Hungry Gap' where it is to crop and thin out to two feet apart. No need to do any transplanting here. This kale can also be sown from June to August for cropping from May to June the following year.

'Dwarf Green Curled' is of a very dwarf habit with closely curled leaves. Remove the heads of all kales early in the New Year and then many side growths will break out. These grow very quickly during a warm early spring. It is these side growths which are used for cooking and not the tough crinkly outer leaves. 'Tall Scotch Curled' is a tall variety with curly foliage and very hardy. Firm the soil around the base of these plants throughout the winter. Draw up soil around the stems.

'Cottager's Kale' grows to a height of two and a half feet. It also needs firming around the base during rough weather; it produces purplish-green shoots after the heads of the plants have been removed, and the shoots are slightly crinkled. It has a most distinctive flavour, quite unlike that of any other vegetable, and it is full of natural iron and very appetizing.

A few rows of 'Hungry Gap Kale' should be grown by everyone because of its extreme hardiness. If all other brassicas, including 'Curly Kale', are killed during a severe winter, 'Hungry Gap' will generally withstand drought, excessive wet and frost, and come through to prevent a total shortage of greens. It will only survive, however, if one can exclude wood pigeons, rabbits and hares. These three are serious pests during a hard winter. 'Thousand-headed Kale' is a strong-growing, hardy and prolific variety. There is no wastage where kales are grown, for every part of every shoot can be eaten, and any surplus plants make nutritious food for all poultry and other livestock.

Summer cauliflowers are difficult to grow in a hot, dry district. They can be grown of course, but require very careful treatment. Cauliflowers must have a rich loamy soil with a great deal of moisture-retaining material incorporated. Prepare the site in autumn with deep digging and put in plenty of good farmyard or pig manure, or good garden compost. Sow the seed in the same way as for cabbage with the same control measures against pests and diseases. Before trans-planting firmly, some bonemeal and wood ashes at the rate of five ounces to the square yard can be raked into the surface soil. Plant out two feet apart each way.

The best cauliflowers are usually produced by sowing the seed in seed boxes in the cold frame during early September and then pricking them out to four inches apart into a cold frame where they remain throughout the winter. The lights must be well covered during severe weather but plenty of air should be given during mild days. The plants are planted out in early April in a sheltered position after hardening off. Instead of using the cold frame, they can be sown in the open ground and then covered with cloches throughout the winter. January and February sowings can be made in frames, in the cool greenhouse, or under cloches. These plants are also transplanted to the open garden during April.

Other sowings can be made in the open during March and early April in the same way as cabbage, and transplanted two feet apart each way. Cauliflower plants need to be transplanted when they are quite small as they are very susceptible to check. Hoe regularly between the rows and plants and give frequent heavy waterings during long dry spells of weather. If the plants are producing their white curds during hot weather, bend over come of the inner leaves to protect these curds from the sun, otherwise they frequently turn yellow or brown. Do this too, if you have cauliflowers or broccoli exposed to frost or spells of very wet weather. Cut cauliflowers in the

early morning when the dew is on them. Some gardeners grow only
one variety called 'All-the-Year-Round'. Seeds of this kind can be
sown at all seasons. There is a new variety which comes from
Australia, and which heads during October and November, called
'Canberra Novelty'. Other varieties are 'Majestic', maincrop; 'Novo',
October and November; 'Early Snowball', 'South Pacific', Novem-
ber; 'White Heart', September and October; 'Early London', August;
'Early Dwarf Erfurt', August; 'Veitch's Autumn' and 'Giant',
September.

THE SALAD CROPS

There are so many varieties of lettuce, so many different sowing
times, and so many methods of cultivation, that the ordinary gardener
can become somewhat perplexed when he studies a catalogue, or
reads some of the articles in the gardening press. A whole book
could be written on salad crops but my purpose here is to show the
ordinary gardener in a simple way how to grow good lettuce and
other salads.

Most people want some early lettuce to cut, say in April or May,
some lettuce through the summer, and perhaps a few during the
autumn. There is not a demand for a large number of lettuce during
the winter. We can safely leave the production of winter lettuce to the
large commercial growers. Enough lettuce can be grown on the
allotment or in the kitchen garden without the aid of a cold frame or
cloches. If the gardener does own these, then he will find them very
valuable aids for producing early and late lettuce.

The best soil for lettuce growing is a deep rich loam. Heavy clay
soils need plenty of strawy farmyard manure or garden compost
worked into them. Light sandy soils will also need a large amount of
farmyard manure or garden compost. All soils for lettuce need to
have the surface soil brought to a fine tilth. Dig the site deeply in
early autumn, putting in plenty of organic manure. Leave the surface
as rough as possible throughout the winter, so that the frosts will
help towards making a suitable soil.

The best varieties to grow for the ordinary gardener are 'Arctic
King', for autumn sowing, 'All-the-Year-Round', 'Continuity' and
'Webb's Wonderful' for sowing through the spring and summer. Only
a small amount of seed is needed at a time, and it is best to sow at
fortnightly intervals for a succession of lettuce. 'Arctic King' is best
sown in late August and allowed to stay in the drill throughout the
winter. When planting out this lettuce, choose a sheltered site which
has been manured for a previous crop. We do not want this lettuce
to be too far forward before the hard weather comes, but we want it

just large enough. I have had a great deal of success with this lettuce by adopting the following growing method.

Having chosen the site, I put down the garden line and draw one drill about a quarter of an inch deep, when the soil is damp. The sowing will be done at the end of August. If the lettuce seed is not sown too deeply, and the soil is moist, it will germinate well and quickly. Most failures with lettuce germination are due to sowing the seed much too deeply, and in dry conditions. Water the drill before sowing if conditions are too dry. Lettuce seed is very light in weight and it resembles grass seed, so sow very thinly. Take a little seed between thumb and forefinger and work along the drill quickly, holding the hand down low so that the seed is not blown away by any gentle breeze.

Cover the seed with soil carefully, press down lightly with the rake head, and then put a clearly printed label at the end of the row. One row will be sufficient for most people, as a quarter-ounce of seed will give about seventy-five medium-sized lettuces for cutting during April and May. Put down a few slug-killer pellets at intervals along the row when the seedlings appear. Annual weeds will grow apace during September and October, so keep these under control by using the Dutch hoe on each side of the row. I have not used any glass cloches but these lettuce are grown in a sheltered position in the extreme south of England. Cloches could be put over the seedlings at the end of October with advantage in other parts of the country.

Leave the plants in the row throughout the winter and plant them out in early spring as soon as possible during showery weather. Plant them in fairly rich soil which has been well manured for a previous crop. A good place to choose is where the maincrop broad beans have been growing and where the roots with their extra nitrogen content have been dug into the soil. Take out the young plants carefully from the row with as little root disturbance as possible. The roots are very easily broken and the plants need handling with great care. If the main tap root is broken a milky fluid runs from it, and when such plants are transplanted they frequently bolt or run to seed without forming good hearts. Plant out firmly with a trowel and choose very showery weather. These plants heart up very quickly once they start making fresh growth during warm spring days. Some are almost sure to run to seed before they can be used, but there will still be plenty for an average family just at a time when they are expensive to buy from the greengrocer.

This variety of lettuce can only be sown in late August or early autumn; it is no use sowing it for summer lettuce. Cut down any which run to seed as they look very unsightly in a well-managed kitchen garden. They can be fed to poultry, rabbits, guinea pigs or hamsters. If there should be a very dry spring, water the plants well at transplanting time and continue this process, never letting the lettuce dry out.

'All-the-Year-Round' lettuce is really misnamed; it is best to grow this variety for a summer lettuce, when it is about the best. Sometimes in the sheltered south in a very mild area, it can be sown in autumn and allowed to stand through the winter, but the results are not usually encouraging. For a summer lettuce, when it is grown on good soil, it is really magnificent. An open position and rich soil are best for 'All-the-Year-Round'. Draw a drill and sow the seed in the same way as for 'Arctic King'. Summer lettuce can be sown at fortnightly intervals from March to September. Only short rows of seeds are needed otherwise the gardener will have far too many lettuce all hearting up at once.

The gardener will sow his lettuces at different intervals and will use quantities of seed according to how many lettuce plants he needs. If he adopts the fortnightly sowing he need not worry if he has a few too many lettuce turning in, as lettuces today are usually easily sold at the greengrocer's shop. There is always a demand for well-grown lettuces with good hearts. 'All-the-Year-Round' lettuces must be planted out when quite small, in showery weather. Leave some plants in the original row and have these and the transplanted ones spaced about ten inches apart. Never allow the original row of plants to become overcrowded as the lettuces grow very quickly.

'Continuity' has purplish-brown partly crinkled outside leaves and light green inside leaves. It makes the salad bowl look very decorative and has a nice flavour. It is grown for its ability to withstand hot, dry conditions, and will remain on the land for a long time without running to seed. Its leaves are very crisp.

'Webb's Wonderful' is another lettuce which withstands hot, dry weather and it is slow to run to seed. It is a very large lettuce with crisp curly leaves. Seedlings should be transplanted about twelve inches apart. 'All-the-Year-Round' and 'Webb's Wonderful' are summer lettuce and both are sown from March until July at fortnightly intervals. All the above varieties of lettuce are known as cabbage lettuces because they are supposed to resemble a cabbage in shape. There is another lettuce with a different shape called a 'Cos' lettuce. This kind of lettuce seems to be less popular than it was, probably on account of its tougher outside leaves, although the hearts are quite crisp. Cos lettuces form large hearts which stand much higher than those of cabbage lettuces. The older varieties of Cos lettuce needed to have their heads tied with raffia, to keep the leaves up together and to encourage the plants to form nice hearts. Many of today's varieties need no tying.

25

There are some very useful lettuces which are half cos and half cabbage. One variety, 'Winter Density', can be used as a summer or winter lettuce. Many gardeners may like to try other varieties of lettuce as well as, or instead of, the ones which have been mentioned. If this is so, a good seedsman's catalogue can be consulted in which they are all described. 'Tom Thumb' is a very useful small variety which can be grown by those with very small gardens. I have grown 'Cheshunt Early Giant' even in a cold county like Lincolnshire, by sowing the seed in a cool greenhouse, hardening off, and then putting the plants out in the open ground in early spring and covering them with continuous cloches until ready for cutting.

There is a further kind of lettuce called a 'loose leaf lettuce'. The best variety in this section is 'Salad Bowl'. It is good to look at, crisp and tender. The beautifully curled, fresh green foliage can be picked as required without cutting the whole plant, for it does not form a heart. It is a good standby during hot dry weather because the plants do not run to seed. New leaves grow to replace those which have been taken.

RADISHES

As with lettuce, it is possible to have a supply of radishes throughout the year. To grow good radishes you need a rich soil, much moisture, thin sowing and quick growing. Grow radishes quickly and pull them when they are of usable size, which means not too large. Sow them in rows and pull as required; this is the way in which they are thinned. Radishes soon get woody and hollow inside, especially on a dry soil, so use them when they are small and young.

Radishes grow well on soil which has been well manured for a previous crop but the soil where they are sown must have plenty of moisture-retaining material in it. The first sowings can be made in a cold frame if one is available. Provide good drainage by forking over the bottom soil where the frame is to stand. Fill the frame with a light loam which has plenty of good well-decayed garden compost mixed with it. Water the soil prior to sowing. Sow during February in drills four to six inches apart. Radishes germinate very quickly, so only leave the lights on until they can be seen pushing through the soil. Afterwards they can be given plenty of ventilation. The well-known variety 'French Breakfast' and one called 'Cherry Belle' are suitable for early cold-frame work.

For the open ground sowings, an early sowing can be made in a sheltered spot at the end of February, followed by continuous sowings at regular intervals to ensure a constant supply throughout spring and summer. Fork over a piece of ground which has been well manured for a previous crop. Tread the site firmly and then rake down to a fine tilth. Put down the garden line and draw drills a quarter of an inch deep. Radish seeds are easily sown thinly because they are of a light colour and fairly large. Cover the seed lightly and firm with the rake head. When the seedlings appear above the surface they are likely to be attacked by the flea beetle, so dust with derris dust in the same way as for the cabbage family. In damp situations radishes are often attacked by slugs, so put down slug-killer pellets.

For early spring sowings 'French Breakfast', 'Cherry Belle', 'Scarlet Globe' and 'Sparkler' may be used. A very nice long, white, transparent radish to sow after midsummer is 'Icicle'. It is a nice sweet radish for those who like a milder flavour. It is ready within twenty days from sowing.

The winter radish 'China Rose' deserves to be grown more widely than it is. It is most welcome for autumn and winter salads. Sow the seeds at the end of July and thin the plants to stand about six inches apart. The roots can be used as required or lifted and stored in sand during November. They grow much larger than other radishes without becoming woody, attaining a length of about six inches and a diameter of two inches. This radish is very appetizing and is best sliced thinly in salad or peeled and then grated.

OUTDOOR TOMATOES

To obtain a good crop of ripe outdoor tomatoes one must have a good summer with long periods of warm weather, with a good shower of rain now and again. If one grows the variety named 'The Amateur', a bush tomato requiring no staking, one is reasonably sure of getting some ripe tomatoes during any summer, and sure of a good crop during a long, warm summer. If a place for a few 'Amateur' tomato plants can be found in front of a white wall which faces south, then this is the best site for them.

It is better if the tomatoes can be ripened on the plant where they can absorb the sun and produce Vitamin C. Towards the end of the season some fruits which are left on the plant may be ripened in a sunny window indoors. These should have a little patch of red on them or some yellow which will indicate that they are mature and ready for ripening. Hard, dark green tomatoes are not easy to ripen and they are best used for chutney.

For those with a cool greenhouse 'Amateur' tomato seeds should be sown in seed boxes in John Innes Compost No. 1, watering beforehand with a solution of Cheshunt Compound. They can also be sown in the same way in a cold frame which is in a sheltered warm position facing south, or where a temperature of 65°F. can be maintained for a little while. The seeds should be sown at the beginning of April and not before, or the plants may fruit in the seed boxes before it is safe to plant them out into the open ground.

Crock the seed boxes and firm the compost before sowing. Tomato seeds can be clearly seen and are large enough to be easily spaced out in the boxes. They could be spaced three inches apart each way. The main difficulty during the early seedling stage, and during pricking out when needed, is the danger of 'damping off'; this is a fungus disease and it can be controlled by the use of Cheshunt Compound, a fungicide. The seeds need to be only just below the surface when sown and require a temperature of 65°F. for germination. After the seedlings have been pricked out where necessary, this temperature can be reduced to 60°F. When pricking out plant fairly deeply by having the bottom leaves just clear of the surface soil. Seedlings may be pricked out into 3-inch pots or into further seed boxes. Water the soil before pricking out with Cheshunt Compound and whenever watering is required. Do not let the boxes dry out, and use the fungicide until the seedlings are growing away, have produced some true leaves, and have become more sturdy with thickened stems.

After a while, move the plants to a cold frame and gradually harden off by ventilating freely. Stand the boxes outside on the open ground for a few days and nights before planting out at the end of May. Very many gardeners who do not have a greenhouse or cold frame buy plants of 'Amateur' or other outdoor varieties from nurserymen. They must be careful to see that the plants are thoroughly hardened off and are healthy before planting them out. Do not buy tall, spindly, yellow-looking plants from a street stall because they are perhaps very cheap. Buy them from a good reputable grower and inspect them beforehand. The plants selected should be sturdy, short-jointed, of deep green colour, with healthy-looking foliage and with at least one truss of flowers already formed.

Outdoor tomato growing is difficult and rather a gamble in most areas. It depends so much on the summer experienced. In the north some shelter ought to be given on the north and east sides of the site chosen. If the plants are facing south with a light-coloured wall behind them to reflect the light and warmth, and enjoy a good summer, a good crop of outdoor tomatoes can be expected even in the north. It is best to grow 'Amateur' as it is so much earlier than other kinds, and it begins to ripen during July and August when we can expect the most suitable weather for tomatoes.

The site for the outdoor tomatoes should be deeply dug during autumn, and plenty of well-rotted garden compost or farmyard manure should be put in the bottom trench. Leave the surface soil rough during the winter for pulverization by frosts. In early spring tread well and rake down finely. Rake into the top surface a dressing of garden lime at the rate of half a pound to the square yard, if the soil is at all acid. Just before planting it would be beneficial to rake in two ounces of bonemeal to the square yard and as much wood ash or bonfire ash as is available. Try to have the bush or other tomatoes some distance away from the potatoes. They are of the same family and both are likely to be attacked by the potato blight, so we do not want one near the other so that both may be infected. Spray with Bordeaux Mixture towards the end of July. Before using, wash tomatoes which may have been sprayed.

Although a site facing south with a white wall behind to deflect the sun's rays and to provide shelter has been suggested, the 'Amateur' tomato can be grown quite well on the open allotment in the south of England. Put down the garden line and transplant, setting plants about three feet apart each way. The 'Amateur' tomato only grows to a height of one foot, so it does not require any stopping or staking. Sometimes the placing of straw or garden peat underneath the plants is advisable in the same way as for strawberries. This prevents those fruits which form low down on the bush from being splashed with soil during rain.

Thoroughly water the box of plants for transplanting before planting out; this enables them to be detached from the box more easily and ensures moisture around the roots. Dig out a large enough planting hole to contain the roots. Use a trowel, handle the plant carefully, and plant firmly. Leave slight depressions of soil around each plant to allow the water to run into the plant and not away from it. Water each plant well after planting out. All varieties of outdoor tomatoes should preferably be grown in a sunny situation, with the rows arranged so that they face due south or south-west.

Because the 'Amateur' bush tomato grows to only a foot in height, it is admirably suited for growing under continuous large barn-cloches. These are generally used, however, to put over the plants later in the season to ripen the last trusses of fruit. Cloches can be used for these tomatoes in any way desired and there are special tomato cloches available. In very small gardens the tomatoes can be grown in large pots. The 12-inch size or larger may be used. Place the pots against a hedge, fence or wall facing south where they will obtain the maximum amount of sunshine and not be subject to draughts. See that the plants never lack water; when grown in pots they very soon dry out.

Very few people seem to grow yellow tomatoes although they are considered by many to be of a finer flavour than the red sort. They also look very attractive when mixed with the red kind in a salad

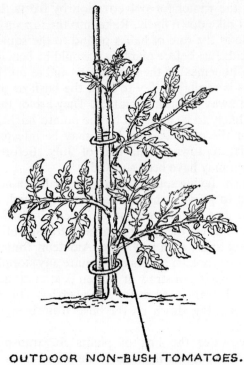

OUTDOOR NON-BUSH TOMATOES.
STAKE, TIE AND TAKE OUT
SIDE SHOOTS

Outdoor Tomatoes

bowl. These can be raised in the same way as the 'Amateur' but when planting out most varieties need to be staked and tied. There is now a yellow variety of the 'Amateur' tomato, 'Yellow Amateur'. For those which need staking put the stakes in beforehand so that they are not driven through the roots. Side shoots are removed regularly and after about four trusses of fruit have set, nip out the growing point of the plants.

Apart from the bush tomato 'Amateur', which is really the best variety of outdoor tomato to grow, there are other outdoor sorts which may be chosen. 'Outdoor Girl' is reputed to ripen ten days before other outdoor varieties. 'Harbinger' is also early, producing clusters of small fruit. 'Moneymaker' is a well-known variety grown indoors or outdoors. 'Peach' is similar to 'Moneymaker' but with yellow fruits of low acid content. 'Golden Queen' has large yellow fruits. In addition to these, there are some ornamental fruiting varieties which are grown in the same way as other outdoor sorts. They have pear-, plum- and cherry-shaped fruits and can be obtained with colours of red, yellow, white and tangerine. They are of low-growing habit and have small-sized tomatoes.

OUTDOOR CUCUMBERS

The only cucumbers which can be grown outdoors are known as ridge cucumbers. They have several good points: they are easily germinated in a cold frame, hardened off and planted out. They produce cucumbers which are not too long, so that the whole of the fruit can be used at one time. They are fairly easily cultivated and have a delicate fresh flavour. Cut them before they become too large and seedy.

Outdoor cucumbers are easily raised by sowing the seeds in pots in a cool greenhouse or cold frame and then hardening off; or they can be bought from a nurseryman. In a cold summer one cannot expect much success with outdoor cucumbers, no matter how well the preparations for growing them are carried out. They are simply plants which need plenty of warmth and a certain amount of moisture.

Seeds can be sown on the site where they are to grow from the middle of May to the end of June, by putting about three seeds to each station one inch deep and thinning to the one strongest plant. A tent cloche with the ends blocked by a pane of glass, a jam jar or a handlight if available, should be placed over the seeds to hasten germination. In a normal summer there should be enough natural warmth in the ground to enable effective growth to take place, either for sowing or planting after the beginning of June.

It has long been the practice of gardeners to make little mounds of soil or ridges and to plant their cucumber plants on to the top of these. This is entirely unnecessary; they are much better grown along the ground. If they are upon little heaps of soil the moisture they need will run away down the sides of the ridge rather than into the roots where it is wanted. If it is thought that the mass of stems and foliage may rot through lying on the ground during a wet season, then small forked twigs to hold up the stems can be inserted into the soil here and there along the length of the growing plant.

Outdoor cucumbers grow well on a soil which has been well manured with farmyard manure or plenty of garden compost. They grow particularly well on good, well-rotted garden compost. Set out the young plants about two and a half feet from one another. If they have been grown in pots, knock out the small plants carefully for the base of the stem is rather brittle and very easily broken. Plant firmly in late May or early June in a fairly open position, but where some protection from the north and east winds is afforded. Leave a depression in the soil around the plant; plant with a trowel and water in well.

We have spoken of the gamble taken when planting out the cucumbers; so much depends upon the kind of summer we have. They may make great rambling plants with plenty of fresh-tasting, succulent fruit, they may make hardly any growth and yield only a few miserable misshapen specimens, or they may produce an average crop with some of the fruit bitter. Do not worry if the first cucumber you cut tastes bitter, because there will always be plenty of nice-tasting fruit to follow.

Not much training of the plants is required. The point of the leading shoot should be nipped out when about eight leaves have been produced; this induces branching. If a shoot grows on and on

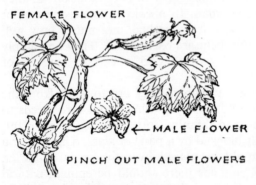

Female flowers of cucumbers do not need pollination. If they are pollinated, misshapen and bitter fruit may result.

Removal of male cucumber flower.

without bearing a cucumber, cut it back to seven leaves. Some slug-killer pellets will need to be scattered around near the plants when they are small; slugs always seem to delight in spoiling young cucumber foliage. Keep down weeds, but be careful not to hoe too near to the roots. Keep the plants well watered during dry periods.

Varieties of outdoor cucumber are 'Bedfordshire Champion', 'Prize Ridge', 'Burpee F.1 Hybrid', 'Crystal Apple' which can be grown in a frame or outdoors (it has the size and shape of an apple), and 'Stockwood Ridge'. There is a climbing cucumber named 'Japanese Climbing'. It is a hardy, vigorous climber and very prolific in a good summer. It can be grown on trellis or poles quite success-fully. The fruits assume a brownish colour when mature, but as they are usually peeled before eating, this does not matter.

ENDIVE

Endive is a most wholesome salad for autumn and winter use. Now that lettuces are very expensive to buy during winter, endive could very well be grown by the ordinary gardener to take the place of winter lettuce. Endive is in season from November to April. In appearance it resembles dark green curled lettuce, but unlike lettuce it must be blanched before it can be eaten, otherwise it tastes very bitter.

Endive is grown like lettuce and on the same sort of soil. Sowings in shallow drills can be made in April for early use, and for late use in June or July. If the weather is very dry during a July sowing, draw the drills, leave them open, and run along the drills with water, using the fine rose on the watering-can. This will give them enough moisture to enable them to germinate. If dry weather persists, water well during the growing period.

When two or three inches high, transplant into good soil and space the plants to one foot apart. When they are almost fully grown, tie the leaves together with raffia in the same manner as for Cos lettuce. This is done to exclude the light and air from the inner leaves. This operation must be carried out after there have been several dry days, for the leaves when tied with raffia must be absolutely dry or they will rot. Other methods of blanching are by inverting a large pot over each plant, and putting a flat stone over each drainage hole, or by lifting in winter and replanting in a darkened cold frame. They can also be lifted, packed into soil in large boxes, and placed in a dark cellar where there are no mice, or under the cool greenhouse staging, in a position where light can be excluded.

Do not blanch all the plants at once, otherwise they cannot all be used. Once blanched they soon deteriorate and start to decay. Blanching takes about four weeks, so blanch a few plants at a time. Endive cannot resist extra-severe frost. There are curled varieties and round-leaved sorts. The varieties are 'Green Curled', 'Moss Curled' and 'Batavian Improved Round-Leaved'. 'Batavian Endive' is slightly hardier than the curled sorts.

MUSTARD AND CRESS

Very little mustard and cress is grown by the amateur gardener today. New, quick and cheap methods of growing on a very large scale have been discovered by the commercial producers, and at 6d. per punnet, which provides enough for a meal for three people, it is hardly worth the gardener's time and trouble to grow.

If it is required, however, mustard should be sown in seed boxes of fine soil mixed with garden peat, three days before the sowing of the cress, because the cress is quicker to germinate and grow than the mustard. Sow little and often for a continuous supply. Mustard and cress can be grown in the cold frame, cool greenhouse or in a warm living-room window. Sprinkle the seed on to the surface and press down with a block of flat wood; do not cover the seeds with soil. Place the receptacles in the dark for a time after germination to encourage long stems, then bring into the light to let the leaves turn green.

Sow the cress three days after the mustard into the same seed boxes or in separate ones. Water carefully without splashing the stems and foliage. Rape is now largely used by many growers in the place of mustard, because it does not bring its seed cases up with the seed leaves. Mustard has a much superior flavour. The variety called 'Finest White' is the mustard used for salads. When mustard is used for green manuring an agricultural type is sown.

'American Cress' or 'Land Cress' needs a moist position in the open garden. It is like watercress in flavour and appearance and it remains green throughout the winter. It does not want to be in stagnant water but should be sown on the north side and where the soil is likely to remain damp. Well water the site, if there is any chance of the bed of cress becoming dry. It grows better if the seeds are sown in mid-August to early October, but it can be sown in the spring. Lightly thin the plants and nip out the points of the growths to encourage branching.

Watercress can be sown in an ordinary garden provided that the bed is kept well watered. Choose a dampish, shady spot if possible. Prepare the site by deep digging and by incorporating plenty of good garden compost for manure and for retaining moisture. If watercress is sown in April and August, and the latter sowing protected with cloches during the winter, watercress can be gathered throughout the year. Sow seed every six months and keep the bed free of weeds. Watercress beds very soon become thickly populated with weeds of all kinds, owing to the damp nature of the site. These weeds will soon choke the watercress plants, preventing successful development. Cut the watercress for the table with sharp scissors; never try to tug pieces out, pulling all the roots with the leaves.

CELERY

Most people will find that celery plants are more easily obtained from a nurseryman than from raising their own from seed. The growing of good celery calls for quite a lot of attention, but if some good sticks are produced it is well worth all the trouble. When raising your own plants from seed, the seed must be sown in heat during February for early crops and in March and April for the main crop. The temperature needed is from 60° to 65°F. White varieties are sown in February and March and pink sorts during April. For the February sowing, sow in John Innes Compost No. 1 in seed boxes after previously watering with Cheshunt Compound and allowing to drain. Put the boxes into the cool greenhouse at a temperature of 60°F. Sow the seed thinly and shallowly.

When the seedlings are large enough to handle, prick them out into seed boxes containing John Innes Compost No. 2, and water with Cheshunt Compound. Handle the seedlings carefully, without bruising the stems or foliage. Space them to three inches apart in the seed boxes. Grow on and gradually harden off in the cold frame, and outside in the open. The March sowing can be made in the cold frame or under continuous cloches, remembering to put the cloches over the sowing site a couple of weeks beforehand. Do not forget to block each end of the cloches with a pane of glass. The last sowing, which will be in early April, is for producing sticks of celery during February and March of the following year. This sowing will also be made under continuous cloches. When pricking out use plants of different sizes in order to obtain a succession.

The wild celery grows in ditches, on marshy land, and in other wet places not far from the sea, so garden celery, which was evolved from the wild celery, naturally requires plenty of moisture during its growing period. It is a good feeder, so it therefore needs an abundance of garden compost or farmyard manure, for plant food and for moisture retention. Celery is planted in a trench and the soil which has been excavated and piled at the sides of the trench is used to earth up the plants, for they must be blanched to make the sticks edible.

Generally a good time to prepare the trench is in February, and to have it ready for planting out the plants during June. Prepare a trench fifteen inches wide for a single row of plants, and about twenty inches wide for a double row. Dig out the trench to a depth of about eighteen inches. If you come to the sub-soil, put this on one side of the trench and the good soil on the other side. Use the sub-soil first when earthing up. Fork over the bottom of the trench and work in a good quantity of well-decayed farmyard manure, or good garden compost. Fork over a layer of good soil on to the top of the manure.

Transplanting into the prepared trench can take place during May, June and July. Plant out to about twelve inches apart and water well in. If you are growing a double row, put the plants opposite each other, and not staggered, otherwise you will have trouble when earthing up. Slugs are very fond of celery plants in spite of their strong flavour. A good plan is to mix some well-weathered soot with the soil that is being used for earthing up. This acts as a deterrent to the slugs and celery fly and provides a small amount of nitrogen for plant food.

As the plants grow, slug-killer pellets will have to be put down as well because the warm, damp conditions necessary for the production of good celery are also very favourable to slugs.

Earthing up is done gradually when the soil is moist and crumbly. Begin by heaping about four inches of soil around the stems of each plant with a hand fork. Do not pack this first lot of soil too tightly around the plants; give an opportunity for the stems to swell and grow. A fortnight later, make the soil friable and heap it up with a spade, wrapping the soil by hand around each plant, but not too tightly. When the plants are about a foot high, tie the stems loosely with raffia a few inches below the top leaves. Continue to earth up gradually as the plants grow. When earthing up, be careful to see that no earth gets between the stems. If the gardener does not mind the extra work involved, the celery sticks may be wrapped with brown or corrugated paper before earthing up. This keeps them nice and clean and well blanched, and it helps to keep the slugs at bay. When a stick of celery has been taken out, replace the soil which may have exposed other sticks nearby, to prevent greening.

When the final earthing has been completed and the plants are fully grown, the earth should be at the top of the stalks, with only the tips of the foliage showing. Remove all side shoots or suckers before each earthing. Do not press the soil too tightly against the plants, use just enough pressure to keep it in place and to ensure that the stalks are in complete darkness. Keep hoeing the banks of soil at the sides of the trenches to keep down annual weeds.

Celery can be fed with dried blood solution, but follow the makers' instructions very carefully. This liquid manure can be given during the growing season about every ten days, but it is no use applying it when the final earthing-up time approaches.

There is one pest and one disease likely to be met with in the growing of celery. This is in addition to attack by slugs or snails. The celery fly is small and it lays its eggs during spring and summer on the upper sides of the leaves. Tiny white legless maggots hatch out and immediately enter the leaves which they feed upon, producing large whitish blisters. Remove and burn blistered leaves as soon as they are noticed. Rags dipped in paraffin may be hung near the plants, or the soil may be dusted lightly with naphthaline. Dust the foliage with derris dust. The leaves can also be very lightly dusted with a mixture of three parts old weathered soot and one part garden lime. Only light dusting must be done or the mixture may burn the foliage. It is best to do this in the early morning when it will more easily adhere to the plants with the aid of the dew.

Celery leaf spot is a fungoid disease which is often transmitted through the seed. Some nurserymen now offer celery seed which has been effectively treated against this disease. If you are growing your own plants, buy only this treated seed. The disease first takes the form of small brown patches dotted with black specks. The fungus soon spreads to leaf stalks and heart and eventually kills the plants. Spray or dust with Bordeaux Mixture, if the disease appears, at fortnightly intervals.

There is a celery which does not need earthing, 'Golden Self-blanching'. It is a dwarf compact variety and the heads are solid and crisp, with a good flavour. It is ready for harvesting rather early in the year, when most people do not want celery. There are many lovers of celery who will welcome celery at any time of the year, and it is a welcome addition to the summer salads. Although it does not need earthing, it is better if it has some brown paper wrapped around the stems and lightly tied with raffia. It is ready for use from July onwards. All other varieties of celery have their flavour improved by being subjected to frost. Varieties of celery are 'Prizetaker', 'White', 'Select Red', 'Superb Pink', 'Golden Self-blanching', 'Market Giant Pink' and there is an American variety which is eaten green without blanching called 'American Green'.

CORN SALAD

Corn salad, sometimes called lamb's lettuce, is a useful plant to grow for winter salad bowls. The leaves are gathered by picking the required amount and the plants still remain productive for some time. The plants can be protected by cloches if there are any to spare. Corn salad grows well on a fairly rich soil and good garden compost suits it well. Make a firm seed bed of fine soil and sow in drills an inch apart and three-quarters of an inch deep. Thin out or transplant to nine inches apart. Sowings can be made from mid-June until mid-September. Water well during dry spells and take control measures against slugs. Two kinds are grown, 'Broad Italian' and 'Large-leaved'.

THE ONION FAMILY

The onion is a very health-giving vegetable. It should be grown by everyone with an allotment or vegetable garden. The so-called spring onions or young onions can be grown throughout the year. Pulled young, with the white bulb and the green foliage eaten raw, they form a delightful addition to the diet. A salad dish without spring onions is like strawberries without cream or new potatoes without mint.

A few years ago, I carried out an experiment with onions. I grew about eighteen different varieties, sowing them at the same time and on the same kind of soil. Thinning them at the same distance apart, I weighed each row of a different variety when they were all mature and ready for harvesting. The result of this experiment was that all of the varieties from a well-known seedsman grew well, and there was not much difference in the weight of the final crop of each. I concluded therefore that it does not matter a great deal which variety is chosen for ordinary garden use.

On my allotment of medium loan and slightly acid soil, onions grown from onion sets have grown very large and of an extraordinary weight, but they did not keep and had to be used fairly quickly. Some seedsmen now offer onion sets which they say are renowned keepers, and maybe they are. Generally, I have found that they do not keep nearly so well as onions grown from seed sown in early spring.

So the best plan for onion growers seems to be the following. Grow a few onion sets (the term 'set' is explained later in this chapter, on page 402), sow some onion seed in the spring and autumn, sow some 'White Lisbon' onions throughout spring and summer for salad use, and grow shallots. I have already spoken of the need to change the site for onions each year. Onions grow best on a deeply cultivated, rich, light loam. There is no need to worry about growing onions to a large size; medium-sized onions are better for use in the kitchen than very large ones. Different varieties of onion vary a little in shape, some are globular and some are semi-flat. Grow the shape which you like the best.

'White Lisbon' is a special type of onion only grown for pulling young, for eating raw, and for salads. Always grow this variety for early spring pulling, as it stands the winter well. Special sorts for pickling and hardy kinds for autumn sowing are also obtainable.

For autumn sowing of onions for transplanting in the spring, sow the seed on a piece of land which has been well manured for a previous crop such as potatoes. Also sow 'White Lisbon' in August on this kind of land.

For the maincrop onions, which are to be spring sown, dig the ground deeply during the autumn. Put in plenty of farmyard manure or garden compost. Never grow onions on badly drained land. Attend to drainage on all land as outlined in Chapter 1. The soil for onions must be retentive of moisture. They need plenty of water so that the swelling of the bulbs can take place; onions always grow larger during a wet summer, so put in plenty of humus-forming material during autumn when the preparation of the site is under way. Always prepare the onion bed for the main crop during autumn, because if onions come into contact with freshly applied manure it often causes them to develop a thick neck instead of the thick bulb which we all prefer. Leave the surface soil as rough as possible throughout the winter. In early spring, tread the onion bed firmly, after raking down to a level, fine tilth. There is no need to roll it with a heavy garden roller as was advocated by many old-time gardeners. The onion bed can always be sufficiently consolidated by treading. A dressing of wood ashes at the rate of half a pound to the square yard and some bonemeal at the rate of four ounces to the square yard will be of great benefit to the onions, if raked into the surface soil a week or two before sowing. Finish the bed with a light covering of garden lime.

In March, rake down the soil again to a fine tilth, and make the bed level. Put down the garden line and draw drills with the rake or hoe to a depth of about half an inch, and twelve inches apart. Sow the

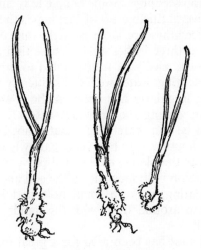

Onion White Rot disease

seeds thinly and cover with soil, carefully pressing down the soil lightly with the rake head. Print the name of the variety clearly on a label which is waterproof and put at the end of the rows. Some seedsmen now offer onion seed which has been treated against onion fly and white rot. If the gardener is sowing seed which has not been treated, then he will need to apply some calomel dust for protection against onion fly. This is dusted along each side of the rows when the seedlings are about an inch high and are still in the looped foliage stage, with the seed case still adhering, and again ten days later. If there is an attack of white rot, a fungus disease, lift and burn affected plants and do not grow onions in the same spot for at least a year. Grow resistant varieties which are 'Improved Reading', 'Rousham Park Hero' and 'White Spanish'.

The main task in the cultivation of onions when they are small is weeding. An unattended onion bed soon becomes full of annual weeds. A small hand hoe, often called an onion hoe, is a good tool for hoeing between the rows and for getting as close to the onion seedlings as possible, without cutting into the small bulbs. This tool will have to be kept very sharp with a file. Go forward through the rows and pull the weeds towards you with a scraping motion, removing them all as you go. After all rows have been hoed, rake away the weeds and put them on to the compost heap. If these weeds are left between the rows and a shower of rain comes, most of them will soon root again.

After hoeing between the rows, hand weeding between the plants will have to be done. Pull out the weeds carefully, trying to avoid dislodging the onion seedlings. Some people may find this task easier if they kneel on several thicknesses of sacking as they work along the rows. When the seedlings are large enough, thin them so that they are spaced at about three inches apart. These thinnings can be used for salads or they can easily be transplanted to other well-prepared land. After transplanting, water well. Subsequently thin the plants to nine inches apart. Regularly hoe between the rows and hand weed between the plants during the growing season. After the seedling stage, hoeing must be done carefully; a Dutch hoe is the best tool for this purpose. It is important to hoe very shallowly and not to loosen the ground too near the plants, as this will prevent the formation of good bulbs. The onion bulb must sit on the soil and not be buried in it. When transplanting, make a small hole and just let the roots trickle in, then firm around them with the hands, leaving the bulb well above the soil.

Well-weathered soot has been used for a great many years for the growing of onions and it is still one of the best fertilizers for them. Dress the rows with it lightly at monthly intervals. It also acts as a deterrent to the onion fly and other pests. During September, for spring-sown onions, ripening can be assisted if the leaves are bent over at the neck and pressed down with the rake lightly. If it is necessary to lift any of the onions while some of the foliage is still green, leave the foliage on the onion until it has withered, otherwise the onions will not keep. When the foliage has been bent over and it is all yellow or withered, ease the onions out of the ground with a garden fork. During a dry September, these onions may be left on the ground to ripen further and dry thoroughly. If the weather is likely to be wet, take them into the shed and then spread them on sacking on the lawn during the first and subsequent sunny days.

Some varieties of onion can be sown in the autumn and left in the open ground to over-winter. Rake down a piece of land that has been manured for early peas or potatoes and sow thinly in rows about

The asparagus pea

A well-grown plant of Swiss Chard

Capsicum, the Sweet Pepper.
Variety: Neapolitan

A pot-grown Egg Plant.
Aubergine, Long White

twelve inches apart. Firm with the rake head after sowing. The best time for sowing these seeds is during the first week in August in the north and during the third week of August in the south of England. When some fairly warm, showery weather comes along in early spring, thin these autumn-sown onions to about nine inches apart. Transplant in well-prepared ground and have the rows twelve inches apart, with nine inches between each plant. Carry out the same cultivation as for spring-sown onions. The varieties which can be used for autumn sowing are 'Ailsa Craig', 'Rousham Park Hero', 'Reliance' and 'Giant Zittau'. The 'Tripoli' and 'Rocca' onions which were used for autumn sowing I have not included, because of their poor keeping qualities.

Maincrop onions for spring sowing are: 'Ailsa Craig', 'Rousham Park Hero' and 'Giant Zittau' for sowing in the spring as well as in the autumn; 'Bedfordshire Champion', 'Brown Globe', 'Cranston's Excelsior', 'James Long-Keeping', 'Superba' (F.1 Hybrid), 'White Spanish', 'Red Weathersfield' and 'Best of All'.

'White Lisbon' onions, the best variety for salads, can be sown from March to August for successional supplies. The most welcome crop of these salad onions arrives in early spring, from July and August sowings. This sowing should be made on a piece of land which has been manured for a previous crop. Make one sowing in July and another in August. Fork over the ground lightly, rake level and tread firmly. Put down the garden line and sow thinly in rows about nine inches apart. These seedlings stand the winter and are pulled during the following spring from where they are sown.

This crop will become infested with weeds like annual nettles and chickweed, if growing on good ground, and frequent use of the Dutch or onion hoe will be required. Hand weeding between the plants must supplement it. These salad onions are not thinned or transplanted. In the spring they make fresh growth and when large enough should be pulled, using the largest first. They are frequently difficult to remove from the soil and are often broken at the base of the plant, leaving the small bulb in the ground. The rows can be watered to make pulling more easy or the plants can be levered out of the soil with the aid of an old table fork or with the trowel.

Salad onion seed may be sown throughout the spring and summer, using the variety 'White Lisbon'. It does not produce a large bulb and is only used for the one purpose. Salad onions can be produced almost all the year round. One can begin with the July- and August-sown 'White Lisbon'; these will be ready during late March and through April and May, if enough rows are sown.

After the shallots have produced their green shoots, some may be pulled and divided; these make excellent salad onions. Then there

26

will be the thinnings from the spring-sown maincrop onions, which are to produce large bulbs for keeping. Further salad onions may be produced from successional sowings of 'White Lisbon' throughout the spring and summer. If some of these sowings are cloched in late August and September, supplies for late autumn and early winter may be gathered.

In the south, some of the spring-sown onions can be left in the ground, if there are a few to spare. These large bulbs will start to root again in autumn and many of them will survive the winter, to send up many green succulent shoots during early spring, before the autumn-sown 'White Lisbons' are ready. These can be lifted in early spring to provide a very tasty salad ingredient. The flavour is unusual and only a few are required at one time.

Onions for pickling should be sown in the usual manner, but on poorer land. Make the sowings fairly shallow and do not thin them. The bed must be kept free of weeds. Sow in March or April and the crop can be harvested in July. Special varieties are used for this purpose and are usually known as 'silver-skinned' kinds. There are 'Silver Skinned Pickling' and 'The Queen'.

Onion sets are onions which have been arrested in their growth and specially treated. On being replanted they will resume growth. As they are much further advanced at planting time than the rest of the onion crops, they frequently make very large onions. They are usually planted during March or April at the same time as onion seed is sown, so they have the same length of season to grow in. Many gardeners do not now sow onion seed for a main crop, but rely on sets to provide enough onions for winter use. If this scheme is followed some seeds will need to be sown for salad onions.

Onion sets are seldom troubled by the onion fly and they are very easy to plant and cultivate. Prepare a piece of land in the same manner as for spring-sown onions, put down the garden line and plant in rows one foot apart during March and April. Space the sets about nine inches apart. Just push the sets firmly into the soil, do not bury them, but have only about half the bulb under the soil. Birds may pull a few out, the roots tend to push the bulb out of the ground or to one side. so one has to keep going along the rows pushing the sets in again, fairly firmly, but without squeezing the bulb too much and without damaging the roots. Keep doing this until the sets have firmly anchored themselves into the ground and are growing away nicely. The only further attention needed during the growing season is the frequent use of the Dutch hoe without going too near the bulbs, and hand weeding between the sets. Remove any flower buds which may appear.

Shallots are another very important crop for the allotment or vegetable garden. If they are moved to a different position each year they are not very often attacked by any pest or disease. Traditionally, shallots are planted on the shortest day of the year and taken up on the longest. This is not a bad plan, either. The shallot is very hardy and it is generally ready for harvesting some time in July. Not many people have a piece of land ready in December for shallot planting. Very often the land is inaccessible because of excessive rain, or it is frozen over. Plant shallots by all means during December, or even in November if conditions are right and the land is at all workable. The next best time for planting is in February, but they can be planted up to the end of April.

Shallots, like so many other crops already discussed, grow well on a piece of land which has been well manured for a previous crop. They also grow well on land which has been well enriched with garden compost. Rake down and firm the site for the shallots, put down the garden line and just press the shallots into the soil, in the same way as for the onion sets. The rows should be about a foot apart and the bulbs spaced about nine inches apart in the rows. They will push themselves out of the soil and the gardener will have to keep pushing them back again until they are showing green shoots and have become firmly anchored.

In July, from six to nine new bulbs will have been produced from each one planted. When the foliage has turned yellow, lift them with a garden fork and leave them to dry thoroughly and ripen on the ground, turning them over several times. Do not store them until they are perfectly dry. Beds of shallots frequently become overrun with weeds during the growing season. They must be hoed carefully and very shallowly, using the Dutch hoe. Hand weed between the plants. If the hoe is thrust into the soil too near to the bulbs the foliage will yellow prematurely, and the resultant crop will be small. Any plants so damaged often take a considerable time to recover, especially during a dry summer. If shallots have to be watered, and this will only be during an exceptionally dry summer, then they must be given some real good soakings and not mere sprinklings. If plenty of garden compost is put in everywhere in the garden, very little watering will be needed. Varieties of shallots are 'Longkeeping Yellow', 'Red', 'Hative de Niort' and 'Giant Exhibition Red'.

Leeks are valuable and useful vegetables and very appetising. To get good leeks, there must be a careful growing programme. Their chief usefulness lies in the fact that they do not have to be stored but can be left in the open ground and dug as required. The leek needs a soil which has been deeply dug and liberally manured with an organic manure such as garden compost or farmyard manure. The site for leek planting should be well prepared during the previous autumn.

Dig in plenty of organic manure and leave the surface rough for the winter. In the spring a light sprinkling of bonemeal may be raked into the surface soil and some wood ashes at the rate of five ounces to the square yard.

If you require massive exhibition roots, then the seed must be sown in seed boxes in February under glass. These plants are hardened off and planted out in May. This method of growing leeks is really unnecessary for the ordinary gardener. For all ordinary garden purposes, and for producing good-sized leeks after Christmas when most people want them, the seed is best sown in the open ground during March. If a grower wants very early leeks but does not possess a cool greenhouse, or does not feel like taking on the pricking-out and hardening-off processes involved, then he can purchase plants

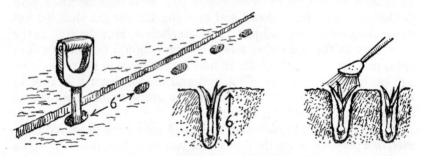

USE DIBBER AND WATER IN

The Planting of Leeks

ready for planting out from the nurseryman, or from other gardeners who have some early plants ready.

The simplest way to grow leeks (and they are always very easy to grow on good soil) is to sow the seeds on a prepared seed bed from early March until mid-April. Sow in drills half an inch deep and six inches apart, although one row of seedlings will be more than enough for the average garden. Leeks are practically disease- and pest-free. The easiest and best way to transplant leek plants is with a dibber. Put down the garden line and plant out the young leek plants six inches apart. Make a hole in the ground about three inches wide at the top and about six inches deep. Drop the young plant into the hole, holding it in the centre and upright, and trickle a little fine soil into the hole with the dibber. Do not fill the holes with soil but leave them wide open. Water in each plant gently with just enough water to wash some soil over the roots. When planting has been completed, the plants will hardly be seen, only a little foliage here and there will be peeping over the top of a planting hole. Gradually the holes will be filled in by the action of wind and rain or the leeks will grow thick

enough to reach the sides of the holes, and they will then be well
blanched.

If the leeks are growing on good soil, with plenty of farmyard
manure or garden compost beneath them, they will want very little
further attention apart from weeding and watering if there is a long,
dry period. Some gardeners shorten the tips of the outside leaves
periodically, so that they never trail on the ground, taking off a couple
of inches at a time. In many years of growing leeks I have never found
this necessary.

When digging the leeks for kitchen use take the largest first and let
the remainder grow on. Lever the leeks from the ground carefully
by getting the garden fork well underneath them. It is best to clean the
soil from them and to remove the rough outside foliage at the spot
where they have been dug, rather than carry a lot of dirt and un-
cookable material into the kitchen. This unwanted material can be
put on to the compost heap at the same time.

All leeks are derived from three main types. These are the 'London
Flag', an early variety and not quite hardy enough for growing in the
extreme north; the 'Musselburgh' or 'Scotch' leek, a hardy sort for
northern gardens, and the 'Lyon Leek', large and slow-maturing, the
best for a late crop. Varieties of leeks are as follows: 'Marble Pillar'
is an early long-stemmed sort which stands well and is useful from
autumn until spring. 'Musselburgh' is good for general purposes; the
'Lyon', of which specially selected seed should be purchased, is very
large, and 'Prizetaker' is also a large type.

Garlic is grown by those who like its strong flavour. The several
sections of each clove should be separated and planted just below
the soil surface from late February until May. The rows should be a
foot apart, leave nine inches between cloves. Lift and dry the crop in
late autumn. Garlic needs a fairly light, rich soil.

Other kinds of onion sometimes grown are Chives, the Tree Onion,
Japanese Bunching Onion, the Welsh Onion and the Potato Onion.
Chives are bought as plants from the nurseryman and planted out
about six inches apart in autumn or spring. They should be lifted,
divided and replanted on fresh ground about every four years. They
grow into grass-like clumps and the foliage is used for flavouring
soups, omelettes and stews. Cut the foliage right back now and again
to produce young shoots which are the best for the kitchen. A stock of
chives can be grown from seed sown in March or April.

'Welsh' or 'Everlasting' onions are not from Wales but from
Siberia. They are bought as plants in spring or autumn and planted out
about nine inches apart. Each plant produces a bunch of 'spring' onions
which are dug and divided for use. Some can be left for increasing the
stock, when they are lifted, divided and replanted in the autumn.

'Potato onions' are planted and lifted like shallots. The bulbs should be set nine inches apart with the tip of the bulb just beneath the surface. Potato onions produce clusters of large cloves on or just below the surface soil. They are of a mild flavour, store well, and are best grown in a warm district.

'Tree onions' are planted three inches deep and left undisturbed except for weeding and watering. They can be left to grow in the same position for five or six years. Plant during late autumn or in March, placing the bulbs about fifteen inches apart. The tree onion produces small onions on the tips of, and at intervals along, the stems. The small onions may be used as they are, or planted as sets to develop into larger onions. The 'Japanese Bunching Onion' is a bulb-less perennial which is like a large Chive plant, but unlike the Chive it does not lose its leaves during the winter.

VEGETABLE MARROWS, PUMPKINS AND MELONS

There are two classes of marrow grown in Britain, the trailing and the bush. Some people find that the bush marrow suits their purpose best, especially in a small garden. The bush marrow makes about a six-feet-round mound of foliage and does not produce a great number of marrows. As marrows are not to everyone's liking perhaps they produce quite enough for most people. The trailing marrow is the best one to grow if you really can use the marrows. Trailing marrows can be trained over walls or along trellis work. Marrows come in different colours and in many shapes. Those with interesting shapes resembling pears and cucumbers are useful if they are to be exhibited. Shape and colour do not matter a lot because they all taste more or less the same. The size they reach is important. Marrows should be cut and cooked when they are small or medium-sized, and young, not left to get old and full of seeds.

The method of growing marrows is the same whatever the variety. Seeds should be sown in April under glass. A cold frame in a warm position will do, or a cool greenhouse. Put the seeds singly on edge, a quarter of an inch deep, in pots of four-and-a-half-inch size. Keep the pots well watered after germination. Seeds may also be sown in the open ground at the end of May. If a few cloches can be spared to help them germinate, so much the better. Handlights, jam jars or other forms of glass may be used to accelerate germination and growth.

Select a fairly open site for the growing of marrows. Dig the soil deeply and put in plenty of farmyard manure or garden compost. This operation is best carried out in March. Plant out in May by putting the plants in about three feet six inches apart for the trailing sort. Marrows must be kept watered if there is no rain, otherwise the fruit will drop. Plants can be pegged down to prevent them being blown out of the ground by strong winds. Put down slug-killer pellets when the plants are young. The trailing marrows can be directed in their trailing by the insertion of short sticks here and there.

Marrows will bear male and female flowers. Although insects will fertilize them in a natural way they can be fertilized by the gardener to make sure of some marrows. The operation of hand-pollinating is simple. To distinguish the difference between male and female flowers, see which of them have a core covered with pollen. These are the male flowers. The female blossoms will be seen to have a baby marrow at the end of the flower near the stalk. Take a male flower, remove the petals, and push the core on to the centre of the female flower; but use a different male flower for each female.

Varieties of marrow are 'Banana Pink', 'Bush Green', 'Bush White', 'Custard Pie', 'Golden Delicious', 'Long Green Trailing', 'Long White Trailing', 'Little Gem' (with fruits the size of a large orange), and 'Zucchini' (F.1 Hybrid).

Pumpkins, squashes and gourds are treated in the same way as marrows. They all need plenty of growing space. When grown on the flat, sometimes a slate or a piece of glass is needed to keep them from the ground. If pumpkins are allowed to climb trellis work or walls, they will need some kind of support such as nets, or the weight of the fruit will bring the plant down and probably break it from the root. It is possible to grow pumpkins weighing a hundredweight or more, but thirty pounds would be a good weight for the ordinary gardener to grow, even if one of that weight were wanted. Pumpkins cooked on their own are rather flavourless and they are usually mixed with apples and lemons and other fruit. The ornamental gourds for flower decoration have already been mentioned (page 288).

Squashes are edible at all stages of growth and they can be hung in an airy frostproof shed for winter use. Some varieties are 'Acorn Squash', 'Hubbard Squash' and 'Golden Scallop Squash'.

Melons are grown like the greenhouse cucumber. A low-span roof greenhouse is very suitable. Seeds should be sown in the first week in January. Use clean 3-inch pots, crock them and fill with John Innes Compost No. 1. Water the soil and allow the pots to drain for a while. Sow two seeds to each pot, a quarter of an inch deep, and keep the strongest plant. Cover with glass and a sheet of paper and germinate in a temperature of 75 to 80°F. When the seedlings appear, remove the glass and paper and stand the plants in full light near to the glass. Pot on into 5-inch pots using John Innes Compost No. 2. Keep the atmosphere moist by syringing frequently with tepid water.

Prepare the beds where the melons are to grow some time before the planting date, to allow the soil to warm. Lay down a layer of inverted turves and on these put the growing compost; this should be about a foot thick. The growing soil can consist of good garden compost or farmyard manure at the bottom and good medium loam with well-decayed garden compost mixed with it for the top layer. The beds should be about two feet wide in the greenhouse. Water the beds well prior to planting out, plant the melon plants firmly eighteen inches apart, and put in stakes to keep them upright. The plants should be knocked out of the pots carefully and then set into the soil with part of the ball of soil above the surface. As watering proceeds, the tops of the roots become exposed and this helps to prevent collar rot. Another safeguard against this disease is to water in the early stages with Cheshunt Compound.

Wires will have to be fixed in the greenhouse for the melons to be trained to. The wire supports should run the length of the house and be about six inches apart. Let the plants run up to the second wire and then stop them; this is to encourage side shoots. Remove those which grow below the first wire. Restrict the growth to about four laterals on either side of the main stem and allow two melons only to each plant. Transfer pollen from male to female flowers in the same way as with marrows. A rabbit's tail, tied securely to a short cane, is a good tool for this job. Bees can be allowed to work in a melon house but they must never be in a cucumber house.

Always use tepid water for watering. Keep the soil around the collar dry, but the roots moist. Syringe the house daily and sometimes twice daily on very hot days. Avoid draughts at all times. Stop watering as flowers open and syringe only once in the afternoon or early evening. When the fruit begins to ripen and change colour, withhold moisture and give plenty of ventilation. The temperature should now be at 70°F. Roots will appear through the top soil; when they appear top-dress with good soil mixed with good garden compost. Leave the top-dressing material in the greenhouse for a few days to get warm before applying. When the fruits begin to swell, dried blood may be given twice at fortnightly intervals. Read the instructions on the packet carefully and apply exactly as directed. As the fruits grow large and ripen they will have to be supported by nets.

In the south, Cantaloupe melons can be grown under continuous large barn cloches. In this case the plants are raised in the greenhouse, hardened off, and planted out under cloches in June. The cloches remain on the plants until all the melons have been gathered by about the end of September.

Varieties of melon are 'No Name', which is of Cantaloupe character with green and yellow marbled skin and thick amber-yellow flesh of juicy texture and excellent flavour. This melon can be grown under cloches, in a cold frame, or in a cool greenhouse. 'English Types Mixed' are a good mixture of the best greenhouse varieties. 'Dutch Net' has orange flesh of beautiful quality and flavour. It can be grown in frames or under cloches. A water melon, 'Florida Favourite', is oval-shaped with green skin and pink flesh.

WHICH HERBS TO GROW

Although there are many herbs which can be grown in our gardens, there are really only one or two which most ordinary English cooks like to use. These are parsley, mint, sage and thyme. Mint we must have for new potatoes, and mint sauce for roast lamb and other purposes. Roots of mint will have to be bought from a nurseryman, but usually there are plenty of people who have beds of mint and who can spare a root or two. Once a rooted piece has been planted in good soil, it rapidly increases. Mint has to be kept in check or it will soon spread all over the vegetable plot. The best way to do this is to make a good bed of soil by digging in plenty of good garden compost ready for a spring or autumn planting. In a small garden, the mint can be confined if bricks are inserted into the soil to make a wall around the mint bed.

There are two kinds of mint usually grown, the spearmint and the round-leaved type. Spearmint is usually preferred because the round-leaved type has hairy leaves. This does not impair its flavour; it grows about four feet high and unlike spearmint it does not suffer from rust. Good garden compost is the only manure required for mint. Be careful not to apply any bonfire or wood ash as mint greatly dislikes potash in any form.

Rust is the great enemy of spearmint. This is easily identified by the orange pustules on the base of the shoots and the rusty spores under the leaves. Flowers of sulphur used fairly regularly in powder form seems to be about the only remedy. Some gardeners have been successful in abating this disease by using the drastic measure of periodically burning away the old foliage. If this is undertaken, straw needs to be worked in among the stems and then set fire to so that it burns rapidly and does not injure the underground stems.

The mint bed should be remade every three years or so. Lift the roots, divide them, and replant on good soil. Additional mint plants can be raised at almost any time of the year except in the middle of winter or during a very dry spell in the summer. Cuttings can be taken in the usual way and put firmly into the open ground. Pieces can be pulled from the parent plant with some roots attached and also inserted in the open ground. Always keep mint beds well watered during dry weather. Early mint can be grown by placing cloches over a few plants in very early spring. Rooted cuttings can be potted into large pots and brought into a warm living-room, where it will delight the housewife who can make some fresh mint sauce instead of using the dried or bottled variety.

Parsley is a wonderful herb to have growing on any vegetable patch. It is very easily grown from seed. As it is a biennial it will run to seed during its second year. Parsley seed is slow-germinating compared with many other vegetable seeds, but if sown in good soil, with plenty of moisture-retaining material in it, it usually germinates very well. Sow in March for summer use and make another sowing in June for winter use. There are two ways of providing enough moisture to last the seeds while they are germinating. Put down the garden line and draw drills half an inch deep, then run the watering-can with the fine rose on along the drills, soaking them well. Sow the seeds thinly and cover with fine soil. Instead of using the watering-can a layer of wet peat can be put along the drills, and the seeds can be sown on top of this.

Parsley needs a deep moist soil, so dig the site deeply and put in plenty of good garden compost. Thin out the seedlings to a foot apart. If you have some distance to travel to your allotment to gather parsley, a bunch can be picked at one time and put into a jug of cold water. This will keep fresh for about a week and can be used as required. Parsley can be grown in a semi-shaded position.

Sage is required for poultry stuffings, stews, baked joints, soups and for many other dishes. Fresh sage can be used in the kitchen or it can be dried and powdered. Sage grows well in a light well-drained soil and very well on chalky soils. Deep digging is not required for sage as it does not root deeply. Dig in some garden compost, rake down the soil to a fine tilth and sow the seeds thinly in April or May.

Sage plants usually grow leggy and a bit unsightly after a few years so it is advisable to make sowings every two years or so. You can grow fresh sage plants by taking cuttings from the old plants. Pull off small pieces about two inches in length with a heel attached, that is, with a piece of the main stem attached to the cutting. Push these cuttings firmly into sandy soil and water well. This is best done in the open ground during May. When the cuttings are growing away nicely, transplant them to where they are required and water them well. When they have become well established in their new positions, nip out the tops of the plants to encourage branching.

Thyme is grown in the same way as sage and it needs the same soil and cultural methods. Thyme is a fine aromatic herb used for seasoning and is excellent with cheese, egg, veal, beef and poultry dishes. There are several types of thyme: 'Narrow-leaved', 'French Black' (which has grey foliage), 'Broad-leaved English Black Thyme' (with green foliage) and Lemon Thyme, with a strong scent of lemon when the leaves are crushed between the fingers.

Plants can be purchased or they can be grown from seed. If the land is not chalky, lime the ground well before sowing. To increase stock, cuttings can be taken of the long tops of the shoots and either inserted in the open ground during April or May or in a box in a cold frame.

HOW TO STORE VEGETABLES

It is not likely that many people will want to dry and store garden peas during these days when there are plentiful supplies of tinned and frozen peas. It is only likely to be done where the gardener has grown too many for his own use and been unable to sell them. Some peas are grown specially for drying. Peas for drying should be gathered when the pods are well filled but before any signs of yellowing are observed. Cut the haulms with a sickle and hang them up in the sun to dry. Complete this operation quickly so that the peas keep as much of their green colour as possible. Stack the haulms under cover for about a month. Then shell the peas and complete their drying in the living-room where there is some heating. Store the peas in airtight jars or tins and inspect them from time to time to see that no dampness has crept in.

Broad beans are usually only stored if wanted as seed. Gather the pods when they are black and brittle but before the seeds have spilled on to the ground. Choose a dry day for gathering the pods and they can be shelled on the spot or afterwards at home. Do not store these, however, in airtight containers as beans used for seed must be able to breathe. Make sure the seeds are thoroughly dry and then put them in a small, dry, clean sack or brown paper bag and store in a place which is airy and frost-proof.

French beans can be gathered and stored for seed in the same way, except that the pods do not usually turn black, but are ready for seed gathering when they are of a brown colour. Although I have not mentioned the growing of haricot beans, they are grown in the same way as French beans. Leave the pods to ripen and turn brown or a straw colour, on the plants. Dig up the plants when the pods are ready, shake the soil from them and hang them up in an airy frost-proof shed. When they are perfectly dry shell the beans and spread them out on to newspaper in a warm living-room to complete the drying. Store in paper bags tied at the neck.

Runner beans are treated in the same way as broad beans for seed-saving purposes. They are preserved for cooking by salting down into stone jars for winter use. The beans are gathered when they will just fit the jars. They are washed and dried and put whole into the jars. A layer of beans is put in and then a layer of coarse cooking salt, and the process is repeated until the jar is full. Well wash and soak the beans before cooking.

Carrots can be stored in sand or leaf mould in boxes. If there is a large quantity, they can be put into a tea chest or apple barrel. They can be left in a frost-proof shed or cellar. Put down a two-inch

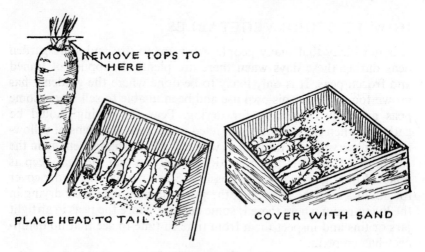

The Storage of carrots

layer of sand and follow with a layer of carrots until the containers are full.

Beetroot can be left in the soil until about Christmas; any remaining after this time should be lifted and stored. Lift with a fork, being careful not to damage any of the roots. Twist the foliage from the beet and shake all soil from the roots. Store the roots in the same way as for carrots, using fairly dry sand, peat or dry earth. Beet need dry and cool conditions for successful storage.

Parsnips can be left in the ground until required, as the frost and snow actually improve their flavour and texture. Turnips and swedes can be stored in the same way as carrots.

Onions are usually harvested during September. The length of time which you can keep onions chiefly depends upon proper ripening. Do not remove the tops from the onions until they have completely withered. Seize an opportunity during dry weather in September to lift the bulbs, lay them on the ground and keep turning them over, to thoroughly ripen in the sun and any drying wind. Some time before lifting bend over the tops of the onions to assist in the ripening process. It is important not to start storing the onions until all the tops have withered and the bulbs are perfectly dry. Look over your crop. Remove any onions which have soft necks or any which are showing a young flower stem. These can be used immediately in the kitchen as they will not keep. Store the rest by removing the withered roots and hang the onions up in nets or put them into boxes or in single layers on shelves in an airy frost-proof shed. Do not keep onions in a stuffy atmosphere and see that they do not get damp.

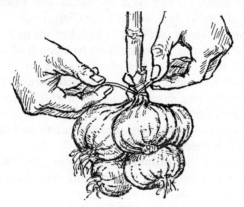

Storing onions by tying them to a cane

Inspect the onions in store from time to time. Shallots can be treated and stored in the same way as onions. Never leave onions or shallots in large quantity in bags for any length of time. They will manufacture heat and start sprouting, the bulb becoming soft in the process.

If you have a great number of tomatoes during autumn or at the end of the summer, and they are not going to be used for chutney, some of them may be stored. Pick the tomatoes to be stored on a dry day and see that they are perfectly dry. The storing method to be described concerns green tomatoes and those just starting to ripen. Wrap each tomato in tissue paper, being very careful not to bruise any of the fruit. Store them in a drawer or dark cupboard at a temperature of about 50°F. Fruits stored in this way will go on ripening until the end of December.

Maincrop potatoes may be stored in several ways. Like onions, they must be perfectly dry and disease-free and be lifted when the haulms have died down. Leave the potatoes on the ground until the skins are dry. As soon as they are dry put them into sacks for transport, but when doing this handle them very carefully; see that none are bruised, for this is the cause of blackness during cooking.

Before storing the potatoes, examine all tubers thoroughly. Reject any diseased or damaged specimens. Potatoes may be stored in the larder or kitchen by enlisting the aid of a tea chest. If they are absolutely dry the tea chest may be nearly filled and the potatoes used from the tea chest as required. In this way the height of the potato store is gradually reduced. Keep a lid on, or some sacking, for the top potatoes will go green if exposed to the light.

After Christmas, the height of the potato pile must not be more than two and a half feet, or they will start developing long shoots. If there is any danger of sprouting, the potatoes must be tipped out and all sprouts must be removed by hand. The potatoes may be stored in a good brick shed which is entirely frost- and rat-proof. Put down a layer of straw, sacking or bracken on to the floor of the shed. Spread the potatoes on to the floor to a depth of not more than two and a half feet. Cover over the potatoes so that all light is excluded. Exclude light in all forms of potato storage. If there is any possibility of dampness creeping in among the stored potatoes, sprinkle them with flowers of sulphur during the storage operation. Examine all stored potatoes every three weeks or so and remove any showing signs of disease.

It is not often that the ordinary gardener or allotment holder will have grown so many potatoes that he will need to make a potato

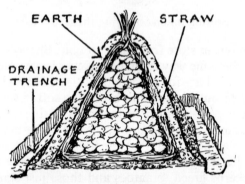

EARTH   STRAW

DRAINAGE
TRENCH

The Potato Clamp: a method of storing potatoes outside

clamp in the open garden or allotment. For those who need to make a clamp here are instructions for doing so. Select a spot for the clamp which is higher than the surrounding land if possible. Mark out this piece of land so that it is three and a half feet wide at the base. Pile up the tubers so that the heap is ridge-shaped, with the sides sloping towards each other and meeting at the top. Make the heap of potatoes about three feet high. Cover with a six-inch thickness of straw, starting from the ground and working to the top. Cover this straw with a six-inch layer of earth and make the sides smooth. Ventilate the clamp by pulling through from the top one or two twists of straw. Dig a shallow trench around the clamp to assist with drainage. In a severe winter the outside soil may have to be thickened to much more than six inches.

Many of the herbs may be dried and stored. Cut the amount of mint required, lay it out in thin layers on thick brown paper, and dry it quickly by placing it in a cool oven at a temperature of about 90°F. If it is dried quickly much of its colour will be retained. When it is very dry and brittle, strip the leaves from the stems and powder the mint by rubbing between the palms of the hands or crushing with a rolling-pin. It may be stored in honey jars with screw tops.

Parsley is dried in a similar way by picking young leaves during summer and autumn. It needs a higher temperature for drying than mint. Dry it in a warm oven. Select only clean leaves, avoiding any which have been splashed by mud during rain storms. Rub it down quickly after drying and store in screw-topped jars.

If sage is cut for drying during June and July, it may be spread on to paper on the lawn and dried in the hot sun. After drying, powder and store in the manner described. Thyme should be cut at the end of May and again in late August, to avoid flowering periods. It can be dried in the same way as sage but it is more difficult to powder. Push it through a coarse sieve and then through a fine one.

SOME UNUSUAL VEGETABLES

Included in this section are some little-known (and some little-grown) vegetables. There are also some of those which are more familiar but only grown by a few gardeners, such as the aubergine or egg-plant, sweet corn and asparagus.

Pole beans are very popular in America and they are grown in exactly the same way as runner beans. The variety 'Blue Lake' has clusters of small, round, fleshy pods which are tender and stringless. This bean has a superb flavour. The small white seeds can be harvested and dried like haricot beans.

The pea bean is grown in the same way as runner beans. The pods may be sliced with the young peas in and cooked like runners, or the half-ripe seeds may be shelled and cooked separately. The pea bean is recommended only for growing in the south as it is not always very hardy. The asparagus pea is grown with the aid of short pea sticks. It grows to a height of one and a half feet and is very decorative with its red flowers and curious square-winged pods. The pods should be gathered when they are about two inches long and cooked whole.

Swiss chard or seakale beet is also called silver beet. The seeds are sown in fairly rich, well-drained soil in about the middle of April. The seeds should be in drills an inch deep and the seedlings eventually thinned to a foot and a half apart. The broad white stems or midribs can be cooked like seakale and the leaves like spinach. The crop is ready for use from late autumn onwards. Rhubarb chard has long stalks of bright crimson with dark green, deeply crinkled leaves. It is highly decorative and very useful for floral art as well as being a valuable vegetable.

Spinach beet is a good substitute for ordinary spinach. The leaves are larger and more fleshy than those of ordinary spinach. A well-cultivated bed of spinach beet will last a year. The best time for sowing seed is in late March or early April. A second sowing can be made in July. Sow the seeds in drills an inch deep and a foot and a half apart. Thin the seedlings to one foot apart. Water the plants well during dry spells and pick leaves regularly, so that fresh young leaves are continually being produced. Old leaves become rather coarse and tough.

Once asparagus has been planted it will occupy a permanent position in the garden. Asparagus is not a crop for the small garden, as it takes up considerable space. A well-made asparagus bed will last up to fifteen years or so. Asparagus plants do not throw up their heads all together in large quantities, they appear here and there along the whole length of the bed, so it follows that a fairly large bed will have to be made in order to gather enough shoots for an average family. The two methods of establishing an asparagus bed are by sowing seed and by purchasing plants. You cannot cut any asparagus until the plants are four years old. Plants can be bought at one, two or three years old.

For raising plants from seed, rake down finely a prepared seed bed and sow the seeds thinly in drills one and a half inches deep and a foot apart. The seeds are slow to germinate and they may be soaked in water for twenty-four hours prior to sowing. Thin the seedlings to a foot apart when they are about six inches high. The seeds can be sown in March and cloches put over the rows, or they may be sown at the end of April when the ground is fairly warm. There are male and female plants but only the male plants are planted out into a permanent asparagus bed during March, when they are one year old. The female plants can be distinguished by the berries they bear.

Wild asparagus grows on the sandy coasts of Britain, so when making an asparagus bed put in some silver sand and a little agricultural salt. The bed should be in an open position and good drainage is important. It does not need to be heavily manured. Dig the bed deeply, mixing with the soil as you go some good garden compost, leaf mould, silver sand and a little bonemeal. A raised bed is best and

Jerusalem artichoke.
White Round

Globe artichoke,
Variety: Grosvert de
Saon

Seakale Beet

Salsify or Vegetable Oyster

should be three feet wide with a two-foot-wide path running on each side of the bed for easy gathering of the plants. Plant two rows of plants on each bed, each about nine inches from the edge.

The roots of the asparagus plant resemble a spider. When transplanting them, build a little mound so that the asparagus plant sits astride it; let the roots fall down each side of the mound and press fine soil around them, carefully filling in all gaps. When planting has been completed, the crowns should be about five inches below the surface. Water them in. When planting, it is important not to let the roots become exposed to the air at any time. You must take care with purchased plants. Have the bed ready for planting well in advance of the time you are expecting the plants to arrive. Once you have removed the plants from the packing you must plant them immediately. Cover each root with soil as you plant; do not set out a whole row before you cover the plants.

Some people like their sticks of asparagus partly blanched. This can be achieved by heaping straw around the base of the sticks. Cutting of the sticks must end about the middle of June to allow some foliage to grow for the remainder of the year. If you were to keep cutting beyond June and through the year, all the plants would die, for no plant can live without foliage. It is through the green chlorophyll in the leaves, with the help of light, that all green plants manufacture their main food, which enables them to live and grow. Do not cut the familiar asparagus foliage or fern for mixing with sweet peas or carnations; let it grow on and tie it to sticks or canes. If the site is exposed to keen winds the stems may snap at the base. When the foliage turns yellow and then brown in the autumn, remove it with shears and then rake over the beds carefully; do not dig the teeth of the rake into the bed, and give a top dressing of farmyard manure or good garden compost. Do not dig this manure in, or the dormant shoots and the roots could be damaged.

In spring prick the beds over very carefully with a hand fork, going no more than an inch deep. Agricultural salt should be applied to established asparagus beds at the rate of two ounces per yard run, in the middle of April. A second and third dressing can be applied at monthly intervals following. Never apply salt early in the year when there is any danger of frost.

The only pest which may attack the asparagus bed is the asparagus beetle which is red, yellow and black. Their larvae eat the young shoots and foliage during July and August. Should any of these pests be noticed, spray with a solution of half a pound of soft soap in a gallon of warm water, adding a quarter-pound of weathered soot and the same amount of flowers of sulphur. This mixture will need a good deal of stirring. Warm water is used for melting the soap. Let

27

the mixture cool before using. Use a coarse nozzle on the sprayer to prevent clogging. If the asparagus bed should occasionally suffer from rust, spray with Bordeaux Mixture. Sometimes asparagus beds are attacked by the carrot fly; should this happen, take the same measures of control as for carrots.

Do not worry about trying to produce huge thick sticks of asparagus such as are often seen on their way from the Vale of Evesham. This entails the use of large quantities of farmyard manure. The medium-sized sticks produced in an ordinary garden taste just as nice and often better, and are perhaps more tender.

Cut the asparagus shoots when the sticks have been blanched about four inches in length. Cut the asparagus with a pointed, sharp knife, being careful not to injure the tops of other shoots which will be near by and just below the surface.

Capsicum or sweet peppers can be grown for salads, for cooking, or for pickling. Sow under glass during March and April and grow on in pots in a cool greenhouse, or plant out under cloches during early June. Sow in a temperature of 60°F. and maintain a temperature of 56°F. If it is your intention to keep them in the cool greenhouse, a 7-inch pot will do for the final potting. Capsicums for pickling are gathered before they begin to colour and while they are still green. 'Outdoor Pepper' is an early sort which can be grown outdoors under cloches. Sow under glass in early April, prick off into 3½-inch pots, harden off and plant out into a sheltered sunny position during late May. Water the plants in and cover with cloches. They are best eaten when the fruits are yellow or half ripe. When fully ripe the fruits are a bright red. Sweet varieties can be obtained in packets of mixed seeds of sweet-fleshed peppers for slicing, salad or stuffing. All are green at first and they change to red or yellow when fully mature.

We often see the egg plant or Aubergine in the greengrocer's shop during October and November, but we do not see many growing in ordinary gardens. This vegetable needs a good warm summer to fruit and ripen well. It is a semi-tropical plant and should be planted in the south of England under a south wall, but in the north it should be grown in a cold frame. The seed, which germinates slowly, should be sown under glass during March. The young plants are pricked off into small pots prior to hardening off and planting out in late June. If the seedlings need watering at any time, use a solution of Cheshunt Compound.

There are purple-, black- or white-fruited sorts but the purple or black are the ones usually grown. Pinch out the tops when the plants are six inches high and limit the fruits to three or four to a plant. It would be difficult to get more than that number ripened during the summers we have been experiencing during the last few years. Gather the aubergines when they are fully coloured in the same way as tomatoes. They can be stuffed with meat and herbs or sliced and fried.

Chicory is excellent for forcing in winter to yield blanched leaves for salads. It can be sown from April to June in shallow drills a foot apart. Thin the plants out to nine inches apart in the rows. Lift the roots in November and store in sand in a cool place. There is only one variety suitable for growing for salad, the 'Large Brussels' or 'Witloof'. It forms a compact close head like a cos lettuce. Chicory is another plant which grows well on soil which has been well manured for a previous crop. When the roots are lifted, pack them into deep boxes and cover the crowns with a twelve-inch layer of sand. The roots must be in absolute darkness. Very little watering is required during the forcing process. When forcing, pack a few roots into boxes or large pots in a warm, dark place but avoid any high temperature. You can cut the leaves for use as soon as they start appearing above the layer of sand. As the wild chicory, with its beautiful blue flowers, grows on the chalklands, it is as well to rake a little garden lime into the surface soil just before sowing time. The leaves produced by the cultivated chicory in summer in the open ground are not edible: only the forced foliage grown in winter is used for salads.

Jerusalem artichokes should be more popular and more widely grown than they are. There should be a place for them on every allotment or large kitchen garden. They are very easily grown and are almost disease- and pest-free. They will grow in almost any kind of soil provided that it is well drained. They are very nutritious vegetables and a great standby during the winter. In an emergency they could take the place of potatoes, although not such a large quantity could be eaten.

The Jerusalem artichoke has many good points. The plants can be left in the ground without fear of damage by frost, and they can be dug and used as required. The plants grow to a height of from ten to twelve feet and so they can make excellent windbreaks and shelter for the site where perhaps outdoor tomatoes, cucumbers or tall peas may be growing. This artichoke produces tubers which are of all shapes and fairly knobbly, although some of the latest varieties have this fault eliminated to a certain extent. Whatever the shape, they are well worth any trouble taken over their preparation for cooking. They are scraped like new potatoes and can be cooked like them. If a white sauce is made, using some of the water in which they were cooked, and served with them, a really delicious dish is produced.

Although these artichokes can be grown almost anywhere, they will give a much better crop if they are planted in a well prepared piece of ground that has been well enriched with garden compost. Planting should be done in February or March and the tubers should be set a foot apart and about four inches deep. The sets may be planted whole like potatoes, or large ones may be cut with about three eyes on each cut portion. Some tubers may be lifted in November and stored in sand for winter use when the ground is frozen.

With globe artichokes it is the scales of the immature flower buds that are eaten. The taste is an acquired one and it would not be worth while for a gardener to grow globe artichokes unless his family liked them, or unless he was required to arrange some large displays of flowers. They take up a great deal of room and grow very tall to form a massive plant. They are magnificent subjects for flower decoration on a large scale. If the flower is allowed to come to maturity it will be a very showy violet-purple bloom which, together with the grey decorative foliage, is ideal for decorations for large halls, or for platform work at concerts.

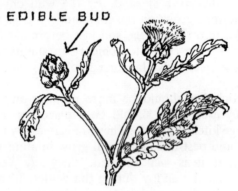

The Globe Artichoke

Globe artichokes require deeply dug soil and a sunny position. They grow well on a good depth of soil over a chalky sub-soil. Wood ashes worked into the top soil are very beneficial. Seed should be sown in February in heat and the plants pricked out, hardened off and transplanted to the open ground during April. If sown in the open ground during April, which is possible in the south, the plants do not form heads until the following year. When sowing in this way, thin the plants to nine inches apart and leave undisturbed until the following spring. The plants are perennials, but they seldom produce any buds worth cooking after the second year, so the usual practice is to sow seeds annually. In spring the final planting distance must be at least three feet six inches between plants. They need little attention during the growing season, except for regular weeding and plenty of watering during dry periods.

If large heads for cooking are wanted, the lateral small buds which surround the main flower head should be removed when about the size of a small hen's egg. These can be eaten raw or they can be fried. The large heads are boiled. The plants will need protection during winter in cold areas. Cut down the tall foliage in late autumn and cover the lower foliage with strawy litter or bracken. A dressing of well-rotted garden compost or farmyard manure can be forked in around the plants at this time. When the strawy litter has been removed in spring, all suckers above three or four are removed; these may be used for propagation. They are inserted into the soil and well watered. They should be planted when they are about nine inches high.

The main flower heads of globe artichokes are gathered and cooked just before they start to open, when the tight heads are beginning to open near the base. When the bud has been gathered the flowering stem is cut down. The summer growth of globe artichokes may be blanched and eaten with salads. It is then known as 'Chards'. Plants should be cut back in July to within six inches of the ground, and watered every week until September, when the resultant growths of foliage are drawn up and tied together with raffia. Some straw is then put round and the growths are earthed up in the manner of celery. Blanching takes five or six weeks and during this period no growth takes place.

Kohlrabi has a distinct nutty flavour and is used as a change from turnips or cabbage, but it tastes somewhat like both of these. The swollen stems should be used before they become too large—they should grow no larger than a cricket ball. The edible portion is that which grows just above ground level. Sow the seed in the open ground in drills, a quarter of an inch deep and fifteen inches apart. Thin out to nine inches apart. Seeds may be sown from April to August and the later sowings may be left in the ground through the winter, after thinning out. The two varieties of kohlrabi grown today are 'Early Purple Vienna' and 'Early White Vienna'.

GROWING MUSHROOMS

Whether the ordinary gardener thinks it worth his while to grow mushrooms, or whether he would do best to leave mushrooms growing to the large commercial grower, is a matter for his own choice. As this is a complete book of gardening, there is room for a short outline of mushroom growing here.

We can gather quite a lot of field mushrooms in various parts of the country, if we rise early enough in the summer, after rainfall. The flavour of mushrooms which can now be purchased from the green-grocers is not much inferior to that of the natural outdoor varieties which we can collect. Mushrooms can be grown out-of-doors only during summer but they can be grown indoors all the year round. With all mushroom growing there is no certainty of success, but if no one ever experimented we should never advance or gain any additional horticultural knowledge.

The great difficulty with mushroom growing used to be the acquisition of a suitable growing compost. Stable manure is difficult to obtain and when obtained, it has to be properly decomposed until it has reached a considerable heat and has then fallen to a moderate temperature again. We now have a special mushroom-growing concentrate called Betasol. This compost enables the ordinary gardener to grow mushrooms without having to obtain quantities of horse manure.

Betasol comes as a dry powder and it is mixed with garden peat or sawdust. Soil can be used but it must be sterilized soil. Mushrooms can be grown in almost any kind of covered-in building which is fairly dry and well ventilated. Greenhouses, frames, sheds, garages or cellars can be used if a temperature of between 50° and 60°F. can be maintained. Mushrooms will not develop properly if the temperature drops below 48°F. or rises above 68°F. If the temperature drops below 48°F. no harm is done, for the mushrooms just remain dormant until the temperature rises. The crop may be grown in semi-darkness or in full light. The direct rays of the sun should not be shining with full force on to the beds.

It is best to put down a bed for mushrooms during early summer if they are to be grown in an unheated building. They will then crop before the cooler weather comes along. With the Betasol mushroom concentrate, what is known and sold as the Grower's Pack contains 7lb. of concentrate. This is mixed by the gardener with the selected filler of either sterilized soil, garden peat or sawdust and it will provide compost for 5 to 10 square feet. These relatively small areas are best made up into fairly deep wooden boxes. Both sufficient spawn and sufficient concentrate for growing fairly large areas are rather expensive. This is about the best way of growing mushrooms, however, on a small scale, because of the near-impossibility of obtaining quantities of suitable horse manure today.

If large beds for mushroom growing are to be made up, they can be in the form of flat beds or beds of a ridge type. Flat beds can be four feet wide and nine inches deep in summer and about a foot deep in winter. If they are made up on to shelves in a shed or garage, they should be nine inches deep and if in cold frames about ten inches deep.

If the mushrooms are to be grown outdoors a ridge-type bed would be the best. Ridge beds need to be two and a half feet at the base, six inches at the top and about two feet high. Mushroom beds outdoors must be on well-drained land. Ridge beds are not left on the same site for longer than three years. There must be some natural shelter from draughts and cool winds and the beds must not be near trees, so that they are continuously suffering from rain drops.

Some people might like to try growing mushrooms on their lawn or in their paddock. Slices of turf can be taken out, measuring about two feet square, during May and June with about an inch and a half of soil remaining on them. Dig out three inches of soil where the turf was removed and fill the space with fresh horse manure. Sprinkle some fine soil on to the top of the manure and put down the spawn according to the spawn maker's instructions. Put the turf back and tread it in well. Water in very dry weather to prevent the turf from browning, but do not over-water.

In midsummer you may raise the turf of your paddock or meadow here and there and insert two or three pieces of spawn and replace the turf. If favourable growing conditions follow, mushrooms may appear in late August, September and early October and continue to show themselves for several seasons afterwards. You may insert spawn alongside cucumber beds, rhubarb beds or anywhere else where a mulch of horse manure has been used, with every hope of success. When gathering mushrooms always pull them, never cut them, and then fill in the hole with a little sub-soil.

Salsify or vegetable oyster is grown in exactly the same way as parsnips. The roots have a delicate oyster-like flavour. The crowbar method, as mentioned for parsnips, is suitable for this crop as absolutely straight roots are desirable. It is an appetizing and nutritious vegetable and it is grown by some people as an alternative to parsnips. Salsify has a cream-coloured slender root. Sow during April and May in drills fifteen inches apart and thin out to six inches apart in the rows.

Salsify is hardy and can remain in the ground during winter, for early spring use. A supply can be lifted for use when the ground is frozen. The variety called 'Mammoth Sandwich Island' is one of the most delicious of winter vegetables. The roots are sweet and can be boiled or sliced and fried.

Scorzonera is very similar to salsify except that it has black-skinned roots. Sow in the same way but thin out to one foot apart. The variety 'Russian Giant' is easily grown and it is a superb vegetable. In preparation for the table, the roots are scalded, scraped and left in water flavoured with a few drops of lemon juice for half an hour. Boil until tender and serve with a white sauce.

Spinach is a wholesome and health-giving vegetable, containing natural iron, for those who like the flavour. There are two kinds, the 'Round Seeded', which is used for spring and summer sowings, and the 'Prickly Seeded', which is sown from July to September. Do not grow spinach unless you are fond of it, for as you can only gather a few leaves at a time from each plant, and as you want a large saucepanful with the spinach pressed down, you naturally have to grow quite a few plants. You have to cook quite a large quantity because it contains much water, and a saucepanful when cooked, is about a quarter of the size it was when in the raw state. Cook it like cabbage and serve with butter and pepper and maybe a white sauce.

Good rich soil with plenty of garden compost is necessary for growing good crops of spinach. It needs plenty of moisture and ample water must be given during any long, dry periods. The first sowing may be made in March, using the 'Round Seeded' variety. Successional sowings may be made until the middle of June. Spinach should be sown in rows twelve inches apart. Make the drills three-quarters of an inch deep, thinning out the plants in the rows to one foot apart. Sow the 'Prickly' variety from July to September and the crop will be used from November until the end of April. Make the autumn sowings on well-drained soil that is not likely to become waterlogged during winter. Varieties of spinach are 'Long Standing Round' and 'Long Standing Prickly'. 'New Zealand Spinach' is quite unlike ordinary spinach, having soft, thick, fleshy leaves with a crystalline appearance. The seeds of this plant should be sown a little later, at the end of April or in early May.

Seakale needs a rich, sunny, well-drained piece of land. The roots should be planted two feet apart each way. The wild seakale grows in coastal areas so seaweed is an excellent manure for it if obtainable. If not, use plenty of well-rotted garden compost or farmyard manure. Tread and rake down the site well and plant two-year-old crowns during autumn or early spring. Remove the pointed buds on each crown and cover with soil. During the growing season, some fish

BLANCHED SHOOTS FORMING

SEAKALE MAY BE
FORCED IN DEEP BOXES

Forcing Seakale

manure at the rate of four ounces to the square yard may be worked into the top soil. Keep down weeds by hoeing throughout the summer and remove flowering stems. Cut down the foliage during October.

Seakale is treated as a forced vegetable. The roots should be dug in winter, the side roots removed and the remainder of the root planted upright in good soil or in well-decayed leaf mould. These roots can be placed under the greenhouse staging, in cold frames or in a cellar or basement of some kind. Moist conditions, darkness and a temperature of 55° to 60°F. are the requirements for forcing this vegetable. The crowns may be forced in the open by covering them with special forcing pots or some other receptacle which can be placed over the crowns to exclude light, and surrounding the whole with strawy farmyard manure.

Sweet corn can be produced satisfactorily in this country if the summer suits it. The harvesting of the crop is a matter of some importance. One has to know exactly when to gather the cobs. They are ready when, if pressed with the finger and thumb, a liquid oozes out which is like fairly thick cream. They are not ready when the seeds are still watery or when the grains are hard. Sweet corn is always chancy in this country, especially during recent summers. If there is enough sun to ripen the cobs sufficiently for cooking, then they make a very delicious vegetable. Any cobs which have been left for the grains to become hard may, after thorough ripening, be used for seed or thrown to the poultry.

Sweet corn must be started under glass. Those with cloches gain an advantage with this crop, as the corn grows better without transplanting. Sow outdoors under cloches during the second week of April. In the north sow at the end of April. The cloches are removed during June. If no cloches are available, sow in John Innes Compost No. 1 in early April, using 3-inch pots and put the pots in a cold frame or in the cool greenhouse. Transplant to the open ground after hardening off during the third week in May.

Sweet corn will grow well on most types of soil only if it contains plenty of organic matter. Prepare the soil during autumn by digging deeply and by putting in plenty of farmyard manure or good garden compost. A week or so before planting, rake into the top soil some bonemeal at the rate of four ounces per square yard. Choose a position which will receive as much sun as possible during the growing and ripening period. Plant in rows running north to south if possible. Good pollination is required and plenty of water. The plants may be mulched with advantage during hot summer weather. When sowing seeds in the open ground, and then covering with cloches, space them to a foot apart for tall varieties and nine inches apart for medium kinds. When planting out from pots into the open ground during

May, put the plants a foot apart with two feet between the rows. Varieties of Sweet corn are 'Kelvedon Glory' (F.1 Hybrid), which produces cobs seven inches in length; 'Prima', which is about the earliest variety; 'Golden Bantam', which produces sweet tender cobs, often appearing in pairs (this is of medium height); and 'Spancross' (F.1 Hybrid).

RHUBARB

Rhubarb is a wonderful stand-by when there is not much fruit around. Rhubarb is a favourite with nearly everyone, but how often do we see it really well grown? It is usually stuck in any odd corner with no attention given it, no manure, and yet is expected to produce fat, succulent stems year after year. To start a good bed of rhubarb, it is best to purchase a few roots from a well-known nurseryman and to get some really first-class varieties. Obtain these in autumn and buy an early variety and a maincrop one. The roots may be planted in November or March. Propagation afterwards is carried out by dividing old crowns in February or March and planting out pieces bearing only a single bud.

The very best early rhubarb is the variety called 'Timperly Early'. You can often pull sticks of this kind when other sorts are only just appearing above the ground. Rhubarb is more or less a permanent crop. The site for it must be well prepared initially. Dig the ground deeply in autumn and put in plenty of well-rotted farmyard manure or garden compost. Fork into the top soil some fish manure at the rate of four ounces to the square yard. Rhubarb requires a slightly acid soil and it is not much good trying to grow it on one of those soils which has only a thin covering of poor soil over solid chalk. You will only get a few thin, tough, green stalks here.

Rhubarb beds can soon get very weedy as the quantity of manure used encourages strong weed growth as well as good rhubarb, so hoe round carefully with the Dutch hoe, but do not go too deeply near the crowns. Do not pull from the rhubarb plants during the first year and during the second year only moderately. In the third year, when pulling can become more normal, pull a few sticks here and there from each plant, do not strip any of them. Never pull any sticks of rhubarb after the end of June. The plants must be left to build up stems and foliage during the rest of the summer, just like the asparagus. From June onwards the stems and foliage are left undisturbed to die down naturally during November. Remove any flower spikes immediately they are seen.

During July, a good top dressing of well-rotted farmyard manure or garden compost may be given, and this can be repeated during the following early spring. Many people like forced rhubarb and a lot of people actually prefer it forced. For forcing, put the roots in a warm dark place from December onwards. Cover with light soil and keep moist. It can be put under a greenhouse staging or in a warm shed or cellar. Plants outside may be covered with very old strawy manure, old leaves or ordinary straw, and then have a cloche with both ends blocked, box or large flower pot placed over them.

Rhubarb grown from seed varies very much in quality and success is not always achieved. If it is thought worth trying, seed may be sown in March in drills an inch deep and a foot apart. Thin the seedlings to ten inches. When a year old the plants may be planted out into the prepared bed in rows three feet apart with two feet nine inches between the plants. Varieties of rhubarb are 'Dawe's Champion', 'Early Albert', 'Hawke's Champagne', 'Timperly Early' and 'The Sutton'. The gardener would do well to grow 'Timperly Early' and any one of the other varieties.

11

Fruit Growing

Apples and pears — stone fruits — bush fruits — strawberries — nuts

Before describing the growing of good fruit we must talk a little
about what are known as the 'fruit fertility rules' for the planting
of apples, pears, plums and cherries.

These cultivated fruit trees are mainly of two kinds and are styled
diploids and triploids. All are propagated vegetatively; this means
by budding, grafting, layering or by growing from cuttings. All
named varieties form what is known as a *clone*; this means that they
are part of one single plant. Therefore, when we know that one
variety of apple will not set fruit with its own pollen, we know that it
will not set fruit with the pollen from any other tree of the same
variety. So to obtain a good crop of fruit we must plant different
varieties that will pollinate each other. The diploids have fertile
pollen and the triploids have poor pollen. The triploids must have
two or more diploids planted with them and, of course, for effective
pollination all the trees must be bearing blossom at the same time.
No amount of good soil, no immunity from frost, no concentration
on good cultural methods will produce a crop unless the trees are
planted in the right company.

No cultivated sweet cherry will set fruits with its own pollen.
Besides this, varieties of sweet cherries fall into groups. Within these
groups, even pollination between different varieties will not take
place. So with sweet cherries we have to plant trees from different
groups pollinating each other, except for a few varieties which are
described as 'universal donors'. With sweet cherries, it is not the
reproductive organs, or the pollen, that are at fault, when there is a
crop failure. It is simply that the trees have been planted together
in the wrong combination. These right and wrong combinations are
called 'compatible' and 'incompatible'. The cooking cherries are
self-fertile and will pollinate nearly all cherries except the very early
flowering sorts.

Plums are divided into three classes. There are those which are entirely self-compatible, those which are entirely self-incompatible and those which are only partly self-compatible.

Pears, like apples, are mainly diploids or triploids but there is a third group called tetraploids. Most of the diploid pears do no set satisfactory crops with their own pollen, so it is better for each variety to be provided with a pollinator.

The difference between a diploid and a triploid lies in the number of chromosomes present in each. A chromosome is a term for the thread-like bodies of definite number formed when a nucleus or growing cell divides longitudinally into parts, from which other nuclei are developed.

A diploid has thirty-four chromosomes and fertile pollen, a triploid has fifty-one chromosomes and poor pollen. The diploids therefore will be more effective as pollinators than the triploids. There are bound to be fertilizing difficulties with trees which have an uneven number of chromosomes. A diploid always has chromosomes in pairs. The diploid groups of fruit trees are generally regarded as the 'normal' kind and the triploids as an 'abnormal' kind.

The apple trees planted and offered for sale fall into these two main groups. It must be stressed that if any of the triploids are grown they must be planted next door to two or more diploids flowering at the same time.

I have recommended 'Bramley's Seedling' as a cooking apple and this is a triploid. 'Laxton's Fortune', 'Cox's Orange Pippin' and 'Lane's Prince Albert', also recommended, are diploids. So if these varieties are planted with Bramley's Seedling all will be successfully pollinated. All apples, whatever the variety, are better if cross-fertilization has taken place.

Pears are in the main either diploids or triploids, but the third small group, the tetraploids, possess sixty-eight chromosomes and set a full crop with their own pollen. They are, however, useless as pollinators for the diploids or triploids. Two well-known varieties of tetraploids are 'Williams Bon Chrétien' and 'Fertility Improved'.

The triploid pears, like the triploid apples, must be planted with at least two diploid varieties. There are two cross-incompatible varieties of pears, 'Beurre d'Amanlis' which is pollinated by 'Conference', and 'Louise Bonne' which is pollinated by 'Seckle' .

All the varieties of plums which are entirely self-compatible may be planted together. The self-incompatible and the partly self-compatible must be planted with suitable pollinators.

Although the sweet cherries are diploids, no single variety is capable of setting fruit with its own pollen. Any single tree planted by itself, or several trees of the same variety planted together, are sure to be unproductive. To further complicate matters, sweet cherries fall into groups and cherries within the same group will not pollinate each other. There is a group, already described as 'universal donors', the members of which pollinate each other and also many members of other groups.

So when planting sweet cherry trees, a variety must be planted next door to a variety from a different group, *provided that their blossoming seasons overlap enough.* The good garden compost, good weather, good culture, an efficient spraying programme, effective pruning and plenty of bees are all wasted if the fruit fertility rules are not adhered to.

If you have taken over an established garden with some fruit trees growing there which have been unfruitful, you may be able to put matters right by planting suitable pollinators. You will have to know the names of the existing trees. On page 469 I give full pollination tables for apples, pears, plums and cherries.

Some good fruit can be grown by most people if they grow the kinds most suited for their particular soil. Have a good look round the area near your garden and notice which fruits are growing and producing the best quantity and quality. Ask local growers about the best ones to grow.

When choosing the site for the planting of fruit trees or bushes, we must take into consideration the expectation of spring frosts. It is the frosts occurring in some years during April and May which do most to prevent the gardener from picking a good crop of fruit. Land which is high in relation to that which surrounds it is the best place in which to plant the fruit. This land has the best chance of avoiding the most severe frost. In a valley or sheltered hollow, especially if it is shaded, the frost will linger. If the blossom in April and May is killed by frost, then there will be no fruit for that particular year. There are some late-flowering apples which nearly always miss the frost.

Good drainage is very important for fruit trees, as it is for all other crops, except for those flowers growing in the water garden. Most soils can be improved sufficiently to enable some fruit to be grown. Apples and pears cannot really be grown successfully on a thin soil overlying deep solid chalk. There is not enough iron in these soils. If you can see wild crab apples, old hawthorns, plenty of wild roses, or large elm trees growing in the area, then this kind of soil will generally grow good apples. All soils for fruit trees should be augmented by the addition of plenty of good garden compost or farmyard manure, then all the essential elements needed for good fruit-growing will generally be present.

We will first of all talk about apples which are such a valuable food supply, and follow on with the other fruits, because some of them need slightly different kinds of soil. We have discussed good drainage in another chapter and this is important for all fruit, so first attend to any drainage problems. Some shelter from gale force winds is desirable for apples so that the chances of the blossom or fruit being blown away are minimized. The best form of shelter is that afforded by some of the coniferous trees. Apples are pruned and trained to assume different shapes and grafted on to various stocks to produce dwarf trees or vigorous-growing ones. The bush, dwarf pyramid or cordon types are the best for small gardens.

The question which the gardener poses for himself, if he is growing apples for the first time, is, 'Which varieties shall I grow?' This decision depends upon many factors. A person with false teeth and tender gums cannot bite into a very hard apple. Some prefer very sweet apples and others like a sharper flavour. Then there are some varieties of apple which will not set fruit with their own pollen, others are only moderately self-fertile while all kinds set fruit better with cross-pollination (see opening remarks). So if you are planting apple trees you must have more than one variety unless your next-door neighbour has a few trees which are different varieties to yours, and which are producing plenty of good pollen and flowering at the same time. Whichever varieties are finally chosen, it would be best to have some early, mid-season and late varieties and to include both dessert and cooking apples. November is the best time for planting apple trees, so unless one is going to wait a year, the site for the fruit trees will be prepared in early spring. It can also be prepared during the autumn previous to planting.

Consult a good nurseryman's catalogue, and having decided the varieties you are going to try, order early and ask for November delivery if possible. I shall talk about varieties a little later. It is better, if possible, to collect the young trees yourself from the nursery, if it is not at too great a distance from your home, and if you have a suitable car for transporting them. Fruit trees are very liable to be damaged in transit.

Prepare the soil in early spring or in the previous autumn by deep digging; this will assist in the important business of drainage. Young fruit trees do not require a heavily manured soil at the outset. If you have reserved a site for your apple trees and you are preparing it during the previous autumn, then it can be manured, and a crop of potatoes can be taken from it during the summer. The land without any additional manure will then be suitable for the young apple trees. If you are preparing the site during spring for an autumn planting, and are leaving it fallow during the summer, then the addition of a light amount of garden compost will be sufficient material to give the soil the right texture and enough plant food.

It is very important, with the growing of apples trees, to make sure that every perennial weed is removed from the planting site. Every piece of dock, dandelion or couch grass, together with any other perennial plant, must be eradicated. It is almost impossible to remove these kinds of weeds later on without digging up the tree. Have stakes and tying materials ready some time before the planting date. With apple trees, planting distances are most important. You should ascertain the type of stock on to which your tree was grafted from the nurseryman supplying. He should also advise you on planting distances between trees.

The following planting distance information should prove useful. These are the distances normally recommended for average soils, but all can be increased, if the room is available, to the advantage of the trees.

Apple Trees

TYPE OF TREE	STOCK	DISTANCE APART IN FT
Standard	Crab or Paradise	30–40
Half-standard	Crab or Paradise	30–40
Bush	Medium to dwarf Paradise or type 1, 2 or 9	12–24
Dwarf Pyramid	Type 2 or 9	4–6: 8ft between rows
Cordon	Type 2 or 9	3–4: 6ft to 8ft rows
Espalier	Type 1, 2 or 9	15–24

When the trees arrive from the nursery you can either plant them immediately, heel them in, or put them in a frost-proof shed, according to the weather. When heeling in, you unpack them carefully, dig a trench deep enough to take the roots, and place the trees side by side in the trench. Cover all the roots with soil and firm by treading. The trees can be left like this until suitable weather occurs. Put them in a frost-proof shed if the earth is frost-bound when the trees arrive. Cover the roots with sacking, straw or bracken.

Before planting the trees into their permanent quarters, drive in suitable stakes after you have taken out the planting hole. Take out a hole large enough for the roots to be spread out comfortably. Fill in the soil around the tree so that when planting is completed the soil is level with the soil mark made when the tree was planted in the nursery. Put the tree near the stake in the centre of the planting hole, spread out the roots carefully, remove any damaged ones with secateurs, and begin to fill in with fine soil, working over and around

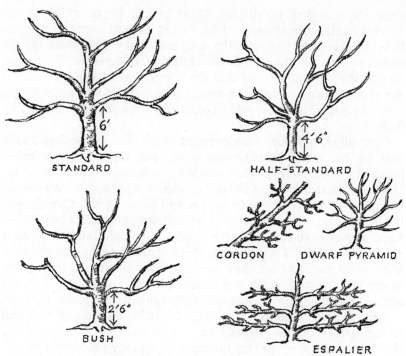

Types and shapes of Fruit Trees

the roots with your hands. Press firmly with the hands at the start, fill in the rest of the soil gradually, firming as you go, and finish the operation by ramming the soil in tightly with a wooden rammer, and by treading. Leave a slight depression around the tree to allow water or rain to seep into the roots. Tie the tree carefully by one of the methods already mentioned for tying trees in the chapter on 'Trees and Shrubs'.

Bush trees can be given a diagonal stake; that is, the stake can be driven into the ground at an angle of forty-five degrees. Cordons will have to be tied to wires, standards and half-standards are best provided with double posts with a crossbar fixed into position to which the trunk of the tree is tied. Keep on attending to ties during the growing season, as the trunks of young apple trees soon thicken. The tying material will have to be loosened from time to time. If there are any rabbits or hares in the neighbourhood, wire netting of one-inch mesh will have to be erected around each tree. This will also apply if an orchard is grazed by sheep or geese.

I am not going to delve into too many scientific reasons for pruning, manuring, special stocks, grafting or spraying. We are going to gather enough information to enable the ordinary gardener to grow a quantity of good fruit. Many people are mystified by the various treatises on pruning of fruit trees. Several forms of pruning have been evolved through the ages and many new ideas on the matter will no doubt be forthcoming during future years. The aim of all pruning should be to see that the branches are evenly spaced and are strong enough to bear the weight of the fruit; to let air and light into all parts of the tree; and to maintain sizeable and good-quality fruit.

Generally it is better to under-prune rather than over-prune. In the past far too much pruning was done, with the result that many hundredweights of fruit which could have been produced were lost. If we disregarded pruning altogether what would happen? We should probably still get plenty of fruit. It would be very small, though, and the trees would be overcrowded. The fruit would therefore be inferior. Small apples have too much core and not enough usable fruit after peeling. The trees, if on vigorous stock, would become too massive. If growing near a house, they would in time cut out the light. They would become unshapely; and diseased wood, not cut away, would spread. You might have to use tall ladders in order to gather the fruit.

Pruning is intended to correct these faults. When pruning is applied to the maiden or one-year-old tree, or to young trees, the pruning decides the shape of the tree to come. It gives the pruner the opportunity to decide how many main branches he requires; it also enables him to see that all parts of the tree, especially the fruiting wood, receives a full quota of light and air. It is correct pruning which makes possible the cordon shape or the dwarf pyramid trees. Only certain varieties can be pruned to cordon or dwarf pyramid shapes. One must adapt one's pruning to the natural growth of the particular variety grown.

It is best to purchase maiden trees; these are one-year-old or two-year-old trees. These may be difficult to obtain today as many nurserymen now sell their trees when they are three years old. This practice, as with so many other innovations, has advantages and disadvantages. If you can plant a one-year-old tree you can build up your own tree into the shape you desire. By planting a three-year-old tree, you obtain a more established tree which has probably built up a good root system; the older the tree the more expensive it is to buy.

When purchasing the bush trees make sure they are growing on the correct stock. Malling No. 1 Stock is normally used for permanent bush trees, but it makes rather too large a tree for a very small garden. Malling Merton No. 3 is a good stock for almost all soils where apples are grown. Malling Merton No. 106 makes a well-anchored stock for a small bush tree; it grows quickly and crops comparatively heavily. Malling No. 9 is a very dwarf stock. It produces a quick-cropping tree, but as the roots are fairly brittle it needs adequate staking.

If you have been able to obtain and plant maiden trees, the object of your pruning in the early stages is to produce a tree with about ten good strong branches evenly spaced. To prune a maiden tree correctly, to form a bush apple tree, you first of all decide how long the main stem is to be. Two feet to two and a half is an average height for most bush maiden trees. The bush tree is the most popular, and one of the most suitable, trees for the average garden.

The first piece of pruning then, on a maiden tree, is the beheading of the main stem in winter, when the tree is dormant. This beheading must be done just above a bud. The top three buds which are left after the operation will grow out into branches or shoots during the following spring and summer. In the following winter, the young tree will have three main branches and these should be cut back to about halfway, just above buds, which are pointing outwards. From each pruned branch, at least two shoots will grow. These are again cut back, so that in three years, twelve branches will have developed, and the trees will probably be bearing a few apples. After five years

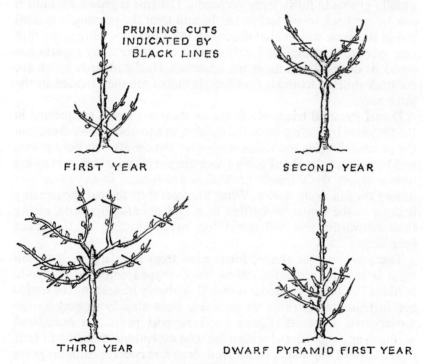

PRUNING CUTS
INDICATED BY
BLACK LINES

FIRST YEAR

SECOND YEAR

THIRD YEAR

DWARF PYRAMID FIRST YEAR

The Pruning of Bush Apple Trees

it is possible to reduce the amount of pruning, and when the tree is ten years old, leading shoots may not have to be pruned at all. When fruiting begins in earnest, pruning will be mainly directed to the supply of fresh wood to replace the older branches.

When a maiden apple tree has been planted in November or early spring, it should be cut back almost immediately; but if a three-year-old tree has been planted late, in about March, it would be better to leave it for the first year and cut back during the following winter, to growth buds which are found below the thicker fruit buds.

Summer pruning should be lightly done, cutting out laterals here and there where they are obstructing sunlight and impeding the ripening of the fruit. These laterals should be cut back about halfway, to within eight buds of their base, during August and September. A popular and easy method of dealing with apple trees is to prune them in the way described for the first five years and to then let them grow almost naturally. Crossing branches, rubbing wood, diseased wood, any branches damaged by storm, are removed when necessary. Entire branches are cut away sometimes, if it is necessary to let in light and air.

Standards, which are far too large for the ordinary garden, are usually grown in fairly large orchards. The tree is grown on until it can be cut back to six feet in height and then the pruning is carried out in the same way as that described for a bush tree. From the fifth year onwards, pruning will only consist of cutting away superfluous wood or diseased and damaged branches. Half-standards which are cut back initially to about four feet six inches are then treated in the same way.

Dwarf Pyramid trees, which are on dwarfing stock, are pruned in the first case by cutting back the maiden tree to about three feet from the ground. During the following winter the shoots that have grown will be cut back to about halfway, cutting to a bud which is pointing outwards. As fresh shoots grow they are treated in the same way during the following winter. When the trees start to bear the pruning is done in the winter by cutting to a bud pointing upwards, rather than outwards; this will avoid too much shading on the lower branches.

There are various shapes for cordon trees in existence. You can grow a row of vertical cordons, of U-shaped cordons, double-U cordons or oblique cordons. It would probably be best for the beginner in fruit tree growing to purchase trees already shaped by the nurseryman. Cordons require good support posts and horizontal wiring. The supports and wiring must be exceptionally strong to bear the strain and the weight of the fruit. Iron and concrete support posts seem to be the best kind to erect; wooden posts will rot at the base in time and then it would be difficult to put in a new post and replace the wires in their previous position.

The cordon is a tree with only a single stem. The side growths are pruned back hard and then short fruiting spurs are encouraged all the way up the stem. Cordon trees take up little room and they enable the gardener to grow several varieties of apple in a small garden. The type of tree chosen will depend upon the size of the garden and its suitability for cordon growing or some other form. Standards or half-standards are not very suitable for the ordinary garden, but as many people have taken over a garden or orchard with these trees present, then we must talk about these as well as the other type.

When apple trees become fully productive of fruit, a certain amount of thinning becomes necessary. It is best to wait until after the natural thinning occurs, which is known as the 'June drop'. Many varieties thin themselves sufficiently during this period. It is usually the very early kinds and those which have short stalks that need thinning by hand. Generally, large cooking apples have short stalks and they often grow in threes, so the centre one can easily be removed. It is very seldom that a 'Cox's Orange Pippin' needs thinning, only perhaps if a cordon tree is heavily laden. Early, mid-season and late trees may be thinned at any time where they are very obviously overladen with fruit.

A problem which frequently occurs for the amateur gardener is the failure to produce fruit, or perhaps only a few fruit one year and more at other times. This can be due to several happenings. Frost may occur when the tree is in full flower and kill the blossom. The fertility rules for fruit planting may not have been observed satisfactorily. These rules must be adhered to. You must plant different varieties that will pollinate each other, and plant these near to each other. You must not plant single trees or blocks of trees of a single variety. Some soils in which the trees are planted may be deficient in all sorts of essential elements, thus causing a lack of fruit. If good garden compost or farmyard manure is given every year as a top dressing on established trees, all the food elements and humus needed will be provided. The top dressings should be put around the trees as a mulch in spring and lightly forked in during autumn, being careful not to dig into the roots. Never put any kind of artificial manure into a planting hole at planting time. If no good compost or farmyard manure is available, fish manure or bonemeal are good organic manures to apply in spring to established trees. Apply to the trees at the rate of three ounces to the square yard. In time the grower will find out which kind of manure his trees will respond to in the best way. Do not put these fertilizers too near to the main trunk, spread it out at a distance.

Sometimes root pruning will induce a tree to fruit. Young trees growing on heavy, rich soils often make excessive growth of branches and foliage, to the exclusion of many fruit spurs. Branch pruning often does not check this growth sufficiently, so root pruning is resorted to. Where a tree can be dug up with a good ball of soil attached to the crown of the tree, the exposed main roots may be cut cleanly and any obvious tap root removed. The tap root is usually

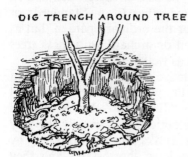 

Root Pruning

the centre root which goes straight down into the soil, often for some distance. After root pruning, plant the tree in another position. After the tree has settled down again with firm planting and watering, fruit spurs may form. This operation should take place during early November. The tree should be marked on its north side, so that when the tree is replanted it is facing the same compass point.

Some trees only bear fruit every two years. Frequently, this is the result of the tree bearing too many fruit spurs in one year, wearing itself out by producing too heavy a crop of small apples. The best way to help the tree to produce an annual crop of sizeable fruit is to cut out one or two main branches each year, to within a few feet of the main trunk. Spread this pruning over four or five winters, so that there are always some branches which may be cut away in this manner. A further remedy is to reduce the fruit spurs and to reduce the number of fruit buds on the remaining spurs. By this method of pruning, nourishment for the tree is concentrated in a few buds, rather than in too many.

When mature trees grow very vigorously but fail to crop, ringbarking can sometimes be done. This should not be resorted to unless it is absolutely necessary. Get an expert to look at your trees before carrying out this sometimes drastic remedy. The object of ringbarking is to encourage a moderate reduction of sap flow.

Other causes of trees failing to fruit are over-zealous pruning or an incorrect method of pruning. Some pests and diseases can be responsible for a reduction in fruit. There are many apple pests and diseases, but not many of them are likely to attack trees which are strongly grown under good conditions of culture.

Apple aphides are of three kinds, the 'black', 'green' and 'rosy'. For control spray with Tar oil wash during the dormant period and dust with derris powder if seen at other times of the year. Apple blossom weevil lays eggs in the young blossom. Spray with liquid derris at the 'bud-burst' stage. The apple capsid bug is an orchard pest which damages leaves and fruit. D.D.T. was the spray recommended for this destroyer of fruit and foliage, together with nicotine, but as these are two poisons it would be better to use liquid derris at a time when the tips of new green leaves are seen.

I am against the over-use of any form of poison in the garden and only advocate a very limited use of those which I think must be used, such as slug-killer pellets. If, however, we want perfect fruit, some form of spraying or dusting will have to be carried out for the control of fruit pests and diseases. We can do much to eliminate pests if we carry out good garden hygiene at all times. Unpack all wood piles, heaps of stone or paving and destroy all pests lurking there in the late autumn. Clean up hedge and ditch bottoms and destroy slugs and snails hidden away in old brick walls or elsewhere.

In September grease bands should be put on standard, half-standard and bush trees. This is to prevent the wingless female winter moths from ascending the tree and laying her eggs among the twigs. *Grease the supporting stake as well as the trunk of the tree,* otherwise the moth may be able to climb the stake and reach one of the lower branches. Use the best fruit-tree grease; examine and replace it from time to time.

For the spraying and dusting of fruit trees, tar oil winter wash, lime sulphur and derris dust appear to be the least poisonous. The aim of spraying should be mainly preventive rather than curative. Therefore a good drenching of tar oil wash during the dormant period aims at destruction of the over-wintering eggs of aphides, apple sucker, and the eggs of the winter moth if a stronger solution is used. The routine tar oil winter wash will now completely control the apple sucker. When using sprays, do so on a still day, keep substances away from the eyes and wear protective clothing. Always follow the makers' instructions very carefully; tar oil wash has the additional power to disperse moss and lichen from the trees.

Do not grow vegetables or any other plants beneath trees which are to be sprayed with tar oil wash. It will probably destroy them and certainly make them unfit to eat. Lime sulphur is reputed to be non-poisonous, but this, I think, depends upon the strength of the solution used. At 'pre-blossom' strength it is slightly caustic, and where a lot of spraying with it is to be done, the face and hands would benefit by a thin covering of lanoline. Eye shields would also be useful. Lime sulphur can be used with safety at any time before the blossom stage but avoid a day of very hot sunshine. Lime sulphur is mainly fungicidal for the control of apple scab, but it is also effective against mites and red spider.

It is only after the blossom has formed that the following varieties of apples are said to be 'sulphur-shy'. Lime sulphur will damage these apples at this stage. They are 'Lane's Prince Albert', 'Newton Wonder', 'Blenheim Orange', 'Charles Ross', 'Rev. Wilks', 'Belle de Boskoop' and 'Beauty of Bath'. There are others, but these are the notable varieties. All spraying should be carried out with a garden syringe or other well-known spraying outfits if possible. The sprays must be directed from all angles, especially when using derris at the fruitlet stage in order to reach the aphides or other pests which we are aiming to control.

A very simple spraying programme for apple trees can be as follows. The spraying year would start in December with an application of a tar oil wash using a $7\frac{1}{2}$ per cent solution. Then follows a lime sulphur spray for scab control; the first is applied at the pre-blossom stage, using one part of lime sulphur in thirty parts of water. Follow this with another spray of lime sulphur at the post-blossom stage, using a weaker concentration of one part in eighty. A further spraying may be made three weeks later at one part in a hundred. In the case of the sulphur-shy varieties already mentioned, Bordeaux Mixture should be used instead.

At other times liquid derris may be sprayed on to the trees following the makers' instructions carefully. Derris dust may be used instead of the liquid. This can be applied if aphides and other insects are prevalent. With the foregoing system of spraying the minimum of poison is used and the very dangerous poisons are not used at all. For woolly aphis the affected parts may be dabbed with neat liquid derris or brushed off with a paint brush saturated with paraffin.

There are many diseases which affect apple trees but these are not likely to appear all at once and they can be greatly minimized with good cultivation methods. How often have we received apples which, when peeled, have revealed brown spots all over the flesh beneath? This condition is called 'bitter pip' and is hardly a disease. The growing conditions are usually responsible for this appearance of the fruit. It sometimes occurs when the season has alternated between drought and excessive wetness. There may be a borax deficiency, when a handful of borax worked into the soil at the base of the tree may put matters right. Prune young trees lightly and avoid heavy nitrogenous manure where this condition prevails.

Blossom wilt, brown rot and canker can all be controlled by

surgery. The symptoms of blossom wilt are a sudden wilting of the blossom during the middle of the blossoming period. Remove all wilted portions and cut back the branches until clean wood is seen. Brown rot is a fungus which attacks trees during the blossom period, causing brown rotted fruit on the trees. Many fruits will fall, and they should be removed and burnt. The wood of the fruit spur may become infected. Cut away any spur or bark infection as soon as seen.

There are one or two sorts of canker; there is 'papery bark canker', where the barks strip away easily, but the worst type of canker is the one where wood is continually dying away, including young laterals.

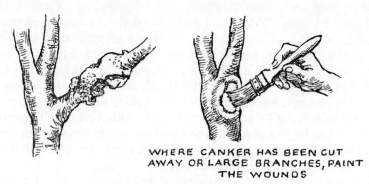

WHERE CANKER HAS BEEN CUT AWAY OR LARGE BRANCHES, PAINT THE WOUNDS

Dealing with Canker on Fruit Trees

Cut away the whole of the soft brown area to good sound wood. Badly-drained land and weak-growing trees invite canker, and so does the lack of scab control. Flowers of sulphur will control any mildew experienced in the orchard.

Some readers might say, 'Why not a recommended list of apples in a chapter on fruit growing?' One cannot really give a select list of apples to suit every person. It is a matter of personal choice, the type of soil, and often the locality. 'Cox's Orange Pippin', first grown in 1850, could be a first choice for almost everyone, although I am told it is not so much favoured in Scotland. It is probably the finest-flavoured apple we have when well grown in a good season. Whichever varieties are chosen, they must be selected by bearing in mind the fruit pollination rules. If any triploids are planted (those with bad pollen) it is necessary to plant at least two diploids with them, and all three must be flowering at the same time.

I will content myself with mentioning a short list of apples suitable for medium-sized gardens which would probably suit most people. 'Cox's Orange Pippin' then, first on the list. 'Beauty of Bath' is a soft, sweet apple; its colour is a bright yellow and spotted and marked with vermilion. It is very early and it should be eaten from the tree or soon after picking. It is ready in August. 'Laxton's Fortune' is a good annual cropper, semi-conical in shape, greenish-yellow, striped red and of excellent flavour. 'Lord Lambourne' is a beautiful apple and a good keeper, staying firm in store until March. It is close-textured and juicy with deep red stripes and an overlying flush. Many people like a russet and 'Egremont Russet' is about the best. It is of good flavour and an attractive golden-brown. The fruits should remain on the tree until almost ripe, they will then store better. All of those are dessert varieties.

Apples must be picked and handled carefully. They are very easily bruised, and even when they have been only slightly scratched, they will not keep long. You cannot make any definite dates for gathering apples; generally if the apples look ripe and you know that it is about the right time for picking any particular variety, place your hand lightly under an apple and press gently upwards; if you then find that it comes away from the bough easily, this is the time to gather your crop. Apples are ready for picking much earlier in some seasons, according to weather conditions. Although only the apples ready should be picked at one time, and the others left to ripen, not a lot of harm will be done if some immature apples are plucked. These often keep as well as the ripened ones.

The newcomer to apple growing, who has seen nearly all cooking apples looking a dark green in the greengrocer's shop, may think that all cooking apples should be green. This is not the case, and many fine cooking varieties achieve as much colour, when ripe, as dessert kinds. If you have some old standard trees which necessitate the use of a ladder for gathering the fruit, place the ladder carefully so that if a branch should break and you cannot avoid falling, you will fall in towards the centre of the tree. Do not rest the ladder against a high outward-growing branch. The network of branches growing out from the centre are more liable to break the fall and save you from more serious injury.

Do not drop the apples into a basket from a height, and never tip them out from the basket when full; take them out carefully by hand, discarding any damaged specimens before storing. Pick the fruit on a dry day and where there is a lot of fruit to be gathered, protect it from the hot sun while awaiting storage.

We will not go into refrigerated storage and gas storage here, as practised by large growers. One of the main conditions which we require for good storage of apples is an even, cool temperature. An apple possesses a high water content, so if it is placed in a dry atmosphere, it will soon begin to shrivel. An attic floor which is frequently used for the storage of fruit is an unsuitable place; this is the naturally warmest and dryest part of the house. A dark cellar with some air circulating is a good storage place. A spare room on the north side of the house which is not too dry could also be used. All storage places must be frost-, mice- and rat-proof.

A shed or unused garage with a north aspect and a cool floor is another suitable storage building. Perfect specimens of apples may be wrapped in newspaper or thick tissue paper. Wrapped apples keep longer but those wrapped must have no blemish and should have the stalks remaining on them. A very large number of apples for storage may be put on to a bed of straw in an outhouse and piled up to two feet deep, using only perfect specimens, then covered with straw, increasing the thickness of this according to the severity of the winter. Examine all apples in store every month or so and discard any that are rotting or liable to do so.

Of the culinary sorts, 'Bramley's Seedling' is still a very popular variety in most parts. It has large, irregularly-shaped fruits which are green with a red flush in broad broken stripes. The trees bear heavily. Two pollinators are needed. 'Lane's Prince Albert' is a large green fruit, striped red, and it is a regular cropper, it makes a good pollinator for 'Cox's Orange Pippin'. For those who require a very large cooking apple for baking or for dumplings, then the variety to grow is 'Peasgood Nonsuch'. It has a delicate white bloom overlying a carmine cheek. It needs a warm rich soil; is harvested in September and used by the end of November. If an enormous amount of fruit is produced some of the branches may need propping. Good pollination can be expected if all of these varieties are grown in one garden. If only one or two varieties can be planted, ask the nurseryman's advice about pollination before ordering.

PEARS

A word of warning before we talk about the growing of pears. Do not on any account plant the variety 'Laxton's Superb'. It is unlikely that you will see this variety listed in nurserymen's catalogues now or in the future. The Ministry of Agriculture have issued an order to the effect that all existing trees of this variety growing in south-east England must be destroyed by 1970. This is to stop the rapid spread of the disease called Fireblight. 'Laxton's Superb' is particularly susceptible to this disease. The disease was first noticed in 1957: since then, over 25,700 trees have become affected. 'Laxton's Superb' was a great favourite among pear growers because it was such a good pollinator. The disease leaves a trail of pear trees and hawthorn hedges with blackened, scorched bark and withered flowers.

There is a great number of pear varieties in existence and we can really only confine ourselves to those varieties which are readily

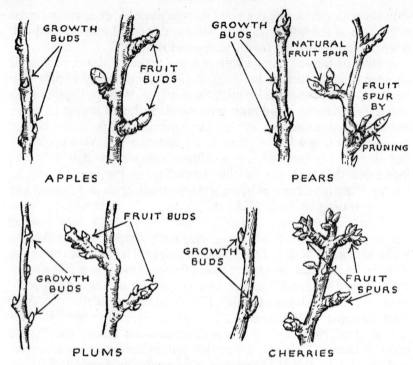

The difference between growth and fruit buds

obtainable from nurserymen today. In very many old gardens throughout the country we see pear trees growing mainly against walls. Many of them have been badly neglected and others are full of scab or canker. Some vigorous-growing varieties manage to survive and produce a few low-quality fruit each year.

Pears have to be planted, like apples, with due regard to the fruit fertility rules (page 428). They require a deep, warm, moisture-retentive soil. Soil that will grow good apples will generally grow good pears. Light, shallow soils over solid chalk will not grow much fruit of any kind and this is the case with pears. Shelter from cold winds is necessary for the choicer varieties of pears and when grown on walls, south-west and south walls are the obvious choice.

Pears generally grow better in the southern half of England but two hardy varieties, 'Williams Bon Chrétien' and 'Conference', can be grown in most parts. As pear blossom appears much earlier than apple blossom, it is more likely to be affected by spring frosts. Pears need to be in a sheltered position so that bees and other pollinating insects are encouraged to visit the blossom.

For ordinary garden purposes buy pears that have been grafted on to quince stocks. Some pears are self-sterile, that is, their flowers need the pollen of another variety flowering at the same time for the blossom to set and produce fruit. There are other varieties which are self-fertile but set their fruit more heavily when cross-pollinated.

Autumn planting is best for pears. Young pear trees are usually supplied today as two- and three-year-old standards and half-standards, two- and three-year-old bush trees, cordons, three-tier espalier and two-tier espaliers. Dig out the planting hole in the same way as for planting apple trees, spread out the roots, and when putting in the young pear tree, take great care to see that the union of stock and scion is not buried. If it is a type of tree which has been grafted to the stock low down, then the tree will have to be planted rather shallowly. Never ruin the growth-regulating stock by planting the scion too deeply, so that it starts producing its own roots.

If planting standards or half-standards, which is very unlikely in the average garden, stakes will have to be put into position prior to planting. Stakes will probably have to be provided for bush trees as well. The best place in which to plant a pear tree in a small or medium-sized garden is against the sunny side of a wall or fence. So when ordering pear trees, choose the type and shape of tree most suited to your purpose. Pears produce fruit spurs quite naturally, so they are very well suited for training as cordons, both oblique and double-U shaped and as espaliers.

The planting distances for pear trees generally recommended are as follows:

TYPE OF TREE	PLANTING DISTANCE IN FT
Standard	25 apart each way
Half-standard	18 apart each way
Dwarf Pyramid	3 apart, rows 5ft apart
Bush	12 apart each way
Espalier	15 apart, rows 5ft
Wall-trained	6 apart
Single Cordon	2 apart
Double Cordon	5 apart

These distances can be increased but they should not be decreased.

The best manuring programme for pears is the application of a good layer of well-decayed garden compost as a mulch in the spring, to be forked in during the winter. If no compost or farmyard manure is available, then bonemeal at the rate of two ounces to the square yard can be applied in early February.

The main principles of pruning pears are the same as for apples. Fruit spurs are thrown out regularly and these will need to be thinned as the trees get old. If pear trees are making very little progress, the leaders may be cut back hard. Pears can be summer-pruned with advantage to the grower. Where there is an over-abundance of foliage shading the fruit, strong side shoots may be cut back to about six leaves and weak ones to four.

During early July pears may be thinned if necessary. It is difficult to lay down any rules regarding the thinning of the fruit. Some trees of about ten years old often bear a heavy crop, dependent on the variety. The grower will learn by experience where to thin or otherwise. Pears are harvested in a slightly different way to apples. The early and mid-season sorts should be picked before the green base colour has turned to yellow. Pears picked too early often shrivel and lose a lot of their flavour. As a guide to correct pear picking, if one lifts the pear up and above the horizontal, and the stalks come cleanly away without breaking, then the fruit is ready for picking. Much pear ripening is uneven so picking should be done in stages.

If one has a large crop of pears and storage is needed, the pears are best stored in a dark, cool place. A cellar is good for storage where there is a temperature of between 40°F. and 50°F. Bring a few pears at a time from storage to ripen fully in a room where the temperature is about 60°F.

Pear trees growing against walls need plenty of water during dry periods. Mulching may be carried out after a good soaking of water. The spraying of pear trees is operated in much the same way as for apples. A tar oil winter wash is used in December. A lime sulphur spray is advisable at the pre-blossom and post-blossom stage. During summer remove any fruit affected by pear-midge maggots. Where a heavy crop of pears is expected, prop up the heavily laden branches.

A short list of pears which would suit most people follows: 'Williams Bon Chrétien', a medium-sized pear, ripening to yellow with russet and pale red. Very sweet and juicy with a fine flavour. A watch must be kept for canker and scab as it is very susceptible to these diseases. Should be picked when green in order to ripen properly. A fairly good cropper.

'Beurré Hardy' is a large-to-medium fruit, russet brown with faint red. It is very juicy and of good flavour. A vigorous grower, it should be picked just before it parts from the bough.

'Conference' is a very popular pear; it has long handsome fruit and it is one of the best and easiest to grow. The flavour is good. It is a clear russet with pale green areas showing through. When the fruit is at its best, the flesh is a pinkish colour. It is not so much liable to an attack of scab as other varieties.

'Doyenne du Cornice' is a beautiful pear with a delightful flavour. It is large, melting and juicy. It is clear yellow with a little russet and some red flush. It is a vigorous grower but a moderate cropper, is liable to scab and is sulphur-shy after blooming. It is ready for eating through November.

'Winter Nelis' has medium-sized conical fruits which are greenish-yellow and russet. They are sweet and juicy with a good flavour. This is a pear which ripens slowly and so will serve a long season as a dessert fruit. This is one of the pears least likely to suffer from scab.

'Beurré Superfin' is a self-fertile variety. It has melting, juicy, conical fruit which are yellow with a patchwork of russet. It is a pear which is not stored and it should be eaten from the tree as soon as the stalk yields to pressure.

QUINCES AND MEDLARS

Just a few words about quinces and medlars seem to fit in here. Many people still make a delectable wine from medlars. Only those people who have acquired a taste for medlars and the wine produced from them are likely to purchase young trees from a nursery, and there are only a few listed. The same may be said of quinces and the jelly, jam and pies made from them.

Medlars grow best on a moist, good soil although they can be grown on most soils. They are grafted on to several kinds of stocks and the nurseryman will advise as to the best stock for the particular soil and site. The medlar makes an attractive standard tree and pruning consists of shaping the tree in early years and thinning out weak, crossing or crowding branches. Manuring can be the same as that given to pears. Gather medlars some time in November during a dry spell. After about a fortnight of storage the medlars are ready for use. Two varieties are the 'Dutch', which is quite decorative, and the 'Nottingham', which is smaller. The 'Dutch' need twenty feet of space in which to grow and the 'Nottingham' fifteen feet.

We often see old quince trees growing in the corner of a farmer's field at the edge of a pond, laden with rich yellow fruit, year after year. This is the sort of position which suits it well, a rich loam with plenty of moisture. Quinces are quite easily raised from layers or from cuttings. If purchasing standard trees from a nurseryman, or bush trees, plant them in autumn. The only pruning necessary is the thinning of overcrowded branches to let in light and air. Quinces are harvested when they have ripened on the tree, and they should hang as long as possible until sharp frosts come along: this is usually towards the end of October. The quince has a powerful scent when ripe and must not be stored with apples or pears or they will take up some of the flavour. Grease-band the trees in October and spray as for apples if any of the pests which trouble the apple are apparent.

Varieties of quince are the 'Pear-shaped', the 'Apple-shaped', the 'Portugal', the 'Bereczki' and the 'Smyrna'.

STONE FRUITS

Most people love cherries and if you have the right soil for them they are not difficult to grow, if you can combat the bird hazard. They must have a well-drained soil and preferably one that overlies a chalk or limestone sub-soil. You cannot grow good cherry trees in a heavy, wet, clay soil. As I have said before, most soils will grow something worthwhile, so with fruit choose the kinds most likely to succeed in your soil.

Those with the right kind of soil for cherries should plant some trees, but they must be careful to avoid any frost holes. Plant the cherries on the highest part relatively to the surrounding land. Where you see good flowering cherries, the ornamental tree, this land is usually suitable, although the flowering cherry will bloom well on a thin soil overlying chalk. Cherries flower early during April and May, and a large number of bees are necessary to pollinate a number of trees. Some shelter from prevailing winds and east winds will encourage the bees to work among the trees.

There are two kinds of cherries grown, the sweet kind and the sour cherries which are the 'Kentish' and the 'Morello'. I do not suppose very many readers will concern themselves with growing the sour varieties, especially in a medium-to-small garden. The Morello cherry, which is used for cooking, has one great advantage over the sweet kinds; it is not attacked by the birds to nearly the same extent as the sweet sorts.

Cherries are grown on various stocks but the wild cherry seedlings are generally used for propagation. Careful study should be made of the 'fertility rules' on page 429; and to ensure cropping, the correct interplanting of the different varieties must be carried out. The sour varieties of cherries are self-fertile. Cherry trees should be planted in November. One of the frequent mistakes made by gardeners is the planting of all subjects too closely. If you are growing some standard cherry trees in a paddock and turning it into an orchard, they must be put forty feet apart each way at least, and they could do with more space. Fan-shaped trees will need twenty feet of space between each one, and sweet cherry cordons four and a half to five feet. The cherry will grow to a tremendous tree with branches which spread outwards when given enough space.

Standard trees are planted when they are four years old and bush trees at two years of age. Fan-shaped trees go in at four years old and sweet cherry cordons at three years old. Where cherry trees are growing in good soil, no manuring is necessary. Cherries must not be given nitrogenous manures, otherwise they rush ahead and no crop is produced. An occasional dressing of wood ashes may be given at the rate of six ounces to the square yard. Garden lime should be applied in January every three years or so where the soil is lime-free. Both sweet and sour cherries should be pruned fairly hard for the first three years to establish plenty of branches. This means cutting back the leaders by half during the first two years and by about one quarter for the next year: all cuts made on cherry trees should be painted over with white lead paint.

Where cherries are grown on walls, the branches should be trained and spaced out a foot apart and radiating outwards to the shape of a fan. These trees are usually summer pruned in July, the one-year-old

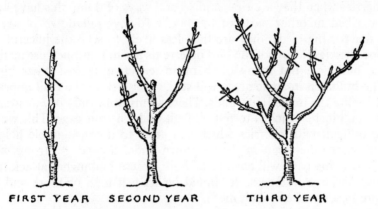

FIRST YEAR   SECOND YEAR   THIRD YEAR
The Pruning of young Cherry trees

side growths being cut back to within five leaves of their base. In early autumn they are pruned back again to within three buds. Any young shoots developing inwards towards the wall should be removed as seen. All varieties of sweet cherries are self-sterile.

Although Morello cherries are not so badly attacked by the birds, they are very liable to brown rot fungus disease. Cut out immediately and burn any branches so affected. Morello cherries will do well on any wall but it is often grown against a north one, if all other walls are occupied. It will grow quite well there. Morellos are difficult to prune because they bear their fruit on young wood, which grew the previous season. Cut out a few of the older branches each October. If a tree grows too high upwards, and beyond its allotted space, it is possible at the end of March to saw through some of the main branches and to paint the cut portions well with white lead paint. Grease-band all cherry trees and give a winter wash of tar oil. Use derris dust as advised for apples.

29

There are many varieties of cherry and if others are wanted which are not in this list, then nurserymen's catalogues can be consulted, always making sure that you plant those which will pollinate each other.

'Early Rivers' has heart-shaped black fruit with a rich flavour. The pollinator is 'Governor Wood'.

'Napoleon' has dark red fruit and the pollinator is 'White Heart'.

'Governor Wood', pollinated by 'Early Rivers', has heart-shaped pale red fruit and it provides beautiful blossom.

'White Heart' is large, well flavoured, and very popular. It is pale yellow with mottled red flesh. It is pollinated by 'Early Rivers' or 'Governor Wood'.

Some method will have to be used to keep birds away from the cherries when they are ripe, and several ways of doing this have been described in other parts of the book. Always put down plenty of water for the birds, they are then less likely to seek the juice of the ripe cherries. Many of the bird deterrents are not of much use against the bullfinch, but many of them are effective against other birds. The bullfinch in some areas will strike long before the fruit appears, stripping the tree of fruit buds. There seems to be only one answer to the bullfinch, which is to put all fruit under a fruit cage. This would be difficult with cherries which can grow to a considerable height, but most other fruit might be grown under a cage. A strong, high wire-netting cage will have to be built, where bullfinches attack fruit trees in large numbers. It should be six feet high or more and the wire netting of one-inch mesh.

PLUMS

Plums, like cherries, come into flower early. They grow well on most soils if it is well-drained. They do not like to suffer from drought during dry summers, just at the time when they are producing their fruit. Plums, like all stone fruits, need some lime in the soil, so if not growing over a chalky sub-soil, garden lime must be added. They should be planted in a sheltered spot so that early pollinating insects can work among the trees.

There are many varieties of stock used for plum growing. One cannot very well advise as to the best one to use for a particular area. When buying plum trees, as with every other tree, you should purchase from an old-established and well-known, reliable nurseryman who will suggest the right tree on a suitable stock, for the kind of plums you want. Always select good straight trunks with clean-looking, well-formed lateral branches. With plums we again come to the fruit fertility rules, and trees must be interplanted with the correct varieties which will pollinate each other. Planting distances are in ft:

TYPE OF TREE	
Standard	20 each way
Half-standard	15 each way
Bush	15 each way
Fan-trained	15 apart, 6 between rows

A site where the least frost can be expected is the best one for plums. Young trees are preferable for planting as then the trees can be shaped to suit the gardener's taste and the tree's position. Trees of four or five years' growth will generally grow away nicely. Plant firmly and put in the supports before planting.

Plums do not require much pruning, only just enough to create the desired shape, and then the removal of crossing branches, weak wood, dead wood or very old wood, when the tree has become too large. If, when the tree has become too large and has outgrown its alloted space, you can bear to remove whole branches laden with immature plums, then this is the right time to prune in these cases. This is done at this period because of the disease called 'silver leaf'. This fungus is less likely to attack during June and July, when the wounds are made by the saw. All saw cuts should be painted over with white lead paint.

When building up a young tree with the initial pruning, try to leave a wide form in the centre of the tree, avoid V-shaped branch junctions here, as trees often break at this point, especially heavy-cropping varieties. With wall plums it is often necessary to carry out some root pruning, try to keep them within bounds. Root pruning should be done in autumn. With trees up to five years old you can dig up the whole tree with a good ball of soil. Remove the tap roots and cut back all fairly thick, solid roots to half their length. Leave all fibrous roots, replant the tree, and ram the soil in very firmly. Water well. With trees which are too large for this operation, dig the soil from around them and sever any roots exposed by driving a sharp spade through them. Care must be taken here on hard solid soil. You can easily give your right hand a nasty jar and be out of action for the autumn digging for a day or two. Sometimes it would be better to use a pruning saw; remove as much of the cut roots as you can.

For pruning wall plums, let the stem grow about two feet high and then train the branches fanwise. Bend down and tie branches to check growth, and lift up and tie to increase growth. Remove any buds which are likely to grow in towards the centre of the wall. An annual mulch of good garden compost will suit plums; they will not require any further manuring. If, as suggested in an earlier chapter, the gardener always puts his bonfire ash on to the compost heap and covers it with further compost, his plum trees are unlikely to suffer from a shortage of potash.

Sometimes small, miserable-looking specimens of plums are seen on market stalls. To avoid producing these, a system of thinning may be carried out. After natural thinning has taken place, plums may be thinned, leaving them about four inches apart. During a good season, plum boughs heavily laden with fruit will need supporting with wooden props, like those used for clothes lines. Plums must be picked carefully with the stalks left on, otherwise brown rot fungus might set in very soon, turning all the plums rotten.

The normal spraying programme for plums is easy compared with that for apples. A tar oil wash is given in December and derris may be used at any time when there is obvious need for it. Silver-leaf fungus is the most serious plum disease. Branches affected should be cut back to clean wood, and the pieces removed should be burned immediately.

There are many varieties of plum, and like apples they are largely a matter of personal choice. Very sharp plums are unpalatable to some people and they take too much sugar for making them enjoyable. However, no one would be without the 'Victoria' variety, raised in 1840. It can be bottled, canned, stewed or eaten when really ripe straight from the tree. When it is ripe it is a beautiful eating plum with an excellent flavour. The tree bears good crops of large oval bright-red fruit with yellow flesh. It is self-fertile. One of the finest eating plums is 'Coe's Golden Drop' which has large fruit of clear yellow with red spots. It is very richly flavoured and thought by many fruit growers to be the best dessert plum. In order to pollinate 'Coe's Golden Drop' we must plant a greengage called 'Denniston's Superb'. It is greenish-yellow with golden flesh of the true greengage flavour. I suppose we must have a purple plum, if only for making jam. 'Early Prolific Rivers' provides heavy crops of smaller purple-black plums ideal for jam-making. It is pollinated by 'Coe's Golden Drop' and 'Denniston's Superb'. 'Marjorie's Seedling' is another blue-black plum, but larger. It is self-fertile.

Damsons are small plums, blue-black in colour, and they are mainly used for culinary purposes. They are very free-growing and hardy and do not require much attention. 'Bradley's King of the Damsons' and 'Merryweather' are two tried and tested varieties which can be grown with confidence.

APRICOTS

Apricots are used to the temperature and sunshine of South Europe and are difficult to grow except on a sunny sheltered wall in the south of England. The apricot blooms during February and March when we are sometimes experiencing some of our bleakest weather with severe icy winds. Protection from these winds must be provided. Apricots need a special kind of soil, well-drained, light, but rich. Some broken mortar rubble and broken brick placed at a depth of two and a half feet will help with drainage and discourage tap-rooting. Mix in good garden compost with the soil as it is put back and rake in a little garden lime on lime-free soils. No further manure will be required until the trees are about ten years old, then a light mulch of garden compost may be given annually in early June.

Many people I have known have raised apricot and peach trees with no scientific knowledge and little gardening experience. They have just put in stones they have saved from the fruit they have eaten and grown a tree from them in any odd corner. Very often trees raised in this way have produced heavy crops of fruit.

Purchase fan-shaped trees or train home-raised plants against a sunny sheltered wall. Plant during November. Fan-shaped trees are planted fifteen feet apart and cordons should be four feet apart. Apricots produce plenty of fruit spurs on old wood and on current growth. They sometimes suffer from some of the branches dying back, which necessitates the whole branch being removed, so plenty of branches need to be encouraged to counteract this fault. Apricots grown against walls must be given plenty of water, for being in well-drained soil the water soon percolates through.

Growths which are needed for future branches should be tied into wires which are running horizontally along on the wall at the back of the trees. Any dying wood which is observed during summer should be cut out immediately. Pruning of apricots consists of removing the shoots which have borne fruit, immediately after picking. This shoot is removed down as far as the replacement shoot, which can be observed. There is also a certain amount of pinching out to be done. On the fruit-bearing shoots, the wood buds would soon overpower the fruit buds if left unchecked. Therefore the tips of each wood-bearing shoot are pinched out with finger and thumb when no more than an inch long; this should be done during May and June.

In the replacement shoot, which is at the base of the fruit-bearing shoot, the terminal bud should be pinched out after eighteen inches of growth. This is done during June and July. Stop all secondary shoots on the replacement shoot, at the first leaf. There will be extension shoots growing at the apex of the fruit-bearing shoot and on young trees; these extension shoots are treated in the same way as the replacement shoot. On established trees pinch out the terminal shoot above the fifth leaf and stop all secondary shoots at the first leaf.

In order to pollinate the apricot a rabbit's tail fixed to the end of a short bamboo cane is thrust into the blossoms in order to transfer the pollen from the anthers to the stigma. Apricots may be sprayed carefully with liquid derris at times when they appear to be infected with aphides. Thin the fruit during June and pick directly the fruits are ripe. Varieties obtainable as fan-trained trees are 'Moor Park', with large, round, deep-orange fruits of excellent flavour, and 'New Large Early' with oval, pale-coloured fruit. 'Moor Park' is a very old variety, first introduced into this country in 1760.

PEACHES

Anyone who has picked his own peach or has been given one by a friend straight from the tree will know that there is no comparison between the flavour of this fruit and one of those bought from the greengrocer. They do not seem to be the same kind of fruit, save in outward appearance.

The growing methods for nectarines are the same as for peaches. A nectarine is like a peach without the velvety skin. A peach will grow in any soil if the drainage is good, but prefers one with plenty of lime and a good top soil over a chalk sub-soil. It will grow well on a south or west wall and it can be grown as a bush tree in the open.

Good peach trees are often grown from peach stones. Keep the stones in damp soil over the winter. In early spring crack them slightly by hand and plant them two inches deep. When the seedlings are large enough they can be transplanted to a wall or in an open sheltered spot and grown as bush trees. Peach trees which are purchased are grown on various stocks and the nurseryman will recommend the best one to grow for a particular site.

The trees will need to be mulched with good compost during June. Fish manure plus potash can be given at a rate of four ounces to the square yard every November. It is necessary to apply garden lime where there is no chalk every three years or so. The site for the peach trees should again be well above the spring frost level because the peach is early flowering. The site for the peach trees should be prepared by excavating to at least two feet six inches. Plenty of mortar rubble or a little garden lime should be well mixed with the soil as it is put back. Some bonfire ash mixed with the top soil is beneficial.

When planting a peach tree against a wall, have the main stem about nine inches from the wall and the fruiting branches are then tied to wire stretching horizontally along the length of the wall. Fan-shaped peach trees are planted eighteen feet apart, bush trees in the open should be twenty feet apart each way. When planting, spread out the roots carefully and plant out in the same way as for apple trees. As with all budded or grafted trees, care should be taken to plant the tree only deep enough for the top soil to come up to the nurseryman's soil mark. Ram the soil in firmly and water in well if the soil is dry. Plant in November.

The peach produces flowers on the previous year's wood and also on a few short spurs. On a young tree allow plenty of branches at the base of the tree and let the centre of the fan-shaped tree fill up later. Peaches are pruned mainly in the same way as apricots. The growths which are tied to the wall should be about four inches away from the wall; this space is given in order to discourage red spider. In winter remove some of the older wood and retain much of the current season's growth. Try to have well-ripened young growths spaced four or five inches apart throughout the fan-shape.

From each shoot which has been retained, laterals will grow out in the following spring. Allow only two or three of these to remain and pinch out the surplus ones when they are about half an inch in length. Leave a good replacement shoot at the base of the fruiting shoot. After the peaches have been picked the fruiting shoot is cut back as for apricots. For bush peach trees growing in the open, prune in April when the trees are in leaf. Cut out old wood and encourage young growths to develop for fruiting. Keep the centre of the tree fairly clear to let in light and air. All varieties of peaches are self-fertile but some hand pollination with a rabbit's tail is helpful. Wall trees can be protected during frosty nights by fixing up some hessian to drop down in front of the trees. As with all wall trees, water and mulch well during very dry weather. If the trees are making too much growth, root pruning may be done during late autumn or on a mild day during winter, in the way already described. In the case of peaches the cuts are made facing upwards and not downwards; this is to encourage fibrous roots to come towards the top soil.

Peach trees should be sprayed with tar oil winter wash during December at bud-burst; and after petal-fall, peaches may be sprayed with lime sulphur at half a pint to two and a half gallons of water. This will counteract peach leaf curl and partially control red spider. Liquid derris may be used at any time against aphides except for when the fruit are ripening.

Peaches should be thinned to one foot apart if sizeable, good-quality fruit are to be obtained. Thin them in stages, first when the peaches are the size of a large pea and finally when they are about the size of walnuts. Pick peaches very carefully as they are so easily bruised. Press lightly underneath the peach and when ripe they should easily part from the branch.

Varieties of peaches are 'Amsden June', which is one of the best outdoor peaches. 'Duke of York' has highly coloured fruit and it is very large and sweet. 'Peregrine' is a favourite variety raised in 1906; it is vigorous and very reliable. 'Royal George', raised during the reign of George I, is a richly flavoured fruit, pale yellow with a rich red cheek. 'Waterloo', raised during the eighteenth century, is a fine-flavoured fruit of medium size and the colour is greenish-yellow with red cheek and mottlings.

Varieties of nectarine are 'Early Rivers', greenish-yellow with a brilliant scarlet flush; 'Ebruge', for those who like an old variety, was raised in 1670; it is rich and juicy and the colour is pale green with purplish-red flush. 'John Rivers' has large, highly-coloured fruit almost covered with rich crimson on a yellow-green ground. All the varieties listed can be obtained from good nurserymen.

BUSH FRUITS

With currants there is one important point to remember, that is, the different method of pruning for blackcurrants compared with the other two. Blackcurrant bushes are encouraged to produce young fruiting wood from the base by removing to its base, old fruiting wood, immediately after picking the fruit.

Red and white currant bushes are pruned by shortening leading shoots to about six inches in winter. Laterals are cut to within an inch of the base to form fruiting spurs. Summer pruning consists of

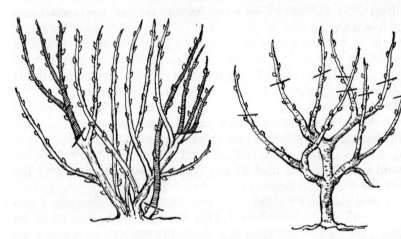

PRUNING A BLACK CURRANT
TWO YEAR OLD WOOD FOR
REMOVAL IS SHADED

PRUNING A TWO YEAR OLD
RED CURRANT BUSH
PRUNING CUTS SHOWN BY
BLACK LINES

The Pruning of Currants

shortening lateral growths here and there to about five leaves. Do not shorten the leaders.

Once this system of pruning is understood, currants are quite easy to grow. Plenty of fruit is usually produced and picked, if you can keep the birds away. Propagation is easy from cuttings. Blackcurrants are very rich in Vitamin C and for this reason alone should be grown in every garden where there is enough room. If you take in plenty of Vitamin C you may be able to bite into one of those delicious hard apples like 'Worcester Pearmain', as Vitamin C helps greatly in the cure and prevention of tender gums.

Blackcurrants succeed in most soils except on the very thin soils overlaying solid chalk. They prefer a good deep soil that contains plenty of humus. For the initial planting of blackcurrants, order varieties which suit your soil and locality from a well-known nurseryman. You will only need a few bushes for a start, because blackcurrant bushes are easily propagated from cuttings. You can keep on increasing your stock from cuttings, as much as you wish.

In preparing the site for the bush fruits for an autumn planting, it is very important to remove any perennial weeds, especially couch grass. This weed loves to ramble through and around the roots of blackcurrants and it is very difficult to remove from around the bushes once it has obtained a hold. Prepare the site for the bush fruit in spring by digging in plenty of farmyard manure or garden compost. Leave the site fallow during the summer, then any perennial weeds which show from time to time can easily be removed. After treading and raking down the soil, plant out the bushes in November. These should be one or two years old. Plant them firmly at a distance of four feet apart in rows six feet apart.

There is another system of growing blackcurrants. They may be treated like raspberries and planted out in rows twelve inches apart. They are then trained to wires so that the plants do not take up nearly so much room as they would if growing as bushes. In the following years these blackcurrants are treated as raspberries by cutting out all wood that has fruited, and by tying in sufficient new shoots to furnish the wire framework. Those remaining are cut away completely.

Once the blackcurrant bushes have become established and are bearing fruit, they will need a good top dressing of organic manure, best applied in early June. This is where a quantity of poultry manure, including the residue of deep litter houses, can be used. This kind of manure is often difficult to use owing to its high content of nitrogen. It is a good organic manure to use for blackcurrants. In addition to nitrogen it contains much phosphate and potash, both needed for the production of good fruit. It should be applied when it has been well weathered, never put on in a fresh state. It is better when it has been well mixed with some garden compost. If this mixture is put around the bushes as a top dressing at the rate of one wheelbarrow load to every six yards of row, each autumn, all should be well. This is in addition to the June dressing.

When blackcurrant bushes are first planted, cut all branches down to almost ground level, leaving only 2 or 3 buds on each shoot. In subsequent years, blackcurrants grown as bush fruits should have at least a third of their old wood removed each year. To propagate insert cuttings nine inches long from one-year-old wood, just above a bud at the top and just below a bud at the bottom. Small trenches can be made about six inches deep and the cuttings laid in these about four inches apart. Cuttings should be placed vertically in the trench and thoroughly firmed and watered in. They should be taken in September or October.

Blackcurrant bushes may be sprayed in December with a tar oil winter wash. In April when the leaves are about the size of a two-shilling piece the bushes should be sprayed with lime sulphur to prevent what is known as big-bud mite. This is easily recognized by the distorted and swelling buds. Currant reversion is a disease which causes bushes to become unfruitful. Leaves decrease in size, assume a dark green colour and become distorted. Pull out and burn diseased bushes and control the big-bud mite, as this pest is probably the cause of the virus spreading. Currant leaf spot is noticed by small brown spots appearing on the leaves in early summer. Sometimes the entire leaf withers and falls away. Rake together all leaves and burn them in autumn where this disease is noticed. Spray with Bordeaux Mixture. Currant rust is a similar disease, again controlled by Bordeaux Mixture. Small yellow lumps appear beneath the leaves in summer with brownish marks on the upper surface. Later on leaves often appear brown or black and drop to the ground.

Keep all blackcurrant bushes well watered and mulched during summer dry spells. Birds are a problem with all currants, not so much with blackcurrants as with the bright red ones. The best way to combat this menace is to build a large, strong fruit cage of wire netting with stout creosoted posts and supports. The other bird-control methods mentioned before may be tried. Good varieties of blackcurrants are 'Amos Black', 'Baldwin', 'Boskoop Giant', 'Sea-brook's Black' and 'Wellington XXX'.

Red and white currants like a lightish soil and plenty of sunshine to ripen their berries. They require a certain amount of potash, so the gardener who puts plenty of wood and bonfire ash on to his compost heap, and then uses this for top dressing his currant bushes, will not keep the plants short of natural potash. Give a top dressing of good garden compost every April, in the same way as for blackcurrants.

Bushes may be ordered and planted when there is about six inches of stem to each one. Red or white currants may be grown as cordons. They can be grown as single, double or triple cordons. Cordons are supported by a fence of three strands of strong wire and each lateral growth usually produces plenty of fruit at the base of the shoot. This fruit-bearing shoot is cut back hard in winter. When the currants are grown in bush form they should be planted about five feet apart each way. Plant two- or three-year-old bushes during November.

For propagation, cuttings are taken which are year-old growths. They should be about fifteen inches in length and should be planted in November. Dig a trench six inches deep and insert the cuttings with all buds removed, except for the top four. Space the cuttings to six inches apart and make firm and water in. Do this work on a mild day.

With the pruning of red and white currants, build up a bush with about eight main branches. For the first four years, shorten the leaders by about half; after this, prune leaders back by a quarter to just above a bud, pointing outwards. Cut back side growths annually in winter to within an inch of their base. Some laterals which are shading the fruit during the ripening period may be cut back by half.

Red and white currants are often attacked by aphides. When seen the bushes may be sprayed with liquid derris. Spray with a tar oil wash in December. Good varieties of red currants are 'Red Lake', 'Laxton's No. 1', 'Laxton's Perfection', 'Wilson's Long Bunch', and 'River's Late Red'. White currants are 'White Versailles', 'White Transparent' and 'White Dutch'.

GOOSEBERRIES

Gooseberries are another fruit which require very good drainage. They need a fairly rich soil and grow best in a medium loam. Prepare the site as for blackcurrants by digging in plenty of well-decayed garden compost. See that all perennial weeds are eradicated, because these are even more difficult to remove from around mature bushes because of the thorns.

There is a lot to be said for growing gooseberries on cordons in small gardens. These trained plants are obtainable from nurserymen. On the cordon system, the fruit is much more accessible and easier to protect from birds. The branches can be trained to a wire fence either upright or at an angle of forty-five degrees. When buying bushes see that they are on a main stem of at least six inches in length.

Gooseberries are very easily pruned by removing annually any overcrowding or crossing branches, and any growing too near the ground level. During the infancy of the bushes, that is the first three years, leaders will require cutting back by half to form a well-shaped, strong bush. On cordon gooseberries, the side growths are cut back to within one inch of their base and leaders reduced by half. The pruning of gooseberries is left until March because of bird damage to the buds.

Gooseberries are sprayed with a tar oil wash during December. To control mildew, spray with lime sulphur immediately after flowering, usually in April. Yellow varieties are sulphur shy and an effective spray for this class is half a pound of washing soda and half a pound of soft soap to ten gallons of water. Liquid derris may be used against pests during the year. Propagation is carried out by taking cuttings in November. Use healthy one-year-old wood which is about fifteen inches long. Cut the shoot just above a bud at the top end and remove all buds except the top three. Insert the cuttings in a trench about six inches deep, make firm and water in unless the soil is very damp.

Dessert gooseberries must be thinned when quite small, leaving the fruit about two inches apart. Gooseberries will benefit from an annual top dressing of good garden compost containing wood ashes during January. A mulch of compost can be put around the bushes in April. Water well during dry periods.

The people who want those hard, green, sour gooseberries which take about a pound of sugar to each tart can have them, but I am only going to recommend three varieties. 'Leveller' is yellow and of superb flavour. 'Whinham's Industry' is red with a sweet flavour, and 'White Lion' is a dessert gooseberry which is a late cropper. Many other varieties may be chosen from the nurseryman's catalogue.

RASPBERRIES

Raspberries are of two types; there are summer fruiting sorts and those which ripen their fruit during autumn. There are yellow as well as red kinds. Raspberries are easy to grow and propagate. Once a row of canes has been planted, the stock can be increased as much as desired, if the plants are kept disease-free. They require a good moisture-retentive soil. Prepare the ground as for blackcurrants by digging in plenty of well-decayed, good garden compost and removing all perennial weeds.

Raspberries need an application of good garden compost along the rows in May; farmyard manure may be used instead. Bonemeal can be given with advantage each autumn at the rate of four ounces to the square yard. Propagation of raspberries is easy; just dig up healthy suckers with roots attached in November, and plant out in separate rows. Raspberries are shallow-rooting plants and healthy canes of medium height with good roots should be purchased and planted in November. Plant them only two inches deep and firm and water well in. Put the canes in eighteen inches apart in rows five feet apart. In February after planting, cut the newly planted canes down to within six inches of ground level.

For the support of raspberries, good posts are needed at either end of the rows and at other points along the rows where they may be necessary. Three single strands of 13-guage galvanized wire, eighteen inches from the ground and between each wire, must be fixed firmly to the posts. The posts are better if they are constructed of concrete or iron. If you are using wooden posts, have them ready and painted with a wood preservative some months before erecting. Old telephone wire is an ideal wire for supporting raspberry canes.

With summer fruiting varieties, pruning consists of cutting down to the ground all canes which have borne fruit, as soon as the fruit

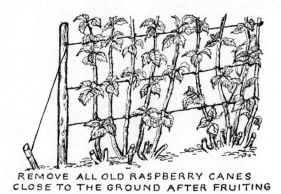

REMOVE ALL OLD RASPBERRY CANES
CLOSE TO THE GROUND AFTER FRUITING

The Pruning and training of Raspberries

has been cleared. Then tie in sufficient young canes to fruit the following year. Cut out the remaining superfluous canes. With autumn-fruiting varieties, all canes are cut down to the ground in late February. Those which arise from the ground subsequently bear fruit on their tips during the autumn of the same year.

Never cultivate or hoe too deeply around raspberries because of their roots which are near the surface. Spray with liquid derris in June when the flowers are open, to kill the larvae of the raspberry beetle. If cane spot fungus puts in an appearance, spray with lime sulphur at one pint to fifteen pints of water. Do this in late April and in early May. Varieties of raspberries are 'Exeter Yellow', a mid-season yellow-fruited sort which is a heavy cropper; 'Lloyd George', dark red; 'Malling Jewel', a mid-season one; 'Norfolk Giant', summer fruiting; 'Hailshamberry' and 'September', the last two, are autumn fruiting.

In gardening circles and nurserymen's catalogues, loganberries, blackberries and other hybrid berries are generally grouped together and it seems the best way to deal with them in this book. All of the berries like a fairly rich soil which is well drained. Dig in plenty of good garden compost where they are to grow. They all need plenty of space as they are very strong growers and some blackberries produce thorny canes twenty feet or more long. Most of these berries are usually trained along a fence in the kitchen garden or elsewhere, or on a plot of land not used for any other purpose. If there is no fence already available, then one like that made for the raspberries must be constructed with an extra strand of wire, making four instead of three. The top wire will be about six feet above the ground and should be reserved for the new canes only, then they will grow

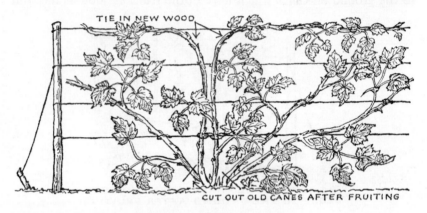

Training and pruning berries

above the current fruiting canes; this will allow the fruit to ripen below without interference and obstruction. After fruiting, the old canes can be cut away and removed, and the new canes brought down, trained, and tied along the wire supports.

Give a mulch of good garden compost each May and water well during dry weather. Plant out one-year-old plants during spring, fifteen feet apart. For propagating these berries, layering is undertaken. Select young canes during the third week in August and layer them with the terminal bud intact. Bury the tip of the cane into the soil at a depth of five inches. A layer of damp peat in the hole will help the tip to root more easily and faster. Sever these layers from the parent plant in November and transplant into their fruiting position in April. Spray with liquid derris when the blooms are open, to kill maggots. The various berries which can be cultivated are two blackberries called Himalaya Berry and Parsley-leaved Berry, Loganberry, Boysenberry, King's Acre Berry, Nectar Berry, which produces very large black-coloured berries which are like Loganberries but are three times as large, Newberry, Phenomenal Berry, Veitchberry, Young Berry (usually called Dewberry) and Wineberry which has amber-coloured sweet berries.

STRAWBERRIES

Now we come to most people's favourite fruit, the strawberry. Considering the high price of present-day strawberries, it would be worth while growing one's own, even if there were only a small patch of garden to spare for them. Once some good virus-free plants have been obtained, the strawberry stock can be increased until you have as many strawberry plants as you care to grow.

Strawberries need good soil containing plenty of organic matter. The land must be well-drained and a soil which is slightly acid seems to suit them best, although I have grown good strawberries in chalk-land. Strawberries should be grown preferably on a slope facing south and protected from winds. As they should be moved to a fresh site after every three or four years, the fairly heavy applications of good garden compost or farmyard manure can be taken advantage of by other crops which follow and which will do well on the vacated strawberry bed. Old strawberry beds make first-class sites for onions, shallots, carrots and broccoli.

Prepare the bed for an autumn planting. Dig deeply and put in plenty of garden compost or farmyard manure. Leave the surface soil as rough as possible for a time. In early autumn tread firmly and rake the soil down finely and level. Some time in autumn or late August is the best time for planting strawberries. They then accommodate themselves to their new surroundings before winter comes. Order good virus-free stock from a reputable nurseryman and have it delivered in time for this early autumn planting. Always use a trowel for planting strawberries. Make the planting hole large enough and spread out the roots well, never have them bunched. Make firm and water well in. When planting has been completed, the crowns of the plants should be just above soil level. The plants need to be a foot and a half apart and in rows two and a half feet apart.

During autumn and early winter, the Dutch hoe will need to be employed to keep down surface weeds around the plants and between the rows. Be careful not to move soil on to the foliage or crown of the plants. Slug-killer pellets will also be needed at this time and again in spring and summer. In early spring, go through the strawberry beds again with the Dutch hoe destroying weeds and aerating the soil. After the surface weeds have been taken away and put on to the compost heap, a top dressing of bonemeal may be scattered around

the plants at the rate of four ounces to the square yard. A high-grade
fish manure will do instead of bonemeal. Stir these organic manures
in with the hoe. This should be an annual dressing.

Keep the Dutch hoe employed during the growing season and water
well during dry spells of weather. When the fruit begins to ripen some
protection from birds will have to be created. Strands of black thread
may be put down, the scarecrow employed, or some good strawberry
netting may be put over the plants. Make sure that the netting used is
well pegged down and put on in such a manner that no birds will be
able to reach the fruit. The new nylon nets are stronger and last
longer. Strawberries may otherwise be grown under a fruit cage or
under large barn cloches.

As the fruit ripens, straw must be put beneath the plants. Some
gardeners prefer garden peat for this purpose, it depends upon which
is readily available and the least costly. The straw or peat is put down
to stop mud splashing and spoiling the fruit during heavy showers
of rain. Most gardeners advocate the removal of all fruit and flowers
during the plant's first year of fruiting, and allowing them to produce
a crop of berries during the second and third year. At the end of the
third year, the plants are destroyed and crops are taken from freshly
planted runners during their second year. By this system you have
rows of one-year-old, two-year-old and three-year-old plants, and
none older than these.

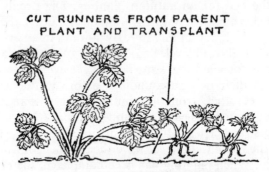

The Propagation of Strawberries

The best runners are produced from parent plants that have flowers
removed. Large numbers of runners may be saved from one-year-old
plants and these are better than those from older plants. It helps if the
runners are pegged down with wires bent in the shape of a hairpin.
Push these into the ground over the stem just behind the plantlets as
they are formed. You can fill pots with John Innes Compost No. 2 to
rim level and peg the runner plantlets into these. From time to time,
remove and destroy any plants which are stunted, small-leaved or

diseased in any way. Strawberries may be sprayed in March with lime sulphur to keep down mildew, red spider and tarsonemid mites. Liquid derris may be used when aphides are noticed.

Strawberries make good crops to grow under cloches; they are earlier, are protected from frost, cold winds, and birds and other pests. Unlike other crops similarly grown, strawberries are not cloched during the winter. Winter frosts seem to invigorate the plants and give them a new lease of life in the spring. The cloches should be put over the plants around the 1st of March. Shading may be necessary later, in very sunny weather. The best types of cloche for this work are the flat-topped or barn types; both are two feet square. Prepare the site for the cloched strawberries in the same way. The strawberry plants are placed a little closer when grown under cloches and can be one foot apart. Spraying is carried out and runners are pinched off until the main crop of fruit has been gathered. Slug-killer pellets should be put down along the rows of all strawberries when in the fruiting stage, because slugs are very fond of ripe strawberries.

The best time to pick is in the early morning; handle the fruit as little as possible as soon as the cloches are removed. After fruiting, give a dressing of organic fertilizer and the beds a good soaking of water to encourage the growth of runners. Varieties of strawberries are 'Royal Sovereign', still the best for all garden purposes; 'Cambridge Favourite', a mid-season sort; 'Cambridge Rival', early; 'Cambridge Vigour'; 'Talisman', a late-ripening kind; and 'Red Gauntlet', which is a mid-season variety.

Alpine strawberries are raised from seed sowing in spring or autumn. They can be sown in a warm border outside or in a cool greenhouse. The plants are transplanted one foot apart with the same distance between the rows. The general practice is to raise new plants from seed sowing every other year. The Alpine strawberries, although smaller, have a much longer fruiting period, from June until October. They do not produce runners.

OUTDOOR GRAPES AND FIGS

Hardy outdoor grapes are trained to walls or fences. Take the leading shoot and train it as far as the height of the support. Lateral shoots should be trained to the right and left. When these shoots produce grapes, the laterals are stopped, two leaves beyond each bunch: non-fruiting laterals are also stopped at the same length. All other surplus shoots are stopped at one leaf. The berries are thinned in the same way as for greenhouse grapes. After leaf-fall all laterals are cut back to two buds from the base. One bud from each will provide the following season's laterals. Good soil preparation is needed with plenty

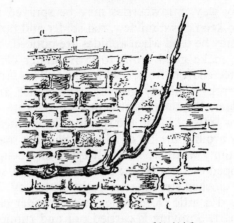

CUT AWAY LATERAL WHICH HAS
FRUITED. RETAIN TWO YOUNG SHOOTS

The Basic Pruning of Outdoor Grapes

of good garden compost incorporated, with an annual top dressing in the spring.

Figs need a lot of warmth and light and will only ripen properly in certain summers; they often only grow really well in the south and south-west of England. The important point about growing figs is that the root run must be restricted. Excavate a hole four feet by four feet and put plenty of broken brick, rammed in hard, in the bottom of the cavity. Fill the hole with good loam containing some garden lime. Figs do well on their own roots, therefore they can be raised from cuttings, suckers or layering. Cuttings one foot in length can be taken in September and planted firmly in a warm spot and well watered. They are ready to plant out two years later. Rooted suckers can be dug out during autumn and planted into their fruiting quarters.

Bonemeal at the rate of two ounces to the square yard can be applied in December and well-rotted garden compost should be given annually in early summer. If not growing on the chalk garden, lime at the rate of four ounces to the square yard should be applied every January. Plant in November eighteen feet apart on walls and sixteen feet apart when grown in bush form. Wall figs are grown on the fan-shaped system and tied into the wires.

Each year weak, crowded branches should be cut away as well as some of the old wood. During the summer prune back some of the branches which are bearing heavy foliage and which are shading the fruit; remove all suckers coming up from the ground. Root prune in late autumn if the trees are growing too vigorously. Water well during dry weather but refrain from watering if the figs are starting to colour.

A fruit-bearing shoot is divided into three sections, at the tip are the embryo figs which produce the following year's crop, halfway down are a few small figs which never mature, and then lower down are larger figs which may ripen in a good summer. It is best to remove the middle-section figs to divert strength to the large figs. Figs must be harvested as soon as they are soft and ready for eating; they cannot be stored and must be eaten soon after picking.

The Growing of outdoor Figs

Sometimes figs need some protection from severe winter weather. If there is only one tree, as is often the case, a covering may be made with sacking or straw. Branches of evergreens may be put over the trees; these will afford some protection and not look out of place. Where fig trees are being planted a warm, sunny, sheltered position is essential. Varieties are 'Brown Turkey', with medium-sized, oval, brownish-purple figs with deep red sweet flesh, and 'Brunswick', which bears pale green figs with a dark blue-brown flush. Both these sorts are mid-season figs.

WALNUTS AND OTHER NUTS

Two kinds of walnut trees may be obtained from nurserymen. The common English walnut does not bear nuts until the tree is from twelve to fifteen years of age. Propagation of French varieties is by grafting instead of by seed, thus enabling the tree to bear in about half the time compared with the English walnut. The best English and other walnut trees are seen growing on the chalklands; if one is contemplating growing some walnuts a site should be selected where there is some good soil and good drainage. Put in plenty of garden lime if not on the chalkland. Mix the lime well in with the planting soil.

Walnut trees require plenty of room. Standards should be fifty feet square and half-standards eighteen feet square. Plant three-year-old trees in November. Dig the site deeply and put in plenty of good garden compost; bonemeal can be applied at the rate of two ounces to the square yard in spring.

For pruning standards the leaders should be cut back during the first two years by about half. Bush trees can be kept within bounds by pinching out the tips of the young shoots when four or five leaves have formed. Thin, weak shoots must be left as these bear the male flowers and pollen. Male and female flowers are produced separately. To get trees to crop as early as possible plant varieties which produce male catkins as young trees. If any fungus diseases appear, spray with Bordeaux Mixture. Varieties of walnuts are *Juglans regia*, the ordinary walnut which makes a large tree reaching twenty-five feet or more in about twenty years; 'Franquette' produces long nuts the shape of a rugby football; 'Mayette Meylanaise' is a good pollinator; and 'Treyve' is suitable for a smaller garden.

Filberts and cob nuts are similar to each other in cultivation, they both do well on chalkland. They need a sunny, open position but protection from north and north-east winds. The most important thing to remember about the growing of these nuts is that pruning must be delayed until March so that the male catkins are left on with the pollen to fertilize the female flowers which appear from mid-February onwards. The nuts are best grown as bushes on a fifteen-inch stem. Plant two- or three-year-old bushes at fifteen feet apart each way. Top dress each autumn with some good garden compost; give lime every third year if not growing on chalkland. When the trees are young, prune like bush apple trees, but after six or seven years when the trees should come into bearing, delay pruning until March when laterals should be cut back by about three-quarters and leaders by about a quarter. Remove all suckers coming from the roots regularly; do not cut back very spindly-looking side growths, as these generally bear the best nuts.

In August prune back the laterals by half. Spray the trees in April with lime sulphur to control the nut gall mite and in June with liquid derris against the nut weevil. Varieties are 'Cosford', oval nuts with thin shells, 'Filbert Frizzled', long nuts of medium size, 'Kentish Cob', 'Pearson's Prolific', large round nuts early, 'Red Filbert', a nut of great antiquity (it was known in 1623), and 'White Filbert', a vigorous grower and good cropper.

In concluding this chapter on fruit growing, I should like to say that if you have fruit trees growing in a garden which is surrounded by other gardens growing fruit trees, then you will have to try to persuade your neighbours to spray and greaseband their trees also. Dig out any old, neglected, diseased trees nearby which can be disposed of and keep a good system of garden hygiene at all times. Do not be discouraged from trying to grow some fruit trees, from stones and pips. Many successful trees have been raised in this way. Peach seedlings raised from stones can begin to fruit in four years. Cherries and plums take about six years and apples and pears from seven to twelve.

POLLINATION TABLES

Many nurserymen now use the new Malling-Merton Stocks for apples and the F12/I stock for cherries. These stocks have given better results during trials than the old Malling Stocks. First-class nurserymen also obtain virus-tested 'Mother trees' from East Malling Research Station in Kent, and use these for propagation purposes. Ask about these when ordering fruit trees.

The following information and Pollination Tables are reprinted from *Scientific Horticulture*, vols. XIV and XV, by kind permission of the Horticultural Education Association.

DESSERT, CULINARY AND CIDER APPLES

All apples show some degree of self-incompatibility; some set no fruit at all when self-pollinated, others can set a fair crop under favourable conditions. Cropping is, however, much more satisfactory and consistent when provision is made for cross-pollination. Although cross-incompatibility has been reported in apples it has not been found among the varieties grown in this country. Apples may be diploid or triploid and the latter are poor pollinators and therefore, in plantations or orchards where these are grown, two diploid varieties should be planted as pollinators to ensure crops from all the varieties unless the pollinating variety chosen happens to be sufficiently self-fertile on its own.

In the following table varieties are divided into seven groups

1 VERY EARLY	2	3	3 (continued)
Aromatic Russet B	Adam's Pearmain B	Arthur Turner	Lobo
Gennet-Moyle T	Baumann's Reinette B	Baldwin TB	Loddington (Stone's)
Gravenstein T	Beauty of Bath	Belle de Boskoop T	Lord Grosvenor
Hume	Ben's Red B	Belle de Pontoise B	Lord Hindlip
Keswick Codlin B	Bietigheimer T	Blenheim Orange TB	Mère de Ménage
Mank's Codlin B	Bismark B	Blue Pearmain B	Merton Pippin
Red Astrachan	Carlisle Codlin B	Bowden's Seedling	Merton Prolific
	Cheddar Cross	Bramley's Seedling T	Merton Russet
	Christmas Pearmain B	Brownlee's Russet	Merton Worcester
	Duchess of Oldenburg	Byford Wonder	Miller's Seedling
	Egremont Russet	Calville Blanche	New Northern
	George Cave	Charles Ross	Greening
	George Neal	Claygate Pearmain	Ontario
	Golden Spire	Cox's Orange Pippin	Peasgood's Nonsuch
	Irish Peach	D'Arcy Spice	Pedro
	Joyce	Devonshire	Potts' Seedling
	Lawfam	Quarrenden B	Queen
	Laxton's Early	Duchess Favourite	Red Victoria
	Crimson	Early Victoria	Reinette du Canada
	Lord Lambourne	(Emneth Early) B	Rival
	Lord Suffield	Ecklinville	Rosemary Russet
	Maidstone Favourite	Emperor Alexander	Royal Russet
	Margil	Encore	St. Cecilia
	McIntosh Red	Epicure	St. Everard
	Melba B	Exeter Cross	Small's Admirable
	Michaelmas Red	Exquisite	Stirling Castle
	Norfolk Beauty	Feltham Beauty	Stonetosh
B=Known to be bi-	Patricia B	Fortune B	Sturmer Pippin
ennial or irregular	Rev. W. Wilks B	George Carpenter	Sunset
in flowering	Ribston Pippin T	Granny Smith	Taunton Cross
	Ross Nonpareil	Grenadier	Tom Putt
T=Triploid	St. Edmund's Pippin	Hambling's Seedling	Tydeman's Early
	Scarlet Pimpernel	Hawthornden	Worcester
	Striped Beefing	Hormead Pearmain	Tydeman's Late
	Warner's King T	Howgate Wonder	Orange
	Washington T	James Grieve	Wagener
	White Transparent	John Standish	Wealthy
	Withington Fillbasket	Jonathan	Winter Banana
Colour sports usually		Kerry Pippin	Winter Quarrenden
flower at the same		King's Acre Pippin	Worcester Cross
time as the variety		Kidd's Orange Red	Worcester Pearmain
from which they		King of Tompkins	S. T. Wright
originated.		County T	Wyken Pippin
		Langley Pippin	

and Culinary Apples

4	5	6	7	8 VERY LATE
Allington Pippin B	Cellini B	Bess Pool	None	Crawley Beauty
Annie Elizabeth	Coronation B	Brabant Bellefleur		
Ascot B	Frogmore Prolific B	Court Pendu Plat		
Bow Hill Pippin B	Gascoyne's Scarlet	Edward VII		
Chelmsford Wonder B	King of the Pippins B	Etoilée B		
Colonel Vaughan B	Lord Derby	Heusgen's Golden		
Cox's Pomona	Merton Beauty	Reinette		
Delicious	Mother (American)	Laxton's Royalty		
Duke of Devonshire	Newton Wonder	Reinette Rouge		
Dumelow's Seedling	Northern Spy B			
(Wellington)	Royal Jubilee			
Ellison's Orange	Thurso			
Golden Delicious	William Crump			
Golden Noble	Winston			
Gospatrick	Woolbrook Pippin B			
Herring's Pippin				
Houblon				
Toybells				
King David B				
Lady Henniker				
Lady Sudeley				
Lane's Prince Albert				
Laxton's Pearmain				
Laxton's Pioneer B				
Mannington's				
Pearmain				
Merton Charm				
Mr. Gladstone B				
Monarch B				
Orleans Reinette				
Royal Show				
Sir John Thornycroft				
Sowman's Seedling				
Superb (Laxton's) B				
Tydeman's Harvest				
Yellow Newtown B				

according to the flowering season. In selecting varieties to pollinate each other, varieties should be selected from within the same group where possible. Varieties may be selected from the preceding or following group and their flowering periods should overlap sufficiently for cross-pollination to take place with the exception of Group 8. Crawley Beauty (culinary) and Medaille d'Or (cider) usually flower when the flowering stage of all other varieties is over and set an adequate crop on their own.

Whilst in most seasons and districts flowering will follow a regular sequence, variations will occur from year to year and also from district to district. It is known that varieties react differently to winter temperatures and this may well cause some varieties to flower earlier than others in some seasons and later, or at the same time, in others; in the same way variation may occur between varieties growing in the eastern part of England compared with those in the western area in the same year.

Among cider apple varieties, biennial bearing and, therefore, biennial flowering is much more common than it is in culinary and dessert apples. It is doubtful whether cider apple varieties are inherently more biennial in their bearing, but the general standard of nutrition in a cider apple orchard is usually of a much lower standard than is found with dessert and culinary apple orchards and this, in part, tends to make many varieties biennial.

Another point which is essential in planning a cider apple orchard is to know the harvesting time of the varieties, as with grazing of orchards it is an advantage to have all the varieties in any one orchard dropping fruit at more or less the same time. Varieties are, therefore, classified into four groups according to the season of harvest.

In the tables of dessert, culinary and cider apples, the varieties are divided into eight groups according to flowering season. No dessert or culinary varieties fall into group 7.

Flowering of Cider Apples

FLOWERING GROUP	VARIETY		HARVESTING GROUP
2 EARLY	Dymock Red		2
	Lavignée		3
	Tremlett's Bitter	*	3
3	Cap of Liberty		2
	Court Royal	*T	3
	Crimson King	*T	4
	Improved Foxwhelp	*	2
	Knotted Kernel	*	3
	Red Foxwhelp	*	2
	Sherrington Norman		2
	Tardive Forestier		4
	Upright Médaille d'Or	O	4
4	Breakwell's Seedling		1
	Bulmer's Norman	*T	2
	Frederick	*	3
	Kingston Black		3
	Kingston Black Improved		3
	Langworthy		2
	Nehou		1
	Porter's Perfection		3
	Reinette d'Obry		4
	Reine des Hatives	*	1
	Slack Ma Girdle		4
	Sweet Coppin	*	3
	Yarlington Mill		3
5	Ashton Brown Jersey	O	4
	Bedan		3
	Brown's Apple		2
	Chisel Jersey		4
	Dabinett	O	4
	Fillbarrel		4
	Fair Maid of Devon		3
	Fréquin Audièvre		4
	Harry Masters' Jersey		4
	Lambrook Pippin		3
	Michelin		3
	Northwood		3
	Silver Cup		3
	Sweet Alford	*	2
	White Close Pippin		3
	White Jersey	*M.S.	3
	White Norman		1
6	Cherry Norman	*M.S.	2
	Dove	O	4
	Strawberry Norman	*T	2
7	Brown Snout		3
	Red Jersey		3
	Stoke Red	*	4
	Vilberie		4
8 VERY LATE	Médaille d'Or	O	4

* Varieties known to need cross-pollination, O=Varieties known to be self-fertile,
T=Triploid varieties, M.S.=Male sterile (ineffective as a pollinator). Harvesting
periods are divided into groups from (1) early to (4) late.

Varieties of pears are less self-compatible than apples and very few fruits are produced from self-pollination. Conference, though sometimes reported as self-fertile, is, in fact, self-incompatible, or nearly so. It may set parthenocarpic (seedless) fruits some of which are normal in shape, and this may account for earlier reports that Conference is self-fertile.

However, parthenocarpy does not always occur and such fruits are often misshapen and of poor market quality. The majority of pear varieties are diploid, though a few are triploid or even tetraploid. Triploid varieties behave in the same way as triploid apples and should have two varieties as pollinators to pollinate both the triploid variety and each other. Two varieties are tetraploids; Improved Fertility, a sport of Fertility is self-fertile; but a sport of Williams' Bon Chrétien known as Double Williams is self-incompatible.

Two incompatibility groups are known in pears. Varieties in these groups are all self- and cross-incompatible, that is, they will neither set fruit with their own pollen nor with the pollen of any variety within the same group. These are:

GROUP I	GROUP II
Fondante d'Automne	Beurré d'Amanlis
Laxton's Progress	Conference
Louise-Bonne of Jersey	
Précoce de Trévoux	
Seckle	
Williams' Bon Chrétien	

Three diploid varieties produce little good pollen and are, therefore, useless as pollinators. These are Bristol Cross, Beurré Bedford and Marguerite Marillat.

The information on perry pears is limited. Preliminary experiments suggest that most varieties are only partially self-fertile in some seasons, therefore provision of facilities for cross pollination is desirable if maximum yields are to be obtained.

In the following tables of dessert, culinary and perry pears, the varieties are divided into six groups according to flowering season. There are no dessert pears in groups 5 and 6 nor any perry pear varieties in group 1. Perry pears are also divided into harvesting groups in the same way as cider apples. Where possible, select from the same flowering group when choosing varieties for mutual cross-pollination, though in many cases the flowering period of varieties in adjacent groups will provide sufficient overlap.

Flowering of Dessert and Culinary Pears

1 VERY EARLY	2	3	4 LATE

Brockworth Park
Maréchal de la
   Cour   T
	Bellissime d'Hiver
	Beurré Alexandre
	   Lucas T
	Beurré d'Anjou
	Beurré Clairgeau
	Beurré Diel T
	Beurré Giffard
	Comtesse de Paris
	Doyenné d'Eté
	Duchesse
	   d'Angoulème
	Easter Beurré
	Emile d'Heyst
	Fondante Thirriot
	Louise-Bonne of
	   Jersey
	Marguerite
	   Marillat M.S.
	Passe Crasanne
	Précoce de Trévoux
	Princess
	Roosevelt
	Seckle
	St. Luke
	Uvedale's
	   St. Germain T
	Van Mons de Léon
	   Leclerc
	Vicar of Winkfield
	Winter Orange
		Baronne de Mello
		Belle-Julie
		Beurré Brown
		Beurré d'Amanlis T
		Beurré Fouqueray
		Beurré Six
		Beurré Superfin
		Chalk
		Conference
		Doyenné Boussoch T
		Doyenné George
		   Bouchier
		Dr. Jules Guyot
		Duchesse de
		   Bordeaux
		Durondeau
		Fertility
		Fondante
		   d'Automne
		Gansel's Bergamot
		Girogile
		Hacon's
		   Incomparable
		Herzogin Elsa
		Jargonelle T
		Joséphine de Malines
		Laxton's Progress
		Laxton's Satisfaction
		Le Brun
		Le Lectier
		Merton Pride
		Napoleon
		Olivier de Serres
		Packham's Triumph
		Petite Marguerite
		Seigneur d'Espéren
		Souvenir du Congrès
		Sucker Pear
		Thompson's
		   Triomphe de
		   Vienne
		Verulam
		Williams' Bon
		   Chrétien
		Windsor
			Beurré
			   Bedford M.S.
			Beurré Dumont
			Beurré Hardy
			Beurré Mortillet
			Bristol Cross M.S.
			Calebasse Bosc
			Catillac T
			Clapp's Favourite
			Doyenné du Comice
			Early Market
			Glou Morceau
			Gorham
			Grégoire's
			   Bourdillon
			Hessle
			Laxton's Victor
			Marie Louise
			Nouveau Poiteau
			Pitmaston
			   Duchess T
			Santa Claus
			Soldat Laboureur
			Winter Nelis

T = Triploid   M.S. = Male sterile (ineffective as a pollinator)

Some Synonyms of Pear Names

SYNONYMS	TRUE NAME
Beurré d'Esperen	Emile d'Heyst
Conseillier à la Cour	Maréchal de la Cour
Beurré Easter	Easter Beurré
Beurré de Mérode	Doyenné Boussoch
Orange Bergamot	Winter Orange
Beurré Bosc	Calebasse Bosc
Belle Lucrative	Fondante d'Automne

Flowering of Perry Pears

FLOWERING GROUP	VARIETY	HARVESTING GROUP
2 EARLY	Hendre Huffcap	2
3	Judge Amphlett	1
	Yellow Huffcap	2
4	Blakeney Red	2
	Brown Bess	4
	Butt	5
	Flakey Bark	3
	Green Horse	4
	Moorcroft	1
	Newbridge	2
	Parsonage	2
	Taynton Squash	1
	Thorn	1
	Winnal's Longdon	3
5	Arlingham Squash	2
	Barnet	2
	Gin	4
	Oldfield	4
	Red Longdon	2
6 LATE	Red Pear	3
	Rock	5

PLUMS

The myrobalan or cherry plums are diploids and are self-compatible. Most other plums, damsons and bullaces grown in this country are hexaploids and may be completely self-compatible, partly self-compatible or completely self-incompatible. All except the completely self-compatible varieties require interplanted pollinators to ensure crops. Cross-incompatibility also occurs, three groups being known.

In a protracted flowering season the time of onset of full bloom from the earliest variety to the latest is about twenty days. In the table which follows, this has been divided into four-day periods and the varieties divided accordingly into five flowering groups. When selecting pollinators for varieties which occur in either compatibility Group A or B, the choice is preferably restricted to those varieties whose flowering group is the same as, or adjacent to, that

Flowering of Plums

FLOWERING GROUP	COMPATIBILITY GROUP A	GROUP B	GROUP C	UNCLASSIFIED
1 EARLY	Allgrove's Superb Black Prince Grand Duke Jefferson Mallard	Blue Rock Utility	Golden Transparent Goliath	Olympia

2	Admiral
	Black Diamond
	Coe's Golden
	  Drop
	Coe's Violet
	Heron
	Late Orleans
	President
		Angelina
		  Burdett
		Curlew
		Farleigh
		  Damson
			Brahy's
			  Greengage
			Denniston's
			  Superb
			Guthrie's Late
			Langley Bullace
			Monarch
			Ontario
			Prosperity
			Reine-Claude
			  de Bavay
			Warwickshire
			  Drooper
				Mitchelson's

3	Bryanston Gage
	Golden
	  Esperen M.S.
	Kirke's
	Late Orange
	Washington
		Early
		  Favourite
		Early Laxton
		River's Early
		  Prolific
		Goldfinch
		Reine-Claude
		  Violette
			Aylesbury Prune
			Bastard Victoria
			Bountiful
			Brandy Gage
			Czar
			Evesham Wonder
			Laxton's Cropper
			Laxton's Gage
			Laxton's Supreme
			Merryweather
			  Damson
			Pershore
			Purple Pershore
			Severn Cross
			Victoria
				Archduke
				Avon Cross
				Laxton's
				  Abundance
				Swan

4	Count Althann's
	  Gage
	Delicious
	Peach
	Pond's Seedling
	Wyedale
		Belgian Purple
		Cambridge
		  Gage
		Cox's Emperor
		Early Orleans
		Stint
			Blaisdon Red
			Bradley's King
			  Damson
			Early Transparent
			Giant Prune
			Oullins Golden
			  Gage
			Shepherd's
			  Bullace
				Liegel's
				  Apricot
				Teme Cross
				Thames Cross
				Wye Cross

5 LATE	Fellenberg
	Frogmore
	  Damson
	Late Transparent
	Old Greengage
	Red Magnum
	  Bonum
			Belle de Louvain
			Belle de
			  Septembre
			Gisborne's
			  Kentish Bush
			Laxton's Blue Tit
			Marjorie's
			  Seedling
			Shropshire
			  Damson
			White Bullace
				Pacific

M.S. = Male sterile (ineffective as a pollinator)

of the variety to be cross-pollinated. A pollinator may be selected from any of the three compatibility groups.

GROUPS OF INCOMPATIBLE PLUMS

I	II	III
Jefferson	President	River's Early Prolific
Coe's Golden Drop	Late Orange	Blue Rock
Allgrove's Superb	Old Greengage*	
Coe's Violet Gage	Cambridge Gage	
Crimson Drop		

In Group I: All pollinations fail.

In Group II: Late Orange × President fails both ways.

Late Orange or President pollinated by Cambridge Gage or Old Greengage set a full crop.

Cambridge Gage or Old Greengage pollinated by Late Orange or President set only 2 per cent.

In Group III: River's Early Prolific pollinated by Blue Rock sets a full crop.

Blue Rock pollinated by River's sets a very poor crop.

CHERRIES

Sweet cherries are not only completely incompatible, but a great deal of cross-incompatibility also exists. This means that no variety of sweet cherry will set fruit with its own pollen nor with the pollen of any variety within its own incompatibility group, but will set fruit when pollinated by any variety in another group provided they flower at the same time. The groups are indicated in the table spread over pages 280 and 281.

The sour and duke cherries, unlike the diploid sweet cherries, are tetraploids. Some are self-fertile, others are self-incompatible and require cross-pollination, but there are no known cases of cross-incompatibility in the sour and duke cherries. Sweet cherries are not suitable pollinators for sour or duke cherries, which, however, are capable of pollinating sweet cherries although most of them flower rather too late to be very useful.

The varieties are arranged in groups so that any variety in one of the flowering groups will flower sufficiently close to any other in the same group, or in the group either directly preceding or immediately following it; for example, the ideal pollinators for Roundel will be found within the same flowering group (group 3), but it could also be pollinated by any variety in flowering groups 2 or 4, provided the

* Four varieties, perhaps bud sports, are distributed as Old Greengage. They are all in Group II. The differences are mainly in flower and leaf characters.

variety chosen is not in the same incompatibility group as Roundel. Thus Merton Heart in flowering group 2, Elton Heart, Emperor Francis in flowering groups 3 and 4 will be found satisfactory.

The table is not complete as there are still varieties which require to be tested and placed in their appropriate incompatibility groups. To provide the intending planter with further assistance in preparing a planting plan for a new orchard, or in fitting new varieties into an existing orchard, the sequence of harvesting the various varieties has also been included in the accompanying tables.

Flowering of Cherries

FOR SWEET CHERRIES	DUKE CHERRIES	DEGREE OF COMPATIBILITY	PICKING (FOR SWEET CHERRIES)
2	Reine Hortense	S.I.	D
3	May Duke	P.S.C.	C
	Royal Duke	P.S.C.	E
	Empress Eugénie	P.S.C.	C
	Belle de Fraconville ...		E
4	Belle de Choisy		D
	Archduke	P.S.C.	E
5	Belle de Chatenay	S.I.	G
	Rote Mai		—
6	Ronald's Late Duke ...	S.C.	G
	ACID CHERRIES		
3	Olivet	S.I.	D
	Ostheimer Weischel ...	P.S.C.	D
4	Kentish Red*	S.I. or S.C.	D
	Wye Morello	S.C.	F
5	Gros-Gobet	S.C.	E
	Montmorency	S.C.	F
	Morello	S.C.	F
	Flemish Red	S.C.	F
6	Coe's Carnation	S.I.	G

S.C.=Self-compatible
P.S.C.=Partly self-compatible (setting only a light crop when selfed)
S.I.=Self-incompatible
* Kentish Red exists in two forms under this name, one is self-incompatible and the other is self-compatible

PICKING SEASON
A—Very Early   B—Early   C—Early mid-season   D—Mid-season   E—Late mid-season   F—Late   G—Very late

Flowering of Sweet Cherries

INCOM-PATIBILITY GROUPS	FLOWERING GROUPS					
	1 EARLY	2	3	4	5	6 LATE
Universal Donors	Noir de Guben E Goodnestone Black C Nutberry Black C	Mumford's Black B Tartarian E. D	Black Oliver C Bullock's Heart D Merton Glory C	Smoky Dun D	Bigarreau Gaucher F Florence F Smoky Heart F	
I	Early Rivers B	Bedford Prolific C Circassian C Knight's Early Black C	Roundel D Tillington Black D	Black Downton D Ronald's Heart E		
II	Windsor E	Bigarreau de Schrecken C Waterloo D Merton Favourite C	Frogmore Early C Merton Bigarreau C Merton Bounty D	Belle Agathe G	Victoria Black A. D Black Elton D	
III		Bigarreau de Mezel (1) D		Emperor Francis E Napoleon Bigarreau E Ohio Beauty F		
IV	Werder's Early Black B		Merton Premier D	Kent Bigarreau E	West Midlands Bigarreau D	
V		Turkey Heart F			Late Black Bigarreau E	

VI		Merton Heart C	Early Amber C; Governor Wood C; Elton Heart D			
VII			Bigarreau de Mezel (3) D		Hooker's Black D	Bradbourne Black E; Géante de Hedelfingen E
VIII			Peggy Rivers C			
IX	Red Turk E					
X	Ramon Oliva B	Bigarreau Jaboulay B				
XI	Guigne d'Annonay A					
XII					Noble F; Caroon A D	
As yet unknown	Rockport Bigarreau B					Cooper's Black F

PICKING SEASON

A—Very Early   B—Early   C—Early mid-season   D—Mid-season   E—Late mid-season   F—Late   G—Very late

31

PEACHES

Peaches are self-compatible; however, a few varieties such as J. H. Hale produce no good pollen.

A list of flowering sequence is given showing the relationship of other varieties to J. H. Hale.

Sequence of Flowering of Peaches in Days

		OPENING OF FIRST FLOWERS
Ginard		1st day
Elberta		
Amsden June		
J. H. Hale M.S.		2nd day
Duke of York		
July Elberta		3rd day
Rochester		4th day
Red Haven		
Hale's Early		
Early Alexander		7th day
Earlyredfre		
Peregrine		8th day
Oriole		9th day
Kestrel		
Diana Grace		10th day

M.S. = Male sterile

BLACKCURRANTS

All the commonly cultivated varieties of blackcurrants are self-compatible and no cases of self-incompatible varieties are known. There is evidence to suggest that insects must be present in sufficient quantity for pollination.

There are two varieties under the name of Invincible Giant Prolific. The true variety, which is similar to Goliath, is a good cropper; the rogue variety, on the other hand, although a vigorous grower, sets only a very sparse crop. The unfruitfulness appears to be due to a form of self-incompatibility of an unusual type, in that the pollen tubes quickly reach the ovules but incompatibility is due to failure of fertilization.

The flowering season, from the first variety to the last, is very short, and there is a considerable overlap of varieties.

The following list places varieties in sequence of flowering:

EARLY   Cotswold Cross
            Malvern Cross
            Wellington XXX
            Baldwin
            Westwick Choice

Westwick Triumph
Mendip Cross
Laleham Beauty
Daniel's September
Boskoop Giant
Supreme
Raven
French Black (including Seabrook's Black)
Blacksmith
Silvergieters Zwarte
Laxton's Giant
Goliath (including Edina and Victoria)
Invincible Giant Prolific
LATE   Amos Black

RED CURRANTS

All the cultivated varieties of red currants are self-compatible.
Sequence of flowering from early to late:

Fay's Prolific
Laxton's No. 1
Red Lake
Earliest of Fourlands
Wilson's Long Bunch

GOOSEBERRIES

All the commonly cultivated varieties are self-compatible. A list
divided into groups according to season of flowering is given. In a
protracted season there are about four days between the opening of
the first flowers of the most forward variety in one group and the
first variety of the next group.

Flowering Sequence of Gooseberries

EARLY	EARLY-MIDSEASON	MIDSEASON	MIDSEASON-LATE
Cousen's Seedling	Bedford Red	Bedford Yellow	Green Gem
May Duke	Crown Bob	Broom Girl	Careless
Warrington	Green Gage	Early Sulphur	
	Gunner	Lancashire Lad	LATE
	Ingall's Prolific Red	Leveller	Howard's Lancer
	Keepsake	Speedwell	(Lancer)
	Langley Gage	Thatcher	
	Whinham's Industry	White Lion	
		Whitesmith	

FOOTNOTE.—Information from a number of different sources shows a considerable
variation in the flowering of gooseberries from place to place. Whether this is due to
faulty nomenclature or to the reaction of varieties to different conditions is not known;
the above list should therefore be taken only as a rough guide to the flowering period of
varieties.

STRAWBERRIES

Most varieties of strawberries are self-compatible and therefore produce good crops without cross-pollination. The garden strawberry arose from the two octoploid species *Fragaria virginiana* and *F. chiloensis*, this latter species produces plants which are wholly pistillate or wholly staminate. A few varieties have been raised which have inherited the pistillate character; these produce little or no good pollen and will only produce good crops of fruit if cross-pollinated by another variety. This necessitates interplanting a pollinator variety which flowers at the same time as the main variety. Two varieties of this kind, Tardive de Leopold and Oberschlesien gained some popularity; they produce little or no good pollen and are seldom, if ever, grown now.

The sequence of flowering of strawberry varieties appears to vary greatly from one place to another and a list in order of flowering is not given.

Flowering of Strawberries

EARLY	MID-SEASON	LATE
Cambridge Favourite	Cambridge Forerunner	Cambridge Rearguard
Cambridge Premier	Cambridge Prizewinner	Merton Princess
Cambridge Profusion	Cambridge Vigour	Sir Joseph Paxton
Cambridge Rival	Early Cambridge	Talisman
Deutsch Evern	Fenland Wonder	
Huxley	Redgauntlet	
Madame Lefebvre	Royal Sovereign	
Perle de Prague		

RASPBERRIES

All the cultivated varieties of Raspberries are self-compatible.
Sequence of flowering from early to late:

> Lloyd George
> Malling Promise
> Malling Exploit
> Malling Jewel
> Norfolk Giant

BLACK AND HYBRID BERRIES

The grouping of the following varieties, all of which are self-compatible, is based on blossom records taken at East Malling only.

EARLY	MID-SEASON	LATE
King's Acre Berry	Veitchberry	John Innes
Loganberry	Himalaya	
Youngberry	Parsley Leaved Blackberry	
	Bedford Giant	

WALNUTS

Walnuts tend to have a longer blossoming period as they mature, so that even in markedly dichogamous varieties there will be some overlap between the male and female flowering times, and self-pollination will be possible. To ensure ample pollination, however, it is necessary to have at least two varieties growing fairly close together. It is reasonably simple to choose a pollinator for a mid-season variety by using a late-flowering variety, as most of the latter are protandrous and their catkins will mature at the same time as the pistillate flowers of the mid-season variety, but there are very few late-flowering protogynous varieties, which can be used to pollinate themselves and other late-flowering protandrous varieties.

Flowering Periods

MIDSEASON (*protandrous*)
Catkins: early to mid-May
Female flowers: early-mid to end May } usually some overlap
    Stutton Seedling
    Northdown Clawnut
    Lady Irene

MIDSEASON (*protogynous*)
Female flowers: early-mid May to early June } complete overlap
Catkins: mid to end May
    Excelsior of Taynton
    Leeds Castle
    Secrett

LATE (*protandrous*)
Catkins: mid to end May } usually no overlap
Female flowers: end May to mid-end June
    Leib Mayette
    Franquette

HIGH BUSH BLUEBERRIES

Most of the information on the pollination requirements for blueberries is available only from the U.S.A. As might be expected from such a large country, where blueberries are grown commercially under very varied conditions and as far apart as the east and west coasts, the information is often conflicting.

Thus the early experiments of Corville (cited by Johnston, 1951) showed that cross-pollination gave better yields in New Jersey. More recent experiments in New Jersey, Massachusetts and North Carolina tend to confirm this result (Johnston, 1951). However, large blocks of a single variety appear to crop satisfactorily in Michigan and Washington (Merrill 1936, Johnston 1951, Schwarze and Myer 1954).

Work has recently started on this problem at Long Ashton Research Station, and the results of the first year, using bushes grown under glass, indicate that there is a large measure of self-fruitfulness though self-pollination results in fewer seeds per fruit. This work needs to be repeated under field conditions. In the meantime, bearing in mind that the need for cross-pollination may well be related to environmental conditions, it is suggested that at least two varieties of blueberries should be planted in each plot or plantation. All varieties appear to overlap extensively in time of flowering.

12

A Garden Calendar

Useful tables for the gardener — the Metric System — garden calendar — conclusion

Garden Weights and Measures

1 bushel	=	40 lbs apples or pears
1 bushel	=	56 lbs potatoes
Punnets	=	1 lb strawberries
,,	=	2 lb ,,
,,	=	4 lb ,,

Surface Measure

144 square ins	=	1 square ft
9 square ft	=	1 square yd
$30\frac{1}{2}$ square yds	=	1 rod
40 rods	=	$\frac{1}{4}$ acre
20 rods	=	$\frac{1}{8}$ acre
10 rods	=	$\frac{1}{16}$ acre
4 roods	=	1 acre
10 square chains	=	1 acre
640 acres	=	1 square mile
1 acre	=	4,840 square yds
1 acre	=	220 yds × 22 yds
$\frac{1}{2}$ acre	=	110 yds × 22 yds
$\frac{1}{2}$ acre	=	220 yds × 11 yds
$\frac{1}{4}$ acre	=	55 yds × 22 yds
$\frac{1}{4}$ acre	=	110 yds × 11 yds

Long Measure

12 ins	=	1 foot
3 ft	=	1 yd
$5\frac{1}{2}$ yds	=	1 rod

40 rods	=	1 furlong
8 furlongs	=	1 mile
1,760 yds	=	1 mile
1 chain (66 ft)	=	4 rods
10 chains	=	1 furlong
80 chains	=	1 mile

Volume

20 oz	=	1 pint
4 gills	=	1 pint
2 pints	=	1 quart
4 quarts	=	1 gallon
2 gallons	=	1 peck
4 bushels	=	1 sack
8 bushels	=	1 quarter
1 gallon water	=	10 pounds
1 cubic ft water	=	$62\frac{1}{2}$ lbs approx.
1 cubic ft water	=	$6\frac{1}{4}$ gallons
1 cwt per acre	=	1 lb per 43 square yds

Some useful figures for the gardener

1 gallon of water	=	10 lbs
1 cubic yd of farmyard manure	=	12 to 16 cwt
1 cubic yd of straw	=	1 to $1\frac{1}{2}$ cwt
1 cubic yd of hay	=	$1\frac{1}{2}$ to $2\frac{1}{2}$ cwt

Common Vegetable Spacings with Decimals and Metric Equivalent

VARIETY	ENGLISH SPACING	DECIMAL	MILLI-METRES
Pea Trench	12 ins wide	12·00	305
Pea Trench	3 ins deep	3·00	77
Broad Bean Drills	10 ins apart	10·00	254
Broad Bean Seeds	9 ins apart	9·00	229
Broad Bean Seeds	3 ins deep	3·00	77
French Bean Seeds	9 ins apart	9·00	229
French Bean Seeds	2 ins deep	2·00	51
Runner Bean Trench	24 ins deep	24·00	610
Runner Bean Drills	24 ins apart	24·00	610
Runner Bean Seeds	9 ins apart	9·00	229
Runner Bean Seeds	2 ins deep	2·00	51
Carrot Drills	12 ins apart	12·00	305
Carrot Seed	$\frac{3}{4}$ ins deep	0·75	19
Beet Drills	15 ins apart	15·00	381

VARIETY	ENGLISH SPACING	DECIMAL	MILLI- METRES
Beet Seed	2 ins deep	20·0	51
Celeriac Plants	15 ins apart	15·00	381
Celeriac Rows	24 ins apart	24·00	610
Parsnip Drills	15 ins apart	15·00	381
Parsnip Seed	½ in deep	0·50	13
Parsnips thinned	8 ins apart	8·00	204
Swede Drills	30 ins apart	30·00	762
Swede Seed	¾ in deep	0·75	19
Turnip Drills	15 ins apart	15·00	381
Turnip Seed	¾ in deep	0·75	19
Early Potatoes, rows	24 ins apart	24·00	610
Early Potatoes, tubers	12 ins apart	12·00	305
Main potatoes, rows	30 ins apart	30·00	762
Main Potatoes, tubers	15 ins apart	15·00	381
Cabbage drills	6 ins apart	6·00	153
Cabbage Seed	½ in deep	0·50	13
Cabbage Plants	24 ins apart	24·00	610
Cabbage Plants, rows	24 ins apart	24·00	610
Brussels Sprouts, plants	30 ins apart	30·00	762
Lettuce Seed	¼ in deep	0·25	7
Lettuce Plants	10 ins apart	10·00	254
Radish drills	6 ins apart	6·00	153
Bush Tomatoes	36 ins apart	36·00	915
Outdoor Cucumber	30 ins apart	30·00	762
Endive Plants	12 ins apart	12·00	305
Celery Trench	18 ins deep	18·00	458
Celery Plants	12 ins apart	12·00	305
Onion drills	12 ins apart	12·00	305
Onion Seed	½ in deep	0·50	13
Onions, thinned	9 ins apart	9·00	229
Onion Sets, rows	12 ins apart	12·00	305
Onion Sets	9 ins apart	9·00	229
Shallots, rows	12 ins apart	12·00	305
Shallots, bulbs	9 ins apart	9·00	229
Leek plants	6 ins apart	6·00	153
Leek plants	6 ins deep	6·00	153
Salsify drills	15 ins apart	15·00	381
Salsify, thinned	6 ins apart	6·00	153
Spinach drills	12 ins apart	12·00	305
Spinach, thinned	12 ins apart	12·00	305
Seakale roots	24 ins apart	24·00	610
Sweet Corn plants	12 ins apart	12·00	305

490 A Garden Calendar

Centigrade and Fahrenheit Conversion Table

CENTI-GRADE	FAHREN-HEIT	CENTI-GRADE	FAHREN-HEIT	CENTI-GRADE	FAHREN-HEIT
100 B.P.	212 B.P.	66	150·8	32	89·6
98	208·4	64	147·2	30	86
96	204·8	62	143·6	28	82·4
94	201·2	60	140	26	78·8
92	197·6	58	136·4	24	75·2
90	194	56	132·8	22	71·6
88	190·4	54	129·2	20	68
86	186·8	52	125·6	18	64·4
84	183·2	50	122	16	60·8
82	179·6	48	118·4	14	57·2
80	176	46	114·8	12	53·6
78	172·4	44	111·2	10	50
76	168·8	42	107·6	8	46·4
74	165·2	40	104	6	42·8
72	161·6	38	100·4	4	39·2
70	158	36	96·8	2	35·6
68	154·4	34	93·2	0 F.P. (Zero)	32 F.P.

Although a Metric System Table and a Centigrade and Fahrenheit Conversion Table have been given, gardeners can still use the measurements which they have always used, even if Common Market regulations prevail.

A GARDEN CALENDAR

This Garden Calendar will show briefly the main tasks which should be carried out during each month of the year. It is meant to act as a reminder and many of the operations mentioned will not apply to all gardens. This Calendar will only contain items which are dealt with in this book, so the reader can turn to any particular section of the book to gain more information about any particular job mentioned in the Calendar.

This Calendar applies mainly to an average garden in the southern half of the country. Gardeners living in some warm, sheltered spot in Cornwall will be a few weeks earlier with their seed sowing and harvesting, while those living in cold parts of the north of England will probably be a few weeks later.

JANUARY

Consult catalogues and send for your seeds. Do not forget those more unusual flowers if you are likely to have some special occasion to arrange for during the year, in your capacity as flower arranger.

Inspect supports for all trees and shrubs and see that they are secure in case of heavy snowfalls. In suitable weather, grass verges can be edged and any new flower beds can be made.

Tread around and make firm any plants loosened by frost. Some hardy shrubs such as forsythia and rhododendron may be layered.

Cut winter-flowering plants and shrubs for flower arrangements.

See that indoor flowering bulbs and plants are staked where necessary and not short of water. Inspect gladiolus corms in store.

Gather pea sticks and bean rods.

Send lawn mower and shears for sharpening and setting if necessary.

Put bracken, straw or decayed leaves round the roots of tender shrubs for winter protection. Erect some form of windbreak or shelter from north and east winds, if not already in position.

Rhododendrons may be top dressed with leaf mould.

Continue with the spraying of fruit trees with tar oil winter wash.

Any necessary root pruning can be done now.

Continue digging through the garden where not completed and put in plenty of garden compost. Shallots may be planted if soil has been prepared and if suitable planting conditions prevail.

If continuous cloches are available, broad beans, early peas, early carrots, lettuce, onions and radishes may be sown under them.

Greenhouse chrysanthemums may be propagated.

Prune outdoor vines. Give greenhouse vines plenty of water and complete all pruning.

Sow Brussels sprouts and cauliflower for early crops. Start them in the cool greenhouse.

Repair or replace any broken tools. Have plenty of labels and stakes ready.

Examine greasebands on fruit trees and renew if necessary.

Unpack and put seed potatoes into sprouting trays as soon as they arrive. Protect from frost.

Garden furniture may be creosoted, painted and repaired.

Seaweed and other manures may be collected.

Clean the greenhouse externally and internally. Clean the glass of cold frames and cloches, paint, putty and repair. Antirrhinums may be sown in the cool greenhouse at the end of the month.

Put down slug-killer pellets in the rock garden, and top dress alpines with chippings or suitable compost as necessary. Remove crowded and straggling shoots of *Clematis florida* and *patens*.

Prune back old growths of *Jackmanii* and *viticella* groups of Clematis.

FEBRUARY

This month will generally show spots in the garden and on the lawn which need draining: mark them for future attention. A good time to make any alterations or improvements in all parts of the garden.

Prune most climbing roses by removing unripe tips and cutting back strong laterals of previous year to three buds.

Clean the rock garden, renovate where necessary.

Prune back hard to within two inches of old wood, young shoots which bore flowers during the previous summer and autumn of *Buddleia davidii* varieties, deciduous *Ceanothus*, *Hibiscus* and *Hypericum* (except *calycinum*). Prune winter jasmine after flowering has finished.

Bulbs which have flowered indoors may be transplanted into the wild garden or elsewhere.

Cut down newly planted raspberry canes to within six inches of ground level, also cut down autumn-fruiting varieties.

Protect apricot and peach blossom.

Cultivate around fruit trees after all spraying and pruning have been completed.

Weather conditions permitting, the following vegetables may be sown in the open garden: parsnip, broad bean, early round peas and shallots.

Keep the hoe going between spring cabbages; autumn-sown onions may be transplanted.

Vegetable seed beds may have their final firming and raking down to a fine tilth.

Sow cauliflower in a cold frame.

Dahlia stools may be brought into warmth for the production of cuttings. Take cuttings of outdoor hardy chrysanthemums.

Sow antirrhinums in a cool greenhouse, also *Ageratum* and East Lothian stocks.

Keep a careful check on ventilation in the cool greenhouse. More may be gradually needed, also an increase of watering.

On a warm border, a sowing of 'French Breakfast' radishes may be made.

Pollinate peach trees in case of a cold spring with a shortage of bees.

Early stump-rooted carrots and turnips may be sown in a cold frame.

Lettuce may be sown in the greenhouse for planting out later.

Try to have all vegetable and flower plots ready for sowing and planting.

Renovate all paths where required.

Soil tests can be made.

A start can be made on neglected lawns. Cut down rough grass and clear before the busy time to come in the remainder of the garden.

Check over all tools in the toolshed and be ready for the spring onslaught.

Sow annual scabious in gentle heat.

MARCH

Any rose bushes which were not planted in November may be planted now and pruned. Complete pruning of gooseberries and red currants.

H.T., dwarf bush, standards and polyanthus roses may be pruned.

Give final preparation to hardy annual border.

Protect all growing plants from slugs.

Clean rose beds and fork in the top dressing of compost.

Give rhododendrons and azaleas a top dressing of good leaf mould.

Plant gladiolus corms in open ground for early flowers.

Look for weed indicators to show the nature of your soil.

Thin autumn-sown annuals.

Give a further top dressing to the rockery where required.

Sweet Williams, double daisies and Canterbury bells may be planted out.

Spray blackcurrant bushes with lime sulphur for control of big bud mite.

Sow maincrop broad beans.

Plant early potatoes on a sheltered border. Sow cabbages, kale, savoy and cauliflower. Sow radish, lettuce and kolhrabi. Sow onions and maincrop leeks.

Plant onion sets. Sow early carrots. Plant seakale sets.

In gentle heat, sow *Primula malacoides*, *Primula obconica* and *Primula sinensis*.

The following half-hardy annuals may be sown in the cool greenhouse: ten-week stocks, *Phlox drummondii*, *Petunia*, *Nicotiana*, *Tagetes*, sweet alyssum, *Nemesia* and *Salpiglossis*.

Start thinning early greenhouse grapes.

Sow seeds of celeriac and celery in the cool greenhouse.

Peaches and nectarines may be sprayed with lime sulphur.

Sow seeds of freesias.

Start the growth of tuberous begonias.

Second-early potatoes may be planted at end of the month.

Prune hydrangeas.

APRIL

Prune back weak and straggling shoots of camellias.

Continue to plant gladioli.

Violets may be propagated.

See that the lawn mower is in order. Oil it, and perhaps give the lawn a first cut.

Make war on all insect pests.

Keep the hoe working everywhere, except near surface-rooting plants.

Well hardened-off chrysanthemums, annual carnations, border carnations and sweet pea plants may be planted out.

Harden off all bedding plants; some may be planted into their flowering positions if the weather is suitable.

Apples, pears and gooseberries may be sprayed with lime sulphur.

Sow dahlia seeds in cool greenhouse. Sow cineraria seeds in the cool greenhouse.

Ivy-leaved geraniums may be re-potted.

Sow hardy annuals.

Sow seeds of 'Amateur' tomato, ridge cucumber and vegetable marrow in cool greenhouse.

Sow in the open ground peas, French beans, beet, carrots, turnips, further onions, spinach, brassicas, lettuce, endive, corn salad and salsify. Chicory, globe artichokes and scorzonera may be sown if required.

Asparagus planting can be undertaken.

Early potatoes may need earthing up.

Plant maincrop potatoes.

Look for pea and bean weevil and black fly on broad beans.

Pinch out tops of broad beans.

Lawn sand may be applied.

Put slug-killer pellets around herbaceous flowers, especially delphiniums and lupins.

Look for woolly aphis on fruit trees and destroy.

Sow seeds of zinnias in cool greenhouse.

Clear garden pools of surface debris and inspect fish.

Carry out necessary tying and staking in the mixed and herbaceous borders.

MAY

Apples, pears, plums, cherries, peaches, nectarines, raspberries and strawberries may be sprayed with liquid derris if required for the control of aphides.

Continue to mow lawn at regular intervals.

Hoe round (except surface-rooting kinds) all shrubs and flowering trees including climbers, water and mulch.

Put out plenty of water for the birds.

Plant out dahlias at end of the month.

Sow zinnias and asters outdoors in the middle of the month.

Sow seeds of wallflowers and most other biennials.

Plant out half-hardy annuals.

Bulbs, including early tulips, may be lifted and planted into spare plot to ripen.

Stone fruits on walls may be thinned.

Put straw or garden peat at base of strawberries and erect some form of bird protection.

Sow runner beans, garden swedes, further turnips and beet for succession. Continue to plant out vegetables grown from seed, as ready.

Tomatoes may be planted out at end of the month.

Earth up second early and maincrop potatoes as required.

Stand chrysanthemums outside on a bed of ashes.

Put down plenty of slug killer.

Damp down the greenhouse and increase ventilation according to the weather. Shade any plants requiring it in the greenhouse.

Burning bush, African marigold and annual scabious may be sown in the open. Many hardy perennials may now be sown outdoors.

Remove tendrils and side shoots from sweet pea plants grown on the single stalk system, and tie frequently.

Thin and transplant hardy annuals as this becomes necessary.

Hoe through raspberry bed and remove any surplus suckers not required for propagation.

Harden off geraniums in pots for planting out at the end of the month.

Keep all pot plants growing in greenhouse and living-rooms well watered as required.

Sow ornamental grasses.

Insert twiggy plant supports into autumn-sown annual border and among other plants.

Vegetable marrows may be pollinated and shoots pinched out.

Mulch raspberries.

Sow broccoli for spring use.

JUNE

Trim back aubrietia.

Much staking and tying will be required everywhere in the flower garden.

Carnations may be ready for dis-budding.

Cut faded roses down to just above an outward pointing bud.

Transplant biennials to nursery bed.

During a dry spell, apply Weedex or sodium chlorate to gravel paths.

Continue to mow lawns regularly and trim edges.

Perennials may be propagated from root cuttings.

Thin any fruit requiring this treatment.

Cut no more asparagus and give a top dressing of decayed garden compost or farmyard manure.

Continue to plant out tomatoes and ridge cucumbers.

Sweet corn may be planted out.

Continue to transplant brassicas grown from seed during showery weather. Make a sowing of an early variety of peas for a late crop. Make late sowings of beet, garden swedes and carrots.

Alpines may be sown.

Syringe carnations and cyclamens daily in the cool greenhouse.

Some shading for the greenhouse may have to be erected.

Make sure you have some choice flowers put by, if you have to make some floral arrangements for a special occasion.

Keep a lookout for any special flower containers which may be on sale at summer fêtes or elsewhere.

Do not use lawn sand or selective killers during very dry spells.

See that all irrigation implements are in order, for the lawn sprinkler may be needed soon.

Do not forget that fish in a pool need more food during summer.

JULY

Often wet and stormy. See that all stakes and supports are secure. Be prepared for sudden strong winds.

Cease pulling rhubarb.

The budding of roses on to briar stocks may be carried out.

If further plants are required, layer rhododendrons and lilacs.

Bearded irises may be lifted, divided and replanted after flowering.

Take pink cuttings and layer border carnations.

Make a start with all formal hedge clipping such as privet.

Begin summer pruning of fruit trees.

Thin apples and other fruits as soon as the 'June drop' is over.

Prune shrubs which have just finished flowering.

Cut out old loganberry canes as the fruit is gathered and tie in young growths. Also do this with other berries. Keep all fruit trees and other trees and shrubs well watered and mulched during dry spells.

Cut sweet peas for the house frequently and do not let them produce pods.

Remove dead flower heads everywhere.

Keep the Dutch hoe employed.

The grass box may be left off the mower and the lawn well watered. The site for a new lawn which will be sown in autumn can now be levelled and raked down.

Lift early potatoes as they become ready and required.

Fill all spare ground with winter greens.

Spray maincrop potatoes with Bordeaux Mixture.

Lift shallots when the tops have died down.

Make a first sowing of spring cabbage.

'Batavian' and 'Broad-leaved' endive may be sown.

Hardy primulas and *Primula malacoides* may be sown in the cool greenhouse.

Sweet peas may be brought down from the supports and re-trained.

Prune blackcurrants and raspberries.

Top-dress greenhouse cucumbers.

Order bulbs for forcing and outdoor planting.

Order hardy annual seeds for autumn sowing.

AUGUST

Rake in suitable fertilizer for a new lawn site.

Sow onions to stand winter and for transplanting in spring.

Sow 'White Lisbon' onions for spring salads.

Strawberry runners which have rooted can be transplanted to fruiting quarters.

Disbud outdoor chrysanthemums.

Try to complete all hedge trimming.

Prune rambler roses and insert cuttings.

Prepare beds for bulb planting by digging in compost and putting down a top layer of leaf mould.

Sow 'Arctic King' lettuce to stand the winter.

Begin to earth up celery.

Propagate hardy flowering shrubs by placing cuttings in a suitable sandy compost.

Dig over and compost any vacant ground where the biennials may be planted.

32

Take out lateral growths on peaches and nectarines.

Clean up old strawberry beds.

Make a further sowing of spring cabbage. Sow winter spinach.

Greenhouse chrysanthemums may have a liquid feed when showing buds.

Cinerarias and greenhouse primulas may need re-potting.

Take cuttings of geraniums.

Evergreens may be propagated by inserting into a rooting medium in the cold frame.

Harvest 'Beauty of Bath' apples.

Any spare moment can be used for mixing compost for autumn-sown sweet peas and other pot plants.

Order sweet pea seed.

Prepare bowls and pots in readiness for forcing bulbs.

Some of the onion crop may be ready for harvesting.

Prepare and clean the fruit store ready for receiving the fruit harvest.

Shorten lateral growths of Wistaria made during the current year back to six inches.

SEPTEMBER

Sow grass seed for new lawns.

Sow hardy annuals to stand the winter for early spring flowering.

Plant all bulbs except tulips.

Pot up bulbs for forcing and bury them outside.

Plant into flowering positions rooted pinks and layered carnations.

Keep the annual border going as long as possible by removing dead flower heads.

Many fruits may be picked.

A good month to take cuttings of shrubs, perennials and bedding plants.

Plant out hardy primulas, primroses and polyanthus.

Biennials may be transplanted to their flowering positions.

Complete the drying and harvesting of the onion crop.

Lift maincrop potatoes as they become ready.

Plant out spring cabbage.

Continue to earth up celery.

Storage of root crops can begin.

Disbud greenhouse chrysanthemums.

Hoe through carefully the autumn-sown onion beds.

Use barn cloches if available to finish ripening the 'Amateur' tomatoes.

Plant hardy lilies.

Have plant-protective material like bracken or straw to hand, ready for any early frosts.

Bring into the cool greenhouse potted chrysanthemums for late autumn flowering.

Gather 'everlasting' flowers and others for preservation.

OCTOBER

Bring in geraniums, either into living-room, conservatory, cool greenhouse or cold frame.

Make a start on the autumn digging programme.

Break up new grassland.

Continue to plant out spring cabbage.

Harvest the remainder of the maincrop potatoes.

Sow sweet peas in the cold frame.

Repair any worn spots on the lawn.

Many herbaceous perennials may now be planted.

Lift border chrysanthemums and pack the stools into a cold frame.

Lift gladiolus corms and dry in the sun. Bring in dahlia tubers, if you intend to store them.

Plant out all spring bedding plants.

Plant tulips.

Top dress the rockery and protect any tender plants against excessive winter moisture.

Pick and store the remainder of the fruit harvest.

A start may be made on the planting of fruit trees.

Prune and train Morello cherries. Prune peaches and nectarines.

Cuttings may be taken of bush fruits.

Protect cauliflower and brocolli from frost, by heeling over or covering the curds with a leaf.

Continue to disbud greenhouse chrysanthemums.

Cloches, if available, may be put over vegetable seedlings standing the winter.

Cut down asparagus stems when the foliage has withered.

Much planting and alteration may now be done in the mixed border.

All chrysanthemums which need protection from frost should now be brought inside.

Pinch out tops of sweet pea plants when about four inches tall.

Collect broad and runner bean seed.

NOVEMBER

Remove bean rods and pea sticks from crops which have finished bearing, clean and store them under cover.

Do as much digging as possible, putting in plenty of good garden compost or farmyard manure.

The best time for planting new rose bushes.

Planting in the water garden can be done.

Plant fruit trees.

Start pruning apples and pears.

Protect fig trees from frost.

Sow long-pod broad beans.

Pick and store late apples.

Inspect all vegetables in store, including potatoes.

Remove decaying leaves from winter greens and put them on the compost heap.

Remove any piles of weeds on the allotment, old finished plants or rubbish of any kind, to prevent harbouring of pests during winter.

Have protective material ready for cold frames.

Protect Christmas roses.

Rake all fallen leaves from the lawn and elsewhere and stack for leaf mould.

Take cuttings of Japanese and incurving chrysanthemums.

Some rhubarb and seakale may be brought into the cool greenhouse for forcing.

Most flowering trees and shrubs can be planted.

Overhaul and clean lawn mower. Clean, repair and oil other tools not being used during the winter.

The planning of next's year's garden can be undertaken.

DECEMBER

Increase the protective material on potato clamps as necessary.

Make sure that no frost can penetrate vegetable and fruit store.

A good time to scrub all pots and paint wooden labels.

New hedges may be planted during mild weather.

Spray all fruit trees with tar oil winter wash.

Continue pruning fruit trees.

Digging and manuring may take place everywhere, when weather is suitable.

Protect trees, shrubs and vegetables from rabbits, hares and wood pigeons.

Prune late greenhouse vines.

Inspect all drainage schemes and clean out ditches.

Continue to gather winter flowers including *Iris stylosa* while in bud, cut holly a few days before Christmas before the birds take the berries.

Lift quantities of vegetables which are left in open ground, put in shed and cover, for use in time of prolonged frost.

Further cuttings of chrysanthemums may be taken.

Keep sweet pea plants growing as hardily as possible by allowing plenty of air during mild days. Give twiggy supports and see that the pots do not dry out.

Slugs may appear during mild, damp days.

Some early carrots may be sown in the cold frame.

Autumn-sown annuals may need frost protection.

Turn off water which leads to outside taps when frost is expected. Listen carefully to weather forecasts.

Make holes carefully in frozen pools to let out gases without injury to the fish (see warning on page 136).

Have a shovel and yard broom handy for clearing snow.

CONCLUSION

This Garden Calendar will help to remind you of urgent work throughout the year. Although here and throughout the book, so much work has been outlined, I hope you will still have plenty of opportunity to rest, to sit back and survey your work, and to enjoy your garden. This means that you shouldn't attempt to accomplish more than you really have time for—try to develop an interesting garden that you can just manage without the weeds taking over.

Index of Plants

General Index

33